Witness to Korea 1945–47

The Unfolding of an Authoritarian Regime

ASIA RESEARCH SERIES 1

Witness to Korea 1945–47

The Unfolding of an Authoritarian Regime

Frank Hoffmann and Mark E. Caprio
editors

Academia Publishers
BERKELEY • DOVER • HAMBURG

Academia Publishers, LLC
Berkeley, California
https://academebooks.com

Cover and interior design by F. Hoffmann.
Typeset in *Academebooks*, *Avenir*, and *Noto Serif CJK KR*.

Set according to *The Chicago Manual of Style*, 17th edition.

This book is available in various print and eBook formats. Order details at:
https://academebooks.com

First edition, 2026

ISBN 978-1-95-606791-0 (Paperback)
ISBN 978-1-95-606707-1 (Hardcover)
ISBN 978-1-95-606708-8 (Kindle eBook)
ISBN 978-1-95-606709-5 (PDF)

Library of Congress record available at:
https://lccn.loc.gov/2022933926

Publisher's Cataloging-in-Publication Data

Names: Hoffmann, Frank, 1962 August 23- author, editor. | Caprio, Mark E., 1957- author, editor.
Title: Witness to Korea 1945-47 : the unfolding of an authoritarian regime / Frank Hoffmann and Mark E. Caprio, editors.
Description: First edition. | Berkeley, CA : Academia Publishers, 2026. | Series: Asia research series, bk. 1. | Includes bibliographical references and index.
Identifiers: LCCN 2022933926 (print) | ISBN 978-1-95-606791-0 (paperback) | ISBN 978-1-95-606707-1 (hardcover) | ISBN 978-1-95-606708-8 (ebook) | ISBN 978-1-95-606709-5 (PDF)
Subjects: LCSH: Korea--Politics and government--1945-1948. | Korea (South)--History. | Gayn, Mark J 1909- | East Asia. | Robinson, Richard D. Betrayal of a nation. | Fascism. | United States--History--20th century. | BISAC: HISTORY / Asia / Korea. | HISTORY / United States / 20th Century.
Classification: LCC DS916.55 .H64 2026 (print) | LCC DS916.55 (ebook) | DDC 951.9/03--dc23.

12.Arrests are carried out on a vast scale, & street arrests, such as one shown here, are grequent. The police halted 3 students, & tied their wrists with a thin twine, pending their removal to police station. One of the 3 was with his wife & child (strapped to her back, on extreme left) & mother. Latter, in protest, tore offher bodice & proceeded to scream & plead with police. Police behavior was noted in United Nations' pre-election report as one of things to watch for. Another was the activities of private armed forces maintained by such men as Syngman Rhee, Kim Koo and others.

CREDIT MARK GAYN

Front cover image: detail of a press photo by Mark Gayn, Seoul, South Korea, fall 1946; above reproduced in full with Gayn's 1948 cutline. In a stunning but for this agitated period emblematic scene, we see unexpected nudity as the last resort of protest by an extremely distressed mother worrying for her son's safety at the hands of police. Gayn's image frame yields a remarkably striking composition. Much like Velázquez, he graciously captures the gazes and movements connecting those present in the unfolding neocolonial drama he witnesses. Yet, the restrictive, politically circumscribed, and censorship-constrained atmosphere of 1940s America made its publication untenable.

Contents

Acknowledgments

e would like to give very special thanks to various individuals for their support in granting us publication rights for texts and images, and cooperating in other ways. Carol A. Robinson deserves special thanks for her enthusiasm and cooperation in the project, and thanks to the author's children Wendy, Linda, and Kermit for their kind agreement. Further, we are especially indebted for the seamless cooperation and exceptional generosity of Anthony Wu, Jennifer Donnelly, and Paul J. Westlake, all in Toronto, for sharing valuable information and for granting the publishing rights to use the Mark Gayn piece.

We would also like to express our appreciation to several institutions that have provided access to their libraries and archives. The Thomas Fisher Rare Book Library at the University of Toronto, the Beinecke Rare Book and Manuscript Library at Yale University, the Hoover Institution Library & Archives at Stanford University, and the C. V. Starr East Asian Library, University of California, Berkeley, deserve special mention.

Last, but certainly not least, we very much enjoyed working with our copy editor James P. Thomas. Himself a Korea expert, he was always there to discuss issues related to this project. His interactive approach and amazing diligence and perseverance played an important role in the book's successful completion.

Frank Hoffmann
Mark E. Caprio

At Long Last

John Merrill

I first encountered Richard D. Robinson's (1921–2009) manuscript, "Betrayal of a Nation," some fifty years ago at Harvard University.

I was writing a master's paper on pre-Korean War political violence in Korea. My professor was Gregory Henderson (1922–1988), a former foreign service officer who had served in Seoul and published a seminal work on Korean politics.* One day, as we were discussing my research, he told me about Robinson and his manuscript on the U.S. occupation of Korea. I fired off a note to Robinson right away explaining my research and asking about getting a copy.

A few days later it arrived. Robinson, it turned out, had retooled himself as a Middle East specialist, gotten a Ph.D., and was teaching International Business at MIT right down the river. Henderson was right. The manuscript was an inside, tell-all account of the occupation that proved extremely useful. When I finished my master's paper, I wrote to thank him and get permission to donate it to Harvard's Yenching Library. Over the years, Robinson's manuscript served as an important source for scholars researching the occupation (1945–1948) and the Syngman Rhee years (1948–1960). A translated version was published in Korean in 1988.

During WWII, Robinson was trained as a Japanese area officer. When Tokyo surrendered, he was suddenly plunked down in Korea. His job was to follow public opinion and maintain contact with Korean political figures. This experience prompted him to write a manuscript

* *Korea: The Politics of the Vortex* (Cambridge: Harvard University Press, 1968).

highly critical of the occupation and its policies—especially its failure to promote democracy and implement social and economic reform. He submitted his manuscript to multiple publishers, but without success, given the political climate of the times.

Robinson left Korea in mid-1947 under something of a cloud. He had uncovered a plot by Korean rightists to provoke an incident that would draw American troops into a confrontation with the Soviets in northern Korea. The plotters hoped the confrontation would eventually bring about reunification. Although occupation authorities wanted to bury the plot, Robinson refused to let it go and was nearly court-martialed. After destroying his manuscript to avoid further complications, he and his wife left Korea by freighter. On the long voyage, he managed to retype the entire manuscript.

In addition to Robinson's account, this volume contains the long Korea chapter from Mark Gayn's (1909–1981) *Japan Diary*. From 1945 to 1947 Gayn worked for the *Chicago Sun* as its bureau chief for Japan and Korea. But he also wrote for other major newspapers and popular magazines. He visited Korea with two fellow journalists just after a wave of strikes and other disturbances in the fall of 1946. Gayn's diary reinforces Robinson's portrait of the occupation—and is even better in conveying its determination to tightly control the press.

The "original sin" of the American occupation was to see Korea as just an extension of Japan, rather than a liberated country. Spurning approaches by the left-leaning People's Committees (Inmin Wiwŏnhoe), which had broad popular support, occupation authorities took their guidance from an army field manual on governing defeated enemy territories. After a hare-brained attempt to retain "experienced" Japanese officials and their Korean trainees, the military government reverted to relying on Korean police who had worked for the Japanese and a highly unrepresentative "translators' government" of English-speaking Koreans.

Haphazard occupation policies soon led to an escalation in violent incidents. Popular unrest exploded in the fall of 1946. Hundreds of police were killed and American tactical troops had to be called out to control the unrest. The scale of protests and violence prompted concern that the situation was spiraling out of control. Fearing that the

American position might become untenable, policymakers decided to disengage. With the U.S.–Soviet Joint Commission at an impasse, Washington referred the Korean issue to the newly established United Nations to provide political cover for bailing out. Soviet disagreement with this development sealed the division.

In April 1948, armed struggle broke out on Cheju-do, Korea's largest island off the southwestern tip of the peninsula. Then, in mid-October, the unrest spilled over onto the mainland as a regiment of South Korean forces rebelled at the mainland port of Yŏsu as they were about to embark for the island. The situation was touch and go for some time. Although the uprising was eventually suppressed, fleeing rebel soldiers scattered into the nearby Chiri Mountains where they continued to hold out. Erupting just a month after the ROK's establishment, the rebellion rattled the new Syngman Rhee government.

The failed policies of the occupation cast a long shadow. Once Syngman Rhee's (Yi Sŭng-man, in office 1948–1960) new government gained its footing, it launched an all-out offensive, determined to punish the North. According to ROK military histories, Rhee personally ordered an amphibious attack on a naval base guarding the approaches to P'yŏngyang. American officials were infuriated but could do little more than complain. Rhee's forces also initiated battles between whole regiments along the 38th Parallel. The South even used partisans to infiltrate into the North by sea. One unit was captured and its surviving members put on trial in P'yŏngyang.

While Rhee indulged himself in endless bluster and bravado, Kim Il Sung (Kim Il-sŏng, in office 1948–1994) was busy preparing to attack—pitching to Stalin (in office 1922–1953) a war to liberate the South, mobilizing the population through a massive fund-raising campaign to buy Russian tanks and planes, and channeling repatriating Korean veterans of Mao's (head of state 1949–1959) forces into the Korean People's Army. In the end, Rhee's foolhardiness only helped Kim win Stalin's approval for eliminating a serious threat to the communist regime in the North.

From a historiographic perspective, the incomplete and corrupted history of the occupation years has continued to also make the current situation more difficult to understand. The consequences of this are nowhere more telling than on the question of the origins of the war itself. Though the conflict is usually said to have started by a surprise North Korean attack in June 1950, its origins stretch back much farther—to the division of the peninsula, the collapse of the U.S.–Soviet Joint Commission, and the establishment of rival regimes, each with its superpower patron and each determined to unify the peninsula on its own terms.

Korea remains a potential flashpoint. Like the question of the origins of the war, American claims about P'yŏngyang's nuclear buildup are only partially correct. Washington officials have bought into an oversimplified view of the nuclear issue. By and large, they are oblivious to how U.S. actions, such as wartime saturation bombing of North Korea and stationing nearly a thousand tactical nuclear weapons in South Korea for several decades, have spurred P'yŏngyang's nuclear push. The perverse action–reaction dynamic we helped set in motion continues to be a prime driver of North Korea's nuclear program.

Together, the Robinson and Gayn accounts present a fuller, much more critical view of the occupation than traditional, airbrushed accounts. An abysmal failure by most standards, the occupation was successful mostly in terms of strategic denial—preventing the southern half of the peninsula from falling under Soviet control.

Richard D. Robinson and Mark Gayn: A Whistleblower and a Journalist

Frank Hoffmann

The accounts of Richard D. Robinson (1921–2009) and Mark Gayn (1909–1981) are the most substantial, intense, and critically engaging descriptions of immediate post-liberation southern Korean politics written in English before 1950. Despite differences in literary genre—one an academic essay, the other a journalistic diary—both texts combine razor-sharp political analysis with the authors' personal eyewitness observations. Both examine the early Cold War politics of the U.S. Army Military Government in Korea (USAMGIK, 1945–1948) and the support of right-wing politicians, and both authors were consequently attacked by McCarthy (1908–1957) and his ilk. Robinson's report makes him a whistleblower in today's terms. A slightly edited 1960 version of his second 1947 manuscript (he had burned the original before departing Korea for fear of being court-martialed by the U.S. Army), it is published here for the first time in English. By contrast, Gayn's journalistic diary, published in 1948, quickly became a bestseller and was soon translated into Japanese, Russian, Polish, and later Korean.

Prelude

In May 1980, following the assassination of South Korea's long-term dictator by his own secret service agency director, the country experienced the extremely violent crackdown of the Kwangju Democratic Uprising and, in turn, the installation of a new fascist boogeyman. That same week German TV aired a special report on the events. Looking back, I remember sitting in the living room late at night with my father as we watched the stunningly gruesome footage in complete silence. Upon rising to leave the room, my father, a former paratrooper in the Nazi Luftwaffe at age seventeen, seemed both upset and triumphant. "You reproach me and leave us, only to go study *that* country—*that* country, where paratroopers slaughter their own people like cattle? If that's not fascism, then I don't know what is." He couldn't have been right—yet he was. The Kwangju Massacre revealed just how little had changed since the 1940s, how the framework of suppression, its enforcers, and its tactics of legitimization were still intact.

Two or three months later, by then in Hamburg, I found myself in M. Y. Cho's (1931–2006) office at the Institute of Asian Affairs. A North Korea expert, gifted essayist, and the wittiest of all political analysts focusing on Asia, Dr. Cho kicked me out of his office in anticipation of the arrival of a man he called "a real VIP journalist." That journalist was Mark Gayn, just in from Tokyo, where he had met with South Korean activists and witnesses of the Kwangju Massacre. As I was on my way out, Gayn walked in, wearing a long gray raincoat on this perfectly sunny and cheerful summer day. Immediately detecting my surprise, he turned to me with a hawkish gaze, making a self-deprecating joke about needing to conceal his youthful body from public sight. Moments later I was out the door. Nearly half a century later, I still vividly recall his lively, curious eyes. "That was Gayn's last trip," Dr. Cho told me later. "He's dying of cancer."

Decades on—May 1998—at the opening of an exhibition of North Korean paintings at Harvard's Korea Institute, two strikingly tall men rushed in. Towering over me, one, a now retired historian, introduced the other as Richard D. Robinson: "He was in Korea with the U.S. Army Military Government when some of your paintings here were produced," adding that I *must* read Robinson's fascinating "Betrayal" manuscript that the Harvard-Yenching Library would have. (Only I never got around to reading it until Mark Caprio shared his copy with me a few years ago.) When we met, Dick, as Robinson liked to be called, was already retired from MIT, no longer lived in Massachusetts, and was only visiting Cambridge to handle some family business. Drawn by his continuous interest in postwar Korea, he visited our exhibition after reading about it in a university newsletter. During the brief stroll through the show, he demonstrated an especially keen interest in the earlier paintings, the ones from the 1940s and 1950s. He told me he had been to northern Korea just once and had seen only works of political propaganda, not art. Eager to describe his role in Korea and account for his interest, he explained with a grin that he had served with U.S. military intelligence—"working with the bad guys"—which at the time sounded to me like a mix of remorse and mockery, or perhaps a joke that former soldiers make. I could not say at the time. We took two or three photos in front of a 1948 Soviet-style socialist realist worker portrait by one of the show's most prominent painters, and that was the last I saw of him.

Richard D. Robinson

Richard Dunlop Robinson was twenty years old when the Japanese bombed Pearl Harbor in December 1941 and the United States joined the fight against the Axis Powers. Robinson had grown up in the city of Yakima in Washington state, but at the time he was living in Seattle as a law school student at the University of Washington. In February 1942 he was drafted into the U.S. Army; a few days later, on his 21st birthday, he arrived at Harvard Business School to participate in a quasi-military training program. Although he published short articles in the *Harvard Crimson* during his two years there,[1] Harvard did not exactly impress him. Half a century later he described his stay at the school back then as "uninspired and non-inspirational," a place with "an elitist, holier-than-thou attitude."[2]

At the end of the accelerated war-time program Robinson was awarded a master's degree in business, and after completing officer's training, he was soon assigned to serve as a longshoreman in the Army's Transportation Corps at the Port of New Orleans in Louisiana. However, feeling out of place in this position and wanting "to do something

[1] See the *Harvard Crimson*, February 26, March 5, March 12, and March 19, 1943.
[2] Richard D. Robinson, "A Personal Journey through Time and Space," *Journal of International Business Studies* 25, no. 3 (Fall 1994): 435 (hereafter cited as Robinson, "A Personal Journey").

of greater value—and perhaps, risk,"[3] he somehow managed to arrange a transfer to a program tasked with preparing personnel for the planned military government of Japan once the country surrendered. As part of the program, in addition to economics and administrative training, Robinson studied Japanese at Harvard and finally at the Army Language School in Monterey, California, completing nearly two years of study—with decent success. "At one point I was even classified officially as an 'interpreter,'" he wrote in an autobiographical sketch. "There would have been a lot of surprised—and puzzled—Japanese!"[4]

Like Edward W. Wagner (1924–2001), who had completed similar training and would later establish the Korean Studies program at Harvard, Robinson was briefly stationed in Japan before arriving in Korea on November 21, 1945. He barely spoke Japanese and knew no Korean whatsoever. Only twenty-four years old but serving as an army officer in the U.S. Army Military Government in Korea, he assumed a leading role as deputy director of the small Office of Public Opinion[5] in the Department of Public Information until his discharge on August 8, 1946.[6] Ostensibly, the Office of Public Opinion existed to provide feedback from the Korean populace to USAMGIK leadership on policy and prospective political trajectories. In practice, it also helped enforce USAMGIK's heavy-handed censorship and exert control over the press. The very month Robinson joined the Office, for example, the Korean daily *Maeil sinbo*, a paper highly critical of USAMGIK,[7] was ordered to cease publication on the pretext of a financial investigation the Office had initiated.

---

[3] Ibid.

[4] Ibid., 436.

[5] At times, the Office was also referred to as the Bureau of Public Opinion.

[6] Regarding the work of the Office of Public Opinion and Robinson's role, see the M.A. thesis by Song Chae-gyŏng, "Migunjŏng yŏronjosaro pon Han'gugŭi chŏngch'i-sahoe tongyang (1945–1947)" [Political and social trends in Korea as seen through the U.S. Military Government Opinion Poll (1945–1947)], M.A. thesis (Seoul National University, 2014).

[7] A full month before the arrival of U.S. troops in Korea—on the eve of Korea's liberation from colonial rule by the Soviet 25th Army—the Japanese governor-general of Chōsen, expecting a Soviet takeover, arranged for the newspaper to be run by Korean journalists close to the communists. Once an important wartime propaganda organ for the colonial government, the paper soon became the most significant critical voice against the U.S. Military Government.

Under Robinson's lead, the Office of Public Opinion ran a survey indicating that by late March 1946, only 51 percent of southern Koreans in the Seoul area preferred the U.S. occupation to Japanese colonial rule.[8] Robinson pinned this grim number on USAMGIK's support for far-right politicians—appointed by them to command the brutal Japanese-trained police—and on the military government's dire economic policies, particularly the botched distribution of food. Another major cause of discontent was trusteeship itself, widely perceived as just another form of colonial occupation. Americans and Soviets alike—including Robinson—considered trusteeship a necessary measure for a newly liberated but politically and economically fractured society. Decades later, in a long interview with Korean TV journalist Kim Hwan-gyun—partially aired on KBS in January 2004 (see fig. 5) and quoted at length in Kim's essay "Why *Betrayal of a Nation* Is Banned in the United States"—Robinson distanced himself from that view. Drawing a parallel to the unwarranted U.S. invasion of Iraq then under way, he remarked: "Right now the Iraq War is happening and anyone who criticizes it is considered unpatriotic."[9] His critique underscores how thoroughly the U.S. has entrenched neocolonial practices since 1945, forging alliances with military juntas and fascist dictators to sustain its imperialist hegemony. Officials consistently justify covert and military interventions as democratization efforts, rebranding them since the Cold War's declared end as "humanitarian interventions"—Bricmont's *Impérialisme humanitaire*. But U.S.-led invasions continue to be followed by failed nation-building efforts. In August 2021, we thus watched panicked Americans and their allies flee Afghanistan—long dubbed the "Graveyard of Empires," where the Soviets had already been defeated in the 1980s. All too predictably, the subsequent U.S. venture to forge a client state had also failed, while critics were muzzled and whistleblowers like Chelsea Manning (b. 1987) court-martialed. After two decades of spin and propaganda, one of those responsible, the "War Czar" himself, the former Assistant to the President and Deputy National Security Advisor for Iraq and Afghanistan,

[8] See Robinson, "A Personal Journey," 436. In his "Betrayal," 132, he has it as 52%.

[9] Richard D. Robinson, quoted in Kim Hwan-gyun, *Pigŭgŭn haengjinŭrobut'ŏ sijak toenda: tak'yument'ŏrisŭt'ŭ Kim Hwan-gyunŭn malhanda* [A tragedy begins with a march: Documentarian Kim Hwan-gyun speaks] (Koyang: Tŭllin Ach'im, 2004), 81 (hereafter cited as Kim, *Pigŭgŭn haengjinŭrobut'ŏ sijak toenda*).

confessed to the *New York Times*: "We were devoid of a fundamental understanding of Afghanistan—we didn't know what we were doing. [...] We didn't have the foggiest notion of what we were undertaking."[10] Tellingly, even the opium-and-heroin trade to the West that flourished through the U.S. occupation fell off only after the Taliban's return.

Read against this neocolonial playbook—ally strongmen, manage optics, sideline critics—Robinson later recounted that his survey of USAMGIK's popularity resulted in his 1946 discharge. A read-through of his report suggests it may have been his political analyses—and not the unfavorable data—that raised the eyebrows of USAMGIK leaders such as Archibald V. Arnold (1889–1973), military governor of southern Korea. According to the 1st lieutenant (now 25 years old), the "reported rising public dissatisfaction with Military Government"[11] could not be reversed, "unless the Military Government follows these general policies"[12]—the lieutenant's very own general policies, that is. Robinson had written the piece at a time when a wide range of political options and solutions still seemed viable, two days before the Joint Soviet–American Commission began its work and before USAMGIK's clampdown of the left. Point three of Robinson's "general policies" instructed USAMGIK to convince Koreans that America's interest in Korea was "solely that of seeing it become a free, democratic, enlightened nation, with whatever economic system it sees fit to choose, *whether it be capitalism, socialism, or communism*. Why? Because it is our own interest as well as that of the Korean people."[13] John R. Hodge (1893–1963) himself, commander of all U.S. forces in Korea, and a man who even asserted the need to personally censor a military propaganda paper like *Stars and Stripes*,[14] lacked the slightest grasp of such a liberal agenda (although he

---

[10] Douglas Lute (b. 1952), quoted in the *New York Times*, December 9, 2019.

[11] Richard D. Robinson, "Suggested MG Public Relations Policy" (March 18, 1946), reprinted in *Migunjŏnggi chŏngbo charyojip: Simin soyo, yŏron chosa pogosŏ, 1945.9–1948.6* [Collection of intelligence materials from the U.S. Military Government period: Reports on civil unrest and opinion polls, September 1945–June 1948], vol. 2, comp. Hallim Taehakkyo, Asia Munhwa Yŏn'guso (Ch'unch'ŏn: Hallim Taehakkyo, Asia Munhwa Yŏn'guso, 1995), 407.

[12] Ibid., 410.

[13] Ibid., 409.

[14] See "John R. Hodge to W. J. Niedergruen" (June 1, 1948), reprinted in *Migun-*

reportedly respected some of Robinson's other work). But Robinson did not stop there. As Chŏng Yong-uk (aka Chung Yong Wook), a historian at Seoul National University, elucidated in his substantive essay addressing Robinson's work and historiographic approach: "By May 1946, his policy proposals became more concrete. In his 'Recommendations' report, Robinson highlighted the confusion and inefficiency of military government policy by dividing the problem into four areas: politics (coping with the far-right and the far-left), the police, rice distribution, and land reform, and he came up with specific corrective measures for each area." When his superiors failed to react to his policy recommendations, "Robinson again raised the issues of police brutality and the role of the police in Korean politics to USAMGIK leadership with renewed urgency in his 'July Report.'"[15]

Back in Washington, a few liberal-minded policymakers in the State Department, including John Carter Vincent (1900–1972) who headed the State Department's Office of Far Eastern Affairs, had already cautioned General Hodge in Korea not "to give any Korean group, such as the Kim Koo [Kim Ku, 1876–1949] Group arriving from Chungking [Chongqing, China], or any Korean individual, such as Dr. Rhee [Yi Sŭng-man, aka Syngman Rhee, in office 1948–1960], the impression that we were supporting such a group or individual as against any other Koreans."[16] As shown in the exchanges between the State and War Departments and the generals and their staff in Tokyo and Seoul,[17] all

---

jŏnggi chŏngbo charyojip: Haji (John R. Hodge) munsŏjip, 1945.6–1948.8 [Collection of intelligence materials from the U.S. Military Government period: Hodge (John R. Hodge) Document Collection, June 1945–August 1948], vol. 2, comp. Hallim Taehakkyo, Asia Munhwa Yŏn'guso (Ch'unch'ŏn: Hallim Taehakkyo, Asia Munhwa Yŏn'guso, 1995), 518. See also Mark Gayn, "Japan Diary: Korea," in this volume, 406.

[15] Chŏng Yong-uk, "Rich'adŭ Robinsŭnŭi Han'guk hyŏndaesa ihae" [Richard Robinson's understanding of contemporary Korean history], in *Haeoe hakcha Han'guk hyŏndaesa yŏn'gu punsŏk*, vol. 2, ed. Han'guk Chŏngsinmunhwa Yŏn'guwŏn (Seoul: Paeksan Sŏdang, 1999), 18 (hereafter cited as Chŏng Yong-uk, "Rich'adŭ Robinsŭnŭi Han'guk hyŏndaesa ihae").

[16] [John Carter Vincent], "Memorandum by the Director of the Office of Far Eastern Affairs (Vincent) to Colonel Russell L. Vittrup, War Department" (November 7, 1945), in *Foreign Relations of the United States: Diplomatic Papers 1945*, comp. United States Department of State, vol. VI, *The British Commonwealth, The Far East* (Washington, DC: Government Printing Office, 1969), 1114.

[17] Bruce Cumings provides an extensive discussion of these exchanges; see Bruce

such advice on building a middle-of-the-road democratic society was either rejected or plainly ignored. As a prominent example, in the circumstances surrounding Syngman Rhee's return from the U.S. to Korea and USAMGIK's support for him, Bruce Cumings has pointed out that "Hodge, MacArthur, Goodfellow, and Rhee conspired against established State Department policy."[18] The justification for such deviation from State Department policies was the inflated "threat of communism," or, in Cumings' terms, "a classic expression of 'nationalist' containment policy" towards the Soviets that "abjured more sophisticated policies designed to win Soviet adherence."[19] Just a few years later, the early Cold War policies practiced in Korea—so pointedly described by Robinson and Gayn—had become the new normal. The aforementioned John Carter Vincent, for example, was wrongly accused by communist witch-hunter Joseph McCarthy of being a member of the Communist Party and consequently forced to resign from the State Department.

Robinson was not the only one within USAMGIK pushing for fairer, more democratic structural change in Korea. Leonard M. Bertsch (1910–1976), a lawyer and Harvard Law School graduate whom Robinson highly respected, dove headfirst into the country's culture and politics and sought to bring together right and left in Korean politics. That explains why Robinson included Bertsch's article as a form of afterword in the last chapter of his "Betrayal" manuscript.[20] Because Bertsch was isolated as a liberal within the reactionary U.S. Military Government, his efforts had already begun to waver by the fall of 1946 and completely collapsed with the assassination of Yŏ Un-hyŏng (aka Lyuh Woon Hyung, 1886–1947) on July 19, 1947. Then just a 1st lieutenant like Robinson, Bertsch was summarily "disposed of" just as

---

Cumings, *The Origins of the Korea War: Liberation and the Emergence of Separate Regimes, 1945–1947* (Princeton: Princeton University Press, 1981), 183–87, 509–10 (hereafter cited as Cumings, *The Origins of the Korea War*).

[18] Ibid., 189.

[19] Ibid., 186.

[20] Chapter X was added in August 1958 as part of some modest manuscript revisions. (Additionally, a "Preface," dated January 1960, was later included to supplement the brief "Introduction" from the fall of 1947.) Bertsch and Robinson, however, also had significant disagreements, such as over the issue of Japanese repatriation. Bertsch believed it was executed far too rapidly, despite taking half a year to complete.

Robinson.[21] As Bruce Cumings sagaciously summarizes the situation, future South Korean president Syngman Rhee "could wait out Leonard Bertsch's studied attempt throughout the summer and fall of 1946 to bring Left and Right together in the middle. The middle could not hold, of course; but within the Occupation and the State Department, neither could the American liberal, anti-Rhee elements. Such people, whether in Korea or elsewhere, ran the risk throughout the postwar period of being accused of playing into the hands of the communists."[22]

Although Robinson was perceived to be stepping over the line with his "Opinion Poll" report and was then discharged from the Office of Public Opinion on August 8, 1946, albeit not before being promoted to captain, he was clearly wanted elsewhere. He immediately started to work for the so-called Historical Section of military intelligence at the XXIV Corps headquarters. Now a civilian employee of the War Department, he worked as a military historian, a position that, he later recounted, alerted him to the ins and outs of the U.S. Military Government's machinations. As he put it, "In my capacity, which gave me access to top-secret political/economic analyses of events in South Korea and the opportunity to meet and interview key Korean actors, I had much reason to note the deliberate falsification of reports regarding the impact of the U.S. occupation upon South Korea." He also noted how provocations from the south, initiated by right-wing politicians such as Syngman Rhee and Kim Ku, that had caused "incidents contributing to the outbreak of the Korean War [1950–1953] in 1950 were omitted from the official account of the U.S. occupation."[23]

Robinson was concerned and alarmed. Witnessing his internal attempts to change the minds of higher-ranking USAMGIK officers being either ignored or harshly rejected—and realizing that the American public had been intentionally misled—he did what seemed the moral imperative: he went public. *The Nation*, New York's liberal weekly, was one of the very few American periodicals that had already published highly critical articles on the situation in Korea. In spring 1947, the

---

[21] See Gregory Henderson, *Korea: The Politics of the Vortex* (Cambridge: Harvard University Press, 1968), 419, footnote 73 (hereafter cited as Henderson, *Korea: The Politics of the Vortex*).

[22] Cumings, *The Origins of the Korea War*, 431–32.

[23] Robinson, "A Personal Journey," 436–37.

Nation ran Robinson's startling exposé in its March 1 issue—a date symbolic of Korea's anti-colonial struggle. It was entitled "Korea: An American Tragedy."[24] Other critical assessments had also appeared elsewhere, including a chapter on Korea in *No Peace for Asia*, a 1947 book by Harold R. Isaacs (1910–1986), which characterized the U.S. Army Military Government in Korea as "bumbling and inefficient" with "no policy about anything"—a "military government, under a military governor general, supported by an army of occupation" that looked to Koreans "like anything but 'liberation.' [...] This was not freedom nor did it look like any prelude to freedom. What Koreans wanted was a government of their own."[25] But Robinson's article, by sharp contrast, identified its author as "a member of the American occupation forces" and disclosed classified information. This made Robinson what today we would call a whistleblower. From the U.S. military's perspective, the publication of Robinson's piece in the *Nation* was considered an act of treason. Among other things, the article disclosed the brutal rape of three Korean women by four U.S. soldiers,[26] General Hodge's policy to "maintain in office notorious Japanese collaborators" such as the directors of the Korean police force, and, as a particular eyesore for USAMGIK leadership, all of the details about Rhee's planned coup d'état (including ousting Hodge), becoming the leader of southern

---

[24] Will Hamlin [pseud.], "Korea: An American Tragedy," *Nation* 164, no. 9 (March 1, 1947): 245–47.

[25] Harold R. Isaacs, *No Peace for Asia* (New York: Macmillan, 1947), 96. Isaacs wrote for *Newsweek* and was a former socialist and Trotskyist who had lived in China and Southeast Asia for many years. He was one of a small group of American journalists whom Robinson had guided through Korea for USAMGIK. Isaacs later joined MIT's political science faculty, while Robinson joined its business school.

[26] The Korean public had already been informed about the barbaric rape—one of the women had held her infant as she was being raped—that occurred on board a train from Mokp'o to Taejŏn on the night of January 7, 1947. A Korean journalist had directly confronted General Hodge regarding the incident during a press conference. Coming so soon after the Moscow Conference, the announcement of the trusteeship, and protests by Koreans across the political spectrum, USAMGIK tried desperately to censor further reporting and to keep such negative developments from being reported back home in the United States. See *Haebang chikhu chŏngch'i sahoesa charyojip, 7: Chuhan Migun pangch'ŏptae charyojip (2)* [Collection of political and social materials from the immediate post-liberation period, vol. 7: USAFIK Counter Intelligence Corps resource collection (2)], comp. Chŏng Yong-uk (Seoul: Tarakpang, 1994), 217–22.

Korea, proclaiming a separate South Korean state, and finally bringing North Korea under his rule by any means necessary, even by instigating a war between the United States and the Soviet Union.

Soon enough, Robinson realized that his choice of "Will Hamlin" as his *nom de plume* for the article was a mistake. "Will" was the name of his father, William D. Robinson (1873–1965), and "Hamlin" was the name of his older brother as well as his mother's middle name. His choice of pseudonym is iconic, for it directly connects his act of insubordination to the very core of his ethical upbringing.

(Fig. 1) The Robinsons in 1936: William D. Robinson, Richard, Marion H. Robinson, and oldest son Hamlin.

(Fig. 2) Robinson with Soviet soldiers at the 38th parallel, winter 1945/46.

There is no question that the underlying moral impetus behind Robinson's *Nation* article and his later attempts to publish "Betrayal of a Nation" was his ethical understanding of society, coupled with his own presumption of taking moral action therein. His exchange of letters with his father showcases his willingness to assume such a high personal risk. Indeed, the very last book that Robinson ever co-authored and co-edited was a volume of his father's writings and sermons.[27] His father, the minister of a Congregational church in Washington state, embodied the roles of both an idealist and a pragmatist. An outspoken critic and progressive thinker, he was not restrained by Christian theology. According to his son, he "did not really believe that any religion or belief system embodied an exclusive *truth*."[28] In his writings, he often focused on ethical behavior and social responsibility in business—themes his son Richard would later explore in academia. Reverend Robinson also did not shy away from political controversies. In a bold critique from 1913, he called out Fordist industrialists, proclaiming, "It is not enough any longer that we insist that employers as a class shall be honest and decent, or even that they shall institute lunch rooms and model tenements for their employees. [...] The time has come when those in control of business should give their minds and energies to the working out of an economic system which will establish more just conditions."[29] As an antidote, he advocated for "inaugurating a system of social control that shall be just and fair."[30]

Days before World War II (1939–1945) ended in Europe, Robinson's father wrote his son a letter criticizing the early signs of the emerging Cold War and questioning the U.S. hypocrisy and self-righteousness in viewing other cultures and political systems: "People say that [...] 'Russia will not cooperate with us.' Isn't that a curious statement? Isn't it just as true to say that we will not cooperate with Russia? We have such an easy way of assuming that what we think, or want, is the absolute standard of rightness."[31] Later, he wrote to his son, then in Korea: "In politics, we are lagging way behind. [...] We are afraid of losing whatever privileged position we may have or think we have."[32] In

---

[27] See Richard Dunlop Robinson and Patricia Elliott Swanson, eds., *In the Process of Creation: The Spiritual Philosophy of Dr. William Dunlop Robinson, 1873–1965* (Gig Harbor: Hamlin Publications, 2004) (hereafter cited as Robinson and Swanson, eds., *In the Process of Creation*).

[28] Ibid., 14

[29] W. Dunlop Robinson, *An Idealist at Large* (Boston, New York, and Chicago: Pilgrim Press, 1913), 22–23.

[30] Ibid., 48.

[31] Letter by William D. Robinson to his son Richard, May 1, 1945, in Robinson and Swanson, eds., *In the Process of Creation*, 20.

[32] Letter by William D. Robinson to his son Richard, February 11, 1946, in Robinson and Swanson, eds., *In the Process of Creation*, 22.

another letter, following the outbreak of the Korean War four years later, his father wrote to Richard, by then in Turkey, "I wonder if the people of Korea would be much worse off under communism, provided it were their own communism. Is that treason?"[33]

Just weeks after the publication of Robinson's *Nation* article, his own colleagues in military intelligence and the FBI were onto him. As a military historian Robinson had access to all sorts of intelligence reports and could thus follow up on any attempts to uncover the identity of the article's author. "There were several investigations," his widow Carol told me. "And in one of these investigations on his piece in the *Nation* he himself was part of the group investigating that case. So, he had to investigate himself. Dick found that hilarious!"[34] Back home in the United States, the War Department's Intelligence Division also continued its investigation. After the *Nation*'s managing editor J. King Gordon (1900–1989) failed to divulge anything about "the case" during an interview with an agent in the Intelligence Division, one of Gordon's colleagues was approached and urged to get the requisite information. The Intelligence Division's Security Group finally discovered that it was Richard's brother, Hamlin Robinson (1915–1982), who had mailed a draft of the article to the *Nation*. Although the investigation was formally never "conclusive," by late spring 1947, Richard D. Robinson was then—unsurprisingly—labeled un-American and a communist sympathizer by the Army.[35]

Robinson, though, was fundamentally just a dedicated researcher committed to his liberal values and ethical principles. His social democratic ideals were considered mainstream in many parts of the world. Yet, even the latest edition of the U.S. *Merriam-Webster Dictionary* still lists terms such as "commie," "communist," "Bolshevik," "Stalinist," and "extremist" as synonyms for "social democrat," underscoring the deeply

---

[33] Letter by William D. Robinson to his son Richard, July 14, 1950, in Robinson and Swanson, eds., *In the Process of Creation*, 26.

[34] Carol A. Robinson in a conversation with Frank Hoffmann, September 27, 2020.

[35] See "Identification of 'Will Hamlin,'" RG 319, Army Intelligence Project Decimal File, 1946–1948, Box 243, National Archives and Records Administration. For summaries on the investigation, see Chŏng Yong-uk, "Rich'adŭ Robinsŭnŭi Han'guk hyŏndaesa ihae," 23–26; and Chŏng Yong-uk, *Migunjŏng charyo yŏn'gu* [Research on U.S. Military Government Source Materials] (Seoul: Sŏnin, 2003), 167–69 (hereafter cited as Chŏng Yong-uk, *Migunjŏng charyo yŏn'gu*).

Robinson as Textbook Case of McCarthyism

Box 243 of group RG 319 at NARA also contains several attachments, primarily copies of letters that led to the second of several investigations mentioned by Carol A. Robinson. A second set of copies of partially identical documents at the Hoover Institution Library & Archives (Box 149, Alfred Kohlberg Papers) complements this collection. These now declassified files constitute a textbook case of McCarthyism.

Richard D. Robinson's letter in reply to Alfred Kohlberg (April 1, 1947):

"I can truthfully say that the reports of the IPR on this part of the world have been notable for their accuracy, your opinion to the contrary notwithstanding. I would like to add that Communist witch hunts such as the one you are now conducting are driving a good portion of the world under the shadow of Soviet Communism. The Far East is the horrible example. A constructive progressive democracy is the only answer. Your answer of suppression has been disproved historically so many times that I refuse to admit its validity."

Alfred Kohlberg's second letter to Richard D. Robinson (April 10, 1947):

"[...] that is the position taken by Mr. Henry Wallace [1888–1965] [...]. I think Mr. Wallace has in mind that a progressive democracy is the type now prevalent in Eastern Europe, Northern Korea and Communist China."

Alfred Kohlberg's letter to Harold J. Noble (same day, April 10, 1947):

"I have never heard of this Mr Robinson previously, but I fear if his interpretation of the history of our occupation of Korea is published, it may not be exactly pro-American. Possibly you would like to forward this to GHQ in Tokyo."

Harold J. Noble's letter to General John R. Hodge (April 14, 1947):

"No reasonable man could charge Robinson with Communist affiliation for refusal to believe Kohlberg's charges, or for refusing to give him his proxy. But a reading of his letter would raise these questions: (1) does the man see events in Korea with any clarity? (2) doesn't his inability to recognize IPR slant on Far Eastern Reporting rasie [*sic*] doubt as to his objectivity as an historian? (3) does not the intemperance of his language raise a reasonable doubt as to his sympathy with the policies and program of the American authorities in Korea? (4) and if the answers to 1, 2, and 3 are 'yes' shouldn't he be investigated for security reasons?"

Surveillance report on Richard D. Robinson by CIC Special Agent William F. Walter (May 31, 1947):

"Investigation was initiated [...]. SUBJECT [...] is using his position to aid, and abett [*sic*] interests, whose concern, and functions, are inimical to the successful completion of the United States Forces efforts of establishing a sound, and stable Government in Korea. [...] SUBJECT has many interests outside duty hours [...]. SUBJECT has also attended a party given on grounds of the Russian Consulate [...]. SUBJECT is usually invited or sponsored through his acquaintance with Theodore Pick [...]. SUBJECT, and his wife have been taking lessons in Russian language from one Madame Yakovleva [...]. Madame Yakovleva is known to be a Communist. [...] SUBJECT is seen often with his wife in the company of various enlisted personnel, driving about the city of Seoul. [...] Investigation is being initiated in United States, to determine exactly the status of SUBJECT is [*sic*] connection with the Institute of Pacific Relations [...]."

These sources show that **Alfred Kohlberg** (1887–1960)—to many "the man behind McCarthy"—had waged a fierce smear campaign against the anti-colonial Institute of Pacific Relations (IPR), a leading international NGO with broad liberal and left-wing participation, and its journal, *Pacific Affairs* (cf. Caprio, 459). Kohlberg was a wealthy New York textile importer, a militant anti-communist, and the architect of the pro–Chiang Kai-shek China Lobby. As discussed later in the section on Mark Gayn (pp. 41–44), he also pressed for a new investigation into the Amerasia case—the journal's editorial staff overlapped with the IPR's under one roof. Following his lead, Joseph McCarthy turned the Amerasia affair into his own political showcase. **Robinson**, then an IPR member, had rejected Kohlberg's "Communist witch hunts," calling instead for a "constructive progressive democracy" in Korea. Stung by the young U.S. military government historian's forthright defense of democratic reform in Korea, Kohlberg forwarded the exchange to **Harold J. Noble** (1903–1953), the ultraconservative son of a Korea missionary, then serving as an adviser to USAMGIK. General John R. Hodge promptly took the bait and ordered Counter Intelligence Corps special agent **William F. Walter** (1913?–2001?) to investigate Robinson—an inquiry that, as Walter's report shows, quickly ballooned into a hunt for even the faintest trace of subversion. The campaign persisted: on September 30, 1953, at the height of the McCarthy era, Kohlberg again petitioned the U.S. Department of Defense, branding Robinson "incompetent" and appending the same 1947 correspondence.

entrenched irrationality of a continuing Cold War-era doctrine of military interventionism. "A deep, abiding, and often unexamined 'consensus,'" as Cumings puts it, "is so rooted in the United States that it is not a matter for conscious reflection, and therefore Americans conceive of themselves as people without ideology."[36] This is by design, Chomsky posits, finding its foundation in *manufactured consent*,[37] skillfully propagated by the American mass media as system-supportive doctrine—aptly explained by the Gramscian hegemonic framework: coercion, *internally* operating through manufactured consent and *externally* through force.

By April 1947, Robinson had been joined by his wife. The military's Counter Intelligence Corps (Army CIC)[38] then assigned a special agent named William F. Walter to monitor him as well as Theodore L. Pick (1912–?), a Paris-born, left-leaning U.S. Army officer who was acquainted with the couple. Their activities and social interactions were under round-the-clock surveillance.[39] Friends of the Robinsons were also subjected to background checks and interrogations. As shown in one of the reports NARA declassified for me in 2021 (fig. 3), the interest of military

---

[36] Bruce Cumings, *Parallax Visions: Making Sense of American–East Asian Relations at the End of the Century* (Durham and London: Duke University Press, 1999), 4.

[37] See Edward S. Herman and Noam Chomsky, *Manufacturing Consent: The Political Economy of the Mass Media* (New York: Pantheon Books, 1988).

[38] On the CIC's role as an exclusive intelligence service for right-wing militaries, see Chŏng Yong-uk's detailed article, "Haebang chikhu Chuhan Migun pangch'ŏptaeŭi chojik ch'egyewa hwaldong" [Organization and activities of the USAFIK Counter Intelligence Corps in the immediate post-liberation period], *Han'guk saron* 53 (June 2007): 443–84. The CIC was indeed such a handy tool for an authoritarian government that, upon the announcement of its withdrawal from Korea in 1948, Syngman Rhee hired American CIC personnel to organize his own "Korean Research Bureau" modeled on the CIC (see ibid., 460–62).

[39] See the two agent reports by Wm. Walter [William F. Walter], "Subject: Robinson, Richard D. (WDC) Chief Historian, XXIV Corps, APO 235" (May 30 and May 31, 1947), RG 319, Army - Intelligence Project Decimal Files, 1946–1948, Box 243, Identification of 'Will Hamlin,' National Archives and Records Administration. In several of his otherwise very accurate studies, Chŏng Yong-uk misreads the abbreviation "Wm." (for William) as "Wynn" and thus misidentifies the CIC agent. CIC did not have a special agent named Wynn Walter. William F. Walter, on the other hand, is listed as a CIC agent in Korea in "Appendix 1: Personnel of the 971st CIC Detachment," reprinted in *Haebang chikhu chŏngch'i sahoesa charyojip*, 10: *Chuhan Migun pangch'ŏptae charyojip* (5) [Collection of political and social materials from the immediate post-liberation period, vol. 10: USAFIK Counter Intelligence Corps resource collection (5)], comp. Chŏng Yong-uk (Seoul: Tarakpang, 1994), 133.

CONFIDENTIAL

CSGID/Secu... Grp
Maj Michael/ml/73917

MID 201

6 January 1948

SUBJECT: Richard D. Robinson

TO: Commanding General
Korean Base Command
APO 901, c/o Postmaster
San Francisco, California
Attention: A C of S, G-2

1. Reference is made to letter Headquarters, U. S. Army Forces, Korea, CIC Headquarters, APO 235, File No. CIC-K-543, dated 10 June 1947, Subject: "Hamlin, Will," which stated that Richard D. Robinson was under investigation, and requested that certain leads be investigated in the Zone of Interior. The result of the Zone of Interior investigation was furnished on 9 September 1947 by this Headquarters to your Headquarters by 3rd Indorsement to above letter.

2. The attached letter was received from a confidential source who believes Robinson was apprehended on arrival at Istanbul, because of his unauthorized route out of Kofea. It is furnished for your information and any action deemed appropriate. Request report of any action taken be furnished Security Group, Intelligence Division, General Staff, United States Army.

FOR THE DIRECTOR OF INTELLIGENCE:

1 Incl
Cpy ltr fr Richard D.
Robinson dtd 10 Aug 47

L. R. FORNEY
Colonel, GSC
Chief, Security Group

ORIS E. McGREGOR, JR.
Major, GSC
Operations Branch
Security Group

For the Record:
Original copy of inclosure filed under Roberts, Rankin IV.

MAILED I.D., WDGS 9 JAN 1948

DECLASSIFIED
Authority NND 775030
By [illegible] NARA Date 12/9/21

RECORD SECTION COPY

(Fig. 3) Robinson under continued scrutiny by the Army, even after leaving Korea for Turkey. Report by Chief of Military Intelligence Division L. R. Forney to Commanding General, Korean Base Command, APO 901, "Richard D. Robinson," January 6, 1948.

intelligence continued even after their move to Turkey.[40] As Jeremy Kuzmarov poignantly argued, the surveillance and harassment carried out by the U.S. Army and the FBI against the Robinsons and their friends was "the military's attempt to silence internal critics."[41]

In July 1947, Robinson ended his tenure as a military historian. More precisely, when his contract with USAMGIK expired on July 15, he simply let it lapse. He subsequently fled Korea with his wife.[42] While their escape may not have been as dramatic as Edward Snowden's (b. 1983) decades later, there are clear parallels. In 2004, Robinson himself elaborated : "Because I was only twenty-six years old, my fear was somewhat tempered. Yet, I felt a sense of crisis. I could be arrested or even jailed for my actions. [...] Regardless, I knew I had to leave Korea soon. [It was all] because I opposed the policies of the U.S. Military Government. I wouldn't describe it as coercion, but the threats were real enough that I felt compelled to leave Korea."[43]

The Robinsons finally boarded a ship to Turkey, the SS *Flying Enterprise*. At a stopover in Kobe, Japan, the U.S. Army tried to arrest Richard, but the skipper refused to hand him over.[44] In a September 1947 summary report titled "Soviet Union Espionage Activities," Colonel John N. Robinson (1893–1978), a World War I West Point graduate of no relation to Richard D. Robinson who had assumed a leading role in Korea as chief of staff of the XXIV Corps at the time, boasted in militaristic jargon how his office "has taken aggressive [...] action to *eliminate* all Americans from *contamination* [italics mine] by

[40] The CIC document from January 1948 (fig. 3) that demonstrates the ongoing surveillance of the couple and USAMGIK's interest in Robinson, was routed through the Presidio in San Francisco to later reach the CIC in Korea: Chief of MID L.R. Forney to Commanding General, Korean Base Command, APO 901, "Richard D. Robinson" (January 6, 1948), RG 319, Army - Intelligence Project Decimal Files, 1946–1948, Box 243, Identification of 'Will Hamlin,' National Archives and Records Administration.

[41] Jeremy Kuzmarov, *Modernizing Repression: Police Training and Nation-Building in the American Century* (Amherst and Boston: University of Massachusetts Press, 2012), 85.

[42] Kermit, his son, told me that this is exactly how his father described their rather adventurous run from the U.S. military to his children—as a flight. (Phone conversation between Kermit H. Robinson and Frank Hoffmann, September 3, 2020.)

[43] Richard D. Robinson, quoted in Kim, *Pigŭgŭn baengjinŭrobut'ŏ sijak toenda*, 80.

[44] See Robinson, "A Personal Journey," 437–38.

the Russians."[45] Part of the colonel's information in his short account was, ironically, derived from Richard Robinson's earlier report on the very same subject.[46] Adding insult to injury—and not without a touch of dark comedy—the Robinsons found themselves on the colonel's "watchlist" of suspected spies, situated right between an Orthodox Russian priest and a high-ranking officer of the Soviet secret police: "ROBINSON, Richard and wife – On good terms with Russians. (Now en route St. Roberts College, Constantinople)."[47]

Robinson and his wife stayed at the Bosporus for nearly a decade before returning to the United States in 1956.[48] Initially, they lived in an Istanbul slum,[49] surviving for a while on various part-time teaching jobs. Later, Richard received a fellowship from the Institute of Current World Affairs (ICWA) to live in Ankara and other cities. This allowed him to analyze and write about human rights, politics, and economics in Turkey and adjacent areas. During that time, he also received a scholarship to study at SOAS in London for nine months. As a result, he returned to the United States as a foremost scholar on politics and economics in Turkish and Middle Eastern affairs. After teaching some courses at Harvard, he eventually became a professor of International

---

[45] Colonel John N. Robinson, "Soviet Union Espionage Activities" (September 19, 1947), RG 319, Office of the Chief of Military History, Investigative Records Repository, Russian Activities in Korea, Box 104, Case ZF016117, National Archives and Records Administration, [2] (hereafter cited as John N. Robinson, "Soviet Union Espionage Activities").

[46] See R[ichard] D. Robinson, "Soviet-Communists-Inspired Espionage in South Korea" (July 1947), RG 332, USAFIK, XXIV Corps, G-2, Historical Section, Box 77, U.S.–U.S.S.R.: The Communist, the Russians, and the American thru Rightist Plots & Miscellaneous Politics, 1946–1947, National Archives and Records Administration.

[47] John N. Robinson, "Soviet Union Espionage Activities," attached "Watchlist," [2].

[48] He and his family, however, had been able to visit the U.S. for his lectures at Harvard Business School as early as October 1952. See Robinson's academic CV: "Robinson, Richard Dunlop," in *Who's Who in International Business Education and Research*, eds. William Shepherd, Iyanatul Islam, and Sankaran Raghunathan (Cheltenham and Northampton: Edward Elgar, 1999), 326–29; Robinson, "A Personal Journey," 442–43; "SS *Exeter*, List of in-bound passengers arriving in Boston, October 13, 1952," in Massachusetts, U.S., Arriving Passenger and Crew Lists, 1820–1963, Roll A3604, Arriving at Boston, MA, 1944–1954, ALL 18, National Archives and Records Administration.

[49] See Robinson, "A Personal Journey," 439.

Management at MIT's Sloan School of Management. Some of his books, including *The First Turkish Republic* (1963) and *International Business Management* (1973, rev. ed. 1978), even became standard reference works.

The original "Betrayal" manuscript, completed in mid-1947, did not survive Robinson's departure from Korea. Fearing apprehension before boarding, he burned it and rewrote the work during the three-month sea voyage to Turkey "from notes, a journal, and memory. The title it bore was *Betrayal of a Nation*."[50] As he noted in the Introduction, the original typescript—now destroyed—had been "several times the length of the present volume."[51] Under McCarthy-era pressures, he delayed seeking publication for years. In 1958 he finally submitted the manuscript to Arlington Books, a nascent nonprofit publishing house in Cambridge, Massachusetts; its editor in chief expressed strong interest and began the editorial process.[52] But publishers were not immune to political pressures either, and—potentially due to official censorship—the project was abruptly halted. Five years later, trusting the liberal spirit of the Kennedy years, Robinson submitted the manuscript to Harvard University Press, which summarily rejected it on the grounds that "it is essentially unpublishable, or it is still too early to publish such an account."[53] In the end, a scholar who would go on to publish roughly twenty academic books saw his candid firsthand account of the U.S. military blocked by the narrow confines of Cold War orthodoxy.

There seem to have been at least two, if not three, versions of the revised "Betrayal" manuscript. Gregory Henderson (1922–1988) may have been the first to extensively reference Robinson's work in his groundbreaking 1968 study *Korea: The Politics of the Vortex*.[54] (Both men were at Harvard at the time and knew each other well.) Henderson's

---

[50] Ibid., 438.

[51] Robinson, "Betrayal of a Nation," in this volume, 68.

[52] Three letters, one with concrete suggestions for revisions by Arlington Books editor in chief Thomas A. Bledsoe to senior editor William R. Polk, and two letters by Bledsoe to Richard D. Robinson, dated August 11 and 13, 1958, in the personal archive of Carol A. Robinson, prove that the editing process had been initiated.

[53] Letter by Harvard University Press associate director Mark Carroll to Richard D. Robinson, Cambridge, May 8, 1963, personal collection of Carol A. Robinson.

[54] See Henderson, *Korea: The Politics of the Vortex*, XII, 408, 413, 416–22, 424, 449, 450, and 456.

references do not match the pagination of the 1960 manuscript, the source text used in this volume. Henderson may have used Robinson's first rewrite, as he explicitly identifies 1947 as the year the manuscript was written. In 1973, toward the end of the Vietnam War, when the U.S. government and military were under public scrutiny for their deception and spread of misinformation, at a time when interest in the history of U.S. engagement overseas was hotly debated in the press and at colleges and universities worldwide, Mark J. Scher also extensively referred to and even quoted Robinson in a biting article titled "U.S. Policy in Korea 1945–1948."[55] Bruce Cumings also employed the "Betrayal" manuscript for his 1975 dissertation, which was later to be reworked into the first volume of his influential *Origins of the Korean War*. So did Joungwon Kim for his monograph *Divided Korea*,[56] published by Harvard University Press. That same year, John Merrill, who authored the foreword to this volume, drew from the work for his own important research and, fortunately, arranged for a copy of the manuscript to be kept at the Harvard-Yenching Library.[57] From its perch on the shelf there, it found its way to a wider but more or less exclusive readership of historians and Korean studies specialists interested in post-liberation Korea.

In 1988, amid the rise of the South Korean pro-democracy movement, Robinson's book manuscript was finally published—not in its original English but as an unauthorized Korean translation titled *Migugŭi paeban: Migunjŏnggwa Namjosŏn* (America's betrayal: The U.S. Military Government and southern Korea)[58] (see fig. 4).

---

[55] See Mark J. Scher, "U.S. Policy in Korea 1945–1948: A Neo-Colonial Model Takes Shape," *Bulletin of Concerned Asian Scholars* 5, no. 4 (December 1973): 17–27.

[56] Joungwon Alexander Kim, *Divided Korea: The Politics of Development, 1945–1972* (Cambridge: East Asian Research Center, Harvard University, 1975).

[57] See John R. Merrill's letter to Richard D. Robinson (Assonet, April 19, 1975), attached to Richard D. Robinson, "Betrayal of a Nation," unpublished manuscript, 1960, Harvard-Yenching Library, Harvard University.

[58] Rich'adŭ D. Robinsŭn, *Migugŭi paeban: Migunjŏnggwa Namjosŏn* [America's betrayal: The U.S. Military Government and southern Korea], trans. Chŏng Mi-ok (Seoul: Kwahakkwa Sasang, 1988). Until 2003, Robinson himself was unaware of this Korean edition. The aforementioned journalist Kim Hwan-gyun presented him with a copy in early 2004. Robinson placed a Post-It note in this copy; it reads: "in Korean *Betrayal of America*." The Korean title, though, might more accurately be translated as *America's Betrayal*, particularly given the heated, anti-American intellectual climate prevailing at the time of its publication.

(Fig. 4) 1988 Korean edition of Robinson's book, published as *America's Betrayal.*
(Fig. 5) Richard Robinson in an interview with Korean journalist Kim Hwan-gyun, aired on KBS TV in January 2004.

Despite being the subject of considerable attention and often cited as a primary source in Korea, the work sparked criticism due to its stance on trusteeship. Although Robinson understood the Korean objection to trusteeship, he did not fundamentally reject the idea, which, along with left-versus-right political polarization, was naturally key to post-liberation Korea (as extensively discussed in his "Betrayal of a Nation"). His perspective did not stray far from the typical post-World War II Western consensus, which saw trusteeship as a necessary step toward independence. Hardly any prominent Western figures, regardless of their political leanings, challenged the necessity of trusteeship during the early months of U.S. and Soviet occupations. Korean critics, of course, had valid objections to such neocolonialist interventions. From January of 1946, the persistent and intense Korean protests began to influence opinions among politicians, administrators, and journalists.[59] Among them was Edgar Snow (1905–1972)—later self-exiled due to McCarthy's attacks. After spending two months in Korea during the winter of 1945/46, the biographer of Mao (head of state 1949–1959) and noted chronicler of the Long March, critiqued that the "[p]rolonged joined trusteeship is both unnecessary and unwelcome." He proposed that both the U.S. and Soviet forces withdraw, suggesting the formation of "a resident joint advisory commission" with "the right of Allied

[59] See e.g. Gordon Walker's report in the *Christian Science Monitor*, January 3, 1946.

intervention."[60] Amid the global wave of decolonization, with nations like India gaining independence from colonial rule after 1945, Snow's proposal illustrates that even critical Western minds offering alternatives could not fully escape endorsing elements of Western supervision, thus maintaining an interventionist stance.

Asserting his paternalistic views, at the Teheran Conference (November 27–December 2, 1943), Franklin D. Roosevelt (in office 1933–1945), the New Deal president known for providing labor unions and socialists with a platform—often causing irritation among the French and British due to his lack of support for *their* colonial claims during the war—told Soviet leader Joseph Stalin (in office 1922–1953) "that the Koreans are not yet capable of exercising and maintaining independent government and that they should be placed under a 40-year tutelage."[61] The underlying racial prejudice that influenced Roosevelt's decisions, particularly his racist attitudes towards Asians, is widely acknowledged today. In a conversation with Stalin at the subsequent Yalta Conference (February 4–11, 1945), for example, he remarked "that the Indochinese were people of small stature" and, as a result, "not warlike."[62] Three decades later, those very people of small stature would stunningly turn the tables in a major conflict against the U.S. giant. The American president raised the issue once more and continued to advocate for an extended period of trusteeship, now suggesting that "in the case of Korea the period might be from twenty to thirty years," comparing it to "the Philippines where it had taken about fifty years for the people to be prepared for self-government."[63]

---

[60] Edgar Snow, "We Meet Russia in Korea," *Saturday Evening Post* 218, no. 39 (March 30, 1946): 118.

[61] Roosevelt, as referenced by Wilson Brown, "Minutes of a Meeting of the Pacific War Council" (January 12, 1944), in *Foreign Relations of the United States, Diplomatic Papers: The Conferences at Cairo and Teheran 1943*, comp. United States Department of State (Washington, DC: Government Printing Office, 1961), 869. FDR's widely publicized anti-colonial stance—cf. Caprio, p. 433—clashed with his actual policies.

[62] Roosevelt, as referenced in "Roosevelt–Stalin Meeting, February 8, 1945, 3:30 P.M., Livadia Palace," in *Foreign Relations of the United States, Diplomatic Papers: The Conferences at Malta and Yalta 1945*, comp. United States Department of State (Washington, DC: Government Printing Office, 1955), 770 (hereafter cited as *FRUS 1955*).

[63] Roosevelt, as referenced ibid. With that comparison, FDR paraphrased a statement from Department of State adviser Tyler Dennett's article, published three weeks earlier: "'In Due Course,'" *Far Eastern Survey* 14, no. 1 (January 17, 1945): 2.

The Philippines remained at that time both practically and formally a U.S. colony, seized by brute force at the turn of the century and subsequently subjected to carrot-and-stick tactics. These approaches involved systemic torture and the relentless murder of Filipino prisoners of war, while the colony's elite, the wealthy *hacendado* class, was bribed into collaborating with the U.S. colonial government. Ultimately, the U.S. role in the Philippines mirrored the Japanese approach in Korea, employing a similar colonial framework of suppression. While Roosevelt did not explicitly endorse conventional colonialism, he still assumed that Koreans, like all formerly colonized peoples, were incapable of self-governance. His comparison of Korea to the Philippines appears presumptuous and inadvertently revealing, particularly as he was a fifth cousin of U.S. President Theodore Roosevelt (in office 1901–1909) and the husband of his niece, Eleanor. Theodore Roosevelt had been responsible for the secret 1905 Taft–Katsura Agreement that allowed Japan to colonize Korea in the first place, expressly in exchange for Japan's agreement not to challenge U.S. control over the Philippines.

Secret deal-making between the two colonizers, Japan and the United States, did not stop there. In April 1941, Washington made a new bid to sacrifice the independence of China and Korea. Now it was FDR's government proposing a secret treaty with the Japanese, adding Manchuria to their colonial portfolio. Effectively nullifying the Stimson Doctrine, the U.S. offered full diplomatic recognition of their puppet state Manchukuo and promised "not to enter the European war" in return for—once again—a "guaranty of the status quo in the Philippines."[64]

In 1945, Stalin recognized that FDR envisioned a semi-colonial arrangement that would violate basic egalitarian and socialist principles, and stressed that the period of trusteeship would have to be short-term.[65] In general, however, the Soviet dictator also agreed with

---

[64] Ambassador Eugen Ott's (1889–1977) telegram to Foreign Minister Joachim von Ribbentrop (1893–1946), "The Ambassador in Japan to the Foreign Ministry," no. 454 (Tokyo, May 5, 1941), in Germany, Auswärtiges Amt, and United States Department of State, comps., *Documents on German Foreign Policy, 1918–1945, from the Archives of the German Foreign Ministry*, Series D (1937–1945), Vol. XII, *The War Years, February 1–June 22, 1941* (Washington, DC: Government Printing Office, 1962), 712. Preliminary talks were held by FDR's long-term secretary of state, Cordell Hull (1871–1955), and Japanese Ambassador Nomura Kichisaburō (1877–1964).

[65] See *FRUS 1955*, 770.

Roosevelt's proposed arrangement. Only after Japan's capitulation, at the Moscow Conference of Foreign Ministers (December 16–26, 1945), with Harry S. Truman (in office 1945–1953) as the new U.S. president, did the United States reduce the number of years for a trusteeship to no more than ten years and finally accept the Soviet's counterproposal for a period of up to five years.[66] In his work, Robinson seems to have been unaware of FDR's earlier suggestions and the full historical background but still finds it shocking "that the United States had proposed a ten-year trusteeship for Korea" and then "wrongly charged them [the Soviets] with having sponsored a Korean trusteeship while" claiming that "the Americans championed the cause of immediate independence."[67]

Another topic that drew criticism for Robinson during the late 1980s, moving from trusteeship, was his stance on land reform. In an April 1946 internal report, he forcefully stated that "land reform is needed, and needed badly," arguing that "a feudalistic state such as Korea today cannot at the same time be a democratic state."[68] But despite his strong convictions, and then still harboring hopes for a future united democratic Korean government, he ultimately suggested that the "Military Government should give merely a strong recommendation to the Korean government, when such is established."[69]

As discussed earlier, Robinson's article in the *Nation* and his later book manuscript were not the product of spontaneous generation. One significant factor was his liberal family background. In February 1946,

---

66 Whereas Roosevelt had envisioned a three-power trusteeship consisting of the United States, the U.S.S.R., and China, thus excluding both of the major European colonial empires of France and Britain, Truman, in agreement with Stalin, wanted to include the United Kingdom, as confirmed by Stalin in late May 1945. See G. M. Elsey, "No. 250: Memorandum by the Assistant to the President's Naval Aide (Elsey)," in *Foreign Relations of the United States, Diplomatic Papers: The Conference of Berlin 1945*, vol. I, comp. United States Department of State (Washington, DC: Government Printing Office, 1960), 310; Harry S. Truman, *Memoirs: Years of Trial and Hope*, vol. 2 (Garden City: Doubleday, 1956), 317.

67 Robinson, "Betrayal of a Nation," in this volume, 92.

68 Richard D. Robinson, "Possible Objections to the Proposed Ordinance for the Sale of Japanese Agricultural Property South of 38° North Latitude" (April 7, 1946), RG 332, USAFIK, XXIV Corps, G-2, Historical Section, Records Regarding the Okinawa Campaign, USAMGIK, U.S.–U.S.S.R. Relations in Korea, and Korean Political Affairs, 1945–48, Box 37, Dept. of Transportation: Railroads of Korea, etc., National Archives and Records Administration, 173.

69 Ibid., 177.

his father reassured and possibly even inspired him: "It takes considerable courage to be honest. [...] I sympathize with you because just now you are tied up with the army. The military mind is not trained for honesty or truth, but for winning whatever contest it is engaged in."[70]

The second essential factor, however, apart from his idealistic–humanistic background and approach (which at once defined the limitations of his political analysis), was that the sources and motivation for the article and book manuscript also derived from his daily work in and for the Military Government itself. In his first position as army officer and deputy director of the Office of Public Opinion in Korea, Robinson reported directly to U.S. military leaders and provided policy recommendations, including repeated proposals for changes in the court system and suggestions for a major police reform. In one report he wrote: "It is pointless to defend the police system as it stands. [...] It all stems from a lack of any definite commitment on the part of MG [Military Government] [...]. It is suggested that a determined effort be made to cleanse the police house [...]."[71] In another 1946 report, an "Investigation of the Police," he makes ten concrete recommendations to the U.S. Military Government "to reform the police along more democratic lines."[72]

Robinson did not just report on injustice and human rights violations in his anonymous *Nation* article and his book manuscript. He also courageously incorporated any evidence he had uncovered into his official reports and proactively engaged when opportunities arose. A poignant example of this is the torture case that occurred in a Pusan police station in July 1946, as described in "Betrayal of a Nation." In his book manuscript, he recounts, "I arrested the torturers on the spot and preferred charges against them for misuse of police authority. The act very nearly netted me a court-martial. [...] The only thing that saved me

---

[70] Letter by William D. Robinson to his son Richard, February 11, 1946, in Robinson and Swanson, eds., *In the Process of Creation*, 22.
[71] Richard Robinson, "Ineffectiveness and Confusion Encompassing the Administration of MG," RG 332, USAFIK, XXIV Corps, G-2, Historical Section, Records Regarding the Okinawa Campaign, USAMGIK, U.S.–U.S.S.R. Relations in Korea, and Korean Political Affairs, 1945–48, Box 38, Report of Directory: New Korea Co. to USAMGIK, etc., National Archives and Records Administration, 3.
[72] Richard D. Robinson, "Investigation of the Police" (July 30, 1946), RG 332, USAFIK, XXIV Corps, G-2, Historical Section, Box 26, USAMGIK: History of National Economic Board 1946–1948, etc., National Archives and Records Administration, 7.

from court-martial was newspaper publicity and the intervention of friends with General Hodge, General Lerch's superior."[73] A review of the report Robinson references, declassified in 2002, further corroborates his actions and reporting during that time.[74]

Robinson was equally forthright in his official reports regarding USAMGIK's top leaders. This shows, for example, in an interview report featuring Economic and Agricultural Adviser Arthur C. Bunce (1901–1953)—"known by all as a 'New Deal' liberal,"[75] as Hodge noted with both spite and relish. Robinson quoted Bunce, a highly respected authority on Korean economics in his view, as saying "that the General [Hodge] is driving South Korea directly into the hands of the communists" and "that to support Dr Rhee, Kim Koo, and the extreme Rightist group would be a disastrous policy and only lead ultimately to civil war in Korea"[76] (see fig. 6). That statement, featured in an official report, likely made its way to Hodge's desk as well.

Whenever and wherever the young man could, he would highlight the injustices and instances of mismanagement that he observed. One of his final reports before fleeing Korea for Turkey was a memo on the looting of significant artworks between November 1945 and May 1946 by Lieutenant Colonel Maurice Lutwack (1906–1979) of Buffalo, the U.S. military governor of Kyŏnggi Province. This is the *they're-nice-pack-'em-up* case reported on by Mark Gayn as well.[77] Robinson wrote

---

[73] Robinson, "Betrayal of a Nation," in this volume, 188–89.

[74] See Richard D. Robinson, "Report on Trip Through the Provinces with American Correspondents," RG 332, USAFIK, XXIV Corps, G-2, Historical Section, Records Regarding USAMGIK, U.S.–U.S.S.R. Relations in Korea, and Korean Political Affairs, 1945–48, Box 41, National Archives and Records Administration, 2. See further Robinson, "Betrayal of a Nation," in this volume, 298–99.

[75] "John R. Hodge to Douglas MacArthur" (January 9, 1948), reprinted in *Migunjŏnggi chŏngbo charyojip: Haji (John R. Hodge) munsŏjip, 1945.6–1948.8* [Collection of intelligence materials from the U.S. Military Government period: Hodge (John R. Hodge) Document Collection, June 1945–August 1948], vol. 1, comp. Hallim Taehakkyo, Asia Munhwa Yŏn'guso (Ch'unch'ŏn: Hallim Taehakkyo, 1995), 427.

[76] Richard Robinson, "Interview with Dr. Arthur C. Bunce, Member of the American Delegation to the Joint–Soviet–American Commission, Economic Advisor to the CG" (January 23, 1946), RG 332, USAFIK, XXIV Corps, G-2, Historical Section, Box 69, Records Regarding the Okinawa Campaign, U.S. Military Government in Korea, U.S.–U.S.S.R. Relations in Korea, and Korean Political Affairs, 1945–48, National Archives and Records Administration.

[77] See Mark Gayn's Korea chapter in this volume, 412–13.

33-

INTERVIEW WITH DR ARTHUR C BUNCE, MEMBER OF THE AMERICAN DELEGATION TO THE JOINT-SOVIET-AMERICAN COMMISSION, ECONOMIC ADVISOR TO THE CG, 23 JANUARY, 1946

....

2. Re Hodge's political policy. Bunce feels very strongly that the General is driving South Korea directly into the hands of the communists and their fellow travelers. He has argued the point with the General but to no avail. Bunce further feels that if a walkout from the legislature comes about, it will be about the final blow for the American occupation. Bunce has sent off a letter to the State Department, with Hodge's concurrence, saying in essence that to support Dr Rhee, KimKoo, and the extreme Rightist group would be a disastrous policy and only lead ultimately to civil war in Korea. Rather, he feels it should be imperative that Hodge's present "middle of the road" policy be maintained. However, he pointed out that unless the General receives some outside help and backing there was danger that he would not continue his present middle of the road policy.

3. MacArthur and Korea. Bunce had just returned from Tokyo where he had talked with Acheson and tried to obtain audience with Mac. He definitly received the impression that Korea was considered by SCAP to be a lemon and that Mac's name must not be tainted by any direct relation with the Korean mess. One of Bunce's objectives had been to interest Mac in coming to Korea and lending his prestige to the Interim Legislature and Dr Kim Kyu Sik's efforts. He got no where. MacArthur is stying clear of Korea. SCAP is supersensitive to any criticism of MacArthur, and it is felt that by associating directly with the Korean situation he would open himself up to some. Hodge is definitly to be the goat. Bunce was very bitter on this attitude of SCAP.

I AND H JOURNAL　　　　　Mr Richard Robinson

(Fig. 6) *"... the General is driving South Korea directly into the hands of the communists ..."* One of Richard D. Robinson's candid reports for the U.S. Military Government, here a summary of a January 1946 interview with Arthur C. Bunce, a New Deal' liberal, like himself.

that "it was well known that" the governor "had looted Kyonggi-do of some 4,000 cases of Oriental goods and objects of art."[78] To be sure, in terms of size, the spoils easily compared to the massive art collection of 4,263 plundered masterpieces amassed by Nazi leader Hermann Göring (1893–1946). Although the Purple Heart recipient was apprehended, stripped of his duties, and removed from the office of provincial governor,[79] Lutwack's massive crime was kept classified and never made public. In fact, not a single article about it can be found today. After leaving the army, Lutwack frequently delivered public talks and lectures on Korea, where he bombastically dished out political and strategic advice—both solicited and unsolicited—often interjecting condescending remarks about the country.

In his secondary role as a military historian, Robinson would once again primarily work on assigned tasks. A good example is his 17-page summary report from July 1947, which was devoted to Soviet espionage in southern Korea, with a focus on the Soviet Consulate in Seoul. This was likely his last extensive report before leaving Korea for Turkey.[80] But his chief task as U.S. military historian during the last twelve months of his stay was to conduct research and write major parts of what was planned to become the official history of the U.S. military occupation and government in southern Korea. Yet, this "History of the United States Army Forces in Korea, 1945–1948"[81] was never fully completed.

---

[78] R[ichard] D. Robinson, "Rumors for the Record as of 3 July 1947," RG 331, SCAP, Adjutant General's Section, Operations Division, Miscellaneous Branch, International Travel Office, Historical Journals, May 1946–May 1948, Entry 1888, Box 10128, National Archives and Records Administration. Because the U.S. Army had attempted to cover up that and other criminal cases, Robinson was forced to use the term "rumor" in his official report. His later "Betrayal" manuscript contains several examples for looting; the Lutwack case, however, is noted only briefly and without revealing the former colonel's name; see Robinson, "Betrayal of a Nation," in this volume, 294.

[79] Lutwack's appointment as governor was terminated on April 25, 1946; see Headquarters United States Army Military Government in Korea, Office of the Military Governor, "Removal Number 83," *Official Gazette, USAMGIK* (May 18, 1946): [1], reprinted in *Migunjŏng ch'ŏng kwanbo / Official Gazette, United States Army Military Government in Korea*, vol. 2 (Seoul: Wŏnju Munhwasa, 1991), 462.

[80] See p. 23, footnote 46 in this essay.

[81] Historical Section, Headquarters XXIV Corps, US Army Forces in Korea, "History of the United States Army Forces in Korea, 1945–1948," 3 parts., manuscript.

Chŏng Yong-uk, who amassed and compiled a significant collection of USAMGIK sources over the past few decades and published numerous scholarly studies on related topics, also conducted extensive research on the writing of the "History of the United States Army Forces in Korea, 1945–1948," with a particular focus on Robinson's role in the process.[82] Chŏng has shown that Robinson authored the bulk of Part Two, half of it alone (i.e., volumes 2 and 4) and the other half with two different co-authors (i.e., volumes 3 and 5). In little more than a year, Robinson produced a staggering 1,100 pages on post-liberation Korean politics and Soviet–American relations.

Internally, Robinson was highly respected and credited for his work. Just two weeks after his article appeared in the *Nation*, but before he was exposed as its author, the Historical Section's chief historian James O. Sargent (1921–1976), Robinson's immediate superior (and his contemporary in age), recommended him for a major promotion: "His long study of Russo–American relations in Korea was commended by General Hodge and taken by the General to Washington. [...] Mr. Robinson possesses admirable qualifications for his position and rating. His services have been sought by other sections in Corps and Military Government," Sargent acknowledged. "In an effort to persuade him to stay with the historical program and because the Section realizes its need of him, Mr. Robinson has been promised a promotion to P-5."[83]

To draft the history using primary sources, Robinson and his colleagues capitalized on their full security clearance and access to G-2 and other intelligence reports. Although Robinson did all that was requested of him, the carefully crafted, multivolume official history ultimately had to navigate through several stages of what can only be

---

Each of the three parts of the typewritten manuscript consists of several volumes. A first unauthorized reprint was finally published in 1988 by Tolbegae: *Chuhan Migunsa / HUSAFIK*, 3 parts in 4 vols. (Seoul: Tolbegae, 1988).

[82] See Chŏng Yong-uk, *Migunjŏng charyo yŏn'gu*, 155–212; Chung Yong Wook, "From Occupation to War: Cold War Legacies of US Army Historical Studies of the Occupation and Korean War," *Korea Journal* 60, no. 2 (Summer 2020): 14–54.

[83] James O. Sargent, "Justification of Civilian Personnel, Historical Section" (March 17, 1947), reprinted in *Haebang chikhu chŏngch'i sahoesa charyojip*, 1: *Yaksayu (1)* [Collection of political and social materials from the immediate post-liberation period, vol. 1: An outline history (1)], comp. Chŏng Yong-uk (Seoul: Tarakpang, 1994), 558.

described as a ludicrous internal censorship process (see fig. 7). In a letter addressed to the Historical Division at the Pentagon—a letter that also introduced Robinson—Section Chief Sargent lamented, "after a chapter is written it has to go through a long process of criticism and with many regrets I have fallen heir to several chapters which were virtually criticized out of existence."[84] Following this, Colonel William J. Niederpruem (1887–1972), chief of General MacArthur's (1880–1964) troop information program and responsible for overseeing the Army's entire history project and print censorship activities in MacArthur's empire, directly reprimanded Robinson's section chief, stating that an academic historical-critical approach and evaluation was entirely off the table: "It does not come within the scope of any account written by a subordinate echelon to pass judgement on the actions or policies of its higher command."[85] In one of his studies, Chŏng Yong-uk thoroughly examines this extensive censorship process.[86] He shows that, inevitably, the United States Army Military Government in Korea and the War Department in Washington routinely flouted their own convoluted regulations whenever anything in their "patriotic" narratives fell short of Metro-Goldwyn-Mayer silver screen standards.

"The 'History of the United States Army Forces in Korea' does not reflect the facts properly, so there is room for distortion," explained Robinson in his 2004 interview. "The official history of the U.S. military occupation of southern Korea—most elements of which are classified as top secret—is very prejudicial and also inaccurately described. The veracity of that history was destroyed because all historical records were written under explicit orders not to criticize

---

84 Letter by James O. Sargent to John M. Kemper, September 17, 1946, reprinted in *Haebang chikhu chŏngch'i sahoesa charyojip*, 1: *Yaksayu (1)* [Collection of political and social materials from the immediate post-liberation period, vol. 1: An outline history (1)], comp. Chŏng Yong-uk (Seoul: Tarakpang, 1994), 555.

85 Letter by W. J. Niederpruem to Albert Keep, May 16, 1946, reprinted in *Chuhan Migunsa / History of the United States Army Forces in Korea*, vol. 1, ed. Kuksa P'yŏnch'an Wiwŏnhoe (Seoul: Sŏnin, 2014), 20.

86 For Chŏng's discussion of the censorship process, see Chŏng Yong-uk, "*Chuhan Migunsa*ŭi p'yŏnch'an kyŏngwiwa naeyong kusŏng" [Compilation process and content composition of *History of the United States Army Forces in Korea*], in *Chuhan Migunsa / History of the United States Army Forces in Korea*, vol. 1, ed. Kuksa P'yŏnch'an Wiwŏnhoe (Seoul: Sŏnin, 2014), 32–36.

DECLASSIFIED
Authority NW21275
RW NARA Date 9/2/08

SECRET

CHAPTER IV

AMERICAN-SOVIET RELATIONS,

THE FIRST YEAR

Perhaps the most significant of the complex and many-faceted problems facing the XXIV Corps in the occupation of South Korea lay in the field of American-Soviet relations. Only 30 miles north of Seoul the 38th parallel of north latitude bisected the country, and to the north of that line lay the domain of the Red Army, [victorious over the Japanese after five days of crashing victories sweeping across the mountains of Manchuria and North Korea. By the 26th of August the Soviet forces had reached the 38th parallel.(1)]

(Fig. 7) Heavy censorship of Robinson's chapters in the "History of the United States Army Forces in Korea, 1945–1948"—a passage about the victory of the Soviets over Japan in Manchuria and their occupation of Korea (prior to that of the U.S. Army) is promptly marked for deletion by later CIA operative W.F. Choinski.

anything related to the United States."[87] In his "Betrayal" manuscript, he adds that "of all the words written on the occupation of Korea [...], at least seventy-five percent were either outright fabrication or highly inaccurate."[88] The military never released the tightly censored, sanitized history to the American or Korean public—even in that cleansed adaptation—as it was judged to reveal too many insider facts concerning its authoritarian, neocolonial playbook in Korea. It was therefore just reproduced in typescript, accessible to only a few high-ranking military

87 Richard D. Robinson, quoted in Kim, *Pigŭgŭn haengjinŭrobut'ŏ sijak toenda*, 66.
88 Robinson, "Betrayal of a Nation," in this volume, 66.

officers and the Intelligence Community. In "Betrayal of a Nation," Robinson distills Part Two of the U.S. Army's official "History," pierces the veil of military censorship, and offers a candid account that frames America's imperialist encroachment and the neocolonial dynamics reshaping postwar Korea, thereby exposing a troubling reality behind the fabricated narratives of democratic liberation in 1945.

Mark Gayn

Born as Mark Julius Ginsbourg, Mark Gayn stood out not only as a journalist in the rich tradition of American muckraker journalism but also as an exceptional analyst. Gayn was a man who breathed life into the narratives of his skillfully crafted reports. A true master at the art of interviewing, he possessed an unpretentious demeanor and engaged with individuals from all walks of life. Whether they were intellectuals, administrators, villagers, workers, revolutionaries, soldiers, generals, fascists, or war criminals, he conversed with people of diverse colors, nationalities, and convictions. Fluent in Russian, English, Chinese, and French, he had a remarkable ability to put everyone at ease. His mastery lay in weaving ironic and revealing twists into his descriptions, often achieved by skillfully using his interviewees' own words to expose their motives and true intentions, or to shed light on the disparities between official narratives and lived realities.

Gayn[89] was born to Russian–Jewish parents in Manchuria, something that was not easily forgiven in the United States during the 1940s, 50s, and 60s.[90] Following years of schooling in Harbin, Vladivostok,

---

[89] A concise, well-evidenced outline of Gayn's life, apart from various obituaries (e.g., Montreal's *Gazette* on December 18, 1981, and the *New York Times* on December 24, 1981), was written by Graham Bradshaw in a pamphlet for an exhibition at the Thomas Fisher Rare Book Library. See Graham Bradshaw and Margery Pearson, "Journey from the East: The Life and Times of Mark Gayn," exhibition pamphlet (Toronto: Thomas Fisher Rare Book Library, University of Toronto, 1986), 1–4. The other major source is Gayn's own early autobiographic book: Mark J. Gayn, *Journey from the East: An Autobiography* (New York: Alfred A. Knopf, 1944).

[90] Typically, conservatives such as Joseph C. Keeley (1904–1968), the biographer of a mastermind of the Cold War, branded Gayn and other foreign-born liberals as "people with strange backgrounds." Joseph Keeley, *The China Lobby Man: The Story of Alfred Kohlberg* (New Rochelle: Arlington House, 1969), 95.

and Shanghai, he left Asia in the fall of 1929 at the age of twenty to study in California. After graduating in 1933 with a B.A. from Pomona College in Claremont, a suburb of Los Angeles, and, a year later, with a B.Sc. from the School of Journalism at Columbia University in New York, Gayn soon became one of the brightest stars in American journalism. Upon completing his studies at Columbia, he returned to Shanghai as a special correspondent for the *Washington Post*. For some time, until the Second Sino-Japanese War (1937–1945), he also worked for Japan's Domei News Service. However, with the outbreak of World War II in Europe, he returned to the United States and applied for U.S. citizenship (see fig. 8). Although he legally changed his surname from Ginsbourg to Gayn in June 1940, his alien status did not change, which prevented him from serving in the U.S. military, not only upon being drafted in October 1940 but also after the law was changed a year later.[91] In November 1943 he was finally granted U.S. citizenship.[92]

Mark Gayn's personality and political viewpoint were profoundly shaped by his family background, linguistic acumen, and diverse cultural and political experiences. The eldest of three boys, his early years were spent in Barim (aka Balin), a tiny town in Manchuria, nestled near the Mongolian border and known for its railway station. At eight years old, his family moved to Harbin with its large, wealthy Russian émigré population, where he attended Western schools. Then, from 1923 to 1926, he experienced his formative teenage years in Vladivostok, amid the tumultuous takeover by the Bolsheviks. Following this, his family moved to a unique extraterritorial enclave—Shanghai's International Settlement. Later, they relocated once again, this time to southern California, and then to New York City. By his early twenties, he had pretty much *seen it all*—more than what most people encounter in a lifetime.

In his autobiography *Journey from the East*—who writes an autobiography in their mid-thirties?—Gayn describes his early life in great

[91] See the draft card of Mark Julius Gayn, no. 2513 (October 16, 1940), WWII Draft Registration Cards for Missouri, 10/16/1940–03/31/1947, Record group: Records of the Selective Service System, 147, Box 114, National Archives at St. Louis.

[92] See the index card for Mark Julius Gayn, no. 5573026, Soundex Index to Petitions for Naturalization Field in Federal, State, and Local Courts Located in New York City, 1892–1989, National Archives at New York City.

460093

ORIGINAL
(To be retained by clerk)

No. ....

UNITED STATES OF AMERICA

DECLARATION OF INTENTION

(Invalid for all purposes seven years after the date hereof)

HEL

STATE OF NEW YORK
SOUTHERN DISTRICT OF NEW YORK

In the DISTRICT Court of UNITED STATES at NEW YORK, N.Y.

I, MARK JULIUS GINSBOURG
(Full true name, without abbreviation, and any other name which has been used, must appear here)

now residing at 308 W. 11th St. New York, NY
(Number and street) (City or town) (County) (State)

occupation Writer(free lance), aged 31 years, do declare on oath that my personal description is:
Sex male, color white, complexion fair, color of eyes dark brown
color of hair brown, height 5 feet 7½ inches; weight 165 pounds; visible distinctive marks none

race Hebrew; nationality Russian
I was born in Statiin Barim, China, on April 21, 1909
I am not married. The name of my wife or husband is ....
we were married on ...., at ....; she or he was born at ...., on ...., entered the United States at ...., on ...., for permanent residence therein, and now resides at .... I have no children, and the name, date and place of birth, and place of residence of each of said children are as follows: ....

I have not heretofore made a declaration of intention: Number ...., on .... at ....
my last foreign residence was Shanghai, China
I emigrated to the United States of America from Shanghai, China
my lawful entry for permanent residence in the United States was at San Pedro, California
under the name of Mark J. Ginsbourg, on October 10, 1939
on the vessel Laxa Maersk
(If other than by vessel, state manner of arrival)

I will, before being admitted to citizenship, renounce forever all allegiance and fidelity to any foreign prince, potentate, state, or sovereignty, and ~~particularly, by name, to the prince, potentate, state, or sovereignty of which I may be at the time of admission a citizen or subject~~; I am not an anarchist; I am not a polygamist nor a believer in the practice of polygamy; and it is my intention in good faith to become a citizen of the United States of America and to reside permanently therein; and I certify that the photograph affixed to the duplicate and triplicate hereof is a likeness of me.

I swear (affirm) that the statements I have made and the intentions I have expressed in this declaration of intention subscribed by me are true to the best of my knowledge and belief: So help me God.

Mark Julius Ginsbourg
(Original signature of declarant without abbreviation, also alias, if used)

Subscribed and sworn to before me in the form of oath shown above in the office of the Clerk of said Court, at New York this 25 day of April, anno Domini, 1940. Certification No. 2-711636 from the Commissioner of Immigration and Naturalization showing the lawful entry of the declarant for permanent residence on the date stated above, has been received by me. The photograph affixed to the duplicate and triplicate hereof is a likeness of the declarant.

(DO NOT ATTACH PHOTOGRAPH TO THIS COPY OF DECLARATION)

[SEAL]

GEORGE J.H. FOLLMER
Clerk of the U.S. DISTRICT Court.
By ...., Deputy Clerk.

No. 290868

Form 2202—L-A
U. S. DEPARTMENT OF LABOR
IMMIGRATION AND NATURALIZATION SERVICE

14—2623
U. S. GOVERNMENT PRINTING OFFICE

(Fig. 8) Mark Gayn's, aka Mark Julius Ginsbourg's, application for U.S. citizenship ("Declaration of Intention"), April 25, 1940.

(Fig. 9)
The Ginsbourg family in Shanghai in the late 1920s. Mark is on the left with his youngest brother Sam sitting on the right.

detail. He indicates that his father, a manager of several large sawmills, had moved from Russia to Manchuria for political reasons—specifically, due to being an outspoken critic of the czar and the brutal monarchy that was "rotten to the core."[93] Gayn writes that his father had "actively protested against government" and "collected money for the peasants and gathered signatures and petitions of protest."[94] In 1903, such actions would normally have warranted placement "on the blacklist of the secret police,"[95] forcing him to relocate across the border to Manchuria. Then again, according to the memoir of Mark's youngest brother, Sam Ginsbourg (aka Jin Shibo, 1914–1979), a staunch Maoist who spent his adult life in mainland China, their father's decision to leave the Jewish ghetto was instead influenced by the suppression of Jews in southern Byelorussia and economic opportunity.[96] Sam describes how their father tracked the economic completion over the construction of the Trans–Siberian Railway and later the Chinese Eastern Railway, so that "[h]e never stayed in any one place for longer than a year or two," and always "dragged his family after him."[97] This nomadic existence was necessitated by the father's work as a timber manager, leading the

---

93 Gayn, *Journey from the East*, 11.
94 Ibid., 12.
95 Ibid., 13.
96 See Sam Ginsbourg, *My First Sixty Years in China* (Beijing: New World Press, 1982), 1.
97 Ibid., 2.

Ginsbourg family to reside deep in the Manchurian countryside for the first eight years of Mark's life. The family would have been regarded as middle or even upper-middle class by income, enabling them to afford a "long list of tutors and governesses," as Mark recalls: "They were German, Russian, English, and American, old and young, dull and stimulating."[98] But the father, engrossed day and night with his lumber business, was not particularly close to his children, as Mark and Sam both attest. Their mother, on the other hand, was very caring, while also passionate about her own education. Even after giving birth to three children, she completed a university education and became a successful dentist, all while raising them.

As a child, teen, and young man, Gayn witnessed bandit attacks, two revolutions, international wars, occupations, economic depressions, and famines—nearly all of them steeped in divergent political ideologies. Between 1923 and 1926, his family's life transitioned from comfort in Harbin to dire poverty in Vladivostok, already under Bolshevik governance. Initially, they couldn't afford shoes or coal for heat. But like his mother and brothers, Mark adapted to the new situation relatively well: "My adjustment from a life of comfort to one of acute discomfort was painless, for I had the miraculous adaptability of youth."[99] Later, his father moved the family to Shanghai, and then followed his son Mark to California. Only the youngest son, Sam, preferred to remain in China.

In June 1945, Gayn, then in his mid-thirties and a U.S. citizen working as a journalist in New York, was arrested by the FBI in what became known as the Amerasia spy case. *Amerasia* was a specialized journal published by Philip J. Jaffe (1895–1980) and another editor for the Institute of Pacific Relations, mostly to be read by students of East Asian affairs. An officer in the Office of Strategic Services (OSS), the wartime precursor of the CIA, had noted that "a striking parallel existed between the text of an article which appeared in the January 26, 1945, edition of *Amerasia* magazine [...] and a document"[100] that he had

---

[98] Gayn, *Journey from the East*, 60.

[99] Ibid., 104.

[100] Senate Reports, No. 2108, 81st Congress, 2nd Session, Serial 11375, *State Department Employee Loyalty Investigation: Report of the Committee on Foreign Relations Pursuant to S. Res. 231* (Washington, DC: U.S. Government Printing Office, 1950), 97 (hereafter cited as *State Department Employee Loyalty Investigation*).

prepared for the OSS, a document classified as "Secret."[101] On March 11, 1945, OSS agents in New York thus entered *Amerasia's* Manhattan headquarters on Fifth Avenue—without any search warrants.[102] The OSS then reported the intelligence it found to the FBI, which proceeded to search and install bugs in Gayn's apartment and the offices of several other journalists working with or for the Institute—again without any search warrants.[103] Although Jaffe, Gayn, and four others were arrested by the FBI, the charges were soon dropped. Without a doubt, the Institute's journalists had referenced classified government documents. Foreign Service officer John S. Service (1909–1999) even admitted to having shared classified papers with Gayn and Jaffe. That, however, was a standard practice at the time, as he explained during the committee hearings.[104] Other copies of classified documents in Gayn's possession had been shared by officers of the Office of War Information (OWI) through an informal agreement,[105] and the articles published in *Amerasia* had in fact passed conventional wartime pre-publication censorship.

The Amerasia case served as a dress rehearsal for the Cold War and the subsequent spread of McCarthyism. Pursuing Alfred Kohlberg's lead, McCarthy took on the case. By claiming that the U.S. State Department had been infiltrated by communist spies in his Wheeling speech of February 9, 1950, Joseph McCarthy took charge of probing and turning the Amerasia case into a major *cause célèbre*. This led to a vigorous and extensive investigation and debate in Congress. But the U.S. Senate Committee on Foreign Relations closed the case, concluding: "It has been charged widely, by Senator McCarthy as well as by others, that the Amerasia case is the key to an espionage ring in the State Department. The evidence clearly establishes that this is not true."[106] That outcome was an embarrassment for the FBI and the

---

[101] The text in question was printed on page 23 of the unsigned *Amerasia* article "Britain's Postwar Plans: The Case of Thailand," *Amerasia* 9 (January 26, 1945), 19–29.

[102] See *State Department Employee Loyalty Investigation*, 97 and 123–24.

[103] See ibid., 134.

[104] John Service himself was fired in 1951 but in 1956 rejoined the State Department after the Supreme Court had ruled that the decision to fire him was illegal. See his obituary in the *New York Times*, February 4, 1999.

[105] See *State Department Employee Loyalty Investigation*, 115–18.

[106] Ibid., 137.

THE PITTSBURGH PRESS

Amerasia Case Skeleton Rises to Haunt U. S.

PHILIP J. JAFFE
EMANUEL S. LARSEN
ANDREW ROTH
JOHN STEWART SERVICE
KATE LOUISE MITCHELL
MARK GAYN

(Fig. 10) Amerasia case as dress rehearsal for the Cold War: photos of four liberal journalists and two State Department employees attacked by McCarthy and his associates, with Mark Gayn on the far right. *Pittsburgh Press*, May 1, 1950.

Department of Justice. The majority of Congress and the general public perceived their actions in the case as an attack on press freedom. As a result, the use of the 1917 Espionage Act to indict members of the press for publishing classified government information fell out of favor. Yet, the very same act that was used against Mark Gayn and other *Amerasia* journalists in the 1940s was unearthed by the Justice Department in the first Trump era to go after WikiLeaks founder Julian Assange (b. 1971), first covertly and then publicly.[107]

Gayn was forever marked as a traitor, as mainstream *Newsweek* reporter Charlotte Ebener (1918–1990) discovered while touring Korea with him. "I never suspected I would be labeled 'Communist' by the Army just because I was on the same planes, trains, and jeeps with Gayn,"[108] she complained, thereby astutely distancing herself from a colleague whom McCarthy had branded as a communist and a spy. In the 1950s, as McCarthy continued his agitation and decisively ignored the decision of the Committee on Foreign Relations, the Amerasia case became the cornerstone of his political career, bringing hardships upon all the journalists and diplomats involved. As a result of his arrest, intimidation, and subsequent actions reminiscent of Nazi-style *Sippenhaft* (kin punishment), Gayn felt forced to leave the U.S. in late 1952 and settled permanently in Canada.

Since then, American authors swayed by conspiracy theories and disinformation have continued to refer to Gayn as a "Russian spy." Such

[107] See *New York Times*, May 24, 2019.
[108] Charlotte Ebener, *No Facilities for Women* (New York: Alfred A. Knopf, 1955), 66.

thinking rests solely on the 1945 Amerasia case, which is now generally understood as an instance of journalistic use of classified OSS, Navy, and State Department documents to report on U.S. foreign policy, not as espionage.[109] The crudest example of what such speculation produced is perhaps Dick Russell's *The Man Who Knew Too Much*, a massive, stultifying cocktail of badly connected conspiracy stories. Tying every conceivable secret service and espionage scandal across the globe to the assassination of John F. Kennedy (in office 1961–1963) and Lee Harvey Oswald (1939–1963)—and that over several decades—Russell patches together page after page of the strangest, most insidiously manipulative speculations and inventions about the "Mysterious History of Mark Gayn"[110] to advance the specious claim of "possible Nagell–Oswald–Gayn connections."[111]

Becoming his most widely read publication, Mark Gayn's *Japan Diary*,[112] spanning over 500 pages, was published in November 1948 by William Sloane Associates and achieved tremendous success.[113] In style and political outlook, Gayn's masterful prose reflects his personal, political, and diverse cultural background. Unremittingly critical and invariably entertaining at the same time, the book became a bestseller that was reviewed in many newspapers and journals, praised by liberals while being denounced by conservatives. It was and continues to be quoted in scholarly circles on issues related to the U.S. military occupation of Japan and Korea. More than ninety pages of Gayn's jour-

---

[109] Three decades later, when the two investigative journalists Bob Woodward (b. 1943) and Carl Bernstein (b. 1944) uncovered the Watergate scandal, they emerged unscathed. Yet, as mentioned, another four decades later, Julian Assange, neither a U.S. citizen nor a resident, found himself on the U.S. Justice Department's most wanted list. The "2025 World Press Freedom Index" thus ranks the United States 57th, worse than Sierra Leone and Romania, but still slightly better than Gambia, Uruguay, or South Korea. See Reporters Without Borders (RSF), "2025 World Press Freedom Index," accessed May 8, 2025, https://rsf.org/en/index?year=2025.

[110] This is one of Russel's subtitles; see Dick Russell, *The Man Who Knew Too Much: Hired to Kill Oswald and Prevent the Assassination of JFK* (New York: Carroll & Graf / Richard Gallen, 1992), 115. Most of Russell's imagined conspiracies involving Mark Gayn appear on pages 113–33 and 143–45.

[111] Ibid., 120.

[112] Mark Gayn, *Japan Diary* (New York: William Sloane Associates, 1948).

[113] Attempts to publish an eight-part article series based on the 1946 Korea tour in the *Chicago Sun* had been rejected. *The New Republic* would later publish one of these reports ("Cold War: Two Police States in Korea," September 15, 1947).

nalistic diary, republished in this volume, chronicle his three-week stay in Korea (October 15–November 8, 1946), in the company of Charlotte Ebener and *New York Times* journalist Foster Hailey (1899–1966).[114]

Gayn had arrived in Tokyo as the *Chicago Sun*'s bureau chief for Japan and Korea in December 1945, but this was his first trip to Korea. His *Japan Diary*, based on a handwritten journal (see fig. 11) now accessible as part of the Mark Gayn Papers in the Thomas Fisher Rare Book Library at the University of Toronto, is not his only publication that addresses post-liberation Korea. Before and after his trip to Korea, he also published several longer and shorter articles about the situation on the peninsula in various papers.[115] His article in *PM* that predicted a civil war in Korea, for example, was quoted and referenced at length

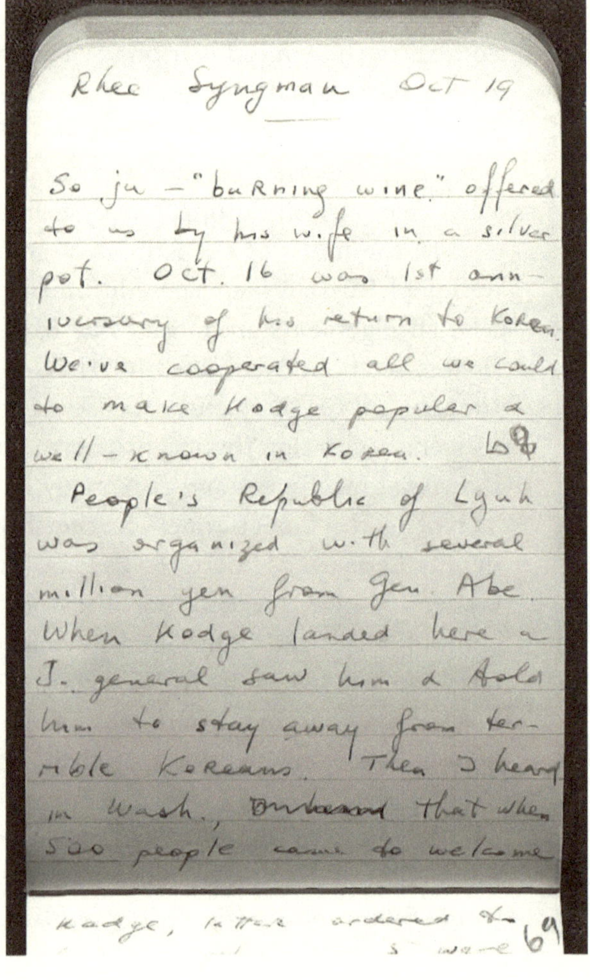
Rhee Syngman Oct 19
So ju — "burning wine" offered to us by his wife in a silver pot. Oct. 16 was 1st anniversary of his return to Korea.
We've cooperated all we could to make Hodge popular & well-known in Korea. 68
People's Republic of Lyuh was organized with several million yen from Gen. Abe. When Hodge landed here a J. general saw him & told him to stay away from terrible Koreans. Then I heard in Wash., that when 500 people came to welcome Hodge, [illegible] ordered [illegible] were 69

(Fig. 11) Handwritten entry for October 19, 1946, in Mark Gayn's journal.

[114] See Gayn, "Japan Diary: Korea," in this volume, 334.

[115] See e.g. his long front-page article on the early days of US occupation and Korean politicians in the LA based Korean community paper *Korean Independence* of November 21, 1945, or his critical reports in the liberal, New York based newspaper *PM Daily*: November 11, 1946 (on mass protests against US-let election procedures), November 2, 1947 (a full-page story "'Liberators' Turned Zones Into Military Bases"), November 3, 1947 (an article predicting civil war in Korea), and November 4 (a report on the failure to carry out land reform in southern Korea).

by Soviet Foreign Minister Andrei Gromyko (1909–1989) in his 1947 address to the United Nations.[116] Two weeks after Gayn's return from Korea, he received a letter from the *Sun*, which, he writes, was recalling him home "and announcing what is in effect a dissolution of its foreign service."[117] Gayn left Japan in early 1947 and shortly afterward settled in Paris to report on Europe, mostly Eastern Europe.

In the midst of the Korean War the Soviets published a slightly abridged Russian language edition of his *Japan Diary* (see fig. 12c).[118] The abridgements are mostly due to censored passages about Soviet figures and political observations liable to give Russian readers food for thought. In his diary entry for October 15, Gayn quotes a U.S. Army officer's accusation that the Russians had stripped North Korea of its industrial machinery and that many Koreans "had fled from the Red Terror in the Soviet zone." In the short entry for October 17, Gayn quotes Leonard M. Bertsch, the abovementioned political advisor to General Hodge, who astutely observed that if a free election were held across Korea, "the Communists would get 20 per cent of the votes in our zone, and five in the Russian zone. The people here would be voting not *for* the reds, but *against* us." In the entry for November 6, Gayn quotes an unidentified Russian characterizing General Hodge's Soviet counterpart, General Chistiakov (1900–1979), as a militarist "no different from any of yours." All such nonconformist observations were omitted from the Russian edition.[119] A Polish edition, *Dziennik japoński*, would follow in 1954 (fig. 12d),[120] published under contract with Gayn.[121]

---

[116] See Andrei Gromyko, "Address by Andrei Gromyko before the General Assembly on the Resolution Establishing the United Nations Temporary Commission on Korea" (November 13, 1947), in *Korea, 1945 to 1948: A Report on Political Developments and Economic Resources with Selected Documents*, comp. Department of State (Washington, DC: U.S. Government Printing Office, 1948), 59.

[117] Mark Gayn, *Japan Diary* (New York: William Sloane Associates, 1948), 446. Cf. Oliver Elliott, *The American Press and the Cold War* (Cham: Palgrave Macmillan, 2018), 50.

[118] Mark Gein [Mark Gayn], *Iaponskii dnevnik* [Japan diary], an abridged translation by I. Boronos, D. Kunina, and N. Loseva, with an introduction by A. Varshavskii (Moscow: Izdatel'stvo inostrannoi literatury, 1951).

[119] Compare ibid., 400, 405, 481, with the 1948 U.S. edition of Gayn's *Japan Diary*, 350, 355, and 431 (or our edition in this volume, 337, 342, and 416).

[120] Mark Gayn, *Dziennik japoński* [Japan diary], trans. Kazimierz Błeszyński (Warsaw: Książka i Wiedza, 1954).

[121] See the Polish book contract and cover letter, May 16, 1956, Mark Gayn Papers,

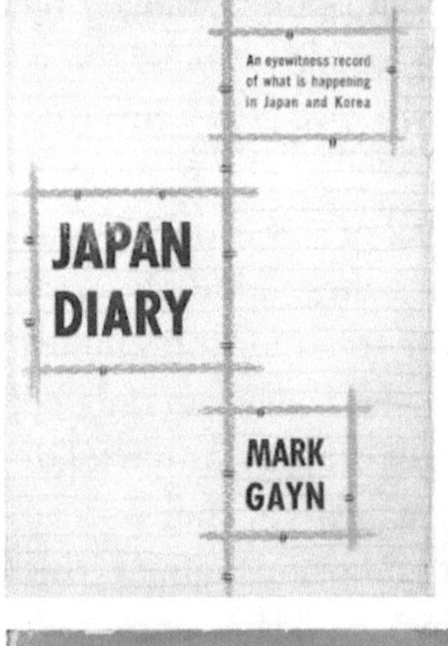

(Fig. 12) Various editions of Gayn's *Japan Diary*:
(a) original American edition, 1948, (b) first volume of first Japanese edition, 1951, (c) Russian edition, 1951, (d) Polish edition, 1954, (e) partial Korean translation, 1986, and (f) a follow-up *Shin Nippon nikki* (New Japan diary) published in 1982.

Along with the 1951 Russian edition, the book was also translated into Japanese by Imoto Takeo (1904–1963) and published that same year in a two-volume edition to outstanding success (see fig. 12b). Almost overnight, it ranked third among the best-selling books in Japan and continued to be widely read decades later. Several other Japanese editions, including some by Tuttle Publishing, which also later republished the English language version, would follow. However, those

MS Coll 00215, Box 97, Folder 31, Thomas Fisher Rare Book Library, University of Toronto.

editions are not to be confused with Gayn's final book, arranged by himself but published posthumously in 1982 as *Shin Nippon nikki* (New Japan diary)[122] (see fig. 12f), a kind of sequel to the *Japan Diary* covering the later postwar period.

In South Korea, as with Robinson's "Betrayal of a Nation," an unauthorized translation of *Japan Diary* was published amid the pro-democracy movement of the 1980s. Also similar to Robinson's publication, the book is quite rare, long out of print, and today can only be found in academic libraries. Back then, I bought a copy for a friend. Like reprints of Cumings' *Origins of the Korean War* and other critical texts questioning the legitimacy of the current and prior regimes, this book was an under-the-table publication that bypassed the censorship review and was sold at a bookstore right in front of Yonsei University's main gate. (In fact, the young bookstore owner would find himself in and out of police custody on a weekly basis.) A second print in 1989 seems to have followed a more conventional process. Both Korean editions, however, titled *Haebanggwa migunjŏng: 1946.10–11* (Liberation and the U.S. Army: October–November 1946)[123] (see fig. 12e), consist of an excerpt, namely the translation of Gayn's long Korea chapter.

Mark Gayn's journalistic diary is dedicated to his wife Sally, also a Russian immigrant, whom he married in September 1941. A year prior, he had entered into a deathbed marriage with another woman, Julia, a friend from Shanghai; she died of tuberculosis shortly after their wedding. Sally also passed away several years later, a mere two weeks before the book dedicated to her was published. Gayn was then still in Greece. Two years after that, he remarried once again, this time to Suzanne Lengvary (aka Suzanne Lengvary-Gayn, 1921–2020), a Hungarian actress twelve years his junior. They had met in Budapest, though Gayn was stationed in Paris for four years.[124] His hilarious recollection of their

---

[122] Māku Gein [Mark Gayn], *Shin Nippon nikki: Aru jānarisuto no ikō* [New Japan diary: The posthumous writings of a journalist], trans. Kuga Toyō (Tokyo: Nippon Hōsō Shuppan Kyōkai, 1982).

[123] Mak'ŭ Kein [Mark Gayn], *Haebanggwa migunjŏng: 1946.10–11* [Liberation and the U.S. Army: October–November 1946], trans. Kkach'i Editorial Board (Seoul: Kkach'i, 1986).

[124] Anthony Wu, who worked with Suzanne's estate after she died in 2020 and sorted out photos and papers that would later go to the Thomas Fisher Rare Book

wedding day poignantly illustrates his sense of humor and his take on "actually existing socialism" (Bahro)—as a bittersweet slapstick of socialism's theoretical potential:

> We were married in Budapest, Hungary, by a portly magistrate who [...] wore a broad red ribbon across his chest. He stood under fly-specked portraits of Stalin, Marx and Rakosi, wished us well, and urged us to "fight for world peace." Later in the day, after a wedding lunch with a few friends, I hurried off to cover the trial of an American and a Briton accused of espionage with the flimsiest of evidence. Still later, Suzanne and I saw an important Soviet hit play, "The Wild West." It featured under-dressed women and zoot-suited men engaged in lewd dancing and fighting, typical, the program said, of life in North America. In the triumphant climax, Wall St. imperialists, plotting to install a Missouri haberdasher as the nation's fuehrer, were caught red-handed by U.S. "revolutionary workers."[125]

Although Mark Gayn had by then been a U.S. citizen for several years, his new wife Suzanne was not allowed to enter the country or gain citizenship due to her alleged communist sympathies. In response to such McCarthyism witch-hunts, the couple emigrated in 1952 to Canada and both became Canadian citizens.[126] Gayn began working for the *Toronto Daily Star* but also wrote for papers like the *Chicago Daily News* and *Le Monde*, and published in important weeklies such as the *Nation* and the *New Republic*. In 1959, he became a staff writer for the *Star* and its Eastern Affairs expert, and in 1966 he opened a Hong Kong bureau for the *Star* as a base to cover the Vietnam War, only returning to Canada in 1972. Occasionally, he would also publish articles in the *New York Times* (e.g., a major cover story in 1972 on a visit to North Korea).[127]

Library collection at the University of Toronto, wrote a highly informative blog post on Suzanne and Mark Gayn. See Anthony Wu, "Reporting East Asia: The Collection of Suzanne and Mark Gayn," updated April 17, 2021, accessed August 28, 2023, https://anthonywuart.com/post/reporting-east-asia-the-collection-of-suzanne-and-mark-gayn.

[125] Mark Gayn, with Suzanne Gayn, "Why We Chose Canada," *Star Weekly Magazine* (May 9, 1959): 10. The play is Alexander Afinogenov's (1904–1941) "Vesterny."

[126] See ibid., 10–11.

[127] See Mark Gayn, "The Cult of Kim," *New York Times Magazine* (October 1, 1972): 16–17, 20, 24, 26, 28, 31–32, and 34.

As we learned, Gayn had moved to the United States in 1929, just as the Great Depression unfolded. For a few months in 1933, he himself experienced the life of an unemployed, homeless man living in an old battered Dodge, driving from day job to day job.[128] Let me quote a passage from his early autobiography that vividly conveys his standpoint as a progressive journalist living through those troubled years. His biting portrayal of American society starts with a line about the bourgeois home–car–refrigerator trinity, a symbol of the gilded cage of political talk that never dares to touch the nation's sociopolitical fabric—bold and loud, yet trapped inside an imperial teacup coliseum. It brings to mind Reynolds' ridiculously innocent yet incisive "Little Boxes Made of Ticky-Tacky," her sly anthem about conformist middle-class life. But as we proceed, Gayn shows how his political outlook extends to his own life in the ticky-tacky empire; America almost seemed to be winning his favor:

> They had their little houses, their cars and refrigerators [...]. Each of these was a symbol of economic independence and a certain social status. For generations their mentality had been molded to admire and venerate the virtues and achievements of capitalism, of private initiative, of self-made men. Both psychology and the bank account had made them bourgeois to the core, and they would have resisted bitterly any encroachments upon their possessions and capitalist prerogatives. But the depression—gradually and inexorably—was depriving them of their property. And with their changed economic status came a change in mentality. [...] There were seeds of revolution and violence [...] in the hearts of countless men in countless Hoovervilles and silent, gloomy industrial towns spread over America's face. I did not like it, and my heart was heavy. [...] Capitalism had to act quickly if it was to survive at all and if America was to remain the land of promise. To me, and to millions like me, Roosevelt was the new Messiah.[129]

Gayn evidently placed his hopes on Roosevelt's New Deal policies, envisioning a just and socially balanced society underpinned by a reformed capitalism with strong social foundations. His political convictions were entirely transparent, manifest in every substantial article he ever wrote.

[128] See Gayn, *Journey from the East*, 191.
[129] Ibid., 192–93.

Drawing from his firsthand encounters with various political systems, he consistently reflected on these experiences. Despite his deep grasp of political theory, he kept his distance from engaging in ideological debates over politics. But for a General Hodge, an Alfred Kohlberg, and later a Joseph McCarthy, any continuation of New Deal policies—which they obtusely imagined as inching towards Soviet-style communism—constituted an unacceptable threat to the American way.

The cases of both, Gayn and Robinson, underline Masuda Hajimu's argument that "it would be a mistake to view the period between 1945 and 1950 simply as a prelude, a transitional period, leading to the era of the Cold War and McCarthyism."[130] With the GOP's bicameral victory and New Dealers' ouster in the midterm elections of 1946, at the very latest, the Cold War was on. Historians Wada Haruki, Gar Alperovitz, and Martin Sherwin, however, have long argued that the uranium bombing of Hiroshima and the later plutonium bombing of Nagasaki started the Cold War in August 1945. Three weeks prior, Truman's secretary of state had speculated that with the dropping of the A-bombs, Japan might "surrender before Russia goes into the war and this will save China"[131]—meaning that Manchuria and Korea would be occupied by the U.S.-backed, right-wing Guomindang regime (led by Chiang Kai-shek, aka Jiang Jieshi, in office 1928–1975), not by the Soviets. One of the ultimate goals in deploying the A-bombs was thus to hasten Japan's capitulation in order to deter Stalin and contain *the Soviets* in East Asia. The gradual Japanese attempts to negotiate surrender through the still-neutral USSR were intentionally ignored.[132] (Yet, the obliteration of two more medium-sized cities—two among many others—did not primarily prompt Japan's surrender; rather, it was Stalin's August 8 declaration of war and the rapid Soviet advance into Manchukuo.) The Korean War later solidified this new Cold War framework and empowered McCarthyism.

---

130 Masuda Hajimu, *Cold War Crucible: The Korean Conflict and the Postwar World* (Cambridge: Harvard University Press, 2015), 54.

131 James F. Byrnes (on July 20, 1945), quoted in Michael Schaller, *The United States and China: Into the 21st Century*, 3rd ed. (Oxford: Oxford University Press, 2002), 256.

132 See "Magic" intercept of message from Japanese Foreign Minister Tōgō Shigenori (1882–1950) to Ambassaor Satō Naotake (1882–1971) in Moscow, "Magic"–Diplomatic Summary, War Department, Office of Assistant Chief of Staff, G-2, no. 1204 (July 12, 1945), Top Secret Ultra, Record Group 457, "Magic" Diplomatic Summaries 1942–1945, Box 18, NARA.

Betrayal of a Nation

Richard D. Robinson

(Fig. 13) August 26, 1945, Koreans look on as Soviet troops parade through P'yŏngyang to disarm the Japanese Army and set up their administrative headquarters. The 25th Army had begun entering northern Korea on August 9, just six days before Japan declared its surrender, reaching P'yŏngyang on the 24th.

(Fig. 14) P'yŏngyang, July 1946, procession to celebrate the implementation of the new Labor Law. The vast, framed Kim Il Sung portrait and the meticulously orchestrated harmony in aesthetic and rhetoric of the banners epitomize the Stalinist project in Korea.

(Fig. 15) September 8, 1945, a U.S. Army M8 armored car enters Seoul, guided by a Japanese Army officer, his imposing *shin guntō* sword attached to his waist. After General Hodge's XXIV Corps had landed in Inch'ŏn, an American reconnaissance platoon under Lt. George Foley arrived in Seoul that same day. Four days prior, Brigadier General Charles S. Harris had arrived with another reconnaissance party at Kimp'o Airfield to prepare the formal surrender of all military forces in southern Korea. He had been instructed by Hodge that "Korea ... was an enemy of the United States [and] therefore subject to the provisions and the terms of surrender." On top of this, Hodge had stipulated that "initially ... the present [Japanese Colonial] Government of Korea will be recognized as the lawful Government." (Photo: Alexander Roberts)

(Fig. 16) Oil portraits of Stalin, British premier Clement Attlee, U.S. president Truman, and Chiang Kai-shek displayed on the wall of the Corean Association for the Progress of Fine Arts (Chosŏn Misul Kŏnsŏl Ponbu) in the fall of 1945. The short-lived art society—founded three days after Japan's surrender to the Allied Forces and dissolved on November 20, 1945—is emblematic of the weeks immediately following liberation. The association's program mandated political neutrality in an attempt to represent Korean culture of all political stripes, and its members included all the major modern Korean artists on the left and the right. Only some well-known pro-Japanese collaborators, such as Pae Un-sŏng (who had studied and lived in Berlin and Paris), were excluded. From October 20th to 29th, the society's headquarters held an *Art Exhibition for the Celebration of Independence and the Welcoming of the Allied Forces*. In the weeks that followed—particularly after the December 1945 Moscow Conference decision on "a four-power trusteeship of Korea for a period of up to five years" (p. 88)—the initial enthusiasm for their liberators vanished. Rightist artists like Ko Hŭi-dong quickly became politically engaged, supporting Syngman Rhee, while leftist artists formed their own groups.

(Fig. 17) Taegu, October 1, 1946, a general strike in protest of the U.S. military government's mismanagement of rice collections and its forceful suppression of the railroad strike then underway. Post office workers in sympathy with the railroad strikers demand the use of Korean language and the "Elimination of Japanese telegrams!" (Photo: Yi Yun-su)

(Fig. 18) Taegu, October 2, 1946, the 10.1 Taegu Uprising of 1946 in full swing. Police and demonstrators exchange fire in central Taegu while the U.S. Army supervises the mass arrests of protesters. The uprisings spread to the Chŏlla and Ch'ungch'ŏng provinces and to Cheju Island, killing 92 policemen and hundreds of civilians. (Photo: Yi Yun-su)

(Fig. 19) Seoul, May 1946, the militant right-wing P'yŏngan Youth Association (P'yŏngan Ch'ŏngnyŏnhoe), a precursor to the Northwest Youth Association (Sŏbuk Ch'ŏngnyŏnhoe), mobilizes its youth to vandalize the offices of the communist *Haebang ilbo* newspaper.

(Fig. 20) Seoul Stadium, March 1, 1947. The March First Day rally is organized by the Korean Youth Party (Chosŏn Ch'ŏngnyŏndang). At lower right, members of the small paramilitary Founding Youth (Kŏnch'ŏng) display the group's fascist insignia: an eagle whose upper half resembles the Hitler Youth's eagle (itself modeled on the Nazi Party's *Parteiadler*) and whose lower part—a perched eagle clutching a fasces—echoes fascist Italy. The participants' white shirts symbolize traditional Korean culture but also link them to the fascist terrorist White Shirts Society (Paegŭisa), whose member An Tu-hŭi—while also an agent of the U.S. Army's Counter Intelligence Corps (CIC)—would later assassinate Kim Ku.

(Fig. 21) Seoul, March 1, 1947—"Nationalist forces, regarded with favor by China's Generalissimo Chiang Kai-shek and the American State Department, clash with Korean communist elements who look to Soviet Russia for approval," commented the speaker for *Pathé News*, a British newsreel at the time, adding that "General MacArthur ... declared that the setting-up of an independent Korea was out of the question."

(Fig. 22) Seoul, June 14, 1947. From left, Generals Hodge, Lebedev, and Shtykov at a meeting of the Joint U.S.–Soviet Commission. (Photo: Acme Newspictures)

Editorial Note

Richard D. Robinson's "Betrayal of a Nation" is published here for the first time in English. Robinson completed a first, more extensive draft in mid-1947. Right before leaving Korea with his wife, he burned that manuscript, fearing he would be searched and court-martialed by the U.S. Army. The text published here is an edited and annotated version of his rewritten, shorter manuscript which he generated immediately afterward, on his journey to Turkey, and which he then slightly revised between 1958 and January 1960, also adding one more chapter (ch. X).

We see this work as a mix of a history by a passionate advocate of social change and a primary source document by a critical U.S. Military Government and Military Intelligence insider and eyewitness. A publisher in 1947 or 1960 would certainly have done more heavy-handed editing than is seen here. But we were committed to a light editing approach, treating the original text as a unique, historical document of the post-World War II era. We thus left all antiquated terms, a few awkward constructions, and a bit of somewhat clumsy grammar in place. For the same reason we did not change Robinson's capitalization of "communist" and his explanation for it (p. 68). With very rare exception, our editing was limited to correcting obvious spelling and grammatical errors (of which there were plenty). We also either corrected and annotated or just annotated mistranslations of organization and political party names (mostly replacing these with more conventional renderings that are commonly used in academic works today). We further, with the usual exceptions, replaced all spellings of Korean and Chinese names and terms with transcriptions according to the McCune–Reischauer and Pinyin systems (Hanja can be found in the glossary) and added, if known, the dates for all mentioned persons in brackets.

Two figures Robinson refers to in his manuscript could not be identified with certainty and a third was too large to reproduce here. All three have been left out. All of Robinson's own footnotes are marked with an asterisk (*), while editor-added footnotes are indicated by Arabic numerals. To complement the text, we have added the ten preceding photographs and their captions (figs. 13–22).

The editors

Betrayal of a Nation

Richard D. Robinson

IN MEMORIAM

Dedicated to the memory of Yŏ Un-hyŏng, assassinated on July 19, 1947, in Seoul, Korea—the victim of tragically unenlightened American foreign policy. As a great liberal democrat championing the cause of his people, he fought totalitarianism and opportunism on both the right and left. And, for that reason, he died ....

"It has been the one song of those who thirst after absolute power that the interest of the state requires that its affairs should be conducted in secret. ... But the more such arguments disguise themselves under the mask of public welfare, the more oppressive is the slavery to which they will lead. ... Better that right counsels be known to enemies than that the evil secrets of tyrants should be concealed from the citizens. They who can treat secretly of the affairs of a nation have it absolutely under their authority; and as they plot against the enemy in time of war, so do they against the citizens in time of peace."

— Spinoza, *Tractatus Theologico-Politicus*

TABLE OF CONTENTS

PREFACE

(1960)

The reader will not get many pages deep before he realizes that this book was written in the latter part of 1947. It was just after my wife and I had made a hurried exit from Korea aboard the ill-starred SS *Flying Enterprise* bound for Turkey that I was able to sit down and write out an account of those tragic first two years of the American occupation of South Korea. At that time there was virtually no interest in Korea among the American public, and precious little knowledge. (The alumni bulletin of a well-known New England college referred to Korea as an island off the coast of China!) Even those publishers who believed my story doubted that a book on Korea would sell. They were possibly right. So, after many futile attempts to peddle the manuscript, it was laid away to rest.

The war in 1950 generated great public interest in Korea, of course, but publication of such a book as this during those bitter years would have merely served to confuse issues and perhaps even to further the interests of the enemy. The manuscript remained on the shelf gathering dust. It was not until 1958, almost exactly eleven years after the volume's completion, that any further effort was made to find a publisher.

Very few changes have been made in the original text. The only major one has been the addition of the final chapter, felt necessary to bring the sequence of events within the compass of easy memory of the reader, specifically up to the outbreak of war in Korea in 1950. Too well known to bear repeating here is the ebb and flow of battle in the Korean War, the seemingly endless conference at P'anmunjŏm, President Rhee's [Yi Sŭng-man, aka Syngman Rhee, in office 1948–1960] attempted disruption of the conference by the release of 26,000 North Korean prisoners, the uneasy truce, and finally the liquidation of virtually all vocal opposition to President Rhee within South Korea.

The true significance of my story is the light that it may shed on these later events, a story which to this date has not been told to the American public.

Harvard University
January, 1960

Richard D. Robinson

INTRODUCTION
(1947)

> Those who find American public opinion responsible for Pearl Harbor accept an entirely false theory. Enlightened public opinion is based on accurate public information. The American people, if kept well informed of their real diplomatic position, do not need an incident to unite them. If foreign policy and diplomatic representations are treated as exclusive, secret information of the President and his advisors, public opinion will not be enlightened.
>
> — *Investigation of the Pearl Harbor Attack.*
> 79th Congress, Document Number 244

If the Pearl Harbor investigation proved nothing else, it proved that democracy is only so strong as the truth that is within the minds of men. During the years of World War II military necessity dictated that certain information be withheld from the public, even that of a diplomatic and political nature. Although this point of view apparently still prevails in many official circles, and secret diplomacy remains very much in vogue, the argument as to the necessity of much of the secrecy is an exceedingly dubious one. In order for Congress to pursue an intelligent course through international despondency, it is essential that the public be much better informed than it is as to the machinations of American foreign policy in all parts of the world, whether that policy be right or wrong, victorious or defeated. This, our authorities make all too little effort to do. The result is an inaccurate press and a misinformed public, a dangerous state of affairs for a democracy. I would estimate, for instance, that of all the words written on the occupation of Korea (1945–1947), at least seventy-five percent were either outright fabrication or highly inaccurate. Congress, itself, obtained a dangerously warped story. It is with this thesis in mind that I write on the subject of Korea. In so doing, I admit to the use of a good deal of still classified information.

Some would call the stark truth in such matters a breach of faith an indication of weakness and disloyalty, even treason, but for myself, I prefer to call it a responsibility to the people of our republic, a responsibility which should be felt by all public servants who see things going awry within their bailiwicks. The American Military authorities in Korea ignored this responsibility. Accurate information relating to Korea was highly classified and not available for public consumption, in most instances for no valid military or security reason. Even the basic political policy document for Korea was stamped "top secret" and kept in a carefully guarded safe. Why? Apparently, the reason was to be found in the deep-seated fear that both our civilian and military authorities felt toward the public—perhaps for good reason; if our activities in South Korea had been reported accurately in the contemporary press, events—and people—might have been altered. But as it was, secrecy prevailed and the American press indulged in fantastic flights of fantasy in reporting events in Korea. These inaccurate press accounts were not without their international repercussions.

Almost any criticism leveled against the military authorities in Korea was considered treason by the powers-that-be. I myself heard Lieutenant General John R. Hodge [1893–1963], the commanding general of the United States Army Forces in Korea (USAFIK),[1] say as much to his assembled staff. The policy was to hide everything in the guise of classified military information which could possibly be construed as critical. Mistakes were rarely admitted to anyone. The official American military history of the occupation, classified "secret" for the most part, was highly prejudiced and inaccurate. I should know; I wrote a good share of it. It told the story in half-truths only, for it was written upon explicit orders not even to imply criticism of anything American. One could rant and rave as much as he wished against the Soviet Union and her doings in North Korea, but not one word could he insert in the record indicating that the American Command in South Korea was anything other than perfect in word and deed. In other words, it is a propaganda document for the benefit—and misdirection—of future historians. If the truth were known, the American occupation of South Korea was incredibly bungled by an incompetent, and corrupt administration—all in the name of American democracy. The claim that the Soviet administration of North Korea was worse than the American regime in South Korea is a doubtful rebuttal, even if we stipulate the truth of the claim—which, I think, we may.

I write not as an outsider, but as one who worked for almost two years as a member of the American forces in Korea, first within the Department of Public Information in Military Government and then as a War Department historian for the occupation in the Intelligence Section of XXIV Corps Headquarters, the highest echelon of command in American-held South Korea. All significant documents pertaining to Soviet–American relations in Korea and to local political developments crossed my desk—from published materials to top secret intelligence reports. To the best of my knowledge, the following is the unbiased truth of what took place during the first two years of our occupation of South Korea.

---

[1] Hodge served as the commander of the occupying U.S. Armed Forces, while Major General Archibald V. Arnold (1889–1973) initially headed the U.S. Army Military Government in Korea (USAMGIK), followed by Archer L. Lerch (1894–1947), and finally William F. Dean (1899–1981). Outranking Arnold, Lerch, and Dean, Hodge appointed them to the highest political positions in occupied Korea. Yet, Hodge could not act independently either; he had to report to the higher-ranking General Douglas MacArthur (1880–1964), the Supreme Commander for the Allied Powers in Tokyo.

The original of this book was several times the length of the present volume, nearly every statement being fully documented from indisputable sources. Unfortunately, General Hodge and his detachment of Counter Intelligence Corps (CIC) agents evidenced such obvious displeasure over this proposed revelation of American mistakes and misdeeds in Korea that the volume was burned to avoid personal incarceration. Would that I had had more courage. This present work is a reconstruction of the more complete version. Fortunately, I was able to take with me a file of the *Seoul Times*, an outspoken daily news sheet published in English in the Korean capital, a very complete day-by-day personal journal, and a few other documents.

The story told here is essentially that of two heroes and two villains playing on a congested stage in front of a most disconcerting audience. The two heroes are the two leading Korean liberal democratic leaders, Yŏ Un-hyŏng [aka Lyuh Woon Hyung, 1886–1947]—now dead—and Dr. Kim Kyu-sik [aka Kimm Kiusic, 1881–1950]; the villains, Communist* leader Pak Hŏn-yŏng [1900–1955] and extreme rightist Dr. Syngman Rhee. The unholy congestion on the stage is a myriad of lesser Korean politicos all clamoring for attention. And as for the audience—politically unconscious Koreans pack the main floor; Americans blink stupidly from the box seats; and hackling ill-mannered Russians hoot unmercifully from the galleries. Such was the occupation of South Korea as the play played on to its inevitably tragic finish.

Aboard U.S.S. *Flying Enterprise*
The Indian Ocean
September 8, 1947

Richard D. Robinson

* The word Communist is used in this book only to refer to Soviet-recognized Communist groups and individuals. It is not used in reference to independent leftists, even those holding Marxist convictions.

CHAPTER I: THE BEGINNING

To paraphrase Kipling in the Korean vein, "North is North, and South is South, and never the twain shall meet." Without realizing the disaster which would follow in the wake of his pen, some poor befuddled strategist once drew a line across a map of Korea, that peninsula of 28 million people and 85,228 square miles* dangling down off the coast of northeast Asia between the Japan and Yellow Seas. The line he traced was the 38th parallel of North latitude. North of that border lay the domain of the Red Army, victorious over the Japanese after five days of crashing victories in a sweep down across Manchuria and the mountains of North Korea. By August 9, 1945 the Soviets were waiting impatiently along the 38th parallel for their American comrades to approach from the South.[2] Well over a month elapsed before such a meeting was effected.

Men and Policy

Meanwhile, on Okinawa, "chaos reigned"—so read the official War Department history until General MacArthur's headquarters changed it. No thought whatsoever had been given to the occupation of Korea by American policy makers. Military Government personnel and Japanese linguists had been trained by the hundreds for the occupation of Japan, but the case of Korea had been virtually overlooked. Apparently, the War and State Departments ignored the fact that the occupation and administration of liberated Korea, a former Japanese colony, would require specially trained personnel. The Japanese had exploited the country thoroughly and relentlessly for nearly forty years. Few Koreans had held high positions in government or business, and those who had were *persona non grata* with the rest of the Korean population. Acceptable trained Korean personnel were few and far between.

* Slightly larger than Minnesota but with a population eleven times as great.

[2] It actually took Soviet troops until mid- to late August to reach the 38th parallel.

The Americans who finally formed the occupying force consisted of veteran combat soldiers of the XXIVth Corps headed by Lieutenant General John R. Hodge, a man of exemplary battle record but, as it developed, having little appreciation of the delicate domestic and international political situation in which Korea was enmeshed. Appended to this combat force as an afterthought were a few Military Government officers and men, sent out to the Pacific from their training center at Monterey, California.[3] These men had been trained specifically for the occupation of Japan. Many were Japanese linguists and had put in at least a year studying all things Japanese. A few of the more fortunate were told that they were going to Korea rather than to Japan prior to sailing from the States. Other shiploads were diverted from Japan at the last minute. These were our trained "experts" who arrived in Korea to guide the Korean people through the difficult years of readjustment. I was one of these "experts." More fortunate than most, I had known where I was going before leaving the United States and had had time to read one outdated book on Korea, the only volume I could find on the subject in the Monterey library. No orientation literature was available at the military government training school in Monterey.

General Hodge's political advisors were little better. He was assigned a third-rate State Department "expert" who was of little assistance.[4] At last, in desperation, the general picked a Navy commander,

---

[3] During the Pacific War, the U.S. military operated Japanese language training centers at various universities across the United States to train people in codebreaking and postwar occupation operations.

[4] Hodge's first political advisor was H. Merrill Benninghof (1904–1995), the son of Baptist missionaries in Japan. Benninghof spoke fluent Japanese and from the early 1930s had served as the U.S. Vice Consul in Yokohama. He later worked as a diplomat in the U.S. Embassy in Tokyo, until December 1941, when the Japanese attacked Pearl Harbor. Bruce Cumings notes that although Benninghof was undervalued by many, as by Robinson, in fact he had an important role in the State Department from 1943 to 1945 in planning the U.S. Korea postwar policy. His tenure in Korea was short. Some time in 1946 he was transferred to Manila, where he served as Consul General, and later to Dairen, then under Soviet control, where he assumed the same role. Hodge's second political advisor was William R. Langdon (1891–1963). Langdon also spoke Japanese and had more experience due to his long diplomatic career in the Far East. In June 1947, after Langdon became U.S. consul general in Seoul, Joseph E. Jacobs (1893–1971) succeeded him. Jacobs had previously served in China and headed the State Department's Office of Philippine Affairs.

the son of a former American missionary in Korea, as his advisor. The sole reason for the appointment was that the general had overheard him speaking Korean to a sidewalk vendor and reasoned that he must know something of Korea if he could speak the language. Unfortunately, many of the close Korean friends of American missionaries in Korea proved to be the well-dressed, English-speaking, wealthy, ultraconservative business men—those who had contributed to the missions. Many of these men had made their fortunes during the Japanese regime and were considered as Japanese collaborators by the rest of the Korean populace. The political philosophy of the newly found political advisor was simple: everyone was fer or ag'n the status quo, and those who were ag'in it were Communists. He was quoted around XXIVth Corps headquarters as having referred to President Truman [in office 1945–1953] on one occasion as a blankety-blank Communist. This was the man who introduced General Hodge to Korean politics.[5]

[5] Robinson is undoubtedly referring to George Zur Williams (aka U Kwang-bok, 1907–1994), who was, aside from Harvard-educated Yi Myo-muk (aka Myo-Mook Lee, 1902–1957), immensely influential in the very early days of the U.S. occupation period. Back in 1945, one of Robinson's colleagues described Williams as "a little condescending and rather intolerant of opposition" (p. 140). The young man had grown up in Korea as the son of Frank E. C. Williams (1883–1962), a Methodist missionary and the founder of a Christian school in Kongju. He then completed high school and medical school in Colorado. During the war Williams served as a medical officer with the rank of lieutenant colonel in the U.S. Navy. He was the military surgeon of the fleet commander who transported Army units under Lieutenant General Hodge to Korea. The well-known political scientist Chong-Sik Lee (aka Yi Chŏng-sik, 1931–2021), formerly at the University of Pennsylvania, interviewed Williams in 1988. Yi reports that "on the day Lieutenant General Hodge landed in Inch'ŏn on September 8, he accidentally discovered Korean-speaking Navy Lieutenant Colonel Williams at the Inch'ŏn pier and immediately appointed him as his special assistant" (p. 319). So, indeed, Williams was Hodge's and Arnold's right-hand man for all things Korean from day one. He spoke Korean fluently and was close to many prominent Koreans. The only others Hodge had at his fingertips were Americans who spoke broken Japanese, like Robinson, and second-generation Japanese Americans. Williams stayed in Korea for only a few months, but during these months he created what many Koreans at the time referred to as the "interpreters' government" (*t'ongyŏkkwan chŏngbu*), a power network with a mafia structure. With the blessing of Hodge and Arnold, he helped over 50, mostly ultraconservative second-generation American missionaries into USAMGIK advisory positions, along with some first-generation ones like his own father. On top of that he and Yi Myo-muk arranged for fascists and extreme right-wing Koreans

And what of the policy for Korea, you say? There was none. It was known that the American forces would accept the surrender of Japanese forces south of 38th degrees North Latitude and evacuate Allied prisoners of war. Beyond that, no one knew anything, least of all General Hodge and his staff. Later it turned out that the War and State Departments knew little more, and what little they did know they failed to pass on to those in Korea responsible for implementing the policy. Let us review for a moment.

The first indication the Korean people had that their desires were being considered by the Great Powers was at the Cairo Conference in November 1943. The so-called Cairo Declaration, to which Great Britain, China, and the United States were signatories, stated, "The aforesaid three great powers, mindful of the enslavement of the people of Korea, are determined that in due course Korea shall become free and independent." This was sufficiently vague so as to be subject to diverse interpretations. The Korean people chose to interpret it as promising independence shortly after the end of war in the Pacific—perhaps a few days after—and on that basis they renewed their campaign of non-cooperation with their Japanese masters. Actually, the Cairo Declaration without a Soviet stamp of approval was like a check that required the signature of a fourth partner before becoming valid. That endorsement was forthcoming at the Potsdam Conference in the summer of 1945 when the Soviet Union gave its unqualified approval to the Cairo Declaration.[6]

---

to get positions of power, such as chief of police. And it was again Williams who, after having travelled through the countryside to interview many Koreans, had advised Hodge to bring back Syngman Rhee as a political leader. See "Interview with Commander Williams, Special Assistant to General Arnold" (October 13, 1945), in *Haebang chikhu chŏngch'i sahoesa charyojip, 1: Yaksayu (1)* [Collection of political and social materials from the immediate post-liberation period, vol. 1: An outline history (1)], comp. Chŏng Yong-uk (Seoul: Tarakpang, 1994), 137–40; Yi Chŏng-sik, *Taehan Min'gugŭi kiwŏn: haebang chŏnhu hanbando kukche chŏngsewa minjok chidoja 4-inŭi chŏngch'ijŏk kwejŏk* [The origins of the Republic of Korea: The international situation on the Korean peninsula before and after liberation and the political trajectory of four national leaders] (Seoul: Ilchogak, 2006), 319–21. See also Harold Sugg, "Watch Korea," *Harper's Magazine* 194, no. 1160 (January 1947): 40–41.

[6] Stalin gave his consent to the Declaration during his subsequent meetings with Roosevelt and Winston Churchill in Teheran the following week.

This was the only real statement of policy General Hodge had in his possession when he received word on August 10, 1945, that he was to direct the occupation of South Korea. At that time, General MacArthur's headquarters erroneously notified him that the occupation of Korea was to be a four-power affair (Great Britain, China, USSR, and the US). It was known, however, that the United States would accept the surrender of Japanese military and naval forces south of 38 degrees North Latitude as the Soviets had already done to the north. Just what the occupation zones for the other powers would be was not known by MacArthur's headquarters, and for good reason; they were to have none.

The 38th Parallel

The quest on of the 38th parallel presented an enigma from the beginning. At the outset it seemed to be merely a tactical demarcation between the Soviet and American forces. In repeated statements designed to dispel suspicions in the Korean mind that all was not quite on the level, MacArthur, Hodge, and Military Government authorities declared that the division of Korea had been determined just prior to the end of the war for purely military reasons. However, as months passed and the 38th parallel increasingly took on an alarming semblance to an international frontier, the Korean public began to speculate. It was known that in the late 1880's, when the Japanese were fearful of expanding Russian influence on the Korean peninsula, the Japanese had proposed to the Russians that Korea be divided at the *39th* parallel into two spheres of influence, the northern part to be exclusively Russia's and the southern, Japan's. The Russians refused the offer, and in 1896 an agreement was reached between the two powers which specified that both parties would respect the independence of Korea and help in the task of rehabilitating the country. The suggestion that Korea be divided into two spheres of influence at the 39th parallel was apparently put forward again sometime just prior to the Russo–Japanese War of 1904–05, but this time by the Russians. However, the Japanese war lords were no longer interested in dividing the spoils. They had visions of seizing all of Korea for themselves, visions which culminated in the Russo–Japanese War from which, much to the amazement of the Western world, the Nipponese emerged victorious.

Soon after this, in 1910 (aptly called the "year of snakes" in the Korean calendar), the Japanese coerced the Korean king into signing a treaty of annexation with Japan which made Korea a part of the Japanese Empire.[7]

It was little wonder, then, that when Korea was divided at the 38th parallel in 1945 older Koreans began remembering this earlier proposed division of Korea along a line of latitude only one degree north of the present division at the 38th. Some began wondering if some secret agreement had not in fact been reached among the Great Powers which provided that North Korea would either become Soviet property or be placed firmly within the Soviet orbit of influence. Dr. Syngman Rhee, Washington representative of the Korean Provisional Government of the Republic of Korea [Taehan Min'guk Imsijŏngbu], publicly accused the Allies of awarding all of Korea to the Soviet Union by secret agreement when Korea was not invited to participate in the UNO charter session in San Francisco in the spring of 1945. The suspicion that Russia was to have at least the northern half of the country remained very much alive in the minds of the Korean people and continued to harass the occupation authorities. Alternately, the Yalta and Potsdam Conferences were cited as the locale of a secret agreement to this effect.

Actually, there was considerable reason to believe that the division of Korea originated with the Yalta Conference of February 1945. At that time the Soviet Union specified her willingness to join in the war against Japan,[8] the date being set for her entry at three months after V-E Day. The division of Korea was envisioned solely as a tactical delineation between American and Soviet forces in the event that a large-scale land battle had to be fought on the Asiatic mainland against the Japanese. Just why the 38th parallel was chosen as the division was open to speculation. The strange thing about it was that no one seems

[7] Although the national seal was affixed to the annexation treaty, Emperor Sunjong (in office 1907–1910) declined to sign the document in person, as requested by Japan in order to meet modern international treaty standards. Sunjung's name was instead added by Prime Minister Yi Wan-yong (1858–1926), whose name thereafter became synonymous with traitor and collaborator in Korean historiography. Since Korea had already lost its diplomatic sovereignty under the forced Japan–Korea Treaty of 1905, the drafting of the consequential annexation treaty was completely in Japanese hands in any case.

[8] Stalin first mentioned this to Secretary of State Cordell Hull (1871–1955) at a conference of Foreign Ministers held in Moscow in October 1943.

to know. The most likely story came from a high State Department official in Korea to the effect that the partition at the 38th originated from a longstanding American–Soviet agreement governing the movement of submarines in adjacent waters, American boats not being allowed north of the 38th parallel either in the Sea of Japan or the Yellow Sea. Thus, the present division of Korea was merely a land extension of this previously-established operational line.[9]

According to the same State Department official, there was a distinct possibility that there was no definite agreement at all as to the partitioning of Korea until just prior to the formal surrender of Japan, at which time the United States was planning to occupy all of Korea. It was calculated by army strategists that three large landing forces would be necessary for such an operation in view of the sizable Japanese military establishment in Korea. Originally, the Tenth Army under Lieutenant General Joseph W. Stilwell [1883–1946] had been assigned the task. However, by reason of MacArthur's requirements for the occupation of Japan, the necessary shipping for the movement of an army to Korea was not available. This shortage of shipping necessitated a rapid change of plans, and MacArthur, over a strenuous objection from Secretary of State Byrnes[10] telephoned from Washington, suggested to the Soviet military authorities that they occupy Korea north of the 38th. The Russians readily fell in with the idea. Apparently, this agreement was reached by telephone, and no records were existent. The reader now knows all—I repeat all—the information on the subject known to the highest officials in Korea in 1945–1947. At best, it was speculation. In any event, it is safe to say that the partitioning of Korea was not envisioned originally as anything other than a mere tactical delineation between the Soviet and American troops, such divi-

[9] Today we know that the plan to divide the Korean Peninsula at the 38th parallel was initially proposed by the U.S. and then accepted by Stalin. Two young officers—Colonels Dean Rusk and Charles Bonesteel—suggested this line of division during a short discussion at a State-War-Navy Coordinating Committee session just days before the Japanese Emperor's August 15 surrender broadcast. They were aware that Soviet troops were preparing to enter the peninsula and could soon occupy all of Korea, while American troops would take several weeks to get there. The main U.S. objective was to keep Seoul in the American zone. The 38th parallel, dividing Korea in almost equal zones of occupation, was thus the best result the U.S. could hope for.

[10] James F. Byrnes (1882–1972).

sion to be dissolved by mutual action soon after the occupation of the country had been completed. (Suffice to point out that after fourteen years, the frontier at the 38th parallel remains.[11])

It has been mentioned that originally Stilwell was to direct the Korean occupation, but that the XXIVth Corps was finally assigned the job rather than the Tenth Army. The shipping shortage was a factor in this decision, but it may not have been controlling. When it became known that Stilwell was to go to Korea, Chiang Kai-shek [Jiang Jieshi, in office 1928–1975] was reported to have objected violently to the idea. Chiang dispatched a letter to MacArthur saying in essence that if Stilwell were assigned to direct the Korean occupation, he (Chiang) would make it as rough for him as he could. Apparently, Stilwell was not considered as being sufficiently in love with the Guomindang [Chinese Nationalist Party, better known as Kuomintang] to be trusted in Korea, China's eastern flank.[12] Since the days when the Dragon Throne demanded annual tribute from the Korean kingdom, China had watched affairs in Korea with a jaundiced eye. As of 1945, an unfriendly Korea would have substantially added to the worries of Chiang's government.

The Fog of War

The fog of war hung heavy as the Americans started for Korea in late August 1945. Even as the XXIVth Corps began its movement from Okinawa to Korea, General Hodge was inquiring of MacArthur's headquarters where the Russians were. He was promptly informed that no

---

[11] With the Korean War coming to a halt through an armistice in 1953, the warring sides adjusted the 38th parallel slightly to create a Demilitarized Zone (DMZ) that separated, and continues to separate, North and South Korea.

[12] Chiang voiced his objections regarding Stilwell in an August 2, 1945, aide-mémoire that he submitted to Ambassador Patrick J. Hurley (1883–1963), who quickly forwarded it on to Washington (*Foreign Relations of the United States*, vol. VII, *The Far East: China*, 144–45). This was the second time Chiang had intervened to replace Stilwell, who objected to the Chinese leader's dictatorial and brutalizing methods. In response, Chiang had sent complaints to Roosevelt and, later, to Truman. In October 1944 Roosevelt had Stilwell replaced by General Albert C. Wedemeyer (1896–1989) as the commander of all U.S. forces in China. But Stilwell, in his new position as commander of the Tenth Army stationed on Okinawa, as announced on August 11 and laid out in the plan for Operation Blacklist, was now to occupy Korea. A few days later Truman ordered MacArthur to send someone else. The choice fell on Hodge.

one knew precisely, but there was a distinct possibility that Soviet forces had moved southward across the 38th parallel and occupied Seoul, the capital city of Korea. The American forces were instructed further by MacArthur that, in the event Soviet troops were in fact found occupying the Seoul area, the landing should be delayed until contact could be made with the local Soviet commander. If an international incident appeared possible from an American landing, the matter was to be referred back to the Supreme Commander.

The first contingent of Americans to set foot on Korea was a small advance party which flew in about September 1 to make arrangements for the surrender ceremony, the location of XXIVth Corps headquarters, and kindred matters. The choice of personnel for this party was an unfortunate one. No sooner had the group arrived than it took over a suite of rooms in the Chosun Hotel[13] in Seoul—the largest and plushiest hotel in Korea—and threw a big party for ranking Japanese military and government officials. Koreans who approached the Americans to discuss their plight were summarily shown the door with a minimum of courtesy. The affair turned into a glorious drunken brawl with the Japanese, which lasted for several days. The episode did little to get Korean–American relations off to a good start.

On September 8, 1945, the main body of the American occupying forces landed on the sticky mud bank fronting the city of Inch'ŏn, the major west coast port in the American zone and the seaport of Seoul. In spite of the many reports from Japanese sources that Seoul had been occupied by the Russians, no Soviet forces were found and the landing proceeded on schedule. The following day, the 9th, General Hodge and his staff landed and drove triumphantly into Seoul to accept the formal surrender of the Japanese military and naval commanders in the Throne Room of the pretentious Capital Building.[14] At 4 PM the 36-

[13] Located in Sogong-dong, central Seoul, near the current Lotte Hotel; following liberation, the hotel's English name, "Chosen Hotel," was Koreanized to "Chosun Hotel" (with a 'u'). It was officially renamed as such in 1949 and is now called the Westin Chosun Hotel.

[14] The Capital Building—the former Japanese colonial Government-General Building—was built from 1916 to 1926 in German Neoclassical style. Much of Kyŏngbokkung Palace was demolished to make way for the construction of this new building, which served as headquarters of the country's colonial administration. After Korea's liberation the building was first used by U.S. occupying

year-old Japanese rule of Korea was at an end. A few words, the stroke of a pen, and a nation was reborn—at least, so thought the Korean people on that jubilant autumn day. The Americans were greeted as heroes.

Those first few days everyone was engaged busily in trying to get his bearings. American intelligence officers were frantically gleaning information about the country, elementary information which should have been given to General Hodge well in advance of his landing in Korea. Delay and doubt ensued. Japanese officials were kept momentarily in office.[15] Trained American personnel were not readily available to take over the direct administration of government, and trained Korean personnel were not readily available. At the same time, the Korean and American press was clamoring for immediate evacuation of the Japanese from Korea. To have given way to such pressure would have meant plunging Korea into immediate chaos. To prove the evil intent of General Hodge, one over-zealous American newspaper correspondent quoted the general as having told his troops prior to landing in Korea that Koreans were the "same breed of cat" as the Japanese. What the correspondent failed to say was that the general was referring only to those Koreans who had collaborated voluntarily with the Japanese in selling their countrymen down the river. This alleged remark by the general renewed the clamor for the immediate removal of all Japanese from official positions. On September 18, President Truman stated: "Such Japanese as may be temporarily retained are being utilized as servants of the Korean people and of our occupying forces only because they are deemed essential by reason of their

---

forces, then by the Korean government as the first seat of the National Assembly, and was finally converted into South Korea's National Museum. Then, to commemorate the 50th anniversary of liberation in 1995, the South Korean government had the Capital Building torn down to reconstruct demolished parts of the Kyŏngbokkung.

[15] General Douglas MacArthur declared this in his Proclamation No. 1, issued on September 7, 1945. Article II ordered all personnel to remain at their posts. That basically kept the former colonial structure and all the Japanese government officials in place. See "Proclamation No. 1 by General of the Army Douglas MacArthur" (September 7, 1945), in *Foreign Relations of the United States: Diplomatic Papers 1945*, comp. United States Department of State, vol. VI, *The British Commonwealth, The Far East* (Washington, DC: Government Printing Office, 1969), 1043.

technical qualifications."[16] The statement did little to quell the mounting criticism. MacArthur soon ordered the American Command in Korea to replace all Japanese in government positions as rapidly as possible "consistent with the safety of operations." By the end of January 1946, after five months of occupation, only 60 of the original 70,000 Japanese administrators remained.[17]

While this wholesale governmental reorganization was going on, the political life of the Korean people, pent up for at least forty years, burst forth in a frenzy of activity. General Hodge commented on September 11, 1945 that the situation was "chaotic, with no central theme except a desire for immediate independence." That this was not quite accurate is indicated in the following chapter. Three days after his landing in Korea, the general, in a laudable effort to calm the populace and at the same time secure much needed intelligence as to political organization and leadership, called a meeting of representatives of all political parties. In part the general said:

> I am a man of the people, born on a farm in the United States. I fought in World War I, and have led troops in the Pacific at New Guinea, on Leyte, in the Philippines and on Okinawa. I tell you this so that you may know where my sympathies are in this nation's disputes.
>
> The Cairo Conference promised Korea independence "in due course." That means that when Korea shows that she is able, she will become self-governing. That cannot be accomplished in one day, or two days, or a few weeks. It will take some time.

[16] It was actually Dean Acheson (1893–1971) who penned Truman's September 18 statement four days earlier: Dean Acheson, "Memorandum by the Acting Secretary of State to President Truman; Annex: Draft Statement Prepared for President Truman" (September 14, 1945), in ibid., 1048; full text, 1048–49.

[17] The "Removal" bulletins issued by the Office of the Military Governor provide a listing of those Japanese government employees and advisors in higher positions. The first Japanese to be released of his duties was the Governor of Kyŏngsangnam-do on September 28, 1945 ("Removal Number 2"). With the exception of a former museum director who stayed longer (see p. 300, footnote 96), the process took seven months. The last five Japanese advisors were released on April 30, 1946 ("Removal Number 83"). See Headquarters United States Army Military Government in Korea, Office of the Military Governor, "Removals," reprinted in *Migunjŏng ch'ŏng kwanbo / Official Gazette, United States Army Military Government in Korea*, vol. 2 (Seoul: Wŏnju Munhwasa, 1991), 266–497, especially 266 and 462.

> If too soon, it will result in a breakdown in the nation. And that is not what you want.
>
> I want you to take back to your groups the counsel of faith. ... young people of all nations like to go out into the streets and march. But the enthusiasm of parades is often misunderstood. I ask you to keep down your demonstrations in number and size. . . . The best demonstration is that of good citizens working at their tasks.

In concluding his speech, the general announced that he planned to interview personally all of the major political leaders. He likewise asked that all parties turn in written statements as to their platforms so that he could ascertain their wishes. So far so good on the domestic front.

Meeting the Russians

Meanwhile, the Americans had established contact with the Soviet Command in North Korea, the 25th Soviet Army with headquarters in the city of P'yŏngyang. This army was a subordinate unit of the Soviet 1st Far Eastern Front just as the American XXIVth Corps was subordinate to General MacArthur's headquarters or, as it was officially known, SCAP (Supreme Commander, Allied Forces in the Pacific[18]). The initial contact which the Americans made with the Soviets in Korea was with the Soviet consul-general, Aleksandr S. Polianskii [1903–1984], and his staff in Seoul.[19] Curiously enough, the Soviet Consulate had been allowed by the Japanese to function all during the war apparently with little interference or restriction. There was some suggestion that the consulate had engaged in subversive activities against the Americans in these early days and had distributed Communist literature. But, the basis for that charge was very insecure, the source of the information being Japanese intelligence reports. Polianskii's first request of the Americans was to fly to Japan to replenish his funds from the Soviet Embassy in Tokyo. The request was granted, as were likewise subsequent requests for permission for other official trips to Japan and North Korea. Later, in the spring of 1947, the Soviet Consulate in

---

[18] Also understood to stand for Supreme Commander for the Allied Powers.

[19] Polianskii, his family, and his staff of diplomats spent the entirety of World War II in Seoul.

Seoul was ordered closed by the American Command following a refusal by the Soviet Government to allow the United States to establish an American Consulate in P'yŏngyang.

Before the American landing at Inch'ŏn, there had been recurrent rumors to the effect that the Russians had moved with force into areas south of the 38th parallel, possibly even into Seoul itself. However, it soon developed that the Russians were not in Seoul—nor had they ever been there—but that they had in fact entered some South Korean towns lying closer to the 38th parallel. One such place was Kaesŏng, Korea's ancient capital, which was first occupied by American troops late in September 1945. Upon arrival there, the Americans found individual Russians wandering about but no units. By questioning the inhabitants, U.S. Intelligence ascertained that prior to the arrival of the Americans there had been quite a number of Russians in the town and considerable looting had taken place—probably no worse, one hastens to add, than the looting by American troops in other places. The few Russians still in the town were politely but firmly asked to get back on their own side of the fence. The town was cleared without incident.

American newspaper correspondents followed the movement to the border like hounds on a scent. Although warned by army public relations officers, according to Richard Johnston [1910–1986] of the *New York Times*, that the Russians were "hostile," a group of American correspondents made a foray north of the 38th from Kaesŏng on the same day the Americans first arrived in the town. By all reports, the Russians received them with open arms and cries of "Amerikanskii tovarishch" [American comrade]. A gay night was had by all. The following evening groups of Russians began appearing at the roadblock which the Americans had established the previous day just north of Kaesŏng. The Soviets could not understand why the Americans refused them a welcome after they had given the American press such a big party the night before. However, they were turned away without incident.

As the Americans occupied one frontier town after the other along the 200-mile frontier, it was found that the Russians had established some eighteen or twenty border outposts. Each was manned by at least a squad of Russian soldiers heavily armed with tommy guns. All movement across the border had been stopped with the exception of those Koreans on foot who managed to bypass the Russian guards under cover of night or by circling through the mountains. It was though a tourniquet that had been applied around the collective Korean neck. Food from the agricultural south could not be used to feed the hungry in the north, and coal and manufactured products of the industrial north could not be brought south to ease the lot of the shivering people of South Korea. The economy of Korea was amazingly well balanced if it could but operate as a unit. But with nothing moving across the 38th parallel, the life blood of the country was effectively choked off and everything thrown out of kilter. This was what the closing of the 38th parallel meant to the people of Korea. For that, the Russians can be blamed, for from the beginning the American Command was ready and willing to open up the border for commerce and travel.

As a matter of fact, within a few days after the American landing in South Korea, General Hodge requested of Polianskii, the Soviet consul in Seoul, that he forward to the Soviet Commander in North Korea, Lieutenant General Chistiakov[20] [1900–1979], a suggestion that liaison officers be exchanged between the two commands in order to expedite negotiations toward the end of effecting an early union of North and South Korea. Chistiakov acceded. Forthwith, liaison detachments were exchanged. No sooner done than the Soviet Commander notified the American Command that the exchange of liaison officers had been premature and that no inter-command negotiations could be carried out until agreement had been reached by their respective governments. For this reason, the Russians were precipitously withdrawn from Seoul, and it was strongly implied that a reciprocal withdrawal of the American officers from P'yŏngyang would be desirable under the circumstances. The desire was complied with. This sudden termination was frustrating to General Hodge who had envisioned the rapid unification of Korea on a local level. Obviously, the Russians intended to settle nothing on a local level until so directed from Moscow. Those directions were not forthcoming until after the Moscow Conference of the Big Three Foreign Ministers of the United States, Great Britain, and the Soviet Union in December 1945.[21]

[20] Ivan Mikhailovich Chistiakov.

[21] The Moscow Conference of the Big Three Foreign Ministers (December 16–26, 1945) brought the foreign ministers of the United States, Soviet Union, and Great Britain together to decide on issues pending from the recently concluded war. For

On the Frontier

When the Soviet liaison officers had first arrived in XXIVth Corps headquarters early in October, they brought with them a strongly-worded protest from the Soviet Command on the subject of alleged violations of the 38th parallel by American aircraft. The security-conscious Russians were nervous about American planes flying over them and continued to be so. Protest after protest came in from the Soviet Command citing alleged violations committed by American aircraft. Again and again it was explained to the Russians that many of the American pilots had never flown into Seoul before and that the Seoul airfield was so close to the 38th parallel that a slight error in navigation put the planes over North Korea. Apparently, the Russians were suspicious of these "lost" American planes, and as a matter of fact they had good reason to be so in some cases. Some of them were reconnoitering intentionally just as were Russian planes over South Korea. The Americans were slow to object, but when a Soviet plane crash landed south of Kaesŏng, a city lying just south of the parallel but well within the American zone, the American Command retaliated in kind and initiated a letter to the Russians protesting the violation of the parallel and inquiring as to why the plane had been over South Korean territory. A mistake in navigation was the explanation, and shortly thereafter permission was given to tow the smashed plane north across the border.

So it was that the pattern was set. Every petty infraction of the 38th parallel occasioned an exchange of letters between the Soviet and American generals. The entire occupation was punctuated by caustic letters flowing back and forth across the border citing violations by one party or the other. Most of these violations were so petty that they smacked of the ridiculous. For instance, a North Korean policeman came south and stole a South Korean cow. This act started a whole chain of events which finally led to an exchange of letters between the two generals. It was General Hodge's idea that local commanders along

---

Korea the ministers established a plan to form a Joint Commission to determine which democratic political parties and social organizations to consult with and how to form a united Korean provisional government, followed by a permanent government. This plan, entailing a period of trusteeship, came to evoke massive opposition among large segments of the population in Korea.

the border, both American and Soviet, should be delegated sufficient authority to negotiate local differences on the ground; for instance, disputes about the exact location of the 38th parallel, the return of the South Korean's cow, and the like. Furthermore, the general envisioned sort of a neutral zone between the two commands instead of an exactly fixed line. But, such was not to be the case. The Russian Command was loath to delegate such weighty responsibilities to local commanders, nor could it accept the idea of a neutral zone when Moscow had directed that it should occupy North Korea south to the 38th parallel. That meant an exact line and not a vague neutral zone.

As a matter of fact, this exact demarcation of the 38th parallel gave both commands considerable trouble. It was only in 1947 that the 38th parallel was accurately surveyed and marked by a joint Soviet-American survey group. Before that time, countless disputes arose as to whether a particular spot was north or south of the all-important invisible line. In the first place, the American and Russian maps differed as to its exact location. There was the port of Yŏngdŭngp'o located on a minute point of land northwest of Seoul. Like the much larger Ongjin Peninsula to the west, the point of land on which Yŏngdŭngp'o lay was bisected by the 38th parallel so that it could be reached only by water or by transgressing on Soviet-controlled territory—at least, so it appeared on American maps. However, when a detachment of American troops attempted to land at the town in October 1945, the Russians shooed them away on the ground that their maps showed the port to be north of the parallel and thus within their zone of occupation. The Americans withdrew, and General Hodge considered the matter so trivial as not to merit further debate.

A slightly different situation arose in the case of the Ongjin Peninsula. This piece of land likewise situated northwest of Seoul, projected southward from the Korean coast in such a way that it was severed from the mainland by the 38th parallel. To reach it by land from the American zone, one had to trespass in North Korea or go by water. As soon as this was ascertained, the American Command requested permission to use a road through North Korea for purposes of supplying the detachment of American troops stationed on the peninsula. After considerable delay, permission was forthcoming to so use the road three days a week at a specified hour. Russian guards would convoy the Americans back and forth. And that was the way it was done.

The Moscow Conference

At an early date it became painfully obvious to all concerned that the Russians were in no hurry to unify the country or negotiate anything on a local level. Perhaps they were motivated by a deep-seated suspicion of American intentions in Korea, the backdoor stoop of the Soviet Union. In any event, the Russian Command refused to accept any American sponsored overtures to negotiate. In December 1945, the matter of Korea was referred to the Moscow Conference of Foreign Ministers, participated in by Great Britain, the Soviet Union, and the United States.

It was not until the Moscow Conference was actually sitting that anyone in Korea knew that the subject of Korea was definitely on the agenda. The decision on Korea was awaited with baited breath. The word trusteeship, the same word under which the Japanese had launched their hated regime in 1910,[22] was heard frequently. Korean politicians without exception began muttering, and General Hodge warned our State Department repeatedly against the use of the word and advised against the whole idea of a trusteeship. On December 26, an unconfirmed report came in that the Soviet Union had insisted on a trusteeship for Korea, and the United States, on immediate independence. By December 28, it was known in Korea that the Moscow Conference had risen and the official communique or some explanation would soon be forthcoming. American personnel were cautioned against discussing the Moscow Decision until its official text had been received.

It was not until December 29, three days after the Moscow Conference, that the official communique was finally in the general's hands, and then it was too late. No amount of explaining was going to stop the rumblings of discontent sweeping the country. Late on the

---

[22] Rather, Koreans were reminded of the year 1905, when Japan turned Korea—assisted by the U.S. through the Taft–Katsura Agreement—into a protectorate (*pohoguk*, Jap. *hogokoku*). A survey of newspapers and magazines from the fall of 1945 removes any doubt that a majority of Koreans, both left and right, directly associated the term *sint'ak t'ongch'i* USAMGIK used to translate "trusteeship" with *pohoguk*, protectorate. More tactful Soviets and Koreans north of the 38th parallel, on the other hand, used the gentler Russian term *opeka* (*опека*) or the Korean word *hugyŏn*—both meaning guardianship—for the very same thing, while reserving the imperialistic sounding *sint'ak t'ongch'i* to reference the U.S. and later the UN in southern Korea.

afternoon of December 29 General Hodge held a dramatic conference with the Korean press in which he attempted to explain away the trusteeship clause. He announced, in essence, that within two weeks the Soviet and American authorities would set up a joint commission. This commission would in turn assist in establishing a provisional democratic Korean Government. This Korean Government, according to General Hodge, could then decide for itself whether or not it wished continued assistance from the Allies in the form of technical advisors and law enforcing troops, but such assistance was not to exceed five years in any event. This, announced the general, had been wrongly termed a "trusteeship." It was further indicated that if the provisional Korean Government so desired, all Allied forces would be withdrawn and the sovereignty of Korea recognized without delay.[23] Up to this point Hodge had been given no hint that the United States had reached an understanding with the Soviet Union on the subject of a Korean trusteeship, not only at the recently-adjourned conference in Moscow, but before that at Yalta.

Unknown to anyone concerned with the initial occupation of Korea, the two Allies had agreed informally early in 1945 at Yalta that a trusteeship should be established over Korea while it was being prepared for assuming the status of an independent democratic nation. Such a period of foreign tutelage was obviously necessary in the face of the acute lack of trained Korean political, administrative, business, professional, and technical personnel, Japanese having filled most of these posts for almost two generations. Moreover, the Korean economy was that of a much-exploited colony geared directly to Japan's war effort. It would have to be reorganized from stem to stern if it were to be divorced from Japan and stand alone. For these reasons, President Roosevelt [in office 1933–1945] and Marshal Stalin [in office 1941–1953] had reached an understanding on the subject. It was known that on one occasion, at the Cairo Conference in 1943, the subject was broached informally by the United States to Generalissimo Chiang, and his concurrence was secured.[24] That these negotiations had taken place

---

[23] Part of the Hodge speech is quoted in Caprio's essay in this volume, 436–37.

[24] Research by Xiaoyuan Liu, who also examined Chinese records on the Cairo Conference, suggests that Chiang and Roosevelt most likely harbored strong

was unknown to War and State Department officials in Korea until well after the Moscow Conference of December 1945. In the meantime, the American Command in South Korea caused itself considerable embarrassment by unknowingly issuing statements contrary to the actual fact.

In the text of the Moscow Decision on Korea, given in full below, the actual word "trusteeship" is mentioned only twice.

> 1. With a view to the re-establishment of Korea as an independent state, the creation of conditions for developing the country on democratic principles and the earliest possible liquidation of the disastrous results of the protracted Japanese domination in Korea, there shall be set up a provisional Korean democratic government which shall take all the necessary steps for developing the industry, transport and agriculture of Korea and the national culture of the Korean people.
>
> 2. In order to assist the formation of a provisional Korean government and with a view to the preliminary elaboration of the appropriate measures, there shall be established a Joint Commission consisting of representatives of the United States command in southern Korea and the Soviet command in northern Korea. In preparing their proposals the Commission shall consult with the Korean democratic parties and social organizations. The recommendations worked out by the Commission shall be presented for the consideration of the Governments of the Union of Soviet Socialist Republics, China, the United Kingdom and the United States prior to the final decision by the two Governments represented on the Joint Commission.

---

differences over the idea of trusteeship for Korea's future after liberation. Roosevelt had seemingly entered the November 23, 1943 meeting expecting Chiang's support on trusteeship, while the Chinese leader supported the idea of Korea's immediate independence after the war. The following passage, taken from the Chinese log, is vague over whether the two sides actually agreed to such a plan: "[The two leaders agreed that] Korea should be granted its independence after Japan's defeat. ... As for the method of helping Korea achieve freedom and independence, the two sides had an understanding that China and the United States should cooperate in assisting the Koreans." Chinese log of the conference, quoted in Xiaoyuan Liu, *A Partnership for Disorder: China, the United States, and Their Policies for the Postwar Disposition of the Japanese Empire, 1941–1945* (Cambridge: Cambridge University Press, 1996), 142; see also 141, 143–44.

> 3. *It shall be the task of the Joint Commission, with the participation of the provisional Korean democratic government and of the Korean democratic organizations to work out measures also for helping and assisting (trusteeship)** the political, economic and social progress of the Korean people, the development of democratic self-government and the establishment of the national independence of Korea.
>
> *The proposals of the Joint Commission shall be submitted, following consultation with the provisional Korean government for the joint consideration of the Governments of the United States, Union of Soviet Socialist Republics, United Kingdom and China for the working out of an agreement concerning a four-power trusteeship** of Korea for a period of up to five years.
>
> 4. For the consideration of urgent problems affecting both southern and northern Korea and for the elaboration of measures establishing permanent coordination in administrative-economic matters between the United States command in southern Korea and the Soviet command in northern Korea, a conference of representatives of the United States and Soviet commands in Korea shall be convened within a period of two weeks.

The italicized portions of the "Decision" certainly implied that the imposition of some sort of trusteeship was a foregone conclusion, not something to be left up to the discretion of a provisional Korean Government, as had been stated by General Hodge in his December 29 press conference.

The blunder of the foreign ministers in Moscow in using the word "trusteeship," the very same word[25] the Japanese had used for their hated regime, was an obvious one. A dozen other terms might have been used—guardianship, period of assistance, guidance, transitional period or the like. But no, it had to be trusteeship, and that hit a psychological trigger in the Korean mind which made the public lose all reason. As wave after wave of resentment swept the country, dangerous tension began building up in Seoul. On December 29, crowds of surly Koreans milled in the streets. Armed American troops tried to disperse them. Most of the shops were closed. There was little laughter

---

* Italics are the author's.

[25] It was not the same phrase, but the meaning came close. See p. 85, footnote 22.

or joy in the Korean heart. At noon all Korean translators and interpreters employed by Military Government held a mass meeting to decide whether or not they would strike. Fortunately for Military Government, the decision was postponed, and before any further action could be taken the Military Governor very shrewdly declared a ten-day holiday for all Korean employees. Without interpreters and translators, Military Government would have been like a great blinking owl whose whoos were neither heard nor understood by the rest of the inhabitants of the Korean woods.

Tension continued to mount. All Americans were ordered to stay off the streets after eleven in the evening. But it was not until December 31 that the pent-up emotion broke loose. Army intelligence had issued warnings of an impending demonstration. Tanks and some light artillery had been brought into the city during the previous night just in case. During the morning of the 31st rumors of coming violence and terrorism were on everyone's lips. All American military personnel were ordered to stay on 24-hour duty. The morning's press conference at Military Government was another dramatic session; the air fairly crackled. General Hodge had received a radiogram from the State Department confirming his interpretation of the Moscow Decision. Again it was patiently explained that the so-called "trusteeship" would not be imposed on Korea without the consent of the provisional democratic Korean Government soon to be established, and even if a trusteeship were established, it would be nothing more than an advisory mission to aid the Korean Government.[26]

The explanations were too late. Thousands upon thousands of people poured into the central part of Seoul. Korean flags flew from every building. The day was bitterly cold, but still the people came—old and young. At two in the afternoon the demonstration started; a great mass of madly cheering people marched past the Capital gates. The city rang with a chorus of "manse!" (Long live Korea!) calls from a hundred thousand throats. The hills echoed with the plaintive melody

[26] On December 31, 1945, Hodge tried to explain this to the Korean people in a press conference and even appealed to Washington to "kill the trusteeship idea," while Syngman Rhee and Kim Ku (1876–1949) reacted by organizing large-scale demonstrations and declaring USAMGIK to be illegitimate. See *Chosŏn ilbo*, December 31, 1945, and James I. Matray, "Hodge Podge: American Occupation Policy in Korea, 1945–1948," *Korean Studies* 19 (1995): 24–25, 36.

of the Korean national song, sung, incidentally, to the tune of "Auld Lang Syne." But despite the crowds and tremendous patriotic fervor of the people, there was no violence or disorder. General Hodge had wisely given orders that there would be no attempt to break up the demonstration. There were roving patrols of armed troops, but these were carried in closed trucks where they were out of sight and would not incite the people. Throughout South Korea similar demonstrations were held. In North Korea, the Moscow Decision had not yet been made public.

As the fervor gradually subsided in South Korea and word got out to the country that the imposition of trusteeship was yet to be decided, life returned to normal. During these troubled days, the American Command let it be known on several occasions that it favored Korean independence, that it had so advised Washington from the beginning, and that a demand for immediate Korean independence had been the American stand at the Moscow Conference. General Hodge had reason for believing that such had indeed been the case. However, on January 27, less than a month later, the Soviet news agency TASS issued a long communique to the Korean press through General Terentii Fomich Shtykov [1907–1964],[27] head of the Soviet delegation to Joint Soviet-American Conference then in session in Seoul, categorically denying these charges. Rather, TASS stated, it had been the United States which had first proposed trusteeship, such trusteeship to be ten years in duration, and that the Soviet Union had favored immediate independence. The compromise reached was a five-year trusteeship. Moreover, TASS claimed, it had been at Soviet insistence that a clause was

[27] A protégé of the Soviet ideological leader Andrei Zhdanov (1896–1948)—for years the most powerful man after Stalin and a kind of Soviet counterpart to America's Joseph McCarthy (1908–1957)—Shtykov was clearly the man in charge of North Korean politics and influenced all related decisions during the entire period from 1945 to 1950. It was then up to Nikolai Georgievich Lebedev (1901–1992), head of the Soviet Civil Administration in northern Korea, to implement Shtykov's directives in the political and administrative system. We should mention that Shtykov left a detailed diary that covers the period he was involved in Korean politics, although part of this record did not survive. A Korean translation was published at the end of 2004. This is supplemented by Lebedev's memorandum, published in a Korean edition in 2016. See *Shwittŭikkop'ŭ ilgi, 1946–1948* [The Shtykov diary, 1946–1948], comp. Chŏn Hyŏn-su (Kwach'ŏn: Kuksa P'yŏnch'an Wiwŏnhoe, 2004); and *Rebedep'ŭ pimangnok* [The Lebedev memorandum], ed. Kim Yŏng-jung (Cheju: Haedong, 2016).

included in the Moscow Decision calling for the early establishment of a provisional democratic Korean Government.[28] General Hodge radioed frantically to the State and War Departments for either confirmation or denial. Meanwhile, public relations officers in Military Government censored the TASS report so that it was not broadcast over the Seoul radio station. The Korean press immediately found out about it and raised the free speech issue in a conference with American authorities on January 29. The Americans had claimed repeatedly that there was no such thing as censorship of legitimate news in South Korea. General Lerch, the Military Governor, stated that, no request to broadcast the TASS release had been received and, therefore, it could not have been censored.[29] However, to my personal knowledge, such a request had been made, and Military Government authorities had ordered that the TASS statement be killed. It all looked to the Koreans very much as if the United States had something to hide.

By this time, answers to General Hodge's radios to Washington had been received. Yes, it was true that the United States had proposed a ten-year trusteeship for Korea, and further, that the proposal had been based on understandings reached at Yalta and subsequent occasions. The American Command in Korea then found itself in the unenviable position of being forced to call itself a liar, which it did as diplomatically as possible. General Hodge informed the State Department that it would be of interest to him to know what the American policy in relation to Korea was, that he—in theory, at least—was supposed to implement. The Department was also reminded of the fact that the Korean press had access to Associated and United Press services, and that statements from Washington should be coordinated with what was said in Seoul.

---

[28] This report is found in "TASS Statement on the Korean Question" (January 23, 1946), reprinted in Ministry of Foreign Affairs of the U.S.S.R., *The Soviet Union and the Korean Question (Documents)* (Moscow: Ministry of Foreign Affairs of the U.S.S.R., 1948), 7–10.

[29] For USAMGIK censorship, see the *History of the United States Armed Forces in Korea*, part 2, chapter 1: "Relations with the Korean Press," online version at https://db.history.go.kr/item/level.do?itemId=husa. *Proclamation No. 2*, issued on September 17, 1945, prescribed "the death penalty in cases of any act against the occupying forces or any act which might disturb the peace," a formulation broad enough to include press reports critical of the U.S. administration.

Public opinion polls run by Military Government at that time indicated that with this exposure of apparent duplicity on the part of the United States Government, American prestige in Korea had hit a new low. If the Koreans were confused, the Russians must have been more so. The American Command had wrongly charged them with having sponsored a Korean trusteeship while the Americans championed the cause of immediate independence. It is probably fair to say that this bit of double play may have jeopardized the entire course of Soviet–American cooperation in Korea. The Russians, already suspicious of American objectives in Korea by reason of the political mumble jumble in South Korea,* no doubt felt that their worst suspicions had been confirmed; the Americans were attempting to increase their own prestige and influence in Korea at the expense of the Soviet Union, even if that meant torpedoing the Moscow Decision. 1946 had gotten off to an inauspicious beginning, not only internationally, but also in the realm of domestic Korean politics.

CHAPTER II: INTRODUCTION TO KOREAN POLITICS

Korean politics were so intimately involved in the play of international forces upon Korea that it was difficult to separate one from the other; they were part and parcel of the same struggle. Although to the American newcomers the Korean political scene initially seemed to present nothing but an unfathomable jungle, it was not long before the tangle was resolving itself and falling into a relatively simple pattern.

Political life in Korea—as in many places—rested on a struggle between the right and left. There was little support for any middle-of-the-road movement. The liberals, the social-democrats, the moderate socialists were very much in the minority and without mass popular support. The Korean people were not sufficiently well educated nor interested in governmental affairs to understand such democratic phi-

* Refer to Chapter II.

losophies or to make such a system as they espoused operative. It will be shown later that both right and left were totalitarian.

To speak of democracy in such an environment was perhaps unrealistic. But neither the State Department nor the American military authorities in Korea seemed to doubt. The Russians, on the other hand, realistically started in North Korea with the apparent assumption that democracy was impractical and would only mean the enslavement of the Korean people by the dominant economic interests. The Russians, therefore, ruthlessly began to destroy these interests; the American began by currying their favor. Both powers mouthed democratic phrases while patiently pursuing undemocratic policies.

Soon after the beginning of the Korean occupation the myriad of political parties cluttering up the scene shook down until there existed four major parties on the left and three on the right. On the left were the Korean Communist Party [Chosŏn Kongsandang] under Pak Hŏn-yŏng, the Korean People's Party [Chosŏn Inmindang] headed by Yŏ Un-hyŏng, the New Korean People's Party[30] headed by Kim Tu-bong's [1889–1960?] Yan'an Korean Independence Alliance [aka North China Korean Independence Alliance, Hwabuk Chosŏn Tongnip Tongmaeng] in North Korea. These groups differed for the most part in only two respects; (1) the degree of Communist control and (2) the historical position and associations of the group. On the right of the political alignment were the Korean Independence Party [Han'guk Tongniptang] directed by Kim Ku, the Nationalist Party [Kungmindang] presided over by An Chae-hong [1891–1965], and the Korean Democratic Party [Han'guk Minjudang] under Song Chin-u [1889–1945]. These groups differed in three respects: (1) their attitude toward Kim Ku and the Korean Provisional Government in exile, (2) their view toward certain economic matters, and (3) the historical associations peculiar to the party.

In both the rightist and leftist camps were found front organizations which posed as "non-political," semi-governmental organs. The

[30] Robinson's manuscript actually named it "Korean Revolutionary Party," which would refer to the Korean National Revolutionary Party (Chosŏn Minjok Hyŏngmyŏngdang), a party that was formed two decades earlier by exiled Koreans in China. While also associated with Kim, Robinson, unless he was misinformed, must have meant to refer to the Chosŏn Sinmindang, formed in P'yŏngyang in February 1946 by the Yan'an faction and headed by Kim Tu-bong.

left had its Korean People's Republic [Chosŏn Inmin Konghwaguk], first directed by Yŏ Un-hyŏng, and later by Hŏ Hŏn [1885–1951].[31] American opposition to the governmental prerogatives assumed by the People's Republic ultimately caused it to lose power and prestige shortly after the occupation opened. Its successor was the Democratic National Front [Minjujuŭi Minjok Chŏnsŏn], likewise led by Hŏ Hŏn. These groups apexed the political organization on the left and served as a general propaganda agency and coordinator of activities. Soon after their inception, the People's Republic and later, the National Front, became tools of the Communists, behind which they could hide their control of the left wing.

---

[31] During colonial times Hŏ Hŏn had become famous as a lawyer and intellectual, as he had defended the signers of the March First Independence Declaration and many March First activists in court. Thereafter he continued to defend journalists, leftists, and communist activists. In 1943 he was imprisoned and tortured. By 1945 he had become one of the most important leaders of the left, and in early September 1945, as Robinson mentioned, he was one of the three co-organizers of the Korean People's Republic. Later, in November 1946, he also functioned as a co-organizer of the Namnodang, the South Korean Workers' Party. Still, USAMGIK reports repeatedly characterize him as a moderate, non-communist leader of the communists. When, on August 11, 1947, USAMGIK issued an arrest warrant against Hŏ and other leaders of leftist and communist organizations, he went underground—but not without sending General Hodge a formal letter of protest. Hŏ Hŏn's letter to Hodge is worth quoting, as it very eloquently describes how USAMGIK's policy was experienced by moderate and leftist activists:

> "Since the eve of 15th of August, all the organizations of the democratic camp have been occupied and closed by force, all of the democratic leaders containing me are sent to the rear for safety [...], most of whom already arrested, and every [*sic*] democratic presses and their staffs have been closed [...]. Even almost all houses of leftist-symphasizers [*sic*] are inspected at dark night by the police or terrorists; and their properties are destroyed at random, their every family members [*sic*], even the oldman, woman and infant, are beaten mercilessly, and not few of them are kidnapped away somewhere by barbarous terrorists. Even the subscribers of the Democratic newspapers are regarded as leftists and thrill [*sic*] under the constant threst [*sic*]."

Quoted from: Hŏ Hŏn to General John R. Hodge (August 29, 1947), reprinted in *Haebang chŏnhu Migugŭi taehan chŏngch'aeksa charyojip* [Source materials on the history of the U.S. Korea policy before and after liberation], vol. 10, comps. Chŏng Yong-uk and Yi Kil-sang (Seoul: Tarakpang, 1995), 218.

In April 1948, Hŏ Hŏn left for northern Korea and was soon later elected to chairman of the Supreme People's Assembly and became president of Kim Il-sung University.

The Korean Provisional Government, organized in Shanghai in 1919 under the leadership of Dr. Syngman Rhee and, later, Kim Ku, was the central focal point about which all right-wing political groups oriented themselves. This so-called Provisional Government made repeated claims to governmental authority in Korea. The anti-trusteeship movement in the early days of the occupation, spearheaded by the rightists, brought about the formation of the Emergency National Congress [Pisang Kungminhoeŭi Chubihoe]. The tongue-twisting National Society for the Rapid Realization of Korean Independence [Taehan Tongnip Ch'oksŏng Kungminhoe] was organized as the provincial organization of this so-called National Congress. A battle between Kim Ku and Dr. Rhee ensued for control of this powerful right-wing group, which soon usurped the political power and prestige of both its parent organizations, namely the Provisional Government and the National Congress.

Although the political organization of South Korea might have been relatively simple, the political ideologies of the diverse groups were not. Very few observers understood why one Korean political group was on the left and another on the right. To begin with, the historical background and associations of the various groups and leaders must be taken into consideration. During the decade prior to 1945, the underground opposition movement against the Japanese was spearheaded by the Korean Communists. Their peculiar cellular organization lent itself best to the resistance movement. All political groups in opposition to the Japanese, both right and left, accepted this Communist leadership and cooperated in the general effort to make the stay of the Japanese in Korea as uncomfortable as possible. As one Korean put it, "Many had leftist mouths and rightist stomachs." Political stratification among politically active Koreans during those early days was a simple one; there were the Communists and the non-Communists. By reason of their leadership against the Japanese, the Korean Communists gained great prestige, even among the mass of Koreans who were, for all intents and purposes, politically unconscious. Actually, the political struggle in Korea was from the beginning sparked by very small politically-conscious groups which tugged endlessly in all directions on the great vacillating amoebic body-politic.

While this Communist-led resistance movement against the Japanese was going on within Korea, Korean groups emerged elsewhere—

in China, in the United States, and in Manchuria. In China and Manchuria, Korean armies were recruited to fight the Japanese invader alongside the Chinese Nationalists and the Chinese Communists. Korean leaders began to come into their own. During the first few months after the Americans landed in South Korea these various groups began filtering back into Korea. Personal followings had been built up by some of them, in some cases in the form of private armies. Deep bonds of friendships were created, which remained even though the individuals did not see eye to eye on political philosophy. Divorced from this historical background, Korean politics seemed like an unholy hodgepodge of strange bedfellows and paradoxical situations.

However, in addition to this historical development and emergence of personal friendships and followings, there were a number of issues upon which the right and left were generally divided. These were as follows:

Primary Issues:

1. *International attitude*. The Korean Communist-left was inclined to consider the Soviet Union as the fountainhead of all good and the United States as the source of all evil. The right considered itself to be the bosom friend of the United States and was not loathe to voice loud criticism of all things Russian. The moderates were inclined to be suspicious of both powers. Obviously, the Korean rightists were much in favor of the Chinese Nationalist Government, the left, in favor of the Chinese Communists. Both Chinese groups reciprocated with special privileges for their Korean friends.

2. *Land reform*. Both right and left favored reform, but the method of achieving it differed. The left believed that all former Japanese land, as well as that of the large Korean landlords, should be confiscated and redistributed without charge to the tenants who worked the land. The rightists, on the other hand, said that Korean landlords from whom land was taken should be reimbursed for their loss and, moreover, the tenants who received the land should pay for it. The fact that the left refused to believe that the right was sincere in supporting land reform of any kind was a factor which entered into the struggle. As a matter of fact, the number of large landowners among the right-wing leaders made one wonder

just how sincere the right was on this score. Land reform was important, for the building up of a large educated middle class was impossible unless the tenants could derive some further benefit to themselves from the land on which they toiled. It was of interest to note that not even the Communist Party favored outright nationalization of the land.

3. *Method of reform.* All political groups, right and left, professed to believe in democratic procedure. Actually, only a very minute group in Korea had any conception of what democratic procedure was. The Communist-left believed in class warfare and revolution; the right, in a police state and force. Both would have liquidated the opposition if given the opportunity. (As Syngman Rhee has done in the post-occupation years in South Korea and the Communists in North Korea.)

Secondary Issues:

1. *Trusteeship.* The right led the movement against imposition of a trusteeship and for immediate independence. The left, on the other hand, believed that a certain period of assistance was necessary in setting up a democratic provisional Korean Government. The Communists probably supported the idea of a trusteeship because they hoped that Communist-controlled North Korea and Communist elements in South Korea could join forces under a Soviet-American trusteeship and gain the upper hand over all of Korea. Similarly, the rightists felt that the Communists would gain under such a trusteeship and, therefore, opposed trusteeship and demanded independence even if only for South Korea.

2. *Pro-Japanese Issue.* The left pounded the right with the charge that the latter was pro-Japanese, that its leaders were Japanese collaborators. There was a certain element of truth in this charge, but it was carried to ridiculous extremes. In order for anyone to have made a living in Korea before liberation, one was forced to collaborate with the Japanese to a greater or lesser degree. The Communist-left also charged the right-wing Korean Provisional Government, which had maintained its headquarters in China from the time of its inception in 1919 to 1945, with having deserted Korea in time of its greatest need and that its leaders had lived a life of

luxury abroad while the left-wing leaders were fighting in the anti-Japanese underground within Korea. (There was an element of truth in this contention.)

3. *Commerce*. The right favored immediate opening of Korea to foreign trade. The left wished such trade to by carefully controlled, evidently fearful of "capitalistic penetration" by the United States.

4. *Industry*. Both right and left favored—at least, in word—the nationalization of major Korean industries. However, the left very obviously doubted the sincerity, and it cited the large industrial interests, of many right-wing leaders.

5. *Social Custom*. Korea was steeped in Confucian moral codes and, as such, had been peculiarly impervious to social change of any kind. The right wing, whether consciously or not, was more or less supporting the maintenance of the social status quo. The left, however, was working for such reforms as the emancipation and equality of women, right of divorce, progressive education and the like.

It should be pointed out before passing on to a more detailed account of Korean political life that a large proportion of the Korean political leaders were nothing but insincere bigots, bandits, and would-be demagogues striving to achieve personal political—and hence, economic—power. They mouthed democratic phrases, but that was all the deeper their democratic ideas penetrated. Surrounding these soldiers of fortune, who were bought and sold daily on the local political market, were whole coteries of followers motivated by the same longing for plunder. The long-suffering Korean people suffered on.

The Korean Communists

The non-Communist left was in control of the Korean peninsula when the Americans landed there on September 8, 1945. However, of necessity, the story of the Korean left wing begins with the Communists. Information as to the early days of the Communist movement in Korea is meagre and confusing. Apparently, the movement had its inception among members of the Korean community in the Russian city of

Irkutsk, located near Lake Baikal in south central Siberia. Here, early in 1920, a group of Korean Communists assembled. On the pretext that they had a sizable following within Korea, the leaders of this Irkutsk group allegedly hoodwinked the Third International out of some 40,000 yuan (several hundred thousand dollars at that time) for purposes of organizing a Korean Communist Party, and thereupon fled to Shanghai to enjoy their plunder.[32]

Meanwhile, in Korea, then under the relatively liberal rule of Admiral Saitō Makoto [in office 1919–1927, 1929–1931],[33] a so-called Korean Laborers' Association [Chosŏn Nodong Kongjehoe] was formed. Actually, membership was not drawn from the laboring classes, but, rather from communistically-inclined professional groups in Seoul. Membership was probably not more than 300. This was in January of 1920. In November of that same year, the All Korean Young Men's Union [Chosŏn Ch'ŏngnyŏnyŏn Haphoe], likewise inspired by Communist doctrines, was organized. This latter organization soon boasted a membership of 30,000, included in which was one Pak Hŏn-yŏng, one day destined to become the leader of the Korean Communist Party. The nucleus of this nation-wide union was the Seoul Young Men's Association [Kyŏngsŏng Ch'ŏngnyŏnhoe], the only section to survive later Japanese police oppression.

In the meantime, the Shanghai group which had originally received official encouragement from the Comintern, began infiltrating into Korea proper in the attempt to build up the popular following which it had previously assured the Comintern was already in existence.

---

[32] The author refers to the Communist Party Fund Case, to Kim Rip's (1880–1922) alleged embezzlement of 400,000 rubles (earlier believed to have been 40,000 yuan) of funds that Han Hyŏng-gwŏn had received on Lenin's order in Moscow. That story about the untrustworthiness of Korean socialist activists also made it into Western research (e.g. Robert A. Scalapino's work) that informed on the Korean socialist movement. More recent research, also making use of a wider range of sources, however, indicates that the money seems to have actually been allocated by Kim Rip—in his position as secretary to Yi Tong-hwi (1873–1935), the founder of the party—to Korean liberal and socialist activities back in Korea as well as to support socialist groups elsewhere in Asia. The rumors and allegations seem to have mostly been spread by members of the Korean Provisional Government in Shanghai and the rival Irkutsk communist group.

[33] Following the March First Independence Movement, Saitō served as Japanese governor-general of Korea (Chōsen) from September of 1919 to 1927 and again from 1929 to 1931, a relatively liberal phase of colonial rule.

Likewise, the disgruntled group which had been left in the lurch at Irkutsk when the Shanghai-bound clique absconded with the Comintern funds began migrating to Korea. The local Korean Communist movement was soon split into two rival camps, one supporting the Shanghai faction and the other, the Irkutsk faction. This was the source of much of the early disunity within the Korean Communist movement and which was later reflected in personal squabbles among the leaders.

By 1924, following a new wave of Japanese oppression, Pak Hŏn-yŏng and others formed a group called the New Thought Research Association [Sin Sasang Yŏn'guhoe]. By this time the original Laborers' and Young Men's Association had pretty well disintegrated as a result of action on the part of the Japanese gendarmerie [Kenpeitai, the Military Police Corps]. There were then two chief opponents in Communist circles: Pak's new Institute and the Seoul Young Men's Association; this latter group being the only portion of the All Korean Young Men's Union remaining more or less intact. Soon thereafter, Pak's Institute changed its name to Tuesday Society [Hwayohoe]. By reason of the malodorous act of the Shanghai group in turning to their own private use part of the money donated to it by the Comintern, this faction ultimately fell into official disgrace. By 1924, most of its major leaders had fallen in with Pak's Tuesday Society. Pak's leadership was forced on them because of the popular following which he had gathered in Korea.

On April 17, 1925, the Korean Communist Party was officially organized. Leadership was divided between one Kim Chae-bong [1890–1944], who headed the main body of the organization, and Pak Hŏn-yŏng, who took over the organizational section of the party as well as the all-important Korean Young Men's Federation [Ch'ŏngnyŏn Ch'ongdongmaeng], a Korean counterpart of the Soviet Komsomol. Apparently, sometime before this took place, Pak had received official recognition through a man known vaguely as Betchinsky,[34] then head

[34] This was Grigori Voitinsky (aka Wu Tingkang, 1893–1953), the new Soviet state's main agent, contact, propagandist, and influencer in China. Since 1920, Voitinsky was critically important to Soviet support of the Chinese communist movement and became the cofounder of the Chinese Communist Party. In his later years he taught at Moscow State University and came to be known as the father of Soviet Sinology.

of the Far Eastern Bureau of the Comintern. Kim Tan-ya [1899–1938], a rather shadowy figure, was allegedly dispatched to Moscow to represent the party in the Comintern (and supposedly was still there as late as January 1947 acting as the real power behind the Korean Communist Party).[35] Soon thereafter, another faction of Korean Communists is said to have petitioned Betchinsky demanding a change in leadership. The petition, however, was denied.

Possibly in contradiction to this, but not necessarily so, were rumors to the effect that in the early 1920's Lenin decided against lending support to the Korean Communists and, instead, aided the Korean nationalists. During the early stages of Stalin's rule, according to the same stories, Russia abided by a secret agreement with Japan and abstained from encouraging Communists in Korea. This support of nationalistic groups would be well in line with later established Comintern policy. In the program of the Comintern, for example, is found this statement of principle:

> The principal task in such countries [i.e., those with "feudal medieval relationships, or 'Asiatic mode of production' relationships"] is, on the one hand, to fight against feudalism and pro-capitalist forms of exploitation and to develop systematically the peasant agrarian revolution; on the other hand, to fight against foreign imperialism and for national independence.*

In any event, at this point in the movement, 1925, the Japanese police stepped into the picture and put a quietus on activities by arresting many of the Communist leaders and effectively breaking up the organization.[36] A later attempt to reorganize the party met the

---

[35] Robinson, or rather the military intelligence report he based his statement on, may have confused Kim Tan-ya with someone else in a position of power between liberation and the Korean War. Kim Tan-ya had died in 1938.

* "The Programme of the Communist International," adopted by the Sixth World Congress on September 1, 1928 in Moscow, *International Press Correspondence* [Vienna] 8, no. 92 (December 31, 1928), repr. in Communist International, *Blueprint for World Conquest* (Washington, DC: Human Events, 1946), 210–11.

[36] The 1925 Peace Preservation Law (Jap. *Chian ijihō*, Kor. *Ch'ian yujibŏp*) sanctioned ten years' imprisonment for anyone who violated it in Korea or Japan: "Anyone who has formed a society with the objective of altering the national polity [*kokutai*] or the form of government or denying the system of private property, and

same fate. Pak was imprisoned a short time but finally regained his freedom and fled to the Soviet Union. Apparently, he remained there from 1927 until 1930, at the end of which time he turned up in Shanghai, only to be re-jailed by the Japanese for Communist activity. Ultimately, he was escorted back to Korea under guard and finally released. This time he retired from active participation in politics and concealed his identity until 1945 under the guise of a common laborer and an assumed name, working the while in the Communist underground.

During the twenty years intervening between the abortive 1925 effort to organize a Communist Party in Korea and the liberation of Korea in 1945, only one Communist group of significance crept into prominence on the Korean scone. This was known as the Marxist–Leninist Party [Marŭk'ŭsŭ Reninjuŭidang], or more simply the ML Party [ML-tang]. Organized in 1935, the group was but short-lived.

On the evening of August 14, 1945, the eve of Korea's liberation, two political groups were meeting in Seoul. One was assisting Yŏ Un-hyŏng in establishing his Preparatory Committee (see below), and the other was discussing the revival of the Korean Communist Party. When the two groups became known to each other, a merger was quickly effected, and two days later, on August 16, all but Yŏ and one other had joined forces to form the Seoul Communist Party [Kyŏngsŏng Kongsandang]. This group is considered to have been at the time of its inception a nationalistic faction willing to compromise with the right wing for the promotion of Korean independence. Likewise, on August 16, Pak Hŏn-yŏng showed up in Seoul, having been most recently employed as a bricklayer in Kwangju, a city some distance south of the capital. With him he carried a membership list of the old 1925 Communist Party and of the anti-Japanese underground, plans for reorganizing the party, and most important of all, the latest instructions from Moscow. Suffice to say that within a short time, by August 28 to be exact, the bulk of the local Communists had fallen in with his leadership and organized the Rehabilitation Communist Party [Chaegŏnp'a Kongsandang]. This Pak-led organization was more pro-Soviet

anyone who has joined such a society [...], shall be liable to imprisonment [...] for a term not exceeding ten years." Quoted in Richard H. Mitchell, "Japan's Peace Preservation Law of 1925: Its Origins and Significance," *Monumenta Nipponica* 28, no. 3 (Autumn 1973): 339.

than its momentary rival, the Seoul Communist Party. By November 1945, the last of the dissenting members of the rival group had been forced to join Pak's Korean Communist Party, but the source of future friction within the party remained, as was made obvious by continued efforts on the part of disgruntled Communists to challenge Pak's leadership. Pak's control was so severely shaken at one time that in 1948 he was forced to repair to P'yŏngyang in North Korea for new instructions and authority.

The Korean People's Republic

As World War II ended, the Japanese authorities in Korea were hard pressed to maintain law and order and to protect the safety of their own persons. Moreover, they wished to find a government acceptable to the Russians, whom they believed would occupy all of Korea. The aid of Korean leaders was enlisted in the hope that some impromptu Korean government could be set up. Shortly before the cease fire order was given ending hostilities in the Pacific, Japanese Governor-General Abe [in office 1944–1945] asked Song Chin-u, later the much-respected leader of the then-moderate right-wing Korean Democratic Party, to form a government. Song refused, and the same request was put to Kim Chun-yŏn [1895–1971], an early leader of the moderate Marxist–Leninist Communist group.[37] Again a refusal was encountered. Finally, on the evening of August 14, Yŏ Un-hyŏng received word that the governor-general wished to see him.

---

[37] In the first half of the 1920s Kim had studied Politics and Law at Berlin University, and organized anti-Japanese Korean student meetings and protests there. He also translated Stalin's booklet on Leninism, then worked for the *Chosŏn ilbo* newspaper as its first Moscow correspondent. He later served as editor in chief of the *Tonga ilbo*. He played an instrumental role in the reorganization of the ML Party and was one of the main leaders of the Korean Communist Party in colonial Korea, for which he consequently spent many years in jail as a political prisoner. He immediately flipped after liberation, however, and supported the right-wing nationalists and Syngman Rhee, who made him his Minister of Justice. But in 1951, when the ROK Army under division leader Ch'oe Tŏk-sin (1914–1989, see p. 232, footnote 79) executed over 700 unarmed villagers near Taegu—known as the Kŏch'ang Massacre—Kim Chun-yŏn was dismissed from office for refusing to go along with Rhee's attempt to cover-up the genocide.

Yŏ was the enigma of Korean politics from the start. His powerful oratory and deep understanding of his people made him a political force with which the Americans were forced to reckon. Originally snubbed and periodically called a "known Communist" by the American Command, he was one of the very few Korean politicos who evidenced sincere concern for the lot of the common folk. He fought totalitarianism and opportunism on both right and left. At times he himself was called an opportunist by both Americans and Koreans because of his apparent vacillation. It is my opinion that Yŏ knew and loved his people far better than most those who stood back and condemned him. It seems likely that at one time Yŏ had approached the Japanese with promises of Korean economic cooperation in establishing the Greater East Asia Co-Prosperity Sphere [Dai Tōa Kyōeiken] in return for the nominal political independence of Korea. No doubt, Yŏ was convinced that this was the only way in which Korea could rid itself of the hated Japanese police, the Western world having long forgotten the Korean cries for help registered at Versailles and The Hague in the early 20's. Yŏ was simply making the most out of a bad deal. It is known that Yŏ had once held a card in a Korean Communist group in Shanghai and that he had visited the Soviet Union in 1921–22. However, there was no evidence—official American statements to the contrary notwithstanding—to indicate that Yŏ ever had been a member of a Comintern-recognized Communist Party.[38] In fact, shortly before the Americans arrived in South Korea, he refused point blank to join Pak's Communist Party. Yŏ was called a "known Communist" on occasion by the American Command simply because he recognized the inevitable fact that Korea would in all likelihood find itself within the orbit of Soviet influence whether it liked it or not, and acted with that fact in mind. He refused to indulge in the hate-Russia campaign

[38] Robinson is mistaken here. When Yŏ saw that the Comintern propagated social equality and assisted the Koreans with funds to support their anti-colonial goals, he accepted such support. In 1920 he first joined the Koryŏ Communist Party (Koryŏ Kongsandang) in Shanghai and later, in May 1921, moved to Siberia to work with the rival Korean communist faction in Irkutsk. In early 1922 Yŏ also attended the Congress of the Toilers of the East in Moscow and met with Lenin and Trotsky. In the first half of the 1920s, both the Shanghai and the Irkutsk groups had been much larger and better organized than the Chinese communists and, in those years, Yŏ had been one of the major figures propagating communism to his fellow countrymen.

sponsored by the Americans or to accede to the leadership of Communists, though he maintained relations with them and on occasions found himself more or less at their mercy. In every case, however, he fought free. His ideal was a rationalist, democratic-socialist state. In an interview with a group of American correspondents in the spring of 1947, the following exchange took place:

> Question: "What are your political convictions?"
> Yŏ: "I am a Marxist."
> Question: "How does that differ from a Korean Communist?"
> Yŏ: "I am a nationalist, and I do not believe in totalitarianism."

He might have added that he rejected force and violence as political devices in a free Korea. Because Yŏ was these things, he was disliked and sniped at by extremists of both camps, although remaining *persona grata* with the Russians. He traveled to and from North Korea without interference from North Korean authorities, apparently by reason of his great personal prestige. On July 19, 1947, he was shot and killed in Seoul, the victim of the tenth assassination plot directed against his life since the American landing in Korea less than two years before. With him died the hope of Korean liberalism. That he was killed just as much by American policy as by the assassin's bullets will become evident as the story of those two years unfolds. The tragic course of events leading to his untimely death began that day in August of 1945 when the Japanese governor-general asked that he form a government.

Yŏ was informed by the governor-general that the Japanese were going to surrender the following day and was requested to form an organization to aid in the maintenance of law and order. Supposedly, the Japanese placed a considerable sum of money at Yŏ's disposal, although this has never been definitely established. Yŏ accepted the offer under five conditions: (1) that food for the coming three months be guaranteed (2) that political prisoners be released; (3) that freedom of the press and speech be guaranteed; (4) that there be no mobilization of students for the maintenance of peace; and (5) that there be no interference from the Japanese. With these conditions, Yŏ apparently intended to isolate the Japanese from direct influence in government. In any event, the Japanese felt that they had no alternative but to accept the conditions.

That same day, August 14, Yŏ and his younger brother, Yŏ Un-hong [1891–1973], drew up a tentative organization which included Song Chin-u* and other leaders who were far from the extreme left. The next day, Yŏ the elder was called before the Japanese Vice-Governor Endō Ryūsaku [1886–1963] and told that the Americans would occupy merely the Pusan and Mokpo areas, two ports in the extreme south. Thereupon Yŏ revised his organization so as to include only Communists and Communist sympathizers, men whom he regarded as acceptable to the Russians. Even so, An Chae-hong, considered to be a moderate rightest in political conviction and affiliation, was invited to participate in the organizational hierarchy.**

The organization which Yŏ so promptly formed, first called the Preparatory Committee for the Establishment of a Korean State [Chosŏn Kŏn'guk Chunbi Wiwŏnhoe], quickly assumed governmental functions not envisioned by the Japanese offer. In mid-August 1945, a few days after its inception, this group adopted the following sweeping resolutions as to its objectives: (1) to establish an autonomous Korea enjoying political and economic independence; (2) to destroy imperialism and residuary feudalistic influence in the state, (3) to be faithful to the principles and ideals of democracy which must materialize in the basic political, economic, and social needs of the nation; (4) to secure a rapid elevation in the living standards of the laborers and peasants; and (5) as a member of the democratic countries of the world, to help establish world peace through cooperation.

As the days went by without the arrival of any American forces, the Japanese administration overcame the initial shock received from the news of unconditional surrender and realized that Yŏ had no intention of following its dictates. The Japanese officials were also under pressure from the Japanese military to disown Yŏ's Preparatory Committee. To reduce the power claimed by the Committee, the Japanese Government-General took the peculiarly Japanese method of ordering its name changed, whereupon, it became the Public Safety Committee. Meanwhile, the Japanese military endeavored to prevent

---

* Who later became the head of the Korean Democratic Party, an ultraconservative group.

** An Chae-hong later headed the Nationalist Party, a right-wing faction—perhaps not quite as conservative as the Korean Democrats.

Yŏ's Committee from exercising even police powers. The Japanese added some three thousand soldiers to the regular police force, transforming them to a civilian status overnight, and attempted to discredit the Public Safety Committee. Yŏ was not, however, to be suppressed. The Japanese had created a Frankensteinian monster which they were unable to control.[39]

When the American occupation was announced, Yŏ grasped the American privilege of free political endeavor, and on September 6, two days before the American landing at Inch'ŏn, in effect constituted his group not only as a political party but as a government, the "Korean People's Republic." The presidency and vice-presidency were offered to the as-yet absent Dr. Syngman Rhee and Kim Ku, respectively, but neither would accept. Later, on January 10, 1946, both were "expelled" from the offices which they had never accepted. Yŏ Un-hyŏng, Hŏ Hŏn and Yi Kang-guk [1906–1956][40] were prominent figures throughout, although Yŏ ceased active participation in the Republic in November 1945 when he launched his Korean People's Party. The People's Republic, on its lower levels of organization, grew in part spontaneously, in part under Japanese direction, in part under Communist control, and in part under conservative auspices. In many places the new groups moved to fill a virtual governmental vacuum. In some cases previously existing revolutionary committees or farmers organizations took over *in toto* the functions of local government and became units of the People's Republic. In other communities, new groups were elected. These local units, known as People's Committees [Inmin Wiwŏnhoe], assumed the prerogatives of government in hundreds of communities throughout Korea and began enforcing the peace, collecting

---

[39] It was around this time that the Japanese Government-General of Korea began to contact the United States forces still in Okinawa by radio to report that the Korean peninsula was being overrun by communists. The U.S. responded by telling the Japanese to maintain control until it arrived.

[40] Yi Kang-guk, a graduate of Keijō Imperial University, and by 1946 one of the three top leaders of the South Korean Workers' Party (Namnodang), had been active as a Comintern agent and agitator in Berlin. Put on the "wanted" list by the U.S. Military Government in Korea in early September 1946, Yi fled to the North, where he was later executed—much like Pak Hŏn-yŏng, the head of the Namnodang. For details, see Frank Hoffmann, *Berlin Koreans and Pictured Koreans*, Koreans and Central Europeans: Informal Contacts up to 1950, vol. 1, ed. Andreas Schirmer (Vienna: Praesens, 2015), 77–81.

taxes, and carrying on other governmental functions. The People's Republic and its constituent People's Committees remained, in theory, non-partisan and set themselves up as the *de facto* government, a fact which was soon to bring the entire organization into sharp conflict with American Military Government in South Korea. At this point, it is safe to say that the Republic was controlled by the non-Communist left and was a sincere effort on the part of Yŏ and others to establish a democratic government both on the local and national levels.

On September 6, 1945, two days before the Americans landed, Yŏ's Provisional Korean Commission called a "Congress of the People's Representatives," and the entire structure was thus welded together and given a shield of alleged popular support. According to a pamphlet issued in English in Seoul on October 5, 1945, by the "Government of the People's Republic of Korea," "the delegates to the congress were revolutionists who had studied Korean problems more than anyone else and who had fought for the cause till the very last day." The statement continued, the "congress was given the power to elect fifty-five People's Committees to found the People's Republic of Korea."

The first contact which the American Command had with this erstwhile government, the Korean People's Republic, occurred on September 8, 1945, when its representatives presented themselves at XXIV Corps Headquarters aboard the AGC Catoctin anchored off Inch'ŏn. It was learned by the Americans that the organization was composed of 130 separate committees throughout Korea and had as its objective the organization of a democratic form of government. General Hodge was advised not to see these men himself, both because of the fact that they were allegedly supported by the Japanese and because it was considered unwise to give even the slightest appearance of favoring any political group at that time. These men did talk with members of the Corps staff, however, and gave from memory a list of Koreans who could be depended upon and another list of those who were said to be Japanese collaborators. They asked about the American point of view toward the various Korean "governments" in exile, assured the Americans of their full recognition of United States Military Government, and offered their own services in a liaison capacity between that government and the Korean people. They showed some concern over the division of Korea at the 38th parallel, about currency inflation, about the discipline of American troops, and about the food situation. They were also most emphatic in expressing their belief that all Japanese should be evacuated from Korea.

By the middle of September 1945, the People's Republic was in control in all major communities of Korea. The country was dotted with People's Committees. It was soon learned that a number of these had seized governmental authority without the sanction of the people. Others, however, had been elected legally and were supported by popular will. It is safe to say that for the most part the local People's Committees in these early days were of the genuine grassroots democratic variety and represented a spontaneous urge of the people to govern themselves. Some Committees were strongly Communistic; others were not. Obviously, almost all were leftist in nature; the peasants and workers demanded long overdue land and labor reforms and protection from the terroristic Japanese-trained police and dishonest politicians. It was natural that these Committees were jealous of the revolution—and it was just that which they had accomplished. They resented orders from Military Government to turn the administration of local government over to American Army officers and their appointed Korean counterparts, many of whom were considered to be Japanese collaborators. It seemed like a reversion to what had gone before. Bloodshed ensued in many communities as local People's Committees defied Military Government and refused to abandon government offices, Koreans and Americans met in pitched battles, and not a few Koreans met violent death in the struggle.

During September, the People's Republic had organized many subsidiary groups throughout the provinces, in part to protect itself. One of these was called the "Student Public Peace Body" [or better, Youth Security Force for the Founding Nation, Kŏn'guk Ch'ŏngnyŏn Ch'iandae], composed, according to American Intelligence, of "radical students, thugs, and criminals—armed as far as possible." It was reported that "the more law-abiding Koreans" felt that no permanent peaceful settlement of Korea's political problems could be effected until these pseudo-political public safety organizations were disbanded. Their fears appear to have had some substance, for when one of the Republic's branches in Pusan was disbanded forcibly on September 28, some 257 rifles, 14 pistols, and 3 shotguns were found.

Many instances of the assumption of governmental functions by unauthorized groups connected in some way with the People's

Republic could be cited. For instance, there was the case of Namwŏn, a small town in North Chŏlla Province. The Japanese had turned over considerable property to the local People's Committee just prior to the arrival of the Americans. Military Government demanded the property, but the People's Committee refused to renounce title. Whereupon, five leaders of the Committee were arrested by the local Korean police. Shortly thereafter, the police chief was captured and beaten by Committee members and the police station attacked by a large crowd of irate citizens. The station was guarded by American troops. When the Koreans refused to disband, the Americans advanced with fixed bayonets. Two Koreans were killed and several injured.

This incident was typical of many such cases, but the People's Republic and its local People's Committees licked their wounds, continued to shout their defiance and quite naturally became more extreme and destructive.

The October 5 statement issued by the "Government of the People's Republic of Korea," already quoted, claimed,

> ... the government of the People's Republic of Korea is the government of the people, by the people and for the people. It stands for all classes. It has nothing to do with communists' dictatorship or capitalists' hegemony; it represents the will of the Korean people and is supported by them. Therefore, American authority should let the People's Republic of Korea take over all the administrative organs as well as economic establishments.

This declaration was a clear bid for power.

Other than the charge of non-recognition of popular sovereignty, the "Government of the People's Republic of Korea" had other complaints against the occupation authorities. Again quoting from the October 5 manifesto addressed in English to the "Dear Citizens of United States!"

> A few days ago the Military Government of U.S. Army in Korea issued a decree that says, "No gathering, no procession or parade should be held without permission of the government authority." Taking General Hodge's message in confidence, we were suspicious about the newspaper release. Suppose the decree is true, our aspiration and agitation will

> be in vain. Do you think it is possible to build a new nation in a democratic way without freedom of speech, without freedom of mass meeting, without freedom of all political activities? U.S. Army is too generous to the Japanese. The Japanese came to Korea penniless and acquired wealth by political and military influence. Koreans have less than twenty per cent of the wealth of all Korea, while the Japanese in this country still enjoy comfort and luxury. As long as present economic conditions continue, the reconstruction is absolutely impossible to imagine, no matter what efforts Americans exercise. The Military Government seems to sympathize with only a few Korean capitalists, ignoring the poor masses. The majority of the population lives below the starvation level and there is no so-called middle class in this country. If a Korean is not rich, he is in poverty. Again, wealthy persons and men of political or upper social positions in Korea are naturally pro-Japanese and often naturalized Japanese. How could any patriots make fortunes under the shrewd Japanese rule? Moreover, under Japanese control, if he was a "respectable gentleman," he could not be a true patriot, because we have been just poor slaves. Our people beg you to recognize the underlying reality of the Korean situation.

Advisors to General Hodge whispered "Communists" and "Russian penetration" into the general's ear. Their view seemed to have some validity. After all, in North Korea, the Soviet command had virtually recognized the Korean People's Republic by authorizing the local People's Committees to maintain law and order. But there was a difference; the Red Army was present in North Korea and had been for several weeks. Hence, the Communists within the Republic and its Committees had the upper hand from the start in North Korea. In South Korea, Yŏ and the non-Communists probably held control at the outset. Apparently, it never dawned on the U.S. command to make use of the popular support generated by the Republic by working with the organization—rather than against it—and by so doing turn it to constructive and democratic ends. Instead, the Republic was destroyed in South Korea and the moderate leftists initially in control were destroyed in the process. The Communists fell heir to what was left organizationally. "We told you so," they must have said. "The Americans are no friends of the People." And indeed, such seemed to be the case. Even Yŏ accepted Communist domination for a time; where else was he to turn? The Americans ignored him.

The American Command sought to undermine the popular prestige of the Republic through a campaign of vilification. On October 10, 1945, Major General Archibald V. Arnold, then Military Governor of Korea, issued the following statement:

> TO THE PRESS OF KOREA
>
> What I say and hand you today must be given a prominent place in the front page of every newspaper. This is a request with the force of an order.
>
> The liberation of Korea from the heel of Japan is of course an occasion for celebrations, for demonstration and speechmaking. Freedom of speech and freedom of press having been given to the Koreans, it is to be expected that many foolish and ill-considered statements will appear in the newspapers under amateur editorship. So long as peace and order are not endangered, and so long as disorder is not fostered and no attempt is made to interfere with the orderly administration of the government, such boyishness even by old men will be allowed to evaporate as smoke in the air.
>
> There is only one government in Korea south of 38 degrees North Latitude. It is the government, created in accordance with the proclamations of General MacArthur, the General Orders of Lieutenant General Hodge and the Civil Administration orders of the Military Governor. It is an organization made up of carefully selected Koreans working under the Military Governor and his officers. It has exclusive control and authority in every phase of government. Self-appointed "officials," "police" groups, big (or little) conferences "representing all the people," the self-styled "Government of the Republic of Korea," the (self-appointed) "Executive Committee for the Republic of Korea," are entirely without authority, power or reality.
>
> If the men who are arrogating to themselves such high-sounding titles are merely play-acting on a puppet stage with entertainment of questionable amusement value, they must immediately pull down the curtain on the puppet show. If some 'peace preservation' groups have sincerely but childishly

acted (without violating laws) to aid law and order, they will now disband and return to proper work to aid Korea [to] feed and clothe and house itself during the coming winter. There is honest work for fair wages for which they are needed. The man power of Korea will have to provide for the basic comfort of the people this winter.

If behind the curtain of these puppet shows there are venal men holding the strings who are so foolish as to think that they can take to themselves and exercise any of the legitimate functions of the Government of Korea let them pinch themselves and awaken to the realities of the situation. Let us have no more of this.

A fraud on the people of Korea has been recently publicized in the free press, namely, calling of a "fictitious" election on the first of March 1946 at which it is proposed that 'all men and women over the age of eighteen, except traitors, will have the right to vote.' Nothing is more sacred to a free people than the right to vote and to elect their own representatives in Government. The right is too sacred to be made a toy of self-appointed statemen who attempt to lead the people with false hopes. The right to vote can only be exercised in the manner and at the times prescribed by the Government for elections. For any man or group to call an election as proposed is the most serious interference with Military Government, an act of open opposition to Military Government and the lawful authority of the Government of Korea under Military Government.

If the people of Korea value the freedom of speech, the freedom of press, and the freedom from many restrictions under which they have long suffered, which freedoms have come to them in recent days, the time has come for the moral leadership of the people to assert itself and prevent the abuse of these freedoms by either foolish or venal men.

The Korean people should prevent any possible threat to the peace and order of their country on the part of irresponsible persons; by doing so they would make it unnecessary for the Government to intervene and exert the power and authority which it possesses.

This heavy sarcasm and thinly-veiled contempt on the part of American Military Government was the answer Yŏ got for his troubles in trying to establish something resembling democracy. And to add insult to injury, Military Government then went about appointing an eleven-man board of advisors, all but two of the appointees being very much on the conservative side of the fence. Though Yŏ was one of the two non-conservatives, he considered the appointment an insult and refused to serve. The group was soon receiving such unfavorable publicity and resembled so much former groups of advisors called in by the Japanese, that the Americans shortly found it wise to forget about the whole project.

By way of an answer to this American activity, the People's Republic published during the third week in October and distributed in Seoul a pamphlet entitled "The Traitors and the Patriots." The pamphlet, largely true, exposed the pro-Japanese and anti-American nature of the Koreans who were acting as advisors to Military Government by quoting from public statements made by them against the Americans during the Japanese rule of Korea. "Communist propaganda," said General Hodge's advisors, some of whom were of missionary origin and were acting to protect their wealthy conservative Korean friends who periodically laid golden eggs for the missions.

That the People's Republic was a potent force at the time cannot be doubted. After an extensive visit to the rural areas, Dr. Horace H. Underwood [aka Wŏn Han-gyŏng, 1890–1951],[41] an advisor to Military

[41] The Underwoods of the typewriter company were the most prominent of the old missionary families in Korea. Horace H. Underwood repatriated to the United States after the war began; he then worked on Korean affairs with the OSS, CIC, FBI, and the Office of War Information. A vigorous anti-communist and Cold War hawk, he had a key role, next to George Zur Williams (see pp. 71–72, footnote 5), as USAMGIK's main country specialist, especially after Williams had left. He also recommended other, mostly ultra-conservative, Christian missionaries and English-speaking Korean Christians (many of whom had openly collaborated with the Japanese, like Underwood himself) for positions in the U.S. Military Government. In his advisor role he actively promoted Syngman Rhee while discrediting all other Korean political leaders, even Kim Kyu-sik, whom his own father had raised as an orphan. In March 1949 his wife Ethel would be killed by leftist terrorists, in an attack seemingly aimed at Mo Yun-suk (aka Marion Moh, 1910–1990), a poet, former pro-Japanese collaborator, and wife of Germanophile right-wing philosopher and Minister of Education An Ho-sang (1902–1999; see Hoffmann's essay on fascism).

Government, a former missionary in Korea and a scholar of Korean history, stated that the Republic was the strongest and most active organization throughout South Korea.[42] By comparison, the leading right-wing group at that time, the Korean Democratic Party, was poorly organized or unorganized in most places, and seemed to have nothing as attractive to offer as free land to the farmers and management of the factories to the workers.

Although the People's Republic under the leadership of Yŏ stopped short of open revolt, it continued to be troublesome to the Military. It defied Military Government's wishes by insisting that it would hold national elections on March 1, 1946, by devoting itself to self-expression rather than union with other political groups, and finally, by refusing at the end of a three-day meeting on November 20–22, 1945 to drop the word ***kuk*** (meaning "republic" or "government") from its name.[43] This last was an act of defiance difficult to ignore, since Military Government had specifically requested that the name be changed to avoid misunderstandings which had arisen about the Republic's status. The leaders had assured Military Government that the name would be so changed. Military Governor General Arnold himself went to the meeting and delivered a brief speech stressing the need for cooperation and order during the following critical months. He pointed out that any possible material aid from Allied sources depended in a large measure upon how the people of Korea conducted themselves. The majority were not convinced. In the resolution of gratitude passed by the meeting for transmission to each of the Allies, the offending word "kuk" was used. Furthermore, on the final day,

---

Their son Horace G. Underwood (aka Wŏn Il-han, 1917–2004)—who was named after his grandfather, the first of the Underwood missionaries in Korea—served as a U.S. Navy lieutenant during WWII and also worked as an interpreter. During the Korean War he interrogated North Korean POWs for the U.S. Marines.

[42] Underwood's report had been submitted directly to Robinson's office: U.S. Army Forces in Korea (USAFIK), MG, Office of Public Opinion, Political Trend No. 11 (December 8, 1945).

[43] ***Kuk*** actually just means country or nation; if combined with ***konghwa***, however, it forms the term for "republic" (***konghwaguk***). What the author, not a speaker of Korean, meant to say is that the U.S. Military Government demanded that the People's Republic drop ***kuk*** in ***Inmin Konghwaguk*** (People's Republic) and replace it with ***tang*** for political party, to become ***Inmin Konghwadang***, which could then be translated as People's Republican Party, or that it choose an entirely different name.

younger and more radical elements ran away with the meeting and shouted down those who wished to comply with the request that the name be changed. In spite of this independent attitude, the Republic did, at this same meeting, publicly resolve to cooperate fully with the American Command until such time as the government was turned over to the people.

Giving more point to the situation was the fact that, immediately after this defiant meeting of the People's Republic, the old Korean revolutionist, Kim Ku, returned to Korea from China bringing with him several members of the self-styled Korean Provisional Government. This meant for the Republic that the issue was joined. It had no choice but to outdo its rival pseudo-government, amalgamate with it, or disappear into the oblivion of history.

Adding to the complexities of the situation at the time was the fact that just prior to the riotous three-day meeting, Yŏ Un-hyŏng, the acting head of the People's Republic and the very man who had carried Military Government's request for a change of names to the central committee, suddenly bolted from the Republic to form on November 12, 1945, what was at first a more tractable middle-of-the-road organization called the Korean People's Party. With Yŏ went many of the members of the parent organization, leaving Hŏ Hŏn, Yŏ's old running mate, and Pak Hŏn-yŏng, the Communist Party leader, as the central figures connected with the Republic. This was the third blow which presaged the final oblivion of the Republic, the first two having been the refusal by the American Command to recognize the Republic as a government or listen to its leaders and General Arnold's press attack against the Republic on October 10. The fourth and final blow was a hard-hitting statement issued by General Hodge on December 12, 1945, specifically denouncing the Republic and reviewing a long list of allegedly broken promises and obstructionist acts. It appears in part below:

> Before the arrival of my forces in Korea there was set up here an organization known as the Chosŏn Inmin Konghwaguk (Korean People's Republic). ... The name connoted, and its actions indicated, that this organization was set up to be a government rather than a political party and its leaders spread the word to the Korean people that it was their new government. This has caused many misunderstandings among the

> people. ... However, because of misunderstandings arising from the name and actions of the Korean People's Republic, some groups operating under its banner have defied and opposed both openly and secretly the efforts of the Military Government of Korea, caused serious delays in establishing economic stability of your country and actually delayed progress toward Korean independence which we all so greatly desire. ...
>
> At the end of the convention (November 20–22) I was greatly surprised and disappointed to find that although they agreed in words to cooperate with and aid the Military Government of Korea, the leaders and representatives had in some ways used the convention to aggrandize themselves further as a Korean government, had intimated that the Military Government is aiding and abetting their organization in its attempted activities as a government, and had left considerable confusion in the minds of Koreans everywhere. In other words, they failed to keep their promise to me that the situation would be completely clarified.
>
> Because of this failure after my long patience, I feel it necessary to the public understanding to announce that, regardless of what it calls itself, the Korean People's Republic is not in any sense a 'government,' and is not authorized to act in any capacity as such. The only functioning government in Southern Korea is the Military Government of Korea.
>
> Therefore, in order to eliminate further misunderstandings and cloaked disorders, I have today directed my occupation forces and the Military Government of Korea that the activities of any political organization in any attempted operations as a government are to be treated as unlawful activities, and that necessary steps will be taken at once to insure that no political organization operates in any way as a government in any portion of the American occupied area without specific authority of the Allied Powers ...

Although the ultra-conservative Korean Democratic Party, the Republic's arch enemy, thought the statement hardly strong enough, the reaction of the People's Republic was immediate and vigorous. The Republic leaders deliberated furiously all night and half the next day and finally released a rebuttal difficult to refute. The main points were:

(1) that the confusion and misunderstandings were due to slanderous advice of pro-Japanese traitors; (2) that the change in name was promised only as an item for discussion at the National Assembly and the body had voted against it; (3) that after the meeting, President Hŏ Hŏn had agreed to all the points of a letter sent to him by General Hodge except the proposal to refrain from using the word "kuk"; (4) that the so-called Provisional Government (Kim Ku's) was tacitly permitted to refer to itself as such, and even to hold "cabinet meetings"; and (5) that such an attitude "might be subjectively consistent, but that objectively it was confusing to the public." The first four of these points were patently true, and the American authorities knew it. The fifth was a bit obscure to say the least.

The Americans acted and forcibly ejected all remaining members of the People's Republic or its constituent People's Committees from governmental posts. In this respect it is of interest and significance to take note of what happened in the east coast province of Kangwŏn. When Military Government authority was first extended over the province in October 1945, it was found that the People's Republic controlled the three easternmost counties along the coast. When county chiefs, appointed by the Military Governor of the province, arrived in these three counties they were promptly jailed. The provincial Military Governor, correctly appraising the situation, directed that locally-elected Republic leaders be recognized officially as government officials. In December 1945, these leaders were ordered by the Americans to disband their People's Committees insofar as the operation of government was concerned and to limit the activities of the Committees to those of a political nature. All agreed to this edict and, further, agreed to take orders from the provincial governor. Everything was going smoothly. But, on December 12, the above-quoted statement from General Hodge was received outlawing the People's Republic from affairs of government. The Provincial Military Governor was forced to fire the officials of the three eastern counties, and from that time on there was nothing but trouble in the area as the American-supported conservative minority attempted to hold power against the left-wing majority. American-sponsored democracy, under such auspices, made little progress.

By the end of 1945, with Yŏ and his associates out of the picture, there was little doubt that the Communists were in firm control of the Korean People's Republic and most of the People's Committees. The moderate leftists, the liberal democrats, had suffered a severe loss of prestige and power. They had attempted to cooperate with the American Command, only to be rebuffed at every turn. As the Communists came more and more into control, the entire organization was corrupted by their graft and by their terroristic acts against rival political groups. The people became alienated, and the prestige of the left wing dropped to an all-time low. The wide popular base upon which the People's Committee organization initially had stood was not thereafter duplicated by any other group in Korea. At the very start, many people had believed that at long last they had come into their own. They became interested in the local Committees and in working out their own governments. Public responsibility was developing. But with the breakdown of the Committees, the people grew bitter and disillusioned and turned back to concentrate on tilling their fields in the struggle for life: "Enough of government" they must have thought. The Communist-dictated pro-trusteeship stand taken by the left wing early in 1946 sounded the death knell of popular left-wing prestige. In the meantime, the right wing was coming into its own.

The Korean Provisional Government

The story of the Korean right begins in 1919 with the Korean Provisional Government. On March 1 of that year, a day still celebrated enthusiastically by all Koreans, a group of Korean patriots gathered in Pagoda Park in central Seoul and read a declaration of independence in defiance of Japanese authority. It was a forlorn bid to attract world attention for Korea's sad plight under the Japanese. Japanese retaliation was swift and terrible. The passive resistance movement which commenced with the reading of the declaration was brutally suppressed, and its leaders forced to flee the country.

Shortly thereafter, a group of these Korean revolutionists met in Shanghai. Among them were Kim Ku, Dr. Syngman Rhee,[44] and Dr.

[44] Like other members of the exile government, Rhee was absent from Shanghai at its formation, arriving only in November 1919 and returning to the U.S. in 1921.

Kim Kyu-sik.[45] The group quickly organized itself into a self-styled Korean government-in-exile, the Provisional Government of the Republic of Korea, with Dr. Rhee as its first president. Its sole purpose was to fight for Korean independence. The newly-formed "government" was soon at odds with itself as to how to carry on the struggle. In sharp contrast to the violent methods expounded by Kim Ku, Rhee pleaded that a more moderate course be pursued and the case of Korea be presented to the world. Representatives of the Provisional Government appealed to Versailles, to the Washington Conference of 1921, and to The Hague. However, by reason of the fact that Japan was an ally and Korea formally part of the Japanese Empire, the feeble cries from these Korean patriots were ignored by the Western statesmen. Dr. Rhee's more moderate attitude became less and less appealing to the impatient group, and Kim Ku was elevated to the presidency shortly thereafter. Thereupon, Dr. Rhee moved to the United States where he became the unofficial Washington representative of the unofficial Provisional Government and headed, during World War II, the American Commission for Korean Independence.[46] Kim Ku, meanwhile, gained considerable fame for his art at assassination and knack at constructing homemade bombs. Former Japanese Foreign Minister Shigemitsu Mamoru [1887–1957] had Kim to thank for his missing leg.[47]

The Korean Provisional Government received the support of Koreans in China, in the United States, and elsewhere. Unofficial relations were maintained with Generalissimo Chiang Kai-shek's Chinese Nationalist Government, at one point receiving its semi-official recognition, according to Provisional Government leaders. (During

---

[45] Kim Kyu-sik earned degrees at Roanoke University and Princeton University. He was then delegated by a Korean youth group to present Korea's case for independence at the post-World War I Versailles Peace Conference in Paris. Later, during the Pacific War, he became one of the leaders of the Korean independence movement and, as discussed here, served in 1946/47 as the Chair of the Southern Korean Interim Legislative Assembly (Namjosŏn Kwado Ippŏbŭiwŏn).

[46] Known in the United States as the Korean Commission.

[47] This incident—reported in newspapers around the world—occurred on April 29, 1932 in Hongkou Park (today's Lu Xun Park) in Shanghai where the Japanese were holding a gathering in honor of the emperor's birthday. A bomb delivered by the Korean Yun Pong-gil (1908–1932) killed and wounded a number of Japanese officials, including Shigemitsu Mamoru. Upon being found guilty, Yun was executed by a firing squad in December of that year.

World War II, *de facto* recognition was forthcoming from the de Gaulle government of France.) In 1936, upon the suggestion of Chiang, the Provisional Government recruited an all-Korean force in China, the Korean Liberation Army or Han'guk Kwangbokkun. General Kim Wŏn-bong [aka Yaksan, 1898–1958], long in opposition to Kim Ku, was appointed War Minister of the Provisional Government as a reward for his capitulation to Kim Ku's leadership. However, real control of the Kwangbok Army remained in the hands of General Chi Ch'ŏng-ch'ŏn [aka Yi Ch'ŏng-ch'ŏn, 1888–1957] and his chief-of-staff, General Yi Pŏm-sŏk [1900–1972]. The training and equipping of this Korean Army was financed by the Chinese Government and was, for all intents and purposes, under Chiang's control. During the closing days of World War II the excesses of the Kwangbok Army under the two General Yis were such, particularly in Shanghai, as to incur the lasting hatred of the Chinese as well as Korean civilians living in China. The Army was used to punish summarily alleged Japanese collaborators. More often than not the "Japanese collaborator" turned out to be merely a political opponent to the Provisional Government. By this time, the Provisional Government was definitely on the side of the conservative moneyed interests and was very vocal about the danger of Communism and the Soviet Union. It offered no program of domestic reform.

Meanwhile, within Korea, a moderately conservative group had been building up informally around the personage of Song Chin-u, a Seoul newspaper man associated with the *Tonga ilbo* newspaper. Just prior to the American landing, Song Chin-u and his so-called "Tonga Ilbo group" sparked the organization of a "Preparatory Committee for the National Congress." Even some leftists, including Communists, were willing to cooperate in the move until the People's Republic announced plans for a national election. When the Americans landed and Military Government was declared, the plans laid by the Tonga Ilbo group were abandoned and, on September 16, 1945, eight days after the American arrival, the Korean Democratic Party was launched with Song Chin-u in the top spot. Shortly thereafter, the party requested that the American Command take measures to return to Korea the leaders of the Provisional Government.

Acting with laudable caution, General Hodge requested that Kim Ku and other officials of the Provisional Government sign written statements to the effect that they would return to Korea as private citizens with no claims to official positions or governmental prerogatives, and would not claim such after arriving in Korea. These statements were duly signed, and American airplanes were furnished to fly Kim Ku and his staff from Chongqing[48] to Seoul. American Military police were immediately stationed at Kim Ku's palatial residence in Seoul to guard the august personage and his staff, even though he had already broken his pledge by modestly announcing upon his arrival, "When I return, the government of Korea returns." Cabinet meetings were announced, and the Provisional Government continued to call itself a government without any objections from American Military Government. Korean guards in the employ of the Provisional Government were allowed to carry arms in spite of the general confiscation of weapons that had been ordered by the American Command. The day after Kim Ku arrived, he was introduced to the local press in the Throne Room of the Capital by the Military Governor himself. The whole affair led one to believe that Kim Ku and his Provisional Government were receiving the semi-official blessings of the American Command.*

Dr. Syngman Rhee, recently of Washington, was already on the scene by this time, having arrived via an American Army plane on October 16. He too was introduced to Korean audiences by American authorities. After a week of political reconnaissance, Dr. Rhee called a meeting of representatives of all political parties on October 23. With American permission, if not encouragement, the session was held in the Chosen Hotel, an American billet for high-ranking Army and civilian officials. The Central Council for the Rapid Realization of Korean Independence [Chosŏn Tongnip Ch'oksŏng Chungang Hyŏbŭihoe] evolved from the meeting. "Unification without principle other than desire for Korean independence" was Dr. Rhee's plea.

---

[48] Chongqing was China's provisional capital during the Second Sino-Japanese War (1937–1945) and, in 1940, also became the seat of the Korean Provisional Government.

* It might be added that during the late fall and winter of 1945, the Provisional Government and supporting political groups were given 4 1/2 hours of radio time per month over station JODK in Seoul as against 30 minutes allotted to the Korean People's Republic and its affiliates. The station was operated by the American Military Government. As of January 1946, headquarters had been established by the Provisional Government in the ancient and spacious Tŏksu Palace in Seoul, whereas the People's Republic had been unable to find adequate quarters for their Seoul headquarters.

However, representatives from the two major left-wing parties, the Communist and People's parties, were conspicuous by their absence.

During the ensuing week, Dr. Rhee approached Pak Hŏn-yŏng and Yŏ Un-hyŏng requesting their participation. Finally, a joint statement of objectives was resolved which called for the rehabilitation and early independence of the country to be achieved through the assistance of the United States and the Soviet Union. By the end of October, representatives from the two left-wing parties joined Rhee's Central Council. No sooner done than the three major right-wing parties issued what amounted to disclaimers of the joint declaration of objectives, saddling the left wing with what might have been interpreted possibly as a pro-trusteeship stand. With that evidence of bad faith, the Communists withdrew. A few days later, Yŏ, disgruntled because Dr. Rhee refused to give the Korean People's Party what he considered adequate representation (not even a strong minority), completed the defection of the left by withdrawing his delegates. This was Dr. Rhee's first and only real opportunity to assume genuine popular political leadership in South Korea during those early years. From that point on he moved steadily toward the extreme right. Using time delegated to him by the American Command on the Seoul radio station as a news commentator, Rhee delivered tirade after tirade against the Korean Communists and the Soviet Union during the fall of 1945. Mud flew in both directions, and the two political camps moved further apart.

But it was the trusteeship issue which really brought about the final parting of the ways. Dr. Rhee and Kim Ku had long been demanding immediate independence for Korea as against the imposition of a trusteeship. More moderate groups of both right and left were inclined to think that perhaps a period of Allied assistance might be the safest and most expeditious means by which a democratic state could be organized. Otherwise, the illiterate Korean peasant would be easy prey for any extremist group which cared to grab power. The extreme left-wing partisans came to favor trusteeship partly because of Soviet dictates on the matter and partly because they saw a Soviet–United States trusteeship as possibly increasing their voice in the affairs of government. Finally, when the Moscow Decision was announced late in December 1945, which seemed to impose a two-power trusteeship on Korea, the Kim Ku–Rhee faction seized upon the opportunity and fired the Korean people against the idea. By constant repetition of the word trusteeship and "fight until death" pronouncements given out hourly by Kim Ku, the mess of Korean people was whipped into a momentary frenzy of anti-trusteeship emotion. And on the crest of that frenzy, the Provisional Government group hoped to ride to power—at least in South Korea.

Personally, I began to suspect the motives for Dr. Rhee's moves when I inadvertently dropped into a meeting on December 16, 1945, being held in Seoul, a meeting ostensibly for the purpose of discussing the food crisis. A group of prominent citizens had volunteered to aid. The discussion I walked in on was far different from that anticipated. My interpreter immediately turned and whispered to me in awed tones, "These are the millionaires of Korea." It soon developed that the group was in the throes of organizing itself as the Economic Contributors Association, the self-avowed objectives of which were: (1) to prove to the public that the wealthy men of Korea were patriotic, and (2) to solicit funds for the Korean Provisional Government. The aim was to be 200,000,000 yen (at least two million dollars as measured by comparative purchasing powers). Dr. Rhee was named as the agent for the Provisional Government in the deal. Promissory notes for large sums were made out on the spot by a number of those present. When I reported the matter to American authorities, I was patently told to forget about it. Somehow, however, news of the transaction leaked out to the local press, and Dr. Rhee was charged with having accepted a large sum of money from the wealthy of Korea, most of whom had amassed their fortunes under the Japanese by exploiting their fellow countrymen. Whereupon, Dr. Rhee publicly denied having had anything to do with such a project. Army intelligence reports as well as my own eyes would have it differently. Exactly what strings were attached to this money I do not profess to know, but I hazard a guess that with the money went the stipulation that the Provisional Government was to be purely a rightist affair—at least in the final analysis.[49] In fact, two

[49] In sight of the Shanghai Korean Provisional Government's (Taehan Min'guk Imsijŏngbu) complex history Robinson's repeated summaries in this text come across as being a bit too simplistic. We should recognize that, over time, the exile government's membership included Koreans holding a wide variety of political views. There had in fact been anarchists, communists, liberal democrats, conservatives, and even fascists. It is mostly the Government's afterlife in southern Korea that is "purely a rightist affair," as Robinson accurately describes it.

months later, on February 7, 1946, all of the leftists and moderate rightists still associated with the Rhee–Kim Ku Provisional Government group walked out in disgust, but that is getting ahead of the story.

On New Year's Eve, 1945, Kim Ku's headquarters served notice that henceforth all members of the Korean police and all other employees of Military Government would take orders from the Korean Provisional Government rather than from the Americans. This was a direct challenge to American authority and could not be ignored. Fortunately, announcements of the coup d'état were intercepted by American officers before reaching the general public. The next day, General Hodge ordered Kim Ku to put in an appearance, whereupon the general gave him such a dressing down that Kim offered to commit suicide on the spot. The general then had to dissuade him from that course of action. A few hours later a statement from Kim Ku was read over the air in support of American authority, but still in violent opposition to the imposition of a trusteeship over Korea.

By this time, the Soviet Government had released the Moscow Decision in North Korea, carefully explaining that the suggested trusteeship was in reality a guardianship. In fact, that term[50] was used in several of the North Korean translations of the Decision. So much so, that the American Command suggested to the State Department that there might be a difference in the official Soviet and American texts of the Decision. Such was not the case, but the Russians continued to use the word "guardianship." At the same time, the Soviet Command in North Korea apparently gave instructions to the Korean Communist Party to support the Moscow Decision and the trusteeship clause. They seemed to consider trusteeship as a *fait accompli* and wished to sell the program to the Korean people. In view of earlier American commitments on the subject of a Korean trusteeship, it probably never occurred to the Russians that any trouble would rise over the issue. But it did. The South Korean public was whipped into a fury by the inflammatory pronouncements of the right-wing leaders. The left saw that it was losing ground fast, particularly after the mass demonstration in Seoul on December 31, demonstrations for which the right wing took full credit. Not to be outdone, the left wing announced a mass anti-trusteeship demonstration for January 3, 1946. On that

[50] The term Robinson refers to is *hugyŏn*. See p. 85, footnote 22.

same day, instructions arrived from North Korea—where the Moscow Decision had just been released—to the effect that the Korean Communist Party would support the Decision, including the trusteeship clause. The South Korean left wing, by this time almost completely controlled by the Communists, reversed its stand at the last possible hour, and the anti-trusteeship demonstration turned into a rather bizarre affair in which both anti- and pro-trusteeship banners were carried by the confused participants. The South Korean political front was now squarely at odds on the issue of trusteeship, or guardianship. The voice of the weak moderate group was lost in the general melee—particularly when early in January 1946 parties unknown assassinated Song Chin-u, leader of the Korean Democrats and a strong moderate influence on the right wing. Later, while under the influence of American whiskey, Dr. Cho Pyŏng-ok [1894–1960], director of the National Police, admitted that he knew that Kim Ku had engineered the assassination out of fear of Song's growing moderate influence among the rightists.

As 1945 ended, the American Command had effectively destroyed the embryonic democracy fostered by Yŏ, had driven Yŏ and his People's Republic into the waiting hands of the Communists, had unwittingly allowed the trusteeship issue to drive a wedge between right and left, and finally had given the wedge an extra tap by holding out a helping hand to Dr. Rhee and Kim Ku—men, who, it soon developed, had no intention of giving the left (whether it be Communist or non-Communist) any voice whatsoever in the affairs of the nation or in creating anything like a liberal democratic state. The Rhee–Kim definition of a leftist was simply anyone refusing to acknowledge their right to lead.

CHAPTER III: THE RUSSIANS AND THE AMERICANS

It was apparent from the Moscow Decision that two separate conferences were called for to settle Korea's ills, one to consider administrative-economic matters of mutual concern to the Soviet and

American Commands and a second to create a Joint Soviet–American Commission for the purpose of establishing a provisional democratic Korean Government. The first of these projects was to be undertaken within two weeks after the promulgation of the Moscow Decision on December 26, 1945. Negotiations were, however, delayed by the Russians for reasons best known to themselves. Finally, at 1 PM on January 16, 1946, the Joint Soviet–American Conference got under way in the Throne Room of the Capital Building in Seoul.

The Joint Soviet-American Conference

The gathering was chairmaned by Major General Terentii Shtykov for the Russians and Major General Archibald V. Arnold, former military governor of South Korea and commanding general of the 7th Infantry Division, for the Americans. Each headed a five-man delegation for their respective countries. The Koreans were allowed no official representation and were barred from all sessions other than the first. This aloofness did little to increase Korean faith in the good intentions of the two Allies. The opening meeting was little more than the usual exchange of pleasantries. Whereupon, the conference got down to the business at hand.

The first matter on the agenda was the agenda, and there matters stood for several days. The Russians proposed a very brief five-point agenda, the most important matters included on which were (1) provisions for shipping South Korean rice and foodstuffs to North Korea, (2) arrangements for shipping North Korean fertilizer to South Korea, and (3) payment for the electric power being generated in the North and used in the South. In sharp contrast to this very limited area of contemplated discussion was a twenty-point agenda submitted by the Americans, a list which included such matters as the opening of the 38th parallel to normal trade and commerce, the movement of persons between the two zones of occupation, the exchange of mail, regulations in regard to coastwise shipping, the operation of rail transportation between the two zones, and the like. A comparison of these two agendas immediately brought into focus the fundamental difficulty which beset the Joint Conference throughout its month-long existence. The Russians placed a very limited and narrow interpretation on the objectives of the Conference and proposed little more than a barter system covering certain specified commodities. The Americans, on the other hand, proposed in essence to reunite the country economically at the earliest possible date. The American twenty-point agenda was finally whittled down to fifteen, and to this the Russians agreed. Such matters as free circulation of newspapers between the two zones, proposed in the original American agenda, were deemed political in nature by the Russians and, therefore, not fit subjects for discussion by the Joint Conference.

It soon developed that the Russians had come with one fixed idea in mind, and that was to get rice for the hungry population of North Korea. Traditionally considered the rice basket of Korea, southern Korea during past years had exported rice to Japan in large quantities. What few realized was that in order to make such exports possible, southern Korea imported a large amount of less desirable grains (from a Korean point of view)—barley, millet, and the like—from Manchuria. The southern Korean farmer bought these grains, sold most of his rice, and realized a cash profit from the transaction. Rice, a must in the Korean and Japanese diet, always brought much higher prices than other grains. With the breakup of the Japanese Empire the importation of Manchurian grains was no longer possible. Therefore, the rice surplus of South Korea vanished like the proverbial Arab's tent. This fact was not grasped by the American economic "experts" when the occupation opened. Someone said that South Korea was a rice surplus area, and without looking further into the case, American Military Government lifted all controls on the collection and distribution of rice—controls which the Japanese had long imposed. A bumper rice crop had just been harvested, and no danger was envisioned by the American "experts." Not only did they not consider the reasons *why* South Korea had been a rice surplus area, but neither did they stop to consider the psychological reaction of the people to a free market in their basic commodity after living for generations under a carefully controlled system of forced rice collection, rationing, and rigid price control. The inevitable happened, and the people went hog wild. Per-capita consumption of rice went up by leaps and bounds. Rice wine and rice candy factories flourished and consumed great stocks of rice. In addition, a flourishing smuggling trade appeared. Rice was smuggled to Japan and traded there for luxury items, which were smuggled back into

Korea and sold for enormous profits. Of the entire 1945 rice harvest, it has been estimated, nearly one-quarter was smuggled out of South Korea.

But even more important than these factors was the fact that the Korean economy was badly out of kilter, a fact which Military Government economists should have recognized at the outset without any difficulty. North Korea was the site for practically all Korean industry which produced those items basic to the farming population, items such as the all-important chemical fertilizers, farming tools, clothes, and shoes. With the 38th parallel closed to all legal commerce, the source of supply for these items was choked off. Critical scarcities began developing within a few weeks' time. With scarcity came higher prices. Naturally, the farmers refused to sell their rice unless they were paid prices commensurate to those of the goods they wished to purchase. The price level of basic commodities began to soar, and a near-disastrous inflationary spiral was on before the Military Government economists had quite figured out what had happened. The situation was aggravated by clever Korean speculators who saw the trend of events and began buying up huge quantities of rice and other goods to hold off the market and sell later at a profit. All of these factors were working rapidly to bring about a real shortage of rice in South Korea when the Joint Soviet–American Conference sat in mid-January 1946. And the winter was a particularly uncomfortable one which, given Korean winters, is saying a great deal indeed.

Military Government cannot claim that it was not adequately forewarned. On December 8, 1945, I myself heard the Korean newsmen at their daily conference at Military Government wax eloquent on the subject of prices and inflation. The correspondents stated that unless something were done immediately to control the situation, there would be very serious rice riots in the very near future. They went on to express the belief that there was actually a surplus of rice in South Korea, but that large quantities were being held off the market by unscrupulous profiteers. The press clamored for direct action by Military Government. It was pointed out that during the Japanese regime each person had been guaranteed a certain ration of rice at a low price. Granted, under such a system a large black market had existed, but each person did get their ration. This was the most pressing problem of Korea, said the press unanimously.

General Arnold's answer to their plea for action indicated a fatal lack of insight. The general naively explained that in a democracy the free play of supply and demand must be allowed to operate unhampered, that any control imposed on that free play would operate against the democratic system of government. The fallacy in such reasoning in the case of Korea was obvious—there was no normal supply or demand. Military Government refused to impose any controls whatsoever, and the people of South Korea went hungry. As late as January 1, 1946, the American Command in South Korea was still announcing that there was surplus rice in South Korea. Fortunately, shortly after this, economic experts—in the true sense of the word—arrived from the United States Treasury Department and put Military Government straight. Instead of a surplus, a very real and possibly disastrous shortage was predicted. Military Government hurriedly placed controls on the price of rice, but at that late date they were largely ineffective. The damage had been done. Cases of actual starvation were reported in Seoul and elsewhere. There were a number of food riots, all of which were promptly reported as "Communist-inspired" by Army Intelligence. These events added an undertone of bitterness to domestic political events as well as to the Soviet–American negotiations.

It is little wonder, really, that the Russians thought that the Americans were lying through their teeth when they suddenly announced in the Joint Conference that there existed a severe rice shortage in South Korea. Only a short time before, the Russians had heard American pronouncements to the effect that there was a surplus. How come? they asked. Figures were produced, including those indicating that per capita production of rice in North Korea was no lower than in South Korea. The Russians countered by saying that the figures did not agree with theirs. The Russians undoubtedly came to the conclusion that the Americans were trying intentionally to undermine the Soviet administration in North Korea by preventing the use of any of the alleged surplus South Korean rice in alleviating the very critical food situation in the Soviet zone. And on this issue, the Conference stalled. The Americans attempted to by-pass the rice issue by talking of other subjects. When the Russians asked for food, the Americans offered fish. The Russians replied that they had plenty of fish in North Korea, that they needed rice. The Americans were in the unfortunate position of having to ask for more than the Russians. Chemical fertilizers from Northern factories were a must if rice production was to be maintained. Electric power, the source of which was the Yalu River hydroelectric development in the North, was the one commodity which had been crossing the 38th without interruption. A continued supply was essential for South Korea. Various other manufactures from the North were badly needed by South Korea. All North Korea wanted, on the other hand, was rice, and that, the Americans did not have.

On this note, the Conference ended. True, certain limited agreement had been reached. Mail was to be exchanged between the two zones. Radio frequencies had been assigned stations in North and South Korea. A limited concurrence had been reached on the subject of the movement of persons across the 38th parallel. It was further agreed that a Technical Transportation Committee, composed of representatives from the two commands, should meet within a month and study measures for developing a unified transportation system for all of Korea through the coordination of rail, water, and highway transportation facilities. All decisions reached by the Conference, however, were subject to the approval of the American and Soviet commanders. General Hodge, acting for the United States, promptly approved the joint decisions. Unfortunately, General Chistiakov, acting for the Soviet Union, saw fit to emasculate and make meaningless the decision on the movement of persons across the 38th parallel. Although apparently accepted by the Russian commander in principle, the Technical Transportation Committee never met, despite periodic prodding from General Hodge to induce the Russians to appoint their delegates and select a time and place for a meeting. In the end, the only significant result of the Conference was the exchange of mail between the two commands at periodic intervals. The exchanges took place at the border town of Kaesŏng, first at odd intervals and then upon American request, weekly.

During the closing days of the Conference, General Hodge had requested of General Chistiakov that the Soviet delegation be instructed to widen its area of discussion so that the economic unification of Korea might be effected. Apparently, by way of an answer, General Shtykov shortly thereafter suggested the early establishment of the Joint Soviet–American Commission, the body charged by the

Moscow Decision with the establishment of a provisional democratic Korean Government. The upshot was that it was agreed to convene the Joint Commission in Seoul on March 6, 1946.

Political Interlude

Before the Joint Soviet-American Commission came into being on March 20—delayed again by the Russians—both Americans and Russians felt it wise to strengthen their position by making a bid for greater popular Korean support. The destruction of the Korean People's Republic by the Americans, the upsurge of anti-trusteeship sentiment in South Korea, the revelation of apparent American duplicity on the subject of trusteeship, and the failure to control inflation had weakened American prestige to a dangerous degree. It dipped to such an astonishing level that a mid-February (1946) poll of public opinion run by my office indicated that a bare 52 percent of the Korean public considered the American administration of Korea better than that of the Japanese! The outcome of that survey was that I was ordered by the Military Governor to undertake no further polls of public opinion of this nature. There was no doubt that the Russians would gain in any political negotiation by this demonstrated American weakness. Early in February an all-out effort was launched to popularize the American effort.

The first problem was that of creating a representative political body in South Korea which would support the American view. It was desired that as wide a representation as possible be lured into the fold. Even the Communists were invited to participate in this first American-sponsored coalition effort. Through the efforts of Lieutenant Colonel Millard Preston Goodfellow [1892–1973], General Hodge's special political advisor for the project, negotiations were launched in January 1946 to bring about the establishment of what came to be known officially as the Representative Democratic Council of South Korea [Namjosŏn Taehan Kungmin Taep'yo Minju Ŭiwŏn]. The purpose of the group, as clarified in the declaration adopted at its first session, was to serve in an advisory capacity to the American commanding general in his efforts to prepare for an interim government of Korea.

Colonel Goodfellow, very much of a Rhee supporter and by mid-1947 an active Rhee agent in the United States, approached the problem from the point of view that the extreme right should be given the overwhelming majority.[51] Each major party was to be given four delegates in addition to four "non-partisan" cultural leaders. Included in the list of parties was the moderate right-wing Chosŏn Democratic Party [Chosŏn Minjudang] of North Korea. If all had accepted, membership would have consisted of eight leftists, twenty rightists, and four "non-partisans." The Communists refused to participate at the outset on the basis that the representation was unfair. Obviously, the North Korean Chosŏn Democrats were in no position to sit. Despite the disparity between the proportion of representation given on the Council to right and left and their actual political power, Yŏ Un-hyŏng and his more moderate Korean People's Party agreed to join the Council, but only on three conditions: (1) that nothing of a political nature be discussed; (2) that the Council would make no decisions but merely give advice; and (3) that it would cease to exist if and when an interim government were established. Colonel Goodfellow agreed to these three stipulations.

On February 11, 1946, the first session of the Representative Democratic Council of South Korea was held with appropriate fanfare in the Throne Room of the Capital Building. Everyone was there—Generals Hodge and Lerch, Kim Ku, Dr. Syngman Rhee, Dr. Kim Kyu-sik—everyone of importance, that is, except Yŏ Un-hyŏng. His chair, one of the four at the head of the long conference table, was removed just before the meeting got under way. The removal of that chair was significant, and all eyes were on the self-conscious American officer who carried it back to its place against the wall. Two representatives of the People's Party were present, but they remained sullen and silent throughout the session and promptly resigned at its adjournment. What had happened?

The day before the opening of the Council, Dr. Rhee, in a public statement which was patently untrue and deliberately calculated to keep Yŏ away from the meeting, made it known that he (Rhee) had *appointed* Yŏ to the Council. This proved to Yŏ what he had probably

[51] Colonel Goodfellow and Syngman Rhee first met in 1942. After the colonel had joined the Organization of Strategic Services (OSS), the wartime predecessor of the CIA, he and Rhee began discussing the OSS using Koreans for sabotage operations behind Japanese military lines. After Japan's surrender Goodfellow was one of those instrumental in Rhee's early return to Korea.

suspected all along; namely, that the Council was not a coalition advisory group, but rather, a right-wing political front. Hourly statements by General Hodge read over the local radio station on the eve of the opening session of the Council exposing this deliberate falsehood by Rhee did not salvage the damage done. Yŏ, now suspicious, was conspicuous by his absence. Soon after the Council's first session, he formally resigned. This completed the defection of the left, and the Council became nothing more than a right-wing political front. Dr. Syngman Rhee was promptly elected chairman and Kim Ku and Dr. Kim Kyu-sik, co-vice-chairmen—all Provisional Government men and Rhee-supporters. (Kim Kyu-sik had not as yet deserted the Rhee camp.) The coalition effort had failed, and the blame rested almost entirely with Colonel Goodfellow and the American Command for working through Dr. Rhee and Kim Ku in organizing the Council. Yŏ had been treated as an unwanted outsider throughout the negotiations. If nothing else had done so, this deliberate sabotage by Dr. Rhee proved Rhee's bad faith in respect to attempting any real political coalition. The prima donna did not care to share the stage with another attraction.

It was at this time that the U.S. State Department finally saw fit to offer the American Command in Korea some advice on the subject of Korean politics. The occupation was now nearly six months old. The gist of said advice was to stay clear of Dr. Rhee and Kim Ku, that negotiations which the Department had had with them over the past few years had been "unsatisfactory," and that it would be highly desirable to give support to younger and more liberal elements who were more closely in touch with the desires of the Korean people. This was the first piece of political advice offered by the Department to General Hodge. A fine time to tell me this, the general must have thought. However, with the opening of the Joint Commission staring him in the face, the general could do no other but give continued support to the Representative Democratic Council. It was impossible to change horses at that late date. Dr. Rhee and Kim Ku now had official advisory positions to the American Command and represented to the Command, on paper at least, the voice of the South Korean people. Both the extreme and the moderate left had been alienated. The situation could not have been worse, but it soon became so.

The American Command envisioned other measures to bolster its waning prestige among the Korean people. On March 7, 1946, a program was announced which called for the sale of former Japanese-owned farmland to Korean tenant farmers. What was planned was a long-term program in which land would be sold to tenant farmers for payment in produce. A 15-year payment schedule was contemplated. No land was to be sold for cash or to anyone other than tenant farmers. It sounded good. Public opinion polls taken at the time, however, indicated that the Korean public did not have sufficient faith in the American Command to trust it with the administration of such a far-reaching program. The sentiment—even among tenant farmers—was overwhelmingly in favor of holding off on any land reform program until a *Korean* Government were established. (Public opinion polls in the villages at the time established this point.) For this reason, the program was dropped. Military Government press releases explained that the matter should be entrusted to a future Korean Government—that it was more democratic that way.

In the meantime, news arrived in Seoul that the Soviet-sponsored regime in North Korea had, on March 5, enacted a sweeping land reform act. The act called for the seizure of all farmlands formerly owned by the Japanese, those owned by "national traitors who had acted contrary to the benefit of the Korean people, those who had cooperated with the political organizations of Japanese imperialists, and those who had left their homes after Liberation." The act further stated that such reform was "designed to prevent ownership of Japanese land, to prohibit individual Koreans from owning land, and to abolish the tenant system. The right to utilize the land will belong to those who cultivate it," declared the North Korean act. The seized land was to be allotted to farmers without cost and the administration of the land would be entrusted to the People's Committees, the local units of North Korean government. Therein lay the proverbial colored gentlemen in the woodpile, for these People's Committees, more political than governmental, seized and distributed the land according to political whims. Ultimately, the unjust and corrupt manner in which the land was distributed reacted vigorously against the prestige of the Soviet regime. However, this wholesale system of political spoils was not envisioned by the people when the law was enacted. The Russians had stolen a march on the Americans, for in North Korea a Korean Government was ostensibly carrying out the reform.

Shortly before this time, the Russian Command had inspired the formation of a central North Korean Government, the North Korean Interim People's Committee. It was tantamount to recognition of the People's Committee organization which had been set up throughout Korea in August 1945 under Yŏ's Korean People's Republic. However, by typical Communist infiltration tactics, the People's Committees in North Korea had become to all intents and purposes the local units of the Korean Communist Party. The one opposition party, the Chosŏn Democratic Party led by moderate Cho Man-sik [1883–1950], was taken over lock, stock, and barrel by faithful followers of the Party line. This occurred shortly after Cho Man-sik's arrest by the Russians, and as of mid-1947 he was still in "protective custody" in a P'yŏngyang hotel. The initial excuse for the arrest was Cho's refusal to endorse publicly the Moscow Decision and its implied trusteeship provision. Without his leadership, Cho's party was easy prey for the political manipulators of the pro-Soviet group.[52]

Thus, when the Interim People's Committee of North Korea was organized in P'yŏngyang in mid-February 1946, the entire network of the People's Committees was Communist-dominated. The two leading figures of this Soviet-sponsored regime were Generals Kim Il Sung (Kim Il-sŏng, in office 1948–1994) and Kim Tu-bong, about whom more will be heard later.

The coincidental organization of central political groups in North and South Korea was interpreted by some as indicative of joint action by the American and Soviet Commands toward the end of bringing

[52] The Soviet detained Cho at the Koryŏ Hotel in P'yŏngyang from early January 1946; the hotel had already been his residence before the house arrest. When the American Delegation of the Joint US–Soviet Commission visited P'yŏngyang in late June and early July of the following year, U.S. Army Major General Albert E. Brown (1889–1984) was allowed to interview Cho Man-sik. When asked about trusteeship, Cho responded that he would have no problem "[i]f Korea will be aided and helped by America alone," but that "[i]t will be very hard for him to support a trusteeship in which the Soviet Union will take part." "Interview with Cho, Man Sik—1 July 1947, at Pyongyang," reprinted in Chŏng Yong-uk and Yi Kil-sang, comps., *Haebang chŏnhu Migugŭi taehan chŏngch'aeksa charyojip* [Source materials on the history of the U.S. Korea policy before and after liberation], vol. 9 (Seoul: Tarakpang, 1995), 666.

about the political unification of Korea. Actually, however, it indicated nothing more than the effort by both commands to consolidate their respective political support in the two zones and, thereby, strengthen their respective hands at the impending conference. By March 1, 1946, the Russians could boast of an operating all-Korean Government to the outside world while the Americans were still playing petty politics.

On February 19, 1946, with the promulgation of Military Government Ordinance Number 55, the American Command pulled another unforgivable boner. The ordinance had to do with the regulation of political parties and required all groups of three or more persons designed to influence the political life of the country to register with Military Government, to keep its books available for audit at any time, to maintain a headquarters at a given address, and to report the names of all party members. This smacked so much of the much-hated Japanese "thought control" laws[53] of past days that the accusation was levelled immediately at the American Command that it was negating its oft-declared principle of freedom of political endeavor. That Military Government merely wanted the information so as to better understand Korean politics was something that the Koreans were unable to appreciate. As a matter of fact, neither could the Americans in Military Government who had objected strenuously to the ordinance prior to its publication. It would only lead to unnecessary furor and be of little assistance to the Americans, they predicted. Actually, one purpose of the ordinance was to drive into the open the activities of the Communist Party, both financially and otherwise. However, the pile of paper which accumulated in Military Government as a result of the ordinance defeated all presumed purposes. There were not enough translators and analysts to sift through the mass of registrations and extract anything of value. In the meantime, Korean public opinion was thoroughly aroused, and countless delegations of Koreans visited Military Government offices complaining bitterly. The American officers concerned were driven to distraction, and were finally forced to modify the ordinance. But the damage had been done.

[53] This is a reference to anti-communist laws of 1928, enforced by the Higher Police Force, the Kōtō Keisatsu (Kor. Kodŭng Kyŏngch'al), better known by the Orwellian term "Thought Police" (Kor. Sasang Kyŏngch'al). From the late 1920s it was utilized to suppress all forms of political opposition and anti-colonial activities in Japan's colonies Korea and Taiwan, and later in its puppet state of Manchukuo.

It was in this political and economic milieu that the Joint Soviet–American Commission met in Seoul on March 20, 1946.

The Joint Commission

The Joint Soviet–American Commission got off to an inauspicious beginning on March 20. Again Generals Shtykov and Arnold headed five-man delegations for their respective countries. On the very first day a dispute arose as to news coverage. The Americans requested daily communiques and freedom to issue unilateral statements. The Russians insisted quite reasonably, that communiques be issued only when something had been decided and that unilateral releases be tabooed. The Americans agreed the following day, but with a modification—that at least one communique should be issued each week. All parties concurred, and with that preliminary tussle over, the Commission got down to the job at hand.

General Shtykov's opening speech on March 20 stated the Soviet position quite frankly. Said the rotund General in part:

> ... With their blood and innumerable sufferings, the Korean people have earned the right for independence and a free way of life.
>
> The Soviet people warmly support this right of the Korean people. The Soviet Union has always championed and will always champion the self-determination and free existence of any nation without exception.
>
> As all of us are convinced, the people of Korea are bent upon and have already shown their determination to create, with the help of the Allied Powers, a free democratic Korean Government, friendly to all the freedom loving nations.
>
> The great aims of creating a democratic independent Korean state have brought to life wide political activity of the whole of all the people of Korea.
>
> The Korean people have formed their democratic parties, public organizations, and people's committees as an organ of democratic self-government.

However, in the way of gradual democratization of the whole of the internal life of the Korean people, there stand serious difficulties, brought about by the furious resistance of reactionary and antidemocratic groups and certain elements, whose object is to undermine the work of creating and firmly establishing a democratic system in Korea.

The task of the US–Soviet Commission is to help the Korean people create a provisional Korean democratic government capable of fulfilling the tasks arising from the democratization and reconstruction of the country.

The future provisional Korean democratic government must be created on a basis of wide unification of all the democratic parties and organizations, supporting the decisions of the Moscow Conference of the Ministers of Foreign Affairs.

Only such a government will be able to abolish entirely the remnants of the former Japanese domination in the political and economic life of Korea, to launch a decisive battle with reactionary anti-democratic elements inside the country, to carry out radical measures in the rehabilitation of economic life, to give political liberties to the Koreans and fight for peace in the Far East.

The Soviet Union has a keen interest in Korea being a truly democratic and independent country, friendly to the Soviet Union, so that in the future it will not become a base for an attack on the Soviet Union.

The task of the Joint US–Soviet Commission deriving from the decision of the conference of the three Ministers concerning Korea consists also in working out, with the participation of the provisional Korean democratic organizations, the measures of aid and assistance *with respect to trusteeship* in political, economic, and social progress of the Korean people, the development of democratic self-government and in establishing the sovereign independence of Korea. *Such a temporary trusteeship corresponds with the fundamental interests of the Korean people, inasmuch as it assures the condition of a most rapid national reconstruction and a revival of an independent Korean state on a democratic basis.**

* Italics are the author's.

This opening speech left no doubt as to the Soviet attitude: trusteeship was a foregone conclusion and only the details need be worked out; a Korea friendly to the Soviet Union was desired; the Soviet Union favored ultimate independence for Korea. Russian–American goodwill was not enhanced by a sniping account in *Time* magazine at this juncture which accused the Soviet delegation of quibbling over hotel accommodations, demanding garage space for their "lend-lease limousines," and generally acting like uncouth barbarians. The story was apparently based on an interview with a single American officer and badly warped in the retelling.[54] The Russians read it and growled.

As already indicated, it was just prior to the Commission meeting that the Americans received a political directive from Washington. This was the first real statement of political policy the Command had seen other than brief suggestions from the State Department. (That directive, promulgated by the State–War–Navy Coordinating Committee, was classified "top secret" and to the best of my knowledge, still remains so.[55]) Among other things, the Command was informed that the United States had pretty much committed itself on the subject of a Korean trusteeship on several occasions. The American delegation on the Joint Commission was directed to accept a trusteeship proposal if made by the Russians. On this score, the February directive quoted an earlier decision of the State–War–Navy Coordinating Committee dated October 20, 1945 (but which had not been transmitted to Korea) as follows: "*The present zonal military occupation of Korea by United States and Soviet forces should be superseded at the earliest possible date by a trusteeship for Korea.*" There were no ifs, ands, or buts about it; there was to be a trusteeship. To those in the know, this all seemed very much like bad faith on the part of the United States. The strategy was obviously that of trying to push the Soviet Union into the role of the villain who was insisting on an evilly-designed trusteeship, a trusteeship long opposed by the United States—at least, so the United States would have the world believe. As the Commission sessions wore on, the Russians understandably became more and more perplexed.

---

[54] Referencing the article "Korea: The Russians Came," *Time* 47, no. 4 (January 28, 1946): 33–34.

[55] See "Policy Paper Adopted by the State–War–Navy Coordinating Committee" (sent January 29, 1946), in *Foreign Relations of the United States, 1946*, vol. VIII: *The Far East* (Washington, DC: Government Printing Office, 1971), 623–27.

The issue was essentially this: The United States insisted that *all* Korean political parties be consulted in the establishment of a trusteeship and of the democratic provisional Korean Government called for by the Moscow Decision. On the other hand, the Russians failed to see the reason for calling into consultation those political parties and leaders which had supported the anti-trusteeship movement in South Korea and failed to support the trusteeship clause in the Moscow Decision. They argued that such leaders as Dr. Rhee and Kim Ku were obviously trying to destroy the effectiveness of the Moscow Decision in their violent denunciation of a trusteeship of any duration or type. All groups which had indicated opposition to the Moscow Decision—specifically, trusteeship—should not be consulted in working out the details of a trusteeship or in establishing a Korean Government, so declared the Russian representatives. Since all political factions in South Korea, other than the Communist Party and its affiliates, were loudly denouncing trusteeship, the Russian view precluded all politicos other than Communists from participating in the formation of a Korean Government. And even the Communists in South Korea had opposed the imposition of a trusteeship, that is, up until January 3. When the issue was relegated to a two-man sub-commission to resolve, the American representative asked his Soviet colleague if he would consider a Korean leader as unacceptable who had at one time denounced trusteeship, but later changed his mind and supported it. Yes, he presumed such a leader would be unacceptable. Whereupon, the American read some statements made by an unnamed leader, first against trusteeship, then in support of it. The Russian again agreed that the man, whoever he was, could not be accepted by the Commission. The American then revealed that he had been reading statements made at various times by Pak Hŏn-yŏng, leader of the Korean Communists. The Russian, obviously chagrined, made no comment.

Soon after this, Arnold called Shtykov in for a private off-the-record *tête-à-tête* during which the American general showed Shtykov a unilateral American statement prepared for release to the press. The threatened release stated the American and Soviet positions, charging the Soviet Union with denying free speech to the majority of Koreans on the issue of trusteeship. This threatened publicity caused the Soviet general to reach for a telephone and call P'yŏngyang. The maneuver worked. The Commission soon came to agreement: any political leaders or parties who would sign the following declaration would be accepted by the Commission for consultation and possible participation in the future Korean Government. This was the famous Joint Communique Number 5.

> The Joint Commission will consult with Korean democratic parties and social organizations which are truly democratic in their aims and methods and which will subscribe to the following declaration:
>
> We, ________________ , declare that we will uphold the aims of the Moscow Decision on Korea as stated in paragraph 1 of this decision, namely:
>
> > "The reestablishment of Korea as an independent state, the creation of conditions for developing the country on democratic principles, and; the earliest possible liquidation of the disastrous results of the protracted Japanese domination in Korea."
>
> Further, we will abide by the decisions of the Joint Commission in its fulfillment of paragraph 2 of the Moscow Decision in the formation of a Provisional Democratic Korean Government; further, we will cooperate with the Joint Commission in the working out by it, with the participation of the Provisional Korean Democratic Government, of proposals concerning measures foreseen by paragraph 3 of the Moscow Decision.
>
> Signed ______________
>
> Representing the ____________ party or organization.

The procedure for inviting representatives of Korean democratic parties and social organizations was to be announced publicly at a later date.[56]

---

[56] In a compromise of sorts, Joint Communiqué Number 5 did not mention "trusteeship" explicitly but referred to paragraphs of the Moscow Decision where this word appeared.

Joint Communique Number 5 was hailed as a major accomplishment, but the jubilance was short-lived. The rightist anti-trusteeship group questioned the declaration on the grounds that it would limit their freedom to oppose trusteeship. General Hodge, in a unilateral statement to the local press—an act in direct contradiction to previous Commission agreements—interpreted the Joint Communique as not infringing upon the freedom of any group or individual to oppose trusteeship, but rather, as providing such parties with an opportunity to air their views on the subject before the Joint Commission. The Russians immediately took issue with this statement. Signing the declaration included in the Joint Communique did not bestow the right to oppose trusteeship; trusteeship was an integral part of the Moscow Decision. The Commission was again at a standstill. The American delegation had assumed that by agreeing to Communique Number 5, the Russians were waiving their objections to hearing the right-wing anti-trusteeship group of South Korea. Such, however, was not the case.

The American delegation used the threat of publicity once again in an attempt to force the Soviet delegation into a more tractable position. General Shtykov asked for a temporary recess while he could refer the matter to Moscow. Within two or three days an answer came back, and it was "no." The Soviet general informed the American Command that he had received orders to withdraw his delegation. Formal adjournment took place on May 6, 1946, but not until the Soviet delegation had placed blame for the breakup of the Joint Commission on statements made by Dr. Kim Kyu-sik in a session of the Representative Democratic Council. Unfortunately, Dr. Kim, in reiterating the views put forward by General Hodge, had stated that by signing the declaration in Communique Number 5, participating parties were merely assuring themselves of the opportunity to speak out against trusteeship before the Joint Commission. By this statement, declared the Russians, the entire Representative Democratic Council and all participating parties had become unacceptable for consultation with the Joint Commission. And on this note, the Joint Commission rose, actually upon an American motion for adjournment. No agreement had been reached.

Within a few days the American Command issued a lengthy press release which placed the full blame for the breakdown of negotiations upon the Russians. The American stand was that of protecting free speech, declared General Hodge. All political factions had the right to say whatever they might, up to and including opposition to the imposition of an Allied trusteeship. To deny them the right to speak their minds on this subject would be to abridge freedom of speech. This position sounded good in the press and to those who thought only superficially. However, the issue was a false one and nearly everyone concerned knew it. There were two lines of reason which made it so.

First, it was fact that the United States had agreed with the Soviet Union on several occasions as to the necessity for imposing an Allied trusteeship upon Korea. When the Joint Commission met, the Russians began with the assumption that there would be a trusteeship—that that had already been decided. In such event, the Russian delegation was perfectly correct in insisting that no one who actively opposed a trusteeship should be consulted by the Joint Commission or allowed to participate in the provisional government. To have done so would have undermined the government at the outset. Nor did the Commission have authority to alter the trusteeship decision; so such hearings would have been quite irrelevant in any event. When the Russians agreed to overlook past sins and hear all those who signed the declaration in Joint Communique Number 5, they apparently assumed that trusteeship was no longer an issue—that signing the declaration was tantamount to agreeing not to oppose trusteeship. When General Hodge, shortly thereafter, issued a unilateral statement saying that signing the declaration did not necessarily imply acquiescence to a trusteeship, the Russians immediately reneged. Dr. Kim Kyu-sik's statement, made apparently in the best of faith, convinced the Russians of American duplicity.

Secondly, there is a line of reasoning in support of the Soviet view even if the United States had not previously agreed to a trusteeship. The Korean people, given their admittedly low educational and cultural level, were easy prey for any ambitious political or economic groups which might appear. Maintenance of a democratic system over any significant period was unthinkable in such an environment. The only possible way to encourage the rapid development of democracy without a long period of oppression and bloodshed would have been to impose an Allied trusteeship upon Korea, a trusteeship which would enforce the peace while the educational and cultural standards of the Korean people could be raised to a point at which a democracy could conceivably survive. If this were the real objective of the Allied Governments, the attitude of the Korean people toward trusteeship was of little consequence. The fact that the group leading the fight against trusteeship (Rhee and Kim Ku) was known to be interested primarily in forcing both the Russians and Americans to retire so as to give it a free hand in exploiting the Korean people to their own selfish ends tended to substantiate this line of logic. These groups intentionally fired the Korean public to a terrific emotional outburst against trusteeship, an outburst fueled by irrational and unrealistic nationalistic fervor. For these reasons, it could be argued that the imposition of a trusteeship, regardless of Korean opinion, was the only way in which the mission of the Allied occupation might be achieved—assuming, that is, that the mission was to create an environment favorable to the development of a democracy. If this mission be admitted, then, Russian opposition to granting the violent anti-trusteeship groups a voice in a democratic Korean Government established under a trusteeship was entirely correct.

For instance, what happened to those who actively opposed the authority of American Military Government in South Korea? Very frequently, warrants were issued for their arrest. Where was free speech there? By American reasoning, those who would oppose the authority of a Korean Government established under a trusteeship should be given the same consideration as those who would support it. And yet in South Korea under American Military Government—which, actually, was a form of trusteeship—this policy was not followed. Even in the United States we have not tolerated those who would oppose the authority of the Government to govern. Free speech is then no longer an issue, for such opposition is equated with subversion—and for good reason. However, the American stand at the Joint Soviet–American Commission in Korea was one of defending the group which expressly declared that it would not recognize the authority of a Korean Government established under an Allied trusteeship. Somehow, by a strange quirk of reasoning, that American position became a defense of free speech. Clearly, it was a false issue manufactured for the occasion to cloud the real issues and discredit the Russians. Perhaps ours was a necessary maneuver to prevent Russian domination of all of Korea, but let us not delude ourselves by insisting that our position was logically sound.

Whether or not the Russians were sincere in their views is uncertain. Not once did they present the arguments outlined here. The reasoning in Moscow may have followed these lines, but if so the Soviet delegation on the Joint Commission sitting in Seoul seemed aware of nothing other than the conclusions Moscow had reached. The Russian delegates in Seoul were thus at a loss to support their views with logical argument. Rather, their minds were those of automats, and their mouths repeated the same old stock phrases, the most familiar being "We must fulfill the Moscow Decision exactly." Had they possessed one man who could have articulated effectively the case as presented above, the American Command could have been trapped in an extremely awkward position. As it was, the United States gained a propaganda victory.

Of course, real explanation of the American stand lay in the fact that the primary mission of the occupation of South Korea was not so much to establish a Korean democracy as to establish a bulwark against the expanding influence of Soviet ideology. General Hodge privately admitted as much on several occasions. The free speech issue was raised to embarrass the Soviet Command so as to put it in the unpopular position of insisting upon trusteeship.

Some of these points were raised in a strongly-worded letter from a young American Army captain in Military Government to two American members of the Joint Commission soon after the adjournment. It was his suggestion that the Russians be approached with the following two proposals: (1) that the Russians and Americans come to initial agreement as to whether a trusteeship was to be imposed and, in the event that it was, to exclude those groups from consultation which *actively* opposed a trusteeship, and (2) that Dr. Syngman Rhee and Kim Ku not be allowed to participate in the establishment of a Korean Government in any event. This suggestion was one of the factors that started the chain of events which eventually brought the Joint Commission back into session over a year later.

Along the 38th

While all this was going on in Seoul, the frontier at the 38th parallel remained very much closed. Negotiations between the two zones of occupation were reduced to petty bickering about this and that. The bickering ranged from the ridiculous to the tragic and covered a multitude of subjects. For instance, there was the wonderful but tragic story of Private Peavy's private treaty. It went like this.

Northwest of Seoul there was an isolated agricultural area lying just south of the 38th parallel. In the early days of the occupation, one Private Peavy was assigned the task of supervising the district for Military Government. In the spring of 1946 trouble developed. The supply of water which normally irrigated the rice paddies in the area had its source in a reservoir located north of the 38th parallel. The North Korean authorities refused to release any of the water, and the situation in the rice paddies became serious. Whereupon, Private Peavy sat down with pen in hand and wrote a letter about it to General Hodge. After going through a dozen different headquarters, the letter showed up in Seoul where it was inadvertently pigeon-holed and promptly forgotten. Other letters from the unhappy private met the same fate. There the matter rested and was all but forgotten. That fall, Private Peavy was passing through Seoul on his way to the United States to be discharged. While visiting friends in Military Government he ran into someone having to do with agricultural problems. By chance, he remembered the water crisis Peavy had reported the previous spring and asked the private what he had done about the situation. "Oh," said Peavy "we got that all fixed up. I promised the Russians 50,000 bags of rice for the water." With that, everyone within hearing distance began remembering strict orders from General Hodge not to communicate with the Russians or make local agreements, as well as orders from Military Government to the effect that no rice would be exported from South Korea. Visions of courts martial floated before their eyes. Seeing the consternation on everyone's faces, Peavy quickly added, "But don't worry none, we never intended to give them any." However, there was a tragic sequel. Not many months had passed before a report came into XXIV Corps Headquarters that North Korean police had raided Peavy's former bailiwick and had kidnapped the major, the police chief, and several other local officials. A few days later, the heads of several of them were deposited on the 38th parallel as a grim reminder of the broken agreement.

Occasional gun fire was heard along the frontier, but rarely were Soviet and American personnel involved. One serious incident did occur in the summer of 1946 which involved troops of the two Allies. One afternoon a messenger came dashing madly into the orderly room of one of the American infantry companies along the 38th to report that North Korean policemen had just crossed the 38th parallel and kidnapped a citizen of South Korea. The young and inexperienced lieutenant in charge quickly organized a party of four or five well-armed Americans to go after the missing Korean. The party advanced across the parallel only to be challenged by a Red Army guard. One of the Americans shot into the ground at his feet. Whereupon, the guard very wisely took to his heels and fled. The Americans fired several other shots in his general direction after calling to him in English to halt. The fleeing guard ran some little distance and then ducked into a house where, it soon developed, a number of other Russians troops were located. Fire was exchanged between the two groups. Shortly thereafter, the Americans noticed that Soviet troops were outflanking them in the bushes and prudently withdrew. This incident occasioned a harsh letter from the Soviet Commander, General Chistiakov, to General Hodge asking for an explanation of this deliberate show of hostility and a report as to what disciplinary action had been taken against the Americans concerned. All the American Commander could do was apologize profusely and report the reassignment of the lieutenant who had led the expedition. The incident was reopened several months later when a badly garbled account reached the ears of columnist Drew Pearson [1897–1969]. He reported an armed conflict of several days' duration between Soviet and American troops.

There was another serious incident in which the Americans were clearly in the wrong. This occurred in connection with the exchange of mail between the two zones of occupation near the border town of Kaesŏng. One day during the winter of 1946–47, American soldiers handling the exchange of mail for the American Command cornered two Soviet officers in the mail car and, at gun point, stripped them of their weapons and other valuables. Official U.S. reports indicated that there was no provocation other than outright maliciousness on the part of the Americans. This incident led to another exchange of letters between the two commands and temporary cessation of mail exchanges.

These particular incidents are related so as to indicate that the fault did not always lie with the Russians. It is of interest to note that accurate accounts of neither of these affairs cited above ever reached the American press. From my personal study of many such cases which took place along the 38th parallel from September 1945 to July 1947, I would estimate responsibility could be divided about half and half. Actually, by far the greater proportion involved neither Russians nor Americans, but were disputes between North and South Koreans, generally members of the police or constabulary. Most frequently, these disputes arose after forays of one group into territory belonging to the other, forays which ended more often than not in shootings, looting, and rape. Occasionally, Americans or Russians wandered inadvertently into territory belonging to the other and were temporarily detained. In no case were Americans mistreated by the Russians. All cases of mistreatment of Americans involved North Koreans in the absence of Russians. In fact, crews of American airplanes which landed unexpectedly in North Korea for one reason or another during this period were treated on all occasions with the utmost of hospitality. (Obviously, I can vouch for nothing after July 1947.)

During the summer of 1946, a Soviet officer was shot and killed on the frontier by South Koreans. It was disputed as to whether or not the Russian was south of the frontier at the time, the Soviet and American Commands presenting varied versions of the incident. Several on-the-spot investigations were made by high ranking Soviet and American officials, and variations in the stories were not resolved. There the matter rested. This incident was the only violent Russian or American death along the frontier during the first two years of occupation.

Another matter inadequately handled by the American press was the inter-command negotiations on the subject of electric power and chemical fertilizers. In both areas the United States Command committed costly errors. As has been stated previously, a very large share of the electric power used in South Korea came from hydroelectric plants lying on the Yalu River in North Korea. One of the earliest subjects for discussion between Generals Hodge and Chistiakov was electric power, specifically, how the Americans were to pay for it. Negotiations dragged on and on. With the failure of the Joint Soviet–American Conference in January and February 1946, the Soviet Commander finally presented a power bill to the American Command totaling several million dollars. The Americans balked and finally suggested that deducted from the bill should be the cost of maintaining transmission lines in South Korea and the amount of South Korean Electric Company capital seized by the Russians in North Korea. Since these two items came to more than the amount of the bill presented by the Russians, North Korea should continue to supply electric power until the credits were used up, the Americans argued. Discussion as to future payment could then be opened. This proposal did not go over well with the Russians. They were willing to give the American Command full credit for the cost of maintaining South Korean transmission lines, but not to deduct the capital belonging to the South Korean Electric Company which had been taken over by the North Korean regime. On that basis, the Russians pointed out, they could claim that all property in South Korea belonged to North Korean companies and vice versa. They went on to observe that payment for electric power did not involve the adjustment of capital, which was an entirely separate subject. The Americans then quibbled about the price, which did seem unreasonably high. Several times the North Koreans threatened to shut off the power in the near future, but such was not done. Early in 1947, tentative agreement was reached as to price, but no payment made. A new power bill was submitted by the Soviets in late spring, 1947, amounting to $4 million. On June 17, 1947, after a Joint Soviet–American Conference on power had met in P'yŏngyang, it was announced that payment for the power consumed would be made by the delivery of specified equipment and materials, the bulk of which, it was anticipated, would be received from Japan in the form of reparations. (Later in December 1947, when it became apparent that delays in the delivery of the specified materials would be "unavoidable because of the extreme shortage in the world markets," General Hodge reopened discussion with the Soviet Command regarding the substitution of other materials or to settle the account in U.S. dollars.)

The fact that practically all of the vital chemical fertilizer plants of Korea were located in the North created a serious problem to South

Korean agriculture. Without those fertilizers, the yield to be expected from the centuries-old rice paddies would be disastrously lower than normal. For this reason, General Hodge began negotiating with the Russians for the purchase of large quantities of fertilizer. There was a prolonged discussion as to price and method of payment. Finally, the differences were resolved when the American Command received authority to establish dollar credits in New York banks for the North Korean administration. At first, the Russians balked a little at this arrangement, apparently because they wished the dollar credits to be setup in the name of the USSR rather than the North Korean government (that is, the Interim People's Committee of North Korea). However, agreement was finally reached on May 7, 1946. Dates were set for delivery of the fertilizer to American ships in North Korean ports. And then the boom fell. Without giving any reason why, the United States Government suddenly withdrew its previously-granted authority to the American Command in South Korea to spend dollars for this fertilizer. This plunged the South Korean authorities into the embarrassing position of having to breach the agreement already reached with the Russians. The situation was explained to an unsympathetic Russian Command. General Hodge pleaded for immediate shipment of fertilizer in view of the impending food crisis, the method of payment to be decided later. However, the Russians wanted cash on the barrel head—in dollars. Payment in Korean yen[57] was offered and

[57] During the colonial period the Bank of Chōsen (Chōsen Ginkō) issued yen banknotes particularly designed for Korea, the Korean yen. These notes continued to be used in the immediate post-liberation era. Following the landing of American troops and two days after the establishment of the U.S. Military Government on September 9, 1945, their value was pegged to the Japanese yen at a rate of 1:1. The following month, the Korean yen was revalued, pegging it to the US dollar at a rate of 15 yen to one dollar. On July 15, 1947, the Korean yen was massively devalued to a rate of 450 to the dollar. Many Wikipedia entries and Bank of Korea booklets now refer to the currency of that time as "Korean wŏn" instead of "Korean yen." Decolonization, though, did not happen overnight. Even a quick look at eBay will demonstrate that the banknotes of that period do not match up to such clean-cut post-liberation currency histories. The *new* Korean 100 yen banknote of the American zone, issued on March 26, 1946, still bore the same image of the Daoist god Jurōjin (Kor. Sunoin), exactly as on colonial period banknotes. The new notes, like the old ones, still carried references to the Bank of Japan and the then vanquished Empire of Japan (Dai Nippon Teikoku). What is more, over the Jurōjin

rejected. A barter was suggested by the Americans, and a list of all goods available for export in South Korea was sent to the Soviet headquarters. They wanted no part of it, and in turn, sent a list of their own making including huge quantities of gasoline and oil. And there the negotiations fell through, and no chemical fertilizers were shipped. By reason of that fact, huge quantities of grain had to be sent into South Korea from the United States in order to avert hunger and starvation, a necessity if American democracy was to have greater appeal than Soviet communism to hungry Koreans. The grain cost the American taxpayer far more than the chemical fertilizer from North Korea would have been.

There was no doubt that the feeling of hostility was growing between the Russians and Americans in Korea in the spring and summer of 1946. The border was as tightly closed as ever. The Russians persistently refused to allow any American newspaper men into North Korea. It was only after long negotiations that even Ambassador Edwin Pauley's [1903–1981] Allied Reparations Commission was allowed to visit North Korea. And then its activities were closely controlled and watched. It was barred from at least two of the most important North Korean industrial areas by reason of fact that these areas were being used as troop demobilization centers, so the Russians said.

Meanwhile, Soviet military strength in North Korea grew; estimates ran as high as 400,000 by June 1946, as contrasted to something like 40,000 American troops in South Korea. When the Soviet forces commenced full dress battle maneuvers just north of the 38th parallel in early summer of 1946, the American Command was well along to succumbing to a bad case of jitters. Plans were drawn up covering every eventuality, including immediate evacuations. General Hodge temporarily suspended the shipment of American families to South Korea—ostensibly because of the cholera epidemic currently raging throughout

---

portrait was the 5–7 paulownia emblem, the colonial coat of arms of the governor-general of Chōsen. While the image of Jurōjin remained on the newly issued currency, those other icons of and references to Japanese colonialism disappeared only after an additional generation of 100 yen notes was issued on July 1, 1946. The Soviet Command in North Korea, on the other hand, allowed the continuous use of colonial period yen until at least December 1947, although it issued the Wŏn of the Red Army Command (*Pulgŭn Kundae Saryŏngbuŭi wŏn*) for its own personnel in order to control corruption.

the American zone, but actually because of the touch-and-go military situation. High military officers in Tokyo referred to Korea as the next Bataan. Fortunately, however, it was a false alarm, the first of many—until 1950. Shortly after the maneuvers, the Soviet military forces were significantly reduced in number, and everyone relaxed. Against this international backdrop, the play of South Korean politics went on before an ever-restless audience.

CHAPTER IV: THE RISE OF KOREAN LIBERALISM

As the occupation of Korea went into its first spring (1946), the main currents of Korean politics were flowing in two well-defined streams: (1) the quiet behind-the-scenes struggle between Kim Ku and Dr. Syngman Rhee for supremacy over the right-wing hierarchy and (2) the contest between Pak Hŏn-yŏng and Yŏ Un-hyŏng for leadership of the left. Meanwhile, the Communists obstinately opposed all American projects, and the extreme right continued to condemn any form of trusteeship. The American Command was caught squarely in the cross fire, though it felt unable to ditch Rhee and Kim Ku.

The power lay with the political extremes by reason of their superior discipline and organization and very real support they were receiving from either the Soviet Union or the United States. The liberal democratic element was left to shift for itself. Little wonder that it failed to retain a separate existence in those early days of liberation.

Communist Capers

Theoretically, American authorities initially accorded the Korean Communist Party the same freedom as given other political groups. But in fact, party members were discriminated against in diverse ways. No known Communists were appointed to governmental posts. Americans who hobnobbed with local Communists were either sent home under suspicion or reassigned to some isolated spot. A Communist who was unfortunate enough to get caught up in the coils of the Korean police was in for a rough time of it and an unfair trial, if any trial at all. Communists were eliminated from the school system, both teachers and students. Several times Communist newspapers were closed summarily without a specific cause.

On September 2, 1946, General Hodge let loose with his first real blast against the propaganda tactics of the Communist Party. He took it to task for starting untrue rumors designed to create chaos and confusion. Shortly thereafter, warrants for the arrest of three top men in the Communist Party, including Pak himself, were issued. The patience of General Hodge had been exhausted by the campaign of vilification directed at the Americans, by deliberate sabotage of American Military Government, by Communist counterfeiting activities, and by out and out espionage against American forces. The only trouble was that the American Command was unable apparently to distinguish between the Communists and the liberal left, which was just the way the Communists wanted it.

The propaganda campaign against all things American was launched by the Communists even before the Americans arrived in Korea. Such propaganda ran from outright appeals for rebellion against American "exploitation" to rumors that vast stores of rice were being shipped out of Korea to the United States. A veritable barrage of verbiage went out of Communist Party headquarters calling on the farmers not to turn in their rice to the government on the grounds that the rice was being either shipped out of the country or turned over to profiteering businessmen. Such charges were patently untrue and the Communists knew it only too well. At the same time, the Party raised a storm of protest over the inadequate food rations being issued by Military Government in the food deficit areas, particularly the large cities. In addition, a deliberate rumor was started that the United States was obligating the future Korean Government for hundreds of millions of dollars by "dumping" huge quantities of American surplus goods in Korea. Actually, the "dumping" consisted of grains, medical supplies, much-needed transportation equipment, and the like, which had been brought in without any expense to a future Korean Government.

But the Communist propaganda tacticians were much more adroit than the Americans. Wherever a real injustice was found to exist—and one did not have to look far to find such—the Communists seized upon it and exploited it to the limit. Very frequently Communist charges of police injustice and brutality, judicial partiality, labor oppression, American corruption, and the like, contained a large element of truth. To deny such charges was tantamount to demonstrating American duplicity, exactly what the Communists were hoping for. Many times the Americans played directly into the hands of the Communists by so denying any or all charges—frequently, even going to the extent of commending those involved whether it was the police, dishonest Americans, or profiteering businessmen. To do otherwise would have been to strengthen Communist prestige, so reasoned the Americans. Actually, this reluctance to effect reforms where they were obviously required gave the more undesirable elements within military government freedom to go ahead and commit any excesses in the name of American democracy—and commit them they did, as will be demonstrated in the following pages. Meanwhile, the charges leveled by the Communists against the Americans and their Korean underlings became increasingly valid. This was General Hodge's conception of fighting communism—deny all, admit nothing, and do less.

To anyone familiar with Comintern tactics, such a policy would appear fatal from a liberal democratic point of view. And so it was in Korea. It was—and is—obvious to any but the most politically unconscious that the arch enemy of the Communist is not the reactionary—but the liberal, the social-democrat, the progressive, anyone genuinely committed to social and economic reform. It is liberal reform the Communist fears most, for it destroys the validity and strength of his appeal. Therefore, in Communist dialectics, reform is a dangerous half way measure, a sop to keep the masses under control and thus avoid the class struggle out of which might emerge a dictatorship of the proletariat. The "Programme of the Communist International," adopted by the Sixth World Congress on September 1, 1928, in Moscow stated in part:*

* *International Press Correspondence* [Vienna] 8, no. 92 (December 31, 1928), repr. in *Blueprint for World Conquest* (Washington, DC: Human Events, 1946), 225–26, and 232.

> "Socialist" reformism, the principal enemy of revolutionary Communism in the labor movement, which had a broad organizational base in the Social Democratic parties and through these in the reformist trade unions, in its entire policy and theoretical outlook stands as a force directed against the proletarian revolution.
>
> ....
>
> All these tendencies [various socialistic schools] take a common stand with Social Democracy, the principal enemy of the proletarian revolution, on the fundamental political issue, viz., the question of the Dictatorship of the Proletariat. Hence, all of them come more or less definitely in a united front with Social Democracy against the U.S.S.R. On the other hand, Social Democracy, which has utterly and completely betrayed Marxism, tends to rely more and more upon the ideology of the Fabians, of the Constructive Socialists and of the Guild Socialists. These tendencies are becoming transformed into the official liberal-reformist ideology of the bourgeois "Socialism" of the Second International.

A close look at the Korean Communist Party exposed its purposes and fundamentally illiberal nature. There had never been a national conclave of representative Korean Communists. "The principle of democratic centralism [totalitarianism] must stand until the members are better disciplined [regimented],"[58] Pak Hŏn-yŏng said on at least one occasion in defense of his autocratic rule of the Korean Communist Party. Pak's leadership of the Party had been challenged from time to time by those Communists who objected to his one-man dictatorship of party policy. At one time, the opposition from the more nationalistically and liberally-inclined Communist elements became so strong that Pak made a quick trip to North Korea to secure advice as to how to handle the situation. Upon his return in mid-July 1946 Pak read the leaders of the dissenting faction out of the party. No vote was taken on the subject other than by the Central Executive Council, and then not until after Pak had announced to his colleagues that he had been given secret information to the effect that the Russians would occupy all of Korea within three years. (He was off by only one year;

[58] The insertions in brackets in this and the above quote are in Robinson's original typescript.

the attempt was actually made, of course, in June 1950.) Whereupon, he warned all his fellow Communists that it would be well to do nothing to alienate the Russians in the interim, such as displaying disloyalty to his leadership. Anyone objecting would be dealt with severely at a later date, Pak threatened. Needless to say, much of the dissension came to an abrupt end.

Orders to the party organization emanated from the central Communist headquarters in Seoul. If these orders were not carried out, disciplinary action against the delinquent members followed. Duty to party was considered to be above that to one's family or country, and blind obedience was required of every member, for there was no opportunity to discuss, object to, or vote on official party policy or officers. This was the "democratic centralism" of the Korean Communist Party.

On May 6, 1946, American investigators[59] entered the Chikazawa Building in downtown Seoul, wherein was housed the presses for one of the Communist Party newspapers as well as Communist Party offices.[60] The paraphernalia of a full-blown counterfeiting operation was found, including paper, ink, plates, and bogus money. All told, some twelve million yen (about $120,000 on the basis of comparable purchasing power at the time) had been run off. Directly involved were a number of Communist Party members and two-party officials. The case was unusual in that it was one of the few involving Communists in

[59] Robinson refers to agents of the U.S. Army Counter Intelligence Corps (CIC).

[60] The Chikazawa Building (Kor. Kŭnt'aek Bldg.), later to become the headquarters of the *Kyŏnghyang sinmun*, was located at 74 Sogong-dong in Chung-gu. It housed, among other leftist publications, the communists' *Haebang ilbo* paper. The high-end Komori printing presses utilized here were not just located in the Bank of Chōsen's longtime banknote printing facility; they were, in fact, the very same colonial-era presses now being redeployed under USAMGIK's supervision to once again print Japanese-looking banknotes, while jointly being used by leftist publishers for their literature. Robinson's take, with his Office of Public Opinion directly involved in handling this case, is surprisingly uncritical, possibly because his office was not fully informed. It has been argued, both in the past and presently, that all evidence was orchestrated to allow USAMGIK to utilize this as a showcase trial to heavily manipulate Korean public opinion, subsequently leading to the shutdown of leftist presses and the complete discrediting and criminalization of all labor union and leftist demands and activities. Cf. Im Sŏng-uk, "Migunjŏnggi Chosŏn Chŏngp'ansa 'wijojip'ye' sagŏn yŏn'gu" [A study of the Chosŏn Chŏngp'ansa 'Counterfeit Banknotes' case during the U.S. Military Government] (PhD diss., Hankuk University of Foreign Studies, 2015).

which a fair hearing was held. General Hodge personally directed that the defendants be tried as individuals, not as members of the Communist Party, though the general announced publicly that the Party had seriously implicated itself by its acts and utterances. Party organs dubbed the whole affair a police frame-up. As the trial came to its conclusion, the defendants rose and sang the "Red Flag Song." On one occasion during the trial, on July 29, a mob tried to free the defendants. In the melee which followed one man was killed and fifty were jailed. That the Communist Party had been directly involved was obvious to all. In view of the overwhelming evidence, all the defendants were convicted.

While securing evidence against these men on the counterfeiting charge, investigators discovered evidence of still more serious activity from the military point of view—evidence that the Communist Party had been indulging in well-organized espionage against the American forces. Such had been suspected for a number of months, and various documents picked up by CIC had tended to substantiate the charge. But evidence uncovered on this May 6 raid of the Chikazawa Building confirmed the suspicion beyond all reasonable doubt. During previous months the Communist Party had been sending out blank forms to all subordinate units and cells on which they were to return a report of American military activity in their respective areas. Such subjects were covered as troop strength, types of units, locations of headquarters, movements, weapons, transportation, port facilities, and the like. As General Hodge commented at the time, "We are well cased." No concrete evidence was unearthed indicating the final destination of the information, but in the minds of the American authorities, there was little doubt that the intelligence had been ordered by the Soviet Union—all of which brings up the relationship between North and South Korean Communist parties and the Russians.

The first evidence indicating close liaison between North and South Korean Communists came at the time of the first trusteeship disturbances in the late 1945 and early 1946. As already reported, on January 3, 1946, the Communist Party suddenly switched its stand on trusteeship from one of opposition to support. This bewildering change of spots occurred so rapidly that the January 3 Communist-sponsored demonstration began in an anti-trusteeship vein and ended a few hours later as a pro-trusteeship movement. Just what had happened was suspected at the time by the American authorities, but it was not until later that those suspicions were established as fact. Verification came in the form of a document, intercepted at the 38th parallel, from Communist headquarters in North Korea to subordinate units specifying what the view of all Communists should be on the subject of trusteeship—another example of "democratic centralism" in the determination of policy. The document was dated January 3, 1946, the very day on which the South Korean Communists had obviously received some kind of orders on the subject.

The next piece of evidence confirming the existence of close liaison between North and South Korean Communists came at the time of the Chikazawa counterfeiting case when the books of the party were seized for investigation. Upon examination, it appeared that the bulk of party funds had come from an unknown Mr. X. Contributions and donations from party members were listed, but there was, in addition, a limitless reserve. Whenever cash began to run low, an entry appeared which indicated that money was being drawn in the name of the unknown Mr. X in amounts as needed. Apparently, there was another set of books not intended for American eyes and which American eyes did not see. The books seized in this raid were quite different from the financial statements submitted by the Party some time before to Military Government as required by ordinance. Expenditures covering trips of specified individuals to North Korea and to Japan were revealed for the first time. Other papers seized during this same raid included a number of passes authorizing the bearer to enter North Korea, some of which were signed by Pak Hŏn-yŏng and written in both Russian and Korean.

Evidence tending to indicate other international affiliations of the Korean Communist Party was meagre. On two occasions official Party documents were seized which made passing mention of its subservience to the International Communist Party, an apparent reference to the Comintern. It was known that Japanese Communist Party leaders had passed through South Korea in the early days of the occupation, during the process of repatriation, and that contact had been made between them and Korean Communist leaders. It was suspected that an exchange of money had taken place at the time. Occasionally, Communist Party leaders were observed going to and from the Soviet Consulate in Seoul. Korean Communist headquarters journals reported a few meetings with American Communist Party members, for the most part, American GIs. At a later date, one of these men was searched upon his entry into the United States. On this person was found a letter signed by Pak Hŏn-yŏng and addressed to the National Secretary of the American Communist Party recommending the bearer for special consideration by reason of aid rendered in Korea. Also found in his possession was a carbon copy of an article on Korean labor which had appeared in a Korean paper published in Los Angeles as an anonymous front-page story.[61]

In late October 1946 the so-called master plan of Communist strategy was released to the press by the American Command. Its authenticity was substantiated by at least two highly reliable sources, one being an agent within the ranks of the Communist Party itself. The plan called for the military training of not less than 500,000 North Koreans and the infiltration of as many agents as possible into South Korean governmental agencies, especially the police. During the same period, the Communist Party in South Korea was to strive for the greatest possible membership, establishing branches in every administrative level. As soon as an adequate organization had been achieved, several moves were to be carried out simultaneously. Members would begin to go underground. Various Communist-sponsored organizations were to disassociate themselves publicly from the Party. Implied was either a takeover by subversion and/or overt aggression from the North. This "master plan" allegedly was first written in December 1945 by Party leaders.

As a matter of fact, a number of North Korean agents—some trained in Russian-staffed North Korean political and military schools-were apprehended in South Korea. Several submarines of unknown origin were sighted off the island of Cheju, a left-wing stronghold. It was suspected that agents were landed, as well as printed propaganda. From time to time vessels were apprehended attempting to smuggle cargoes of propaganda leaflets down along the coast and into South Korea. And finally, the unanimity of opinion on any and all subjects

---

[61] In chapter IV—a chapter authored by Robinson in his role as military historian—of part II, volume I, of the internal (then classified "secret") US government publication *History of the United States Army Forces in Korea, 1945–1948*, the paper is identified as the weekly Los Angeles *Korean Independence News*. See Historical Section, Headquarters XXIV Corps, US Army Forces in Korea, *History of the United States Army Forces in Korea, 1945–1948*, part II, vol. I (Manuscript, 1949), 313–14, National Archives and Records Administration.

voiced by official Soviet spokesmen, by North Korean leaders, and by organs of the South Korean Communist Party and its affiliates left little doubt in anyone's mind as to the source of inspiration.

The entire Communist program was designed to bewilder and confuse. On no occasion did the Communists respond to American invitations to participate in the affairs of government. They spurned responsibility and were content to sit back and criticize and condemn.

Late in September 1946 the American Command revealed documents proving that the *Chosŏn inminbo* (Korean People's Press), the official South Korean organ of the Communist Party, had been receiving day-by-day instructions from North Korea as to just what to print and when to print it. In the particular document captured there were orders for each day of September, including instructions to publish handbills, arrange newspaper and radio programs concentrating on the Soviet victory against Japan, and to "send propaganda agents into the provincial districts to stay a long time." The document stipulated that almost every conceivable "anniversary" of Soviet conquest was to be observed by demonstrations. Favorable mention was made of the August 15 demonstration and of the riot on July 29 relative to the Chikazawa counterfeiting trial. The document went on to give orders to the South Korean Communists to oppose Military Government's proposed Interim Legislative Assembly and the establishment of the $25 million American credit for Korea, which was then under discussion.

In early September 1946, after several long statements denouncing the Communist propaganda factory, General Hodge ordered the arrest of Pak Hŏn-yŏng on several charges up to and including espionage. At the same time, the general ordered the closing of three Communist newspapers on the charge of violating General MacArthur's occupation proclamation Number 2 (dated September 7, 1945) which, among other things, specified the death sentence for anyone endangering the life, safety or security of, or committing any act hostile toward, the occupation forces. The three papers so suspended were the *Chosŏn inminbo*, the *Hyŏndae ilbo* (Modern Daily News) and the *Chungang sinmun* (Central Times of Korea). The first-named was the official South Korean Communist organ, and the latter two were normally far leftist in their editorial policies. The deliberate lies propagated by these three papers had long taxed American patience and interfered with the administration of government. In addition to the warrant for Pak's arrest, the general also ordered the arrest of Yi Chu-ha [1905–1950], vice-secretary of the Korean Communist Party, and Yi Kang-guk, chief of the business section of the Communist-dominated Democratic National Front. None of these men were apprehended, and the *Hyŏndae ilbo* and the *Chungang sinmun* were eventually allowed to reopen.

The true color of the Korean Communists was shown in their constant refusal to participate in any coalition move to effect reform in South Korea, but that story comes later. Suffice to say here that revolutionary Communism thrives on confusion, chaos, injustice and oppression, and abhors socialistic and democratic reform. This elementary Communist dogma should have been known and understood by the American authorities. It was not. The Communists rubbed their hands in glee and kept up their incessant clamor against all things American—and with telling effect. In the meantime, the right-wing extremists were also running wild, thanks to tacit support from their American well-wishers.

Right-Wing Plots

As previously related, Dr. Syngman Rhee and Kim Ku were returned to Korea in the fall of 1945 in American airships, sponsored by the American Command, protected by American guns, and awarded a degree of freedom given to no other Korean political figures. Kim Ku, as head of the "Korean Provisional Government," laid claim to governmental authority in Korea. As a prerequisite to his return to Korea, the Americans had insisted that he sign a written pledge that he was returning as a private citizen and not as an official of any "government." Notwithstanding this agreement, soon after his arrival Kim began calling "cabinet meetings" of his Provisional Government. On New Year's Eve, 1945, his attempted coup d'état, previously described, incurred the momentary wrath of General Hodge. However, the wrath was not so great as to preclude his being used as one of the mainstays for the American-inspired Representative Democratic Council, a coalition effort, which failed because of American snubbing of left-wing leaders and deliberate intrigue by Messrs. Rhee and Kim Ku.

Dr. Rhee was named president of the group probably because his name had achieved greater prestige among the Korean people than any other and because he had mobilized the moneyed interests of South

Korea behind him. Nevertheless, Kim Ku still retained in his hands the reins to greater effective political power, for he held the presidency of the Provisional Government. Moreover, his violent anti-trusteeship stand had given him a momentary lead in political organization over his erstwhile opponent for rightist leadership.

Dr. Rhee, however, was not to be outdone. An extreme individualist and obviously convinced of his own divine right to rule, Rhee was already working on projects of his own which would soon undermine Kim Ku's political power and make him very much a second fiddle (and indirectly lead to Kim's death in 1949).

To understand this clash of personalities requires a thumb nail portrait of these two men. Kim Ku, the venerable (69 years old) revolutionist and author of countless assassination plots, placed his faith in force and violence. His hard, pockmarked features, verging on the stoic, were leathery and dark, much resembling those of a Great Plains Indian. He had no children but operated a large house and grounds in Seoul, co-inhabited by a bevy of concubines. Kim spoke no English, nor had he adopted many of the Western ways of doing things. His person was protected by a flotilla of paid gunmen.

Handsome, seventy-year-old, white-haired Dr. Syngman Rhee, the idol of Korean females, and who in private conversation frequently referred to General Hodge as "my son," was superficially quite different from Kim Ku. As the graduate of several American schools and a long-time gadabout amid Washington society, his veneer was distinctly Western. This veneer included an Austrian-born wife who deplored Korean cooking and dress and who ruled the roost—including the good doctor—with a none-too-subtle hand. Her status was disputed, for the doctor already had a Korean wife with prior claims when he joined forces with the present Mrs. Rhee. The Korean wife no longer lived in the Rhee household, but was nevertheless, supported by the doctor. On the surface Kim Ku seamed to represent the old traditional Korean way; Dr. Rhee, the spirit of a new youthful Korea. But that was as far as it went. Actually, the difference was not so great as it might seem, though Dr. Rhee obviously had the more polished veneer, the greater learning, the more agile brain, and the more pleasing personality. But the political philosophies of the two men were quite similar in all essential respects. "Might makes right," "the end justifies the means," and "to hell with the people" summed up their philosophies—if such sentiments could be dignified by the term philosophy.

Both of these ambitious old men, although rivals for top rightist billing, were forced to maintain superficial harmony between themselves for purposes of public impression. But behind that public level, the struggle for control was intense. For reasons already explained, Rhee started behind in the race, but he had one big advantage, either through design or historical accident, his name was the most revered and respected name among the Korean villagers. In the minds of the people, he occupied a place somewhat akin to that of a legendary hero. Without political organization, however, Rhee could not capitalize on this advantage. Quickly coming to the realization of this fact, Rhee launched a campaign to place himself at the apex of the right-wing organization. Kim Ku might sit at his feet as a not-too-trusted deputy, but that was all.

No sooner had Dr. Rhee arrived in Korea (one month prior to the arrival of Kim Ku and his Provisional Government) that he set up the tongue twisting Central Council for the Rapid Realization of Korean Independence. Although originally intended to be a union of both right and left without principle other than a common desire for national independence, this organization soon became a purely right-wing federation. Shortly thereafter, Dr. Rhee launched out in tirade after tirade against the Communists and the Soviet Union. By so doing, he no doubt felt that he would curry favor with the Americans and receive their tacit support, as well as cause tension between Americans and Russians which could be used to his advantage. There were no other reasons, for surely in the circumstances then obtaining, no true patriot would have seen anything constructive coming from these highly emotional denunciations of everything Russian.

Early in 1946, as already described, Rhee's Central Council for the Rapid Realization of Korean Independence joined with Kim Ku's Anti-Trusteeship Committee to form what came to be known as the Emergency National Congress, a body claiming to represent all the people. The leftists refused to participate, although invited. When the moderate rightists and moderate leftists under Messrs. Kim Kyu-sik and Kim Wŏn-bong likewise deserted, the Emergency National Congress became merely a coalition of extreme right-wing groups. Even so, it still maintained the fiction of being a national congress and a non-political group representing all the people. Dr. Rhee and Kim Ku occupied the number one and two spots, respectively. But the balance of power was still with Kim Ku because of the superior organization he had mustered about him, in part a holdover from his years in China. Coincidental with this activity, it will be recalled, Dr. Rhee was elected president of the American-inspired Representative Democratic Council. This placed him in an official advisory capacity in relation to General Hodge and greatly added to his prestige.

It soon developed that the right wing lacked the mass organization on the provincial level to compete with the left. Meetings of all right-wing bigwigs were called and plans were laid to achieve a wide popular base for the top-heavy organization. From these meetings emerged the National Society for the Rapid Realization of Korean Independence. Actually, it was Dr. Rhee's older Central Council with a few minor additions. This innovation was more or less forced on Kim Ku by reason of the fact that the Society grabbed a head start in organizing on a provincial level. As late as the April (1946) organizational conclave of the new National Society, however, Kim Ku still had sufficient power to wangle the top spot away from Dr. Rhee.

Shortly thereafter, Rhee commenced an exhaustive barnstorming tour of the provinces. The road over his entire route was literally lined with Korean police, and for some reason. At least one plot against his life was kept from fruition by these precautions. Schools were dismissed and the children marched off to hear him speak, obviously with permission of the local American authorities. This, I myself saw in many communities. The village and town elders turned out *en masse* to greet the white-haired politician.

At the same time, down through the channels of the Korean police came orders to arrest all leftist leaders. This put the left-wing organization in an uproar and temporarily to flight. Many leftist organizers wisely took to the hills. Warrants for their arrest were issued, on the basis of their allegedly illegal seizures of governmental authority the previous fall, opposition to the government grain collection program, or on no charges whatsoever. Leftist leaders were jailed by the hundreds. All of this I duly reported to Military Government authorities after a lengthy tour through the provinces. However, all was vigorously denied by General Lerch, the Military Governor, and by American police supervisors. In any event, in the absence of active left-wing opposition, conservative village elders and the landed gentry (the Korean *yangban*) moved rapidly to fill the void by organizing local units of the National Society for the Rapid Realization of Korean Independence in support of Rhee's grassroots appeal. By direct personal contact with these new groups, Dr. Rhee's political power soared. In June he returned to Seoul to attend a second conclave of the National Society, this time attended by representatives from all over South Korea. Dr. Rhee knew his strength and demanded that he be named as number one man. He was named president by unanimous acclaim. This time the vice-presidency went to Kim Ku.

At this point, Dr. Rhee set up his General Headquarters for National Unification as the "non-political" headquarters to spearhead the independence and anti-trusteeship drive. Both right and left were "ordered" by Dr. Rhee to participate. Naturally, no groups other than those of the extreme right did so. This move was an undisguised attempt to undermine the position of Kim Ku's Emergency National Congress and to throw another hurdle in the path of the American-inspired coalition negotiations currently taking place between the moderate left and moderate right, negotiations which were showing some signs of progress at this juncture and hence constituted a danger to Dr. Rhee's growing power.

Labor was not over-looked by Dr. Rhee's energetic organizers. The National Federation of Labor Unions [Taehan Tongnip Ch'ongsŏng Chŏn'guk Nodong Ch'ongdongmaeng] was conceived and setup in competition to the left wing's National Council of Korean Labor Unions [Chosŏn Nodong Chohap Chŏn'guk P'yŏngŭihoe; short: Chŏnp'yŏng]. The latter was far in the lead, but every effort was made to destroy it. The police were enlisted in the campaign. On this score I quote Dr. Arthur C. Bunce [1901–1953],[62] economic advisor to General Hodge and a member of the American delegation on the Joint Soviet–American Commission:

[62] Bunce spoke Korean fluently. He had lived in northern Korea from 1928 to 1934 as a Secretary of Agriculture under the allied Canadian Missionary Association, developing new farming methods for the northern Korean region and leading a cooperative movement for farmers. After his return he earned a PhD degree in Agricultural Economics and worked as an East Asia expert for the U.S. Federal Reserve Board. In February 1946 he was sent to Korea as Hodge's Economic and Agricultural Adviser; one of his foremost concerns was land reform.

> Police activity with regard to disputes between the two parties [right and left wings] has taken the form of assistance to the National Federation of Labor Unions [right-wing labor organization] in a policy of hands off where they have been concerned. On the other hand, the National Korean Labor Union Council[63] [left-wing labor organization] has been subject to strict police surveillance exercised towards them and certain punitive measures such as the arrest of members for distributing handbills and roundups following strike activity.[64]

Typical of labor activities undertaken by the right wing was that in Samch'ŏk, one of the most important industrial areas in South Korea. On July 24, 1946, I interviewed the man responsible for organizing labor in the area for Rhee's National Society for the Rapid Realization of Korean Independence. By his own admission he had been a large factory owner under the Japanese and head of the Financial Association in the area, the organization through which the Japanese kept the farming population under control. According to his own statements made to me on that date, labor unions should not be encouraged and certainly not for economic purposes; they should be mere political adjuncts. He frankly admitted that he did not believe in collective bargaining—this, from the right-wing labor organizer in one of the most important industrial areas in South Korea. When I made inquiry about what had happened to the left-wing unions in the district which I knew had been very strong only a few months previous, he replied that the left-wing labor leaders had been imprisoned for dabbling in politics and operating a school for the workers. Later that same day I went on a tour through the cement and chemical works at Samch'ŏk. The workers gave our group unfriendly glances and edged away whenever we tried to approach. No one would say anything about their political sentiments; the workers were obviously frightened. Such was the labor organization to which the American Command gave its full stamp of approval. It is little wonder that the workers turned more and more toward communism. But to get back to our story.

After the June meeting of the National Society for the Rapid Realization of Korean Independence in which he had been named

63 This is the just mentioned National Council of Korean Labor Unions.
64 The insertions in brackets in this quote are in the author's original typescript.

president, Dr. Rhee returned to the provinces to further strengthen his political organization. As he did so, a new character entered the political stage in Seoul in the person of one Sin Ik-hŭi [1894–1956], an accomplished politician and Minister of Home Affairs in the cabinet of Kim Ku's Provisional Government. Sin and his personal following had been wooed away from Kim Ku and into Rhee's National Society. Sin's value lay in his unique ability and finesse in promising everything to everybody at one and the same time and getting away with it—at least, for the moment. Sin the opportunist saw the balance of political power swinging to Dr. Rhee and promptly jumped on the bandwagon while the jumping was good. With him came his "Political Task Force" [Chŏngch'i Kongjaktae] a group initially formed under the Provisional Government by Sin (in his capacity as Minister of Home Affairs) to organize support for the Provisional Government. This desertion of Sin and his group from the cause of Kim Ku constituted a personal victory for Dr. Rhee. However, Sin was soon to prove an unruly bedfellow.

In June 1946 rumors were picked up by watchful CIC agents that Sin Ik-hŭi and his flock of political faithfuls were preparing the ground for a coup d'état at the expense of American Military Government. Such plans called for a march on the Capital Building and a mass sit-down strike in the Capital's front yard in a move designed to force the Americans to evacuate and turn authority over to Sin and Rhee. Plans were changed several times. It finally developed that the August 15 celebration commemorating the first anniversary of Korean liberation would set off the insurrection. Learning of the pending move, American CIC agents apprehended Sin and a group of his lieutenants and escorted them to CIC headquarters for interrogation. Sin admitted hearing of the plot, but denied that he was a participant. Did he have a list of those men sponsoring the move? Dr. Rhee had the only one. When asked whether or not Dr. Rhee and Kim Ku had given their approval to the contemplated coup, he replied that they had not. At this, the American Command announced to Sin that he would be held personally accountable for any adventures launched by the rightists. The August 15 demonstration came and went without undue disturbance. A few handbills were distributed among the crowds of demonstrators announcing the formation of a new government with Dr. Rhee at its helm, but few took serious notice of them. Later, when Dr. Rhee and Kim Ku were interrogated, both disclaimed any knowledge of the venture. News of the plot was as much a surprise to them as to anyone else. American intelligence officers received this information with a tongue-in-cheek attitude and promptly reported that it was quite likely that Dr. Rhee had known of the move all along and had approved of it as sort of a trial balloon to see what the American reaction would be. A more serious effort to establish a Korean rightist government in the Capital was predicted for the future. The prediction was not an idle one, as later events showed.

By this time, Sin Ik-hŭi, now a lesser official in Rhee's National Society, was causing trouble within the organization. Without consulting the national officials of the Society, he brought public charges in the name of the Society against several leftist leaders who had allegedly libeled the Society. This act incurred the displeasure of the leaders of the Society because they had not been consulted beforehand. A number of the higher officials in the National Society resigned in protest. This move called for Rhee's personal intervention. He promptly returned to Seoul from his tour of the provinces, asked for the resignation of all the officers of the Society, and called for another national convocation. Dr. Rhee's prestige and power was such by this time that a mass resignation of officers quickly followed. Furthermore, at the September 1946 session of the National Society, Rhee's control was so complete that he could force the adoption of an entire slate of candidates for office, including his man Sin Ik-hŭi. As for Rhee himself, he accepted the presidency only after announcing in no uncertain terms that he was no longer going to play the "role of a doll." He would give orders and the members would follow them. To quell the disquieting rumors that all was not well between himself and his redoubtable colleague, Kim Ku, Dr. Rhee announced that they stood as one man. Kim Ku quickly parroted this sentiment. Rhee had won complete control of the right-wing extremists.

The political scene had now shaken down so that Pak Hŏn-yŏng and his Communists stood on one side and Dr. Syngman Rhee and his National Society for the Rapid Realization of Korean Independence on the other. In the middle, caught between the two fires, were Yŏ Un-hyŏng and Kim Kyu-sik, now squirming this way and then that to break free of extremist control, but really without any effective, popular organization backing them. For a moment, they found temporary shelter in the blessing of American support, and therein lies the story of the rise of Korean liberalism—and of its final demise.

A Liberal Hope

By late February of 1946, as we have said, the State Department had belatedly given forth some advice on the subject of Korea. In essence it was a warning against Dr. Rhee and Kim Ku. This advice came too late, for the American Command was already involved in the Representative Democratic Council and the Joint Soviet–American Commission. Any sudden change at that juncture would have weakened the American position in the Joint Commission.

But it was late spring of 1946 that the first real directive arrived from Washington relative to *domestic* Korean politics. The American Command was instructed to work towards a middle-of-the-road or slightly left-of-center political coalition as the first step in establishing an interim Korean Government in South Korea. Dr. Rhee and Kim Ku were to be definitely on the outside. In view of this long-overdue State Department advice and the mounting evidence of the duplicity and ambition of Rhee and Kim Ku, a shift in political policy by the American Command was made necessary. However, so many Korean politicos had been alienated in the early days of the occupation by roughshod American action in support of Kim Ku and Rhee that change was difficult. The extreme right wing was the only political faction friendly to the Americans. All other factions had been snubbed by General Hodge on one occasion or another. The sincerity of the Americans was openly doubted by the middle-of-the-roaders and moderate left-wingers due to the forced breakup of Yŏ Un-hyŏng's Korean People's Republic, the apparent sanction of the many excesses committed by the Korean police, and the appointment of many questionable characters to Military Government administrative posts. The Korean Communists, of course, maintained a hostile attitude toward the Americans from start to finish as matter of principle.

On or about February 1, 1946, the last remaining remnants of the liberal element deserted Kim Ku's Provisional Government. On this date Kim Kyu-sik and Kim Wŏn-bong, former "cabinet ministers" of the erstwhile government, led their factions out from under Kim Ku's leadership. The move was made when it became apparent that Kim Ku and his henchmen had organized the Emergency National Congress only as a means of grabbing more complete control over the right wing. The liberal elements, led by the two rebel Kim's, could not stomach further obeisance to Kim Ku and his gunmen. Kim Wŏn-bong and his Korean National Revolutionary Party, one of the oldest of Korean political groups, found themselves forced into the Communist-dominated camp ruled by the Democratic National Front. Kim Kyu-sik agreed to participate in the Representative Democratic Council of South Korea and became one of its vice-chairmen. This desertion by the liberal elements left Kim Ku's group more than ever on the extreme right. And when Yŏ's representatives were withdrawn from the Representative Democratic Council and Kim Kyu-sik became inactive, the Council likewise moved to the right extreme of the political spectrum. A void was left in the middle.

It was March 1946 when General Hodge finally gave permission to his political advisors to start negotiations for the organization of a truly representative political group, one which would be middle-of-the-road, if not slightly left-of-center. This was per State Department advice. The first hurdle to overcome was the resentment and animosity aroused in the more liberal elements by past American acts. These delicate negotiations were left in the hands of a second lieutenant, Leonard M. Bertsch [1910–1976], newly-appointed political advisor to General Hodge.* That he soon became *persona non grata* with the general and assigned only more menial tasks stemmed from the lieutenant's genuinely liberal philosophy which the general's mind seemed completely unable to grasp.

Obviously, the two men most suited to lead a coalition movement were Yŏ Un-hyŏng and Kim Kyu-sik, moderate leftist and moderate rightist, respectively. Effort was concentrated on bringing the two men together. It was soon ascertained that Kim Kyu-sik was more than willing to cooperate in such a coalition movement. He had long since

* Leonard M. Bertsch, now of Akron, Ohio. See his article "UN Victory in Korea Poses Question of Rhee's Future," *Foreign Policy Bulletin* 30, no. 2 (October 20, 1950): 2–3, the text of which is given in Chapter X.

become disgusted at the overly ambitious and dictatorial leaders of the extreme right wing. However, Yŏ was a horse of another color. He had been deliberately rebuffed by the American Command in the early days of the occupation and more or less ignored since. He had little reason to trust the Americans. On the other hand, he was tired of Communist domination. On this basis, the Americans appealed to him, but still he hesitated. He was doubtful as to the strength of his political backing in the event he incurred all-out opposition from the Communists. Moreover, he no doubt saw Korea as one day being inevitably under Soviet influence; he would think twice and then again before antagonizing the Russians completely by deserting the Communists and openly aiding the Americans. It is now safe to say that Yŏ, being the liberal that he was, wanted nothing more than to cooperate in a coalition movement with Dr. Kim Kyu-sik. He said so privately on more than one occasion. But his realistic mind made him suspicious and doubtful. To maintain a middle-of-the-road liberal organization would need very real American protection. The extremes were armed and organized. Both would snipe at any moderate movement with both words and bullets. During this period Yŏ was kidnapped, beaten, and warned not to participate in a coalition effort. Several attempts were made on his life. It was rumored that Kim Ku had actually placed a price on his head. The situation was such that he received permission from General Hodge to maintain an armed body guard.

Yŏ Un-hyŏng and his younger brother, Yŏ Un-hong, met with American representatives on numerous occasions throughout the spring of 1946. But Yŏ the elder still refused to participate in a coalition movement of political moderates. He was frankly suspicious and worried. It became apparent that Yŏ would have to be forced to come to a showdown with the Communist elements within his People's Party before he would agree. American efforts were then concentrated on Yŏ Un-hong. Not only was he Yŏ's brother but also one of his political lieutenants. It was thought that if Yŏ the younger could be persuaded to denounce Communist control of the Korean People's Party and break away from it, Yŏ the elder might be induced to do likewise—particularly when he saw the large non-Communist backing he would have. Yŏ the younger was finally convinced and on May 9, 1946, three days after the breakup of the Joint Soviet–American Commission, Yŏ

Un-hong publicly announced his withdrawal from the Korean People's Party and the formation of a moderate left-wing group, the Social Democratic Party [Sahoe Minjudang]. The move, said the younger Yŏ, was occasioned by the intolerable stranglehold which the Communists had on his elder brother's party. This move caused a momentary furor in Korean politics, but when the dust had settled only a handful of second-raters had deserted the Korean People's Party.

The Social Democratic Party never achieved very wide influence itself, but it did finally accomplish what had been desired. Younger Yŏ's denunciation of the Communist control of the People's Party brought the issue to a head within that party. Yŏ Un-hyŏng was finally talked into meeting with Dr. Kim Kyu-sik for preliminary discussions. The group was quickly enlarged to four, both men extending an invitation to one other. Yŏ brought Hŏ Hŏn, non-Communist leader of the Communist-controlled Democratic National Front. Kim Kyu-sik showed up with Wŏn Se-hun [1887–1959], leader of the moderate element in the extreme right-wing Korean Democratic Party. During the ensuing month, July 1946, informal discussions continued with General Hodge's second lieutenant political advisor present as mediator upon unanimous invitation of all four men. Kim Kyu-sik commented at an early meeting that but for the effort of Lieutenant Leonard M. Bertsch they probably would never have gotten together at all. On July 22, 1946, the Coalition Committee membership was expanded to ten, five rightists and five leftists. Dr. Kim and Yŏ were appointed co-chairman. The left-wing delegation was named by the Democratic National Front and the right-wing delegation by a combined meeting of the Representative Democratic Council and the Emergency National Congress.

The initial task facing the Committee was the adoption of a joint statement of principles which, it was hoped, would lead to the reconvening of the Joint Soviet–American Commission and the establishment of a legislative organ, if not for all of Korea, at least for South Korea. However, on July 30, 1946, the Coalition Committee seemed destined for an early death as the entire left-wing delegation absented itself from a scheduled meeting. In direct contradiction to an agreement prohibiting unilateral press statements by either delegation, the People's Democratic Front had released on the previous day the "minimum requirements necessary for the unification of the left and right factions." Apparently, the left wing felt that by absenting itself it could force the rightist delegates either to accept their ultimatum or take the initiative in ending the coalition effort.

The Communists probably hoped to accomplish the latter, and there was considerable evidence indicating that such was indeed the case. On June 10, 1946, Pak Hŏn-yŏng, the South Korean Communist leader, had retired to North Korea for direction. Upon his return to South Korea on July 22, Pak's attitude on the subject of the coalition was crystallized, no doubt under the impact of orders received in the North. Immediately thereafter, he set about to wreck the negotiations. On July 29, the following impossible conditions were dictated by the Communist-controlled Democratic National Front; it is doubtful if Yŏ was even notified beforehand:

> (1) to work for the reconvening of the Joint Commission in unanimous support of the Moscow Decision and to support the movement for the speedy establishment of a free, democratic provisional government in cooperation with the North Korean National Front.
>
> (2) to attain a land revolution and to nationalize important industries.
>
> (3) to purge the country of pro-Japanese and treacherous elements and to take concrete steps to exterminate terrorism while, at the same time, liberate our patriots who have been imprisoned since the end of the war and, in other ways, actively extend the democratic movement.
>
> (4) to plan for the immediate transfer of political authority from Military Government to the People's Committee meeting in South Korea, which is an organ of self-government such as the North Korean political organization.
>
> (5) to oppose the organization and constitution of a legislative body or any advisory organ of Military Government.

Obviously, the right-wing delegation, as well as the American Command, could never agree to points 4 and 5, and Pak (who had no doubt dictated the demands) must have known it. The unqualified support of the Moscow Decision specified in point 1 undoubtedly implied unqualified support for an Allied trusteeship as well. By this move, the Communist-controlled left probably hoped to stick the fatal knife into further coalition efforts.

The following day, July 30, the right-wing delegation met as scheduled only to find the left-wing delegates absent. Yŏ conveniently claimed ill health. "I have lost my appetite," he announced. He doubtless felt it best to stay clear until he could see the lay of the land. Did he have enough left-wing support to launch out on a course completely independent of any Communist support? That was the question. It further came to light that Pak had cautioned Yŏ not to "play the American game," and had predicted that the Coalition Committee would be another fiasco and that all rightist opposition in Korea could be eliminated in short order if southern leftists stood firmly by their compatriots in the North. Pak's attitude toward the coalition effort before going to P'yŏngyang, the North Korean capital, had not been unfriendly, even though non-committal. After his return, however, it became painfully clear that a resolute and positive opposition to the coalition effort on his part was the result of instructions received in P'yŏngyang. Yŏ informed General Hodge that he had told Pak that he, Yŏ, was too far committed to Dr. Kim Kyu-sik and the coalition effort to slacken or discontinue his efforts to effect political unity in the South and, further, that he would stay with the project until some conclusion was reached.

It was speculated at the time that some deep fear or mortal enmity of Pak must have come to the surface in this encounter—perhaps threat of assassination, for Yŏ hinted that it was essential to the success of the American coalition program that Pak be dealt with drastically at this juncture. Yŏ was asked why he himself did not expose the Communist intention to sabotage the unity effort. His answer was that large labor, farmer, and youth elements in South Korea divided their allegiance between him and Pak, and that if an open break came between the two of them at that time it would hurt the unity movement. Rather, he suggested, if Pak could be made to lose face at that moment, he (Yŏ) might be able to win a considerable portion of these elements over to his and, therefore, the American side. General Hodge's private comment was that Yŏ either lacked the moral courage or was too far secretly committed to the Communists to have a showdown with Pak and was looking for the Americans to extricate him from his uncomfortable position.* Earlier, it had been suspected by the Americans that the Communists were blackmailing Yŏ with some documents indicating that he had carried on certain negotiations with the Japanese before World War II which would finish him politically if made public. An American officer was even dispatched to Japan to search Japanese Government files and interview high Japanese officials on the subject. No information whatsoever was found, however, which indicated that Yŏ was anything other than a patriotic Korean.

Possibly because he found himself unable to straddle the ever-widening gap between the two divergent political groups even within his own Korean People's Party, Yŏ tendered his resignation from leadership of his party on August 13, 1946, and retired to the country. This act threw the People's Party into an uproar and forced a decision on the Communist call for a merger of the three principal left-wing parties along North Korean lines. A few days later, the matter was resolved in the high councils of the People's Party by a 48 to 31 vote in favor of the merger, with 53 abstentions. It was later suspected that the outcome of this balloting had been effected no little by the payment of over two million yen to those voting in favor of the merger, the money having come from Communist Party coffers. By mid-September 1946 Yŏ had withdrawn his resignation, and, with the exodus of the more vocal Communist members into the Namnodang, the new South Korean Workers' Party,** he had regained control of his old party. In fact, on September 15, Yŏ announced that he would make a new start as chairman of the People's Party and warned the Communists to keep their hands off.

While Yŏ was joining battle with the Communists and trying to consolidate the moderate left behind the coalition movement, the extreme right was, like the Communists, doing its level best to torpedo the unity discussions. Late in June 1946 Dr. Syngman Rhee had announced the formation of his General Headquarters for National Unification and "ordered" all parties to participate. It was a move

---

* The order for Pak's arrest was not issued until September 1946 (see pp. 161–62).

** The South Korean Workers' Party [Namchosŏn Nodongdang, short Namnodang] was set up as a popular front movement which claimed to represent all leftist elements. The Communists had been forced to go underground in September 1946 when warrants were issued for the arrest of Communist leaders.

patently designed, to undermine the Coalition Committee as well as to seize personal control of the right. The American Command attempted to dissuade Rhee from his course, but to no avail. Meanwhile, Rhee was understandably loath to commend the Coalition Committee or in any way indicate his support of it. He was doubtlessly more than a little offended at the cooling American sentiment towards himself. None of the left-wing parties responded to Rhee's call. Instead of being a headquarters for national unification, Rhee's organization became the headquarters for right-wing unification. But to return to the story.

On July 30, 1946, the left-wing delegates had absented themselves from a scheduled meeting of the American-inspired Coalition Committee. In view of the unauthorized publication of the five left-wing principles for unification the previous day, the rightists retaliated in kind and announced their principles as follows:

(1) We will exert our efforts through unification of both wings, including North and South Korea.

(2) We will issue a joint communique demanding the reconvening of the Joint Commission.

(3) The problem of trusteeship will be solved probably by the interim government, under a compromise among the United States, the Soviet Union, and the spirit of Korean independence.

(4) A conference of representatives of the people should be held not later than six months after the establishment of an interim government. The representatives ought to be selected by general election.

(5) A formal government should be established not later than three months after the conference of elected representatives.

(6) Freedom of expression, organization, assembly, press, travel and suffrage should be protected to assure us a fair, just, and representative general election.

(7) All systems and laws concerning politics, economy, and education should be drafted on the assumption of a society based on equality, and they should be legislated in the conference of duly elected representatives.

(8) Pro-Japanese and national traitors will be tried immediately after the interim government is established. A special court should be set up for this purpose.

A full meeting of the Coalition Committee did not occur again until early September 1946. It took repeated appeals from Kim Kyu-sik, General Hodge, and the final parting of the ways of Yŏ and the Communists before any measure of real unity was attained. The right-wing delegation remained the same throughout, but the final delegation of leftists, still headed by Yŏ, underwent radical change. A group of anti-Pak Hŏn-yŏng Communists and representatives of Yŏ's recently-cleansed People's Party comprised the final leftist delegation. Just prior to final agreement, Yŏ disappeared. Later, it developed that he had visited North Korea to discuss the coalition movement with North Korean political leaders. Finally, on October 8, 1946, the Coalition Committee issued a joint statement of principles:

(1) A democratic interim government should be established throughout North and South Korea under the guidance of the Moscow Decision of the foreign ministers.

(2) A joint commission of both the left and right wing should be formed to pursue the reconvention of the Joint Soviet–American Commission.

(3) The democratization of the country should be hastened by redistributing farmlands by confiscation, nationalizing many large industries, enforcing a labor law, setting up constitutions for district governments, stabilizing currency, and establishing a national life insurance program.

(4) Instances and cases of traitors and collaborators should be investigated by a legislative committee or organization and action taken determined by this body.

(5) All political prisoners now in custody both in North and South Korea should be freed. Terroristic actions should be outlawed.

(6) The delegates of the unification conference should write the plans for the legislative organization, and the latter should be responsible for their enforcement.

(7) All freedoms—of meeting, speech, press, travel and voting—must be granted.

The extreme right-wing Korean Democratic Party lost no time in opposing the principles of the Coalition Committee. "Anti-trusteeship is not clearly declared in the first article of the seven principles," objected the Korean Democrats. Party spokesmen then objected to the third principle calling for the confiscation of farmlands. "This will bring great financial difficulties to our state," they announced. With that, liberal Wŏn Se-hun, a member of the Coalition Committee, resigned from the Korean Democratic Party. On October 15, 1946, Dr. Syngman Rhee expressed his dissatisfaction with the Coalition principles. In the first place, the principles favored the Communists. Secondly, he considered trusteeship and the disposal of farmlands as matters for discussion only after an interim government had been established.

The Coalition Committee was now a thing of reality, but it remained to be seen if the American Command would act on its suggestions and protect its leaders adequately from the onslaught from both right and left.

CHAPTER V: MOBS, RIOTS, AND MURDER

The second year of occupation opened in September 1946 amid the resounding discord of political struggle. The left soon was to wage open warfare against the American regime. Meanwhile, the right, vary of possible success in the newly-resumed Russo–American correspondence on the subject of Korea, was laying careful plans for an insurrection the next spring (1947). Amidst this reversion to violence and intrigue, the Korean liberals paradoxically had their heyday. But all the while, there was a somber undertone, an undertone which promised that one day the position of the liberals would be made untenable by the joining of a mortal struggle between right and left extremes. This undertone was the Korean National Police, the greatest political force in South Korea by the fall of 1946.

The Korean Police

As already recounted when the Americans landed in Korea, they found the Korean People's Republic the keeper of law and order. The hated Japanese police and their Korean underlings had been forced out of office and replaced, for the most part, by Koreans largely of undisputed patriotism. This, the Republic had done. Naturally, some opportunistic and lawless elements took advantage of the rapid changeover, but on the whole, things were progressing rather smoothly considering that a radical social and political revolution was in process. The effect of American opposition to the Republic and its displacement by poorly trained Americans and ill-chosen Koreans was, in effect, to turn back the revolutionary clock and to annul much progress. The first step in undermining the prestige of the Republic was to take away from it the police power it had assumed during the interim between Japanese and American control.

At the outset. General Hodge and his staff admittedly knew little or nothing about Korean personalities. With a population, fifty percent of whose family names were either Kim, Pak, or Yi, the situation was just a bit confusing. The upshot was that the American Command unwillingly chose Dr. Cho Pyŏng-ok and Chang T'aek-sang [1893–1969] to occupy the top spots in the National Police organization. Cho was appointed National Director and Chang, Chief of the Seoul Metropolitan Police or Division "M." Both men were active members of the extreme right-wing Korean Democratic Party. Chang had once signed a petition addressed to the American Command from the Korean Democrats asking that Kim Ku's Provisional Government be brought back to Korea and recognized as the legitimate government. Both men had been well known in missionary circles, Dr. Cho having taught at one of the mission-supported schools in recent years. (His doctorate was from Columbia University.)

That Dr. Cho and Chief Chang had prospered during the Japanese occupation did not increase their popularity. In addition, the fact that they tolerated—if not encouraged—all kinds of police excesses, corruption and political partiality in the enforcement of the law soon acted to destroy whatever popular prestige that remained to them. For instance, after the shooting spree between rightists and leftists in Seoul on March 1, 1947, one of the top American police supervisors commented to me that he would not be surprised at all if Cho and/or Chang had deliberately started the whole affair. He went on to explain that there was enough evidence in his files on these two men to hang them several times over and that, further, there was no hope of reducing police irregularities so long as the two men held power. The American police supervisor then commented that the only reason the pair had not been removed long before was because of a direct order from General Hodge not to do so.

Having selected this pair to head the police organization, the Americans commenced recruiting officers and men. Those with past police experience—experience by necessity gained under the Japanese—were preferred. Hence, in the beginning the vast majority of both officers and men were former Japanese-trained policemen. Later, the percentage dropped, but even as late in mid-1947 the upper police brackets were still filled with these Korean quislings. An interesting coincident occurred on this score in December 1946. A very close Korean friend of mine was boarding an American plane in Seoul for the island province of Cheju. He looked about and found seated next to him a Korean whom he recognized as having worked for the Japanese secret police during the war. In fact, the gentleman had been assigned by the Japanese on one occasion to follow my friend about in order to check on his anti-Japanese activities. This former Japanese police agent, one Sin U-gyun, was making the trip to Cheju as the new, American-appointed police chief for the island. Sin did not last long; he was caught in February 1947, operating in league with smugglers. He had realized the neat profit of over half a million yen (about $5,000 in comparable purchasing power) in three months' time. The very large percentage of police officers who had held office under the Japanese was conclusively demonstrated by the ultimatum served on General Hodge by the National Police on July 2, 1947. The Interim Legislative Assembly had just proposed a piece of legislation which would bar from public office all those who had held office under the Japanese.[65] General Hodge was

[65] The Interim Assembly passed the Special Ordinance on National Traitors, Pro-Japanese Collaborators, and Profiteers (*Minjok panyŏkcha, puirhyŏmnyŏkcha, kansangbaee taehan t'ŭkpyŏl chorye*) in early July 1947, only to have it vetoed by the American Military Government. See *Seoul sinmun*, July 4, 1947, and Mark E. Caprio, "The Politics of Collaboration in Post-liberation Southern Korea," in *In the Ruins*

informed by the National Police that either he vetoes the law or the police throughout South Korea would oppose the administration of the law. A year before, on August 15, 1946, General Lerch, the Military Governor, had said, "We now have a democratic police force."

The police organization was set up on a national basis, provincial governors and city mayors having no control whatsoever over the police within their areas. All American supervisors could see was police efficiency. The machinery for an autocratic police state was thereby constructed. Yŏ Un-hyŏng and others objected vigorously when the National Police organization was set up; first, as to the personnel selected and, secondly, as to the type of organization. They saw it not as a police force so much as a political force endangering any move in a liberal direction.

The police force of South Korea as of mid-1947 was approximately 25,000 strong, almost 10,000 more than the Japanese had maintained in South Korea. The prison population in South Korea was close to 22,000, almost double the highest number ever held by the Japanese in South Korea. The excuses given were the political unrest in the country and the lack of training on the part of the average police recruit. True, the turnover in the police force was very large, partially because of the enmity felt by the general public towards the police. In the spring of 1947, the director of the Women's Police resigned for no other reason than the fact that she refused to be a party any longer to what was going on; she had her own reputation of which to think.

A police academy was established to train new officers and men, but the old Japanese-trained clique still ruled, and with stubborn American support. The Communists accused the police of being shot full with Japanese collaborators. Therefore, of course, it would be poor strategy to admit any of the charges or to make any effort to alter the situation, so believed General Hodge and his associates. Actually, the police did more to ruin the reputation of the United States in Korea and the way of life for which it stands than any other one thing, thereby immeasurably strengthening the Communist appeal. A study of police tactics indicates the reason.

---

of the Japanese Empire: Imperial Violence, State Destruction, and the Reordering of Modern East Asia, Barak Kushner and Andrew Levidis, eds. (Hong Kong: Hong Kong University Press, 2020), 27–49.

In the first place, the police were not politically impartial as the American Command insisted. I know from personal observation and investigation that on two occasions blanket arrest orders went down through Korean police channels calling for the arrest of *all* leftist leaders and "agitators," the purpose being to aid organizational moves by the right wing. The American authorities denied that such was the case, so I will give American Military Government the benefit of the doubt and assume that the orders originated with Dr. Cho and his *Korean* colleagues. School teachers were jailed summarily for the mere mention of the subject of communism in their classrooms. On numerous occasions the police were guilty of intimidating the press. In quelling disturbances, the police invariably were found with uniformed companions from the rightist Great Korea Democratic Young Men's Association [Taehan Minju Ch'ŏngnyŏn Ch'ongdongmaeng][66] in reality an organization of armed thugs. This last was denied repeatedly by Messrs. Cho and Chang, but time after time I personally have seen these political strong-arm men utilized for police purposes. On one occasion, such rightist "youth" actually *arrested* a left-wing labor leader before American witnesses.[67] In many communities, the American Military Government authorities delegated to the local police the power to grant permits for meetings. Suffice to say that a *legal* leftist meeting rarely took place, and distinction between Communist and leftist was rarely made. In many areas the power to grant licenses for the publication of newspapers, handbills, pamphlets, and the like was also delegated to the Korean police. When these facts were reported to Military Governor General Lerch, he refused to believe that the power had been so delegated or was being misused.

---

[66] In his manuscript Robinson referred to the "Young Men's Association" and Charlotte Ebener named it the "Great Korea Association," while Mark Gayn called it the "Great Korea Young Men's Association." Yet, despite the variant English renderings, their descriptions identify the same right-wing youth group. Established in April 1946, it was likely the most violent among all the many politicized paramilitary youth organizations (see p. 190). We could easily classify it as a terrorist organization, as USAMGIK did in April 1947, when it ordered the association to disband.

[67] This is a hinted reference to Mark Gayn's and Charlotte Ebener's firsthand depictions of the incident. See Gayn's diary herein, 352–58; Ebener, *No Facilities for Women*, 57–59.

Whenever right-wing leaders toured the provinces, the roads were lined with armed policemen and meetings were well guarded. Such service and honor was rarely, if ever, accorded the leaders of the left. A typical example of how the police "protected" left-wing meetings occurred in 1947 in Seoul. Protection had been requested by the leftist leaders, and the meeting place was encircled by Korean police. Shortly after the session got underway, a group of rightists gathered and began pelting stones in through the open windows. The police looked amused. The fire was returned by the leftists. Some of the policemen, caught in between the two lines of fire, were hit, and thereupon began aiding the rightists in stoning their political opponents. The upshot was that the police escorted several of the leftist leaders off to jail for disturbing the peace. Such was the substance of the official American intelligence report based on witness evidence.

It was required that a certain percentage of all grain raised by each farmer be turned over to Military Government for a fixed price. This grain, largely rice, was used to supply food rations in the food deficit areas. The quotas for the individual farmers were set by local boards appointed with American approval and composed of high police officials, village elders, businessmen, and large landowners. Some months before the harvest, the quota for each individual farmer in the area was determined. From this decision, *no*—I repeat *no*—appeals were allowed. The farmer either turned in the amount of grain demanded or went to jail where he was more frequently than not, severely beaten and refused trial. I once asked a local police chief if the board ever made a mistake in setting a quota. "Never," he said. "We never make mistakes." I made a number of personnel investigations of alleged rice hoarding cases in which farmers had ended up behind bars. In almost all of these cases, there was reason to believe that the farmer's crop had not been as large as had been expected, and that in fact he did not have enough rice to sell to the government to fill his quota. I sat in the offices of local police officials and heard relatives of jailed men come in and beg to be allowed to fill the prisoners' quotas with excess rice which they themselves had—only to be denied. Meanwhile, American Military Government insisted that opposition to the grain collection program stemmed wholly from Communist propaganda spread among the farmers. This was only a half-truth. The other half was that the police administered the program arbitrarily, harshly, and unjustly, often with partisan political objectives in mind. Communist propaganda fell on increasingly fertile ground. By the end of 1946 it was unwise for unattended Americans to walk alone in the country at night.

And then there was the subject of the schools. In Seoul and the other large cities were numerous student strikes and other disturbances. Without doubt, agitators from both political camps circulated among them from time to time firing their prejudices and emotions. In Seoul, the police became increasingly active in the school yards and college campuses. Alleged Communist agitators and trouble-makers were expelled, jailed, and beaten—but rarely tried. Faculty purges of left-wing influence were common. Friction increased in intensity so that by the fall and winter of 1946 little real education was being accomplished in the classrooms.

Actually, much of this "Communist-inspired" agitation did not have its source in Communist agitation at all, but in very real grievances, such as the lack of books, poorly trained teachers, inadequate food and heat, undue police interference, the desire for student government, and the arbitrary administration exercised by certain American supervisors—particularly in the case of Seoul National University, the largest of the Korean institutions of higher learning. The situation was investigated in the spring of 1947 by an American officer especially delegated by XXIV Corps G-2 Section. He soon returned with a report citing Communist agitation as only a minor, secondary cause of disturbances in the schools. The report was ordered rewritten. The new version described the basic grievances as merely fictitious propaganda raised by the Communists. Little was done except to appoint a missionary as head of the Department of Education in Military Government. Soon after that, the advisor to the Seoul City Department of Education, an American civilian, issued a vigorous denunciation of undue police interference in the schools and a plea for an intelligent and constructive approach to the whole problem of education by the American Command. General Lerch, the Military Governor, acted by asking for the advisor's resignation.

Police officialdom was rife with graft and corruption. This situation was not unique to the police, for such activities had been encouraged by the extremely low level of governmental salaries established by an economy-minded Military Government. Initially a large percentage of the salaries paid to Korean employees of Military Government would not even cover the cost of living. Graft was necessary if an official were to live. Some few had private fortunes from which they could draw. The fact that many of the top police officials not only lived on their meagre salaries, but became very wealthy men during the first two years of occupation was *prima facie* evidence of large payoffs somewhere along the line. For instance, Dr. Cho came into office with a very modest personal fortune. Two years later, U.S. Intelligence reported that he had twenty million yen (about $200,000 by comparable purchasing power) in his bank account.

Black market operations either in rice or American goods provided a major source of income. One of the top national police officials made a private fortune by shipping rice illegally into Seoul and selling it at enormous prices to the hungry populace. Another of the top officials was caught red-handed by American investigators dealing in stolen cameras. The American Command deemed it best not to prosecute, and the guilty official continued to hold office. After the Taegu Riots in the fall of 1946 (see next section), the homes of the murdered policemen were examined. An average of three *sŏk* (143 U.S. gallons) of rice was found in each. It was impossible that such a large amount could have been acquired legally. Obviously, there had been a large-scale police shakedown operating in the area. Then there was the case of the police chief in Kangnŭng, an east coast town just south of the 38th parallel. Because of the high value of chemical fertilizer in South Korea, attractive profits could be realized by smuggling it in from the North, a very easy feat so long as the local police chief got his fair share at no cost. And then there was the case of the *Life* photographer who "lost" his choice camera in Seoul. One of his friends, a member of the inner circle at XXIV Corps Headquarters, ventured the thought that in his opinion only one group would have enough gall to steal anything so important as a camera belonging to an American correspondent—and that would be the police. Sure enough, a visit to the police station and a certain amount of persuasion produced the camera.

One of the largest police rackets was worked on Korean merchants selling black market American goods. Such merchants were forced to pay protection money in order to avoid police raids and confiscation of their stock. For instance, to sell, buy or barter American cigarettes was a cardinal offense in Korea by American law. However, sidewalk vendors directly across from XXIV Corps Headquarters in Seoul openly sold American cigarettes with no thought of concealment. How it was done was obvious; the Korean police were bought off regularly, and there was considerable suspicion that such buying off was not confined to the *Korean* police.

The Korean police operated on the well-known, pre-war Japanese legal principles of arresting a suspect without warrant, torturing him into confessing—whether guilty or not, and then locking him in a dark, rat-infested, evil smelling jail for an indefinite period of time with or without trial. Regardless of what the legal authorities in Military Government claimed, prisoners generally were not allowed to consult a counsel, in fact, not to consult anyone; they were held *ex communicato*. Supposedly, prisoners were to be served with specific charges upon being arrested and either given a hearing or released within ten days' time. Actually, many prisoners were never served with any specific charges or ever brought to trial, even though they might be held several months. This observation is based on interviews with scores of ex-prison and jail inmates. Furthermore, a man was presumed guilty until he could prove himself innocent. There was a case which occurred in 1946 involving a pathetic old man from the hills. He had taken all his savings to make a trip to Seoul in order to have work done on his teeth by a competent dentist. A friend had given him the address of a man with whom he might live during his short stay in the city. The old man was made welcome, but on the very first evening of his stay the police raided the house in search of a group of Communist agitators or some such. The man was arrested summarily along with the men whom the police were after. In this case, the group appeared before an *American* Provost Court for trial. All were sentenced to imprisonment for a number of years, including the old man. His pleas of innocence fell on deaf ears. It was a year later that the old man was finally freed, and only then after an interested American officer had carried the battle to the highest authorities. A number of stories of this sort could be told. It is little wonder that when one spoke of the virtues of American democratic law and justice that the average Korean smiled grimly—and, one suspects, still does.

The police were not above manufacturing evidence when such was needed. In March 1947, Kim Wŏn-bong, a non-Communist left-wing leader, was brought to trial for allegedly having led an "illegal" strike.

The police no doubt felt that this would be as good a time as any to put Kim away for a while. Written speeches were introduced as evidence which presumably he had delivered to a left-wing rally some weeks before and in which such a strike was urged. Fortunately for Kim, he was able to produce witnesses to testify that he had made no such statements. And then there was the wonderful case in which the police were hard pressed to prove that a suspect had been involved in a particular riot. He was, nevertheless, brought to trial. Three "witnesses" were shanghaied off the street. The first witness was called. "Do you recognize this man?" the judge asked, "No, I do not," answered the erstwhile witness. A police sergeant's fist shot out and knocked the man to his knees. Next witness! The process was repeated. Again a denial, a brutal slap, and the witness was taken out whimpering. Third witness! This poor unfortunate had seen the fate of his two companions, and decided to escape a similar ordeal. Falteringly, he recognized the suspect. A conviction quickly followed. The judge was an American officer.

The real payoff on the Korean system of justice came when the American-appointed Chief Justice of the Korean Supreme Court blithely announced in a public speech in the city of Kwangju on June 9, 1946, that: (1) those who supported trusteeship should either die or be sent to Russia, (2) that any judge who advocated strict judicial neutrality on the subject was not qualified to be a justice official, and (3) that it was not right to release those arrested on suspicion of hampering national reconstruction just because there was no clear evidence. He remained Chief Justice under American Military Government. On June 19, 1946, the judge denied that he had ever made such a statement and was supported in his denial by General Lerch—this, in spite of a report to the contrary submitted by at least one American Military Government officer.

Much could be said on the subject of torture. Many of the tricks of the medieval horror chamber were used to extract confessions. One day in Pusan during the summer of 1946 I walked into a police station when the water treatment was being applied to a suspected pickpocket. He was writhing on the floor in agony, tied hand and foot. Acting as any American officer should under the circumstances, I arrested the torturers on the spot and preferred charges against them for misuse of police authority. The act very nearly netted me a court-martial. According to General Lerch, the matter was none of my concern. Apparently, I should have done nothing but report the matter to the proper authorities, meanwhile letting the victim suffer on and learn how American democracy—as interpreted by General Lerch—operated.[68] It should be borne in mind that governmental authority presumably rested in American hands; at this time the United States was temporarily responsible for the administration of South Korea. (The only thing that saved me from court-martial was newspaper publicity and the intervention of friends with General Hodge, General Lerch's superior.) But this incident was minor compared to much which went on. In October 1946 the police were combing the country for the leaders of the Taegu Riots. It was suspected that one of the leaders was hiding in a particular part of Taegu. Unable to unearth him, the police seized his aged mother. They announced that she would be held and tortured every day until her son gave himself up. Either he did not choose to do so or was not alive, for he failed to show up. A few days later the beaten and bloated body of the mother was delivered to her home for burial.

On June 30, 1947, the Korean Civil Liberties Union—inspired by a recent visit to Korea by Roger Baldwin [1884–1981], director of the American Civil Liberties Union—charged the police with having tortured a 19-year-old girl witness in Kimje, North Chŏlla Province. On July 7, Dr. Cho admitted many police misdeeds in that particular province but defended them by declaring that the police were acting from patriotic motives. He did go on to promise that all persons responsible for terrorism, including policemen, would be punished.

When such cases were reported to Military Government authorities, the American retort was often to the effect that this type of brutal treatment was the only thing a Korean understood. On August 1, 1946, Colonel William Maglin [1898–1958], American Director of the National Police, and Colonel A.S. Champeny [1893–1979], Deputy Military

---

[68] Robinson's highly critical report of this incident to Generals Lerch and Hodge (in line with his description here) is included in his August 1946 report. See Captain R. D. Robinson, "Report on Trip Through the Provinces with American Correspondents" (dated August 1, 1946), 2, RG 332, United State Army Forces in Korea, XXIV Corps, G-2, Historical Section, Records Regarding USAMGIK, U.S.–U.S.S.R. Relations in Korea, and Korean Political Affairs, 1945–48, Box 41, National Archives and Records Administration.

Governor, made such a statement in my presence in rebuttal to arguments which I had presented. Such views, of course, negated everything for which the United States stood, as well as being unsound.

But even the callous arguments of these gentlemen did not stand in face of the fact that brutal treatment was reserved generally only for suspected Communists and left-wing "agitators." It was true that in some cases extreme rightists were arrested, but rarely were they convicted or held in confinement for long. However, in the spring of 1947, a case occurred in Seoul so brutal that the police had to act. Kim Tu-han [1918–1972], the head of the earlier mentioned right-wing youth corps, the Great Korea Democratic Young Men's Association, and a group of his colleagues seized two members of the rival left-wing Korean Youth Vanguard [Chosŏn Ch'ŏngnyŏn Chŏnwidae].[69] On April 20, 1947, the pair were horribly tortured and finally murdered. The bodies were discovered, and the police were forced to act by the pressure of public opinion. In July, well after public interest had cooled, the sentences were announced. Kim Tu-han, the ringleader, received a fine of 20,000 yen (about $200 by comparable purchasing power) *or*—I repeat, *or*—imprisonment for 160 days. In other words, for a rightist to torture and murder, the price was $100 per head—cheap enough at half the price. No one doubted their guilt. By way of comparison, I cite a few sentences meted out of leftists. On April 5, 1947, two men received two years each for "disturbing the general peace." On the same date, two others received sentences of two and one years, respectively, for fomenting an "illegal" strike. On November 16, 1946, two men received six months at hard labor each for *attending* an "unauthorized speech." At the same time, three others were awarded similar sentences for the possession of "illegal" handbills. On November 9, 1946, 23 strikers were given sentences ranging two months to four years each. On November 7, 1946, a sentence of two years at hard labor was meted

---

[69] It should be noted that Kim Tu-han himself had earlier been a leading member of the Korean Youth Vanguard group he now fought. Kim was the son of Kim Chwa-jin (1889–1930), an early anarchist and the most successful military leader of Korean partisan troops in Manchuria fighting the Japanese. During colonial times Kim Tu-han had made a name for himself as a fist fighter and gangster boss in Seoul. From 1947 he seems to have been one of Rhee's hatchet men to organize assassinations, deliver threats, etc. He later became a parliamentarian and member of the Rhee and Park governments.

out for "organizing a strike against Military Government." Another received 90 days for an "unauthorized meeting;" another 90 days for "demonstrating against Military Government." On October 4, 1946 "writing against United States Military Government" netted the unlucky author one year at hard labor. And so it went.

Dozens of other cases could be cited as evidence in condemnation of the Korean police and in demonstration of the support awarded them by the American Command. Suffice to say that by the end of 1946 it was plain to all but the most stupid that South Korea was a police state. American Military Government no longer ruled; the Korean police was in power, and the Korean people hated them at least as much as they had hated their Japanese forebearers. At the top of the organizations stood Cho Pyŏng-ok and Chang T'aek-sang, appointed upon the advice of American missionaries and supported completely by General Hodge, but, nevertheless, two of the most venal men it has ever been my pleasure to know. I once asked a close political advisor to General Hodge why the general insisted that these two men continue to hold power. He thought for some moments and then answered that it was probably a combination of things but important among them was the fact that they had been loyal to the American Command and had fought against the Communists at every turn. The political advisor paused and then added, "But the greatest factors are the inability of the military mind to admit a mistake, and General Hodge's own stubborn bull-headedness." When Roger Baldwin, the above-mentioned director of the American Civil Liberties Union, visited Korea in mid-1947 and objected most strenuously to the antics of the Korean police in the name of American democracy, General Hodge radioed the War Department that Baldwin had apparently been "taken in by Communist propaganda." Hodge admitted, however, that "Baldwin appeared to be reasonably fair *despite the cause which he espouses*."* The general was obviously still oblivious to the effects of the policy which he had been pursuing. But we are ahead of our story; the scene is the fall of 1946.

* Italics are the author's.

The 1946 Fall Riots[70]

On September 24, 1946, O Pyŏng-mo, the representative of the South Korean Railroad Workers Struggle Committee to Improve Labor Conditions [Namjosŏn Ch'ŏldojongŏbwŏn Taeugaesŏn T'ujaengwiwŏnhoe] made the following announcement to the press:

> We presented the following demands on September 14 to the responsible officials of the Transportation Department,* to which they promised to reply by September 21.[71] We have not yet received any official reply, and we feel that they are only trying to postpone the date of an answer. We started to walk out on Tuesday [the 24th][72] because we do not expect to receive any official reply under normal working conditions.
>
> The demands:
>
> 1. We demand four hops of rice per laborer per day and three hops per day for our families.
>
> 2. We oppose the daily payment system. [Previously, a monthly salary system had been used. The new daily payment system had been instituted recently to minimize absenteeism.]
>
> 3. We demand an increase in the living cost allowance by 800 yen per month and an extra 600 yen per month for family allowance. [At the most this would be $4 and $3, respectively, on the basis of comparable purchasing powers.]

---

70 What Robinson calls the 1946 Fall Riots is also referred to as the 10.1 Taegu Uprising of 1946 (*Taegu 10.1 sagŏn*), Taegu October Incident, and Autumn Uprising of 1946. Bruce Cumings, using the name Autumn Harvest Uprisings, discusses these at length in the first volume of his *Origins of the Korea War*. See Bruce Cumings, *The Origins of the Korea War: Liberation and the Emergence of Separate Regimes, 1945–1947* (Princeton: Princeton University Press, 1981), 351–81 and 548–52.

* The Korean railroads were a government corporation operated under the Department of Transportation in Military Government.

71 Since the US Military Government functioned as the workers' employer, the railway worker's union negotiated directly with the head of the Department of Transportation, Lieutenant Colonel Arthur J. Cornelson (1909–1996); Cornelson rejected all demands. The resulting nation-wide "September General Strike" that originated from this labor strike was therefore directly aimed at the US Military Government.

72 All insertions in brackets in this quote are in Robinson's original typescript.

4. We oppose the planned cut in the number of employees. [An economic measure proposed by Military Government.]

5. We demand lunch every day as formerly.

6. We demand enforcement of a democratic labor law.*

On the morning of September 25 workers in the large Pusan railroad yards walked off the job. Engines were driven into the sheds and their fires extinguished. Rail transportation was quickly paralyzed throughout South Korea. The strike spread like wildfire from one industry to another. The Printing Union struck in sympathy, and only a handful of newspapers appeared on the streets of Seoul. Said General Hodge in part on September 28:

> I regret deeply and am much disappointed that the splendid Korean railway workers have been misled by radical agitators into an illegal strike against the Korean Government and the Korean people. I regret that any fine Korean workers have been misled into such a gross violation of good labor practices as to go on strike *without first formally presenting demands* and going into negotiations with their employers and the mediation board.
>
> I have reliable information that the strike has been fomented by agitators to discommode and discredit the American forces in Korea. In view of other information and the vicious propaganda aimed against the United States Forces that has recently been spread by certain groups in South Korea, there is little doubt but that this is the primary aim of the agitators. ...**

By way of proof that General Hodge was giving vent to a falsehood—very possibly an unintentional one, but nevertheless, a falsehood—by charging that no prior demands had been made by the workers before going on strike, I would refer the reader to the September 25, 1946, edition of the *Seoul Times*, a right-wing paper printed in English in Seoul, which quoted the September 14 demands. The fact that both right- and left-wing labor unions were participating in the general strike by the time General Hodge made his statement was

* The strikers' employer in this case was the Department of Transportation, American Military Government.

** Italics are the author's.

indicative of the fact that the strike was not entirely Communist-inspired. The strikers were simply objecting to recent changes made in the method of payment, to a decrease in railroad employment, to inadequate rice rations, to the inadequate cost of living allowance (cost of living having risen several times), and the maladministration of the labor ordinance. These appeals found general approbation among the laboring classes. The strike continued to spread. By September 30, large numbers of electrical workers were on strike, one of their demands being the recognition of the right to make employee contracts by collective bargaining.[73]

General Hodge's appeal—despite the falseness of it—achieved the desired result. It made the right-wing labor unions suspicious of the motives of the left and, thus, the ranks of labor were split. Soon thereafter, back-to-work orders were issued from rightist headquarters. The left, however, was determined to make the strike an effective one, and pitched battles took place in some areas. The district surrounding the Yongsan Railway Station in Seoul and the Seoul car shops took on the appearance of a battlefield as strikers holding forth in the car foundry tried to turn away returning workmen. At least one railroad policeman was killed and 14 others wounded. In all, sixty persons were injured by gunfire, clubs, and rocks. The Korean police marched in and arrested more than 2,000 strikers. At the same time some 3,000 right-wing labor union members returned to work, guarded by the police and several thousand uniformed thugs belonging to the rightist "Youth" Association. Simultaneously, all the employees of Seoul City Hall walked off the job and issued a declaration stating that they had made their demands one month previous to the mayor of Seoul but had received no answer. On October 2, transportation service within the city of Seoul came to a halt when the tram car motormen and conductors struck. The police announced that of the 2,000 strikers jailed in Seoul up to this time, some 800 had been released when they signified their willingness to return to work. In the meantime, rightist labor headquarters were trying to induce their workers to go back to work. Gangs of their hired thugs, armed with sticks and clubs, roamed downtown streets and industrial areas in Seoul with the announced

[73] It is estimated that around 250,000 workers participated in what had now become a general strike.

purpose of breaking up any leftist agitation. The police gave them a free hand. The situation was soon under control in Seoul, but elsewhere trouble brewed.

On October 4, the Taegu Riot broke loose, Taegu being one of the largest cities of South Korea. The Korean police had shot and killed a railroad striker the previous day. On the morning of the 4th, strikers carried the body of the dead man through the streets of Taegu, bouncing it up and down on a canvas stretcher for all to see. A huge crowd collected, sullen and angry. The procession converged on the central Taegu police station. The police attempted to stop the crowd by force of arms, and a brutal battle ensued. Fifty-three policemen were mutilated and killed, and an undetermined number of rioters met violent death. Even wounded policemen who had been taken to hospitals for treatment were dragged from their beds and slain. The people were hungry for blood. As soon as American troops arrived on the scene, rioting stopped, martial law was declared, and order quickly restored. But the very brutality of the attack against the police was a measure of the frequency and degree of police misdeeds and the temper of the public.

Throughout South Korea the people were rebelling violently against the Korean police. It was a full-fledged revolution. Martial law was declared in two provinces, and 8,000 persons were arrested in one province alone. In the meantime, the rioting spread. There was an attempt to cremate the police chief in Sŏngju, a town one hundred miles southeast of Seoul. At Waegwan, ten miles northeast of Sŏngju, the chief of police, five policemen, and seven rioters were killed. The police station was retaken by police reservists. At Yŏngch'ŏn, rioters burned the post office and police station.

Police retaliation was quick and terrible. Mass arrests took place. Measures were used to exact confessions which would make even the most hardened squirm. The police were nervous and adopted the policy of shooting first and asking questions second. The worst of all occurred in the town of Chŏnju on the afternoon of December 16, 1946. The local left-wing youth groups had asked permission to hold a meeting. The police had granted permission with some misgivings, but specified that the session should end at 4 PM. The stipulated deadline came and went and long-winded speakers were still rattling away. The police moved in, stopped the speakers, and ordered the audience to go home. The spectators began to do so. However, a small group of students decided to form a parade. *According to an eyewitness American CIC report*, the paraders were unarmed and at no time presented a disorderly or threatening appearance; they were merely marching through the streets. The police became nervous in view of past events and quickly threw up a series of street barricades. A large crowd of people returning homeward from the meeting—as well as a number of innocent passersby—were caught between two such barricades. The police ordered them to disperse. Because they were trapped in the middle of a city block, the crowd could not find an exit. The police began firing into the air. The mob milled around. The jittery policemen lowered their fire into the crowd and followed this with a horseback charge into the screaming people. Clubs and rifle butts flew. When the street was cleared, twenty persons lay dead—including men, women, and children. This incident was reported by CIC to American authorities. No action was taken to discipline the police concerned.

It is admitted that there was considerable truth to General Hodge's charge that the situation had been exploited for all it was worth by Communist agitators. But strangely enough, among the thousands of arrests made during the strike period, not one individual was found who was other than a bona fide resident of South Korea. General Hodge's oft-repeated charge that North Korean agitators engineered the whole thing seemed to be unfounded. Regardless of the truth of some of the general's observations, his method of attack aggravated the situation. He had issued a statement which was not wholly in line with the facts; the strikers *had* presented legitimate demands to their employer, the Department of Transportation, before striking. No action had been taken by the authorities. Only after a second warning did the workers strike. And then, instead of giving the Korean police and right-wing thugs a free hand to beat up strikers and make wholesale arrests, immediate steps should have been taken to mediate the trouble. Because this was not done, the Communists were able to exploit the situation and so fan the temper of the people that the strike became an outright rebellion against the authority of the police. In the one case where such a sane policy was pursued—in South Chŏlla Province, *a Communist stronghold*—very little violence broke out. The police were ordered to stay clear. American-operated sound trucks appealed to the strikers. Mediation was immediate. Despite Communist efforts, the people could not be induced to commit acts of violence.

It was true as General Hodge explained that "sabotage and murder are criminal offenses in all nations of the world and are still to be so considered in Korea." On the other hand, it was General Hodge himself who refused to agree to any reform. On that score, I remember a report submitted by an American Military Government officer after making an exhaustive study of the police situation. This was well before the 1946 fall strikes. The report was a wholesale condemnation of police activities, adequately supported by case histories. He predicted trouble in Pusan, Taegu, and Seoul where police activity had been particularly obnoxious. Among his final recommendations he suggested: (1) American police supervisors in each province to whom all prisoners would have the right to appeal and who would act as police inspectors; (2) the use of the writ of *habeas corpus*; (3) the right to defense counsel; (4) higher salaries for policemen so as to discourage graft; and (5) the establishment of a civil liberties commission to make continuous investigation of police activities throughout South Korea. Upon reading the report, General Hodge's first comment was, "This man sounds like a Communist."

However, after the Taegu Riot, even the general sensed that all was not quite as it should be in his kingdom, and the Joint Korean–American Conference was hurriedly convened to study the matter.

The Joint Korean–American Conference

On October 24, 1946, General Hodge announced that he had accepted an offer made by the Coalition Committee to serve with American officers and civilian experts as a committee to investigate conditions leading to the recent disturbances in southern Korea. All Koreans and American having knowledge of benefit to the Committee were invited to appear before it. Major General Albert E. Brown headed the American delegation, Dr. Kim Kyu-sik and Yŏ Un-hyŏng, the Korean. Actually, Yŏ did not attend the conference until well along in the sessions, and then only sporadically. By the end of October 1946, the Joint Korean–American Conference was in session. Its agenda included such subjects as enmity toward the police, the presence of former Japanese collaborators in Military Government, the effect of interpreters in government, corruption of some Korean officials, agitators against the best interests of Korea, the rice collection program, and inflation. It was decided that before the Conference reached any conclusions a thorough investigation should be made. It was emphasized that the sole objective of the inquiry was to determine facts and make appropriate recommendations, not to prosecute anyone.

The subject of Korean personnel in Military Government and the Japanese collaborationist issue were discussed at the initial sessions, but it was decided that these subjects should be resolved by the Interim Legislative Assembly soon to be seated. Most of the ensuing sessions of the Joint Conference were devoted to discussion of the Korean police. Among those heard on the subject by the Conference were Colonel William H. Maglin (American advisor to the Director of National Police), Dr. Cho Pyŏng-ok (Director of the National Police), Chang T'aek-sang (Chief of the Seoul Metropolitan police), and Ch'oe Nŭng-jin [1899–1951] (Head of the National Detective Bureau). The real fireworks occurred when the last-named gentleman appeared. Ch'oe had been hurling accusations against Dr. Cho and the police in general via the local press, and he aired his sentiments before the Conference in no uncertain terms. In so doing, he admitted the Japanese collaborationist charges and accused the police of undue brutality, corruption, and political partiality. A few days later the Korean members of the Conference rose in alarm when Ch'oe was summarily discharged from his post upon orders of Dr. Cho. His discharge had nothing to do with his testimony before the Conference, both Dr. Cho and General Lerch chorused. Whereupon, Dr. Kim Kyu-sik condemned the entire proceedings. All they had heard had been police officials telling how well they were doing their jobs, exclaimed Dr. Kim. The American delegation chief, General Brown, replied that anyone was free to appear before the Conference. However, it was obvious to all that to appear before the Conference and give testimony against the police would be tantamount to committing suicide. The upshot was that a secret agreement was reached advising General Hodge to discharge Chang T'aek-sang immediately. This was concurred in by two of the five American delegates as well as the entire

Korean delegation, including the moderate right-wing representatives. The Korean delegates further adopted by unanimous vote a resolution asking for the dismissal of Dr. Cho. Kim Kyu-sik appended a note to this resolution explaining that if anyone was to blame for past police excesses it was Dr. Cho, not Chief Chang. The Americans voted unanimously against this second resolution, so it was submitted to General Hodge only as a Korean suggestion concurred in by the moderate right and moderate left. These decisions were not made public.

Further decisions on the subject of the police were made known to the press on December 5, 1946. As a result, General Hodge announced that Military Government had been directed to raise the standard of efficiency of the Korean police. Practical measures would be taken which would gradually eliminate those policemen whose actions were incompatible with the established principles of democracy, announced the General. He went on to say that instructions had been reiterated to the Korean National Police to prevent the abuse of authority and to eliminate brutality and torture. "Special measures [never revealed]* have been taken to prevent utilization of the police for political purposes," the general declared. He finished by promising an improvement in police training standards as well as police salaries.

On the subject of Japanese collaboration, it was stated that Military Government had been directed to search the records of all Korean personnel for possible collaboration with the view that the more notorious collaborators be discharged as rapidly as possible and replaced by patriots. In the remainder of the cases, dossiers were to be prepared and held for future action by the Interim Legislative body which would define exactly what constituted collaboration. It was further announced by American authorities that steps had been taken to improve the agencies disseminating public information so that the smallest farming and fishing villages would be reached by timely, pertinent information from the various departments of the Government. Finally, General Hodge issued a statement to the effect that agitators who had "illegally fomented" the recent riots and who had "deceived the people" were being tried by the courts. At the same time,

* The insertion in brackets is in the author's original typescript.

it was added, those against whom there was no evidence would be released. The cases tried were to be "reduced to the smallest possible number of persons consistent with the preservation of law and order."

This is what General Hodge claimed to have done by way of fulfilling the desires of the Joint Korean–American Conference. What was actually accomplished was quite another matter. The recommended removal of Messrs. Chang and Cho was completely ignored, and the pair continued to hold office. There was no evidence of any measures having been taken to eliminate those policemen whose actions were deemed incompatible with the principles of democracy and humanity. There was no discernible decrease in the use of police brutality and torture or in the utilization of the police as a political weapon. Police salaries still remained at a miserably low level, thereby requiring that policemen indulge in graft to stay alive. There was no record of any search having been made of the files by Military Government to ferret out undesirables from its service, and no dismissals were made on that basis. Actually, all Military Government had to do was to refer to old newspaper files and translate some of the statements made under the Japanese regime by a number of its most trusted officials. (The subject of public information will be treated in Chapter IX.) As for the trial and confinement of strikers and rioters, I would again refer the reader to the files of the *Seoul Times*. Several death penalties were handed out—later, commuted by General MacArthur—as well as numerous sentences of several years of hard labor. As of June 1947, it was estimated by advisors close to General Hodge that there were something like 7,000 prisoners in South Korea who could be classed as political.

Such was the way in which the American Command kept faith with the Korean people, with the Coalition Committee, and in particular with Yŏ Un-hyŏng. It is little wonder that with this American inactivity, the power of the extreme right wing began to grow. The American do-nothing policy which envisioned a Communist threat behind every liberal bush made it impossible for the liberal movement to live. It was caught in the cross fire between the two extremes. Sensing the weakness of American policy, Dr. Syngman Rhee and Kim Ku, in collaboration with the Korean police, began laying plans for insurrection.

CHAPTER VI: DEMOCRACY AND REVOLUTION

Passers-by had long noted that changes were taking place in the main rotunda of the great domed Capital Building in Seoul. The barren marble grandeur of the place was being marred by bustling workmen. Soon it became apparent that a legislative chamber was being constructed. This was the first public evidence that a legislature was being considered for South Korea. Initially, it had been hoped that the Joint Soviet–American Commission would reach agreement and move to create an interim Korean Government, including the necessary appurtenance of democracy, a legislature. However, with the breakdown of negotiations in May 1946, the American Command began to think in terms of some sort of legislative assembly for South Korea alone. The Coalition Committee took on new importance, for this was apparently the group which should supervise the organization of such a legislative body.

The American Command felt that a legislature was necessary for a number of reasons, among which were: (1) the need for practical training in democratic procedure for Korean politicians, (2) the desire for an all-Korean body to lift part of the responsibility of government from American shoulders, (3) the political advantage to be gained over the Russians who had established no such representative legislative body, and (4) the demands of a restless Korean public who saw Japan well on the road to recovery and democratization. As the political situation in South Korea became more and more tumultuous, Generals Hodge and Lerch became more and more anxious to place the burden of responsibility on Koreans. Such matters as the Japanese collaborationist issue, the Korean police, Communist agitation, and the grain collection program were rapidly draining the last dregs of American prestige. The Joint Korean–American Conference had been a temporary stop-gap measure, but when its recommendations were for all intents and purposes ignored, a new clamor arose. By this time, however, the new Southern Korean Interim Legislative Assembly was sitting, and the American Command could simply refer the discontented to this group of "representative" Koreans.

Embryonic Democracy

The stage was set shortly after the Joint Soviet–American Commission broke up by a public letter from General Lerch to General Hodge suggesting the establishment of an interim legislative body for South Korea. General Hodge quickly placed his stamp of approval on the proposal, saying in part, "While it is my legal duty to retain the ultimate authority and the ultimate responsibility for South Korea until the establishment of a provisional government under the Moscow Decision, I believe that it would be beneficial and a step forward to create a legislative body." The general went on to specify, "This body would not and could not be considered as a step toward the establishment of a separate government for Southern Korea. Any such legislature could exist only as long as Military Government exists in South Korea. When North and South Korea are unified under the Provisional Korean Democratic Government, the functions of this interim legislative body would be taken over by the Provisional Government and this body would cease to exist."

Meanwhile, the Communist Party made known its opposition. Party leaders stated, perhaps more frankly than they themselves realized, "We believe such a body is not suitable for us, and we oppose such an organization." Party spokesmen went on to say, "We cannot establish a legislative body unless a united Korean democratic interim government is organized. It is unreasonable to organize a legislative body without the organization of a complete government." Commented the Communist-dominated People's Democratic Front, "It is regrettable that the establishment of this organization cannot have the unanimous support of Korean nationals who sincerely have the interests of their fatherland at heart." Shortly thereafter, the Front crystallized its opinion on the subject and came out in wholehearted condemnation of the proposed legislative body. The Communists feared that the legislative body would act to correct some of the basic injustices and errors of the current administration, thereby weakening the Communist appeal.

In mid-summer, 1946, the American-inspired proposal for the legislative body was referred to the Coalition Committee for detailed planning. Unfortunately, however, the Coalition was in no position to do any planning on any subject at that time. It will be remembered that on July 30 the left-wing delegation had walked out, and the Coalition Committee was currently non-existent, thanks to Communist insistence on the five impossible demands already enumerated.* Negotiations dragged on and on. News of the proposed legislative body, which had initially caused quite a flurry in the indigenous press, disappeared from public discussion. But finally, on October 8, 1946, the Coalition Committee achieved initial success, and its seven basic principles for cooperation [*hapchak 7-wŏnch'ik*] were published, among which was one dealing with the proposed interim legislature.[74] The Committee unanimously recommended to General Hodge that such a body be created for South Korea. The general received this action with enthusiasm. "I regard the establishment of an interim legislature as the greatest step forward to date on the road to Korean national unity and independence," announced the general. Military Government was promptly directed to prepare an ordinance covering the subject. "The ordinance is being drafted to give full consideration to the recommendations of the Committee concerning the legislative body," the American Commander said on October 9. He went on to outline the powers which the legislature would possess:

> This body will be the law-making body for South Korea. It will have authority to review present and future high appointments in the government. It will be a forum for full and free discussion of Korean problems. It will foster free expression by the people and will be a sounding board for public opinion in Korea. It will be a place for the public meeting of the minds of patriotic Koreans who are interested in their nation. In general, I shall leave to the legislature the determination of future policies affecting the Korean people, including such vital things as collection and distribution of grains, imposition of taxes, and redistribution of land. It is to

* See this volume, 173-75.

[74] See *Haebang ilbo*, October 7, 1946, and *Tonga ilbo*, October 8, 1946. These astounding agreements included: (1) and (2) reestablishing a provisional democratic government, (3) promoting land reform that would distribute confiscated land to farmers free of charge, (4) letting the legislative body deal with pro-Japanese groups and traitors, (5) releasing political activists that had been arrested, (6) allowing the Coalition Committee to form a new legislative body, proposing alternative interim legislature, and (7) guaranteeing freedom of speech and freedom of the press.

be expected that the legislature will follow the will of the people. The seven basic coalition principles enunciated by the Coalition Committee are their own recommendations, and do not in any way bind or restrict freedom of action or decision by this legislative body.

By mid-October 1946 the basic ordinance establishing the Southern Korean Interim Legislative Assembly was published in the *Official Gazette* by Military Government.[75] Although the printed ordinance bore the date of August 24, the first copies were released to the Korean press on October 12. It is of significance to remember that those suggestions by the Coalition Committee which were to be incorporated in the ordinance were not even agreed upon until well after October 1. The purpose of the project, as specified in the basic ordinance, was to "increase the participation of democratic elements in the government by the establishment of an interim legislative body ... pending the early establishment of a unified Korean state with a provisional democratic government of all Korea as provided in the Moscow Agreement."

Section III of the ordinance established the Legislative Assembly as "an organ of government." It was to consist of ninety members, 45 of whom were to be elected and 45 to be appointed. Elected members were to be chosen in each province and in the independent City of Seoul on the basis of one member for each 550,000 population or major fraction thereof; provided, that from each province and from the City of Seoul a representative-at-large be elected. The 45 appointed members were to be selected by the American Command so as to represent "equally and fairly major democratic elements of Korean life, economic, political, and intellectual." The duties and powers of the Assembly were outlined in Section V of the ordinance which stated in part that the duty of the Assembly should be the enactment of ordinances affecting the general welfare and interest on matters referred to it by the Military Governor. "It shall also have the power to review all past appointments of the Military Government above class four civil service status and

[75] See Headquarters United States Army Military Government in Korea, Office of the Military Governor, "Ordinance Number 118: Establishment of Korean Interim Legislative Assembly," *Official Gazette, USAMGIK* (August 24, 1946): 1–4, reprinted in *Migunjŏng ch'ŏng kwanbo / Official Gazette, United States Army Military Government in Korea*, vol. 1 (Seoul: Wŏnju Munhwasa, 1991), 442–45.

confirm and consent to all such future appointments," the ordinance stated. It declared farther, "Ordinances enacted by the Assembly shall have the force and effect of law when concurred in by the Military Governor. In case the Military Governor does not concur in any ordinance, he will return it to the legislature with a written statement of reasons for non-concurrence." Three-fourths of the members was specified as constituting a quorum. Debates on the Assembly floor or in committee meetings were to be free and the members were not to be held legally responsible for their utterances during the course of such debate. The Assembly, however, was empowered to adopt rules of conduct and measures for punishment of its members. Section VII required that any person elected to the Assembly be Korean, be past his or her twenty-fifth birthday, and have been a bona fide resident of the province or area represented for at least one year immediately preceding the election. Persons who had held positions as provincial or municipal councilors or above the rank of bureau chief under the Japanese administration were specifically declared as ineligible for Assembly seats.

The idea of this first interim legislative body was that it should enact immediately a general suffrage law which would pave the way for the early establishment of an entirely elected body. The ordinance specified that members of this future assembly should be elected by and for the people of the provinces south of the 38th parallel and the independent City of Seoul by universal suffrage regardless of sex. However, of the members of this first assembly, only half were to be elected and those, not by universal suffrage but by the ancient Oriental headman system. The village elders or the family heads were to meet and select a delegate to represent their village or community in a district meeting. At this meeting, representatives were to be named for a county meeting. Finally, county delegates would meet and select the Assembly representatives for the province. For instance, in Seoul—a city of probably close on to 1.5 million persons—the final electorate which actually chose the assemblymen for the city consisted of 564 men. This system was selected by the American Command for several reasons: (1) it followed traditional Oriental custom in such matters; (2) it made it possible for the Assembly to meet within the near future by making unnecessary elaborate election machinery; and (3) it would assure a conservative delegation. After all, the community elders were generally conservative, elderly, property-owning gentry. The American Command was more than impatient to get the election over and done with so that the Legislative Assembly could swing into action and absorb responsibility—and blame—for the critical problems of the day; namely, the grain collection, police, and Japanese collaborationist issues. Orders were issued for immediate elections.

The elections were all over before most Koreans—and Americans—knew what was happening. Dr. Rhee's summer-long tour of the provinces to organize local chapters of his personally-controlled National Society for the Rapid Realization of Korean Independence, coupled with the police-inspired rout of leftist leaders and organizers throughout the provinces, gave the extreme right wing a clear field. The disrupted state of left-wing channels of communication and the lack of advance publicity, together with the method of election, acted against the left wing so that out of the forty-five representatives finally elected, only two were leftists—and those two were from the all-leftist island province of Cheju. Later, these two leftists, on orders of the People's Democratic Front, refused to take their seats.

In the meantime, the Coalition Committee, charged by General Hodge with the task of nominating forty-five members to be appointed by the American Command, was balking. No list of nominees had been submitted. The entire Coalition Committee, both right and left, expressed dissatisfaction with the manner in which the election had been carried out. Irregularities and inadequate publicity were charged. On November 5, 1946, Kim Kyu-sik, co-chairman of the Coalition Committee and a moderate rightist, sent an open letter to General Hodge condemning the elections and asking the general to invalidate the results. Dr. Kim expressed thanks to the American Commander for his continuous sympathy for, and assistance to, the Coalition Committee and voiced the hope that a proper decision would be made by the general regarding the elections in which. Dr. Kim regretted to see, only men of one political stripe, including many who had been Japanese collaborators, had been selected. The letter continued, "Because of police investigations there was no chance for the leftist members in the elections. As a result, no competent patriot was elected. The results of the elections have produced impressions of an undemocratic nature and have caused disappointment to the people." In concluding, Dr. Kim wrote, "I hope that your pre-eminent judgment will find a suitable way to either partly or entirely invalidate the results of the elections."

Yŏ Un-hyŏng, the other co-chairman of the Coalition Committee and representative of the moderate left, let it be known in no uncertain terms that the price for his continued cooperation with the Coalition Committee and with the American Command would be the invalidation of the elections and the heads of the two top police officials. Dr. Cho and Chief Chang. Yŏ was just about fed up, and so also was Dr. Kim Kyu-sik. Debate ensued in XXIV Corps Headquarters. Finally, on November 26, General Hodge announced the invalidation of the elections in the City of Seoul and the east coast province of Kangwŏn by reason of alleged "illegal procedures." Preparations were started immediately for new elections in these two places. The Coalition Committee was invited to provide election supervisors. One of General Hodge's intelligence officers commented at the time that Yŏ's continued cooperation, and perhaps that of the entire Coalition Committee, had been bought with the invalidation of the Seoul and Kangwŏn elections and the agreement to remove Police Chief Chang from his job. Actually, the latter was not removed, and, as for the new elections, the same men were re-elected with two exceptions, and those two were of the same political complexion as the men they displaced. That rightists would be elected was inevitable under the electoral system which had been chosen, given the watchful eyes of Rhee-controlled police.

Nevertheless, the Coalition Committee, determined to make the most of an admittedly bad situation, submitted a list of forty-five men to be named by General Hodge to the Assembly. The bulk of this group consisted of moderate leftists and moderate rightists, with only a handful included from the Rhee–Kim Ku group of the far right, the group which had seized all but two of the forty-five elected seats. The general, persuaded that a moderate group was required to balance the right-wing extremists already elected, agreed to appoint the Committee's nominees. The original list submitted by the Committee had not included such heavy weights as Yŏ, Kim Kyu-sik, and others. However, the Committee was finally persuaded to include these names, and the list was released.

But Yŏ was disgusted. Not only did he refuse to sit in the Assembly, but he announced once again that he was retiring from politics. When Yŏ queried American authorities as to why something had not been done to remedy the intolerable police situation as demanded by the Joint Korean–American Conference, he was told that such matters were within the jurisdiction of the Legislative Assembly and that the undesirable police officials could be removed by legislative action. "That *might* be so," murmured Yŏ doubtfully—and with good reason as later events demonstrated. In a statement to the local press on December 5, 1946, a week before the Assembly finally sat, Yŏ said, "I have been trying to accomplish the establishment of our new Korea, but no good results have been accomplished by my efforts." Therewith, he admitted his failures and asked the people's forgiveness for mistakes made. He was retiring from the political field, he said, but as a private citizen he would "continue working unfailingly for the establishment of a Korean nation." To many it sounded like the statement of a disillusioned man who was apologizing for having cooperated with the Americans at all. Exit Yŏ Un-hyŏng from the good graces of the American Command. Henceforth, he was a "known Communist" in most reports from Korea to the State and War Departments.

Only one of the big five of Korean politicos was, therefore, a member of the new Legislative Assembly, namely, Kim Kyu-sik. Rhee and Kim Ku chose not to become candidates for membership, apparently feeling that it would endanger their political prestige to be forced to take definite stands on the many controversial issues facing the Assembly. Pak Hŏn-yŏng, the Communist leader, was in hiding, a fugitive from justice, having been charged in September with espionage and inciting to revolt against constituted authority. And Yŏ was sullen and disillusioned. Only Kim Kyu-sik would agree to participate as one of the appointed members. The final membership of the Legislature gave Rhee's National Society for the Rapid Realization of Korean Independence and the ultra-conservative Korean Democratic Party a slight margin over the less extreme elements of the right and moderate left. A handful of extreme leftists, but not Communists, were included among the appointed members. The power balance favored the moderate right. At a later date, from a safe distance—specifically, Washington, D.C.—Rhee accused General Hodge of having packed the Assembly with Communists and Communist sympathizers!

After several postponements, made necessary by the election mix-up, the Southern Korean Interim Legislative Assembly came into being. It was the twelfth minute of the twelfth hour of the twelfth day of the twelfth month (December 12, 1946) when the Assembly was called to order in its first formal session in the newly-appointed legislative chamber in the Capital. Dr. Kim Kyu-sik had been named temporary chairman in an informal preliminary session the previous day. It was obvious that the elderly Dr. Kim, sick as he was with recurrent kidney trouble, was the only man in the Assembly who could rule over the unruly backbiting delegates. In fact, the Assembly was in a turmoil even before it had convened. The twenty or so Korean Democrats who had been elected were angered over the list of men named to the Assembly by General Hodge. In a move designed to force the American Command to name extreme rightists to replace the moderates and leftists composing this list of appointed assemblymen, the Korean Democrats decided to boycott the Assembly. With a quorum required of three-fourths of the entire membership (68), this defection—together with normal absenteeism and the two elected Cheju-do leftists who refused their seats—would have made it impossible for the Assembly to conduct business. However, Military Governor Lerch moved at the last minute to forestall such tactics by summarily changing the basic ordinance so that only a bare majority constituted a quorum. Cries of anguish went up from the Korean Democrats. "Autocratic and arbitrary law!" they cried, and with some merit. However, their boycott no longer provided them with any bargaining power; the Assembly could exist without them. A few days later the tardy Korean Democrats showed up in their seats bristling with a chip-on-the-shoulder attitude.

At this point, everyone gave a sigh of relief and began thinking optimistically that perhaps something might really be accomplished after all. The Assembly quickly chose its officers, Dr. Kim becoming the permanent chairman. The next step was that of seating the members. To do so would require a study of their qualifications, for the basic ordinance had set up certain prohibitions—for instance, those who had held high office under the Japanese were specifically barred from membership. Accusations of Japanese collaboration were hurled back and forth. A committee was appointed to investigate the matter, but the committee had no stomach for this delicate job—considering among other things, the attitude of the police on the subject—and referred the whole thing back to the Assembly. The Qualifications Committee finally suggested that all qualifications other than those having to do with Japanese collaboration be considered immediately and that the Japanese collaboration issue be postponed for later debate. Over left-wing objection, the matter was so resolved, and all members were forthwith declared qualified and sworn into office. Rules of conduct were adopted and standing committees appointed. Acting as a quasi-official steering committee during this hectic organizational period was a Legislative Liaison Committee composed of American advisors and Assembly leaders.

The first real issue between the Assembly and the American Command arose over the authority to be granted the Assembly. It had been made clear on several occasions that final authority on all matters still rested with General Hodge and the Military Governor. The basic ordinance establishing the Assembly gave the Military Governor absolute veto power. At the same time, General Hodge had announced on at least one occasion that such veto would not be exercised unless the Assembly passed legislation directly counter to declared United States policy or attempted to seize power from the American Command. "After all, you can't vote us out of Korea," said the general. Other than that, the Assembly was to have full authority. However, within a month after the Assembly had been launched on its stormy existence, it was in conflict with General Lerch, the Military Governor. Some of the Assembly rules, said the general, were matters of constitutional concern and others infringed upon the duties of the executive branch of government, namely the Military Governor. And with this. General Lerch exercised his veto on a number of proposed rules. However, the immediate issues were resolved amicably, and everyone was happy again—that is, everyone except Dr. Kim Kyu-sik who became troubled periodically over the matter.

It was hoped by the American Command that the Assembly would move rapidly to solve the food problem, the police issue, to pass "laws" under which a new legislature, entirely elected by universal suffrage, would replace the current Assembly. However, as of July 1947 the Interim Assembly had accomplished little of a constructive nature. More and more it was becoming merely a sounding board for political bickering and a tool for the extreme right. Absenteeism among members grew to such extent that a quorum (forty-five out of the ninety members) was rarely present. It passed two major pieces of legislation, one having to do with child labor—a subject upon which all could readily agree—and a second having to do with local elections. The story of the political bickering on the floor of the Assembly is mentioned further in the following pages. Actually, the major accomplishment of the Interim Legislative Assembly was to furnish Korean politicians with some idea as to the machinery of representative democracy. But the public lost interest, for during the Winter and Spring of 1947, the right wing was making a strong bid for power which far overshadowed the activities of the embryonic legislature.

Revolutionary Comedy

Ever since the formation of the ill-fated, American-inspired, Representative Democratic Council in February of 1946, Dr. Syngman Rhee and Kim Ku had been working busily to perfect their political machinery. They realized that the left wing had the stronger political organization and had set out to widen their own political base by a nationwide organization. With the assistance of the Korean police, the National Society for the Rapid Realization of Korean Independence had succeeded in building a powerful political organization throughout South Korea by the summer of 1946. Meanwhile, Dr. Rhee had displaced Kim Ku as the reigning monarch of this organizational success. The Coalition Committee, which at first appeared a challenge to Rhee's political fortunes, seemed doomed to ultimate discord as the summer wore on and it failed to get together. Using Sin Ik-hŭi's trial balloon insurrection which temporarily excited American CIC agents late in the summer, Dr. Rhee and his lieutenants began laying plans. The Joint Soviet–American Commission had failed and the chance of an international agreement on the subject of Korea was looking dimmer all the while. In view of these facts and the probability that the United States was getting tired of both the Russians and the Koreans, it was held as a distinct possibility that the American forces might be induced to pack up and go home, or at least the American Military Government. Rhee saw his opportunity. If he could convince the United States of the futility of prolonging Military Government control, he might induce the United States to place himself in power in South Korea.

By early fall, 1946, Kim Ku was resigned to playing second fiddle and found himself the recipient of orders. Dr. Rhee announced to his colleagues that he would go to Washington—and possibly, also London and Chongqing—to carry the case of Korean independence directly to the Allies concerned and to the United Nations. He expressed the belief that any further effort in Korea was useless and that General Hodge was already acceding somewhat to the Soviet view on trusteeship and turning a cold shoulder to the right wing. Rhee gave orders that during his absence plans should be carried ahead to intensify the anti-trusteeship drive. The right-wing delegation would withdraw from the Coalition Committee; the Legislative Assembly would be used as a sounding board for the anti-trusteeship campaign; the American Command was to be attacked for its uncertain attitude on trusteeship and alleged favoritism to Communistic groups. An all-out drive was to be launched for the recognition of a separate South Korean government—often hinted at by Rhee but never quite expressed openly because of adverse public opinion relative to making the division of the country a permanent one. The final step would be an outright insurrection against the authority of American Military Government. Kim Ku and two others were named to lead the rebellion. It was anticipated that the Americans would be forced to arrest the leaders, whereupon Rhee would start an intensive propaganda campaign from Washington demanding the removal of General Hodge on the basis that he was acting against the interests of Korea by favoring the Communists and ignoring Korean patriots, and, further, was playing into the hands of the Russians. Rhee planned to play up Kim Ku and the other jailed leaders as martyrs placed on the sacrificial block by General Hodge. If the campaign were successful and General Hodge removed, Rhee would then try to bring enough pressure to bear on the general's replacement so as to persuade him to authorize a separate South Korean government with himself (Rhee) at the helm. If such could be accomplished, then the problem of extending the control of that South Korean government over North Korea could be considered.

As a distinct possibility within Rhee's mind was war between the Soviet Union and the United States even if he, himself, had to instigate border incidents to bring conflict about. This is not idle speculation on my part; these plans were known by American intelligence agents—but not until later. Rhee also felt that this was a propitious time for him to go to the United States by reason of the Republican victory in the 1946 Congressional elections. He commented privately several times that now that "his friends" were in power again he would have no trouble getting his ideas across to the right people.

One other factor in the planning was money, a commodity much needed by Rhee and his cohorts in large quantities. Some of the 200,000,000 yen fund contributed by wealthy Koreans to the Provisional Government via Rhee in December 1945 probably remained. In addition, there was some money which had been made available to the Representative Democratic Council by Military Government, money to be used by the Council in its official advisory capacity. Some of this cash, likewise, probably found its way into the Rhee campaign chest. But still, what remained of these resources was not adequate. The entire right-wing organization was directed to collect yen for Rhee's projected "non-political diplomatic mission" to the United States. Banks and business houses ordered their employees to contribute a certain amount of their salaries or wages—this, regardless of the donor's feelings toward Rhee and his project. Sin Ik-hŭi toured the country with the seal of the Home Affairs Ministry of the Provisional Government in his pocket. The impression was created that the collection was a semi-official one, so much so that Military Government saw fit on one occasion to announce that no *official* collection of funds was being made. It was estimated that by the end of the year the immediate goal of 30,000,000 yen (approximately $300,000) had been surpassed.

The next problem was how to get this money out of Korea. Strict American directives prohibited the exchange of Korean yen into American dollars. At that time the exchange rate for military purposes was pegged at 15 yen to the dollar. This was the only legal rate of exchange even though the comparable purchasing power would have placed the exchange rate at least at 100 yen to the dollar. An illegal transaction of some kind would have to be arranged. Rhee first approached local Chinese bankers for an off-the-record exchange. It was agreed that the exchange rate should be something like 120 yen per dollar. Just a few days prior to Rhee's departure for the United States, the bankers upped the rate to 200 yen for one U.S. dollar. Rhee balked. At this point his American missionary friends came to the rescue. Several mission-supported institutions pooled their dollar credits in the United States and "donated" to Rhee's accounts in the United States a large sum of money. Rhee, in return, "contributed" large sums of yen to the institutions concerned in Korea. The rate of exchange was 100 yen for one American dollar. The whole transaction was illegal from start to finish, regardless of the high motives which may have moved the mission-supported institutions to participate. Actually, it was the only way in which they could transfer their much-needed dollar funds in the United States to yen accounts in Korea. The occupation authorities had very foolishly left no legal channel open to them through which to effect a transfer. The transaction was brought to the attention of General Hodge, but he failed to see anything to warrant prosecution. American legal experts thought differently, one commenting, "A GI would break rocks a helluva long time for the same offense." As a matter of plain fact, directives on the point were painfully clear. The *only* legal transaction would have been one made at the Army Finance Office by exchanging dollars for yen at the rate of one to fifteen. The exchange of yen for dollars by anyone else and the use of any other exchange rate was specifically prohibited.

Thus, it was that Rhee left Korea for the United States on the morning of December 2, 1946, ostensibly for the purpose of pleading the case of Korea before the United Nations. A special United States Army plane was provided upon orders of General MacArthur's headquarters (over the objections of the American Command in Korea). Several hundred thousand dollars with which to finance his activity awaited him in American banks. Kim Ku, watched over by the ever-watchful Mrs. Rhee, was holding the fort in Korea and carrying on with the well laid-out program. In Washington, Rhee's lobby was already active in carrying forward the policy of undermining General Hodge and clamoring for immediate Korean independence and/or a separate South Korean government.

This Rhee-controlled lobby in Washington was an interesting assortment of persons. Officially, it was known as the Korean–American Council. During his many years in Washington as the unofficial representative of the Korean Provisional Government (then headquartered in exile in China), Rhee built up a circle of Korean and American supporters in the United States, largely recruited from wealthy business groups. Their aim was purely altruistic, so they claimed, but their business connections were of interest. One such man was John W. Staggers [1878–1957], a preposterous Washington attorney, long associated with Rhee. On occasions his name had been linked in left-wing newspapers with that of a company designed to develop Korean trade possibilities. Another was Jay Jerome Williams [1893–1961], a retired public relations man. Still another was Millard Preston Goodfellow, the proprietor of the *Brooklyn Eagle* and formerly a political advisor to General Hodge in Korea. Rhee in a speech delivered in Korean in the spring of 1946, mentioned Goodfellow along with Dr. Robert T. Oliver [1909–2000] of Syracuse University and himself as being the interested parties in the establishment of the Korean–American Trading Company, a company designed to "monopolize Korean foreign trade." As one American observer commented at the time, "Dr. Rhee has the uncanniest ability for putting his own foot squarely in his own mouth." Dr. Oliver was by profession a college professor. He achieved his initial fame on the subject of Korea by writing numerous letters to the editors of various newspapers, particularly the *New York Times*, in support of Dr. Rhee. This activity finally brought him to the attention of Rhee,[76] and he was offered a substantial fee to come to Korea (for the first time in his life) and act as a Rhee advisor. He did so—ostensibly to participate in the Military Government educational program. Shortly thereafter, he was nudged gently out of Korea by the American Command when he broke his pledge not to participate in local politics, a pledge which had been a condition for his admission into Korea.

Another member of the Rhee circle in Washington was Samuel Dolbears [1886–1972] who was reported to be interested in Korean mineral concessions. Korean leftists accused Dr. Rhee on occasions of having already sold Korean mining rights in anticipation of the day when he would head a Korean government. Perhaps the most active and energetic of all of Dr. Rhee's cohorts in the United States was Miss Im Yŏng-sin [1899–1977]—in the U.S. better known as Louise Yim, chairman of the Korean Women's Nationalist Party [Taehan Yŏja Kungmindang]. As president of the Chungang Professional School for Women [Chungang Yŏja Chŏnmun Hakkyo] in Seoul she had emerged as a professional gatherer of donations and as such has been eminently successful in the United States. Her wide acquaintance amid social and

[76] In fact, Robert T. Oliver, who had taught speech at Bucknell University, only began writing on Korea *after* he was introduced to Syngman Rhee in August or September 1942 by his colleague, the Reverend Edward L. Junkin (1894–1982).

political circles made her an invaluable ally. All during 1946 she acted as an unofficial Korean delegate to the United Nations. Actually, she represented nothing more than the rightist Representative Democratic Council of South Korea. Dr. James S. Shinn [1905–?], field director-general of the Korean–American Council and a former California physician, was another member of the Rhee political family. Still another was Im Pyŏng-jik, in the U.S. known as "Colonel" Ben C. Limb [1893–1976], an old-time Rhee associate. Finally, Rhee's Stateside force of well-wishers and supporters included many key figures in the McCormick and Hearst newspaper constellations. This was the force that Rhee enlisted in his campaign. This roster summarizes many U.S. military intelligence reports on the subject.

On the way to the United States, Dr. Rhee asked for, and received, an audience with MacArthur. The details of the meeting have never been disclosed. Upon his arrival in Washington on December 9, 1946, Rhee told the press that he planned to remain in the United States for one month with the immediate objective being to "have the needed Korean unification considered by the United States and also to enlist the assistance of American authorities in establishing and recognizing a Korean government. Korea wants her own government and wants it now," stated Rhee. On December 11, in an apparent rebuttal to these statements made by Rhee, Undersecretary of State Dean Acheson announced, "The American policy toward Korea is the same as always—to bring about a unified, free, and democratic country—and we intend to stay there until we are successful." While Im Yŏng-sin was renewing her plea to have the case of Korea reviewed by the United Nations, Dr. Rhee bluntly declared that Koreans would no longer be patient without some definite date set for the realization of their independence. Rhee hastened to add that he was only trying to "uphold the principles of democracy" in obtaining "United States' support for settlement of the Korean independence question." He went on to announce, "We want Communists and pro-Japanese elements as well to have representation in the government. We are fighting only those who are trying to sell out Korea. Korean patriots," he said, "have made four or five attempts under Military Government sponsorship to induce Communist leaders to come into the government but their sole aim is either to control or to destroy the unity of the people." The eventual aim of the Communists, Rhee concluded, was to "have certain powers say that the

Koreans cannot govern themselves and, therefore, the only solution of the problem would be a trusteeship."

Of course, Rhee was entirely correct insofar as the motives of the Communists were concerned, but his own motives by this time were under considerable suspicion in XXIV Corps Headquarters in Seoul. On January 6, 1947, General Hodge felt compelled to deny publicly the impression created by "certain elements" that the United States was actively working toward a separate government in southern Korea. "Either through lack of knowledge of facts or through malicious intent to deceive the Korean people, certain elements are creating the impression that the United States now favors and is actively working toward a separate government in southern Korea and that the Korean Interim Legislative Assembly is a completely independent body designed as the forerunner of that government. Both of the above assumptions are incorrect." And with that, the general reiterated once again American policy in respect to Korea. In the context of events, the reference to "certain elements" was an obvious reference to Rhee's entourage.

An exchange of letters between the American and Soviet Commands in late December 1946 had made it clear that the reconvention of the Joint Soviet–American Commission in the near future was a distinct possibility. The American Command was proposing to the Russians as a basis for reconvening the Joint Commission that "anyone fomenting or instigating active opposition to the work of the Joint Commission or to either of the Allied Powers or to the fulfillment of the Moscow Decision" should not be consulted by the Joint Commission or allowed to participate in the future democratic provisional Korean Government. To Dr. Rhee and the extreme rightists, this American proposal was definitely not acceptable. They had committed themselves to an irrevocable anti-trusteeship stand whether or not the Joint Commission decided on the imposition of a trusteeship. Furthermore, Rhee was soon to come out in the open and frankly demand the establishment of a separate South Korean government. On January 13, 1947, John Z. Williams [1911–1986], director of Korean Affairs in the State Department, announced that the trusteeship provision of the Moscow Decision to which the Koreans had reacted so violently in some cases was now "becoming better understood" by the Koreans, the implication being that the United

States favored such a trusteeship. If designed to draw Dr. Rhee out, it was not without success.

Radiograms flowing between Dr. Rhee's Washington headquarters and that in Seoul were intercepted by the American Command in Korea. The implication in them was that widespread and violent demonstrations would soon take place against trusteeship. General Hodge felt compelled to step in and warn the Korean people. On January 17, the general said in part, "It has come to my attention that there are extensive plans underway by certain Korean groups to instigate widespread demonstrations in South Korea against the Moscow Decision, against the so-called trusteeship, coupled with attempts to discredit the American effort in Korea. This appears to be tied in with ill-advised propaganda that if South Korea is given a separate government it can itself unite all of Korea and solve all the international problems without outside help." In a thinly-veiled reference to Dr. Rhee and Kim Ku, the general said, "Through internal dissension and ill-advised political activity on the part of several Koreans who disregarded international aspects during sessions of the Joint Commission last spring, the establishment of a Korean provisional government has already been delayed several months." The general was, in effect, blaming the breakdown of the Joint Soviet–American Commission on the right-wing anti-trusteeship campaign. "Ill-advised actions by Korean groups may operate against the interests of Korea in future international conferences," the general concluded.

At the same time, Im Yŏng-sin, one of Rhee's Washington lobbyists, petitioned the United States Congress for self-government for South Korea—this, in face of Soviet-American correspondence on the subject which would seem to indicate an early reconvention of the Joint Soviet-American Commission. In her petition, Miss Im said, "Subversive elements have taken advantage of the situation and are plotting civil war for early this year. Hostilities are scheduled to begin in the zone occupied by the United States endangering United States soldiers in a crossfire." This was nothing but a threat, for the only scheduled hostilities then planned were those of the right-wing extremists—as later events proved. Then, in perhaps the greatest public cleansing of hands since Pontius Pilate, Rhee cautioned his countrymen against indulging in any demonstrations. "They might be interpreted as antiforeign," said he from Washington on January 16. Apparently, the time was not deemed ripe.

On January 20, 1947, Rhee's Representative Democratic Council withdrew its representatives from the Coalition Committee. The reason for this act was given in the following words: "The Coalition Committee of rightists and leftists has become an organization far different from what was intended and is performing a mission which lies outside its real duties. The attitude of the Committee on the problem of so-called trusteeship is very unclear, and we have decided to call back our representatives." Dr. Rhee quickly endorsed this action.

On the same day, January 20, Rhee's forces moved to sabotage the Southern Korean Interim Legislative Assembly. The plan was this. A strongly worded anti-trusteeship resolution was to be introduced in the Assembly by forty-two Rhee followers. If it failed to pass, they would demand the resignation of Kim Kyu-sik so that he could be replaced by an extreme rightist, someone more amenable to the Rhee cause. Failing this, the forty-two dissenters would walk out of the Assembly, leaving it a mere shadow of its former self. Dr. Kim Kyu-sik, forewarned, absented himself to the country, and the stormy sessions which followed were presided over by the vice-chairman. Dr. Kim did not wish to become embroiled in the highly partisan debate which would ensue and in which he would be forced to take a definite stand on the controversial trusteeship issue, which, as he saw it, would not be resolved in the final analysis by Koreans anyway. More moderate elements in the Assembly persuaded the forty-two to hold off for two or three days, and the vote was postponed.

Meanwhile, General Hodge rushed to the firing line and addressed the Assembly personally. In strong words he urged against any precipitous, ill-advised action and once again explained American policy—that the United States would occupy South Korea until all of Korea were independent under its own democratic government. A resolution on the floor of the Assembly charged the Americans with conniving with the Russians in imposing a trusteeship over Korea. This, the general denied. The trusteeship issue had yet to be resolved by American and Soviet negotiators, the general pointed out. But his appeal was ignored, and two days later the resolution came up for a vote. Leaders of the ultra-conservative Korean Democratic Party circulated on the floor of the Assembly talking to the members. Chief Chang of the Seoul

Metropolitan police and some of his cohorts were present to help persuade those who showed signs of wavering. Rightist youth filled the galleries, cheering madly those Assemblymen who spoke in favor of the resolution, hissing and shouting down those who rose to oppose it. Finally, the moderate and leftist delegates absented themselves from the chamber in disgust. As they left, crowds of rightist youth outside in the hall jeered and chanted "traitor" until the representatives had passed out of earshot. Needless to say, the anti-trusteeship resolution was passed by acclamation, 44 to one. Moderate rightist and Coalition Committee member Wŏn Se-hun bravely cast the lone vote in opposition. The next day. General Hodge added his voice to those in opposition. "I regret that there are erroneous statements contained in this resolution, apparently brought about through misunderstandings or misinterpretation. It is very unfortunate that the resolution should state incorrectly the position of the United States," said the general.

This activity drew further State Department comment. Again the Department expressed concern over the fact that the activities of "dissident political groups" in Korea might very likely interfere with the establishment of independence as provided by Allied agreement. The dissident elements were not identified by name other than the fact that they were "rightists." Rhee, however, added his ten cents' worth by saying that by "rightists" the State Department undoubtedly was referring to the Representative Democratic Council of which he (Rhee) was president. At this point, January 25, 1947, it became known that Rhee's National Society for the Rapid Realization of Korean Independence had reached two decisions: (1) that the Coalition Committee had to be broken up because it was dividing the people and hindering the movement for independence by inducing the public to support trusteeship, and (2) that the Interim Legislative Assembly was not a step toward independence and therefore should be opposed. On January 27 it was announced that all major right-wing groups had cancelled their signatures previously affixed to the declaration in Joint Communique Number 5 which had pledged their support of the Joint Soviet–American Commission.

By this time, right-wing organizational activities were well under way in Korea. The Coalition Committee had been effectively sabotaged and the Legislative assembly torpedoed—at least, for the time being. Meanwhile, the Anti-Trusteeship Strife Committee [Pant'ak

Tongnip T'ujaeng Wiwŏnhoe] had been formed to organize the campaign. On January 27, Rhee was named "supreme advisor" to the new committee, with Kim Ku as chairman. Meetings were being held more and more frequently in Kim Ku's Seoul residence. Local units of the National Society for the Rapid Realization of Korean Independence were being utilized to prepare the details for a nationwide uprising. Representatives and messengers from all over South Korea were transforming Kim Ku's home into a veritable beehive of activity. American authorities were plainly worried. The worry became more acute as Rhee brought the campaign into the open with a hard-hitting press statement from Washington on January 25. It was a reply to the State Department's accusation that dissident rightist elements were interfering with the establishment of Korean independence.

Rhee swung wide in this January 25 statement. He charged what he termed "obscure elements" within the State Department of "blocking the fulfillment of the American pledge to bring independence to Korea." He stated that the policy of the State Department was contrary to the desires of General MacArthur. By way of explanation, he said that MacArthur favored giving the South Korean rightists greater consideration and less to the Korean Communists. Rhee went on to take a swing at General Hodge by charging that the general was favoring leftists and that the United States Military Government in South Korea was continuing "efforts to build up and foster the Korean Communist Party." Rhee went on, "There are only a few Communists in South Korea despite the active encouragement given them by American Military Government. The Interim Legislature, which the so-called Coalition Committee established, was packed, through Hodge's appointment, with a solid block of leftists after the rightists had won 43 out of 45 seats in the general election," Rhee charged with little regard for the truth. Seeking further to substantiate his charge that Hodge was favoring communism, Rhee displayed a cablegram from the All Korean Students' Association [Chŏn'guk Haksaeng Ch'ongyŏnmaeng] which stated that the general had refused the students permission to demonstrate on January 21 against trusteeship, but had "previously allowed the Communists to demonstrate for trusteeship"—just where and when was not mentioned by Rhee. The message further stated that Communist demonstrators had confiscated student handbills against trusteeship and replaced them with posters saying "Annex Korea to Russia." It is curious that no such posters were reported by or to American intelligence officers in Korea during the period mentioned.

With those wild accusations, Rhee and his lobby continued to press the Korean case in Washington and within United Nations' circles. They openly sought establishment of a separate government in South Korea which, they claimed, would be able to solve Korea's ills without outside help and establish Korean independence. Just how relevant international problems were to be solved by an independent South Korea was never specified. By reason of that omission the suspicion grew in no few American minds that Rhee might actually be in cahoots with the Korean Communists and the Soviet Union in a concerted move to get the United States to evacuate South Korea. It was even whispered about that Rhee's price had been a promise that he would be the first Korean president. In view of later events, however, it seems clear that these suspicions were nothing more than flights of fantasy. Nevertheless, there seemed to be no other explanation for Rhee's continued campaign for the recognition of a separate South Korean government in view of the Russian colossus only forty miles north of the gates of Seoul—unless, that is, he was counting on the continued presence of American troops in South Korea and the extension of his South Korean government over North Korea by force of American arms. That thought also occurred to worried American intelligence officers and, using post-1950 hindsight, for good reason.

Radioed messages between Rhee's Washington and Seoul headquarters flowed more rapidly than ever. A number were obviously in code. One spoke of the "tiger painting," another of the "second phase of the Lerch plan," and so on. Mrs. Rhee and Kim Ku were still directing things from the Korean end. From the headquarters of the Anti-Trusteeship Strife Committee in Seoul on February 9 went the following radiogram to the governments of the United States, China, Britain, the Soviet Union, and France, and to General MacArthur:

> We have the honor to communicate to you that we, as representative of 30 million Koreans, oppose unconditionally the Section on trusteeship of the Three Foreign Ministers' Decision at Moscow. We want immediate independence of Korea which was promised by the Conference of Potsdam and by the Cairo Declaration.

The campaign continued. On the subject of alleged reports from official American sources in Korea to the effect that the American Command was attempting "to explain" the trusteeship proposal to the Korean people, Rhee commented publicly from Washington on February 11, "The proposal is an insult to the Korean people" and "a desecration of the faith of the Americans who died for freedom." He continued, "The Korean people cannot believe that the hundreds of thousands of American dead who paid the highest price for their belief in liberty, freedom and democracy would visit the insult of trusteeship upon a friendly people who have known forty centuries of self-government." General Hodge and the United States Military Government in Korea had tried before to persuade the Koreans to accept trusteeship, Rhee contended, "but the more they try, the more resistance they will encounter." Rhee then emphasized the differences between MacArthur's policies in Japan and those of Hodge's in Korea. "There is a fundamental contradiction of policy in regard to Japan and Korea," he declared. "On the one hand is General Douglas MacArthur's announcement that a new election will be held in Japan "to obtain another democratic expression of the people's will." On the other hand, is the continued failure of the Military Government in South Korea to establish the rudiments of a democratic and independent government there. Korea, eighteen months after its liberation, continues to be ruled by a military dictatorship," Rhee finished.

What Rhee did not trouble going into was the reasons why American Military Government had been unable to make any progress toward democratization in South Korea. The trusteeship issue, raised by Rhee and Kim Ku, had been one of the basic reasons for the inability to effect Russian–American accord on the subject of Korea—this, by General Hodge's own words. Moreover, it had been Rhee's own group which had refused to cooperate in establishing a truly democratic regime in South Korea in that the Rhee–Kim Ku controlled South Korean police made such an impossibility. The sabotage of the Coalition Committee and of the Interim Legislative Assembly by Rhee's group bared its true color for all to see. Rhee and his colleagues wanted control of the government, and they did not care particularly how they seized it; this much they had in common with the Communists.

The argument about differences in policy pursued in Japan and Korea was a weak one at best to anyone who was at all familiar with the situation. The political environment of the two countries was very dissimilar. In Japan existed an educated electorate and thousands of trained officials and technicians, including not a few truly democratic leaders—witness the liberal democratic movement in Japan in the late twenties. Moreover, the country was united geographically and was well integrated. In the case of Korea, one had a country suffering from geographical disunity and political disintegration. The mass of people were illiterate and had access to no reliable information or system of communication. The Americans had been at a loss to find public officials sufficiently well trained to assume responsibility and reliable enough to be trusted with any degree of authority. Moreover, there was no liberal tradition. Korea may have been self-governing for forty centuries—which goes back to a prehistoric era—but it certainly had never known democracy or anything even resembling it. For the past forty years it had been under Japanese domination. Before that, the Yi dynasty had headed a corrupt and autocratic government. Rhee's arguments simply did not stand if one were sincerely interested in setting up a democratic state in Korea. Of course, the secret was that Rhee was not so motivated. Rather, he possessed an overweening ambition to set up an autocratic South Korean government with himself in charge. His approval of police activity in South Korea and disapproval of the Coalition Committee gave amble evidence of his views on civil liberties and the rights of political groups opposed to him.

General Hodge had had enough, and on February 15, 1947, he left via plane for Washington. Commented Rhee on the general's sudden departure for the United States, "Hodge may get a new attitude toward the Korean leftists. Unless he changes his policies toward the Korean Reds, I do not think he can succeed there." Rhee went on to explain that the recent appointment of An Chae-hong to the newly established post of Civil Administrator for Military Government "again exemplifies this." How Rhee could construe the appointment of An Chae-hong, a former supporter of his own cause and always considered a moderate rightist, as indicating undue partiality toward the Korean Reds by General Hodge was left unexplained.

By this time, Rhee's activities had extended to London with the arrival there of "Colonel" Ben C. Limb [Im Pyŏng-jik], a member of Rhee's Washington lobby. The British Foreign Office was taken entirely by surprise when Limb showed up in London and refused to have anything to do with him. To the press, however, Rhee announced that Limb was contacting the British Foreign Office to ascertain its attitude on the proposed trusteeship and other Korean questions. At the same time, Rhee made it known in Washington that he would discuss Sino–Korean problems with Chiang Kai-shek on his way back to Korea. But by this time, it was rumored that the Korean impasse would be included in the agenda of the impending conference of foreign ministers at Moscow and that large-scale American economic assistance would be offered to South Korea in the near future. Rhee decided to postpone his departure for the Orient and capitalize on this lucky turn of events. In order to bring the Korean situation to a head, as well as to scare Rhee out of his anti-trusteeship and separate South Korean government fixation, General Hodge announced to the press that there was indication that the Soviet Union might be recruiting a North Korean army of 500,000 persons, a charge immediately denied by official Soviet spokesmen, though apparently in bad-faith.

American counterintelligence agents were busy in Seoul. It was known that the discussions taking place at Kim Ku's Seoul residence were reaching their final phase. It was reported on February 27 that Kim Ku and Cho So-ang [1887–1958], representing the Provisional Government, and Kim Sŏng-su [1891–1955][77] and two others representing the extreme right-wing Korean Democratic Party, were meeting to plan the foundation of a separate South Korean government. It was suspected by American authorities that March 1, 1947, the anniversary of the 1919 Korean passive resistance movement against the Japanese, would be selected as the date for the insurrection against American authority. The American Command warned rightist leaders in no uncertain terms.

Two demonstrations were planned to celebrate March 1 (known as Samil Day to Koreans) in Seoul, one by the rightists in Seoul Stadium and the other by the leftists atop Namsan Mountain, one of the hills adjacent to Seoul proper. Everything proceeded calmly at the outset except for a minor disturbance at the rightist rally when a few persons in the crowd attempted to introduce a resolution calling for the establishment of the Provisional Government as the legitimate govern-

---

[77] On Kim Sŏng-su, see Mark Gayn's Korea chapter herein, 389, footnote 56, and the end of his November 5 entry, 420–21.

ment of South Korea. Korean police, under direct orders of American officers, moved in and quietly removed the more vocal of the group. Those on the speakers' platform, forewarned by American authorities that they would be held directly responsible, chose to ignore the disturbance. However, when the rightist conclave adjourned, the rightist youth formed a parade and marched to the bottom of Namsan, arriving there at exactly the time when the leftist meeting was breaking up. Fighting ensued, deliberately started by the rightists and possibly by the police. Truckloads of armed policemen were already on the spot even before the two rival groups met. The three-way battle among police, rightists, and leftists ended in considerable gun play. Two men were killed and several wounded. American GIs added to the general excitement. One of General Hodge's staff later told of seeing an American soldier firing his weapon gleefully into the air. When the officer asked him why in the world he was doing so, he replied, "Oh, I just heard some shots and figured I might as well shoot some too." Fortunately, no Americans were actively involved. The police finally gained control of the situation and American authorities heaved a collective sigh of relief for there had been considerable doubt as to just how the police would act. Later, I was told by one of the American inspectors in the Department of Police that he would not be at all surprised to learn that Chief Chang T'aek-sang and Dr. Cho Pyŏng-ok themselves had instigated the shooting. In any event, the relief was short-lived, for it soon developed that the date for the insurrection had been postponed.

Trouble had developed among the right-wing leaders. Mrs. Rhee and Kim Ku were at odds. Kim resented her authority and was trying to take over the political machinery in the absence of Rhee and reassume the position of leadership which had been his in the old days. A split developed. Many of the provincial right-wing leaders got cold feet and decided to call the whole thing off without conferring with Kim Ku. When the final resolution establishing the Provisional Government as the legal government came up for adoption even Kim Ku's aged feet grew a bit numb, and he refused to sign it. When March 1 arrived no one knew quite what they were doing, least of all Rhee in Washington. It soon developed, as already indicated, that the whole plot had been planned prior to Rhee's departure from Korea the previous December, and Rhee, not knowing of the dissension among his lieutenants in Korea, acted on the assumption that everything was going according to schedule. It had been agreed previously that in order to strengthen the Provisional Government, Kim Ku would step down from the presidency and Dr. Rhee would take over the top spot. Apparently, at the last minute, Kim Ku refused to live up to this agreement, and no announcement as to the change of leadership was forthcoming on the appointed day from Kim Ku's headquarters. Nevertheless, Rhee, acting according to the prearranged schedule, announced on March 6 from Washington, "It is reported from Korea that I am again to be called for the presidency of my country in this, it's a time of great trial." On the same day, spokesmen for the Anti-Trusteeship Strife Committee in Seoul stated, "The argument on Korea at the Conference of the Four Ministers at Moscow, despite the United States Government's backing, may be unfavorable in its result, so all the Korean people must prepare and wait for the command of the supreme guide." It was not disclosed, however, just who the "supreme guide" was. In any event, the insurrection had been postponed pending events in Moscow.

On March 7, 1947, American counterintelligence agents searched the Seoul headquarters of Rhee's National Society for the Rapid Realization of Korean Independence and of Kim Ku's Korean Independence Party, as well as the residence of Kim Ku. A large number of propaganda documents were seized. Copies of a proclamation dated March 3, 1947, were found which stated in part, "Those Military Government officials [Korean]* who dare violate any direction of the Korean Provisional Government should be punished severely." In addition, there was a document proclaiming the establishment of the Provisional Government as the legal government of South Korea. Very few copies got out to the public, and the entire incident was quickly forgotten. Soon thereafter, a radiogram from Rhee to Kim Ku was intercepted saying, "Hold the problem of a Korean provisional government in abeyance until I return to Korea. In the meantime try to unify all rightist groups." The Gilbert & Sullivan insurrection was over.

It was mid-March of 1947, and Dr. Rhee was still in Washington. His announced one-month's stay in the United States had extended into three. The reason for this extension was not long in coming to the

* The insertion in brackets is in the author's original typescript.

surface. It was rumored that discussions were under way for an American-financed economic rehabilitation program for South Korea of no mean proportion. The sum of $600,000,000 was mentioned in the press. In addition, there was talk of terminating Military Government in South Korea and replacing it with an all-Korean government directed by an American civilian as high commissioner. Associated Press commented on March 22 that such a program would seem to constitute a "sweeping victory for Dr. Rhee who for the past few months has been urging changes along the lines outlined." Commented Rhee when asked for his reaction, "It is possible to establish a Korean democratic government that would be a model for Asia and an inspiration to China. So far, the development of democracy in Korea has been hindered rather than helped." Rhee went on to predict the establishment of an "interim independent government" within the next thirty to sixty days. The State Department quickly denied any such program.

In Korea the repercussions were intense. Korean newspapers which printed Dr. Rhee's prediction of a separate South Korean government, followed by the State Department's denial, were severely censored by right-wing groups. Newspaper editors were beaten by right-wing thugs for daring to cast aspersions on the integrity of Rhee in such a fashion. In one case, editors of the Korean Press, one of the two leading Korean news agencies, and the Korean correspondent for United Press were abducted from their offices by rightist strong-arm men, carried to the headquarters of Rhee's National Society for the Rapid Realization of Korean Independence, tried before a self-styled tribunal on the charge that they had committed treason against the Provisional Government of the Republic of Korea and severely beaten. Other newspaper men were threatened and warned not to print anything uncomplimentary to Rhee's cause. The South Korean police did nothing to prevent this intimidation of the Korean press. On April 10, the State Department was again forced to deny publicly a statement made by Rhee, this time a claim that President Truman had promised Korea—through Rhee—a loan of $600,000,000. The contemplated loan program for Korea would "likely involve far less than $600,000,000," said Department spokesmen in denying Rhee's claim.

By this time, however, Rhee had left Washington and was in Chongqing as a guest of state of Chiang Kai-shek. From China, Rhee blandly announced that the loan would be granted as soon as the

Korean Government was formally recognized. The doctor arrived back in Seoul on April 21 aboard a special Chinese government airplane. MacArthur had given permission for his return over the strenuous objections from the American Command in Korea. Seoul was decked out with posters acclaiming Rhee's "diplomatic success." The impression that he had been largely responsible for the impending financial assistance to South Korea and for Secretary of State George C. Marshall's [1880–1959] introduction of the Korean problem at the Moscow Conference of Foreign Ministers then in session was not allowed to wane. In the absence of American denials that he had instigated any such moves, Rhee's barometer of popular prestige nearly burst its bubble. Kim Ku was at the great man's feet once again, bowing his obeisance. Mrs. Rhee was all smiles.

CHAPTER VII: POLITICAL INTRIGUE

While the Korean right wing was consolidating under Dr. Rhee's leadership and raking a strong but abortive bid for power, the left was split wide open.

It all began in September of 1946 when the Namnodang, the South Korean Workers' Party, was launched with the long-talked-of merger of the Communist Party and the Communist elements of Yŏ's Korean People's Party and the New Korean People's Party[78]—the latter, a lesser left-wing group with headquarters in North Korea. This combination paralleled a similar development in North Korea where simultaneously the Workers' Party of North Korea [Pukchosŏn Nodondang] appeared. The formation of these two labor parties marked the end of the on-the-surface existence of the Korean Communist Party. Henceforth, it operated underground, maintaining the fiction that its organization had been dissolved in the formation of the North and South Korean

[78] Robinson's manuscript refers to the party as the New Democratic Party. However, the party in question was the Chosŏn Sinmindang, the New Korean People's Party.

workers' parties. Actually, these parties merely formed a convenient front behind which the Communist Party could operate and by which it could gain control of all the left. The South Korean Workers' Party, then, early in the fall of 1946, became the Communist-dominated front modestly claiming to represent all leftist groups. The earlier organization apexing the Communist-controlled left, the Democratic National Front, became merely a propaganda agency. It did maintain its separate identity, but only to provide the Communist-controlled left with the fictional existence of a "non-political" front.

Schisms in the Left

This move to form a South Korean Workers' Party split the ranks of the left, and precipitated a crisis in the People's Party. When the inner sanctum of Yŏ's People's Party voted in mid-August 1946 to join the Communist-inspired merger, Yŏ Un-hyŏng resigned. With him went the non-Communist left—or the "patriotic left" as American observers in Korea were wont to call them. Yŏ's group claimed that the others had merely voted themselves out of the People's Party, but that the party still existed. The Communist-dominated group contended that by their vote to join the South Korean Workers' Party, the People's Party had been dissolved. Whatever the logic of the question might be, the fact remained that a nationalist group under Yŏ continued to exist which called itself the Korean People's Party.

Both factions had their trouble, however. The Communist Party was again threatened with a schism between Pak Hŏn-yŏng, the National Secretary, and a good portion of his followers. The most powerful opposition to Pak's autocratic leadership was spearheaded by Yun Il [aka Yun T'aek-kŭn, 1893–?], a Communist from the South Korean port city of Pusan. He had been ousted from the Communist Party during the previous summer (1945) because of his disinclination to follow Pak's orders. In late September 1946 Yun Il showed up in Seoul as the chairman of a meeting of dissident Communist Party members. He told American CIC agents at the time that he intended to call a national Communist meeting, a meeting very much opposed by Pak's group which felt that its power would be threatened if party representatives were ever brought together in a general meeting. Yun also told the Americans that he intended to convince the Communist

Party to operate in a legal manner and not to follow dictates originating outside of Korea. What happened to these plans was never known. The 1946 fall strikes and riots intervened and momentarily eclipsed all else. Furthermore, it was quite apparent that even this anti-Pak group did its level best to exploit the strikes and attendant violence to Communist ends. Fear of retaliation might well have put the quietus on the anti-Pak faction, just as Pak had attempted to instill the fear of the Russians in Yŏ at an earlier date. In any event, Pak apparently retained firm control of the party, even though forced to operate underground by reason of the American warrant out for his arrest.

So late in November 1946 the South Korean Workers' Party was formally organized under the leadership of Hŏ Hŏn, the same man who had emerged earlier as leader of the People's Republic and of the Democratic National Front. The new party marked a resurgence of the extreme left-wing faction whose power in the political field had been on the wane since early September when Pak Hŏn-yŏng had gone underground to evade arrest.

Just prior to the organization of the South Korean Workers' Party, Yŏ Un-hyŏng had proposed an unconditional merger of his group with the new organization. The proposal had been ignored, possibly because the extreme left no longer trusted Yŏ in the face of his past defections. Yŏ then made a start to organize the moderate left under the banner of a new group, the Social Labor Party [Sahoe Nodongdang]. The members of this new party, however, were more or less out on a limb in that they opposed both the South Korean Workers' Party and the right-wing groups. It was again the case of would-be liberal democrats being caught between extremists. The result was a great scurrying for cover. A mass resignation of Social Labor Party leaders took place early in December 1946. For the most part, they had belonged to the former People's Party, and their withdrawal was prompted by a desire to reactivate the old People's Party with Yŏ as chairman. A few weeks later, the central committee of the Socialist Laborites split on the issue of continued separate existence from the Communist-dominated South Korean Workers' Party. Communist money probably influenced the voting. Yŏ Un-hyŏng pulled his favorite maneuver and again retired to the country. He appeared no longer capable of bridging the gap between Communist and left-wing liberals. Most of the leaders of the so-called "Convention group" of dissident Communists were still on the sidelines under acute pressure from North Korea. Specific threats against their personal safety had been made to virtually all the prominent leftists so as to prevent their affiliation with the Social Labor Party.

Dr. Kim Kyu-sik, moderate rightist and chairman of the new Interim Legislative Assembly, commented publicly in December 1946 that he would endeavor to extend the organization of the Legislative assembly into an all-Korean Assembly formed by a general election in North and South Korea. Dr. Kim's plan, if successful, would in effect have destroyed the organization of the People's Committee—then directly under the South Korean Workers' Party—and the Interim Peoples Committee of North Korea, the organ of central government in the North established under Soviet sponsorship. The Democratic National Front, the propaganda organ for the Communist-left in South Korea, was quick to denounce the plan. The American Command, at the same time, announced that it had no objection to such unification attempts of individual members of the Interim Legislative Assembly acting in an unofficial capacity and that it was sympathetic to all such efforts which might aid the reunion of South and North Korea.

As the first step in Dr. Kim's strategy, the coalition movement was to be accelerated in South Korea. The seven principles of the Coalition Committee were to be disseminated throughout the southern provinces. Emissaries were to be dispatched to confer with North Korean political leaders. Ch'oe Tong-o [1892–1963], vice-chairman of the Legislative Assembly, was mentioned as a likely member of the diplomatic mission.[79] When asked about the unfavorable attitude the Russians would probably assume in the negotiations, Dr. Kim seemed to think that the difficulties would somehow be overcome. Obviously, both the extreme right-wing forces of Dr. Rhee and the extreme left-wing forces of Pak Hŏn-yŏng's had much to lose from the success of such a

[79] Kim Kyu-sik and Ch'oe Tong-o were brought north after northern troops had captured Seoul in the early days of the Korean War. Although Kim died the same year, Ch'oe served in a high political office in North Korea until his death. His son Ch'oe Tŏk-sin (see p. 103, footnote 37), however, became South Korea's Foreign Minister after Park Chung Hee's (in office 1961–1979) military coup d'état in 1961, and later the ROK's ambassador to West Germany. Interestingly enough, in 1986 he moved to P'yŏngyang with his wife to then assume a political office in North Korea.

venture—or even from the favorable publicity such an effort by the Coalition Committee would receive. Therefore, both groups moved to destroy the Coalition Committee. Rhee denounced it, and the Representative Democratic Council withdrew its delegates. The left assailed the unfortunate Committee and by threats and sabotage prevented the Committee from achieving any notable success. This was the ground upon which Rhee and the Communists saw eye to eye; no liberal middle-of-the-road movement could be allowed to succeed in South Korea.

During this period, the extreme left under Hŏ Hŏn and Pak Hŏn-yŏng was on its best behavior, perhaps content to sit by and watch the right overreach itself in its attempt to seize power from Military Government and thereby gain the hostility of the Americans. However, to keep the record straight, the left did make demands for the withdrawal of the warrant for the arrest of Pak Hŏn-yŏng, for the transfer of governmental authority to the People's Committees, and for the dissolution of the Interim Legislative Assembly and, of course, of the Coalition Committee. Leftist organs also criticized the anti-trusteeship vote forced by Rhee's group in the Legislative Assembly and denied that the Assembly spoke for the Korean people on the issue. On the other hand, this extreme leftist element made its first conciliatory gesture towards the Americans. On January 25, 1947, the Democratic National Front declared that it was ready to cooperate with Military Government and publicly endorsed (although conditioned by eleven demands) Military Government Ordinance Number 126 which provided for the election of provincial and local officials. The demands made by the Front included the election of provincial, city, country, and township People's Committees, with the principle of obedience of lower committees to higher committees prevailing. The leftist proposal would have eliminated the Legislative Assembly and made no provision for a central law-making body, but did call for general suffrage, including women, and the participation of all political parties. A further proposal was the creation of an appointed general election commission to insure fairness of the elections.

In mid-January 1947 the explosive trusteeship issue took precedence over all other news in the Korean press and among local political circles. The subject had been aroused by a speech made by General Hodge on January 4, by the publication of the exchange of letters between Generals Hodge and Chistiakov relative to the reopening of the Joint Soviet–American Commission,* and by the statement of a State Department official to the effect that the majority of Koreans looked favorably on the idea of a trusteeship. The extreme left seemed to gain at least momentary strength from this turn of events in their favor. The Communist-dominated organizations under the banner of the Democratic National Front praised General Chistiakov's letter highly and generally endorsed General Hodge's reply, but took issue with the latter over the fact that the right-wing anti-trusteeship parties which had signed the declaration embodied in the Joint Commission's famous Communique Number 5 would be consulted by the Joint Commission and allowed to participate in the formation of the Korean Government. The less extreme Social Labor Party praised the American Command as showing an "inclination to take a sincere attitude in the interpretation of the Moscow Decision."

On February 22, 1947, Yŏ Un-hyŏng came back on the scene with the expressed intent to emerge from his quasi-retirement and to journey throughout South Korea in an effort to reorganize his old People's Party. Yŏ admitted that approximately half the former membership had been lost to the South Korean Workers' Party, but he indicated a belief that his former leaders would join him. He felt assured of 100,000 loyal followers. Yŏ was reported as having commented that the South Korean Workers' Party had instructed its provincial branches to bar him from addressing their meetings. In the meantime, the Coalition Committee was expanding its activities under Kim Kyu-sik's able guidance. It had enlisted the active support of a number of organizers and administrators and was canvassing South Korea for support. Its intelligent middle-of-the-road approach was appealing if the people could be reached.

At this juncture, early spring of 1947, there was no doubt that the strength of the moderate right and left was gaining despite American inaction, the crossfire between right and left extremists, and an unfriendly police. The plans of the extreme right for seizure of governmental power from American Military Government had turned out to be a comedy of errors and poor judgement. Both Rhee and Kim Ku had lost considerable face in the episode, as likewise had their organizations.

* See this volume, 242–45.

This was before the return of Rhee from his "diplomatic success." Obviously, this was the time for the left-wing extremists to stage another show of power to forestall any possible political corps by the moderates.

March 22, 1947

The date chosen was March 22. South Korean industry, communications, railroads, and some phases of government and maritime operations were disrupted in varying degrees by the general strike called on that date, a strike secretly conceived and initiated by the Communist-dominated National Labor Union Council [mentioned above]. In fifteen hours' time the strike spread from its point of origin in Pusan to six of the leading cities of the Chŏlla provinces (leftists' strongholds) and to Seoul, Taegu, Inch'ŏn, and several smaller communities in Southwestern Korea. The strike was not without violence, but it did not assume large-scale proportions. There were eleven reported dead with an unknown number of injured. Violence broke out in Seoul when members of the rightist "Youth" Association began to operate strike-bound streetcars under police protection. Of course, this show of police partiality was just what the Communists had hoped for.

An ultimatum, apparently prepared previously, was reserved until the strike had passed its initial phase and was served on General Hodge during the morning of the 22. The following demands were made:

(1) The reinstatement to their former jobs of all members of leftist unions who had been reduced in rank or discharged and steps to prevent factory lockouts, unemployment, and redaction of personnel.

(2) The increase of wages to meet rising prices.

(3) Four *hops** of rice daily to laborers and office workers and three *hops* to "ordinary men."

(4) The dissolution of the General League of Great Korean Laborers (the right-wing labor organization, the National

* A *hop* of rice equals 0.63 of a cup.

Federation of Labor Unions and right-wing youth groups. (These groups were charged with terrorism.)

(5) The dismissal and punishment of persons of bad character in Military Government and the police organization. (In this category were listed pro-Japanese, profiteers, and oppressors.)

(6) The release and reappointment to their old positions of those imprisoned for striking, demonstrating, displaying posters, and participating in meetings.

(7) The release from imprisonment of certain labor leaders and the cancellation of the warrant for the arrest of Pak Hŏn-yŏng, the Communist leader.

(8) Immediate security for the freedom of the trade union movement.

The political nature of these demands was at once obvious. Only four of the eight were really legitimate demands concerning labor. The ultimatum stated that the laboring people of South Korea had undertaken a twenty-four-hour strike in order to strengthen by action the demands made. The petition concluded with a threat of a violent, long-term strike should suppressive measures be taken or persecutions occur before or after the present strike. The authors of the petition arrogantly placed the responsibly for the consequences of such action upon General Hodge. Further, it was desired that the issue not he obscured again by charges that the future strike was being called without due warning.

Chang T'aek-sang, Chief of the Seoul Metropolitan police, issued an order for wholesale arrest of leftist leaders, including Kim Wŏn-bong and other high-level leaders of the Democratic National Front, the left-wing Labor Union, the South Korean Workers' Party, and leftist youth and farmer associations. With leftist leaders in jail or in hiding, rightist youth moved into various left-wing headquarters in Seoul on March 23, confiscated documents, stole office equipment, and generally smashed up the offices. The police did not intervene until March 25, two days later. All told, 2,718 persons were arrested, many being left-wing leaders other than those affiliated with the labor unions responsible for the strike. Leftist organs screamed against Military Government. They denounced the "ferocious outrages ... wicked heinous, unpardonable savagery perpetrated upon a people plunged into horror by the undemocratic police who (with others) have stolen into the organs of Military Government!"

Investigation by Korean newspaper men revealed some curious things about that arrest order. When General Lerch was questioned by the press on the subject, the general allegedly replied that it had been entirely a Korean affair. When An Chae-hong, the Civil Administrator, was approached, he claimed that he had been helpless, that the arrests had been ordered by "high American authorities." Later, Cho Pyŏng-ok, Director of the National Police, reputedly said that although he had been in agreement with the arrest of the leftist leaders by reason of their opposition to Military Government policies, he had been "helpless" to do anything about the arrests. The obvious implication was that he had been ordered to make the arrests by the Americans. At this juncture, an American officer from Military Government—and, incidentally, a member of a missionary family of long standing in Korea—visited Kim Wŏn-bong in the local jail and extolled him to leave the Democratic National Front. Replied Kim, "This is no place to discuss such a matter."

The center of the controversy raged about the figure of Kim Wŏn-bong. The name of 50-odd year-old Kim was known to virtually every Korean child as an intrepid champion of Korean independence. In the early twenties he had organized a Korean group in China to plead and fight Korea's cause. This had been an anti-Kim Ku Provisional Government group until the late thirties, at which time, upon suggestion of Chiang Kai-shek, Kim Wŏn-bong buried his misgivings and joined forces with Kim Ku. By way of reward for his capitulation to Kim Ku's leadership, Kim Wŏn-bong had been appointed War Minister in the Provisional Government. When the Provisional Government staff returned to Korea in the fall of 1945, Kim Wŏn-bong came with it. Most of his followers, however, entered North Korea and joined Kim Tu-bong's Yan'an faction, a Korean group which had been fighting the Japanese in North China alongside the Chinese Communists and which later had gained the favor of the Soviet regime in North Korea. Kim Wŏn-bong retained his position in the Provisional Government until the organization of the Emergency National Congress in February 1946, at which time he—along with the four other leaders of the liberal group within the Provisional Government, including Dr. Kim Kyu-sik—walked out in an act of rebellion against Kim Ku's highhanded assumption of authority. Kim Ku's anti-trusteeship campaign was then at its height, and the old revolutionist was attempting to consolidate his hold over the right wing by fair means or foul. This was more than the liberal group could stomach. After this exodus of the liberals, Kim Wong Bong and three others ultimately accepted chairmanships in the Democratic National Front. Dr. Kim Kyu-sik, another member of the group, stayed clear of political parties, first participating in the Representative Democratic Council, then in the Coalition Committee, and most recently as chairmen of the Interim Legislative Assembly. Kim Wŏn-bong was a philosophical communist, but had steadfastly refused to join the Korean Communist Party. He, like Yŏ, was a nationalist and a moderate and therefore refused to accept the totalitarianism and Soviet authority inherent in the Communist Party. However, he had no political refuge other than the Communist-controlled Democratic National Front. He was never offered any significant post by the American Command. Kim Wŏn-bong obviously did not relish the idea of being under the Communist thumb, but there appeared to be little he could do about it. On April 9, 1946, I met Kim Wŏn-bong quite by accident in the home of a Korean friend. At that time, he was working desperately to effect a reconciliation between certain rightists and leftist elements. The move failed, and he found himself completely subject to Communist dictates if he were to remain politically active. No doubt, personal threats helped keep him in line, his name being a valuable asset to the Communists. It was reliably reported that his wife, an extremely powerful influence over his thinking, was more than a little perturbed by this hold which the Communists had over her husband. At times, Kim was even handed Communist-prepared speeches to read on public occasions, although generally he refused to utter more radical statements.

Kim Wŏn-bong's arrest in March 1947, following the twenty-four-hour strike, made it all the more impossible for him to leave the Communist Party fold. The Americans had irrevocably lost what might have been a powerful ally. Even his trial, held some weeks later, was a farce. The police, in a desperate effort to prove his complicity in the strike, introduced as evidence copies of speeches purported to be addresses delivered by Kim urging the strike. Actually, they were Communist texts of speeches which he was supposed to have delivered, but which he refused to do. He probably knew vaguely that such a strike was scheduled to take place sometime, but that was all. The mere fact that when he had been picked up by the police on the morning of March 22 while he had been waiting impatiently at Seoul Station to board a train—not even knowing that the trains were strikebound—was perhaps prima facie evidence of his innocence. Fortunately, the case was dismissed, but the damage had been done.

When representatives of the World Federation of Trade Unions arrived in South Korea in late March 1947, they found all leftist labor leaders either in jail or fugitives from justice.* This caused the American Command considerable embarrassment, and all of a sudden no one seemed to know just who had issued the blanket arrest order following the twenty-four-hour strike. Unfortunately, however, Dr. Cho Pyŏng-ok had had the temerity to announce the arrest order in the Korean press at the time. The American Command was caught red-handed, for it was obvious to all that it must have been fully aware of what was going on and had taken no steps to prevent the arrests. Just why there should have been any arrests at all for a twenty-four-hour strike, in which the only violence was started by the police, defied explanation. The sentences finally meted out to the labor leaders involved ranged as high as five years at hard labor.

The Tragedy of Yŏ Un-hyŏng

Both the extreme right and extreme left were now temporarily out of the picture; both had lost considerable face during the winter months of 1946–47 through ill-conceived activity. And Rhee's temporary surge of prestige when he arrived back in Korea on April 21, 1947, from his "successful diplomatic mission," was but short-lived by reason of the reconvention of the Joint Soviet–American Commission on May 22. The opportunity for Yŏ Un-hyŏng to step forward once again into the political limelight was at hand.

---

* At this time the WFTU was still a respectable organization in which Western labor was participating.

On May 24, 1947, Yŏ's efforts brought about the formal launching of the Working People's Party [Kŭllo Inmindang]. By dropping the name and organization of the old Korean People's Party and Social Labor Party, Yŏ may have felt that he could escape Communist domination and alliance with the Democratic National Front, though why so much importance should be attached to names was difficult for an outsider to appreciate. It appeared that Yŏ was aspiring to leadership of the moderate left in one final desperate attempt. The new party was formed initially from Yŏ's old followers who were with him in the Korean People's Party and from former members of the Social Labor Party. In spite of Yŏ's strenuous protests, the latter group (which included a sizable number of anti-Pak Communists) forced through a series of resolutions a few days after the party's birth, resolutions calling for alliance with the Communist-controlled Democratic National Front, as well as the left-wing Women's Association, Youth Association, and Farmers' Union. Within days, control of the new Working People's Party had been wrested from Yŏ's hands. Once again it was demonstrated that the moderate left was in an impossible position in the Korean political arena.

In a May 1947 discussion between Yŏ Un-hong (the younger Yŏ brother) and members of the American Command, the former pointed out that the Working People's Party was anti-Pak Hŏn-yŏng but contained many Communistic elements. The elder Yŏ apparently felt that he could not bar Communists from his party without inciting a general exodus of his following to Pak's camp. This new party constituted Yŏ's third attempt to break loose from Communist control. The first had been his desertion from the Korean People's Republic and the formation of the Korean People's Party. Next had been his resignation from the Korean People's Party and the formation of the Social Labor Party. And the third and final effort had been his withdrawal from that group and the formation of the Working People's Party. Wherever Yŏ went, the Communists followed, infiltrated into the group, and dragged the party back to the political fold ruled by the Democratic National Front.

Yŏ was truly in an impossible position and by the summer of 1947 he had achieved the dubious fame of being the most shot-at man in South Korea, having been the intended victim in nine such plots against his life. In one of the later attempts, part of his home had been demolished by a bomb. It was obvious that he was a thorn in the side of both the extreme left and the extreme right.

About this time a bribery scandal broke into public consciousness. According to Dr. Syngman Rhee, Dr. Kim Kyu-sik was directly involved. This confirmed the final parting of the ways for the two. Dr. Kim immediately indicated a desire to resign from further active participation in politics, including chairmanship of the Interim Legislative Assembly. On May 12, 1947, he requested the Assembly to grant him a ten-day leave of absence, and forthwith he retired to the country to think things over. With him went Yŏ Un-hyŏng. Strategy was planned. The two champions of liberalism in Korea determined to pool their forces and their effort to fight the extremists in any way they could. No help could be counted on from the American Command, which had steadfastly refused to take any effective measures to curb police excesses, excesses which were increasing every day. Neither Yŏ nor Kim dared move without an armed bodyguard. Both requested permission to carry weapons and to arm their guards. The two men refused Korean police "protection" for obvious reasons.

On May 21 Dr. Kim returned to Seoul and submitted his resignation to the Assembly. The American Command was forced to act in order to salvage the Legislative Assembly, for it was painfully obvious that it would rapidly fall apart if Dr. Kim walked out. Moreover, if the Assembly broke up, the American hand at the impending sessions of the Joint Soviet–American Commission would be weakened immeasurably; the American would have no political structure in South Korea upon which to rely. With the help of careful moves by American manipulators—unknown to Dr. Kim—an impressive vote of confidence was awarded the tired doctor in the Assembly as his proffered resignation was rejected unanimously. By this adroit maneuver in forcing a show down, Dr. Kim had gained considerable power. Shortly thereafter, he withdrew his resignation.

It was at about this time that General Hodge was visited by a delegation of middle-of-the-road liberals. The group included Dr. Kim, Yŏ, An Chae-hong (the Civil Administrator for Military Government)* and Wŏn Se-hun (a member of the Legislative Assembly and a mainstay of the Coalition Committee). An ultimatum was placed before the

* As such, An was the top-ranking Korean in the administration.

general: either Dr. Cho Pyŏng-ok and Chief Chang would be removed from the police force, drastic measures taken to curb police excesses, and Korean personnel on the payrolls of Military Government thoroughly combed for undesirables, or the entire group would no longer cooperate with the American Command. It was a shrewd move, for the Americans were in no position to lose the support of this group in view of the fact that the Soviet delegation to the Joint Commission was momentarily expected to arrive in Seoul. Why the ultimatum was never carried out by the quartet, given the fact of American inaction, was never explained. Civil Administrator An Chae-hong approached General Hodge a few weeks later for permission to fire Dr. Cho and Chief Chang. Said the general, "You have full authority to fire the two men if you wish, but *mind you*, I don't want you to." As one American observer wryly commented, "What kind of a statement was that?" An and the others, in the face of uncertain American support and certain police reprisal, thought better of the entire project and no more was heard. Perhaps it was the announcement of the reconvention of the Joint Soviet–American Commission which caused these leaders temporarily to forget their threat of non-cooperation. In any event, nothing was done, and Dr. Kim retained his position at the head of the Legislative Assembly and An, his post as Civil Administrator.

The reconvention of the Joint Soviet–American Commission on May 21, 1947, brought a burst feverish political activity with the left-wing parties working in almost complete unity under the banner of the Democratic National Front. This unity was in marked contrast to the wide cleavages in the right wing caused by differences in opinion as to the wisdom of consulting and cooperating with the Joint Commission. The Korean Communists, having the support of the Soviets and being in absolute control of North Korea where all opposition had been effectively squelched, were busy organizing and grinding out propaganda. They hoped to win over to their side the majority of the common folk who genuinely desired the establishment of a Korean Government, even though this might come through the Joint Commission and carry with it a tentative trusteeship rider. These left-wing advances came at the expense of Rhee and Kim Ku who were achieving a notable lack of success in keeping the people dancing about their "anti-trusteeship" banner. The left-wing political parties and social organizations—claiming to be about seventy in number, but with much overlapping—were all being kept in line through the Democratic National Front and all were to approach the Joint Commission with the same platform: (1) that the structure of the new government should be that of the People's Committees, (2) that reactionaries and pro-Japanese elements should be eliminated, and (3) that the new government established under the Joint Commission should carry out land reform and labor legislation in conformity with that of North Korea. While the Joint Commission remained in session, no serious split in the forces of the extreme left could be tolerated.

Meanwhile, Kim Kyu-sik and Yŏ Un-hyŏng were attempting to strengthen the Coalition Committee which they hoped to use in much the same way as the Communists were using the Democratic National Front—namely, as a propaganda organ and "non-political" front behind which to recruit various and sundry groups. By early June 1947 the move had not achieved notable success. The opposition from the extremes was too strong to allow headway. Even though Yŏ reluctantly acquiesced to the inclusion of the extreme right-wing Korean Democratic Party, he failed to receive the approval of the now Communist-dominated (anti-Pak) Working People's Party. There appeared to be little hope that other leftists in the Coalition Committee could be induced to join forces with even that part of the extreme right which had agreed to consult with the Joint Commission—this, in spite of the fact that such union would give the moderates the lower-level party organization without which they could not hope for permanent success. The moderates probably felt that this was no time to compromise. The Joint Commission was in session, and if it were successful in establishing a provisional Korean government—as was optimistically predicted by all—it seemed very probable that the moderates would come into their own. Certainly, the Americans would agree to go no further left in search of governmental leadership, and the Russians would go no further right. And, with this thought in mind, the political structure of South Korea crystallized. The Communist-left supported the Joint Commission without qualification. The moderate group, spearheaded by the Coalition Committee, emphasized the early establishment of a provisional government representative of the people. The rightist extreme under Rhee and Kim Ku flatly opposed the work of the Joint Commission and refused to have anything to do with it.

At this juncture it seemed as though the moderates might come out on top in any Soviet–American compromise. Even Chang T'aek-sang, the much-maligned chief of the Seoul Metropolitan police, saw this and made a hurried visit to the home of one of the American political advisors. He arrived one evening in full regalia—police limousines, motor-cycle patrolmen, guards, and what have you. After being ushered into private conference, he made known his mission. He would no longer fight against Kim Kyu-sik and Yŏ but, rather, would join forces with them, the reason being that Rhee was "finished." Commented Chang, "Rhee's main fault is that he acts first and thinks later—if at all." If one wanted evidence of police partisanship, he need search no further than this frank confession.

On June 14, Yŏ visited Generals Brown and Shtykov, the heads of the American and Soviet delegations on the Joint Commission. He asked for the creation of an interim government without fail. Three days later, Kim Kyu-sik, Wŏn Se-hun, Yŏ Un-hyŏng, and a number of others announced a joint move on their part to concentrate political power in South Korea and to work out principles for the establishment of a Korean provisional government. On July 3, the first meeting of the so-called "Current Affairs Counter-Action Committee" was held at an undisclosed place in Seoul. Yŏ's political organization had disintegrated by this time by reason of continued rightist and Communist attack and American rebuffs. However, Yŏ's immediate personal following was doing its best to approach the problems of the day intelligently through study and thought, the fruits of which were to be submitted to the Joint Commission for its guidance in establishing a provisional government.

Although a threat to the Communists by reason of his liberal democratic convictions, Yŏ was no longer a challenge to their power. The right wing, however—currently doing its level best to destroy the Joint Commission in the hope that rightists might then be put in charge of a separate South Korean government of its own choosing—was plainly worried by the inroads Yŏ was making among the ranks of right-wing leaders. Rightist parties one after the other were splitting on the issue of supporting the Joint Commission. Both the Korean Democratic and Korean Independence parties had so split. Yŏ was picking up ground at the expense of Rhee and Kim Ku.

And then, a fatal bullet finally found its mark. On July 19, Yŏ Unhyŏng was shot and killed in Seoul by unknown assassins, the victim of the tenth plot against his life over the past two years. I leave it to the reader's judgment as to who had the greater motive for bringing about bis death—Dr. Rhee or Pak Hŏn-yŏng. The police and the American Command immediately charged the Communists with his murder. Regardless of whom the Korean police succeeded in convicting for Yŏ's death, Yŏ was gone, and with him died the vigorous hard-fighting core of Korean liberalism—almost before it had lived. Dr. Kim, Yŏ's close friend and colleague during those last tragic months, was old and sick and tired. Those who knew and understood wondered how long he could keep up the pace. Had the death knell of Korean liberalism been sounded with the untimely murder of Yŏ? (Using the hindsight of eleven years, one can only answer in the affirmative.)

Of significance was a July 8, 1947, meeting of the Christian Association in Seoul. Kim Ku had just spoken. Dr. Kim Kyu-sik, the following speaker, had been announced. A heated debate broke out as to whether the group should listen to Dr. Kim's scheduled address or not. The so-called Christians finally approved a hands-over-ears motion introduced by a brother who insisted that they not listen to any address by "that materialistic Dr. Kim." After the vote against him. Dr. Kim quietly retired.

Rhee at the Cross Roads

Dr. Syngman Rhee was facing a dilemma in the spring of 1947. It was fairly certain by then that the Joint Soviet–American Commission would reconvene, a tentative working agreement being then under discussion by the two powers concerned. Rhee's campaign for the establishment—either legally or by force—of a separate South Korean Government seemed doomed to failure if the Joint Commission succeeded. Rhee knew full well that the Russians would demand that he be barred from participation in any future Korean Government and that the Americans certainly would not be overly zealous in defending him in the light of past events. Rhee achieved a momentary gain from his alleged "successful diplomatic mission" to Washington, which according to his enthusiastic faithful, had resulted directly in the pending financial assistance to South Korea by the United States as well as the discussion of the Korean problem at the Fourth Meeting of the Council of Foreign Ministers in Moscow [March 10 to April 24, 1947].

However, Rhee's gain was short-lived. The financial assistance program was postponed until after the conclusion of the Soviet–American negotiations in Seoul. And the American stand at the Moscow Conference turned out to be far different from that desired by Rhee. In addition, American Military Government was taking steps during the spring of 1947 toward establishing a new legislative assembly, this one to be *wholly* elected on the basis of universal suffrage. There was considerable doubt as to whether Rhee's legislative delegation in this new body would be anything like its present strength—strength which was sufficient to prevent passage of any objectionable legislation, such as the confiscation of farmlands. Rhee thus faced three problems: (1) the unlikelihood of any American moves to establish a separate South Korean government or to render large-scale financial assistance to South Korea in the near future, (2) the reconvention of the Joint Soviet–American Commission on a basis not acceptable to him, and (3) moves by Military Government to establish a new legislative assembly which would threaten his control over that august body. What next?

On April 2, 1947, Rhee had announced that among the first acts upon his return to Korea would be a campaign for the passage by the Legislative Assembly of a universal suffrage law. Such a law would open up the way for a general election and the establishment of an interim government in South Korea. What Rhee actually envisioned was a separate South Korean Government. Yŏ had announced soon thereafter, on April 22, that while he supported the principle of universal suffrage the election should be carefully supervised so as to insure its fairness. In view of ever-present threat of police power, Yŏ was suspicious of Rhee's motives.

The Interim Legislative Assembly, however, was in no mood to vote itself out of existence regardless of what anyone might think. General Lerch recorded his impatience with the slothfulness of the Assembly in a sharply worded warning to the Assembly early in May 1947. If the Assembly did not pass a law calling for universal suffrage in selecting a new Assembly by July 31, Military Government would do so in the form of an ordinance, the Military Governor declared. At this juncture, Rhee, apparently reconciled to his fate, issued a laudatory statement on the subject. Said Rhee on May 9, "Let us lay aside for the time being the problem of the ... Provisional Government and concentrate, instead, on the forthcoming proposed general election ... We should have an election to form a government to constitute what will be the first step toward establishment of a united South-North Korean Government. As far as the ... Provisional Government is concerned, let us lay this problem aside unsettled, as it is possible for us to transfer its historic mission to a congress and government elected through popular representation. ... However, if our plan fails to materialize through any international interference, we can then fight under the above government's banner for our independence." Rhee was holding the door open for a rapid retreat. What would constitute "international interference" was left unexplained.

General Lerch again reiterated his impatience with the Legislative Assembly for not enacting a general election law so that Military Government could proceed with the establishment of an entirely elected body. He pointed out in a letter to Dr. Kim Kyu-sik, chairman of the Assembly, that in the course of a debate a few days previous in the United States Congress on the matter of assistance to the Greek and Turkish Governments, one Congressman had insisted that there be no help to either of those governments until the officials of the government had been selected by popular vote in a general election. The general concluded, "I hope that as soon as the matter of aid to the Greek and Turkish Governments is settled, the Congress will take up the matter of aid to the Korean Government. I do not want it possible to have objections raised to aid to Korea on the ground that its legislature is not elected." On the same day, Rhee warned that should the legislators fail to form a legitimate congress for "individual reasons, they would suffer blame for interfering with the restoration of the nation's sovereignty." Rhee was still thinking in terms of a separate and independent South Korean Government.

By this time, debate had begun in earnest in the Interim Legislative Assembly on the proposed general election law. Two sections of the proposed law very nearly broke up the Assembly. These had to do with qualifications for office seekers and minimum age requirements for voters. It was proposed that candidates who had held office or had gained financially an inordinate amount under the Japanese regime should be barred and that the minimum age requirements should be 20 years for voters and 25 for office seekers. The extreme rightists rose in indignation and demanded a less stringent qualifications provision and age minimums of 25 for voters and 30 for candidates. The move was designed to prevent the Korean youth—believed to be overwhelmingly leftist—from voting. Debate raged in the Assembly for a full month. Dr. Kim threatened to resign unless the lower age limits were adopted. Finally, the issue was settled by a compromise on age minimums of 23 and 25 for voting and candidacy, respectively. The stringent qualifications provision on the subject of Japanese collaboration was adopted, thanks to the pressure of public opinion. And with that, the general election law was passed.

Reaction was immediate and drastic. The Korean National Police demanded that General Hodge veto the measure on the grounds that it was "too partial and too strict" in reference to the Japanese collaborationist clauses which would ban many of the top police officials from public office. They did not wish to lose their jobs. The petition presented to General Hodge stated that were the new law put into operation in its present form, police all over South Korean would be ordered to oppose it. Several members of the Interim Legislature who had been instrumental in getting the measure passed requested permission to carry weapons for protection. Was this Rhee's way to squelch the proposed general election? Fortunately for the American Command, the entire issue could be shelved temporarily pending events in the Joint Soviet–American Commission, in session in Seoul since May 22.[80] But the issue remained unresolved.[81]

This strategy disposed of the general election threat for the time being. Dr. Rhee considered his other two problems: (1) the unlikelihood of any American moves to establish a separate South Korean government or to launch a large-scale financial assistance program to South Korea in the near future by reason of the Soviet–American negotiations on Korea, and (2) the reconvention of the Joint Commission on a basis not acceptable to him. His decision was, very simply, to wreck the Joint Commission so that the United States would be forced to pick up its plans to establish and finance a separate South Korea.

[80] A celebratory opening session had been held two days earlier.

[81] At the same time, the Interim Legislative Assembly debated and agreed upon a Special Ordinance on National Traitors, Pro-Japanese Collaborators, and Profiteers, which the Military Government vetoed. See p. 181, footnote 65.

CHAPTER VIII: ON THE HIGHER LEVEL

As previously recounted, the Joint Soviet–American Commission had risen from its first series of meetings on May 8, 1946, in complete disagreement. There had been no perceptible meeting of the minds.

By August 1946 an American letter had been dispatched northward to ask that the Soviet delegation reconsider its stand and resume negotiations. It was not until late in October that an answer was forthcoming. The Soviet Commander discussed the attitude of the Soviet delegation concerning the consultation of democratic parties and social organizations by the Joint Commission, the point upon which the Commission sessions had broken down. The Soviet Commander stated that he wished to resume negotiations and carry out fully the Moscow Decision. Although his letter recognized the right to freedom of expression on the part of Koreans in presenting their views to the Joint Commission, it did not recognize the right of Koreans to oppose the Moscow Decision or the work of the Joint Commission.

Compromise

An American letter dated November 1, 1946, reiterated the American position of allowing Koreans freedom of expression concerning the establishment of their own provisional government. However, it was agreed that the Joint Commission could exclude from consultation those individuals, parties, and organizations who fomented or instigated mass opposition to the work of the Joint Commission or to the fulfillment of the Moscow Decision. Korean rightists did not like the tone taken by this American note to the Soviet Commander—least of all, Dr. Rhee.

When the first exchange of correspondence on the subject was made public in November of 1946, Rhee must have realized that the Americans were conceding ground to the Russians, ground upon which the Joint Commission might one day reconvene. As a matter of fact, General Hodge commented publicly at the time, "Based upon my observations and discussions of the subject with Koreans for almost a year, I am convinced that those Koreans who oppose the 'trusteeship' provision in the Moscow Decision have a highly erroneous concept of what it means. ... I fear that many Koreans have never really studied the Moscow Decision and have greatly misinterpreted its terms." This must have sounded in Rhee's ears very much like rationalization for a new American stand on the subject of trusteeship. That a change had indeed taken place in the American view was confirmed when further inter-command correspondence was released in January 1947.

At that time, a Soviet letter of November 26 and an American reply of December 24, 1946, were made public. The Soviet letter proposed reopening the Joint Commission by resolving the political consultation issue as follows:

> 1. The Joint Commission must consult with those democratic parties and organizations which uphold fully the Moscow Decision.
>
> 2. Parties and social organizations invited for consultation with the Joint Commission must not nominate for consultation those representatives who have compromised themselves by actively voicing opposition to the Moscow Decision.
>
> 3. Parties and social organizations invited for consultation with the Joint Commission must not and will not voice opposition nor will they incite others to voice opposition to the Moscow Decision and the work of the Joint Commission. If such be the case, such parties and social organizations by mutual agreement of both delegations, will be excluded from further consultations with the Joint Commission.

The United States' answer of December 24 proposed certain modifications designed to further clarify the exclusion clause. The American counterproposals, sent over General Hodge's signature, were as follows:

> *Proposal No. 1*, to be interpreted as follows: Signing the declaration in Communique Number 5 will be accepted as a declaration of good faith with respect to upholding fully the Moscow Decision and will make the signatory party or organization eligible for initial consultation.
>
> *Proposal No. 2*, I consider it the right of a declarant party or organization to appoint the representative which it believes

> will best present to the Joint Commission its views on the implementation of the Moscow Decision. However, should such representatives for good reasons be believed to be antagonistic to the implementation of the Moscow Decision or to either of the Allied Powers, the Joint Commission may, after mutual agreement, require the declarant party to name a substitute spokesman.
>
> *Proposal No. 3*, it is suggested that it be reworded as follows: Individuals, parties and social organizations invited for consultation with the Joint Commission shall not after signing the declaration contained in Communique Number 5 foment or instigate active opposition to the work of the Joint Commission or to either of the Allied Powers or to the fulfillment of the Moscow Decision. Those individuals, parties, and social organizations which after signing the declaration contained in Communique Number 5 do foment or instigate active opposition to the work of the Joint Commission or to either of the Allied Powers or to the fulfillment of the Moscow Decision shall be excluded from further consultation with the Joint Commission. The decision excluding such individuals, parties, and social organizations shall be by agreement of the Joint Commission.

Coincident with the publication of these letters, a spokesman for the State Department declared that the trusteeship provisions of the Moscow Decision, to which the Koreans had reacted so violently, were now becoming "better understood." He went on to point out, "(The fact) is becoming more widely appreciated in Korea that the Allies who made the great sacrifices in breaking the power of Japan over Korea are, unlike the Japanese before them, committed by the Moscow pact to a limited period of control over Korea's destiny—up to five years."

Rhee's National Society for the Rapid Realization of Korean Independence quickly denounced this change in American views. Society spokesmen said that the contents of the American reply to the latest Soviet letter not only disregarded the will of the Korean people but also degraded the United States by reason of its inconsistent policy. Shortly thereafter, from Washington, Rhee accused General Hodge of supporting trusteeship and launched his campaign to force the general's dismissal or, failing that, to bring about the establishment of the Provisional Government as the legal government of an independent and separate South Korea.

By this time, the Moscow Conference of the Big Four Foreign Ministers had been announced. It was rumored that Korea would be a subject of discussion. In mid-February 1947, General Hodge left Korea suddenly for Washington. Actually, just prior to his departure a new letter from the Soviet Command in North Korea had arrived which virtually agreed with the American proposals transmitted in General Hodge's letter of December 24. Nevertheless, the general had no sooner arrived in Washington than he announced that further negotiations between the two commands appeared "hopeless." "I feel that I have done all I can on a local level," declared the general in Washington.[82]

Hodge further charged that Russian radio had carried reports that Koreans from 17 to 25 years of age were being drafted in North Korea. On the basis of a North Korean population of ten to eleven million, this mobilization could mean a North Korean army of 500,000. Dr. Rhee, likewise in Washington, took up this vein of thought and charged that the Russians were drilling and equipping 500,000 Korean troops in North Korea for incorporation into the Red Army. It will be noted that this was not what Hodge had said. Actually, the truth of the matter was still different. There were no intelligence reports which proved conclusively that a forced conscription of North Korean youth had ever been undertaken by the Russians or their Korean underlings. On the other hand, there was considerable evidence indicating that a North Korean army had been formed on the basis of voluntary enlistment. Nevertheless, the figure of 500,000 seemed exaggerated, for the most reliable American intelligence reports indicated a North Korean force of not over 200,000. General Hodge's apparent exaggerations may have had the purpose of scaring Dr. Rhee into a more cooperative attitude.

---

[82] Once in Washington, as noted by Robinson, Hodge reported that his attempts to come to terms with the Soviet Command in northern Korea did not succeed. U.S. newspapers actually carried that story on February 25, 1947, three days before General Chistiakov's mentioned letter to Hodge. We might thus understand the letter as a reaction to Hodge's attempt to blame the Soviets for the failing talks on Korean unification. For the correspondence between Hodge and Chistiakov, see *Korea's Independence* (Washington, DC: Government Printing Office, 1947), 20–32.

While in Washington General Hodge helped Secretary of State George C. Marshall pen a new American note on the subject of Korea, this one to be presented to Vyacheslav Molotov [1890–1986] during the impending Moscow Conference of the Big Four Foreign Ministers. When this news leaked out, Dr. Rhee added his views. "The Koreans consider themselves as an independent nation and are determined that their fate will be decided by themselves," he announced. He added that if the foreign ministers at Moscow attempted to decide Korea's future there would be "no guarantee that the Koreans will cooperate."

The American policy during this period was to assume the worst; namely, that no further progress would be made with the Russians toward eventual unification of North and South Korea. On that basis, the United States decided to proceed with the rehabilitation of South Korea. Dr. Rhee interpreted this policy as one moving towards a separate South Korean government. In the meantime, rumors of pending large-scale economic assistance to South Korea began to circulate. On March 10, 1947, Assistant Secretary of State John H. Hilldring [1895–1974] gave voice to the official American policy. After reviewing the general plight of Korea, he pointed out that a weak Korea, unable to sustain her own independence, "would be a fertile ground for some new disturbance by openly inviting rivalry for her control and, later, domination by some strong outside power." He went on to point out the unique and important nature of the Korean situation arising from the fact that "there, as nowhere else in the world, the United States and the Soviet Union face each other directly and with identical commitments. Here alone, we are mutually obligated by agreement to work out between ourselves the initial steps in establishing a free and independent state." The State Department spokesman continued, "In the United States zone, we have the opportunity to demonstrate to the Koreans, to the Russians, and to the rest of the world what American democracy can accomplish in rehabilitating the economic, social, and political life of a country impoverished by four decades of bondage." This and subsequent statements made it clear that the United States was determined to make South Korea a model for all of the Far East to behold. Unfortunately, South Korea was far from exemplary as a *New York Times* editorial in mid-March 1947 pointed out. "To lay the principal blame on Moscow, however, is not to exempt the United

States from its fair share of the blame for Korea's plight. From the first landing our occupation record in Korea has been one of confusion, delay, and neglect,"[83] declared the editorialist.

On the eve of the Moscow Conference of the Big Four Foreign Ministers, State Department officials stated that the United States had decided for the time being to give up its struggle to obtain Soviet cooperation in Korea and was preparing a long-range program for South Korea. The plan called for the expenditure of more money and for an all-elected Korean legislative assembly. Just how much money would be called for was not specified.

This development was what Rhee had been awaiting the past two months in Washington and no doubt motivated him in calling off further effort to establish the Provisional Government in office without consent of American authorities. There was also little doubt that Rhee considered himself as the most likely candidate to head any American-sponsored South Korean Government. He hurried off to Korea, stopping only long enough on the way to re-establish relations with Chiang Kai-shek. What Rhee did not know was that this publicity regarding a separate South Korean government and economic aid for South Korea was a strategic move by the United States designed to force the Soviet Union to reopen negotiations on the subject of Korea on a high level.

Meanwhile, the last letter from the Soviet Command in North Korea to General Hodge early in 1947 had remained unanswered because the U.S. desired a new international agreement before proceeding further on the local level. The Moscow Decision was felt to be too ambiguous for dealing with the literal-minded Russians. Furthermore, it was made clear by General Hodge and other authorities that United States troops could not evacuate South Korea until such time as the Moscow Decision had been fulfilled.

In April 1947 it became known that a change of Soviet Commanders in North Korea had occurred. General Korotkov [1898–1982], replacing General Chistiakov, entered the game for the Russians. The coaches in the Kremlin gave no reason, but many took it as an indication of an approaching change of policy on the part of the Soviet

[83] The quote is from a short piece titled "Help for Korea" on page 24 of the *New York Times*, March 19, 1947.

Union, the Russian strategy of picking a goat to explain away an error being a well-known one.

The Korean problem did not actually come up for debate at this new Moscow Conference, but formal notes between Marshall and Molotov were exchanged on the subject. Marshall's letter of May 2 outlined the situation:

> I have considered your letter of April 19, 1947, in which you accept our proposal to reconvene the U.S.–U.S.S.R. Joint Commission and suggest that the Commission resume its work on May 20 of this year. I have also noted your statement that resumption of the Commission's work shall be "on the basis of an exact execution of the Moscow Agreement on Korea."
>
> In order to avoid any future misunderstanding with respect to the phrase "exact execution" I wish to take clear my interpretation of the phrase. In my letter to you of April 8, I stated that the Joint Commission should be charged with expediting "its work under the terms of the Moscow Agreement on a basis of respect for the democratic right of freedom of opinion." In making this statement I had and have in mind the well-known position of the Government of the United States that Korean representatives of democratic parties and social organizations shall not be excluded from consultation with the Commission on the formation of a provisional Korean government because of opinions they might hold or may have expressed in the past concerning the future government of their country, provided they are prepared to cooperate with the Commission.
>
> You mention three points which the Soviet Government believes to be of primary importance in its policy towards Korea. Your statements concerning the importance of establishing a provisional democratic Korean government on the basis of widescale participation of Korean democratic parties and social organizations has from the beginning been accepted by the United States Government as basic to its policy of assisting in the establishment of a self-governing sovereign Korea, independent of foreign control and eligible for membership in the United Nations.

> I interpret your second point with respect to the establishment of "democratic authority agencies" throughout Korea as referring to local, provincial, and national government agencies chosen, as you state, by means of free elections on the basis of a general and equal electoral right.
>
> I welcome the assurance contained in your third point with regard to the importance you attach to aiding in the restoration of Korea as an independent democratic state and in the development of its national economy and national culture. The United States Government has under consideration a constructive program for the rehabilitation of the economy of Korea and for its educational and political development.
>
> In order that I may direct the United States commander in Korea to make preparations for opening the sessions of the Joint Commission in Seoul on May 20, 1947, may I receive an early confirmation that we are mutually agreed as to the basis on which the Commission shall resume its important work?
>
> I am furnishing copies of this letter to the governments of China and the United Kingdom.
>
> Please accept, Mr. Minister, assurance of my highest esteem.

The reference to the Korean economic rehabilitation program envisioned by the United States seemed something in the nature of a threat. The Soviet Union could either come in or stay out as it saw fit.

Molotov answered within the week. In so doing, he cited General Hodge's letter of December 24, 1946, giving the three American proposals for reconvening the Joint Commission, after which Molotov wrote, "To expedite the resumption of the work of the Joint Commission and the formation of the provisional Korean democratic government, I am ready to accept the above amendments proposed by the American Commander. I hope that, thus, there no longer exists any reasons for delaying the convening of the Joint Commission." On May 13, Marshall assured the Soviet Foreign Minister that there was no longer reason for delay and announced that he was instructing the American Commander in Korea to make immediate preparations for reconvening the Commission in Seoul. And with that, the scene shifts from Moscow to the Korean capital.

On May 15, 1947, the pending reconvention of the Joint Commission was announced officially. The following day, the proposed United States economic aid program for South Korea was shelved for the duration of the Commission sessions. There was small flurry just prior to the reopening of the Commission when the Soviet Command requested permission for a TASS reporter to accompany the Soviet delegation to cover the Commission sessions. General Hodge retaliated by asking permission for American newspapermen to accompany the American delegation to P'yŏngyang when the Commission proceeded to North Korea to consult with North Korean parties and organizations. To this, the Soviet Commander replied that such permission would be forthcoming for *one* correspondent. Before passing judgment, General Hodge referred the matter to the local American newspaper colony. The correspondents hashed it out and finally decided that it would be better to have one man in North Korea than none at all and so advised the general. However, Hodge saw fit to refuse permission to the TASS man and consequently no American press representative accompanied the Joint Commission when, at a later date, it adjourned to North Korea.

On May 22 the curtain was raised on the long-awaited reconvention of the Joint Commission. General Shtykov again headed the Soviet delegation. However, in place of General Arnold, who had headed the American delegation at the initial session, was General Brown. In the first meeting, General Hodge rose to greet the Russians. Said the general in part: "It is agreed in correspondence between our nations that the Joint Commission shall carry out the provisions of the Moscow Decision working under the principles of democratic freedom of expression and opinion. The American delegation, headed by General Brown, has been so instructed. The first and most pressing task of the Joint Commission is the establishment of a Provisional Korean government for all Korea ..." General Shtykov rose and replied, declaring in part, "We are certain that on the basis of the fulfillment of the Moscow Decision, Korea will develop along democratic lines and become an independent state and will join the family of the peace-loving nations as an equal member." So far, so good.

However, On May 23, the first blunder was pulled. This time it was James K. Penfield [1908–2004], a State Department advisor to the American delegation on the Joint Commission and a personal representative of Secretary of State Marshall. At a meeting of Dr. Rhee's Representative Democratic Council, Penfield declared that Koreans might denounce trusteeship when a Korean Provisional Government was set up and, therefore, that it was quite probable that trusteeship could be avoided. From the Soviet point of view, negotiations were right back where they had been left a year before. How that statement by Penfield could be reconciled with the following statement made by Assistant Secretary of State Hilldring in March, less than three months before, was left unexplained: "In brief, this agreement [the Moscow Decision][84] provided for setting up a four-power trusteeship, which, during a period of not more than five years, would guide and protect the people of Korea and prepare them for membership in the United Nations." Furthermore, in the Molotov–Marshall correspondence the United States had agreed that resumption of the Joint Commission's work should be "on the basis of an exact execution of the Moscow Agreement on Korea," providing that such execution did not abridge the freedom of expression of any group agreeing to cooperate with the Commission. How a group could agree to cooperate with the Joint Commission charged with implementing the Moscow Decision and, at one and the same time, oppose a trusteeship which was imposed by the Moscow Decision—according to Hilldring's own statement—defied logic. And yet, that was the American stand, according to Penfield. Little wonder that the Russians accused the Americans of double talk.

Even so, Penfield's statement had failed to convince Messrs. Rhee and Kim Ku. It was soon apparent that they were doing their level best to break up the Joint Commission.

Sabotage

On May 20, two days before the Joint Soviet–American Commission reconvened in Seoul, Rhee announced that his group could not attend the Joint Commission without amendment of the trusteeship clause in the Moscow Decision of 1945. Two days later, Kim Ku and Rhee issued a joint statement demanding clear definitions of the words "trusteeship" and "democracy" as used in the Moscow Decision. It was pointed out that trusteeship and independence were incompatible, and further,

[84] The bracketed insertion in this quote is in Robinson's original typescript.

that the Soviet and United States Governments held different concepts of democracy. The two revolutionists inquired as to which type of democracy would be used in Korea and commented that if both ideologies were included in the future Korean government it would be hopelessly split by internal conflict. That there was considerable merit in these arguments could not be disputed. If the discussion had been kept on that level, there would have been no objection from the Americans. However, four days later, May 24, the State Department felt compelled once again to deny rumors being spread by Rhee among official circles in Seoul that he had been given secret assurances by the State Department that a separate South Korean government would be established. Obviously, such statements would make the Russian delegation sitting on the Joint Commission more leery than ever of American motives in South Korea. The next day, Rhee vigorously denied that he had stated anywhere at any time that there existed a *secret* agreement between the State Department and himself. However, in his denial he made it quite clear that an *open agreement* had been reached whereby the United States would declare an independent South Korean government as soon as the Interim Legislative Assembly adopted an election law and a general election was held. "No one can deny the act that spokesmen of the United States Department of State in Washington agreed to this plan and General Hodge will tell you that he openly agreed to support it," stated Dr. Rhee angrily. In affect he had called everyone from the Secretary of State and General Hodge on down an out-and-out liar.

In the meantime, Rhee's political fences were being mended. He would need all the forces he could muster if he were to torpedo the sessions of the Joint Commission successfully, thereby forcing the Americans to treat South Korea as a separate entity. All rightist "youth" associations announced on May 23 that they would band together in a single organization under General Chi Ch'ŏng-ch'ŏn. General Chi had been commander-in-chief of the Korean Kwangbok Army in Nationalist China which had been recruited and organized by Kim Ku's Provisional Government upon request of Chiang Kai-shek. General Chi had returned from Chongqing to Korea in the company of Dr. Rhee on April 21, 1947 and since that time had been busily at work effecting a merger of rightist "youth." Essentially, it was a military organization under trained and experienced military leadership. And this was not all.

Late in May of 1947 a group of visiting American newspapermen by chance dropped into the Korean National Youth Corps [Chosŏn Minjok Ch'ŏngnyŏndan] training center situated in the ancient walled town of Suwŏn, some thirty miles due south of Seoul. What they learned could scarcely be believed if it were not for the fact that at least three highly reliable American witnesses reported similarly. The story was essentially this. For the past year, under American Military Government auspices, the Korean National Youth Corps had been training "youth" (ages 18 to 30) in the ways of patriotism. An American Army officer, Lieutenant Colonel Ernest E. Voss [1895–1969], had been appointed to direct the movement. (In the *Far East Stars and Stripes Weekly Review* for June 15, 1947, it was stated quite frankly that the Association had been born under the official sponsorship of the United States Army Military Government.)[85] The head of this movement was "General" Yi Pŏm-sŏk, formerly, the second-in-command of Kim Ku's Kwangbok Army. As of July 1947, some 70,000 men had received training at the Suwŏn training center. The objective by the end of 1947 was 100,000, according to official releases. American Military Government had contributed some five million yen to the movement and several times that amount in equipment. The Suwŏn training center was actually the officer candidate school for a *rightist* army. Cadres of these men had been sent to all areas of South Korea to recruit and train subordinate groups of Korean "youth."

The head of the Suwŏn training center, the visiting press men found, was a German-speaking Korean who had been a resident of Germany from 1931 to 1935 and an open admirer of the Hitler Youth movement.[86] The group of American correspondents were greeted

---

[85] In an earlier article of February 23, 1947, p. 2, the paper already stated that "the movement was started by the military government authorities" in March 1946.

[86] This was the fascist Kang Se-hyŏng (aka Sche-Hyong Kang, Sze Hyong Kang, 1899–1960). During the late Weimar and early Nazi period he was a student and Korean language lecturer at Berlin University. Kang's main interest, both during colonial times and after liberation, was indeed the introduction of Hitlerjugend-style education and organizational structures to Korea and the Korean community in Japan. Mark Gayn also discusses the Nazi-style cadre school and U.S. funding thereof. In Gayn's diary entry of November 7, 1946, Kang Se-hyŏng is referred to as one of Yi Pŏm-sŏk's "right-hand men." See also Hoffmann, in this volume, 465.

with, "Sprechen Sie Deutsch?" During the ensuing conversation, the school director admitted that the Association was patterned after the *Hitler Jugend* [aka Hitlerjugend], and that the objective was to train a Korean army to perpetuate the "glorious traditions of the Kwangbok Army." The school was strictly "non-political," the director claimed, but went on to say that Kim Ku was a regular lecturer. He also volunteered the information that though the recruits came in with various political ideas, they all graduated with the same.

This was Military Government's answer to the Communist threat. It was an army of 100,000 South Koreans led by the most brutal and opportunistic elements of the extreme right. To this force could be appended approximately 25,000 South Korean policemen and a few thousand Coast Guardsmen and constabulary men. This last group was the official "internal security" force (administered by the Department of Security in the American Military Government) of South Korea, but in reality, it served merely as a shield to hide the real South Korean Army, the National Youth Corps.

When all of this was reported in *Time* magazine (June 30, 1947),[87] XXIVth Corps and Military Government public relations offices went into a dither. A few days after the story broke, XXIVth Corps Public Relations Officer commented to me with a worried frown, "This will set our public relations in the United States back at least twelve months." He then admitted that he could issue no denial for the story was true. However, Military Government saw fit to lie its way out by denying the veracity of the account. Both General Yi Pŏm-sŏk and the head of the Suwŏn training center denied they had ever made the statements attributed to them. The Korean National Youth Corps was purely a patriotic movement designed to train the Korean youth in the ways of good citizenship, the authorities chorused. The fact remained that it was a rightist army, well trained and armed. And U.S. army officers had been involved.

The Korean middle-of-the-road liberals were fully aware of this apparent duplicity on the part of the American Command. They saw American public support for their efforts on the one hand and Ameri-

[87] Robinson refers to an article by the photojournalist Carl Mydans (1907–2004), "Korea: A Scout Is Militant," *Time* 49, no. 26 (June 30, 1947): 25–26. See also fig. 32 on p. 463 in this volume.

can efforts to create an organization to destroy them on the other. And listening in were the Russians.

During the last week in May 1947, Dr. Rhee told American correspondents, "More good can come to Korea if this present joint conference breaks down than if it comes to agreement. I shall be misunderstood if I put it that bluntly, but those are my convictions. If I were General Hodge, and especially in view of President Truman's new policy, I would not waste time talking to the Russians. At a moment's notice my people will demonstrate to a man if I raise my voice." On June 18, Dr. Rhee declared publicly that the Joint Commission would create a "chop suey government, neither clear-cut Communist nor clear-cut American type of democracy." Rhee went on to tell newsmen that the two powers occupying Korea should let the Koreans establish a government "their own way." "If the Koreans make a mess of it in two or three years, then the big powers should step in," he declared, knowing full well that once Korea was cleared of Allied forces that it was very doubtful if any would return—at least, United States forces. Dr. Rhee's stand made sense only on the basis of one of two assumptions: (1) that he was in league with the Russians and the Korean Communists or (2) that he was presupposing war between the Soviet Union and the United States. Otherwise, his views were contrary to both his own interests and those of an independent Korea. The idea that if the Americans cleared out of South Korea he could somehow come to terms with the Russians was naïve in the extreme. Rhee, of all people, was the most unlikely candidate for Soviet cooperation.

On June 20, the Anti-Trusteeship Strife Committee announced its absolute adherence to the line taken by Dr. Rhee and Kim Ku. The Committee pledged its absolute renunciation of trusteeship and its decision not to participate in the Joint Commission consultation. And with this, right-wing parties began to split over the issue, the more extreme elements voting to follow the non-cooperation stand taken by Dr. Rhee—this, in spite of the warning from the Chief of the American Delegation to the Joint Commission that "a few Korean leaders" who were hesitating to support the Commission faced "the loss of their following to more thoughtful leaders."

The right-wing extremists made one more stab to disrupt the Joint Commission proceedings, this time with a show of force. On June 24, Sŏ Yun-bok [1923–2017], the Korean marathon runner, returned from his Boston victory to receive a tumultuous welcome in Seoul. During the ensuing ceremonies conducted in front of the Capitol Building some unknown person shouted "anti-trusteeship" into the microphones which were broadcasting the affair over a nation-wide hookup. This interruption appeared to be a prearranged signal for anti-trusteeship demonstrations throughout the country. In Seoul, they were already under way. Several thousand people, excited to a frenzied pitch by pamphlets and loudspeakers, gathered in front of the gates to the Tŏksu Palace where the Joint Commission was in session. The Korean police and United States Military Police managed to disperse the crowds temporarily, but not until mud and stones had been hurled at the Soviet delegation as it drove through the Palace gates. Later in the day, still larger groups of demonstrators collected. American Army tanks and armored cars were called out to patrol the streets and keep the demonstration in order. During the afternoon of that uneasy day, a student delegation of three visited General Brown at the Tŏksu Palace. They demanded the recognition of "an independent government to be established by Kim Ku." They declared passionately that they would murder "various individuals" if trusteeship were forced upon them.

The American Command, through General Brown, immediately denounced the disorders and their purpose. The Russians protested the outrage committed against them at the Palace gates. Other demonstrations flared up sporadically in scattered communities throughout South Korea, but the failure of the anti-trusteeship leaders to secure the mass support on which they had counted indicated that the Korean people were more and more pinning their hopes on the success of the Joint Commission. Clearly, they preferred a united Korea rather than an independent South Korea under Rhee.

During the early summer, American intelligence agents had picked up disturbing rumors and scraps of information which, when pieced together, seemed to indicate that Rhee and Kim Ku were planning further violence. General Hodge was finally moved to send open letters to the two Korean leaders. In part, the general wrote to Rhee, "I have information purporting to come from the inner circles of your political organization that you and Kim Ku are planning terroristic activities and disruptions of the Korean economy at an early date as a protest measure against the work of the Joint Commission." Rhee promptly denied that he and Kim Ku were doing anything of the sort and declared publicly that the general's accusation once again confirmed his "misgivings" that the American Commander in Korea would "never understand the Korean people and their leaders." Kim Ku quickly echoed this vein of thought. (Incidentally, the letters sent to the American Command by the two men were composed on the same typewriter. One suspects that Kim's letter was written for him.) A few days later a mass meeting of right-wing leaders protested General Hodge's charges, demanded that General Brown either withdraw his statement that the Soviet delegation had been pelted with stones and mud during the anti-trusteeship demonstration or submit evidence to prove the veracity of the report, and insisted upon the release of several right-wing leaders who had been jailed for inciting the demonstration. It had been announced previously by Civil Administrator An Chaehong that outdoor political demonstrations or rallies would be forbidden during the Commission sessions. Later, right-wing leaders demanded that the American Command name its informant in Rhee's inner circle. The Americans maintained a discreet silence.

In mid-July Rhee defied the Joint Commission by publicly urging the establishment of a Korean Government, either as a successor to the Provisional Government or as appointed by an executive committee to be selected. The status of such a government would be merely a transitional one until an election could be held, Rhee declared. Referring to the preference expressed in some circles for the formation of a Korean government through the Joint Commission, Rhee commented, "We believe that we should do with our own hands that which should be done by us without relying upon others. If the results of the Joint Commission are in accordance with our expectations, then we can give up our plans to set up a government. On the other hand, if the results do not prove satisfactory to us, it is better that we go our own way." The fact that the overwhelming bulk of political parties had indicated a desire to cooperate with the Joint Commission by this time was no deterrent to Rhee's plans.

Stalemate

Despite Rhee's efforts, the Joint Commission seemed to be making some progress. In fact, it seemed as though Rhee was destroying himself politically in the eyes of his Korean countrymen as well as in those of the Russians and Americans. He was banking everything on the failure of the Commission. As long as progress was being made, his stock was down. From the liberals of the moderate right and moderate left and, of course, from the Communist-controlled left came a flood of statements pledging wholehearted support to the work of the Commission. The Coalition Committee added its voice to those of the other well-wishers by saying, "The successful establishment of a unified democratic provisional government in Korea on the basis of the Moscow Decision reached at the Three Ministers' Conference in 1945 is our sole objective." Dr. Kim Kyu-sik optimistically predicted that the Commission would achieve its objective. He went on to state that all true patriots of Korea would cooperate unanimously with the Joint Commission in order to achieve complete freedom for Korea. This was, in effect, a backhanded jab at Rhee. Yŏ Un-hyŏng likewise enthusiastically endorsed the work of the Commission.

Nevertheless, the American Command did not see fit to consult the Coalition Committee as to the American stand at the Commission until June 18, almost a month after the Commission had reconvened. Commented General Brown when reminded that it would be wise to discuss matters with the Coalition Committee, "We haven't got time to talk with Korean politicians." *Therefore, the American delegation sat on the Joint Commission without once having conferred with its own Korean advisory group.* It is little wonder that feelings were deeply wounded by this snub, and the Coalition Committee lost considerable prestige in the public eye.

Within a week after the Commission had gotten down to work on May 22, agreement had been reached as to procedure. The initial stage of the work was limited to the study of plans towards establishing a provisional government. Three sub-committees were set up to work simultaneously on three different phases of the task; namely, the question of consulting Korean political parties, the structure of the future Korean government, and the problems relative to the composition of the government. Each sub-committee was to be presided over alternately by a Russian and an American. Agreement had also been reached on the subject of press releases. The rules adopted previously in the 1946 session had been modified so that unilateral statements could be made provided no "secret" information was given out.

As the sub-committees went to work, the same old reefs were quickly struck and thereon the Commission stuck fast. The problem of consulting political parties was again the issue. The Russians continued to insist that those leaders or groups participating in the anti-trusteeship campaign should not be consulted and, by implication, not allowed to participate in the future Korean government. The Americans, on the other hand, insisted that all groups should be included which signed the statement included in Joint Communique Number 5 declaring their intent to cooperate with the Commission and abide by its decisions.

While this debate was going on, plans were being developed for consulting with the political parties and social organizations for North and South Korea. On June 13, 1947, Joint Communique Number 11 was issued by the Commission which outlined the procedure for consultation. At this point, it should be noted that no agreement had been reached as to which political parties would be received for oral consultation before the Commission or allowed to participate in the future government. However, it had been agreed that the initial step in consultation could be taken. Thereupon, all groups which signed the pledge to cooperate with and support the Commission were asked to fill in a questionnaire having to do with the manifold problems with which the future Korean government would be confronted and the methods for establishing such a government.

Contained in Joint Communique Number 11 were three documents: "The Method of Consultation with Korean Democratic Parties and Social Organizations in Northern and Southern Korea," a questionnaire on the "Structure and Principles of the Provisional Korean Democratic Government," and a second questionnaire on the "Political Platform of the Future Provisional Korean Democratic Government." The first of these, the document on consultation, set forth in detail the conditions for consultation and the procedure and schedule to be followed by the parties and organizations in submitting applications and in filling out the questionnaires. All parties and organizations were asked to make known their views regarding the provisional government and its platform through their central organs only so that a single set of answers would be filed for each group. Applications for consultation, including the signed pledge to abide by the decisions of the Commission, were required to be in the hands of the Commission secretariat, either in Seoul or P'yŏngyang, by June 23. Answers to questionnaires were called for by July 1.

Within twenty-four hours, more than eighty political parties and social organizations in South Korea had sent representatives to the Tŏksu Palace requesting the necessary documents and forms. Extreme rightists under Dr. Rhee and Kim Ku had made it painfully clear by this time that they would have nothing to do with the Commission. All in all, 463 political parties and social groups signed the required declaration and submitted applications for consultation. Of these 425 were from the American zone of occupation in South Korea and 38 from Korea north of the 38th parallel in the Soviet zone. Although Koreans both north and south of the parallel were asked to submit applications under identical conditions, there was a sharp contrast between the lists of applicants from the two zones.

All organizations in the North listed themselves as members of the National Front and as affiliated with the North Korean People's Committee, the organ of central government in the North. The groups applying from South Korea represented all shades of political opinion. More than two-thirds of the South Korean applicants were of the right, middle-of-the-road, or moderate left. Less than twenty-five percent admitted affiliation with the Communist-controlled Democratic National Front, as measured by both numbers of organizations and total membership claimed. Applicants from South Korea represented a broad cross-section of Korean society, including 39 political parties, 101 civil organizations, 54 cooperative, economic and business associations, 43 professional, scientific, and technical societies, 40 cultural groups, 35 labor unions, 34 young men's organizations, 31 religious bodies, 19 relief and welfare agencies, 15 farmers' unions and agricultural associations, and 14 women's societies. The North Korean list included three political parties, 18 labor unions, five cultural groups, three religious organizations, two welfare groups, two civic organizations, and one each of the following: farmers' union, consumers' cooperative, and women's, youth, and technical associations. The claimed membership of all 463 organizations applying for consultation totaled about 70 million, of whom only some 14 million were from North Korea. In view of the fact that the total population in South Korea was but 18 million—the overwhelming majority of which were politically inactive—the claimed membership of 56 million for South Korea was an amusing one, even assuming large overlapping memberships.

A July 12, 1947, press release from the American delegation on the Joint Commission charged that the "large number of applications stemmed in part from the Soviet refusal to agree to any definition regarding political parties and social organizations, or to any limitation on applications with respect to membership or types of organizations." Of the 463 applicants for consultation, 435 submitted answers to the questionnaires concerning the provisional charter and political platform of the future Korean government by the July 5 deadline—moved up from July 1. This posed a tiresome job of translation and tabulation for the Commission staff.

In naming their representatives for consultation, two political parties had presented an interesting dilemma for both the Soviet and American Commands. The Chosŏn Democratic Party of South Korea (distinct from the Korean Democrats) named as its representative Cho Man-sik, the North Korean leader who had opposed Soviet polices and had been placed under house arrest early in 1946 in a P'yŏngyang hotel. At the same time, the Democratic National Front, likewise of South Korea, had selected as its delegate Pak Hŏn-yŏng, the South Korean Communist leader who had been under warrant for arrest by order of General Hodge since early September of 1946.

The curtain rang up on the oral consultation with political parties and social organizations on June 25. A total of 425 Korean delegates were present for the impressive ceremony in the legislative chamber of the Capital Building in Seoul. On the dais sat Generals Brown and Shtykov. Below them were seated the other members of the Joint Commission. General Brown spoke explaining what had been accomplished and what remained to be done. Said the general in part, "This meeting is the first formal step towards oral consultation with the leaders of Korean democratic parties and social organizations. Such consultation will be carried out in the best democratic traditions in order that the voice of the people may be given paramount consideration in the creation of a provisional government. Inasmuch as the people make known their desires through parties and organization, the importance and seriousness of the task of their designated representatives is very great." It was explained that it would be impossible for the Joint Commission as a whole to consult with each representative and that, therefore, sub-committees would be formed to expedite the work. Oral consultation was to deal specifically with necessary explanation or elaboration of the written answers submitted on the questionnaires. Representatives invited for oral consultation were to be notified of the time and place of consultation. And with that, General Shtykov rose and closed the meeting.

A few days later, the performance was repeated in P'yŏngyang for benefit of North Korean groups, but not without certain bizarre circumstances. When the American delegation arrived in P'yŏngyang, only Russian officials were on hand to meet it at the station. No Koreans were in sight. The streets were deserted, and shops were closed. Russian movie cameras whirred away recording the "welcome" accorded the Americans. Later, it was learned that upon the arrival of the Soviet delegates several days earlier, a lively demonstration had been staged, likewise duly recorded by camera. Prior to the American arrival orders had been issued clearing the streets of all Koreans. American personnel were permitted to move freely throughout P'yŏngyang although shadowed everywhere by Korean police. To the amusement of local onlookers, the Americans annoyed their persistent pursuers by photographing them or hiding in doorways and whistling at them. The North Korean police were kept busily occupied shooing curious folk away when Americans paused to take photographs. The North Koreans were generally friendly toward the American visitors and obviously curious, but hesitated to be seen with them when police were present. On one occasion, several Americans browsed through a small bookstore in which a considerable stock of Soviet literature was for sale. The Americans made several purchases, but as they turned to leave, they were accosted by plain-clothes North Korean policemen and a Soviet agent. The books were seized and minutely examined, apparently to ascertain if they contained any secret messages. Finding nothing, the officials handed the books back, and the Americans went about their business. Learning of the Soviet literature for sale, other Americans frequented the shop later on that same day. The following morning the shop was found boarded up and the proprietor in jail, no doubt under suspicion of espionage. General Brown, in a press statement thanking the Soviet Command for its courtesies, half-humorously mentioned that the security of the Americans was at all times "assured by North Korean Police and armed Soviet escorts."

During the stay in North Korea, American delegates met and talked with a number of North Korean political leaders. Most of them simply parroted stereotype phrases. By July 7 both delegations had returned to Seoul and regular Commission sessions were again under way. General Brown, in a unilateral statement to the press, announced that despite continuous debate for over five weeks no formula had been found to harmonize the Soviet and American views on the principle of broad consultation of Korean groups. The practical application of the principles had led to Soviet objections to certain parties and organizations, objections which had not yet been resolved. Those certain parties and organizations were the anti-trusteeship bloc in South Korea, some of whom had signed the declaration to cooperate with the Commission.

In the meantime, the Commission turned its attention to the answers which had been received on the questionnaires. These could be divided roughly into three distinct camps of political thought—right, left, and moderate—on the basis of the following three subjects: (1) appropriate name for the country, (2) principles of government, and (3) the method of establishing the provisional government and administrative organization. Those holding rightist views wished the country to be called the Taehan Min'guk (Republic of Korea), desired a division of government into executive, legislative, and judicial branches, and urged establishment of a government by general election which would include choice of a president. Those inclined to the left proposed that the nation be called the Chosŏn Inmin Konghwaguk (People's Republic of Korea) and the government be established "according to the proposals of representatives of individual parties and social organizations." The left agreed with the right as to desirability of separating the governmental powers into three branches. Moderate parties favored "Republic of Korea" as the name of the new country and otherwise agreed with the rightist suggestions.

The basic and all-important problem of land reform brought a sharp split. Leftists and moderates favored confiscation of former Japanese-owned farmlands and the holdings of the large Korean landlords without compensation and free distribution of that land to tenant farmers. The rightists favored land reform but demanded just remuneration for confiscated land and payment by the tenants.

The Joint Commission, however, was at a standstill. The ship was stuck on the same rock on which it had originally foundered. No agreement could be reached as to which Korean political groups and social organizations were qualified for participation in the Commission activities. The Russians still insisted upon the exclusion of those groups and leaders in South Korea which had participated in the anti-trusteeship movement even though they might sign the required declaration pledging support of the Joint Commission. The Americans insisted with equal vigor that these admittedly anti-trusteeship groups should be consulted, a view which was hopelessly illogical for reasons already discussed, e.g., because the United States had already committed itself to a Korean trusteeship. The date for oral consultation with Korean politicos was indefinitely postponed, but the delegations continued to sit in Seoul and stare at one another. Neither delegation seemed to care to assume the responsibility for actually moving for adjournment. The discussions continued into the summer. The Joint Commission even found itself unable to agree upon the text of an explanation to the other two powers involved—Great Britain and China—of why no decision had been forthcoming and no further steps taken toward establishing the provisional democratic Korean government called for by the Moscow Decision of 1945. A heavy cloak of hopelessness and futility settled down over the forlorn people of Korea.

CHAPTER IX: NORTH AND SOUTH KOREA, A COMPOUND TRAGEDY

Except as it bore on political events, little had been said thus far relative to actual administration of government in the two zones of occupation. Suffice to say at the outset that both were bad, both being designed to further short-run Soviet and American national interests first and those of Korea second, public statements to the contrary notwithstanding. American Military Government in the South was out to stop any infiltration of Soviet ideology. The Soviet-sponsored government in North Korea was designed primarily to suppress an influx of American influence. It was probably safe to say that neither administration, if it had been transplanted to its homeland, would have been tolerated for long—at least, one liked to think so. To judge the Soviet Union by the miserable record in North Korea was as fair as to judge the United States for the ghastly fiasco perpetrated in South Korea under the name of American democracy. Neither was a fair test. When it was announced in 1947 that the State Department would soon assume direct responsibility for all civil affairs in Korea, thereby replacing the War Department, one American observer in Korea commented, "Well, there is one consolation; things couldn't be any worse." (The actual transfer of authority took place on August 8, 1947.)

What the Russians Did

Countless sensational newspaper accounts have been written on the subject of Soviet activities in North Korea behind the iron curtain which dropped into place with a resounding crash in August 1945. The approach here will be a little more moderate, being based entirely upon personal observations, interviews with North Koreans, and upon American intelligence reports. There is no doubt that the Soviet administration was harsh and unjust in much that it did. Being no apologist for the Soviet Union, I make that charge at the outset. With the same breath, however, I would hasten to condemn the American administration in South Korea on the same basis and almost as vigorously. Both regimes offended a democrat's sense of justice and humanity, not to mention intelligence.

When the Red Army arrived in North Korea in August 1945 People's Committees associated with Yŏ Un-hyŏng's Korean People's Republic were in control of the situation, just as they were in South Korea. While the Americans refused to have anything to do with this erstwhile grassroots government, the Russians realized the potentialities of the situation. The Japanese administration was promptly ousted, and the People's Committees were taken over as organs of local government. As soon as plans could be completed, Communists infiltrated into those committees of a non-Communist nature and eventually took control. Within a very few months, the People's Committees in North Korea became Communist-dominated in every sense of the word. The process of communization was complete by February 9, 1946, when the first central government was set up, the Interim

People's Committee of North Korea. By this time, organized political opposition had been eliminated through fair means or foul.

The story of North Korean politics can be told in terms of three names: Kim Il Sung, Kim Tu-bong, and Cho Man-sik. The first of these, "General" Kim Il Sung, was of vague origin.[88] It was suspected by many—and on the basis of considerable evidence—that he was a Soviet citizen, not Korean. The first anyone heard of the general was during the last year of World War II as the leader of a Korean guerrilla band in southern Manchuria. When the Red Army came marching down through Manchuria, he joined forces with it and was the first Korean leader of note to appear in North Korea. Upon arrival in P'yŏngyang in mid-August 1945, he announced bluntly by radio—with apparent Soviet sponsorship—that his group had been fighting the Japanese a long time and now the Korean people would obey his orders. For a time, the Korean people appeared to confuse him with the original General Kim Il-sŏng who fought in the mountains of North Korea against the Japanese invader many years before. This older general had achieved in the early twenties a legendary fame comparable to a Korean Robin Hood. He had then faded into oblivion. It was said that though the Japanese had closed in on his mountain hideout he had escaped to Manchuria. One school of thought suggested that the general carried a young son in his arms during his flight to Manchuria, and the North Korean leader of the same name was that son. Another point of view was that all of the original general's lieutenants took the name of Kim Il-sŏng to bewilder the Japanese pursuers, and the present leader was one of these young lieutenants. However, no one with whom I talked, or who wrote on the subject, claimed to recognize this new General Kim II Sung as ever having been in Korea before. It was known that he spoke excellent Russian and not-so-good

---

[88] Robinson's short biographical sketch of the later DPRK leader, which he himself acknowledged to be in part based on some "vague" speculation, reflects the standard South Korean and U.S. depictions of Kim until well into the 1970s. Kim's name adaptation was actually not unusual for independence and communist activists during those years. Later studies also clarify in detail how Kim had been a young but major anti-Japanese guerrilla leader in the Chinese North-East (which was after liberation, of course, blown out of proportion in North Korea). Because of the growing military dominance of the Kwantung Army, at the end of 1940 he and his remaining men were forced to retreat to Soviet Far Eastern territory, where they joined the Red Army.

Korean. He admitted having attended the Leningrad Officer Academy and having been cited by Stalin for his fight against Japanese imperialism. He was, in 1945, 33 years old—obviously much too young to be the old general himself. Nonetheless, the young general appeared in February 1946 as the head of the Interim People's Committee of North Korea.

A second member of the North Korean trio was "General" Kim Tu-bong. For some years before the war, he had been the rallying point for Koreans in North China—specifically, Yan'an—who wished to fight against the Japanese for the independence of Korea.[89] It was reported on good authority that he had held a general's commission with Mao Zedong's [head of state 1949–1959] Chinese Communist forces. When the Russians marched into North Korea, he soon followed with his Yan'an Korean Independence Alliance. There was no love lost between Kim Tu-bong and Kim Il Sung, the former being reported as a sincere Korean patriot first, a Communist second—if at all. Actually, there was considerable doubt whether he was actually a Communist Party member even as late as mid-1947. But the Russians were forced to permit him a position of leadership by reason of his powerful organization and tremendous prestige. While Kim Il Sung was a virtual unknown in North Korea before being shoved forward by the Russians, Kim Tu-bong was a hero to young and old alike, a living legendary figure. Kim Tu-bong's forces were augmented after his arrival in North Korea by many of Kim Wŏn-bong's following from Nationalist China. It will be remembered that Kim Wŏn-bong had accepted the post of War Minister in the cabinet of Kim Ku's Provisional Government upon the request of Chiang Kai-shek, a post which he soon renounced after returning to South Korea.

The third major North Korean leader was Cho Man-sik, founder of the Chosŏn Democratic Party, quite distinct from the ultraconservative Korean Democratic Party of South Korea. The Chosŏn Dem-

[89] A key Soviet asset, Kim Tu-bong became nominal head of state in 1948. North Korean sources did not, in fact, refer to Kim as a "general"; he had been the political leader of the (Yan'an) North China Korean Independence Alliance rather than commander of its armed wing. Much of his prestige instead stemmed from his scholarship: by the 1920s he was already a leading linguist, known for his work on language reform, the Korean alphabet, and grammar. By the standards of traditional Confucian society, which still persisted, a professional, Soviet-style revolutionary and political cadre—which Kim Il Sung epitomized—was a social role that continued to lack popular legitimacy.

ocratic Party was originally a moderate, perhaps slightly left-of-center group. Cho had great popular prestige, probably greater than any other North Korean. Russians wisely left him more or less alone during the first few months of occupation, content to infiltrate their puppets slowly into the hierarchy of Cho's party. The crisis finally came when Cho refused to support the trusteeship provision in the Moscow Decision, but neither did he violently oppose it. Nonetheless, this attitude was counter to Soviet policy and brought the matter of Cho's status to a head. Despite his prestige, Cho was placed in "protective custody" in a P'yŏngyang hotel. From February 1946 on he was under 24-hour-a-day guard by Russian soldiers. Strangely enough, the Russians granted permission to American officials to talk to him on several occasions. There was no indication that he was being maltreated.[90] Perhaps the Russians awaited the day when their incessant propaganda designed to smear his reputation would have so destroyed his popular prestige that the Soviet puppets could feel that he might be disposed of safely. As of mid-1947, Cho still wiled away the hours in his hotel room. Most of his lieutenants had long since fled to South Korea. The tragedy was that most of them had sold out to the extreme right, leaving Cho with but little organized support.

These were the big three of North Korean politics. It was reported that Kim Tu-bong of North Korea and Kim Wŏn-bong of South Korea were closely allied and had agreed to join forces in the event that North and South Korea were unified. This could have only meant that Kim Tu-bong would throw off the Soviet harness and Kim Wŏn-bong, the control imposed on him by the Communists in South Korea. Both men intensely disliked Pak Hŏn-yŏng, the Korean Communist leader. If North and South Korea had been unified, possibly these two men would have emerged as the leaders of the new Korea, with a program along national, social-democratic lines and quite opposed to the Korean Communist Party. Among those assisting would have been Dr. Kim Kyu-sik. This assumed successful conclusion of the Joint Commission negotiations and precluded a civil war (neither of which conditions, of course, obtained).

As a result of the forced political amalgamation in North Korea, there existed only three political parties: the Workers' Party of North

[90] See p. 136, footnote 52.

Korea, the Yan'an Korean Independence Alliance or New Korean People's Party,[91] and the Korean Democratic Party—the last-named being very much changed from the original party of that same name under Cho Man-sik. All of these groups belonged to the Democratic National Front of North Korea and were controlled by the Communist Party. Theoretically, the Korean Communist Party—as in South Korea—ceased to exist with the formation of the North and South Korean Labor Parties in the fall of 1946. Actually, the Communist Party effectively controlled all other North Korean parties by infiltration, police intimidation, and economic measures designed to paralyze political opposition. Included in the political amalgamation were the various Christian groups in North Korea, that section of the country having been the focal point for much missionary activity in Korea. Several Korean Christian leaders had been arrested. For instance, there was the case of the director of the Presbyterian Seminary in P'yŏngyang who suddenly disappeared in November 1946. A few months later, another seminary official made official inquiry as to the director's whereabouts. He likewise disappeared. In view of the activities of certain of the South Korean missionaries, the Russians may have had good reason to be suspicious of these self-styled "Christian democrats," but that argument certainly did not justify arbitrary liquidation.

A charge often made against the Russian regime in North Korea had to do with the excesses committed by Soviet troops against the Koreans. Several explanatory remarks should be made. In the first place, the initial Soviet force in North Korea contained a large number of relatively green recruits from Mongolia whose standard of living was even lower than that of the Koreans. There was no doubt that these ill-trained troops gave the Russians a black eye, and deservedly so. The Soviet Command finally became so irritated that authority was given to the Korean police to shoot any Russian soldier caught committing crimes against the public. Several deaths ensued. Shortly thereafter, the Military Police contingent was increased, and discipline became better. After those first few months, stories of individual excesses by Russians became rare. Moreover, during that initial period, a large percentage of the stories of Soviet rape, looting, murder and the like had their origin

---

[91] See p. 93, footnote 30.

in Japanese sources and were designed deliberately to foment trouble between the Russians and Americans. Also, many of the incidents involved not Russian troops but North Korean police and constabulary men. It was very doubtful that the actions of individual Russian soldiers were any less commendable than those of American soldiers in South Korea. Finally, it should be kept in mind that the size of the Soviet garrison in North Korea all along was several times that of the American in South Korea.

Still another charge leveled against the Russian regime was that it stripped North Korean industry and exported large amounts of North Korean foodstuffs to the Soviet Union. Without doubt there was considerable stripping of industry, but it was selective and not on such a grand scale as had been the case in Manchuria. Instead, the Soviets seem to have made considerable effort to assist Korea in reviving industry, to which end Japanese skills were conscripted, Japanese prisoners of war employed, and Soviet technical help brought into the country. There was evidence indicating that nearly all the major industries in North Korea were maintained in operating condition. Moreover, it was probably safe to say that we Americans would have preached less on this score if its industrial potential had been largely annihilated by war and if the United States were geographically contiguous to a conquered area in which was found valuable industrial equipment. Moreover, the vast majority of Korean industry was Japanese-owned and probably considered legitimate spoils of war by the Soviet Union, though in fact Korea was later promised this Japanese property as reparations from Japan for past suffering under the Japanese yoke.

The story relative to Russian exports of food from North Korea no doubt arose from the fact that the Red Army lived almost entirely off the land. This practice inflicted great hardship upon North Korea, but not so much that the North Koreans were eating any worse than South Koreans up until late fall of 1946. There was no reliable evidence that any food has been exported from North Korea to the Soviet Union.

According to many American newspaper accounts, the Soviet Military forces in North Korea were engaging in warlike activities along the 38th parallel during the entire occupation. The rumor of impending war between the Soviet Union and the United States was always strong in Korea, abetted no little by those who apparently believed they would benefit from such a conflict—specifically, the forces of the extreme right under Dr. Syngman Rhee and Kim Ku. Actually, there was no evidence up to mid-1947 which would have led one to believe that the Red Army was—or had been—making any offensive preparations. On the other hand, there existed considerable indication that the Soviet Army had prepared defensive positions along the 38th parallel to repel an attack from South Korea. In the beginning and up through the spring of 1947, Soviet forces in North Korea probably numbered close to 250,000 as against the 40 to 50,000 American soldiers in the South. It was reported upon the best of authority, however, that North Koreans had objected so vigorously to such a large army living off the land that the Soviet Command reduced the force, first by twenty-five percent, and then later, in 1947, even further. Early in the spring of 1947, it became known that the 25 Army Headquarters in P'yŏngyang had been reduced to a mere shadow of its former self and had become merely a corps headquarters.

Thus far, we have been talking about what the Russians did not do. What they did was another story. Their propaganda mills in North Korea focused on three programs above all else; namely, land reform, labor legislation and "democratic" elections. The North Korean Land Reform Act, partially described previously, was enacted by the Interim People's Committee of North Korea on March 5, 1946.[92] Because of its general interest, the entire law is reproduced below in translation:

---

[92] The rough English version reproduced by Robinson is very likely an internal USAMGIK translation of the 1940s. A more polished translation of the "North Korean Land Reform Act" (Pukchosŏn t'ojigaehyŏge taehan pŏmnyŏng), now entitled "Law on Agrarian Reform in North Korea," can be found in *Kim Il Sung: Works*, vol. 2 (P'yŏngyang: Foreign Languages Publishing House, 1980), 93–95. For an online digital reproduction of a northern Korean edition from 1946, see the digital copy at the National Library of Korea: https://tinyurl.com/NKland46. The draft translation Robinson reproduced in his manuscript is again reproduced here, as it documents USAMGIK's specific interpretation of such important North Korean documents. This is nicely exemplified in the translation of the essential part of Article 1. The USAMGIK translation reads: "It is designed to *prevent ownership* of Japanese land, to *prohibit individual Koreans from owning land* [italics our's], and to abolish the tenant system." The much smoother official DPRK translation reflects a completely different spirit: "The aim [...] is to abolish the land ownership of the Japanese and of the Korean landlords and the tenant system."

Article 1. The North Korea Land Reformation Act is the result of economic and historical necessities. It is designed to prevent ownership of Japanese land, to prohibit individual Koreans from owning land, and to abolish the tenant system. The right to utilize the land will belong to those who cultivate it. The agricultural system of North Korea will be administered by farmers who are not subordinates of any land owners.

Article 2. Land which will be seized and allotted to farmers includes:
(a) Land formerly owned by Japan, individual Japanese, and Japanese groups;
(b) Land owned by national traitors who acted contrary to the benefit of the Korean people, those who cooperated with the political organizations of Japanese Imperialists, and those who left their homes after liberation.

Article 3. Land to be seized and distributed to farmers without cost includes:
a. That of persons who possess more than 5 *chŏngbo**;
b. Land cultivated only by tenants;
c. Land continually cultivated by tenants, regardless of area;
d. That of churches and other religious groups owning more than 5 *chŏngbo*.

Article 4. Land which will not be seized includes:
a. That owned by schools, scientific laboratories, and hospitals;
b. That owned by those who distinguished themselves against the Japanese, as decided by the Interim People's Committee of North Korea, and those who have contributed to Korean cultural development.

Article 5. All land mentioned in Articles 2 and 3 will be given to the farmers without cost.

Article 6.
a. Administration of the seized land will be entrusted to the People's Committee.
b. Land cultivated by owners themselves will not be seized.

* Approximately 12 acres.

c. Landowners who intend to cultivate their own land will be authorized to possess land in another county in compliance with this ordinance.

Article 7. The procedure of distributing land to farmers will be completed when the Provisional People's Committees issue licenses and register the farms.

Article 8. Land allotted in accordance with this ordinance will be mortgage free.

Article 9. All debts of employees and farmers, who borrowed from landowners whose land will be seized under this ordinance, will become invalid.

Article 10. Land allotted under this ordinance will not be sold or purchased, given away for tenant farming, or mortgaged.

Article 11. Domestic animals, farm implements, and buildings will be seized in accordance with Article 3, to be distributed by the People's Committee to farmers who previously possessed no land according to Article 6. Buildings will be utilized by schools, hospitals, and other social organizations.

Article 12. Orchards formerly owned by the Japanese government, individuals, and groups will be seized and placed in the hands of the Provincial People's Committee. Orchards owned by Korean landowners will be seized according to Article 3 (a) and entrusted to the Provincial People's Committee.

Article 13. All forest, other than those owned by small farmers, will be seized and placed in the hands of the North Korean People's Committee.

Article 14. All establishments owned by landowners affected by this ordinance will be seized by the Interim People's Committee of North Korea.

Article 15. All land reforms will be conducted by the Interim People's Committee of North Korea with provincial, county, and district People's Committees in charge of local reformation. Administration of small villages will be conducted by village committees elected by the people.

Article 16. This ordinance will be effective on the date of publication.

Article 17. Farm reformation will be completed by 31 March. Permits to own land will be issued by 20 June.

It will be noted that this law called for confiscation of former Japanese-owned farmland as well as that belonging to Korean landlords. Distribution of the land was left up to the People's Committees, and therein the Russians made a very large mistake. The law was so badly administered that a large proportion of the farming population—including tenants—were alienated. The distribution of land became a political weapon. It will be noted further that this law did not specifically transfer title of the land to the tenant farmers but merely the use of it as administered by the local People's Committees. The fundamental urge of the Korean tenant farmer to own his own little plot of rice paddy which he and his forebearers had sweated over for centuries was not satisfied; the land still was not his. Furthermore, the forced collection of rice proved so heavy that the farmer in fact realized little benefit from the reform. For instance, during the late spring of 1947, thousands of refugee Korean farmers arrived in the American zone from a rich dry farming belt near the Yalu River in North Korea. The reason for their flight was that the authorities had made off with their draft animals, without which the farmers could not meet the high quotas of grain which the government insisted they turn in. In order to escape persecution at the hands of North Korean officials, the farmers had fled southward.

On June 24, 1946, a labor law was enacted by the Interim People's Committee of North Korea.[93] Again, because of the interest attached

[93] Like the Land Reform Act translation discussed earlier, this text appears to be derived from an unpublished USAMGIK draft. The English version is somewhat unsophisticated; for example, instead of "maternity leave," it employs a rudimentary phrase: "when women [...] become pregnant, they shall be allowed 25 days [*sic*] of vacation." We have retained the original translation as a historical document to reflect the mindset and information available at the time. However, we added Article 26, which was omitted in Robinson's manuscript. For a more polished and accurate English translation of the "Labour Law for the Factory and Office Workers in North Korea" (Pukchosŏn rodongja mit samuwŏne taehan rodong pŏmnyŏng), refer to *Kim Il Sung: Works*, vol. 2 (P'yŏngyang: Foreign Languages Publishing House, 1980), 247–51. A digital reproduction of the 1946 Korean edition (located at: Captured Korean Documents, Doc. No. SA 2009, RG 242, National Archives and Records Administration) can be found at: https://tinyurl.com/NKlaborlaw1946.

to such Soviet-sponsored legislation, the translated text of the law is reproduced for the reader.

> *Article 1.* All persons who work for national and social groups, for cooperative societies, and in private offices shall work 8 hours a day.
>
> *Article 2.* Laborers engaged in dangerous occupation and those who work in underground projects need work only 7 hours a day.
>
> *Article 3.* Boys between the ages of 14 and 16 shall work no more than 6 hours. Boys shall not undertake dangerous work or work on underground projects.
>
> *Article 4.* Boys under 14 years of age shall not work in any productive enterprises.
>
> *Article 5.* Aside from certain exceptions, no one shall work over the maximum hours.
>
> *Article 6.* The amount of compensation shall depend on the occupation, position, and technical skill of the laborer.
>
> (a) Compensation for laborers who work in national (i.e., public) enterprises or offices shall be decided by the Interim People's Committee of North Korea.
>
> (b) Compensation for laborers who work in private offices shall be decided by the labor contract.
>
> *Article 7.* Laborers who are engaged in the same occupation and have the same technical skill shall be paid equally regardless of their ages and sex.
>
> *Article 8.* Compensation paid through the contract system shall be decided according to the quantity of standard articles produced by the laborers. Quantity of the standard articles shall be decided by the managers and vocational groups.
>
> *Article 9.* Compensation for laborers working overtime and those working on holidays shall be computed on a time-and-a-half or more basis.
>
> *Article 10.* Wages of laborers shall be paid monthly, the day to be designated by the manager of the company.

Article 11. January 1, March 1, May 1, August 15, and December 31 are holidays. Every Sunday is a general holiday. The People's Committee of every locality is authorized to set up six more holidays a year according to the customs of the territory.
Note: The pay of salaried workers shall not be reduced because of these holidays.

Article 12. All laborers shall be given at least two weeks of vacation a year. Boys and girls below 16 years of age shall be given at least one month vacation. Those who are engaged in dangerous occupation shall be given at least two weeks of extra vacation. Wages shall be paid by the employers during periodical or supplementary vacations. The amount shall be based on the average wage earned during the previous twelve months.

Note: Supplementary vacations to be awarded shall be decided by the General Vocational Alliance and should gain the approval of the Interim People's Committee of North Korea.

Article 13. Every laborer, upon the agreement of the employer, shall be allowed to take a short vacation. During that period, he shall not be paid.

Article 14. When women who work in offices become pregnant, they shall be allowed 35 days[94] of vacation before giving birth and 42 days after birth.

Article 15. If a woman is pregnant, and if she requests lighter work, she shall be allowed to do easier work after six months of conception till her post-birth vacation ends. During that period, her wage shall be paid according to the average compensation received by her during the last six months.

Article 16. If a woman has a child ranging up to 1 year old, she shall be allowed to suckle the child twice a day, 30 minutes each time. Wages for suckling time will be paid in accordance with her average wage.

Article 17. Women who are pregnant, or have a child to be suckled, shall not be permitted to work beyond the regular hours, nor work nights.

---

[94] Robinson's manuscript had this as "25 days," likely a typo; the law did allow 35 days.

Article 18. All laborers and officials shall be insured as follows:
(a) Subsidy to laborers who have temporarily lost their working power.

(b) Subsidy to women during their vacation for child births.
(c) Subsidy for funeral services.

(d) Subsidy to those who cannot work due to abnormality or sickness acquired while at work.

(e) Payment of annuities and social insurance to those families who have lost their supporters shall be made as follows:

1. All public offices and enterprises shall give between 5 and 8 percent of their regular pay wages as annuity and social insurance.
2. All private offices and employers shall give an amount equal to 10 to 12 percent of their regular payroll.
3. Insured laborers and officials shall pay 1 percent of their wages. Only those who pay the aforesaid insurance premium for over seven months will be authorized to benefit under the insurance policy.

Article 19. The Bureau of Industry shall, with the Vocational Alliance, formulate social insurance regulations and determine the methods of paying insurance.

Article 20. The Bureau of Industry shall, with the Vocational Alliance, study the problem of setting up the organization required to administer social insurance and endeavor to create such an organization.

Article 21. The Health Bureau shall be entrusted with the responsibility for cleaning up the surroundings of all industrial organizations and studying ways and means of inspecting them.

Article 22. The Vocational Alliance, Financial Bureau, and the Bureau of Industry shall construct a table of wages and standards. They shall also establish a salary scale for workers and technicians who are engaged in all national (i.e., public) organizations and civil services.

Article 23. All controversies between employers and employees shall be settled by negotiation between employers and the

> Vocational Alliance. If agreement is impossible, the People's Court shall make the final decision.
>
> *Article 24*. All laborers and officials shall observe the labor regulations. Directors of industrial organizations and employers are authorized, after consulting the representative of the Vocational Alliance, to dismiss those laborers who do not report their absence or ignore the labor regulations.
>
> *Article 25*. A special committee shall, with the participation of the Vocational Alliance, be organized to study the problems of insuring laborers and the payment of annuities to non-employees and aged laborers. The period for the activation of the committee is six months.
>
> [*Article 26*.] This ordinance shall be effective from the date of publication. 24 June 1946

It will be noted that the right to strike was not declared in the law. In fact, Article 23 implied that to strike was illegal by saying, "All controversies between employers and employees shall be settled by negotiation ..." There was no reliable information as to how this labor law was enforced. A statement by the American representative in the delegation of the World Federation of Trade Unions, which visited both North and South Korea in April 1947, cast some doubt on labor freedom in North Korea when he declared, "I do not understand how any labor movement can be free with soldiers standing around with tommy-guns." Of course, he then went on to condemn the labor policies of the Military Government in South Korea, and for good reason as we shall see. Regardless of the degree of control apparently present in the North, the bulk of evidence indicated that the run-of- the-mill worker was materially better off in the Soviet zone than in the American zone, particularly if he were apolitical and content merely to live and let live.

In November 1946 the first North Korean elections were held. Theoretically, voting was free and universal, and 99.16 percent of the possible electorate cast ballots. The number of qualified voters was 4,516,120 out of a population of around eleven million. TASS reported that 3,459 members of provincial, municipal, and district committees were elected, of which 1,102 were members of the Workers' Party of North Korea, 351 of the Korean Democratic Party, 253 of the Young

Friends Society, and 1,753 who professed no party. The method of voting was very simple; one either voted for or against the single official slate of candidates. In the event a candidate did not receive a majority vote, another candidate was selected. Evidence indicated that in no case did more than one man run for a given office. In South Korea, of course, the American-sponsored elections were little better. As already pointed out, the headman system was used so that the general public had no ballot at all, contested or otherwise. Also, the lack of advance publicity, plus police action against the left wing, made it virtually impossible for the left to win any seats other than the two for the island province of Cheju. The reader may select for himself the more democratic system. It should be added, however, that the American Command had the good grace to add forty-five appointed members to those elected in order to make the legislative body a more representative one. But such a process was still far from democratic. Furthermore, only a few isolated *local* elections had taken place in South Korea. What elected bodies existed at the time of the American arrival—specifically, the People's Committees—had been arbitrarily shoved aside in the establishment of Military Government.

The Soviet administration did not make the early American mistake of declaring a free market and relaxing all controls over basic living commodities, including rice. A rigid control was maintained from the beginning. There were forced collections of harvests from the farmers, controlled distribution, and price fixing. In this way, as under the Japanese, the people were assured of a minimum ration at a reasonable price. Anything they desired above could be purchased on the black market. In the American zone, however, all controls were relaxed at the outset, and a cruel inflation was soon under way. During the first year the price of rice in Seoul, for instance, rose from 47 yen per *sŏk* (47.65 gallons) to 14,000 yen. On December 30, 1946, Hugh Borton [1903–1995], Chief of the Japanese Affairs Division in the State Department, said that evidence indicated that Russia was doing a better job of feeding Koreans in its zone than the United States was doing in South Korea. But by early 1947, the import of large amounts of American grains and other foods probably had made the South Korean diet superior to that of North Korea.

Major industries were nationalized in North Korea under the Interim People's Committees, and apparently operated more or less satisfactorily. The Russians entered into at least two agreements relative to North Korean industry, and the Interim People's Committee of North Korea and the Chinese Government signed what amounted to an international treaty governing the usage of power generated at the Sup'ung Dam hydroelectric plant on the Yalu River. The Soviet agreements had to do with new facilities in the northeastern Korean port of Wŏnsan—a warm water port. The controlling corporations were the Wŏnsan Oil Company and the Soviet–Korean Transportation Company, in which the Soviet Union held important interests. These corporate entities and the Sup'ung power agreement had the approval of the Interim People's Committee of North Korea, a government which actually was not a government and certainly not empowered to enter into or approve any international agreement.

The sum total of the evidence indicated that the harsh treatment awarded to a large segment of the population of North Korea by Soviet puppets did great harm to the prestige of the Soviet Union; witness the continued migration of North Koreans southward, a migration which rose to at least 6,000 per day during the summer of 1947. The movement northward was negligible. As Cho Man-sik once commented to American visitors, practical communism had lost its appeal among North Koreans, and the real danger was in South Korea where the people had not tasted the inhumanity of the system.

American Military Government, an Assessment

The first act the American Command in South Korea did—after snubbing Yŏ's People's Republic—was to announce that the hated Japanese officials would be kept in office for the time being.[95] Ensuing furor was such that General Hodge soon received orders to relieve high-ranking Japanese officials without delay. The episode got the Americans off to a bad start. It will be recalled that the Russians had made no such blunder in the North. Japanese officials in South Korea were replaced by ill-trained Americans and poorly selected Koreans, often named upon the advice of missionaries. Many of these Koreans were relatively wealthy, English-speaking, Western-dressed, politically-ambitious opportunists, included among which was a large sprinkling of Japanese

[95] See p. 78, footnote 15.

collaborators. Typical of such selections was the eleven-man advisory council named by the Military Governor in the early days of the occupation. Selected upon the advice of certain missionaries, the council included some of the most callous collaborators—so much so that public opinion soon forced Military Government to forget about the whole project. In those early days, any Korean who could speak English and wore a respectable Western-style suit of clothes was hired by Military Government. The Korean capital was as full of carpet baggers as the American South after the Civil War.

Also, during those first two years, the food program—in spite of large-scale imports of American foodstuffs—was very badly administered. As previously mentioned, the first move had been to lift all commodity controls in the name of American free enterprise capitalism. The fact that the economy was neatly severed at the 38th parallel apparently was overlooked. Inflation soon forced Military Government to act. By that time, the spring of 1946, it was too late to save any of the 1945 harvest, and starvation faced hundreds of thousands, and some well authenticated cases of actual starvation were reported. There was no food to distribute, but somehow the crisis passed without disaster. The immediate shortage facing agriculture was chemical fertilizer, the former source of supply being North Korean industry. Last minute negotiations with the Russians failed because the United States Government suddenly forbade General Hodge to spend American dollars for it. This lack of fertilizer and a very bad flood in late spring of 1946 caused that year's harvest of rice to drop 18 percent below the five-year average of 1940–44. This decrease made necessary large imports of cereals from the United States during the latter part of 1946. The American taxpayer paid the bill, a bill which would have been very much lower had the United States gone through with its fertilizer purchases from North Korea. The mistake was not repeated, however, and large shipments of chemical fertilizer arrived from the United States for the 1947 crop.

The next problem in relation to food was that of collecting the harvest from the farmers so that it would flow into the rationing channels. The low prices offered by the government motivated the farmers to hide their harvest and sell it on the black market for higher prices. The idea soon developed to provide the farmer with incentive goods for surrendering his produce to the government. The idea was good, but after the promises had been made, an adequate supply of such goods was not made available. The plan nonetheless worked with moderate success, chemical fertilizer from the United States being one of the items bartered with the farmer in exchange for his crop. Another item with which Military Government tried to bargain was American candy. Nine million pounds of candy were imported into South Korea from the United States. The farmers were not interested. The upshot of all the effort was that the quota of rice was still not collected in many areas in the fall of 1946. In at least one instance, armed American troops participated in the rice seizure program, for seizure was what the program culminated in. When an American GI shot a Korean farmer squarely in the back and killed him, a public furor was created. Orders went out that no more American troops would be so utilized.

Nevertheless, the police moved in on the recalcitrant farmers. For instance, in one province alone over one thousand farmers had been arrested as of January 20, 1947, for alleged failure to fulfill 1946 rice quotas. The American Command charged the Communists with inciting the opposition to the rice collection program. No doubt, the Communists, as always, exploited the situation to their own ends, but the basic trouble remained: The government was not paying the farmer enough for his rice in relation to the prices of other commodities. Furthermore, as previously explained, the quotas for the individual farmers were arbitrarily fixed by local boards of landlords and police officials. The quotas were frequently wrong, but very seldom adjusted. The hatred felt by the average farmer toward the police became intense.

Instead of assigning grain collection to the police, the Americans at the outset should have asked the Farmers' Association and other farming groups to participate. Strangely, in American eyes all such groups were Communist dominated. Probably they later became so, but largely because of past American acts against them. Furthermore, farm prices should have been set commensurate with the prices of other goods. Finally, a decent system for the distribution of incentive goods—such as fertilizer, clothing, seed, farm tools, and the like—should have been established. As it was, a large quantity of the already insufficient supply of incentive goods found its way into the black market, the proceeds frequently going into police pockets. Moreover, of that rice collected by the police and other government officials, a large quantity likewise went into the black market. On March 28, 1947, a spokesman for Dr. Rhee's headquarters called for improvement in the grain collection system, which was leaving the farmer little or nothing. He pointed out that even the Japanese did not touch the summer grain. This observation came from a right-wing spokesman, not a Communist.

Nonetheless, by mid-1947 it was safe to say that the people of South Korea were eating better than those in the North, due to the import of American foodstuff. It was revealing to note, though, that despite the fact that the per capita production of rice was almost the same in North and South Korea, and even though a large Russian army was living off the land in North Korea and importing nothing into the country, the people of South Korea had been worse off in respect to food up until then. This observation constituted a ringing indictment of American Military Government. Finally, after 18 months of fuss and worry, the Military Governor saw fit to establish a National Economic Board to coordinate all economic planning and to call in some competent practical economists. From that day forward, the economic ship of South Korea gradually righted itself.

Not only in food production, but in the entire scope of agriculture, Military Government failed to produce. During the first winter of occupation, 1945–46, large amounts of fire wood were cut from the hillsides. The scarcity of coal, the inaccessibility to North Korean fuel supplies, the severity of the winter, and the inability of Military Government to control the fire wood situation, combined to bring about the denuding of many Korean hills. Spring rains rapidly developed into flood proportions, thereby destroying a good proportion of the summer grain harvest and permanently destroying a considerable acreage of rice land. The situation became worse by the year. The remarkable reforestation work of the Japanese was not continued. Little land reclamation work was set in motion. And then there was the disastrous slaughter of cattle. Again, Military Government acted too late in controlling the situation. Hungry Koreans slew their cattle by the thousands. By the second year of occupation, few were left. In South Korea were a number of very excellent agricultural stations. However, the results of the work accomplished by them rarely went beyond a file in someone's office. Any sort of program for the introduction of new and better farming methods was almost non-existent. Such was the administration of agriculture in South Korea—great dreams, few accomplishments.

Second only to the food and agricultural program in mismanagement by Military Government was the matter of land. On October 27, 1945, not two months after the Americans had landed, Military Government announced that Koreans might negotiate with Japanese individuals for the purchase, lease, or other use of residential and business properties and farm lands. Loud cries of horror were soon heard. It was obvious that those Koreans who had amassed large fortunes by collaborating with the Japanese regime would buy up most of Korea. After all, something like ninety percent of invested capital had been Japanese-owned, as well as a very large percentage of the best farmlands. Instead of bringing Korea out of the feudalistic era, such a program would have thrust the country deeper into it. Military Government officers had not considered this aspect of the problem. Soon thereafter, this ordinance was rescinded, and title to all Japanese property was vested in American Military Government while the matter was restudied. Cultivated farmlands so vested amounted to some 700,000 acres, or about 12.5 percent of the total cultivated area in South Korea (5.6 million acres). This 12.5 percent included a very large percent of the best rice paddy land.

In March of 1946, Military Government came out with a new plan in respect to farmlands. This time, the tenant working on former Japanese land would have the option of buying it. No land would be sold for cash. Rather, the farmer would pay by giving a certain annual percentage of his crop to the government over a fifteen-year period. After generations of virtual slavery, the tenant would now be allowed to purchase the land over fifteen years. That there was little popular enthusiasm was perhaps understandable. In the first place, the Japanese had promised a similar program and failed to make good. In the second place, who was to guarantee that such a program would be kept in force over the span of fifteen years when a Korean government had not even been established? Furthermore, public opinion polls taken among the farmers at the time indicated that they did not have sufficient faith in the ability of Military Government to administer such a reform fairly. Shortly thereafter, orders came from Washington specifying that Military Government did not possess the authority to transfer title to *any* Japanese property, including farmland—that that right belonged exclusively to the future Korean government, whenever such was set up. Military Government, thereupon, announced that it had decided that it would be more democratic for land reform to wait upon the desires of a Korean government. In the meantime, all formerly Japanese-owned farmlands were held in custody by Military Government's New Korea Company. The single reform effected during the occupation in respect to land was the regulation of tenant rents, the maximum being set at 33 percent of the crop. Formerly, rents often absorbed 50 percent or more of the principal crops raised.

In July of 1947, a new policy was announced relative to formerly Japanese-owned small business holdings and residences which provided for the sale of such properties to "competent, patriotic Koreans." The move was deemed a necessary one so as to put such property into effective and productive use. Proceeds from the sale of such property were to be safeguarded by Military Government for transfer to the future government of Korea. The program was designed to give more stability and security to small business, as well as eliminate a good deal of the graft accompanying the former manager-system under which Military Government appointed Korean managers to operate such properties.

The industrial program of South Korea was lacking in raw materials and trained technicians. At one time. Military Government suggested that Japanese technicians be brought back to Korea, but the Interim Legislative Assembly vetoed the idea.[96] A large percentage of

---

[96] The *G-2 Periodic Reports*, which also list the numbers of Japanese remaining in the North and South, consistently note that around 50 Japanese technicians continued to work in northern Korean factories. A son of one such technician, Satō Tomoya (b. 1931), wrote on his experiences in P'yŏngyang after Korean liberation, which included teaching at a school for Japanese children, in his memoir, *Heijō de sugoshita jūninen no hibi* [My daily life over twelve years in P'yŏngyang] (Tōkyō: Kōyō, 2009). He reports that some Japanese remained even through the Korean War, with a number of them being killed in the U.S. aerial attack on the North Korean capital. For further reading on Japanese citizens who remained and died in North Korea, see Mizuno Naoki and Mark E. Caprio, "Stories from Beyond the Grave: Investigating Japanese Burial Grounds in North Korea," *Asia-Pacific Journal: Japan Focus* 12, no. 9 (March 2, 2014): 1–13. Online: https://apjjf.org/2014/12/9/Mizuno-Naoki/4085/article.html.

The situation in southern Korea was no different. Apart from the industrial sector and the administration, we even find cases in the cultural field. Arimitsu Kyōichi (1907–2011), for example, the young director of the Government-General

the raw materials needed for the rehabilitation of South Korean industry were to be found only in North Korea. But the 38th parallel effectively choked off this source despite American protestations to Soviet authorities. Also, the wanton destruction of machine tools by the American forces early in the occupation had held back Korea's industrial rehabilitation. The trouble was that General Hodge had been under orders to destroy *all* industry capable of turning out munitions despite the fact that much of the machinery could have been converted easily to useful peace-time production. In any event, the occupation was only a few weeks old when American troops began destroying the very considerable wartime industrial development lying about five miles inland from the port of Inch'ŏn, the future site of the Army Service Command in Korea (commonly referred to as Ascom City). In addition, there was the case of Korea's largest scientific laboratory. Army medical authorities selected the impressive marble-encased laboratory buildings as a suitable site for the 29th Army General Hospital. Tons of fine scientific apparatus were loaded onto trucks by American GIs, later to be dumped into sheds. What was not destroyed by the rough handling and exposure to the weather was hauled off by looters. A year later only a very small fraction of the original equipment remained. Another sad story was that of the destruction of Korean books by American GIs who were billeted in a Seoul library. Granted, these incidents were but passing episodes, but they should have prevented Americans from becoming too moralistic about the Russians.

By 1947, American Military Government was operating a planned socialistic economy with the ownership of most industry either held in trust by, or actually vested in the government. In addition to former Japanese-owned industrial and business properties not yet sold under the new program, as well as former Japanese owned farmlands, there were a number of government monopolies such as the railroads, tele-

---

Museum of Chōsen (Chōsen Sōtokufu Hakubutsukan), was in fact detained by USAMGIK to assist with the reopening of the museum as the new National Museum of Korea (Kungnip Chungang Pangmulgwan) and with the training of Korean experts. Colonial legislation had limited such occupations to Japanese nationals. Arimitsu remained in Korea until early June 1946. See Arimitsu Kyōichi, "1945–46-nyŏne issŏttŏn naŭi kyŏnghŏmdam" [My personal account of 1945–46]," trans. Kim Sŏng-nam, *Han'guk kogo hakpo* 34 (May 1996): 7–27.

phone and telegraph systems, power generation and distribution, and radio broadcasting.

Closely connected with industrial rehabilitation was the rebuilding of commerce. Here again a number of near-tragic mistakes were made. For some inexplicable reason. South Korea was for the first year or so prohibited from carrying on any commerce with foreign countries, thereby effectively strangling Korean foreign trade. Why? No one in Korea seemed to know—at least in the Department of Commerce where I made specific inquiry on the subject at the time. (The largest shipment of Korean goods during the first year appears to have been one to the United States consisting of over 4,000 cases of art treasures looted by an American Army colonel from museums, shrines, temples, and private homes. He was a provincial governor at the time and for a small fee would reduce fines and sentences or perform other requested favors. The Army CID[97] finally caught up with him, and he was promptly relieved of duty and sent home on "sick leave." The Command decided not to prosecute because of the bad publicity which would ensue.)[98]

In 1947, trade agreements were permitted with China and with the United States. Naturally, all such trade was carefully controlled by Military Government so as to conserve Korea's limited exports and to make certain that what was imported was of the greatest possible value to Korea. A list of priorities was established, and only certain goods could be brought in. Since the dollar exchange rate was so out of line with relative purchasing power, the only way to effect an exchange of goods was by direct barter or through the United States Commodity Corporation. In both cases, transactions had to receive the prior approval of Military Government. It is of interest to note that by mid-1947 the Department of Commerce in American Military Government was under investigation for alleged large-scale embezzlement and graft by American military officials. The offending officers were later removed quietly and sent home, although it was thought at the time that the corruption extended up into the highest levels in Military Government. A convenient fire on March 17, 1947, destroyed many of the records involved in the allegedly illegal transactions.

[97] Criminal Investigation Division (CID).

[98] See also Mark Gayn's Korea chapter herein, the November 6, 1946, entry, and Hoffmann's essay on Robinson and Gayn in this volume, 31 and 33.

Perhaps one of the most important fields of activity into which American Military Government entered was that of education and public information. But here again, the story was a sorry one. The trouble began with the selection of ill-trained Americans who had little or no understanding of the problems confronting them. If democracy were to take hold at all in Korea, it was essential that the education and public information programs reach the vast majority of the South Korean public—and do so without delay. It was an obvious truism that democracy could not long endure on the basis of an illiterate and unenlightened public, but too few American policy makers appeared to realize the fact, obvious or not. Both the Departments of Education and Public Information combatted communism, not with any constructive policy but with mere negation and opposition. Student strikes were invariably interpreted as Communist-inspired. Students objecting to American Military Government policies were arrested promptly by the Korean police. Early in 1947, thirteen Korean "universities" and eleven high schools, with 17,000 students, went on strike. Their common slogans were "Reject police interference in schools" and, "We demand self-government of schools." This was said to have been the biggest school strike in the history of Korean education. One of the initial issues was the American-sponsored amalgamation of a number of separate colleges into Seoul National University. The move was no doubt a well-advised one from the point of view of efficiency and raising educational standards, but the way in which the amalgamation was effected did offend a great number of teachers and students. Other strike issues were the lack of food, inadequacy of text books and equipment, police interference, the desire for self-government, poorly trained teachers, and arbitrary dismissal of teachers who seemed too radical for the American Communist witch hunters. Actually, many of the teachers who were dismissed on such grounds were merely good liberal democrats. The Communists had succeeded in smearing the names of some of these liberals so as to induce the Americans to order their removal; the liberal-democrat being the Communist's most feared adversary. On February 12, 1947, the American educators very foolishly allowed Dr. Cho Pyŏng-ok, the Director of the National Police, to order striking students back to their studies. Said Cho, "The policy of the authorities is to deal severely with groups or individuals who agitate strikes or the leader who acts on orders to interrupt the attendance of good students." This was an obvious threat. On February 19, the police produced the famous letter, allegedly signed by a Soviet Army major, to the leader of the South Korean Workers' Party ordering agitation against the American Command, including school strikes. This move was designed to prove the Communist nature of the strike. A week later the letter was exposed as a fraud cooked up for the occasion by the South Korean police.

On March 31, 1947, it was announced that five students had been sentenced by an American Provost Court to one year's imprisonment each for holding an unlicensed meeting against the Seoul National University plan. Some of the students' demands were finally met, including the appointment of Korean directors to the National University and other institutions and less police interference with school affairs. But the real showdown came on May Day, 1947. A number of the more radical students—found on the campus of any large school—participated in the May Day celebration staged by the Communists. Close to 800 students were promptly arrested by the Korean police, arrests being made upon request of the educational authorities. Chief Chang of the Seoul Metropolitan Police admitted as much in an early May press conference. Such a ferment of public opposition to these arrests was raised that on May 9 Chief Chang was forced to issue an order forbidding further arrests of students on school campuses. In addition to the arrests, a large number of students were expelled from school by the Department of Education. The army advisor to the Department of Education in the city of Seoul could keep quiet no longer. In defiance of Military Government, he issued a public denunciation of the unjustified arrest and expulsion of students for merely participating in the May Day celebration. A few days later he was dismissed from his job by Military Governor General Lerch. Such was the manner in which American democracy was taught in the Korean schools.

To keep the record straight, it should be added that some progress had been made by mid-1947 in revising textbooks (a large quantity having been printed in the United States), in training teachers, in sending selected groups of Korean educators to the United States to study American schools, and in advancing adult education. Several hundred thousand adults had been taught in night school to read and write the simple Korean alphabet. At the same time, it should be noted that the educational facilities in South Korea were totally inadequate. In the spring of 1947 my Korean houseboy applied for entrance into middle school. *Five hundred out of ten thousand* applicants were to be selected. Korean youth were desperate for education, but only a very small percentage of the potential students could be accommodated. Furthermore, the middle schools were so expensive that the average Korean boy could not afford to attend.

The progress in developing a public information program was likewise largely unsuccessful. The bulk of the Korean people—largely farmers—could not be reached by any means, whether it be radio, newspaper, or word of mouth. Seeing the desperate need for a large-scale and well-integrated program if the Korean people were to be made aware of governmental activity or given any feeling of responsibility toward a government of their own making when such seemed possible, an American Army colonel went to work to convince the American Command to do something. Both General Hodge and General Lerch agreed, and the colonel went to Washington with the outline for a grandiose plan in his briefcase calling for the importation of radio transmitters, of thousands of cheap radio sets, of much-needed newsprint and Korean type, of presses, of trained public relations personnel, and just plain salesmen. Official Washington emasculated the program, and the farsighted colonel who conceived the whole idea became *persona non grata* in Korea, apparently because he was suspected of radical tendencies. After all, he wanted to take the government to the people.

A short time later, a young American public relations official working for the Seoul City Government submitted a program for setting up a system of public discussion groups throughout the city, sort of a town meeting idea for thrashing out public issues. In addition to constituting something of an escape valve, he envisioned a number of very helpful citizen-initiated suggestions emanating out of these public discussions. Military Government dismissed him from his job on the grounds that he was a rabble-rouser. And so, the Korean citizenry remained happily unaware and disinterested in governmental or national affairs.

Incidentally, the political education section of the Department of Public Information was controlled by an ex-missionary and an ex-army chaplain, neither of whom had the slightest concept of the importance or significance of their jobs. The main function of the Department was that of preaching to any Koreans who would listen. According to such sermons, the United States was completely devoid of strikes, racketeers, corruption, black markets, political dishonesty, insincere politicians, and profiteers, and had an economy which was completely *laissez-faire* in nature. On July 4, 1946, I made the following remarks to the Korean–American Cultural Society, remarks which indicated that all was not perfect in the United States and which were quickly reported by American counterintelligence officers as controversial and subversive.

> I am rather afraid that we Americans are too prone to preach to others. Actually, we need less preaching to others and more effort at home in the United States to fight against those who would use American democracy to further their own selfish interest—a fight, however, waged through words and the ballot box, not by violence and force.
>
> It is true that within any free democratic country a constant effort must be made against those who would destroy democracy and freedom. In the United States today we are faced with many groups trying to promote their own interests above those of the rest of the country. The problem of Korea and the United States may not be too different.
>
> Neither independence nor democracy solves anything in itself. They merely create the opportunity for a people to live under a government and leaders of their own choosing. However, without constant vigilance by educated and enlightened citizens and popular control exorcised through a representative democratic government, independence from a *foreign* master can all to easily merely mean the substitution of a *domestic* master. With independence comes a grave responsibility for every citizen.

On the subject of police and security, a great deal has already been said. There was ample evidence to indicate that the Korean police were politically partial, corrupt, and medieval in their methods of treating prisoners. But time after time, General Lerch praised the Korean police as one of the finest in the world. In spite of the recommendations made by the Joint Korean–American Conference in the fall of 1946, there was no improvement in the administration of law and justice in South Korea other than the release of a few political prisoners.

The American Command all along contended that of the 22,000 persons in prison in Korea, there were no political prisoners—all were criminals. Strangely enough however, some 1,056 political prisoners were released by the end of June 1947. A Military Government press release said that none of the prisoners had committed serious crimes and that their release had been decided upon by the American Command after Korean courts had assumed trial function formerly performed by American Provost Courts. Dr. Rhee charges that this release of prisoners was indicative of how American policy tended to favor Communists. "These young men (referring to the released prisoners) will easily obtain arms, and we will be helpless," Dr. Rhee said. At the time, all persons convicted by American Provost Courts for crimes not involving violence were scheduled for ultimate release. Non-violent crimes included such offenses as participating in an unlicensed meeting, going on an illegal strike, and the like. Interestingly enough, delegations of extreme rightists protested the release of these political prisoners. On one such occasion, an American representative observed, "But your party has gone on record as saying that there were no political prisoners in South Korea." The other three elements of the South Korean security forces—the Constabulary, the Coast Guard, and the Korean National Youth Corps—need not be discussed at length here. Suffice to say that the Constabulary—ostensibly the South Korean Army—was small in comparison to the real South Korean Army, the Korean National Youth Corps, which boasted close to 100,000 trained men by mid-1947. That it was a weapon of the extreme rightist could not be disputed.

Although the reader may be more than a little disillusioned at this stage, the record of Military Government in South Korea was not all bad. The work of the Department of Public Health and Welfare was particularly outstanding. An unprecedented cholera outbreak during the summer months of 1946 taxed the Department to the utmost, but the work it accomplished probably did more to incur Korean goodwill than almost any other activity of Military Government. American doctors shamed Korean medicine into adopting higher standards. When Korean doctors would refuse to treat a patient because he was dirty or ailing from a deadly disease, American doctors would give treatment without apparent worry about their own well-being. Large scale inoculation and DDT dusting programs were completed with a high degree of success.

Perhaps the most spectacular American activity of all was the civilian supply program and large scale American economic assistance in the form of such items as grain and food of all kinds, drygoods, fertilizers, medicine, petroleum products, and clothing—to mention only a few. A total of $91 million was given by the United States Government to the Korean people to improve their standard of living under the civilian supply program from May 1946 to March 1947, and the aid continued. After the initial breakdown of negotiations between the Russians and Americans in 1946 on the subject of Korea, a plan to make the American occupation zone self-supporting within the next three years was drafted by the U.S. War and State Departments. Although Soviet–American negotiations on Korea were resumed in May 1947, Secretary of State Marshall made it plain on more than one occasion that the United States proposed to go ahead with or without the Russians. On July 4, 1947, Marshall said that Congress would be asked for an initial $78 million appropriation for recovery measures in addition to the War Department's request for $137 million for food, medicine, and other materials with which to cope with both disease and unrest in the American occupation zone. The Korea recovery plan was aimed largely at restoring railways, highways, and the chemical and textile industries. The program called for American supervision somewhat along the lines of aid to Greece. On December 30, 1946, Edwin M. Martin [1908–2002], Chief of the State Department Division of Japanese and Korean Economic Affairs, wisely observed that it was America's first job in Korea to see that Koreans had enough to eat. "A country threatened with starvation is not a fertile ground in which to develop an understanding of or desire for democracy." He went on to comment that the ability to get American supplies into Korea during 1947 might be the deciding factor. "If we are pennywise on this, we will be a pound foolish regarding our position in the Far East," he added. By mid-1947 the entire economic program in Korea was coordinated by a National Economic Board operated by competent personnel. That part of the economic picture was hopeful.

American Military Government's Department of Labor was created late—not until July 1946—and only after specific orders from Washington to do so. Since all labor unions were considered Communistic by American military authorities, they were very loath to create any agency to deal with them, feeling that by doing so the labor unions would be awarded undesirable prestige and official blessing. Pressure from Washington finally brought action. During the ensuing year a number of very laudable labor ordinances were enacted by Military Government, even though sabotaged by the Korean police. The first such ordinance was promulgated upon the establishment of a Department of Labor in Military Government on July 23, 1946. In substantial accord with the policy of the United States in labor matters, the ordinance gave workers in Korea the right, through self-organization, to form and join labor unions and to designate representatives of their own choosing for the purpose of negotiating terms and conditions of their employment without interference from employers or their agents. The ordinance did not make strikes illegal or impose a compulsory mediation system. How the American Command, therefore, construed ensuing non-violent strikes as illegal remained unexplained. The law did not even require strikers to present their demands before going on strike. It did set up a National Mediation Board which could mediate when presented demands by workers' committees after local negotiations with employers had broken down.

A second labor ordinance was enacted soon after the 1946 strikes and riots. This law provided that the basic work week for employees in industry, commerce, and government should be a maximum of 48 hours and that no employer should work his employees in excess of that number of hours except as provided in Section II. That section specified that an employee might work up to 60 hours per work week if compensation at the rate of not less than one and one-half times the regular compensation were paid. This section further provided that employment in excess of 48 hours per week should be pursuant to a collective bargaining agreement between the employer and a labor union or other organization representing the employee, or, lacking such collective bargaining agreement, should conform to a specific agreement between the employer and employee. Each legal holiday, except Sunday or other legal days of rest, was to be counted as eight hours of the permitted work week. Every employee subject to the ordinance was entitled to not less than 24 consecutive hours of rest each week. Certain types of labor were specifically exempted; particularly, those of a seasonal nature. Every employer was directed to maintain records of the persons employed by him and of the wages, hours, and other conditions and practices of employment. Any person who willfully violated these provisions was upon conviction of a first offense to be fined not less than 20,000 yen nor more than 100,000. Upon conviction of a second offense, he was to be subjected to a fine of not less than 20,000 nor more than 200,000 or to imprisonment for not more than six months or both. Upon conviction of a third offense, he was subject to such penalty as a Military Occupation Court should direct, but the sentence was in no event to be less than three times the fine or imprisonment, or both, imposed upon the last previous conviction. In addition, a Child Labor Law was passed by the Interim Legislative Assembly in the spring of 1947.[99]

The attitude of the police toward labor's rights was accurately reflected on March 24, 1947, in a statement by Chief Chang of the Seoul Metropolitan Police when he issued a stern warning to all laborers, declaring that ring leaders responsible for agitating future strikes would henceforth be punished more strictly and severely than before. As indicative of the attitude of the American military were these sentences given to persons responsible for the March 22 strike in Seoul, previously described. Nine men were sentenced by American Provost Court—one for five years imprisonment, two for three years each, one for two years, one for one year, three for six months, and one for 90 days. The charge on which basis these men were sentenced was that of rioting, instigation to strike, and staging an unlicensed meeting. Two other men received sentences of two years each on the charge of disturbing the general peace. It would be interesting to watch the reaction in the United States if a group of American labor leaders received similar sentences on such charges. Incidentally, the alleged "riot" was no more than that which attends any strike when the police rush the strikers.

Another activity of Military Government deserving passing mention has to do with the Department of Foreign Affairs. As of July 1947, this Department had accomplished the staggering task of evacuating some 882,689 Japanese nationals from Korea and repatriating to Korea 1,999,551 Korean nationals from areas bordering the Pacific to which

---

[99] The Child Labor Law (Misŏngnyŏnja Nodongbohobŏp) was signed by the military governor on May 16, 1947, but no adequate machinery was set up to enforce it. See "Statement of the Military Governor," *Summation: United States Army Military Government Activities in Korea* 20 (May 1947): 14–15.

they had been displaced by the Japanese. The early movement of Japanese out of Korea was not a happy sight. The movement took place through the southern port of Pusan onto waiting LSTs[100] and hence, to Japan. The sight on those Pusan docks in mid-winter 1945–46 was a pathetic one. The refugees were provided with no shelter and no warmth. They were allowed to take with then only what they themselves could carry, and even that was looted by American soldiers—looted, incidentally, with official approval. For a time, a young humanely-minded American lieutenant was in charge of the night loading operations. Taking pity on the sad plight of these defeated people, he ordered some of his men to help the elderly men and women down the long docks and onto the ships. Some were so sick they had to be carried; others could barely stagger along. The weather was bitterly cold. The lieutenant did his best to expedite the movement and minimize the suffering. One night, a colonel came to inspect the movement. When he saw American soldiers helping the Japanese with their many bundles and children, not to mention the sick, he thundered, "Who's in charge?" The lieutenant confronted him. "What do you mean by having Americans help these yellow-bellied bastards?" he shouted. "If they can't get on the ship by themselves, let them lie where they fall." And such was done. The lieutenant went off in the night and wept bitterly at man's inhumanity to man. Fortunately, news of the treatment being accorded Japanese refugees in Pusan reached the ears of American newspapermen. Upon threat of adverse publicity, the American Command reformed its ways. The Commanding General in Pusan was sent home "for reasons of ill health."

Other than this one black mark, the repatriation program was well-handled by the Americans. The problem was made even more difficult by the Soviet refusal to cooperate in any orderly movement of repatriates in and out of North Korea. The Russians simply shoved their unwanted Japanese down over the 38th and let the Americans take care of them. Despite repeated protests from the American Command, the Russians continued to evacuate the Japanese in this haphazard and cruel manner. For instance, in mid-winter of 1945–46, the Soviet Commander in the North Korean city of Hamhŭng ordered all Japanese to get out within a few hours' time. Trains were furnished

[100] LST stands for "Landing Ship, Tank," also known as tank landing ship.

part way to the border. From there, they walked—men, women, and children, healthy or sick. At the 38th parallel, Russian sentries stripped them of all their remaining valuables. Those Japanese who did not follow orders and remained behind in Hamhŭng were deprived of their food ration cards and soon starved or froze to death.

The Chinese acted little better than the Russians. Although the United States furnished transportation as rapidly as it could to repatriate Koreans from China, the Chinese Nationalist Government meanwhile confiscated practically all Korean property except the shirts on the Koreans' backs. Korean communities were looted. Any who resisted were maltreated by Chinese officials. The Chinese did not want any Koreans to remain and were not at all loathe to let one and all know about it through act and deed. Despite these atrocities committed by the Chinese Government against Korean residents—atrocities which drew the fire of the Korean press and Korean political parties on more than one occasion, and even official American protest—there was no record of Dr. Rhee's ever having approached his good friend, Chiang Kai-shek, on the subject in behalf of his unfortunate countrymen.

American Military Government was subordinate to XXIV Corps Headquarters. The former controlled the administration of government; the latter, matters of policy. The first Military Governor was Major General Archibald V. Arnold. Early in 1946, Major General Archer L. Lerch, former Provost Marshal General of the United States Army, stepped into the job. Under the Military Governor were a number of departments and offices, each responsible for a particular phase of administration. In addition, there was the Southern Korean Interim Legislative Assembly, over which acts the Military Governor had complete veto power. Finally, there was the provincial government level. There were nine provinces in South Korea plus the independent city of Seoul, both Seoul and the island of Cheju having been given provincial status by act of Military Government. The channel of command ran directly from provincial governor to the central government.

In March of 1946, General Lerch announced his intention of Koreanizing the government. American Military Government officers would more and more move into the background, thereby allowing their Korean counterparts to carry on. In September 1946, the Military Governor announced that the time had come when Korean directors should take full charge of their respective departments, and the Americans should function only in an advisory capacity. And with that, the Americans moved out of the Capital Building to an annex, leaving Koreans in full charge of the roost. To head this Korean organization, An Chae-hong, the already introduced moderate rightist and member of the Coalition Committee, was appointed to the post of Civil Administrator on February 10, 1947. In the spring of 1947, the United States Army Military Government in Korea (USAMGIK) became the Interim Korean Government of South Korea. In this manner, American Military Government washed its hands of all responsibility for what its Korean officials did. A fundamental rule of organization is that he who holds authority likewise is responsible for what goes on. But not so in South Korea. One approached a Korean official on a matter and received the answer that he did not have the authority to act. Upon approaching an American advisor, one was told that the Koreans were in charge. As Roger Baldwin put it, "We started out not with the idea of democratizing Korea but of Koreanizing it. We would pick Koreans—the wrong kind—for administrators, then wash our hands of responsibility for what they do."

Military Government on a provincial and local level was both good and bad. Local government—municipal and county, controlled initially by small Military Government detachments—was largely in Korean hands by mid-1947. However, the provincial governments remained under close American supervision. One could cite many cases of American excesses—such as the sadistic major in Pusan who personally supervised the torture of police prisoners, of the purchase of women by American officers, of the provincial military governor who looted his entire province of art treasures, of brutal treatment of Japanese civilians at the hands of Americans, of forcing prisoners (including those held only for investigation) to work on private projects, the pocketing of public funds, of justice being bought and sold. On the other hand, many cases of good American works can be cited: the sewer system and public market inspired by an American lieutenant in Wŏnju, the outstanding work of an American Army doctor in Pusan, the colonel in Chinju who through his own enthusiastic and kindly leadership instilled a city pride into his people, the sergeant who ran the large industrial area of Samch'ŏk, the three GIs who governed the little town of Nonsan and launched a sports program for the townspeople.

Such persons as these did much to establish goodwill among the Koreans.

However, as Raymond Cromley [1910–2007] reported in the *Wall Street Journal*,[101] the average American GI in Korea was not exactly an ambassador of goodwill. He held obvious contempt for the Koreans and everything Korean. "The Koreans are no damn good," he announced on every and all occasions. I myself was told by high military officials that all the Koreans understood was harsh and brutal treatment, that they did not respond well to kindness and justice. Few American Military Government officials had any interest in the Koreans, their culture, their history, their problems, their country. All many Americans asked was, "Why in hell did I sign up for Korea; when can I go home?" Regulations laid down by General Hodge helped little. It was strictly forbidden for an American to go into a Korean home even if invited, to invite Koreans into his home, to enter Korean restaurants, to ride in a Korean car or date a Korean girl. Special permission in writing from XXIV Corps Headquarters was required for each occasion of this sort. There was no place in Korea where Americans and Koreans could mix socially and get to know one another. The first question CIC agents asked when inquiring into one's loyalty was, "Does he have any Korean friends?" My wife and I were threatened with court martial for joining a group of American newspapermen in a banquet in a Korean *kisaeng* house.

And the American Command did little on a personal level to better Soviet–American relations. Those Russians who came in contact with the Americans in South Korea were visibly unimpressed by American democracy as applied there by the United States. The spring of 1947 was the saddest time of all for amiable relations on a personal level. American personnel were no longer allowed to associate in any fashion with the Soviets in Seoul without specific written authority from the American Command. Those Americans who manifested the least show of friendship for or interest in the Russians immediately became objects of suspicion and the subjects of CIC investigation. In this connection can be cited the case of an American Army sergeant of Russian extraction. He conceived the idea that he could do his part in

[101] See Ray Cromley's article "Failure in Korea: Lack of a Definite Plan, Inexperienced Personnel" in the *Wall Street Journal* of January 16, 1947.

promoting friendly relations between Russia and the United States by offering to give English lessons to some of the Soviet liaison personnel living in Seoul, and secured official permission from XXIV Corps G-2 to do so. As a result of the lessons, he became quite friendly with a number of Soviet officers. In the natural course of events, he introduced several of his American associates to the Russians and a number of friendly social occasions ensued. In mid-June of 1947 the sergeant was transferred permanently out of Korea. Why? I happen to know that it was solely because he had been the center of the American social group in which the Soviet officers had been circulating. It was felt by the authorities that if he were removed from the scene, the group would disintegrate. The American Command did not wish the Russians to have any American friends. Added to this episode was the case of the American official in American Military Government's Department of Commerce. Knowing that the Russians had a collection of motion pictures, the American asked one of his Russian acquaintances to show some pictures of Soviet agriculture, industry, and the like to some of the people in his department. The Russians did so. No sooner done, than the American responsible for the showing received an official reprimand from General Hodge.

On June 17, 1947, one of the Soviet liaison officers in Seoul commented to me that he had long been a student and great admirer of all things American, but that after his experiences in South Korea he had been thoroughly disillusioned. "I have—what do you call it—the kiss of death," said the Russian. "Anyone who associates with me gets into trouble." He commented that it was very strange that *his* superiors allowed him to see all the American motion pictures he wished but that the American Command would not let any Russian films be shown to interested Americans. "What is your general afraid of?" he asked me. The Russian went on to remark that it would be best that we met no more, that he liked me, but that any show of friendship would only get me into trouble—and so it would. I hasten to add that none of the Soviet personnel I met in Korea ever attempted to pump me for information. Rather, they were friendly, frank, and extremely sociable. On one occasion, after a long discussion as to the possibility of war between the Soviet Union and the United States, one of the Soviet officers said very gravely, "The Russian people do not want war—believe me, they do not want to fight anyone. They are tired of fighting.

All they want to do is to live and laugh again." However, such discussions had become a thing of the past by the end of 1947. Anyone who looked at a Russian automatically became a "known Communist." Little latitude was allowed for curiosity and personal friendship. Are Americans so naïve and weak and the Russians so strong and superior that social intercourse inevitably leads to an undermining of an American's patriotism? Admitting a few defections, one would have thought that we had much to gain and little to lose by personal association with the Russians.

Summary

If in this chapter I have seemed unduly harsh on American Military Government in Korea, it has not been without premeditation. Perhaps this account will shake some of the superiority, smugness, and complacency which has made the American a close runner up for the most hated person on earth. American administration of South Korea was intolerably bad. The Koreans know it and the Russians know it, not to mention a small minority of Americans who ate their hearts out trying to rectify some of the mistakes. If one contends that the cases cited here are exaggerated or isolated, he dodges the truth. Granted, the Russian administration of North Korea was equally bad, perhaps worse, from the American standpoint. But there is scant solace in that. If I have not dealt in such great detail with the North Korean administration, it is because the details were not available and because the lesson for Americans lay in South Korea, not in the North.

* * * * *

And so, as the Russians and the Americans argued and bickered *ad infinitum*, the Koreans suffered on. The 38th parallel was still closed to all but a select few. Armed American and Soviet guards faced each other across the invisible line. A Korean army trained in North Korea; another trained in South Korea. The policy of neither the Russians nor the Americans was right nor just. The Korean villager still sweated and toiled from dawn to dusk over land which was not his under a government which he did not like. Political extremists fought it out in the large cities while the ordinary citizen was trying desperately to make ends meet and keep out of the hands of a police force which he bitterly hated and tremblingly feared. American democracy and Soviet communism had come to Korea; both had made a horrible unholy mess of the country. The Japanese, the former masters of Korea, must have been smiling to themselves to watch the fiasco. As one Japanese commented wryly, "We couldn't do much with Korea either."

The Han

July 15, 1947

Over across the stretch of white sands, against the dark mountains, the Han River flows lazily to the sea—a gleaming thread in the late afternoon sun. The mountains are fast becoming cloaked in a purple haze as the shadows lengthen. A soft evening breeze stirs the leaves and grasses. It is a Korean summer evening—beautiful in it is primitive natural splendor. On a distant hill a group of mud huts seems like so many dark mushrooms. Far across the river bottom, an oxcart leaves its trail of dust in the evening air. High on the lonely mountain directly opposite is a small Buddhist temple, a dark speck against the sky. Even now I seem to hear the temple bells far away on the breeze calling the lonely monks to prayer. Below me to the edge of the river's sand, stretch rice paddies—green with the new crops. A group of villagers are wading through the mud, laboriously pulling up weeds from among the rice shoots. Back bending labor, but necessary if one is to eat. As I watch, they straighten up and for a time stand looking out toward the river and the mountains, faces lifted as if pleading with their ancient deities to protect their crop. Theirs is an ageless trinity—man and the earth and that unknown power of life and universe. As I write, the shadows lengthen and threaten to engulf my world. I have seen my last day in Korea die.

CHAPTER X:
POSTSCRIPT FROM A DISTANCE – IN MILES AND TIME

August, 1958

Negotiation

Satisfied that no further results could come from the joint commissions sitting in Seoul, the United States, on August 26, 1947, proposed to the U.S.S.R., the United Kingdom, and Nationalist China that "the four powers adhering to the Moscow Agreement meet to consider how that agreement may be speedily carried out." Attached were seven proposals:

> 1. In both the U.S.S.R. and U.S. zones of Korea there shall be held early elections to choose wholly representative provisional legislatures for each zone. Voting shall be by secret, multi-party ballot on a basis of universal suffrage and election shall be held in accordance with the laws adopted by the present Korean legislatures in each zone.
>
> 2. These provisional zonal legislatures shall choose representatives in numbers which reflect the proportion between the populations of the two zones, these representatives to constitute a national provisional legislature. This legislature shall meet at Seoul to establish a provisional government for a United Korea.
>
> 3. The resulting Provisional Government of a United Korea shall meet in Korea with representatives of the four powers adhering to the Moscow Agreement on Korea to discuss with them what aid and assistance is needed in order to place Korean independence on a firm economic and political foundation and on what terms this aid and assistance is to be given.
>
> 4. During all the above stages the United Nations shall be invited to have observers present so that the world and the Korean People may be assured of the wholly representative and completely independent character of the actions taken.
>
> 5. The Korean Provisional Government and the Powers concerned shall agree upon the date by which all occupation forces in Korea will be withdrawn.

6. The provisional legislatures in each zone shall be encouraged to draft provisional constitutions which can later be used as a basis for the adoption by the National Provisional legislature of a constitution for all of Korea.

7. Until such time as united, independent Korea is established, public and private Korean agencies in each zone shall be brought into contact with international agencies established by or under the United Nations and the presence of Korean observers at official international conferences shall be encouraged in appropriate cases.

On September 4, 1947, the Soviet Union made known its rejection of the proposed four-power conference. Its principal argument was that according to the Moscow Decision "the measures to assist the formation of a Provisional Korean Democratic government were to be carried out by the Joint Commission consisting of representatives of the Soviet command in North Korea and the United States command in South Korea. The Soviet note went on to point out, "for the consideration of the four governments, including the British and Chinese governments, according to the Moscow Decision, there should be submitted the recommendations worked out by the Joint Commission prior to adoption of a final decision." The letter then placed the blame on the U.S. delegation for the inability of the Joint Commission to reach any positive decision. It was observed that on August 26, the Soviet delegation had introduced a new proposal for the establishment of a consultative organ—"the Provisional General Korean People's Assembly of Representatives of Democratic Parties and Social Organizations of All Korea." It was further stipulated that the U.S. proposals concerning Korea were unacceptable on the grounds that they would "entail the further division of Korea inasmuch as they envisage the establishment of separate provisional legislative assemblies in the south and in the north of Korea." The vital task before the Commission, the note explained, was to achieve as rapidly as possible "the establishment of a single, even though provisional, organ of authority—the General Korean Provisional Democratic Government." It observed, "The American proposal does not correct the situation now existing in Korea—the division of the country into two zones, to the liquidation of which all efforts should be directed—but on the contrary consolidates this abnormal situation." And for these reasons, the U.S. note was rejected.

A few days later, on September 17, 1947, U.S. Secretary of State, George Marshall, announced publicly the U.S. intention to take the question of Korea independence to the UN General Assembly. He charged that the Soviet Union, by refusing the right of free speech to all Korean political groups, had obstructed any move toward Korean unification or the establishment of a government. (As we have seen, this issue was not quite as black or white as Marshall's statement seemed to indicate.) He concluded that inasmuch as further attempts to solve the Korean problem by bilateral negotiation would serve only to delay establishment of an independent and united Korea, the U.S. government would present the Korean problem to the UN. And on September 23, the General Assembly voted to place this question on its agenda. The essence of the U.S. proposal which ensued was that a UN commission be sent to Korea, consult with the Koreans, hold a prompt election of delegates to a national convention, establish a government complete with the machinery for maintaining law and order, and then evacuate all foreign troops.

Apparently in an effort to forestall UN action, the Soviet delegation on the Joint Commission still sitting in Seoul, introduced on September 26 yet another proposal—"to give the Koreans the possibility of forming a government themselves, without aid or participation on the part of the United States of America and the Soviet Union, on condition that American and Soviet troops be withdrawn from Korea." The Russians proposed further, "If the government of the U.S.A. should agree to the proposal for the withdrawal from Korea of all foreign troops at the beginning of 1948, the Soviet troops would be ready to leave Korea simultaneously with the American troops." According to *New York Times* reports at the time, this proposal was enthusiastically received in South Korea. In fact, sometime later, in February 1948, Kim Ku and Kim Kyu-sik, South Korean rightest leaders, both came out in open support of the formation of a national Korean government following the withdrawal of foreign troops, as the Soviets suggested.

It might be argued that withdrawal of Soviet troops would have left a Korean Communist army of between 200,000 and 500,000 in

North Korea, an army backed up by the Chinese Communists, whereas a power vacuum would have been created in South Korea. In such a situation, the North Koreans might have been lured into taking over all of the country. But this argument overlooks the fact that a Korean army had been organized in South Korea—though unofficially—and that the U.S. troops would move back only so far as Japan and Okinawa. If the United States had been able to stabilize South Korea politically during its two years of occupation by means of a popular interim government, under which an official Korean army could have been built up, then the U.S. position would, of course, have been much stronger. In such case, we might well have been in a position to accept the Soviet proposal. It should perhaps be borne in mind that it was not entirely the fault of the Russians that the American command had failed to accomplish stability and strength in South Korea.

The American answer to the Soviet proposal which had been made in Seoul and embodied in an October 8 note from Molotov to Marshall, came from Washington. It declared in part, "In the opinion of the United States government the question of withdrawal of occupation forces from Korea must be considered an integral part of the solution of the (whole) problem." Later, on November 13, Andrei Gromyko [1909–1989], in an address before the UN General Assembly on the resolution to establish the United Nations Temporary Commission on Korea declared, "The General Assembly cannot adopt this decision in the absence of representatives of the Korean people." He blamed the breakdown of negotiations in Seoul on the U.S., primarily because of its insistence on consulting with "anti-democratic parties and organizations which, moreover, had fought against the Moscow Agreement" and on its refusal to consult with certain "democratic parties and organizations of South Korea." And then he named as examples of the latter category the National Council of Korean Labor Unions, the Korean Women's Federation [Chosŏn Punyŏ Ch'ongdongmaeng], the Korean National Youth Corps, and the National Federation of Farmers' Unions [Chŏn'guk Nongmin Chohap Ch'ongyŏnmaeng]. He reiterated the Soviet desire to fulfill the exact terms of the Moscow Decision, including a trusteeship, and the opposition of same by the United States.

Because of the untenable position into which the United States had permitted itself to be maneuvered, these Soviet charges were virtually impossible to answer, particularly when backed up by an offer of bilateral withdrawal of all troops. John Foster Dulles [1888–1959], in answering Gromyko in the General Assembly on November 13, all but admitted the weakness of the U.S. case by saying that in the UN First Commission the Soviet Union had claimed that there were no duly-elected representatives of the Korean people in South Korea, that it was only in North Korea that such representatives could be found. "Therefore," Dulles observed, "the essence of such a proposal (that is, to consult Korean representatives) would be to bring here, at some time or other—I do not know when—some representatives of North Korea, and no representatives of South Korea where two-thirds of the Koreans live." In making such a statement, Dulles implied that the U.S. could not produce any "duly-elected representatives of the Korean people" from South Korea. In fact, of course, the U.S. was suffering under such a handicap, but through no fault of the Russians. We had had over two years to organize and conduct an honest and adequate popular election in South Korea, but to that date we had not done so.

Dulles' rejection of the Soviet proposal for immediate bilateral troop withdrawal was more convincing:

> It is perfectly obvious—any sensible person knows it, and it was the promise of the Moscow Agreement of 1945—that the orderly procedure was to have the troops there to maintain order, because there was no government in Korea to maintain any order whatsoever. You first have to have a government with the normal processes for maintaining order. As quickly as their purpose is accomplished, the troops are withdrawn. If you try to withdraw the troops before that has happened, it is certain that there will be chaos and probably civil war, and a very bad time indeed for the Koreans, whom we are ostensibly trying to help.

His point was also well taken when he observed that although the Soviet delegates in the First Commission had charged that South Korea under the U.S. Military Government was "hell on earth" in comparison with the "virtual paradise of North Korea," still it had been the Soviets who had objected to a U.S. proposal that a UN commission be sent to

Korea "to see for itself what was going on." The U.S. record was plainly bad, but the Russians seemed to feel even more uncomfortable about their "paradise" in North Korea.

Elections

The upshot was that the General Assembly acted favorably and established the United Nations Temporary Commission on Korea (UNTCOK). In so doing, the Assembly directed that the Commission invite "elected representatives of the Korean people to participate in the establishment of a government and of national independence." It resolved further, "that in order to facilitate and expedite such participation and to observe that the Korean representatives are in fact duly elected by the Korean people and not mere appointees by military authorities in Korea there be forthwith established a United Nations Temporary Commission on Korea, to be present in Korea, with right to travel, observe and consult throughout Korea." The Commission was informed that all occupying forces should be withdrawn at the earliest possible date following re-establishment of Korean national independence. The General Assembly recommended that elections be held not later than March 31, 1948 "on the basis of adult suffrage and by secret ballot to choose representatives with whom the Commission may consult regarding the prompt attainment of the freedom and independence of the Korean people and which representatives, constituting a National Assembly, may establish a National Government of Korea." The number of representatives from each voting area was to be proportional to the population.

In that the U.S.S.R. had objected to, and abstained from voting for, the establishment of UNTCOK, Soviet authorities refused Commission members entrée into North Korea, and the Ukrainian Soviet Socialist Republic, which had been named a member of the Commission, refused to appoint a representative to participate in its activities. Hence, the Commission was unable to discharge its mission and the matter was referred back to the United Nations. UNTCOK itself had voted five to three against the idea of recommending that national elections be held in Korea. The five favored "consultative elections" to choose Korean representatives to confer with the UN.[102] The Commission chairman, K. P. S. Menon [1898–1982] of India, was reported as being highly critical of the state of civil liberties in both zones of Korea.[103] Several members appeared "skeptical about the possibility of holding anything resembling free elections." The U.S., nonetheless pressed for national election, even if held only in the South.* The upshot was that the Interim Committee of the General Assembly passed a resolution dated February 26, 1948, charging the Commission to proceed "with the observance of elections in all Korea, and if that is impossible, in as much of Korea as is accessible to it." The representatives so elected were authorized to establish a "National Government of Korea." On April 23, UNTCOK issued the following communique:

> In order to comply with the provisions of the resolution passed at its twenty-second meeting, on 12 March
>
> HAVING SATISFIED ITSELF as a result of its extensive field observation in various key districts of South Korea that there exists in South Korea in a reasonable degree of a free atmosphere wherein the democratic rights of freedom of speech, press and assembly are recognized and respected
>
> The United Nations Temporary Commission on Korea *resolves*:

---

[102] On October 7, 1947, the *Chosŏn ilbo* reported that its poll found 58 percent of Korean adults were opposed to establishing a separate South Korean government. USAMGIK surveys found comparable results.

[103] Menon had an affair with the right-wing poet Mo Yun-suk (see p. 114, footnote 41). Mo—then still legally married (though separated) to the German-educated fascist scholar and future ROK minister of education An Ho-sang—mounted a calculated charm offensive, fully coordinated with Syngman Rhee, to sway K. P. S. Menon (India's first foreign secretary and, from early 1948, chair of UNTCOK) toward endorsing South-only elections. Menon later admitted Korea was "the only occasion in my service when I allowed my heart to prevail over my head," a revealing concession that a staged romance was instrumental in UNTCOK's decision to hold separate elections in the South—a turning point that helped lock in Korea's partition. Furthermore, Hugh Deane writes that the U.S. "virtually blackmailed India," threatening to withhold support in the First Indo-Pakistani War unless India voted for separate South Korean elections. See K. P. S. Menon, *Many Worlds Revisited: An Autobiography*, 4th enl. ed. (Bombay: Bharatiya Vidya Bhavan, 1981), 259; Hugh Deane, *The Korean War 1945–1953* (San Francisco: China Books, 1999), 64.

* See Lawrence K. Rosinger, "Election Leaves Korea's Future in Doubt," *Foreign Policy Bulletin* 27, no. 31 (May 14, 1948): 1–3.

> To confirm that it will observe the elections announced by the commanding general of the United States Forces in Korea to be held on 10 May 1948.

As the United Nations undertook these steps, several significant developments unfolded in Korea. Late in February 1948, it was reported that rightist Kim Ku and moderate Kim Kyu-sik had both proposed a joint meeting of North and South Korean leaders to discuss unification of the country and the creation of a national government. On March 25, the North Korean radio voiced agreement to such a North–South conference and extended an invitation to certain Southern leaders, mostly leftists but including the two Kims, to participate in such a conclave in P'yŏngyang in late April. After their return to South Korea from the conference the two Kims expressed satisfaction with the conference resolutions, which were embodied in a joint communique:

1. A nation-wide political conference shall be held following the withdrawal of Soviet and American troops.
2. A unified Provisional Government shall be formed.
3. A nation-wide election shall be held.
4. A constitution shall be enacted.
5. A formal central government shall be formed.

The defection of Kim Ku and Kim Kyu-sik from Rhee now seemed complete. Uppermost in their minds must have been the well-founded fear that given Rhee's control of the South Korean police, an election could be equated with a personal victory for Rhee and the elimination of all effective opposition, themselves included.

The UN-supervised balloting on May 10, 1948, was boycotted not only by the South Korean Communist-led left wing, but also by rightists grouped about the two Kims. Therefore, the election went by default to Rhee with virtually no effective opposition. The left attempted to discourage people from voting, while the U.S. authorities and Rhee's organizations—including the police—exerted every effort to get out the vote. According to official reports, something like 74%

of the electorate cast ballots.* It was ominous that the entire Korean police was alerted allegedly for possible action in forestalling a North Korean effort to create disturbances and, in addition, a civilian "community protective corps" was organized shortly before the election. Undoubtedly, these were Rhee's "youth" groups with which we are already familiar. Curiously, the latter were reported dissolved two weeks after the election. Why was all this organization needed with several thousand armed U.S. troops on the scene? Despite these efforts, most of the candidates elected were so-called "independents," which was interpreted by many informed observers as a direct rebuke to Dr. Rhee. Nonetheless, this fact did not prevent the First Congress of the Republic of Korea, which convened on May 31, 1948, at first naming Dr. Rhee as its chairman and later, following the adoption of a constitution, as the first president of the Republic.

In his opening address from the chair, Dr. Rhee told Parliament in part,

> We deeply regret that our brethren of the five provinces in the North were not able to elect their representatives to participate with us in this Assembly. However, 4½ million refugees from the North participated in the national election, and some of them have been elected as members of this House. Moreover, we have reserved a certain number of seats for the representatives freely elected by our people in the North to come and occupy them so that they will fully share the responsibilities and privileges with the rest of us. In this, we count on the support of the United States and the United Nations so as to achieve our common objective as speedily as possible.

He went on to point out that the main objective of the Congress was "to adopt a constitution based on democratic principles and to establish a government according to that constitution and to form a national defense force for the security and defense of our country and provide for the relief of our sovereign people." He observed that the U.S. military

---

* Eighty per cent of the eligible voters registered and an estimated ninety-two point five per cent of these voted. See *Korea, 1945 to 1948: A Report on Political Developments and Economic Resources with Selected Documents*, comp. Department of State (Washington, DC: U.S. Government Printing Office, 1948), 15.

government would turn over its functions to the new government and withdraw, and then added, "The American forces of occupation, we hope, will remain for security purposes until our government has organized its own security force. ... There is no doubt that whenever we request the withdrawal of the American forces, they will evacuate at once."

A few days later, on June 12, the Korean National Assembly adopted a formal resolution addressed "To our fellow countrymen in North Korea," suggesting that they hold "a general election soon in a free atmosphere in accordance with the UN resolution as we did, elect true representatives of the people, and send them to the National Assembly to sit with us."

The story of Dr. Rhee's rise to undisputed power in South Korea was now at its climax. A democratic republican constitution was enacted on July 12, and on July 20, under authority of that new constitution, the National Assembly elected Dr. Syngman Rhee first president of the Republic of Korea. Dr. Rhee promptly named as his first prime minister, General Yi Pŏm-sŏk, former commandant of Rhee's Officer Training School in Suwŏn and an open admirer of Nazi Germany. General Yi appeared to be the prototype of Rhee's rightist "youth," which had done so much to bring Rhee to power by intimidating and terrorizing the opposition.*

All that remained now was for the functions of government to be transferred from General Hodge to Dr. Rhee. Dr. Rhee, in a letter of August 9 to the general, so requested and the general concurred. And so, on August 15, the new government was inaugurated and formal negotiations commenced for the transfer of all governmental functions from the South Korean Interim Government [Namjosŏn Kwado Chŏngbu], which had been operating under U.S. military authority, to the Republic.

Meanwhile, a parallel development had been taking place in North Korea. In August 1948 a second joint conference of North and South Korean political leaders had been held in P'yŏngyang in order to provide some claim for legitimacy for the establishment of a People's Republic in North Korea. An election followed on August 25, which was not observed by UNTCOK, and the "Supreme People's Council of Korea" was convened in P'yŏngyang. South Koreans allegedly occupied 360 of the 572 seats in the Council, but appeared to represent only small

* See this volume, 260–61.

Communist factions in the Southern zone. The Soviet command in North Korea then proceeded to divest itself of any ostensible governmental authority and of all responsibility for the resolution of difficulties between the military commands of North and South Korea, such as the electric power problem, which by June 1948, still remained unresolved. In one note the Soviet command declared, "The Soviet command cannot fulfill the function of an intermediary between the American command and the People's Council of North Korea."

On September 18, the Soviet Union notified the United States that "pursuant to a request from the Supreme National Assembly of Korea," dated September 10 and addressed to both the Soviet and U.S. governments calling for simultaneous immediate withdrawal of Soviet and American troops from Korea, the U.S.S.R. had ordered the evacuation of all Soviet troops from North Korea, said evacuation to be concluded by the end of December 1948. It was hoped that the U.S. would reciprocate by a similar move in the South. The U.S. replied, "... the U.S. government regards the question of troop withdrawal as part of the larger question of Korean unity and independence, concerning which its views will be presented at the appropriate time by the U.S. delegate to the General Assembly of the United Nations." In fact, the withdrawal of U.S. occupational forces from Korea was completed by June 29, 1949, following which only a small U.S. military advisory group remained.

On October 21, 1949, the UN General Assembly adopted a resolution to renew the UN Commission on Korea, giving it the additional function of observing and reporting "developments which might lead to or otherwise involve military conflict in Korea." Following North Korean broadcasts appealing for national unification, the Commission, on June 10, 1950, sent representatives to the 38th parallel to meet with a North Korean delegation, but with no positive results. The North Koreans claimed that they were only messengers and could engage in no discussion.

Meanwhile, on June 26, 1949, 73-year-old Kim Ku met his death by an assassin's bullet. The assassin? A young Korean army officer.[104]

---

[104] Unknown to Robinson, An Tu-hŭi (1917–1996), the assassin, had in fact worked as a Korean agent for the U.S. Counter Intelligence Corps (CIC), the same agency

Korean police quoted fellow officers as saying that their colleague had argued with Kim Ku over a report that Kim intended to use part of the Korean army for "his own purposes." What these purposes might have been, the police did not specify. The next day, Rhee charged that his death was due to a divergence of opinion within Kim's Independence Party. *The New York Times*, however, reported "highly placed Government sources" to the effect that Kim's death was the outgrowth of a plot in which he had planned a military coup against Rhee's government. Kim had been convinced apparently that the creation of a separate South Korean government would cause a permanent partition of the country and might well lead to armed conflict. Rhee seemed willing to subject the Korean people to these dangers if such satisfied his ambition, and it did. But for Kim Ku, though by no means a political moralist, such a sacrifice of Korean national interest was too much—hence, his joint efforts with Kim Kyu-sik to affect some sort of *modus vivendi* which might lead to national unification. Neither Kim wished to see a Korea united by force and placed under a Rhee dictatorship. Their position was no doubt compounded of fear, personal dislike, and patriotism. These two men, who had started so far apart politically, had been virtually thrown into each other's arms by pressure from the Communist left and the Rhee-dominated right.

War

Early Sunday morning, June 25 (Korean time), North Korean forces moved across the 38th parallel. The war many had long expected was begun. It was soon apparent that "the weakness of South Korean morale and military resistance" severely handicapped the Western position. Within a matter of days, the former South Korean minister of home affairs, Kim Hyo-sŏk [1893?–1966], shifted his allegiance to North Korea and accused President Rhee of having ordered on June 25 the invasion

---

that had surveilled the author and his wife. Also a founding member of the fascist terror group White Shirts Society (Paegŭisa), An Tu-hŭi was backed by Syngman Rhee and only spent one year in prison for the murder. In a 1955 essay An stated that Kim Ku's talks with the North regarding Korean unification had been his sole motivation for assassinating Rhee's rival. But in 1992, he confessed that the head of the Rhee administration's new South Korean Counter Intelligence Corps, modelled after the American CIC, was behind Kim's assassination.

of North Korea.* In view of past plots, there was some reason to believe that had the North Koreans desisted, Rhee would have eventually initiated the fighting on the theory that the United States would have been obligated to support South Korea, and ultimate victory would have meant the extension of his authority over all of Korea. To remove any lingering ambition Rhee might have had along this line, the United Nations, on October 12, 1950, in effect resolved to limit the authority of Rhee's government to the area south of the 38th parallel.

The final words of our story are best told by Leonard M. Bertsch, who did so much to further the effort to affect political unity in South Korea between the moderates of the right and the left, a unity on which might have been built a genuinely popular, liberal state dedicated to the welfare of the Korean people. Shortly after the Korean War was on, Mr. Bertsch wrote as follows:

UN Victory in Korea Poses Question of Rhee's Future **

The October 12 decision by the UN's Interim Committee of Korea—which would limit the authority of President Syngman Rhee's Republic of Korea to the area south of the 38th parallel and ask General Douglas MacArthur to set up a UN-sponsored civil authority north of the line—may have profound influence on the struggle for peace and unity in Korea. The Seoul government promptly notified the UN that this proposal was "unacceptable" as both "wrong in principle and untenable in practice."

The difference of opinion thereby brought into the open reflects a basic problem of the utmost importance for Korea's future. Many observers, including influential governments such as those of India, Britain, and Australia, oppose extending the authority of the Rhee regime to all of Korea because they think that it will be unable to carry out the social reforms and gain the popular support which, as John King Fairbank [1907–1991] pointed out in the October 13 issue of the *Foreign*

* See Blair Bolles, "Can U.S. Quarantine Korean Conflict?," *Foreign Policy Bulletin* 29, no. 37 (July 14, 1950): 1–2.

** This article appeared in the *Foreign Policy Bulletin* 30, no. 2 (October 20, 1950): 2–3, and is reproduced here with the permission of the *Foreign Policy Bulletin* and the author.

Policy Bulletin, is so urgently needed if Communist guerrilla resistance is to be suppressed.

In justifying their position, however, the Rhee spokesmen point out that their regime was organized under the auspices of the UN, was recognized by the General Assembly as the only legal government in Korea and is therefore entitled to assume control of the North. They also contend that the Korean Assembly, elected in June 1948, provided for 100 seats to be assigned to the North after unification.

Against these arguments, opponents of Rhee make two principal points. The first is the recognition was based on the UN commission's acknowledgment of a lawful government, established "over that part of Korea" in which it was able to observe elections. It is argued that there was a reservation of intent to seek a more fundamental solution whenever the reunion of the two zones became possible.

The second point is based on Rhee's record. The original intent of the Korean Assembly was to establish a president with strictly limited powers, according to the French model. Rhee, however, was able to make the cabinet responsible only to himself. Thus fortified, the administration proceeded to dissipate the assets of the state—a considerable quantity, thanks to the confiscation of Japanese property—while the Korean *won* plummeted from an actual exchange rate of 100 to the dollar down to a rate of 1,500. Dr. Arthur Bunce, the ECA Korean administrator, served upon Rhee a long series of Washington-directed complaints that went unheeded. While couched in diplomatic terms, they in effect blamed the venality of the administration for the waste of American aid funds. Finally, in April 1950, American Ambassador John Muccio [1900–1989] delivered an unprecedented open rebuke, denouncing Rhee's attempt to cancel the approaching elections.

During 18 months of his rule, President Rhee frequently jailed Korean personnel of the UN Commission—on spurious charges or on none—warned the Koreans against cooperating with the Commission—and hampered that group with heavy-handed censorship. Legislators were summarily imprisoned for petitioning the Commission to remove foreign troops, a request which, however unwise, was a reflection of the popular will and a legitimate political activity. Other legislators were imprisoned for attempting to restore the cabinet's responsibility to the Assembly.

In the elections of May 30, 1950, despite overt police activity and "youth group" pressure, Rhee's party, the National Society, won only 10 of 210 seats. Twenty-two seats went to the Democratic Nationalist Party, a rightist group, once led by Rhee but now influenced more by such leaders as Shin Ik Hi [Sin Ik-hŭi], Lee Chung Chun [Chi Ch'ŏng-ch'ŏn], and Hong Kil Sun [Hong Kil-sŏn, 1904–1980], returned émigrés from China, who give their deeper loyalty to the memory of Kim Koo [Kim Ku], the assassinated former president-in-exile. Most seats, however, went to opposition parties, and heavy votes went to men known to have incurred the president's disapproval. The conclusion of the press and former representatives was that the elections constituted a condemnation of-the administration and at the same time gave heartening evidence that the people were beginning to learn self-government.

Unless political maturity has begun to develop, however, it would be futile to eliminate Rhee only to have another arbitrary ruler seize personal power. The evidence, fortunately, does not warrant a defeatist view. As the Koreans weight possible sources of leadership, the most obvious will lie among the following of Cho Man Sik [Cho Man-sik], founder of the Chosun Democratic Party [Chosŏn Democratic Party]. Cho himself has been a Russian prisoner since January 1946 and probably has little chance of living to reach freedom. His party, which swept the free local elections in the North in 1945, has several leaders surviving in the South. Among these Lee Yun Yung [Yi Yun-yŏng, 1890–1975] is probably paramount. The party adheres to a vaguely religious egalitarianism.

The fate of another Korean leader, Kimm Kiusic [Kim Kyu-sik], is also in doubt. Left in Seoul last June without means of escape, he may have prejudiced his cause by his coerced collaboration. Kimm's National Independence Federation,* which invoked the open enmity of Rhee, has the quiet approbation of most Korean intellectuals, including many whose announced allegiance, for obvious reasons, has gone to Rhee. Among Kimm's followers are Won Sei Woon [Wŏn Se-hun] ** and Lyuh Woon Hong [Yŏ Un-hong], both of whom were

* Developed out of the Coalition Committee.

** A former member of the rightist Korean Democratic Party and then associated with Kim and Yŏ [Lyuh] on the Coalition Committee.

elected last May in crucial areas adjacent to the capital. Lyuh is the younger brother and possible political heir of the assassinated Lyuh Woon Hyung [Yŏ Un-hyŏng].

Korea may well be on the road toward self-government. If the social and intellectual ferment is permitted to seek its own channels of expression, new leadership will also appear, including authentic spokesmen for the peasantry. Whether or not these hopeful potentialities will be allowed to develop, however, depends to a large extent on the polices which the UN Commission adopts toward the Syngman Rhee government and the success it has in encouraging and safeguarding the emergence of various rival groups and interests.

Japan Diary: Korea

Mark Gayn

(Fig. 23) Dr. Syngman Rhee, the newly elected President of the Korean Republic (thus far limited to the U.S.-controlled half of the country). Prominent in the liberation movement for 35 years, Rhee was chosen on July 20 [1948] by vote of 180 to 16, in a legislature almost completely dominated by the parties he controls. Rhee was educated in U.S., and has been married for 14 years to Francesca Donner, an Austrian he met in Geneva.

CREDIT MARK GAYN

(Fig. 24) Kim Ku, the second of the Big Three in Korea politics. Former Pres. of Korean Government-in-Exile in Chongqing, Kim Ku had opposed elections which gave victory to his rival, Rhee, and in April [1948] journeyed to the Soviet zone of Korea, to add his voice to that of communists opposed to the balloting. A staunch conservative, like Dr. Rhee, Kim Ku has specialized in anti-Japanese terrorism, and is credited with organizing the famous Hongkou Park bombing in Shanghai in 1932, in which a number of Jap. Diplomats (including Foreign Minister Shigemitsu Mamoru, who signed Japan's terms of surrender) and officers were wounded or killed. CREDIT MARK GAYN

(Fig. 25) Kim Kyu-sik, the third of Big Three, has joined with Kim Ku in opposing Rhee and the election, on the ground that it was rigged up by the Rhee political organization, and also travelled to the Soviet zone. A moderate conservative, Dr. Kim ... briefly headed a moderate political coalition and an Interim Assembly set up under American auspices in 1946. He promptly ran into difficulty with Dr. Rhee and other right-wing politicians, and eventually took political refuge in a hospital. Dr. Kim was educated at Roanoke, Va., and at Princeton, sold bibles and farm machinery in exile in China, and later taught English at University of Chengdu in China.

CREDIT MARK GAYN

(Fig. 26) Typical county police chief. He has served for 14 years under Japanese, and according to testimony of American officers, such policemen still regard confessions extracted through torture as legitimate evidence. CREDIT MARK GAYN

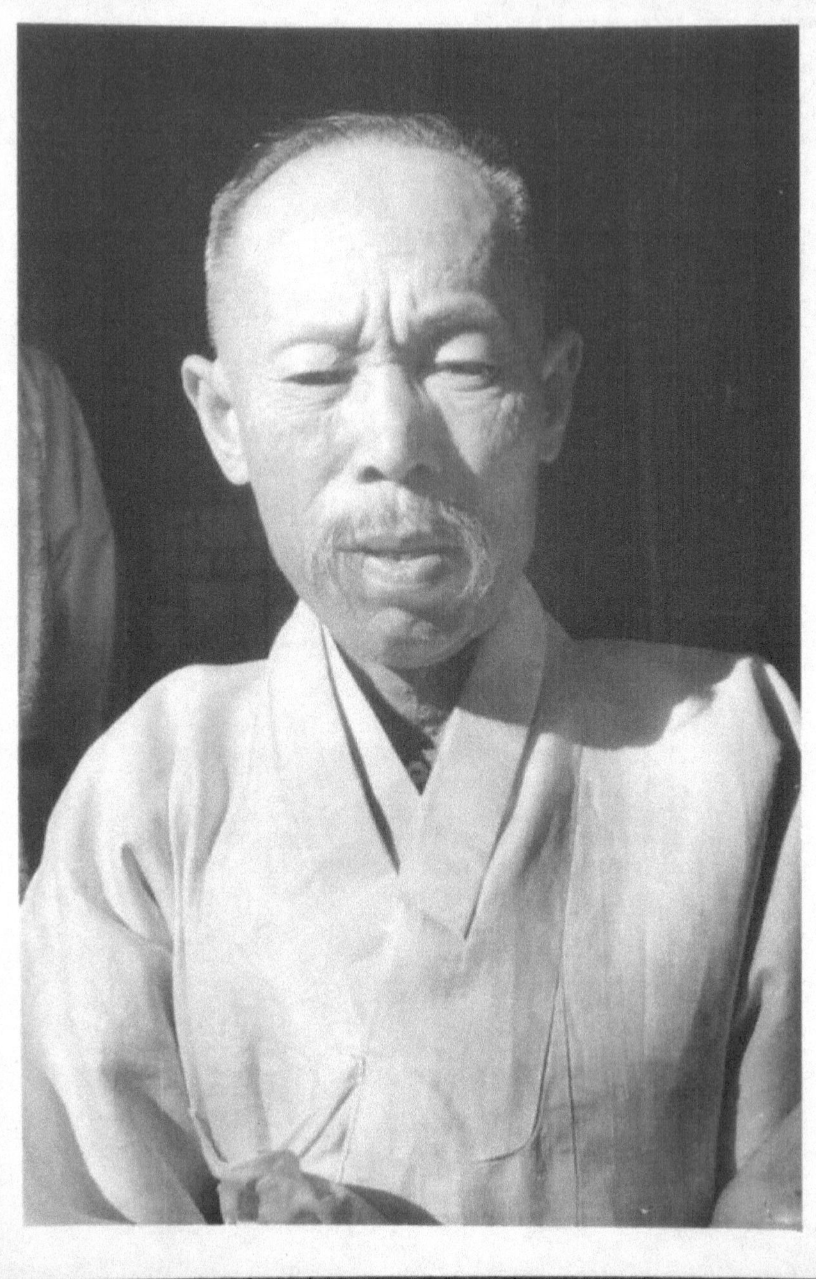

(Fig. 27) Korea is a country of great landlords, who managed to retain their holdings through the decades of Japanese rule, and now vigorously oppose the redistribution of land such as was carried out in Japan under U.S. Army guidance. This landlord owns 20,000 acres of land, serves his guests brandy which he brought from a visit to Paris, has a Japanese-educated son who had turned leftist. CREDIT MARK GAYN

Editorial Note

The following text by Mark Gayn appeared on pages 347 to 443 of his *Japan Diary* (New York: William Sloane Associates, 1948). Gayn's "Korea" chapter actually runs for another forty pages. These additional diary entries, written after his departure, contain no more direct observations and lack some of the vividness and insight of his earlier firsthand accounts from Korea. Accordingly, we have not included these pages in this volume.

Written by a gifted writer and thoroughly edited back in 1948, his book contained only a handful of minor typos requiring spelling or grammar corrections. Gayn made a few factual mistakes and mix-ups, though, which we have either annotated or corrected and annotated. Otherwise, we left the text and its basic formatting intact. Consistent with the Robinson text—and with the usual exceptions—we standardized romanization: Korean in McCune–Reischauer; Chinese in Pinyin (Hanja listed in the glossary); and Russian personal names in ALA-LC. Furthermore, when known, we added dates for all mentioned persons in brackets. All the footnotes in Gayn's text are our editorial annotations.

The preceding five photographs from the fall of 1946 (figs. 23–27) are by Mark Gayn, as are the cutlines reproduced here. (As was customary for press photos until well into the 1980s, these were glued to the reverse of the photos.) Gayn produced these cutlines in the summer or fall of 1948, two years after his visit to Korea. This leads us to speculate that the photos and their accompanying descriptions were intended for inclusion in his book, published in mid-November of that year. Yet his New York publisher did not include any photos. Small head-and-shoulders crops of the Syngman Rhee, Kim Ku, and Kim Kyu-sik portraits had already appeared in Gayn's articles in the New York *PM Daily* on November 3, 1947, and May 6, 1948. The other two photos, along with the one featured on this book's cover, have, in all likelihood, never been published before now.

The editors

Japan Diary: Korea

Mark Gayn

October 14, 1946 TOKYO

Leaving for Korea tomorrow, with Charlotte Ebener [1918–1990], of *Newsweek*, and Foster Hailey [1899–1966], of the *New York Times*.[1] A sudden hitch developed three days ago, when Brigadier General A. P. Fox [1895–1984] summoned me to the Office of the Deputy Chief of Staff, announced that he was sitting as a court-martial officer, and demanded that I reveal the names of my informants for a recent article. The story was a belated report on that fantastic conference in May when a group of colonels objected to purging war criminals from Japan's big business. Headquarters apparently was far less perturbed by what the colonels had to say than by the fact that one of them had talked to a reporter.

I was told that I could inform no one—not even my editor—of the summons, and that I was not entitled to legal counsel. General Fox also told me I could not leave Tokyo. I refused to answer any questions

[1] While in Korea, Ebener only published an unsigned, one-column wrap-up on the 1946 Fall Riots: "Korea: Master Plan," *Newsweek* 28, no. 19 (November 4, 1946): 50. Years later she published her own report about their Korea trip. See Charlotte Ebener, *No Facilities for Women* (New York: Alfred A. Knopf, 1955), 55–72. Hailey does not seem to have published anything more than the article "Prominent Leftist Arrested in Korea" for the October 21, 1946, issue of the *New York Times*; it is the same story that Gayn renders in lively detail in his diary entry of October 20. But Hailey did include a short chapter on Korea in a later book that also discusses his experiences during this trip and offers a broad political analysis of the peninsula. See Foster Hailey, *Half of One World* (New York: Macmillan, 1950), 40–50.

without guidance from the *Chicago Sun*, and promptly filed a long report to Chicago. The next morning, the *Sun* notified me it had taken action with the War Department. And yesterday morning thirteen correspondents, led by Russell Brines [1911–1982] of the Associated Press, and Crane [1901–1963] of the *New York Times*, filed into General Baker's [1891–1968] office, and demanded an explanation. The right to protect one's sources of information is one of the basic elements of a free press, and no correspondent is willing to make any concessions on it. Ten minutes after the group left Baker's presence, General Fox telephoned me to tell me I would "no longer be required in this investigation."

KOREA

October 15, 1946 SEOUL, KOREA

The trip from Tokyo, in an old army transport, was uncomfortable and uneventful. I slept most of the way and did not wake up until the plane started coming down to a landing. The airport was buzzing with activity—bombers and transports warming up, fighters taxiing all over the place, trucks, jeeps, bulldozers at work. It was a regular army base with little civilian nonsense about it.

A young lieutenant gave us a lift to Seoul in a sedan. We drove along a wide dirt road, and watched the face of poverty—the straw-and-mud huts sagging at the corners; the bare yards; the lean mongrels lying in the sun; the men with enormous loads of straw and branches on their backs; and the women with jars and bundles finely balanced on their heads. Charlotte and I agreed that, in contrast, China looked well-to-do.

The lieutenant spoke of the Koreans with contempt. He said they were dirty and treacherous. We were watching a flight of fighter planes cavorting over villages to the west. The planes dived in a mock attack, re-formed in the sky, and then dived on a new target.

"Psychological warfare," the lieutenant said. "That's the only way to show these gooks we won't stand for any monkey business."

Major Buel A. Williamson [1926–2020],[2] the red faced, stout Public Relations Officer to Lieutenant General John R. Hodge [1893–1963], our commander for Korea, made a stab at affability. He made me think of a real estate agent, appraising visitors to his office to see if he would earn a commission. His face fell when I said I did not want to see General Hodge until I had had a chance to look around and understand the picture a little better. Briskly, Williamson made us fill out a long questionnaire, and assigned us to billets.

Hailey and I were put in a room in the Chosun Hotel,[3] a colonels' billet known hereabouts as "Frozen Chosun." Charlotte was sent to a women's billet. The Chosun is a weird compound of a mid-Western, small-town hotel, an army barrack, and a Korean roadside inn. It is large and shabby, filled with the smell of garlic, and serviced by Korean bellhops who understand nothing of what you are saying, but smile hopefully. Both Foster and I went to sleep.

We woke up in time for dinner. Charlotte was already waiting downstairs with two local correspondents, Stanley Rich [1924–2005] of the United Press and Roy Roberts [1887–1967] of the Associated Press. Both are nice, keen boys, and while we ate our dinner, they gave us a general survey of the situation.

The biggest story, they agreed, is the bloody riots which have been sweeping the countryside in our zone. General Hodge has called them "disgraceful agitated riots." There is apparently some reason to think, however, that the economic distress and the universal hatred for the Korean police, which we have taken over from the Japanese,[4] have had something to do with the uprisings. No Americans have yet been attacked, but at least sixty Korean cops have been killed.

Later Charlotte told us of her billet. She was put in a room with a woman who violently objected to Charlotte, on the ground that the

[2] Major Buel A. "Pappy" Williamson. According to one source, Williamson made it a point to brief every visiting reporter before they had a chance to form their own opinions. See Oliver Elliot, *The American Press and the Cold War: The Rise of Authoritarianism in South Korea, 1945–1954* (Cham: Palgrave Macmillan, 2018), 43.

[3] See Robinson's "Betrayal of a Nation," in this volume, 77, footnote 13.

[4] See ibid., 78, footnote 15.

room was reserved for CAF 9's. (CAF is a civilian salary rating, going up to 15). Charlotte explained that under army regulations, she was CAF 14. The woman promptly called her darling, told her they had had no water in the house for eight days because the Russians had stolen a turbine on the Yalu River, in North Korea, and warned Charlotte against the Korean servants. They steal everything in sight, she said, to support their relatives who had fled from the Red Terror in the Soviet zone.

"When things come to such a pass," the woman said, "they have to be resolved one way or another. Even if it means war now!"

October 16, 1946 SEOUL

Spent the day making rounds of the XXIV Corps, the Military Government, and the Joint U.S.–Soviet Commission.[5] Discovered, with some surprise, that orders had been sent down the chain of command to give me no information. Two of the men I met especially interested me. One was Lieutenant Leonard Bertsch [1910–1976], the rotund and bespectacled political adviser to General Hodge. A doctor of philosophy from Holy Cross and a lawyer from the Harvard Law School, Bertsch, I suspect, fancies himself as a sort of "American Century" Machiavelli. His primary concern is Korean politicians, and he is saturated with their lore. Bertsch's current assignments in intrigue are two: he is trying to split the Korean Communist Party, and he is promoting a coalition of moderates of both the right and the left. Bertsch is a delightful talker, one reason being that he remembers, and quotes, every *bon mot* he has ever uttered.

The other man was Dr. Arthur C. Bunce [1901–1953], a Treasury official on loan to the State Department on loan to General Hodge, with the personal rank of Minister. Bunce spent six years setting up

[5] The Joint Commission was organized per directive of the Moscow Decision of December 1945. The Soviet Union and United States delegations met in Seoul and P'yŏngyang between March and May 1946 and then from May to October 1947 in an attempt to form a unified provisional Korean government to be followed by a permanent government. The Commission's failure delivered the Korean issue to the United Nations Security Council. Discussed in detail in "Betrayal of a Nation," chapters III, VI, and VIII.

rural YMCAs in North Korea, and he speaks a fluent Korean. The difference between Bertsch and Bunce is vast. Bertsch is immersed in political scheming to the exclusion of all else. Bunce considers Korean problems in terms of social and economic forces. He is the first man I have met here who speaks with genuine affection of the Koreans. He is also the first to lay emphasis on social reform, and not on the Soviet menace.

There is an atmosphere of violence, intrigue, and uncertainty about this place. Seoul may not look it, but it talks and acts like an armed camp on the eve of an insurrection. It is hard to analyze this impression, for it is compounded of things both seen and intangible. Such things as the submachine gun next to my jeep driver, news of yet another uprising, or an officer's lament, "I've got six more months to go. The Russkys will be here before then."

I find that fear of communism, rather than a desire to reform or rehabilitate, forms the solid base of our policy for Korea. I am told that when we came here on September 7 of last year,[6] we found that a progressive Korean government had been formed thirteen hours earlier. Bertsch and many others feel that, with all its defects, the government — known as the People's Republic[7] — could have been converted into a staunch and useful ally. Instead, we branded the People's Republic red, and wasted two precious months driving it underground.

This was more than a functional conflict between our own Military Government and a native government with roots in the resistance movement. Their very ideas were different. The Koreans thought of themselves as a nation liberated. To this day we appear uncertain whether we had come to liberate or to occupy. The Koreans wanted to be rid of the collaborators. We not only kept the collaborators in office (for we were understaffed), but also we actually began our "liberation" by ordering the hated Japanese governor general, his officials, and his

[6] It was on September 7, 1945, that General Douglas MacArthur announced Hodge would be in charge of Korean affairs, but it was only the next day, September 8 (Korean time), that U.S. forces landed at Inch'ŏn and established USAMGIK.
[7] The Korean People's Republic consisted of local government formations that coalesced just after Japan's surrender on August 15, 1945. See Robinson's "Betrayal of a Nation," chapter II, 103–19 in this volume.

police to stay on the job as if nothing had happened. The People's Republic wanted social reform. The Americans vetoed any drastic social or economic changes.

But, having suppressed the People's Republic, we turned to the other extreme. We imported an aged rightist by the name of Syngman Rhee [Yi Sŭng-man, in office 1948–1960] all the way from Washington, and made him and other rightists our counselors, and the bearers of our hope. Rhee, Bertsch assured me, is not a Fascist. "He is two centuries before fascism—a pure Bourbon." Yet Rhee was allowed, and even encouraged, to build up a political machine. Rhee's followers took key posts in our Military Government, from police chiefs to county masters. They also set up a network of mass organizations, from women's clubs to terrorist bands.

Rhee's was a one-track mind: he wanted independence for Korea. But he saw an independent Korea as a feudal land, with himself at the head. He spoke for every Korean when he demanded that the country, now split along the 38th parallel into a Soviet and a U.S. zone, be reunited. But he spoke for no one but the landlords when he opposed land reform, social security, or civil freedoms.

Like many other politicians in East Asia with whom we have allied ourselves, Rhee did not fight Japanese collaborators; he embraced them. They hated the same things he hated, and they saw in him the promise of continued well-being. And since we—General Hodge and the Military Government—depended on Rhee and trusted him, and since we were terribly shorthanded, we condoned a government by collaborators.

"The Koreans in the Military Government," one official told me today, "represent a conspiracy of insufferable corruption. People we now use to govern Korea are rightists who happily did Japan's dirty work. There are now men in the Korean police force who actually were decorated by the Japanese for their cruelty and efficacy in suppressing Korean nationalism."

We did, I was told, issue a stern order for the purge of collaborators. This was mistranslated so skillfully by our Korean interpreters in the Military Government that when the hour of purge came, it was discovered that in all of our zone the order could be applied to only one official.

I was also told this: One day early last spring, it dawned on our policy-makers on the Potomac that our Korean allies—and our own blunders—were losing us Korean good will at a catastrophic rate. If on September 7, 1945, our men landing in Korea were greeted with hosannas, now a Military Government poll of public opinion showed that the Koreans in our zone preferred the Japanese to us.

Thus our command here was ordered to sever its bonds with the extreme right. Instead, every effort was to be made to form a coalition of moderates, both left and right, who would and could give the Koreans a measure of reform.

The job was delegated to Bertsch, and he cast about for a conservative who could head the coalition. Bertsch's choice fell on Kim Kyu-sik [1881–1950],[8] the U.S.-educated moderate rightist who knew the language of reform, and could even clothe it in fine Elizabethan English. To win over the leftists, Bertsch persuaded the great leader of the wrecked People's Republic, the silver-haired, silver-tongued Yŏ Un-hyŏng [1886–1947],[9] to enter the coalition as co-chairman. The first meeting of Yŏ and Kim took place in Bertsch's own house on June 14, 1946.

Although Bertsch sounded confident, there seemed to be two oversized flies in his ointment. One is the feud between General Hodge and Major General Archer Lerch [1894–1947],[10] Military Governor. Lerch's men told me Bertsch was "an upstart," with whom "it's impossible to work." The other fly is the inability of the military here to readjust their minds to the new policy. Directive or no directive, they feel that only a "strong man," like Rhee, can stop communism. Bertsch's plan may remain a scrap of paper unless the military, in and out of the Military Government, agree to carry it out.

[8] See ibid., 120, footnote 45.

[9] Yŏ Un-hyŏng was an early leader of the Korean communist movement and an important figure in the Korean independence movement during the Pacific War. He was selected by the Japanese on the eve of liberation to form a provisional government body. In July 1947, he was assassinated by a member of the White Shirts Society (Paegŭisa), as was Kim Ku (1876–1949) two years later. Yŏ is discussed at length in "Betrayal of a Nation."

[10] Major General Archer L. Lerch, U.S. military governor in Korea from December 1945 to his death in September 1947.

Late at night talked Roy Roberts into going for a walk. The streets were still crowded, and there was much more electric light than one sees in Tokyo. We walked down to Ponjŏng,[11] the main shopping street. The shops were closed, and women peddlers, in their brightly colored little jackets and long white skirts, were hurrying home with their bundles balanced on their heads. What amazed me was the number of drunk Koreans and GIs. I saw an American arguing with a Korean. The soldier was holding the Korean by the lapels of his coat and shouting, "I'll show you, you goddamned gook!" The Korean did not seem to be frightened. Roy stepped in and said to the soldier, "Go easy, boy." Then the GIs companions, who were watching from the sidelines, came up and pulled him away. Roy said such incidents are frequent and generate much resentment against the Americans.

At night there was some scattered gunfire outside our wall, and we could see some Korean policemen running down the street with pistols on the ready.

October 17, 1946 SEOUL

After lunch Charlotte and I went to see Bertsch in his office in Tŏksu Palace, where the U.S.–Soviet Joint Commission holds its sessions. When Bertsch came in, a little late, he began to search for a lost button, some missing papers, and a mislaid corps insignia. At the same time he conducted a conversation with five different people, making little sense but being very witty. Finally, over the protests of his secretary, whom he called Blossom ("Every woman under seventy is Blossom to me."), we took Bertsch up to the roof.

Bertsch's topic for today was the Communist Party. He said it lost some strength as a result of police repression and the party's approval of Allied trusteeship for Korea, but he thought it still had some 18,000 members in our zone and at least 100,000 active sympathizers.

[11] Ponjŏng is the Korean reading of the area's colonial period Japanese name Honmachi, which is now called Myŏng-dong. Gayn and the U.S. Military referred to it as Bun Chong—a five minutes' walk from Hodge's headquarters.

Like some other officers I have talked to, Bertsch felt that one of the secrets of Communist strength lay in our own mistakes. "If a free election were held today," he said, "the Communists would get 20 per cent of the votes in our zone, and five in the Russian zone. The people here would be voting not *for* the reds, but *against* us."

The Korean Communist Party, Bertsch said, was formally organized in 1922, and admitted into the Comintern in 1926. After that, the party disintegrated into a flock of rival "clubs"—"Tuesday," "The Northwest M-L" (for Marx-Lenin), and "Seoul." In 1937, there was a reorganization, and, as Bertsch put it, "The Seoul Club was anointed as the bearer of the true word."

Sometime this year Bertsch obtained the membership lists of the old factions, and had gone to work trying to split them apart. He sounded well pleased with his handiwork, but from another source I have heard that there had been only one defection from the Communist Party. A small clique of Communists called on Syngman Rhee, and asked for his blessings and cash. If they join up with Rhee, these "converts" will be of little use to Bertsch's coalition.

October 18, 1946 SEOUL

In the morning Bertsch took Charlotte and me to see Kim Kyu-sik, the man he had chosen for head of the new moderate coalition. On the way, Bertsch told us that Kim came of "the standard poor but respectable parentage," studied at Roanoke, Virginia, and taught English literature to the Chinese. Bertsch went to special pains to tell us that U.S. Army doctors had found Kim to have "a satisfactory life expectancy." I did not grasp the point until much later, when Bertsch, with bitterness, told us of a State Department official here, who, at a banquet, referred to Kim as "Mr. Kim Kyu Sickly." Since Kim is, in fact, no athlete, the pun achieved some irritating fame.

Far in the outskirts, we drove up a steep hill, and stopped before a lovely Japanese-style house, guarded by a Korean policeman and an American MP. Japan-fashion, we removed our shoes, and were taken to a spacious sun room. There were three men already in the room—a

Colonel Shaw [1922–1950],[12] Chief of the Labor Division in the Military Government; a natty, young Korean named Mun;[13] and Kim himself.

Kim struck me as a grotesque figure. He is very short, and tremendous around the waist. He was wearing a beautiful gray gown, which made him look feminine, and American zippered felt slippers. His lap was covered with a rug. As we came in, he was filling a two-foot-long reed pipe with a tiny brass head with tobacco out of a GI pouch. Once he began to talk, I was charmed by his cultured and smooth flowing speech.

While Kim talked to Mun, Bertsch was explaining the significance of the conference. This appeared to be another of his Machiavellian shenanigans. The Korean Federation of Labor[14] had been driven deep underground after last month's strikes, but it still remained a powerful force. Mun, the Federation's only officer still at large, was now being wooed into supporting Bertsch's coalition. Mun, I thought, looked uncomfortable.

When Kim turned to us, he quickly established his own position. He was a moderate rightist. He favored State control of the major industries, farm reform, and social insurance. From this vantage point he proceeded to attack both the right and the left, reserving his sharp-

---

[12] William Hamilton Shaw was born and raised in Korea. After going to the United States to pursue his education, he returned to Korea after the Pacific War to help establish a Korean Naval Academy.

[13] His full name was Mun Ŭn-jong (dates unknown).

[14] Here and throughout the chapter the author consistently mixed up the names of the left and the right-wing labor organizations in his English rendering: Gayn's left-wing "Korean Federation of Labor" would better be termed the National Council of Korean Labor Unions (Chosŏn Nodong Chohap Chŏn'guk P'yŏngŭi-hoe, short: Chŏnp'yŏng). Organized in early November 1945, it was an all-Korean labor organization that included workers in northern Korea, with a membership of around 600,000 (Gayn reports later in this text that there were 270,000 members in the South). Right from its inception, it fought for a minimum wage, an eight-hour work day, and the prohibition of child labor, among other things. Notably linked to the communist movement (Mao Zedong, Kim Il-sŏng, Pak Hŏn-yŏng were elected honorary chairpersons), it was the one labor organization that represented the overwhelming majority of industrial workers in a single labor organization. Rhee's right-wing "Labor Association," on the other hand, which Gayn mentions and terms the Great Korea Laborers' Association, should be referred to as the (Korean) National Federation of Labor Unions (Taehan Tongnip Ch'ongsŏng Chŏn'guk Nodong Ch'ongdongmaeng). Also compare "Betrayal of a Nation," 166–67 and 235–36.

est barbs for Rhee. He felt that the United States and Russia blocked the creation of a democracy in Korea by splitting her in two. He thought the rightists were losing popular support by bickering. He believed the leftists, "pre-occupied with sabotage," were missing a golden chance to sweep the country in the election scheduled for the end of this month.

Later, Kim told us a bit about his father, who had served at the court of the Korean kings. Kim himself was born in 1881, spent much of his childhood with American missionaries, and at the age of sixteen was taken to the United States by a rich uncle. After seven years of study, he returned to Korea only to go into exile in 1913. He tried to start a secret officers' training camp in Mongolia, but gave it up when the funds promised by the Korean underground failed to arrive. After that Kim went into business, selling hides in Mongolia, Bibles in North China, and power engines in Shanghai.

Kim's interest in a Korean revolution seemed sporadic. From time to time, he went abroad to plead Korea's case. But most of the time he was either a merchant or a teacher, including a stretch at the ultra-conservative Central Political Institute of the Guomindang [Chinese Nationalist Party, better known as Kuomintang]. In 1942 he was appointed Minister of Information of the so-called "Korean Provisional Government" in Chongqing, which barely stayed alive on a Guomindang subsidy. By November 1945, when a U.S. Army plane took him to Korea as "a private citizen," he was vice-premier of the government-in-exile.

Over lunch, Bertsch talked excitedly of the greatness which destiny held in store for Kim. I had the impression that, perhaps subconsciously, Bertsch was trying to make up for the drive and excitement that were so conspicuously lacking in Kim. There is a strange relationship between the two men. Bertsch talks as if he were a disciple of Kim the prophet. Yet, now and then, the schemer in Bertsch wakes up, and then Bertsch is a political puppeteer. What is happening, I think, is that each man is using the other for his own ends. Kim is shrewd and ambitious, and he hopes Bertsch may help to make him president of the Korean Republic. Bertsch, apart from the delight of playing god, may also be considering the possibility of becoming an adviser to the Korean Government, headed by his friend Kim.

In the afternoon, Charlotte, Foster, and I went calling on Syngman Rhee.

Like Kim and most of the other self-respecting politicians, Rhee lives in a building put at his disposal by a Korean multimillionaire. An armed policeman opened the gate for us, and we waited in a large compound filled with other armed men, until word came down from the hill. Then we walked up the steep, well-kept path, and halfway up the hill Syngman Rhee met us. He had thought that Bertsch was with us, and sounded disappointed when we said he was not.

In the small western-style living room, whose main decoration was a huge multi-colored pagoda, we had a chance to look Rhee over. He is a thin man, with sparse white hair, pale lips and almost no eyebrows. His eyes are concealed behind thin slits of eyelids, so that most of the time he looks as if he is asleep. (Charlotte, in an irreverent aside, whispered, "Doesn't the old boy look like a mummy?") But Rhee was not asleep. His mind was alert and busy, and his words were vigorous.

He sat erect in his chair and threw bait out, to see what we would bite. He attacked General Hodge, the Communists, and the famous Moscow decision of 1945,[15] which proclaimed a U.S.–Soviet trusteeship for Korea. When he found out we had seen Kim, he damned him with praise. He alternately praised and attacked the Military Government, and referred bitingly to U.S. Army corruption.

I was trying to understand what makes Rhee what he is. He has been away from his native land for thirty-five out of his seventy-three years, and when he returned he spoke what was described to me as "a Hawaiian brand of pidgin Korean." Yet he is a political boss without peer in Asia, except perhaps for Chiang Kai-shek [Jiang Jieshi, in office 1928–1975]. With what must be a sixth sense, he has mastered the complexities of Korean politics, and he plays the game ruthlessly, skillfully, and to his own advantage.

He had long been a legend and a symbol in Korea, and he has made the legend pay. There is much talk of the "assessments" his agents

[15] See "Betrayal of a Nation," 82–83, footnote 21, and pp. 85–92.

collect throughout our zone. I was told of a Women's Patriotic Convention in Pusan, at which 1,500 delegates were "assessed" 200 yen each in honor of the great man's visit to the city.

Much like the Japanese and the Germans, Rhee talks in terms of a "Great Korea" and the "Korean Folk." His main political instrument is the *Han'guk* (or Korean Folk[16]) Democratic Party [aka Korean Democratic Party], an organization of landlords and rich collaborationists.

Rhee has a Master's degree from Harvard and a Doctor's from Princeton. Yet his English is labored, and he puts sentences together with an effort. I wondered by what inner strength he had impressed his ideas on General Hodge and men of the Military Government. Listening to Rhee, I thought he was a sinister and dangerous man, an anachronism who had strayed into this age to use the clichés and machinery of democracy for unscrupulous and undemocratic ends. I have been in Korea only seventy-two hours, and it may well be that my impressions are wrong. But I have begun to think that it is not Hodge who is the most important man in the U.S. zone, but this old, pale man with half-closed eyes.

Rhee was now in the middle of a passage on Hodge:

"When General Hodge landed here, a Japanese general saw him and told him to stay away from the terrible Koreans. Then I heard that when five hundred people came to welcome General Hodge, the Korean police fired on them and killed five men. General Hodge has also said that the Koreans and the Japanese are the same breed of cats.[17] It was unfortunate that Hodge got his information from a Japanese

---

[16] Gayn's translation is off. *Han'guk* does not imply any sense of "folk;" it is no more than one of two most common names for Korea. In subsequent references to Han'guk Minjudang, we changed the author's translation to Korean Democratic Party which then also matches Robinson's translation.

[17] William R. Langdon (1891–1963), acting political advisor in Korea, claims that Hodge was just referring to Korean collaborators and Korean policemen in Japanese services and, in that context, he said that "Koreans consider them the same breed of cats as Jap policemen." See "The Acting Political Adviser in Korea (Langdon) to the Secretary of State" (November 26, 1945), in *Foreign Relations of the United States: Diplomatic Papers, 1945*, comp. United States Department of State, vol. VI, *The British Commonwealth, The Far East* (Washington, DC: Government Printing Office, 1969), 1134–35.

general. ... " The door opened, and an Occidental woman came in with a small silver pot. This was Rhee's Viennese wife, who had been his secretary before he married her. She was described to me as "Rhee's greatest liability, because she thinks he is the greatest man in Korea, and he agrees with her." I had expected a fat old ogre. This woman was slim, handsome, and poised. She made small talk, and poured a white liquid out of the pot. This was *soju*, or burning wine.

"This is almost my first anniversary here," said Rhee. "I arrived in Seoul on October 16 of last year. You could call this an anniversary celebration."

We took a sip of *soju* and choked and gasped as it burned our throats. Mrs. Rhee talked of servant problems and the high cost of living.

"Last March," said Rhee, "I went south, and told immense crowds: 'We're trying to save our country from a sell-out. The best thing is to tell every Communist to change his heart. Those who oppose us, let them go home, to their fatherland.' This created a tremendous stir in the south.

"Last May, General Hodge asked me to cooperate with the new coalition. But I couldn't change my stand. So I said I'd stay silent. I've now kept silent for five months, even though the program of the [Bertsch] coalition is contrary to the principles of democracy. The men of the coalition, for instance, want to confiscate all land and redistribute it among the sharecroppers. I say land reform must be left to the Provisional Government, when we have one."

I told Rhee I was planning to go south. He produced three large calling cards, and on them wrote notes of introduction. They were to the governors of three provinces.

"All these are my friends," he said. "They'll get *good* information for you."

Dr. Bunce was waiting in the crowded bar of the Chosun Hotel when we got back. He is a charming, mild-mannered man, with a ready store of anecdotes and a tremendous background in world—and Korean—rural economics. Over the dinner, he expressed his conviction that the best way to meet the challenge of communism is through social reform. He is very pleased with the new turn of policy here, and with the coalition. If a progressive regime could be established in Seoul, he said, the Communist administration in the Soviet zone would willy-nilly have to come to terms with it.

October 19, 1946 SEOUL

Once again Major Williamson said he was unable to get a jeep for us, and once again we were sitting disconsolately in the Chosun lobby when a Korean delegation came in to see Foster, in the apparent belief that he was publisher of the *New York Times*. They wanted to know if we were in Foster's entourage, and when I said no, their faces fell. They rose just as fast when they discovered we met Rhee yesterday. The delegation, two men and a woman, came in behalf of one of Rhee's numerous political satellites, the Representative Democratic Council [of South Korea], which, local wits told me, was so called because it was neither representative nor democratic.

The delegation was led by a fat and voluble man with a shining Phi Beta Kappa key. He said, "I am Pak, Brown '05, you must've heard of me," and to make him happy I said yes, indeed I had.[18] With him was a shabby looking man who once studied at the University of Iowa, and a Mrs. Kim Sŏn [1896?–?], who said she represented the Women's Patri-

[18] Brown '05 was Paek Sang-gyu (aka Sangkyu Pak and later Pack Sang Kyu, 1880–1957), a wealthy Korean landlord and economics scholar. (Why he was enrolled under the name Pak at Brown University in 1902 is unclear. Paek later changed the spelling to Pack, most likely due to the proximity of the pronunciation of his name to that of the English verb *pack*.) It was also Paek who, together with Yŏ Un-hyŏng's younger brother Yŏ Un-hong (1891–1973), greeted General Hodge on September 8, 1946, on his landing at Inch'ŏn Harbor. Paek and Yŏ acted as representatives of the Preparatory Committee for the Establishment of a Korean State (Chosŏn Kŏn'guk Chunbi Wiwŏnhoe), the first major political coalition aimed at forming an independent state after liberation. (See also Robinson's "Betrayal of a Nation," 107.) General Hodge, however, did not want to discuss any self-governing options with Paek and his committee. Paek then became the vice president of the Korean Red Cross and a member of the National Assembly. In 1951 Paek was abducted to the North, where he, like many other prominent former South Korean personalities, was given an office in the Council for Promotion of Peace and Unification of Korea (Chae Puk P'yŏnghwa T'ongil Ch'okchin Hyŏbŭihoe).

otic Association and the Women's Nationalist Party,[19] both of the Rhee camp.

The trio talked of the subversive Communists and the treacherous nationalists, who once worked with Rhee but were now forming their own little cliques. It soon appeared that there were wheels within wheels in Rhee's machine. All three readily agreed that the banker who had given his house to Kim Kyu-sik was enjoying wealth "generally regarded as ill-gotten." But there was disagreement when it came to the multimillionaire who had given his house to Rhee.

Brown '05 said, "He's a nouveau riche, an economic upstart. Why, he made his fortune in the last six or seven years, as a Jap contractor."

His male companion agreed: "The man is wallowing in wealth."

But Mrs. Kim Sŏn dissented. "No," she said sharply. "He's a patriot. He also has a very fine mind."

The men beat a hasty retreat, and Mrs. Kim Sŏn proceeded to tell us the story of her grandfather, whose land in North Korea once yielded 20,000 bushels, but the Communists had now taken this land away and given it to his tenants, and all he was allowed to keep was land producing 200 bushels a year.

At this point, Foster showed up, and Charlotte and I fled. Behind us, we could hear the rich baritone: "I'm Pak, Brown '05, you must've heard of me. . . . "

After lunch, Charlotte, Foster, and I wandered over to a Korean newspaper office and looked up a man named Muk.[20] He was an English speaking editor, recommended to us as both impartial and well informed. We had already met some Korean rightists, and Bertsch was lining up more of them for us. Now we wanted Muk to get us interviews with labor and farm union people, and with some leftist politicians.

"That will be difficult," said Muk. "They've gone underground."

We said, "You don't understand. We aren't looking for Communists. We just want people left of center."

"They're underground or in jail."

---

[19] Full names: Korean Women's Patriotic Association (Taehan Yŏja Aeguktan) which, after the March First movement, was established in California, and Korean Women's Nationalist Party (Taehan Yŏja Kungmindang).

[20] Muk is a rare surname in Korea. Gayn was inconsistent with transcriptions and may have meant Mr. Mok.

Muk explained that since the railroad strike, three weeks ago, the Korean police had arrested many scores of leftist leaders, closed up leftist newspapers, raided union offices, and handed over the headquarters of the Korean Federation of Labor[21] to a rightist group (which, we later learned, was controlled by Rhee).

We kept pressing, and Muk, after consulting some reporters, finally said he would try to find Hŏ Hŏn [1885–1951],[22] one of the five leaders of the defunct People's Republic. Bertsch had already told us that he was trying to win Hŏ Hŏn's support for the coalition. The army still could find no jeep for us, and so we walked across the sprawling city, down dusty roads and filthy alleyways, until we reached a two-story building. Muk went in, and returned in five minutes to tell us that Hŏ Hŏn was upstairs, in a conference of leftist groups called to form a united leftist front to oppose Bertsch's rightist coalition.

We went upstairs to a huge, bare, ugly room with dirty white walls. There were two long tables. At one a dozen people sat in conference. At the other two men waited for us. Hŏ Hŏn is a handsome, graying man of sixty, with a smiling face. His hands were trembling. The other man had a stern face and a tremendous neck and shoulders. He said he was Kim Wŏn-bong [aka Yaksan, 1898–1958], War Minister in the defunct government-in-exile in Chongqing and now head of the Korean National Revolutionary Party [Chosŏn Minjok Hyŏngmyŏng-dang].[23] I gathered that he had moved leftward since his Chongqing days. Both men talked readily, but occasionally one of them would go over to the other table to join in the discussion there.

In the three hours that we were with him, Hŏ Hŏn said two things of especial interest. One was his spirited defense of trusteeship.

"Korea," he said, "has been under Japanese domination for so long that she has to prepare herself for independence. But during this period she must also be secure. Therefore, it's desirable to have a trusteeship—

[21] See pp. 343, footnote 14.

[22] See Robinson, "Betrayal of a Nation," 94, footnote 31.

[23] Kim Wŏn-bong, a military leader and founder of the egalitarian, anarchist group Ŭiyŏltan (Righteous Brotherhood), had always leaned more to the left. During his long exile in China, he had co-founded the Korean Nationalist Revolutionary Party in 1935 with Kim Kyu-sik and Cho So-ang (1887–1958). Facing possible imprisonment and the target of death threats in the South, he would—like Hŏ Hŏn—decide to stay on in the North after the April 1948 Joint North–South Conference in P'yŏngyang.

but not under one power. We have had too much trouble in the past dealing with single nations, China, Russia, and Japan. ... The trouble with the U.S. Military Government is that it doesn't understand the situation, and makes blunders. One of these is the inability to see that most of the Korean leftists are nationalists and not Communists. Yet, all of them are being oppressed alike."

The second item dealt with the current wave of arrests.

"On the morning of September 30," Hŏ Hŏn said, "I heard 500 or 600 shots outside of my house. This was the beginning of the raids, carried out jointly by the police and Rhee's terrorists. They concentrated on the railroad union, but they also raided other union offices, beat up people, wrecked the furniture, and took the places over.

"In all, 3,000 people were arrested here, and of these 1,700 were kept in jail. Today 1,400 remain imprisoned. The morning the raids started, I went to General Lerch. I said, 'Did you order the arrests and the shooting down of the people, or are the police doing it on their own?' Lerch didn't answer."

He pulled a piece of paper out of a pocket. "For six months I've been trying to get a house to live in. There were 60,000 Japanese homes distributed to Koreans by the Military Government, but I can get nothing. I have an authorization, but I still can't get the house. Korean rightists in the Military Government say, 'You're a Communist. You've lots of counterfeit money. You can buy anything.'"

"Now I'm told that if I support the coalition, I'll be able to get a house. It's such tactics that alienate the Korean people."

Kim Wŏn-bong now returned from the other table, and Hŏ Hŏn left us. Kim talked softly, and his gentleness looked odd beside his powerful hands, or the tale of violence he told us. "Hŏ Hŏn is a lawyer," he said. "I'm a professional revolutionary." As a youth, he fled to China, studied in Chiang Kai-shek's Whampoa Military Academy, and then served as an officer in the great Chinese Northern Expedition in 1926–27. Ever since he has been in the Korean underground, in Shanghai, Manchuria, and North Korea. By the time the war ended, he said, he had 3,000 guerrillas under him.

The only other guerilla force, he said, was Communist-led and based in Manchuria. It made two major raids on North Korea, in 1935–

36 and again in 1940, attacking Japanese installations. It totaled about 3,000 men. The Communists also had a small, tight, and active underground within Korea. It was led by Pak Hŏn-yŏng [1900–1955], who is now top leader of the Communist Party in our zone, and has gone into hiding. Pak had served three jail terms for anti-Japanese activity by the time he was twenty-five. In 1926, while in prison, he feigned insanity and managed to escape. He fled to Russia and spent three years at the Lenin University in Moscow. In 1929, he returned to Korea and was arrested the minute he landed. On release from prison in 1936, he became a worker in a brick factory and an underground leader.

Hŏ Hŏn now returned to us, and the two men began to fire loaded questions at us. Can we have a democratic election, they said, when thousands of leftists are in jail? Can we have an election when labor unions are barred from politics, and the police terror is at its height? Can the coalition of Kim Kyu-sik and Yŏ Un-hyŏng be taken seriously when Yŏ Un-hyŏng's entire People's Party[24] is in jail or hiding? Can the Military Government expect cooperation from the Koreans when even such a meeting as that—they pointed at the other table—could be raided at any minute?

We did not answer. All we wanted to know was if the two men could arrange a meeting for us with some leftist labor or farmer leader. Very firmly, both said no, because any man leaving his hiding place would be arrested on sight. We kept insisting, and finally it was agreed that a special guide would lead us to some hideout tomorrow.

October 20, 1946 SEOUL

Our difficulties continue. Yesterday we had drinks with an officer from Military Government, and invited him to have lunch with us today. This morning he sent word down he would not come, for he had been seen with us yesterday and severely reprimanded.

Although there are several jeeps assigned to Williamson's office, they seem to be available only when we go to "approved" interviews. Today, finally, I demanded to see Hodge at once so that I could register

[24] Korean People's Party (Chosŏn Inmindang).

a formal protest. Williamson then backed down and said he would have a jeep for us this afternoon.

After lunch Charlotte, Foster, and I picked up Muk, our interpreter, and went off to our rendezvous with a leftist. Somehow everything went wrong, and at the end of an hour we were still looking for our special guide. Foster, who had another appointment, left us. We kept making stops, while Muk, with a conspiratorial expression which we felt was overdone, went into buildings to investigate.

Eventually he emerged from a four-story office building, and beckoned to us. We walked to the top floor, passed through a small door cut in a wooden partition and guarded by a middle-aged man, walked through another office, and found ourselves in a small room, with a man sitting behind a desk. We recognized him instantly. He was Mun, the labor leader to whom Bertsch introduced us at Kim Kyu-sik's house.

Mun still looked very dapper and diffident, and I did not particularly like him. He told us the story of the Korean Federation of Labor, which for thirteen years had been an underground organization fighting the Japanese, and which a month ago had 270,000 members in our zone. Now, once again, it has been driven underground. Mun also talked of Rhee's Labor Association, and of how factory owners and Military Government officials ordered workers to become its members.[25] This, Mun said, plus the low wages and short rice rations, provoked last month's disastrous strikes.

Thus far the interview had not been particularly exciting, and Charlotte was openly bored. Mun spoke in a low monotone, and much of what he said—especially about the rightist terrorism—cried for substantiation.

"The worst of the terrorist bands," Mun was saying, "is Rhee's Great Korea Young Men's Association.[26] It works with the police. Together, they . . . "

We were sitting around a small, round table. To my right was a door which, I assumed, led to a corridor. Now, in the middle of Mun's

---

[25] See pp. 343, footnote 14.

[26] Quoting Mun Ŭn-jong, Gayn means to refer to the Great Korea Democratic Young Men's Association (Taehan Minju Ch'ŏngnyŏn Ch'ongdongmaeng); for further details, see Robinson's "Betrayal," 183 and 190.

sentence, there was a terrific crash, and the door came open, sagging on its hinges. I looked quickly but saw nothing. Then slowly a bayoneted rifle appeared in the doorway, and began to make a swing in our direction.

In a few moments, a sturdy young Korean in civilian clothes came out cautiously and aimed a pistol at us. Next to him, a uniformed policeman materialized behind the bayonet. The two men walked into the room, and behind them came a band of young men, of the type one meets in tough Chicago or New York neighborhoods.

The man with the pistol walked over to Mun and placed him under arrest.

To me, the whole scene was unreal. It is true I was warned by Hŏ Hŏn yesterday that this would happen. But Mun was no subversive. Bertsch himself told us Mun was a moderate, and when we first met Mun, he was being chaperoned by an American colonel.[27] Things like that simply could not happen in the American zone. It must be, I reasoned, one of those unauthorized raids of which we had heard so much.

I asked the man with the pistol for his credentials. He took out a card showing that he was a Detective Sergeant Kim Ho-ik [?–1949],[28] Korean National Police. I asked him if he had a warrant. He said yes, there was a warrant. Mun was being arrested on General Hodge's orders, for leading the railroad strike. Unfortunately, the warrant had been left at the police station. I said I would stay around until the warrant was produced.

Sergeant Kim sent a youth out, and we all settled down to wait. From time to time, the sergeant slapped Mun on the back and laughed. Mun remained noncommittal. Charlotte suggested that she go out, contact General Hodge, and find out if he had issued an order for

---

[27] Mun Ŭn-jong, Executive Chairman of the National Council of Korean Labor Unions, had in fact been a communist ever since the early 1930s and would co-found the Namnodang, the South Korean Workers' Party, just a month after meeting with Gayn.

[28] Having studied law in Japan and joined the police force immediately after liberation, Kim Ho-ik was handpicked by police chief Chang T'aek-sang (1893–1969) as the officer in charge of all left-wing spy cases. After Gayn and Ebener had run into him, Kim continued to be promoted to become the Metropolitan Government's chief information officer. But he was assassinated in August 1949, apparently by the Namnodang.

Mun's arrest. We arranged that if I was not there on her return, she would proceed to the main police station.

After about fifteen minutes of waiting, the sergeant lost patience. He began to shout that I was interfering in the arrest, and who was I, and what was I doing there anyway. Through Muk, I explained that I was a reporter; that his band broke in claiming it had a warrant, which it seemingly did not have; and that I had no intention of interfering in anything the sergeant wanted to do. I would merely tag along, and report all I saw. I also told him to lower his voice.

Sergeant Kim then ordered Mun to stand up, and we all filed out of the room. On the landing just outside, I saw thirteen kneeling, frightened men, guarded by four of the youths in civilian clothes. The sergeant arrested one of the thirteen, and told the rest to go. We walked downstairs, and I waited in the doorway with Mun and the sergeant.

It was a long wait, and soon my attention was drawn by the youngsters. They had all gone into the street and were pushing people out of the way. One of them pushed an old man resting a huge load on his back against a tree, and the man fell. The boy was about sixteen, and he was as hard as they come. I went out with Muk and asked the youngster if he was a detective.

"No," he said, "I'm a member of the Great Korea Young Men's Association."[29]

"What are you doing here?"

"We're helping the police to catch leftists."

"How many of you are there here?"

"Eight—"

An older youth ran up to the youngster and ordered him not to talk to me. At this point, a car drove up, and the sergeant got in and began to talk earnestly to a stout, middle-aged man in a police uniform. Later, I found out this was Chang, chief of the Seoul Police. After a few minutes, Mun was put in the back of the car, with Chief Chang. I asked Chang's permission to come along, and he nodded at a seat next to him. Muk sat in front.

---

[29] See p. 353, footnote 26.

We drove up to the main police station and walked in, past armed sentries and a roomful of youngsters engaged in horseplay. Mun was taken upstairs, and Muk and I followed him.

Sergeant Kim sulked in a corner. After a while Mun told me that back in August he had gone to the town of Taegu, was arrested as a vagrant, and was released on September 24 on Colonel Shaw's orders. He returned to Seoul, and was promptly set upon by a band of young terrorists, who beat him up so badly that he was hospitalized until five days ago.

Mun told me he was thirty-six, was first jailed by the Japanese at the age of eighteen, and had spent eight years in prisons and ten years in underground union work.

"Until two hours ago," he said in a matter-of-fact voice, "I was the only officer of the Labor Federation still at large. Both our president and vice-president are in hiding."

Muk told me Mun is a leading moderate in the labor movement, and has often been used by the U.S. Army to settle labor disputes. He also said that Mun had decided not to join Bertsch's coalition. "Kim Kyu-sik is a good man," Mun explained, "but he doesn't know what the common people want, and the common people don't know what he stands for."

A policeman asked Muk and me to go to Chief Chang's office. We found Chang sitting in a corner, with his hands folded placidly over his stomach. An American officer came up to me, and said he was Major F. E. Richardson,[30] chief of the Police Division of the Military Government for Seoul. He said he had been ordered by General Hodge to investigate the incident. Richardson was very affable, and told me he had been an investment banker in Chicago. While I was telling him of the incident, another uniformed American came in and introduced himself as "Whitaker, Counter Intelligence."[31]

[30] Major Francis E. Richardson served as military advisor to the Korean police through 1948.

[31] This was CIC's Technical Sergeant Donald P. Whitaker (1900?–1987), spelled with a single T (Gayn's 1948 edition spells the name with a double T). From 1946 to 1962 he probably was—alongside the infamously brutish and corrupted intelligence officer Donald Nichols (1923–1992)—the most important CIC and later CIA agent residing in Korea. Whitaker was married to a Korean and was one of the few

After I finished, Richardson said smoothly, "Have you lived in the Orient before?" and when I nodded, he said, "Well, you know then that the police don't operate our way. They are cruel and undemocratic." This discussion went on for some time, with me saying that I thought we could expect the police in our zone, and under the direction of such men as the major himself, to obey some of the Military Government directives, and Richardson saying that we could not expect much progress overnight.

"And anyway," I said, "I'm a little puzzled by the use of members of a private terrorist band in a police arrest." Richardson said he had never heard of the Great Korea Young Men's Association.[32] "Have you?" he asked Chief Chang. Chang said he had not. "Are you sure you're not mistaken?" Richardson said to me. "You don't speak Korean." At my insistence, Sergeant Kim and Mun were brought into the room. Richardson said to the sergeant: "Mr. Gayn charges that you've been using some private hoodlums to make this arrest. You know that if this is true, you'll be severely punished. Is it true?"

Sergeant Kim said it was not true; I was certainly mistaken. He said he had seen no young men in the room. Later he recalled seeing some, but insisted they must have been passersby. When I suggested that no passersby were likely behind locked doors on the fourth floor of an office building, Kim guessed they might have been Communists.

Richardson said to me: "You must've made a mistake." Sergeant Kim decided to go on the offensive. Pointing at me, he said I had interfered with the arrest and ordered him out of the room. I was still wondering how to cope with that one, when Muk, my wonderful, quiet, courageous Muk, spoke up. "Major," he said, "I was translating for Mr. Gayn. Not once did he say anything of the sort to the sergeant."

At this point Whitaker came to life. "What's your name?" he asked Muk. "Where do you work?" He then proceeded to question Muk on his position, his relation to me, and his work for any other correspondents. While they were talking, a policeman brought a folded note for me. It was from Charlotte, and it said: "Sit tight. Talked to Hodge who

---

U.S. intelligence officers who learned to speak Korean early on. In a civilian capacity he soon became central to the 971 CIC. Having become close to Premier Chang Myŏn (in office 1960–1961), Park Chung Hee (in office 1961–1979) expelled him from Korea in 1962 on charges of plotting to overthrow his new military junta.

[32] See p. 353, footnote 26.

says he will investigate. Don't go away until Big Brass investigates." In another five minutes, a policeman told me I had visitors. I went out, and saw Charlotte and Foster.

Charlotte told me hurriedly that Foster had telephoned Hodge, who said he knew nothing of the arrest; Dr. Bunce, who said, "Lord, more of their stupidity;" and Colonel Shaw, who said in exasperation, "But I've just gotten Mun out of jail. I guess I'll have to get him out again."

Whitaker now wanted to know if I had interfered with the arrest, and both Charlotte and Muk had the answer. I, in turn, wanted to know about the Great Korea Young Men's Association,[33] and everyone, Richardson, Whitaker, Chief Chang, and Sergeant Kim, was denying knowledge of it.

A memory that was turning in the back of my mind now came closer, and I caught it. I said: "O.K., Major, this has been going on long enough. How much would you bet me I could find you a room full of the Great Korea boys right in this building?" Then, for fear that someone would send a word of warning out, I rushed downstairs to the room where I saw the young men at horseplay. Behind me came the whole group. The first person I saw downstairs was the youngster to whom I talked after he had pushed an old man. I headed for him and he began to run down the basement steps. I caught him and brought him before Richardson.

"Here's one. Ask him if he's a cop. Ask him what he's doing in a police station."

Richardson asked him. The boy said he was a member of the Great Korea Association, assigned for duty to this station. I asked him who gave him his orders, and he said they came from his "leaders," who were in the other room. I went in, spotted some more boys who were in on the arrest, and dragged them out. It was becoming very embarrassing.

"Did you know of this?" Richardson asked Chief Chang. Chang shook his head vigorously. Richardson said to me. "An honest arrest has been made. But a mistake has also been made in using these young men. I didn't know of this. But I'll instruct Chief Chang not to use such

[33] As before, see p. 353, footnote 26.

help in the future." He thought briefly. "I'll recommend that a special board sit to decide on the sergeant's negligence."

I asked him what he intended to do about the thirty or forty youths in the room, and Whitaker said he would "investigate." He had three of the "leaders" brought out. They were small, compact men of about twenty-five, in well-cut Western clothes and trim overcoats. They looked like a Hollywood idea of underworld killers, and I wondered if they got their inspiration in movie houses. "Come on," Whitaker said curtly, and marched out with the three men.

Richardson offered Charlotte and me a lift to the Chosun. In the jeep he told us there had been some trouble up north, in a town called Kaesŏng, just this side of the 38th Parallel. Early this morning bands of twenty to thirty armed men each, raided ten police boxes, killed a Korean police officer and a detective.

"In some troubled areas," Richardson said, "the police were shorthanded, and so the Military Government gave them authority to recruit sons of well-known shopkeepers to patrol the streets and help the police. You know, act as a stabilizing influence."

As for Mun, Richardson said he was arrested on charges of involvement in the recent railway strike. I did not remind the major that Mun had spent the last two months either in jail or in a hospital.[34]

October 21, 1946 SEOUL

This morning had an appointment with Muk to see some Korean professors. When Muk did not show up, I asked an American friend to check. He learned that Muk was visited by an agent of Counter Intelligence, told that General Hodge did not want him to work for correspondents, and ordered to leave town. Muk left at once.

Heard that the press conferences given by Military Government officers for Korean newspapermen are worth attending, for the Kore-

[34] The very next day, October 21, 1946, Foster Hailey reported in the *New York Times* about Mun Ŭn-jong's arrest; see also footnote 1 in this text.

ans ask sharp questions on current problems. Asked an officer in the Military Government to arrange a visit for me tomorrow.

He put his arm around my shoulders, said he hoped I would not mind his frankness, and told me I could not attend. When I asked why, he explained:

"General Brown[35] will be there to answer questions tomorrow."

"I don't mind."

"No, you don't understand. You haven't been introduced to General Brown yet, and it wouldn't be protocol for you to come to his press conference until you are."

I said, "Oh, is that all? I'll come fifteen minutes earlier, and you introduce me."

"You still don't understand," he said. "I can't introduce you to General Brown until you've met General Lerch." "All right," I said, "I'll come an hour earlier, and you introduce me to both Lerch and Brown."

"No, no," he said patiently. "I can't introduce you to Lerch because you haven't yet met General Hodge. You know, everyone here's talking about it. It isn't right. You must follow the rules, you know."

I promptly walked over to Major Williamson's office and asked for an interview with General Hodge.

In the afternoon the three of us were taken to a former Japanese textile plant, now being operated by the U.S. Military Government. We had been trying to get to the port of Inch'ŏn, where, we were told, we would find more typical sweatshop conditions, but Major Williamson could find no jeep for us. The plant we saw was obviously a show place for visiting firemen. But even as a show place it was instructive. Of its 1,300 employees, nearly 900 were little girls. They all said they were fourteen, but they were either lying to keep their jobs, or they were so undernourished they looked no older than nine. We walked past the endless rows of looms and the endless lines of little, pale-faced children, and our guide, an American officer, was telling us of the great strides in industrial rehabilitation being made under the management of the Military Government.

---

[35] U.S. Army Major General Albert E. Brown (1889–1984) was Chief Commissioner of the American Delegation in the Joint Commission meetings with the Soviet Union from June 1947 until the talks ended in October.

As we were leaving, I took one of the workers aside and asked him if there was a labor union at the plant. The Korean manager, hand-picked by the Military Government, hurried back to us. "I can answer all your questions," he said. "Union? Yes, we have a union." It was, as I expected, Syngman Rhee's Great Korea Laborers' Association. "We used to have the Federation of Labor, but they were a bunch of trouble makers. We threw them out, and the Great Korea Association came in.[36]

Saw General Hodge. The conservation was "off the record," and I could write no story on it. All I could say was that he dwelled on the difficulties, human, political, and economic, facing the United States in South Korea. Hodge is a handsome soldier, with an alert face and a long jaw. From time to time the conversation lagged, and at such points I raised myself in my chair and said, "Well, general, it was . . . " But each time he resumed talking. When I finally left him, I realized what had happened. It was an hour to the minute since I went in. Apparently, there was an hour assigned to me on the calendar, and the general was being punctual.

Later Charlotte and I paid a formal call on General Lerch, the Military Governor. He opened the interview by saying, "You know, I'm peeved at you." I thought he was joking, but he was not. He was in deadly earnest. "I'm very peeved at you. You've been here a week, and you haven't thought it necessary to call on me. There's such a thing as military protocol. When you arrive in town, you must call on the commanding officers."

Lerch talked of Korea's scarcities, and of the supplies ordered in the United States but not yet received. He impressed both Charlotte and me more favorably than Hodge had. This morning we heard more details of the feud between Hodge and Lerch. Theoretically, Lerch, as Military Governor, should be the most important man in South Korea, and Hodge should devote himself solely to the command of the tactical troops. But Hodge is a lieutenant general and Lerch is only a major general, and Hodge keeps butting into political and economic problems which lie within Lerch's province.

---

[36] See pp. 343, footnote 14.

I was told, however, that Lerch is just as opposed to reform as Hodge, and just as friendly to the Korean rightists. One of the officers we talked to told us of entering Lerch's office just as another American visitor was leaving.

"See that man?" Lerch said. "He comes here from Tokyo, and tells me there are too many little children working in factories, and we must change this and change that. I told him, 'As long as I am Military Governor, we change nothing.'"

Mun was released this afternoon, after a perfunctory examination.

At night Charlotte and I packed for our trip north, to the 38th Parallel. We're going to do our best to cross the line into the Russian zone.

October 22, 1946 PAECH'ŎN[37]

Early in the morning, Charlotte, a Captain G. of Military Intelligence, an Army driver, and I started north. Just ahead of us was another jeep with a Nisei[38] lieutenant. The countryside is restless and military men prefer to travel in groups. The two drivers kept their carbines close at hand, and the officers wore automatics in shoulder holsters. Quite suddenly we came to a cleft in a mountain, and the bustle of Seoul was left behind. At once the road became bad, and we began to bounce wildly, gritting our teeth and bobbing our heads like toys with springs where necks should be. The jeep ahead of us sent back a thick cloud of fine yellow, choking dust.

By all accepted standards, the road from Seoul north is the world's worst. For centuries an ox cart route, it has now become a scarred and rutted ribbon of dirt, winding across rice paddies. Most of the bridges

---

[37] Named Pakchon in the 1948 edition, Gayn later clarifies (p. 372) that it is located 23 miles from Kaesŏng, directly at the 38th parallel. It must therefore be Paech'ŏn-gun—in Hanja written with the 'white' character that is otherwise pronounced 'paek.' In 1945, U.S. maps labeled it as Paekch'ŏn.

[38] Nisei (second generation) was the name of a Military Intelligence Service unit primarily composed of second-generation Japanese Americans who were trained as linguists.

were washed away in last year's great flood, and no effort has been made to restore them. ("Why should we make the Russian advance any easier?" an officer asked me later in the day.)

We drove at a steady thirty miles an hour, slowing down only in the villages. As we roared by, the women in their bright red and yellow and green silk dresses, and old men in their invariable white gowns and tiny black straw hats perched on top of their heads scattered into the bushes. At the first river the bridge was down, and the ford made a wide detour across an uneven, pebbly bottom. We splashed across, bumping in and out of holes and taking in water. A few feet away, a middle-aged man carried an old man, with a white beard and the incongruous hat, piggy-back. The younger man had carefully rolled up his trousers, but it did not really matter for the water was well up to his hips. Neither man looked at us. Only a few miles further, an ox blocked our passage. When we honked, the ox came closer, lowered its head, and tried to gore the radiator. Both the radiator and the beast were rescued by a flock of farmers.

The harvest time was over, and the road was now hemmed with straw mats, covered with rice, garlic, and red pepper out to dry in the sun. The whole countryside was dotted with these patches of red and white, and occasionally there was a crunching sound as our wheels went over a protruding mat. *Kimchee* [Kimch'i], with which every Korean spices his rice, seems to consist predominantly of garlic and red pepper, and its aroma hovered over each village.

Captain G. is a silent, sullen man of twenty-nine. He glumly evaded our questions on the peasant riots. But the signs of unrest were difficult to conceal. In nearly every village, we ran through a patrol of Korean policemen, with their Japanese fur coats and carbines. Occasionally, around a turn, there was a road block, with half a dozen policemen questioning and searching the rare traveler. And once, some twenty miles out of Seoul, we waited patiently until a U.S. Army tank, standing guard at a bridge, slowly crawled to one side to let us through.

Beyond Mungson,[39] on a ridge high above a broad river, we turned off the road into a U.S. Army camp. It consisted of about twenty Quonset huts set on a bare mountainside. Even an amateur could see that a few field guns set here would command the river and its ap-

[39] Possibly Munsan-ŭp, today part of P'aju City.

proaches for many miles. The men in the camp looked grimy and preoccupied. It is no more than forty miles from here to the Soviet outposts on the 38th, and war is on every mind.[40] "No." said an officer, "I'm not bringing my wife out. I'd hate to have her caught here."

Far below the camp, on a small, narrow beach, a Korean policeman waited for a ferry coming across from the other bank. The current was strong, and the crew pushed hard on the single oar. The ferry—an oversized, badly leaking junk—ran onto the beach. From it a heavily loaded truck rolled ashore. The policeman halted the vehicle, and ordered the men out. He examined their passes, patted their sides and legs for concealed weapons, looked through their wallets.

Captain G. explained: "He's looking for Communist spies." Later we rode the ferry, and Captain G. talked shop with the Nisei lieutenant. Both agreed that the Korean policemen were something terrific. "I saw a truck hit a kid on a bicycle," the lieutenant said. "So a cop comes up, and instead of giving hell to the truck driver, begins to belt the kid on the head, first one side, then the other."

"Oh, that's nothing," said the captain. "The other day, the cops caught some guy with 40,000 yen and asked him where he got it. He said he had sold his property and was now going to Seoul. So they made him kneel and started asking him questions. Every time he'd open his mouth to answer, they would kick him in the groin. They sure beat hell out of him before he admitted he was a Communist.

At Kaesŏng, which five centuries ago was the capital of Korea, we waited for the other jeep which we had somehow left behind. As soon as our jeep stopped, the entire street, as far as the eye could see, came to life with hundreds of children rushing toward us. They clustered around the jeep, fingered our clothes, hopefully pulled and tugged at everything that might come off. Occasionally the captain bellowed, and the kids backed off, but not for long. Not far from us, as a sort of huge island in the middle of the street intersection, stood an ancient, moss-coated tower. It was now circled with barbed wire, and we noticed that

---

[40] The war in the Pacific had barely ended when fears among civilians and military personnel surfaced that World War III was imminent. In addition to Korea, other areas of conflict, such as the differences between the U.S. and the Soviet Union over Iran and a looming Berlin crisis, also contributed to these fears.

many of the supporting posts were fresh. We knew already that two days ago Kaesŏng had an uprising, that its jails were packed, and that some three hundred of the more important "leftists" had been shipped to Seoul. The police stations were heavily guarded by uniformed policemen and by tough youngsters in civilian clothes, much like the boys I met in Seoul two days ago.

The second jeep did not show up, and we decided to move on. We were now running along the 38th Parallel. Somewhere between Kaesŏng and Paech'ŏn, we met another jeep. It halted to unload a slight, blond captain, with a pistol strapped across his chest. The two captains walked back out of hearing and had a conference. Then the newcomer, a Captain K., said, "See you tonight," hopped into his jeep, and roared off in a cloud of dust.

We arrived in Paech'ŏn, tired and filthy and much after the dinner hour. We rolled into the compound of what was once a Japanese hotel, and was now the billet and headquarters of Company Fox. The company commander, a trim, compact captain, met us with exemplary courtesy. We splashed some water on our faces, drank up our host's last remaining liquor, and then addressed ourselves to a steak dinner. There was a strange atmosphere in the place, as if everyone was watching us. Questions on what was happening in Paech'ŏn or along the border were ignored. We stuttered along until we hit on two safe subjects: the University of Wisconsin, of which Charlotte is a graduate, and the hot springs which feed the hotel baths.

Later that night, six or eight officers and I went down to a typical Japanese bath pool, filled with steaming sulphurous water. The army's vaunted efficiency is sorely missing in Korea, and the billet—among so many other things—lacked electric light bulbs. We undressed and washed in the dim light of two flashlights. Someone said, "I wish I were back home, in California." Another young, wistful voice joined in: "Me, for Iowa." One voice after another called the roll call of states represented in this shallow Japanese pool, in a Korean no man's land, a few miles away from the nearest Soviet outpost. After the bath, we stumbled up the dark stairs. Captain G., who, I suddenly realized, had not left me alone since we left Seoul, slept on the other cot in the room. There were some panes missing in the window, and a cold wind blew in. Around midnight I was awakened by the sound of shots very close by. The captain also woke up, and I asked him what the shots could be. He said he had not heard any.

October 23, 1946 RUSSIAN ZONE IN NORTH KOREA

After it was agreed at Yalta to divide Korea in two along the 38th Parallel, someone unhappily remembered Ongjin. A peninsula on the western edge of Korea, Ongjin—or most of it, anyway—lies on our side of the 38th. Unfortunately, the only way to enter Ongjin by land is through the Soviet zone. Thus, by agreement, American supply convoys were allowed to cross the dividing parallel, make a 23-mile run inside the Soviet zone, and then re-enter the U.S. zone at Ongjin. After a brief stay the convoy has to retrace its route the same day.

Our convoy started forming very early in the morning, while the sun was still down. We shivered in the penetrating chill and dashed down to the pool, to wash and shave in its hot water. Our group had grown, and the little Captain K. whom we met on the road was now with us. We learned that he is S-2, or Regimental Intelligence Officer, and guessed that he was watching us. We all had tall mounds of hot cakes and enormous soup bowls filled with coffee. Then we pulled on all the warm clothes we had and got into the jeeps.

The convoy had four jeeps and a truck with oil drums. We started early, for there was a long, hard run along the 38th before we got to the Soviet border gate. Once again we bumped and bounced, choked in the heavy dust, and shivered in the cold. We passed through the town of Yŏnan, where there had been a bloody uprising the previous week. We also passed through many villages, where the road blocks were busy and each police station resembled a fort.

Then we reached a belt devoid of villages and travelers. We skirted a hill and came to a sudden halt before a GI with a submachinegun pointed at us. The man looked trim, tough, and competent. Across the road from him were a couple of Quonset huts and a few incurious GIs. Even Charlotte, who is young and good looking, aroused no visible interest. This was U.S. Outpost No. 7.

The Quonset huts were bare, neat, and very cold. The mess hall was a tent, with the flaps open and the wind whistling over the rough table and benches. We squatted in the sun and talked to a GI. "No," he said, "this place is not too cheerful. I wouldn't want to get stuck here very long. As it is, we're supposed to stay here only two weeks, and I've already been here three. It's too damn lonely, and nothing to do. And them Russkys sitting up there." He pointed his thumb at the hill behind him.

At 9:45 A.M. we got back into the jeeps and drove a few hundred yards to the border gate. The gate was a wooden bar suspended over the road. Just behind it was a small sentry box and a Russian soldier with a rifle. He wore a thin shirt which had long lost its original white, and his trousers had a big patch of a different color. It was hard to tell his age, for he had the peasant's ageless face.

At ten, a Red Army truck drove up to the gate. It was a Studebaker, filled with officers and men. Three or four of the officers approached us. They looked neat, and each wore a string of tinkling medals. One of the officers, an extraordinarily handsome youth with a fat briefcase, saluted and engaged us in conversation. He talked first in Russian, then in German. Our officers responded in English and French. A common ground was found briefly in Korean and Lettish. The American officer, who spoke a little Lettish, explained his family had come from Latvia. "America," said the Russian sententiously, "is an interesting country. It has peoples of many races and nationalities," We readily agreed. After a while the conversation floundered. We stood and smiled at each other, and the Russian said to his neighbor: "Many new faces today." Then he nodded decisively, and said, "Well, let's go." The sentry raised the gate, and we entered the Soviet zone.

The instructions to the U.S. convoys are specific. The vehicles are to follow a definite route, they must not stop, and they are to average twenty-five miles an hour. We had heard that on the previous Wednesday one of the jeeps turned off at the wrong road, and the Russians in the escorting truck promptly fired a shot overhead. The errant driver quickly backed out and took another turn. Some weeks earlier, another jeep managed to break its axle on the road. The Russians quickly transferred its occupants to another vehicle, and when the convoy returned four hours later, the jeep had been repaired—with the Red Army's compliments.

A few miles beyond the border we passed by an airfield, with a swarm of Russian Yak pursuit planes warming up. At the gate to the field, a large group of Red Army officers and men watched us with smiles. Behind them, on the guard house, there was a large sign in Russian: "Soldier, keep your secrets. The enemy is watchful." Next to the field there was a cluster of shabby buildings that must have once been occupied by the Japanese garrison. Now they were tenanted by Russians, there were flowers in the windows, fresh laundry flapped in the wind, and children played in the bare yard under the eyes of young, breasty Russian women. Another half-mile, and we reached a huge wooden arch, decorated with flags and portraits of Joseph Stalin [in office 1922–1953] and Kim Il Sung [Kim Il-sŏng, in office 1948–1994], the ranking leader of North Korea. Kim is a youngish-looking man of about thirty-five, with stubby hair, a determined chin, and, reportedly, the assumed name of a famous guerrilla said to be dead.

We were now in Haeju, one of Korea's few large cities.[41] We soon realized that we were in a sign-painter's paradise, for nearly every lamp post, every fence and building was decorated. Sometimes it was merely a brief slogan, or the crossed hammer and sickle. Sometimes it was a string of twenty-one stars, for the twenty-one points of Kim's program of national reconstruction. Sometimes it was a portrait of Kim. But we also passed by a two-story building nearly hidden behind the portraits of four Red Army marshals who had fought against Japan. And here and there we saw intricate—and excellently done—political drawings. Some showed a farmer turning in his rice at a state collection point. Some showed the same farmer stomping vigorously on snakes with unmistakable capitalist heads. Some portrayed Kim talking to children, or the trinity of farmers, workers, and Red Army men, or a group of Asiatics. All through the town there were hundreds of colored posters, urging the populace to vote in the forthcoming local election, or appealing to women to assume their responsibilities as citizens. The posters gave the city a gay, carnival air.

---

[41] Gayn's 1948 edition misnames the city "Kaijo" (Kaijō), the Japanese name for Kaesŏng, while it should have been Kaishū (Kor. Haeju). In 1945/46 Haeju was roughly 20% smaller than Kaesŏng. Until the Korean War Kaesŏng had been part of South Korea. But this stop on Gayn's trip was undoubtedly Haeju in the Soviet zone. Charlotte Ebener, who took this same trip with Gayn and is mentioned regularly by him, reproduced Gayn's mixup in her own description that appeared seven years later. See Ebener, *No Facilities for Women*, 62.

We rolled down the road and made a sharp turn into the main street. A Korean traffic policeman let us through, but halted the jeep behind us. Within a few seconds the Russian truck appeared on the scene, the Russian officer bounced out and impatiently waved the convoy on. The policeman sheepishly stepped back.

The streets of Haeju were packed with shoppers, vendors, children, farmers come to market with their produce, students milling in front of their schools, ox carts, bicycles, and an occasional horse-drawn cart of the Red Army. Here and there a Russian soldier ambled by, as often as not with a Russian woman by his side. There were a few policemen and militiamen, but there was no display of police force. As our jeep went by, children cheered and shouted in Russian, "Americansky." Some thrust out their fingers in a "V for Victory," and one dissident tot stuck out his little finger in the common Asiatic expression of contempt.

The shops seemed to be well stocked and well patronized. In one store we spotted smudged portraits of Stalin, Roosevelt [in office 1933–1945], and Churchill [in office 1940–1945 and 1951–1955], and above them the three Allied flags, including the Stars and Stripes. There were several Red Army PX's, one of them displaying children's garments in its window, and two others labelled "The Red Army's Vegetable and Provision Store." They looked small and rundown; were they American, they would, beyond the shadow of a doubt, have led to some passionate Congressional oratory.

It took half an hour or more to cross the town. Then our jeeps passed the last flag-bedecked arch, and once again we were in a world of dust, terraced fields running up hillsides, and tiny villages, with their red pepper, garlic, peasant carts with huge wooden wheels, and bolts of brightly colored silk laid out on display along the main street.

In an hour we completed the run through the Soviet zone and approached the exit gate, to the Ongjin Peninsula. The Red Army truck, lost in the dust for most of the way, caught up with us. We stopped by the gate and watched the two Russian guards—lean men in thin, dirty shirts. One of them was probably near forty, the other looked no more than sixteen. Both were probably billeted in a Korean school near by—an ugly box decorated with a huge banner in Russian: "Let's Not Allow the Arsonists of a New War to Disrupt the Peace We Have Won. Let's Maintain Our New Peace."

Though the road was no better, we picked up speed. In ten minutes we reached a cluster of neat houses and Quonset huts. This was U.S. Outpost No. 4—a couple of officers, a handful of men, a few trucks, and an overpowering feeling of impending crisis, in which a Russian tide would sweep over the helpless Americans. The commanding officer, a young lieutenant, took us to his house across the road. There were a few Korean laborers, busily hammering and sawing. "Those goddamned gooks," said someone, "they just pretend they are working." The Koreans were fixing up the living room—a bright room with a small fireplace and a bar with two tall stools. We washed and went to the mess hall for lunch. There were two middle-aged engineers eating with us. They talked of weather and of dust, but said nothing of themselves. Later we saw them testing field phones.

After lunch we walked uphill to the Quonset huts and stretched out in the sun. Next to me was a young, pink-cheeked, alert lieutenant, who, we soon found out, is the Military Governor of the county. We struck up a conversation, and he talked readily of the smuggling junks, intercepted on their way from North to South Korea; of a Patriotic Youth Association, being formed by the U.S. Army's interpreter here; of rice, fertilizer, and prices; and of taking a bunch of policemen to the mainland a few days earlier, to break up a riot. "We went in," he said, "and found the city completely empty. The police stations were a mess. The cops had fled. The townsfolk were hiding. We took over the stations, and then started . . . . "

He was in the middle of a sentence, when one of the Military Intelligence people with us—a very young corporal—came up to the lieutenant, tapped him on the shoulder, and said: "Sir, could I speak to you for a second?" They walked behind the Quonset hut, and when the lieutenant returned, his face was flushed, and he talked no more. We took pity on him, and asked no questions.

Instead, we watched a painfully blue sky for the plane which we could hear but not see. "Must be the Russkys," said a sergeant, and cranked the handle of the field phone.

We tried to talk to some of the other men, but two Military Intelligence men broke up every conversation. They were not offensive, but very obvious. We were glad when the time came for the return trip. Again we waited by the border gate, until the Russian truck arrived. Then we rolled back, through the villages, through Haeju, and past the

Russian airport. In another hour we were back at the first border gate, and the Russian officer smiled broadly and said, "Well, I guess we'll see you in another week." Everyone saluted formally, the gate was raised, and in another minute we were back at Outpost No. 7.

It was late afternoon when we returned to the hotel, and the air was cold. Our teeth beat a tattoo, and our bodies were numb when we climbed out of the jeeps. We thawed out in the pool, had dinner, and then gathered in the commanding officer's room, which he had gallantly surrendered to Charlotte.

The previous night I had talked to the commanding officer of writing an article on him and his unit, and we had agreed that he would try to remember the landmarks, the anecdotes, and the human touches. Now he smiled apologetically and said he could remember nothing. It was plain that, although he wanted to see his name in print, he would not talk.

This went on for half an hour, until Charlotte exploded. "Look, fellows," she said, "this is getting to be silly. Remember? We're American correspondents. I've been in Manchuria with the Russians, and in North China with the Chinese Reds, and in Chongqing with the Guomindang, but I've never been treated like this. You're watching us all the time, and you make a secret of things which have no business being secret. Like rice collection. . . . "

I was sitting in the corner and writing in a notebook. I set down the answers. "In this country," said one captain, "everything is secret." Then Captain K. came in with a longer, more passionate reply. He was about to go home to Minnesota, become a dentist, perhaps be married and raise American children.

"We like correspondents to visit us," he said, "but not for news. The army is doing a competent job, and it doesn't want any interference. The American people are too dumb to understand what's going on here. We can't wait until they wake up to our problems. The army will tell the people what they ought to know. I am not the only one who feels this way. I happen to know that this also represents the views of my regimental and divisional commanders."

He went on and on in a high-pitched, angry voice. He denounced the press for misreporting, and wanted to know why we thought our reporting would be any better. He called the U.S. Congress "a farce," and insisted the army had to make its own policy in Korea, for there was no time to wait for decisions in Washington. He snorted as he spoke of the meddling, ignorant, inconsiderate American people. We all felt very uncomfortable, and gradually the group broke up.

We went to bed early. I climbed into the sleeping bag and read a magazine condensation of *The Hucksters* by the light of a flashlight, and thought of the unreal people in the unreal city a world away. The cold wind still blew through the missing window panes, and with it came the shreds of a monotonous Korean tune, sung by a man. The hot spring gurgled near by. Dogs barked. Then all was silent.

October 24, 1946 PAECH'ŎN–KAESŎNG

Left Paech'ŏn after a substantial breakfast, topped by a real stateside Macintosh apple which made me homesick. We took off in a convoy of three jeeps, with Captain K. leading. I take it that he will keep an eye on us until we leave his territory.

We made the twenty-three miles to Kaesŏng in thirty-six minutes, which must be some sort of a record for this kind of road. At Kaesŏng, we spent the morning talking to Japanese repatriates, returning home from Manchuria and North Korea by way of our zone. Most of the Japanese looked amazingly neat and fit, considering the trials behind them.[42]

We questioned four Japanese—including the wife of a Japanese brigadier general—on the conditions in the Soviet zone. Captain K. supplied the interpreter, a Nisei Intelligence officer. The Japanese said that the Russian troops behaved badly in the early months of the occupation, but that discipline was restored with the arrival of Soviet Military Police.

One of the Japanese, a teacher who on the side ran an orchard yielding an income of 400,000 yen a year ($26,000 at the current

---

[42] At the end of World War II, it is estimated that there were 700,000 Japanese in Korea and approximately 850,000 in Northeast China. Many of those in northern Korea and Manchuria (known as Manchukuo from 1932 to 1945) had to travel through northern Korea into southern Korea before repatriating to Japan. See also Robinson's, "Betrayal," 302–3.

exchange rate), complained that the Communists had redistributed all the land. "Men who used to work for me now have my orchard."

From the outset, we began to run into difficulties with the interpreter, who insisted on censoring both the questions and the answers. I wanted to know if it was true, as Seoul rumor had it, that the Soviet garrison in the capital of North Korea was being reduced. "This I will not translate," said the interpreter.

The same thing happened when Charlotte wanted to know if the Japanese had seen any Chinese Communist troops in North Korea. It happened again when I asked for a physical description of Kim Il Sung, the Communist leader. I blew up.

"We must've seen a thousand portraits of Kim Il Sung across the line yesterday," I said, "and his appearance cannot be a secret to us. A picture of Kim Il Sung must be in the files of every large American newspaper. What's going on? What is it that the Japanese can know, and the American correspondents cannot?"

Captain K. turned red, and told the interpreter to translate the question. The Japanese said Kim Il Sung looked about thirty-five years of age, was about five and a half feet tall, always wore civilian clothes, and was an impressive speaker.

From the camp we drove to the city to see Major John Stein [1917?–2008?], Military Governor for the province, who was noted for his excellent administrative record, a magnificent moustache, and a loaded pistol with which he seldom parted. At the city hall Captain K. asked us to wait in the reception room, and went ahead into Stein's office. He returned ten minutes later and said the major was waiting for us.

Stein did have a magnificent moustache and a pistol in a shoulder holster. I assumed it was loaded. A huge man with bushy hair, he towered behind a writing desk meant for a Japanese executive.

"Come in, come in," he boomed. "Pull up the chairs and put your feet on the table."

We sat down and asked him if he could tell us the story of rice collection in his province.

"You ought to get that in Seoul."

"Could you then tell us the mechanics of rice collection?"

"You can get that in Seoul too." Charlotte asked him if any preparations were being made for the election, now a week off.

"I never talk to the Korean press," said Stein. "I won't talk to the American press."

"O.K., Major," I said. "Let's call this a social visit. We just dropped in to pay our respects. Thanks very much for seeing us." He rose and said goodbye, and we went out into the outer office to wait for Captain G., our guide from Seoul, who had the keys to our jeep. Captain K. came out and said the major did not want us in the building. We got into Captain K.'s jeep and drove to his office atop a hill. The captain took us into his own bare room, pulled two clippings from his desk—one from *Time*, the other from the Chicago *Tribune*—and began to denounce the press.

"Goddamned lies," he said, "all lies. I can't tell you how much harm they've done here. Did you write this one?" He waved the *Tribune* clipping before me.

Charlotte said mildly, "Captain, he works for the *Sun*, not the *Tribune*."

"Oh," said the captain, "well, it doesn't matter. All the papers are alike. There's a war on here, and the goddamned reporters are meddling in our work. . . . "

Captain G. finally arrived, and we drove the hundred miles back to Seoul in silence.

October 25, 1946 SEOUL

In the morning Charlotte and I went to the National Police Division of the Military Government to try and get a picture of the unrest sweeping our zone. We were taken to an enclosure, where copies of American police reports were being kept. There was a huge wall map, with little labels showing the trouble spots. The labels were grouped in three clusters: one near the 38th Parallel, in the areas we visited; another in a city called Taegu, in the heart of our zone; and the third in the extreme south, around the city of Pusan.

For the next two hours we scribbled feverishly. What we had before us, in the form of laconic two- and three-line reports, was the face of a revolution. It was a face covered with blood, and contorted with pain and agony. As most revolutions, this one was based on deep distress—on a hunger for land, food and justice.

It was a full-scale revolution, which must have involved hundreds of thousands, if not millions of people. In Taegu alone a third of the 150,000 inhabitants took part in the uprising. It was here that the fuse of the revolution was set off last month. The railroad workers went on strike, followed by the phone and metal, textile and electric workers. As each strike was suppressed by the police, another one took its place. Students went out into the streets to demonstrate, and then the whole city was aflame.

From the city, the revolution spread into the countryside and was taken over by the sharecroppers. The farmers refused to surrender their rice to the police. They attacked the homes of the landlords, and then the police stations. They tore off jail doors to release arrested sharecroppers, they burned the records, and stole the weapons.

Arrayed against the revolution were the police, the rightist organizations, and the U.S. Army. In one town after another, right-wing leaders offered their aid to our local commanders, or actively participated in the mass roundups of suspects. As for us, we did far more than just transport the Korean police to the trouble areas, or supply arms, or maintain preventive patrols. Our troops—come here as liberators—had fired on crowds, conducted mass arrests, combed the hills for suspects, and organized posses of Korean rightists, constabulary and police for mass raids.

It was amazing to recall again that despite our active involvement, no harm had come to a single American. To me it was a remarkable stroke of luck or an indication of stern discipline in the ranks of the rebels. The revolutionists wanted no trouble with us. They were merely settling their scores with the men and forces which oppressed them under our rule, as they did under the Japanese. By today, about 75 policemen have been killed, and 200 to 300 were missing.[43]

This was the face of the revolution:

September 26: two men killed in strike at ——.

September 28: two cases of dynamite stolen at ——. Railroad, phone and metal workers on strike at ——.

---

[43] Had the U.S. Army not intervened against the revolution from below in the fall of 1946, "Korea would have been thrown into civil war then instead of four years later." Bruce Cumings, *The Origins of the Korea War: Liberation and the Emergence of Separate Regimes, 1945–1947* (Princeton: Princeton University Press, 1981), 369.

October 1: Communications workers on strike at ——. Clerks operate street cars in Pusan. Stores and schools on strike in Seoul. Thirty leaders of streetcar strike arrested. Demonstrations in Seoul. A food demonstration at Taegu. One civilian killed, six policemen injured. Four hundred policemen disperse demonstration.

October 2: Fifty thousand rioters at Taegu seize all police stations. Jail broken into. Homes of policemen raided. U.S. troops in control with tanks. Thirty-eight policemen dead. Post office burned down at ——. County government buildings and former Japanese houses destroyed at ——. Five thousand demand food in front of a county office at ——. Uprisings spread through province of ——. U.S. troops on patrol trying to arrest all leaders and agitators. Korean police reinforcements reach Taegu.

October 4: In the early morning, U.S. troops retake police stations at ——. Colonel Gundy, U.S. Army, with 150 troops, made 15 arrests, recovered 40 weapons, rescued all but 37 policemen at ——.

October 7: At night, 500 attack police station at ——. Police fought from half-destroyed buildings until rebels fled. At Taejŏn, right-wing leaders pledge support to U.S. commander. In Pusan, half a squad of U.S. troops assigned to each police station. Number of arrests: 254. Several thousands attack city hall at ——. Rioters dispersed by police and U.S. troops; 7 rioters killed, 8 injured. Student plot discovered, 13 leaders arrested. U.S. troops and Korean police repulse mob with machineguns at ——. Number of agitators arrested: 18 . . . 25 . . . 17 . . . 7 . . . 8 . . .

October 8: Mob of 200, mostly women, demand more rice at ——. Three hundred men being surrounded in hills north of ——. U.S. troops dispatched.

October 10: Report from Taegu—"Have borrowed gymnasium, cell block, and office space from Taegu prison to relieve pressure on police jails. Capacity of 1,200 prisoners held there while being investigated."

October 11: Leftists set fire to right-wing homes near Pusan. From Taegu: "*Do not believe it safe to withdraw reinforcements until after coming election.*"

October 12: A Korean police lieutenant and five policemen, investigating unlawful meeting, accidentally shot and killed a labor leader at ——.

October 14: Detachments of fifty men each sent to —— to comb hills for suspects, and to show force to villages. Hundred men held for investigation, hundred escaped to hills.

October 20: A democratic leader killed in Kaesŏng (where we saw Major Stein yesterday). Fifty-four leftists arrested. Jail full, and now using school as arrests continue. District station at Yŏnan captured by rebels; 64 rifles stolen. Rebels seize police station at Paech'ŏn (where we stayed two nights), but station retaken by U.S. troops. Arrested: 11 at Paech'ŏn, 100 at —— , 117 at ——, 150 at ——, 43 at ——, 23 at ——, 13 at ——, 20 at ——. Three hundred and fifteen prisoners being moved from Kaesŏng to Seoul. "Choy Chang Ki[44] attacked a police station, and then committed suicide. ... "

We kept making notes, and a worried colonel hovered over us. From time to time, he disappeared into the office of the American chief of the Police Division, Colonel William Maglin [1898–1958]. We had already heard of Maglin. He is a son of a New York City police captain, a West Pointer, Commandant of a Provost Marshal school at Fort Custer. A professional policeman, he has served in the French, Italian, and Mexican police. The worried colonel came to us and said Maglin wanted to see us. We found half a dozen American officers in Maglin's office. They sat in two neat ranks, and stared at us. We took the two chairs facing Maglin. He is a tall, square-shouldered, handsome man in his forties.

Maglin told us of the steps taken to democratize the Korean police. Swords, he said, have been replaced with clubs. A bar with the word "Service" has been placed above the police badge. Policemen have been told to abstain from political activity. The police have been barred from keeping people in jail without charges for more than forty-eight hours, though this could be raised to a maximum of ten days by using the "vagrancy" charge.

"You must remember," said Maglin, "that when we took over last year, 12,000 out of the 20,000 men in the police force were Japanese. What we did, after sending the Japs home, was to push the Koreans up, and then build up the force by incorporating all the young men who

[44] Ch'oe Ch'ang-gi; identity unknown.

had been helping the police. In this manner, we have brought up the police strength from 20,000 to 25,000 men.

"Many people question the wisdom of keeping men trained by the Japanese. But many men are born policemen. We felt that if they did a good job for the Japanese, they would do a good job for us. It would be unfair to drive men trained by the Japanese out of the force."

October 26, 1946 SEOUL

Charlotte and I told Major Williamson we wanted to go south, to Taegu and Pusan. He said we could not because there were no accommodations for correspondents. During the argument, we discovered that General Baker's office in Tokyo had pulled a fast one on us. I applied for permission to spend thirty days in Korea. Charlotte wanted to stay a fortnight. Someone cagily predated our travel orders, so that by the time we arrived here, my time had been reduced to fifteen days, and Charlotte's to ten. Now Williamson agreed to give me a ten-day extension, but told Charlotte she would have to leave Korea in a few days. Since we expected to spend at least two weeks in the south, we obviously did not have enough time.

I told Williamson that unless I had my permission this afternoon I would file two messages to the *Sun*. One would be an article describing army censorship methods here. The other one would be a request to my editor to file a formal protest with the War Department.

In the afternoon Williamson informed us that General Hodge had granted us permission to go south, but that Charlotte would have to leave Korea as soon as she returned to Seoul.

Had lunch with Bertsch. He talked of the coming election to the Interim Legislative Assembly,[45] which in effect will be the Korean Government for our zone. The Assembly will have 90 members, of

[45] This was a 90-man assembly—half elected, half appointed—empowered to propose legislation, over which the United States Military Government retained veto power. This veto was exercised to cancel the assembly's July 1947 effort to bring colonial-era collaborators to justice. See also Robinson's discussion, 181–82, 198–200, and elsewhere.

whom 45 will be elected. The rest will be appointed by General Hodge, on Bertsch's recommendation.

The elections, Bertsch said, had already begun in many areas, a bit ahead of schedule, and he intended to seek their annulment. "The fact is," he said, "that the people know nothing of the elections, and the thing might prove embarrassing to us in the end." (We later checked with Military Government, and discovered that they did not know the elections had already begun, and were still waiting for orders to publicize it to the Korean people.)

Bertsch also said he has come to doubt that the left will win. "By the very nature of the election," he said, "the forty-five elected men will be old and reactionary. It will remain for the forty-five appointed men to be the solvent." Bertsch said he knew Rhee would get many of his henchmen elected, but the system of appointed seats would give Kim Kyu-sik the balance of power.

As we left the Chosun Hotel, a colonel approached Bertsch with a radiant smile. "Say," he said, "I understand you're recommending men for the Interim Legislature."

"Yes."

"Well, I know a wonderful guy. His name is Na,[46] and he is the president of the Horse Racing Association. He wants very much to serve in the Legislature. You'll do me a great personal favor if you meet him."

"O.K.," said Bertsch. "Send him to me with your card. I'll talk to him."

"I believe in the inevitability, and necessity, of conflict with Russia," said Bertsch, as we were walking down the street, "just as the conflict with Germany was inevitable and necessary. We should proceed in two phases: atomic preparedness and democratic reform in the occupied countries."

We are leaving for Pusan by air the day after tomorrow.

---

[46] The name is spelled "Rah" in the original edition. This may have been Na Yong-gyun (1896–1984) of the Korean Democratic Party.

October 28, 1946 PUSAN

By the time we got to the airdrome, we found our transport filled to capacity with unscheduled, but high-priority Korean politicians. A colonel with whom I had played poker at the "Frozen Chosun" then put Charlotte and me on a small, rickety plane carrying a U.S.O.[47] company to Pusan. It was fiercely cold, and poor Charlotte, who promptly went to sleep, and who had nothing over her thin uniform but a light, bright, unmilitary red coat, kept whimpering through the trip.

Why the single, sand-coated strip at Pusan is called an airfield is a mystery. There was only one seemingly unused Quonset hut, and not even a phone. The transport that brought us in took one quick look at the place, and took off again. We picked a ride to Pusan with a colonel, who had a jeep waiting for him. Pusan, we found, is a shabbier version of Seoul. It is a city of 350,000 people, rutted streets, rundown stores, and buses made out of old automobile chassis drawn by apathetic horses. It is a sad, sad place, filled with dust.

I registered at the U.S. Army's Railway Hotel. Later we went to the Public Relations Office to look for a Captain Hooper [1905–1985] who was supposed to take care of us here. The captain was out, and we proceeded to the Military Government to talk to Lieutenant Colonel H. O. Benton [1894–1977], Deputy Military Governor. We learned that there were 1,300 political prisoners in the province, that rice shortages loomed large in the riots, and that the Military Government made every effort to operate through the Koreans themselves. "You know, this is their country."

On the way out, we asked a major, sitting importantly behind a desk, the name of the Korean provincial governor. The major could not remember it.

Now we went back to the Public Relations Office to see if Captain Hooper was back. We met him in the entrance, and his smile was distinctly below zero. He told us that he had just returned from the airfield, where he had gone with two other officers to meet us. When

---

[47] U.S.O., the United Service Organization, provided entertainment and other services for military personnel.

the scheduled transport arrived we naturally were not aboard. Since then the three officers had been scouring the town for us. Hooper was very anxious to learn where we had been, and with whom. He insisted on escorting us to the Railway Hotel, where, inevitably, we found the other two officers waiting for us. One of them was Lieutenant James[48] of Military Intelligence; the other a Captain Davies, a company commander assigned to us "for security."

Our first hours together were quite strained, for we resented being under surveillance, and the officers were angry because we managed to get away from them. Eventually, Davies' wife, an extraordinarily pretty girl, arrived, and we had a silent dinner together. After dinner, Davies took Charlotte to her billet, and James remained with me. It was six o'clock in the evening, there were no books or newspapers in sight, and James and I found few subjects of common interest. We had a couple of drinks, and he suggested going to a movie. It was a very poor whodunnit, and when we left the theater I said so.

"It stinks," said James tersely. "I saw it last night."

October 29, 1946 PUSAN

After breakfast Charlotte and I, with our two escorts, went back to Military Government. This time we had a chance to observe the machinegun nest over the arched driveway, the Korean policemen who examined the papers of all Koreans entering the compound, the floors worn so badly even the boards under the linoleum showed grooves, and the numerous helpful signs in English: "Care for Fire" and "Way in Meeting Hall," with an arrow pointing towards the auditorium.

We spent most of the morning with Chief of the Home Affairs Division for this province, C. V. Bergstrom [1905–1962].[49] He is an easy-going, good-looking man of about forty who had served for ten years in the city government of Milwaukee, and intends to enter politics there when his term here is ended.

[48] John E. James (dates unknown), 224th CIC Detachment.

[49] Carl V. Bergstrom, then Home Affairs advisor to the provincial government of South Kyŏngsang Province, was in Korea with the United States Naval Reserve (USNR). He had been a traffic consultant for the city of Milwaukee before the war.

The election procedure, Bergstrom explained, was decided by the Military Government's Advisory Council, whose members were nominated by the Korean governor. The governor, I recalled, was the "friend" to whom Rhee gave me a letter. The procedure was complex. In the first-level election, already held, family heads in each village chose two representatives to the county meetings, being held today. Each county meeting would pick two delegates to go to a provincial meeting.

"You know," said Bergstrom, "strategically, this is the proper time for the rightists to hold the elections. All the leftists are either in jail or in the hills."

We arranged to go this afternoon to the neighboring county seat of Tongnae to watch the election.

Our escorts, who sat in on all our interviews, including the one with the Military Governor himself, were with us at lunch. Davies was telling us about his first day in Korea. He had landed at Inch'ŏn, and was ordered to proceed with his unit to a town on the southwest coast. The trains, of course, were packed, and many Koreans rode the roofs. They kept throwing refuse down, and some of it came in through the open windows. The exasperated GIs finally sprayed the ceilings with tommygun fire.

"You should've seen those guys slide off."

Tongnae is a fair-sized, undistinguished town of one-story buildings, a gray brick private bank, a busy market, and the inevitable dust. We drove up to the county office, and met the County Master—a slim, handsome and altogether very impressive Korean. He was wearing a well-cut Chesterfield overcoat, in which he looked more like a diplomat than a rural administrator.

The election was already in progress, and we walked to a temple-like building where it was being held. A large blackboard carried the names of the seventeen voters present who would choose two of their number to go to the provincial election in Pusan. The board gave the men's professions—six farmers, five village headmen, two landlords, a sake brewer, a fire department chief, a monk, and an organizer for Syngman Rhee's Korean Democratic Party. ("He used to be no good before," the county master said of the last man, "but he has now changed his mind.")

We were especially interested in the farmers, and we asked the County Master to find one for us.

The man was small and round-faced, about forty-six, and wearing Western clothes. At once we discovered that though he listed himself as a farmer, he was also the headman of his village. He owned some land, which he rented out to sharecroppers. "I belong to no party," he added, "but I lean to the right."

We asked him about the riots. "We had none in my village," he said proudly. "As soon as I heard of riots in other villages, I organized a vigilante unit, armed it with clubs, and had it patrol the village. I control the village, and there were no disturbances."

We were not satisfied with the man. We wanted a real, down-to-earth peasant, who knew the feel of the soil in his fingers and got up before the sun to plough his field. We went into the temple, and began to look for another farmer. There were three tables—one with four official witnesses, another with two official watchers, and a third with two detectives. We found that one of the official watchers was both a farmer and a candidate for election, and we took him out.

He too was a curious specimen. He owned only two and a half acres of land, but he rented two-thirds of it out to three sharecroppers. The man looked well-to-do, and it was obvious it was not farming that gave him his look of affluence.

"Father," he said laconically. "My father is a landlord. Thirty-six acres."

We waited.

"I also hold some offices. I'm president of the Farm Credit Association, president of the Deep Sea Fisheries Association, and president of the Association to Suppress Disturbances."

There had been no riots in his village, because the police arrested eight men and they confessed plotting an uprising. He then formed his Association to Suppress Disturbances, with about a hundred and fifty members—"mainly elderly people." Until recently, the two most important organizations in his area were the Farmers' Union[50] and the

[50] National Federation of Farmers' Unions (Chŏn'guk Nongmin Chohap Ch'ong-yŏnmaeng).

Youth Alliance,[51] but now they were inactive, and their leaders were in jail or in hiding.

We asked him who in his opinion was Korea's outstanding man. "Syngman Rhee," he said without hesitation.

We talked to yet another "farmer," an old man in a black silk gown. He told us he owned no land and declined to go into any details. Instead, he told us of a riot in his village, where the Farmers' Union demanded a redistribution of land. The unpleasantness ended with the arrest of "three or four hundred people." The old man then encouraged the remaining citizenry—the substantial folk—to form a vigilante unit.

"The Military Government," he said shrilly, "shouldn't be so lenient with these trouble-makers."

We had had enough of these fraudulent farmers. Now we talked to the County Master. The Farmers' Union, he said, used to be very important, and nearly all of the 20,000 sharecroppers in the county belonged to it. "However," he said, "it made a lot of rash promises: land reform, clean government and such, and it couldn't keep them, and it gradually lost support. Now it's inactive, and its leaders are in jail."

Word came in that the voting was over, and we all went to the temple. The police chief was standing by the ballot box and surveying the scene with a hard eye. The two detectives were now reinforced by two uniformed policemen. Benches were brought in, and about fifty people trooped in and sat down. The County Master took a key out of an envelope and opened the box. Then he removed the ballots one by one, and read the two names written on each. A clerk wrote the names on a blackboard.

The organizer for Rhee's party won with seven votes. There was a tie, with six votes each, between the president of the Association for the Suppression of Disturbances and the old "farmer," to whom we talked. At once, the old man was proclaimed winner. Bergstrom asked the reason for the choice, and the County Master said, "He's the older of the two."

After dinner I decided to see if I could lose my escorts. I pleaded a headache and went up to my room. An hour later, when I came down,

[51] Meant is the left-wing Korean Youth Vanguard (Chosŏn Ch'ŏngnyŏn Chŏnwidae).

the boys were gone. In the lobby I saw a Military Government officer whom I had met earlier. I told him about the election we witnessed, and he shook his head.

"This is quite an election," he said. "First, they let Syngman Rhee's boys decide the procedure. Second, to make sure nothing slips up, they hold the election in a series of four levels, so that the undesirables might be eliminated. Third, they let only family heads, or heads of ten families, vote.

"They put all the possible opposition in jail, or drive it into the hills. Then they leave us nine days to announce and explain the election to the illiterate farmers. You can't beat the machine. It includes everybody in power, from the village cop and the landlord to the provincial governor.

"The machine is the same we found when we got here. For our purposes it's an ideal setup. It's organized military fashion. All you have to do is push the button, and somewhere some cop begins skull cracking. They've been learning the business under the Japs for thirty-five years. Why should anyone expect them to unlearn all they know now?

"Most of our junior officers are sick of being partners with this gang. All they want is to get word of what's going on here to the people back home. Maybe they can do something to stop this crooked show."

October 30, 1946 PUSAN

Went to see Major Atkinson [1915?–?],[52] Chief of the Police Division. He said he had an appointment elsewhere and could not talk to us. We said it was all right; we would talk to the Korean police officers. Atkinson hesitated, but finally agreed. We started with the deputy chief, a small, stocky man, holding on tight to his police cap. Atkinson apparently forgot about his appointment. He stayed, and kept making surreptitious gestures to the deputy and his interpreter. Finally, he called a clerk out of the room, and a few minutes later the clerk returned and said something softly to the deputy chief.

[52] Louis B. Atkinson.

But by that time we had learned that there were 3,450 policemen in this province; that most of the Korean policemen hired after the U.S. Army arrived here had served in the Japanese Army; and that nearly all the high Korean police officers had been trained by the Japanese. The deputy chief had spent all his adult life in the Japanese police force, the chief spent twenty-two of his thirty-eight years under the Japanese; the chief of detectives was also Japanese-trained.

Now Atkinson took over. The new policemen, he said, were trained in law, history, and culture, and although the Koreans are not as sharp witted as the Chinese, they have the merit of sincerity.

The riots, he said, had been organized by "agitators imported from north of the 38th Parallel." They stumped the country, demanding high wages for the workers and land for the sharecroppers. In the past six months, there had been only three complaints of police brutality. They were investigated, and found to be untrue.

He refused to tell us how many people had been arrested in the province, how many were presently in jail, or how many outside agitators had been apprehended. "I couldn't tell you for fear of making a mistake."

We talked to the Korean governor, to whom I had a letter from Rhee. A little man with a puzzled expression on his face, he told us that he had started as a teacher, next became manager of the Tongnae Bank (which we saw yesterday), and became governor nine months ago. We told him we wanted to visit a village, and specified the things which interested us. He looked more puzzled than ever, but finally suggested the village of Waya, on the other side of Tongnae. The village has a landlord named O who owns 7,500 acres, and it has had a riot. We are going with Dr. Han [1902–1982],[53] a Korean graduate of the Chicago and Princeton Theological Seminaries and Bergstrom's interpreter. I am beginning to think that Dr. Han is a very important man, for both the Korean governor and the American Military Governor defer to him.

We spent the afternoon in the Agriculture Department, headed by a Major Fowler.[54] The major, a stout, loud-voiced professional

[53] Han Yŏng-gyo taught at Yonsei University and later became president of Pusan Yonsei Vocational College.

[54] USAMGIK records indicate that Gayn's "Major Fowler" was likely Capt. Joe L. Farrow (dates unknown).

soldier, has been in Korea a month and spent the war years running an army camp in Texas. I wonder what in his background qualified him for the crucial job of collecting rice in a hungry and restless Korean province.

The major knew little, and we finally prevailed on him to bring out his Korean associates. They told us the province was short on rice and on the essential commodities needed by the farmer. The hungry, they said, do not consider American wheat, which they are now getting, as a substitute for rice. The black market is rampant, with the price of rice ten times the official rate.

Midway a Captain Price, who is in charge of rice collection under Fowler, came in. He was a young man—not more than thirty—good looking and alert. He has been in this province for a year.

"Last year," he said, "someone in Seoul blundered and proclaimed an open market in rice. By the time they woke up and vanished and there was hunger. We collected only a fifth of what we should have.

"Our relations with the farmers are not so good. The Japanese took rice out of this country, but at least they brought in grain from Manchuria. Now the farmers give up rice to feed the townfolk, and get nothing in exchange. The farmer is worried, and he has transferred his hate from the Japanese to us.

"When we came here, we found the Korean People's Republic in control. This was in violation of our orders to let the Jap officials stay on in their jobs. So we broke it up. I feel that the People's Republic, the Farmers' Union and such are no longer a problem. What happens is that the old men organize their people, arm them with clubs, and protect installations. This is very gratifying to us.

"Three weeks ago I was sent to a county where they had some riots. I fired the County Master and the police chief, organized a posse and raided some houses, raided the headquarters of the Farmers' Union, and helped to get Syngman Rhee's Korean Democratic Party going."

We asked him if anything was being done about land reform.

"Land reform?" he said brightly. "That's not important. Remember that the present system is the system they're used to."

October 31, 1946 PUSAN

The provincial election was being held today, and the building was crowded with policemen. While we waited for the session to start, we talked to Military Government officers about the Korean Advisory Council, chosen so as "to reflect public opinion of all the people." Because the American Military Governor depends so much on it, it has become more than an advisory body. It nominates all Korean officials, and recommends the dismissal of those it does not like.

Of the Council's 23 members, we were told, 20 are professed rightists. Its president is the provincial boss of Syngman Rhee's Korean Democratic Party. We learned, without surprise, that the man had been a Japanese collaborator.

While we waited, we picked at random an elector and questioned him. He was a mill owner and a landlord, with seventy sharecropper families. When we asked him about the Farmers' Union, he perked up.

"I've had much trouble with the union," he said. "All my tenants belonged to it. They demanded that the land be redistributed, and the Farmers' Union be represented in the elections. We had to break it up."

There were about a hundred and fifty people sitting in the auditorium. Policemen at the door examined the credentials of the new arrivals. The Korean governor, unshaven and looking very old, sat near the ballot box. The show was obviously being run by his deputy, who looked much like a cop in plain clothes. Dr. Han was translating for Colonel Gillette [1901–1989], the Military Governor.[55]

"This is a historic occasion," said Gillette. "There've been elections before. But this is the first one pointed toward a democracy. Your very presence here indicates you're representatives of the people. We've had

---

[55] Colonel Francis E. Gillette's internal reports and related documents about political life and the anti-government riots of those years have been collected in Korea: F. E. Gillette, *Migunjŏnggi chŏngbo charyojip: Chillet'ŭ (F.E. Gillette) pogosŏ, chŏnbŏmdae chaep'an kirok, 1946–1948* [Collection of intelligence materials from the U.S. Military Government period: Gillette (F.E. Gillette) reports and war crimes tribunal records, 1946–1948], 2 vols., compiled by Hallim Taehakkyo, Asia Munhwa Yŏnguso (Ch'unch'ŏn: Hallim Taehakkyo, Asia Munhwa Yŏn'guso, 1996).

very few reports of dishonesty or intimidation. I've also had reports of great public interest. You're truly intelligent and able. ... "

A Korean rose and said he wanted to make a comment. There was some confusion at the table. "We can't have electioneering here," said Gillette. "You can ask a question." The Korean deputy governor, tapping the face of his watch impatiently, said something sharply. The man sat down. No one else rose to speak.

"I think he's an anarchist," explained my neighbor. The audience, he said, consisted mainly of county officials and Military Government personnel.

There were seven men to be elected to go to Seoul—one representative-at-large and six others. The name of the representative-at-large was announced, and there was applause.

"What's his name?"

"Kim Ch'ŏl-su."

This was the president of the Advisory Council, head of Syngman Rhee's party, a former Japanese collaborator.[56]

I sat in an office, and could not help hearing a conversation at my desk. A high American officer was approached by a U.S. Army captain and the Korean governor's secretary. The problem was patronage.

"I've had to remove the County Master in my district," said the captain.

"He was a leftist," said the secretary. "He wasn't firm."

"We can't decide whom to appoint in his place," said the captain.

There was a long pause.

"How about appointing the county's candidate who failed to be elected today," said the high officer. "He's a rightist, isn't he?"

---

[56] Here Gayn undoubtedly confuses Kim Ch'ŏl-su (1896–1977) with Kim Sŏng-su (1891–1955). Kim Ch'ŏl-su was at the time just the chief secretary of the Pusan branch of the Korean Democratic Party. Kim Sŏng-su, on the other hand, was one of Korea's wealthiest industrialists, founder of the *Tonga ilbo* newspaper, colonial-period collaborator, and chairman of the hand-picked eleven-man Korean advisory council that Archibald V. Arnold (1889–1973), as military governor of Korea, had set up on October 5, 1945. (The council was again abolished on March 29, 1946, months before Gayn's trip to Pusan.) Gayn later meets and describes Kim Sŏng-su; see end of his November 5 entry (pp. 409–10). It is unlikely that even Gillette would have interrupted one of East Asia's richest and most powerful men if he had indeed been the one speaking.

November 1, 1946 WAYA VILLAGE, CH'ŎLMA COUNTY

On our way to the village, we stopped at Tongnae to pick up a guide. Dr. Han told me he knew the town well; he had worked at the bank for ten years.

We followed the highway for a few miles, turned off into a rutted country road, and finally got on a country path. The only traffic we saw was men with heavy loads on their backs, and ox carts with their tremendous iron-bound wheels. Twice we forded rivers, bouncing hard on the boulders. After that we climbed up to a high plateau. It was a beautiful scene—a wide, sparkling river below, the rugged Ch'ŏlma mountains, and on every side of us the carefully terraced paddies that were no more than ledges crawling up the steep mountainsides.

Waya was a narrow village, hemmed in between a mountain and a river. Above it, dominating it, lay the magnificent mansion and family mausoleum of landlord O, who himself had gone to the safety of Tongnae. We drove the length of the village, until we came to the one-story, whitewashed building of the county government.

The County Master was a tall, lean man of about fifty, in a white robe and a white silk suit under it. He had close-cropped white hair, and a growth of bristle on his chin. We talked to him in the small back room, and the happy shouts of hundreds of children massed around our jeeps came in from without, and at times drowned our conversation.

Waya has 570 people, four out of every five of them sharecroppers. In all, 3,900 people in sharecropper families live on 1,350 acres of rented land. The biggest landlord is O, who has 75 sharecroppers in this county alone. The current price of land runs at about $1,300 an acre, and there are few sales. The County Master himself was a farmer, cultivating four acres, some of which was rented. He was elected to his post by the seventy heads of family groups in the county. He also got as high as the county-level in the election to the Interim Legislature.

Up to this point we were getting the information we wanted. James mumbled that he was hungry and walked out. We obviously were not discussing any dangerous subjects. But the atmosphere changed as soon as we asked the County Master about the Farmers' Union and the Youth Alliance. He became uncertain and evasive. Union leaders, he said, sometimes came to see him, but "they never talked like Communists." He had never heard of any "imported agitators." The union, he thought, was primarily engaged in protecting sharecroppers from landlords who might try to evict them or raise the rent.

One morning three weeks ago, he said, the police station here was raided by forty or fifty young men, most of them from this village. They had no weapons, and there was no violence. The three policemen did not resist. The young men occupied the station for an hour, and then left. Later, Major Atkinson arrested about twenty men. All were sharecroppers. Since then, all the officers of the Farmers' Union and the Youth Alliance have either been arrested, or have escaped. Only their wives and young children remained.

We asked him to name a member of the Farmers' Union, or just a sharecropper, to whom we could talk. The only two names he would give us were those of former headmen. "You don't want to talk to any sharecroppers," he kept repeating. "The people here are so ignorant, you'll learn nothing."

He followed us when we walked out of the office. In the yard, he took Dr. Han aside and whispered to him earnestly. I asked Han what the County Master wanted.

"He asked me to talk to the Military Government people, and get the Youth Alliance members out of jail. He said they weren't Communists. They were just young boys who followed the lead of others."

Han paused. "I think," he said, "that the reason he didn't want to give you the names of Farmers' Union people was because he's a leftist himself. He doesn't trust Americans."

When we got to the jeeps, James and the GI driver had just finished eating. They picked up the paper and the empty cans, and tossed them into a ditch. There was a great rush of children, screaming and yelling and trampling on each other. Then the pile unfolded itself, and there was a little boy, crying bitterly. His hand was covered with blood. I saw only a nick, and gave him some candy as consolation. However, blood kept flowing over his hand and finally I pried his fingers open, and saw that he had a deep gash on the inside of his thumb, probably cut with an open can. Davies bandaged the finger tenderly with his handkerchief, and volunteered to take him to the school, which had a first-aid kit. The County Master said in a hostile voice, "I'll take care of him," and led the boy off.

The police station was a tall, airy room, with windows on three sides, and a jail cell on the fourth. The cell was three feet wide and six long, and had no window. There were three young policemen in the room, one rifle, and, scattered here and there, inspirational posters reading, "Service" and "Order."

The chief was a man of about twenty-six, with alert eyes and a jaw much wider than his forehead. He seemed nervous, and kept buttoning and unbuttoning his coat. He told us he had been a policeman for five years under the Japanese.

His story of the troubled night differed from that of the County Master. He said five hundred rioters had surrounded the station, and the three policemen within gave up quickly. The crowd then listened to speeches attacking the system of rice collection. There was no violence. The crowd left some youngsters behind to guard the station, and went on towards Tongnae, taking the policemen along. The latter were dropped off at a vacant house, and discovering that no one was guarding them, walked out, and sent a warning to Tongnae.

Major Atkinson was summoned, and a force was dispatched to the village. The police met the marchers on a country path that night, and opened fire. Four of the marchers were killed, the rest fled. By the following noon, Major Atkinson had arrested 45 men—20 of them in Waya village. All of the arrested men were from this county.

"We're now checking on every man in this village to find out if he had been active in the Farmers' Union."

I remembered Colonel Maglin's assurance that the blacklists had been strictly banned. "It must be hard," I said, "to keep an eye on the subversive elements. Do you have any idea who they are?"

"Oh, certainly," the chief said. He slipped a sheet of paper across to me. There were six names on it. "One of them is already in jail," he said. "The others are in hiding. These are the men we regard as unreliable."

Back in Tongnae, we headed straight for the police station and asked to see the jail. The chief, small, flabby and middle-aged, readily agreed. He led us to a wing, into a small, dark enclosure filled with a warm, animal stench. When our eyes grew accustomed to the dim light, we saw before us—separated only by bars—a cell, about 10 feet by 16, with men sitting in rows on the floor. There were 31 men in that cell. In the next cell there were 33, and two men had to stand up because there was no place for them to squat. There were four cells altogether, two with 33 inmates each, two with 31. The chief said the men had been there for twenty-one days.

We stood in front of the cell and listened to the chief's complaint. "I sent a report of our investigation to Major Atkinson seventeen days ago, but he hasn't replied. I tried to borrow a cell in the Pusan jail. They, too, don't answer. These four cells were meant for 30 people. I have 128. Daily I send appeals to the Military Government to move these men. Nothing happens."

The men in the cells listened with impassive faces. A few smiled a crooked smile. We were all Americans, the same kind and in the same uniform that Major Atkinson wore the night he came to Waya village.

We walked back to the chief's room, and he said the food was running a bit low. The bulk of the prisoners were sharecroppers. I asked the chief how many imported agitators there were. He shook his head vigorously, "None."

"What would happen," I said, "if you caught a common criminal? You know, not a sharecropper."

"Unless it's a serious crime, we can't take care of him," the chief said. He thought a moment. "Even if it is a serious crime, I don't know where I'd put him. There's no place."

The chief said he had served nineteen years in the Japanese police force. Never had he been so busy.

From the jail we went calling on O, the landlord. He lived in a maze of compounds, fronting on a narrow lane. Right in front of the gate there was a dead rat. We studied it until Dr. Han returned with O. The latter was a small, old man with a long and scraggly moustache. He was wearing white silk.[57]

---

[57] This is the landlord Gayn photographed; see fig. 27 on p. 332. He subsequently seems to have overstated Landlord O's land holdings in the photo's cutline.

He led us into an inner compound, with a small guest house. Now the sliding wall panels had been pushed open, exposing the clean rooms, with paintings on the closet doors and oiled parchment on the floor. There were two younger men, who helped to answer our questions.

The conversation lagged, and Han told us O had been his friend ever since the bank days, twenty years ago, when Han worked in the bank and O was one of the stockholders. I recalled that the Korean provincial governor had also worked at the bank.

O confirmed that he had about 7,500 acres of land, but complained bitterly and lengthily that he was getting so little rice from it, "it isn't even enough for the beggars who come to my doors." He said he was selling his land bit by bit, "if the price is right. I have a big family. Sixteen people."

In Pusan, at dinner, we told some officers of our visit to the jail. They recounted their own experiences.

"Sometime ago," an officer said, "the Korean police got short-handed, and our troops were assigned to guard the police stations. I spent two days at a station, and I saw an eyeful. I saw cops crack men's shins against sharp-edged wooden blocks. I saw cops put burning wooden slivers under men's nails. I saw more men than I care to remember get the water treatment. They just kept pouring water into a guy's mouth through a tube until he damned near drowned. I saw cops beat a man across the shoulders with a metal rod, and then hang him on a metal hook under his shoulder blades.

"I finally couldn't take it. I went to my commanding officer and said, 'Sir, we've got to stop this. Our soldiers are now guarding the police station, and this is giving us a black eye.' The officer said he agreed with me, but there was nothing he could do. He had orders not to interfere in Korean 'administrative detail.'

"Well, I just went back to my station, and told the sons of bitches to stop the tortures at once. Boy, was I happy when they pulled us out the next day!"

November 2, 1946 PUSAN

In the morning, talked to Colonel Gillette, the Military Governor. He is a shrewd man, high above the run of military administrators. But he too had the blind spots common to the military. He never mentioned the words "land reform" and though he saw clearly some of the abuses which led to the riots, he still blamed the latter on "outside agitators."

He spoke at length of the tremendous educational work being done by the Military Government. He also noted some of the handicaps, one of them being the Hollywood movies available for showing here. "They're mostly gangster pictures," he said, "and the Koreans are beginning to think of us as men with two guns." Somehow, there was a small stock of French movies in Korea, and the people much preferred them to the Hollywood product.

"You mustn't think too harshly of us here," he said as we left him. "I used to run a CCC camp[58] in Louisiana when Huey Long [1893–1935][59] was in power, and some of the things I saw there would make Koreans look like amateurs."

I did not comment, but I have little patience with this argument. Whenever any shortcoming becomes so glaring as to require comment, it is pointed out that things are not ideal back home—corruption, strikes, race riots. With equal justice, this argument could be used to condone all that happened in Hitler's Germany.

Outside of Gillette's office we ran into a major who is in charge of the educational work in the province. He was a harassed-looking, middle-aged man. We told him we were leaving Pusan tonight. He said he was sorry we did not have a chance to see some of the great work being done by his department.

"I tell you what," he said. "You got a few hours. Why don't you visit some school here. I've been a physical education instructor for thirty years, and I tell you, I've never seen boys do better gymnastics."

I told my escorts that I had to pack, and went up to my room. Pretty soon there was a tap on the door, and a man came in. He was an

[58] Civilian Conservation Corps (CCC) camps were established as part of Roosevelt's New Deal in 1933 to put young men to work during the Great Depression.
[59] Right-wing politician Huey Long was Governor of Louisiana from 1928 to 1932 and was known for his verbal attacks on Roosevelt and the left.

American civilian attached to the army. "I heard there was a correspondent around," he said, "and I've been waiting for you to get back to your room. I want to talk to you privately."

He was a mild, low-voiced man who spoke unemotionally of the things that troubled him. There were two of them—the low morale of the troops and the poor supply service. He has been here a year.

"Some congressmen went through here," he said. "They heard that the PX stores were bare of supplies, and they raised holy hell. The next thing you knew, the supplies appeared in some of the bigger towns. But in the smaller places, today, fourteen months after we landed here, we still lack cigarettes, beer, tooth paste, and electric light bulbs. Most of the military men I've met are lousy administrators. There are all kinds of alibis—no ships and stuff. There are plenty of ships that come here to pick up the boys going home. There's no reason why they can't send supplies here aboard the ships.

"The lack of supplies only makes it harder for us to deal with the problem of morale. This is not the disciplined war army. This is a peacetime army of boys of eighteen and twenty, who have had only eight weeks of basic training before they came here. Except in the big towns, nothing is being done to keep up their morale. No radios, few movies, little athletic equipment.

"Even window shopping is discouraged. In Chinhae[60] entire areas are off limits to GIs. You can drive through in a jeep, but the moment you get off, an MP will pick you up. Association with Koreans is frowned on. You may have a Korean friend, but you can't take him for a ride in your jeep, or even invite him to your billet. The boys never get a chance to meet the Koreans and learn something about them, and pretty soon the Koreans are 'goddamned gooks,' and you try to see how close you can drive to a gook to scare him to death without touching him. You ought to write this up. A lot of guys here would be grateful to you. Newspapermen never get here, and we sort of feel lost."

An hour before train time, Charlotte and I went to Bergstrom's house to say goodbye. We had just finished our first drink when a tall,

[60] Chinhae Naval Base near Pusan had been Japan's major naval base in Korea before 1945 and was taken over by the United States upon arrival; it was the scene of a number of anti-U.S. incidents by Koreans.

balding American in a civilian suit and a loud tie came in. This was Mr. Flaherty [1914–1990],[61] the Military Government's legal officer. Flaherty, we learned, was a Boston lawyer, served in Korea as a major, and on demobilization decided to stay on. He said he had land in Massachusetts, but he loved Korea, and would just as soon go to Tongnae and settle down there.

After that the conversation followed its carefree way. We said, "We've visited the Tongnae jail, and it was jammed."

"They're jammed everywhere."

We said something about the Tongnae riot.

"There's been no riot in Tongnae."

"What do you mean no riot, Mr. Flaherty? Why are all those people in jail?"

He said, with a happy grin. "Oh, we just put them in on a charge of conspiracy. We can jail anyone on that charge. Hell, I've just come back from the riot country. The cops would bring a man before me and say he is a rioter. I'd say, 'How do you know?' They'd say, 'He has just confessed, in the back room.' Well, it's easy to get a confession the way the Korean cops work."

We told Flaherty of our visit with O the landlord. "I know the guy well," he said. "I've been his guest many a time. Have you visited his place in Waya village? It's a real palace. They serve you delicious food on gold plate or on solid silver. And if O likes you, he'll bring out some choice liquor that he brought with him from France fifteen years ago."

From O, the conversation naturally shifted to land reform. Charlotte said that once the reform bill passes, O might have to sell his land to the State for redistribution among his sharecroppers.

For the first time, Flaherty showed agitation. "That's impossible. You can't take a man's property away from him. I know what I'd do if you tried to take my land in Massachusetts away from me."

November 2, 1946 (night) TAEGU

After a ride on the Pusan-Seoul Express—which is shabby, jerky, unbelievably overcrowded, and evil smelling—we got to Taegu. We were

[61] Gordon Flaherty.

met by Lieutenant Lewis [1928–2015], adjutant to Colonel Potts [1907–1996], the regimental commander. Lewis was a portly young man with a steel helmet, and a pistol strapped to his leg. His martial appearance impressed us until we learned that Taegu was quiet,[62] and Lewis himself has been here only eight weeks. He spoke to us with a politeness that somehow bordered on insult.

Charlotte was put up in a Red Cross billet. I was put up with a Major Arne Stenslie [1890–1968] of Devil's Lake, North Dakota. I was now so accustomed to the constant surveillance that, on a hunch, I asked the major how long he had been with Regimental Intelligence. He answered promptly, "Two months."

November 3, 1946 TAEGU

Picked up Charlotte after breakfast. She told me that last night, at dinner, she asked the other girls if they were in town during last month's riots. There was a stony silence. Charlotte tried a few more questions, but there was no answer. At midnight, after she had gone to bed, one of the girls came in and said: "Honey, please don't think that we're rude, or that we don't like you. It's just that we had orders not to talk to you about the riots."

Later we met Lieutenant Hitchcock [1922–2020],[63] Public Information Officer for the Military Government here. He is a young and pleasant fellow, interested in the work he is doing. He brought us our first news of the election in this province: of the seven successful candidates, six are Syngman Rhee's followers, and the seventh is "some sort of a neutral."

"You know," said Hitchcock, "the results amaze me. I thought that since most of the people here are sharecroppers, the leftists would

---

[62] As described in Gayn's October 25, 1946, entry, Taegu, of course, had not been quiet. Now declassified USAMGIK reports also tell us that a month earlier Taegu's main police station had been stormed by rioters and several of the policemen had been tortured and killed, with this same Colonel Russel J. Potts having refused to send in U.S. troops to intervene in a timely manner.

[63] Wilbur W. Hitchcock.

run away with the election. Instead, the rightists won, and the leftists got nothing."

The courts, he said, are working overtime trying the rioters. The Military Commission which deals with major crimes is still on its first case. But most of the work is done by the U.S. Army Provost Courts, in which the judge is at the same time the counsel for defense and the prosecuting attorney. My ideas on justice are pretty orthodox, and this combination somehow frightens me.

Every defendant, Hitchcock said, had been advised that he could have an American defense counsel. But the sharecroppers' reaction has been as expected. "Very few men have asked for counsel, and you can't assign one to each defendant. There are too many of them."

In the afternoon, Charlotte, Hitchcock and I drove fifteen miles out of Taegu, stopped in a hamlet, and walked into the first yard. There was a man sitting in front of his hut. Our interpreter told the man we were newspapermen, and could we talk to him, please.

The hut, windowless as most of the Korean country houses are, was made of yellow mud. It was set in a small yard, no more than thirty feet long. The highway, laid atop a dam, towered over the yard and the hut. The man was dressed in a ragged white jacket, under which he wore a thick vest. He was peeling an apple, and watching the road through the bamboo fence.

We started talking to him, and pretty soon other people started coming in. Before we knew it, there were eleven men squatting on the ground around us, and twenty or thirty kids, and more men and women sitting on the road behind the fence. The village meeting was on.

The place—the hamlet of Yŏnho in Kosan county—was poverty-ridden.[64] Of its seventy families, sixty were sharecroppers. The men in the yard averaged just over an acre per family. They agreed that half an acre was needed for each mouth. The man with the apple had five children and only an acre of land, and that was not enough. To keep alive, he worked for other farmers. I asked them if they would buy land if the government gave them credit and cut the price, which in this area

---

[64] The village, east of Taegu, was Yŏnji (Yŏnji maŭl) in Yŏnho-dong, part of what was until 1981 Kosan county (Kosan-myŏn).

ran upward of $1,600 an acre. They all laughed. "No matter how low the price," said one, "I couldn't buy it."

Under the Japanese, they said, they could borrow money from the Rural Credit Association at 24 per cent a year. But now the Japanese were gone, and the only source of credit was the local landlords, who charged up to 60 per cent, when they wanted to lend money. This village was so poor few men in it were able to get a loan.

The land belonged to men who lived in Taegu. The biggest landlord was a man named Sŏ. They called the names of their landlords out, and most of them said Sŏ. Then we came to what seemed to me to be the highlight of the day. I said, "You pay your landlord a third of the crop in rent?"

There were immediate protests. "No, we pay half the yield." I said, "There must be some mistake. Don't you know of the Military Government order limiting all land rents to one-third?" They said, no, there were some rumors of that, but is certainly was not true in this village. Nor in the next one, a voice said on the road. Nor in the next county, said someone else.

The man with the apple explained, "We take all our rice to the Military Government. The Korean clerks give us credit for half the value, and credit the landlord with the other half."

There could be no clearer proof of the alliance between the Korean personnel of Military Government and the landlords. And I thought it significant that it was in this general area that the worst riots had taken place.

We now talked of the election. The man with the apple thought most of the family heads had voted. Two men next to me said this was the first they had heard of the election. Hitchcock said indignantly to them: "That's impossible. I sent out the election posters myself. You must've seen them." The men admitted they could not read. I remembered then a passing remark I heard in Seoul that 80 per cent of Korean farmers were illiterate. I asked the people around me how many of them could read and write. Two or three said they could; the others could not.

I said, "How then did you write in the names of your candidates in the election?"

"Others wrote the names in for us."

"Was the headman one of the men who helped you?"

"Yes, he helped everyone."

"Was he himself elected?"

They all caught on. They laughed and said, "Yes."

But Hitchcock's mind was still on the posters. That was his job—telling people of the election—and he wanted to know what had slipped up. We drove back to the office which the headman shared with a barber. There, on the barbershop wall, were two large posters. "See," said Hitchcock, "what did I tell you?"

The barber was outside. We asked him when the posters were put up. "I helped to put them up myself," he said. "That was the evening before the election."

November 4, 1946 TAEGU

The Military Commission was sitting in a large, airy, and fairly clean room. The five judges—a colonel, two majors, and two captains—sat on a high dais, with the flag and an iron stove behind them. In the center of the room stood the witness chair. The two defendants sat with their counsel on the judges' right. There were nine benches for the public, but these were occupied only by us and the wives of the defendants. Later I was told that "anyone can come in here and see the trial, provided they're solid, reputable people. We don't want any mobs here."

One of the defendants was an alert, handsome man of forty named Hwang. He lived in Manchuria until 1942, when he returned to Taegu, and owned first a liquor store and then a fruit stall. The prosecution said he was one of the minor ringleaders of the riot.

The other man was named Chang, and by profession he was a brothel owner. Chang was tall, slim and about fifty-five. In his Korean trousers tied at the ankles and a Western coat worn directly over his undershirt, Chang looked sloppy.

Both were accused of murdering a recently retired police captain.

As the witnesses followed each other on the stand, it became clear that the brothel owner had had an old grudge against the police captain.

When the Japanese surrendered, the brothel owner's brother moved into a Japanese house.[65] Sometime later, the police ordered him out and assigned the house to the police captain. Now, when the riots began, the brothel owner went to the police captain and told him to get out of the house by nightfall.

Then a crowd of sixty or seventy men, allegedly hotly led by Hwang, swept through the alley, and the brothel owner guided it into the police captain's yard. The captain hid himself, and the crowd contented itself with wrecking the furniture. The brothel owner was shouting jubilantly, "We've got the house back," and, to the crowd, "Please don't damage the house."

A woman found the police captain in his hiding place, and the crowd began to beat him. His wife, a small, old woman, threw herself over him in an effort to save him, but she was pulled off, and the police captain was dragged into the street and beaten to death. Then an American tank appeared in the lane, and the rioters threw the body into a Buddhist temple, and dispersed.

The defendants had a Korean lawyer, who, with his each word, helped to hang them. His questions were stupid, his witnesses evasive. One witness, who was meant to clear Hwang of all guilt, looked terrified by the scene. He kept saying, "Had I known I would be a witness, I would've looked around, but I'm just a carpenter." His failure to testify, I thought, condemned Hwang. The damage was compounded by the tragically poor interpreting.

After recess we went to a Provost Court, a bleak and dusty room where a lone American officer—a lieutenant colonel—was trying a ragged young Korean. There were only four people in the room—the judge, the defendant, an interpreter, and a Korean policeman with a rifle.

Just as we sat down on the dirty bench, the judge pronounced his verdict: one year at hard labor. The boy tugged at his long, unkempt hair and said, "This is a very harsh sentence." Then he began to cry, saying that he was not a rioter, and that his old father depended on him

[65] Following Korean liberation, the vacated Japanese residences were hot items, with different groups vying for ownership. Leftists accused any Korean who sought to acquire them as being a pro-Japanese collaborator, while the U.S. military claimed them for its own use.

for a livelihood. The colonel said he knew all that, and would put in a recommendation for leniency in the court report to the provincial Military Governor.

The guard took the young Korean away. The interpreter left. There were only the three of us in the room. Charlotte and I sat on the bench and looked at the colonel. After a while he began to speak. First he told us of the case: the boy and four men had heard that the head of the rationing board had concealed seventeen bags of rice for police use. They talked it over, and decided to get the man to surrender the hoard. They had lured him out into the street, and were talking to him when the police appeared. The four men fled; the boy was caught.

The colonel said: "I realize that this is a very light sentence, and in other provost courts in this building he would have gotten five years. But I think a year is enough."

We walked to the colonel and stood facing him. "This is a bad job," he said. "I don't like any part of it. We sort of get assigned to it between jobs. Anybody who passes through and has no definite assignment gets a job on a provost court. I don't like the idea of having to decide what a young man is to do with his time for the next year or two. We're just infantry officers, not legal people. I try to treat these people leniently. But some officers just give them five years as a rule. I'm soft hearted. I guess it takes a little longer to get callous."

He paused again. "There're still three thousand cases to be tried in this town alone," he said. "In so many of them people just pay off old grudges, and you can't tell where the grudge ends and the evidence begins."

We stopped at the Provost Court office, which channels the cases to the judges. There was a crowd of happy officers there, headed by the major in charge. They told us that up to this morning one hundred ten cases have been tried in the provost courts in town, and an unknown number by the six courts operating elsewhere in the province. The major thought the dock would be cleared in thirty days.

The others cried, "Want to bet?"

The Army's Criminal Investigation Department, the major said, could not investigate the cases fast enough, and it became necessary to admit Korean police testimony.

"The Korean cops," the major said, "still function under the Jap rules of evidence. You have to have a confession. How you get it doesn't matter. We see these jokers brought in all beat up, with lacerations. Each has made a confession. We finally had to try indoctrinating the Korean cops, and now many prisoners are set loose."

"We still get funny ones," said a captain. "The other day they brought in a guy who confessed murdering a cop. Quite by accident, we discovered that the murdered cop was still walking his beat."

I found that some 6,500 people had been arrested in Taegu—not one of them an "outside agitator." I also learned that the police chief had to be fired for "softness" during the riots, and the new chief was made of a harder mettle. He had served in the Japanese police force for ten years. He was teamed up with a Captain Tyree,[66] U.S. Army, who, we were given to understand, was no softie himself.

Before we left, the major invited us to attend another trial later in the day. Although no case had been scheduled, he said he would arrange a trial for us.

"Come a little later," he said, "and see our justice function. Quasi-justice, I guess you can call it."

In the evening, two officers who had taken an active part in suppressing the Taegu uprising told us its tragic story.

One day about five weeks ago two schools had a football game, followed by a fight. The police came to restore order, and after they were done, a student was dead. This provoked resentment, and student groups met clandestinely to plan protests.

Meanwhile, a railroad strike was in progress in the Taegu railway shops. On the night of October 1, with the permission of the Military Government, some 4,000 workers gathered in front of the railroad station in support of the walkout. One of our informants who was on patrol duty in the area said the meeting was orderly.

The meeting was to disperse at 10:00 P.M. Long before the deadline, police units began to move up. "The Korean cops," said the other

[66] We have not been able to identify the "Captain Tyree" Gayn mentions. During and after the Taegu Uprising of 1946, the U.S. Army liaison to the Taegu police was Major John C. Plezia (1913–1984). The only well-documented "Captain Tyree" we can locate is a captain at sea in the U.S. Navy, associated with USS *Bowfin* (SS-287); we find no evidence that he served with Army authorities in Taegu in 1946.

officer "were trigger-happy that night. They were shooting all over the place. When they got through dispersing the crowd, there was a dead man."

There were shots through the night, and in schools and factories meetings of indignation were in progress. With daylight, the town was out in the streets. "It was the craziest thing you ever saw," said the first officer. "Everyone was out—workers, students, farmers from the countryside, school kids marching in long columns. They all marched toward the police station, and then most of them just squatted in the street and waited. I walked through and nobody even gave me a dirty look."

The students brought a body, which they said was the body of the student killed by the police, and laid it before the police station. Then they submitted two demands to the frightened police chief: disarm the police, and release the political prisoners. The chief accepted the first demand, but said he could do nothing about the second without the permission of the U.S. Army. By this time, the policemen were climbing over the wall into the adjoining American compound, and were being sent back because "we didn't want to take sides in this mess."

In the late morning, the crowd poured into the station, destroyed the files, and released a hundred prisoners. Little other damage was done. The rioters remained in control of the building for an hour. During this hour, meetings were bubbling up all over the town, with the workers and the farmers reciting stories of police brutality.

Around noon, a U.S. Army major ordered the crowd surrounding the police station to disperse by 3:00 P.M. Before the deadline, army tanks and armored trucks began to patrol the streets. The enormous crowd broke up slowly. But as each splinter drifted away, it swept over other police stations and the homes of policemen. Many policemen were beaten to death and their relatives injured.

That night American patrols began to find policemen's bodies in the dark streets or vacant lots. Seven bodies, two still alive, were found in a park. All had been mutilated. A few had been castrated. Injured policemen sent to the city hospital received no help. "We soon discovered," one of the two officers said, "that the leading Korean doctors were in cahoots with the rebels. We put them in the clink too."

Order returned to Taegu on the third day. On that day, 1,100 police reinforcements arrived in town, and the policemen who had gone into hiding returned to duty. "Every grudge that any cop ever had against anyone was now being paid off." One truckload of prisoners after another began to roll toward the jail. When this was filled, schools and offices were taken over. Among the arrested were teachers, and lawyers, farm and labor leaders, and all prominent members of the People's Party, whose leader, Yŏ Un-hyŏng, was even then advertised as a co-chairman of Bertsch's moderate coalition.

From Taegu, violence spilled over into the countryside. The farmers were rougher on home soil than they were in Taegu. Cruelty was more extreme, and sometimes county offices as well as the police stations were attacked. In some places American patrols made tentative pokes, and hastily retired. At these points, the committees of sharecroppers governed for many days. From this province, the wildfire of revolution spread to other provinces. For a time the uprising in South Korea appeared to be a match for some of history's great peasant revolutions. By today, it appears to have been crushed.

After dinner there was a reception for a visiting general, and all the officers had gone upstairs. I begged off, saying I had to put my notes in order and pack. I was typing when there was a gentle tap on the door, and a young captain came in. He wanted to know if he could read in my room. I said yes. He sat down and pulled *The Nation* magazine[67] out of his pocket. He did it with such a conspiratorial air that I said: "That's dangerous stuff you're carrying around with you." He said eagerly, "I have to hide it. If anybody sees it, I'll get hell. A friend of mine wrote a letter to *Stars and Stripes*,[68] complaining about the chow. They're investigating him now."

[67] *The Nation* published several critical reports about the role of the U.S. Military in southern Korea. Richard D. Robinson's anonymous article that would be published the following year was not the only such piece. For example, in February 1946, Andrew Roth (1919–2010) who, like Gayn, had been arrested in the so-called Amerasia spy case, published a piece that had characterized General Hodge as a pretentious and prejudiced man who called Koreans "the same breed of cat" (cf. p. 346, footnote 17) and who gravely misjudged the political situation in Korea and thus "surrounded himself [...] completely with rightist supporters." Andrew Roth, "Korea's Heritage," *Nation* 162, no. 5 (February 2, 1946): 122, and "Cross-Fire in Korea," *Nation* 162, no. 8 (February 23, 1946): 222.

[68] *Stars and Stripes* is a newspaper published by the United States military. During the 1940s it was published in various regional editions, one of them the Far East edition, which also reported on the riots in Korea from a pseudo-objective viewpoint.

He read and I typed. After a while he said, "Are you having much trouble getting information?" I told him it was not too bad.

"You know," he said, "the day before your arrival, some of the officers here got orders not to talk to you because your papers (the Chicago *Sun* and *Newsweek*) 'have not demonstrably proven their patriotism.' But it's always the same. A correspondent from the New York *Herald Tribune* came here right after the riots. They kept telling him they had no spare jeeps for him and finally gave him a small plane. But you can't cover the riots from that. Then all the men in the office were ordered to give him nothing outside of the official releases. A friend of mine didn't know of the order, and gave the guy some dope. They bawled hell out of him."

We left Taegu by train at 11:00 P.M.

November 5, 1946 SEOUL

At noon Charlotte and I went to the Public Relations Office for our mail. Major Williamson was affable. "Going back to Tokyo tomorrow, Charlotte?" Charlotte said she was staying for another day or two for some interviews we had arranged. Williamson turned red. "You can't stay here. I told General Hodge you're leaving. You must leave."

For a moment Charlotte looked as if she was going to burst into tears. "Look, Major," she said. "I don't understand any of this. I'm an American reporter. This is the American zone. What's the idea of running me out?"

Williamson said: "For one thing, we don't have quarters here. The families of the officers are arriving, and we've no place to put them up."

"That's a lot of bunk, Major," said Charlotte. "The billet I'm in now is practically empty, and the families are not due for weeks. I assure you I'll be out before they arrive. All I want is to interview some of these Koreans."

"You've got to leave," Williamson said firmly. "Tomorrow. There's nothing to argue about."

Our next chat was with the Korean head of the Bureau of Contacts in the U.S. Military Government. He was ordered to get interviews for us with Korean leaders whom we had not met yet. Above all, we wanted to see Kim Ku, the patriotic assassin and head of the defunct government-in-exile in Chongqing, and Yŏ Un-hyŏng, head of the People's Party and cochairman of Bertsch's coalition.

"I'll get you an interview with Mr. Kim Ku," said the Contact Man.

"We also want to meet Mr. Yŏ."

"Apart from Kim Ku, I'll also get an interview for you with Mr. Syngman Rhee."

"We've met Mr. Rhee already. We want to meet Mr. Yŏ."

"Look," he said. "You want to talk to gentlemen. Mr. Rhee is a gentleman. Mr. Kim Ku is a gentleman. Mr. Kim Kyu-sik is all right. But Mr. Yŏ is a Communist, a gangster. You don't want to see him."

"Don't you worry about that," I said patiently. "We've met the gentlemen. We now want to meet the gangsters. You just get us an appointment with Mr. Yŏ."

The Contact Man shrugged his shoulders. "I don't even know where to find him. But I'll get you an interview with Mr. Kim Ku."

I wanted to talk again to Hŏ Hŏn, the left-wing leader whom I saw on my fourth day in Korea. I mentioned it to an American in Military Government. He said: "I doubt if Hŏ Hŏn will want to see you today. A few days ago he finally came out openly against the coalition. He was picked up by the cops, beaten up, and then released with the explanation that it was a case of 'mistaken identity.' He's in no mood to talk to Americans."

There are few problems more pressing in our zone than the police excesses. So sharp has become the public criticism that Military Government has found it necessary to set up a special American–Korean Commission to consider corrective steps. I looked up the list of the members and experts and picked out a name. I went to the man and asked for information. He agreed to give it to me, on the understanding that I would not use his name.

"Let me give you a typical example of what's happening," he said. "In a village not far from here, sixty-two men were arrested on the charge of plotting to attack a police station. Among them was a doctor. The other day, the doctor's relatives finally got to an influential American officer and persuaded him to drive out to the jail and check the reports of brutal treatment. He did. He found the doctor dead of torture. Another man died later, with his face smashed to a pulp. The third had his back broken. A report was turned in to General Hodge. He said: 'This is the way police have traditionally operated in the Orient. What can we do?'

"One reason for the brutality is that the bulk of the police have been steeped in Japanese practices. The Commission has been given these statistics which help to explain what's wrong with the police. Of the one hundred forty police officers with the rank of captain, more than one hundred ten have served with the Jap police. In Seoul, every one of the ten precinct police chiefs is Japanese-trained. So are eight of the ten provincial chiefs in our zone.

"Our army has been concerned solely with the maintenance of order. It took over the Japanese police machinery, without understanding this important psychological fact: under the Japs, the really dirty police work was done by Korean underlings, and this is why the Korean people hated the Korean cops worse than they hated the Jap bosses for whom these cops worked."

The ten American military governors in our zone are meeting here with General Lerch to discuss the election results. Lerch, I am told, is highly pleased with the outcome of the election. He told a meeting, in approximately these words:

"We've been ordered by directives from Washington to play along with the moderate groups. The elections, resulting in an overwhelming victory for the right, show that Washington was wrong."

In the evening Charlotte and I drove out to the Rhees for dinner. Once again we passed through the screening board of policemen at the gate, and walked up the hill to the brightly lit house on top.

Rhee seemed happier than he was the first time we met him. I told him I saw his men win the election in two provinces. He said simply, as if he was a feudal sovereign speaking of his domain: "My people are with me."

There were three other guests—an aide to General Hodge, his woman friend, and a small, middle-aged, silent Korean whom I did not identify until later. The American officer talked to Rhee in terms of familiarity and friendship, and I wondered of the propriety of General

Hodge's aide visiting the man whom General Hodge—at least on paper—had been ordered to shun.

It was right in the middle of a mouthful of hot cabbage-and-pepper *kimchee*, with which the Koreans spice their food, that I realized who the silent Korean guest was. This was Kim Sŏng-su, Rhee's financial angel, Korea's fourth richest man, a great landlord, an educator, and one of the most powerful bosses of the Korean Democratic Party. Kim has been described to me as a political Dr. Jekyll and Mr. Hyde. He is a university president, has helped numerous youths to get an education, and believes he is a model citizen. On the other hand, he is accused by many Military Government officers of having been a collaborator before Japan's surrender, and of having urged young Koreans drafted into the Japanese Army to "die for your fatherland." Kim sees no need for drastic reform, resolutely opposes it, and because of his tremendous influence can do much to block it. Kim is one of the powerful figures behind Syngman Rhee, and much of what Rhee champions was born in Kim's mind.[69]

November 6, 1946 SEOUL

At noon Charlotte went to the Air Transport Command and discovered that she could not get passage until she had taken a whole series of shots, including one for cholera. By the time she got through with the shots, no seats remained on tomorrow's plane for Tokyo. When Williamson found out she was not leaving, his face turned purple, and he started stuttering. "What will I tell General Hodge now?" He ended by going over to ATC himself to check on Charlotte's story. I told Williamson I would take off for Tokyo the day after tomorrow.

In the afternoon we again called on Kim Kyu-sik. He was still swathed in his gown, felt slippers, and robe, but he was a different man.

[69] Kim Sŏng-su founded and headed Korea University (Koryŏ Taehakkyo), one of South Korea's most prestigious universities. Kim was also the founder of the *Tonga ilbo*, which (together with the *Chosŏn ilbo*) was the leading nationalistic newspaper in the Korean language during the colonial period. For a detailed study on Kim, see Carter J. Eckert, *Offspring of Empire: The Koch'ang Kims and the Colonial Origins of Korean Capitalism, 1876–1945*, 2nd ed. (Seattle: University of Washington Press, 2014).

There were force and anger in his voice as he talked of the election. He said he had just sent a letter to General Hodge, suggesting that the results be annulled, wholly or in part, or the coalition be permitted to name all the ninety members of the Interim Legislature, instead of only forty-five.[70] He called the election fraudulent, said he agreed with his co-chairman Yŏ that no fair election could be held as long as all the leftist leaders were in jail, and revealed that two months ago he had urged General Lerch to establish special safeguards for a fair election. His plea was ignored.

Syngman Rhee's men won forty of the forty-five seats. Kim Ku, another extreme rightist, whom we are seeing tomorrow, took three seats. Yŏ Un-hyŏng, co-chairman of the coalition, managed to get two, on an isolated island. ("The governor there is an honest man.") Kim won nothing.

Now Kim was spelling out for us the story of this, Korea's first "democratic" election. In many provinces, the decision on who was eligible to vote was left to local headmen. In hundreds of villages, the election consisted of a friendly chat between the headman and a selected list of family heads. (Headman: "We're having an election. Do you want to vote for me?") In hundreds of cases, the village and county heads dispatched servants to the prospective voters, asking for the loan of their name seals, which were then stamped on ballots filled in by the officials. No adequate notice of elections was given, and in many cases the date was left to the discretion of local officials. In dozens of instances, men who questioned the validity of the election were jailed on the charge of sedition. Although the Military Government expressly called for a secret election, countless thousands of illiterate voters had their ballots filled in by helpful headmen, who by the oddest coincidence were among those elected. Though the Military Government

---

[70] A carbon copy of Kim Kyu-sik's letter is among the Mark Gayn Papers in Toronto. Kim, in his role as chairman of the Coalition Committee, not only asked that the election results be annulled, he also provided Hodge with a partial incident list of election rule violations in Seoul and each of the provinces. Several of the listed violations were *ab initio* cases, as Kim termed them, where the winning, right-wing candidates had been staunch collaborators with the Japanese colonizers and their war efforts, who should have been banned from running for office from the very start. Letter by Kim Kyu-sik to John R. Hodge, November 4, 1946, Mark Gayn Papers, MS Coll. 215, Series 8 (Books), Box 100, Folder 25 (Politics), Thomas Fisher Rare Book Library, University of Toronto.

specified that all persons over eighteen years of age were entitled to vote, in practice only family heads were allowed to vote.

"In Kangwŏn Province," Kim said, "the entire election was conducted not by the authorities, but by Syngman Rhee's party. Naturally, all the three elected men were his henchmen. All three were notorious Japanese collaborators.

"In Seoul, the morning of the election, the city hall entrance was covered with the posters of Syngman Rhee's party. All the three elected men are its members. Two of the three are known collaborators. In Taegu, which you've just visited, one of the elected men is a known collaborator. In Pusan, the head of Syngman Rhee's party was elected. He is a collaborator.

"I know that the American military governors attended the provincial elections, and then reported to General Lerch that they had seen no undemocratic practices. As a matter of fact, they didn't. It wasn't necessary to be undemocratic on the provincial level, when all the dirty work had already been done on the village and county levels."

Here, as in Japan, carpetbagging supplies one of the less savory aspects of the Occupation. One well-placed officer told me he knew of "at least one hundred and fifty cases" of Americans who "came to do good and remained to do well." This may be just a figure of speech, but I am flabbergasted by the open and unashamed talk of business ventures by army officers. A lieutenant in the Bando Building,[71] where General Hodge has his office, told me that once he is out of the army, he will remain here "to look after my interests." It developed that these included a million-dollar glass factory whose purchase in behalf of Korean investors he is already negotiating in Detroit—in contravention of all military regulations. ("I keep sending home a couple of hundred bucks a week—as 'poker winnings.' Christ, I don't play that kind of poker.") Charlotte went to a dance the other night, and four majors at her table openly boasted of their business deals.

But all of these seem unimaginative beside the story of a high Military Government officer who visited a Korean museum, examined

[71] Gayn's 1948 edition had this as Honta Building, a simple transposition error—he meant Hantō, the Japanese pronunciation of the Chinese characters for peninsula, in Korean *pando* resp. *bando*. The Bando Hotel was the predecessor of the Lotte Hotel in Sogong-dong, central Seoul.

its treasures, calmly said, "They're nice. Pack 'em up," and then shipped most of the collection back home to the United States.[72] The army allowed him to go home, but stopped the last eighteen cases before they left Korea. My informants said they did not know why the officer was not prosecuted, unless it was the reluctance of Generals MacArthur and Hodge to have a scandal comparable to the malodorous scandals in the European theater.

In my room tonight, I had a long session with an American high in the Seoul hierarchy. I had met him here casually, but we had close mutual friends and we trusted each other. To both of us, I suspected, the talk gave an opportunity for soul-searching. He wanted to know how much I had learned on my visit, and I wanted to match my impressions against his.

"I've been here since October of last year," the visitor said. "I know that right up to last spring we had no policy for Korea. It's hard to believe that, but it's true. The best proof is a statement of policy sent by General Hodge to Brigadier General Charles Harris [1894–1993],[73] deputy Military Governor, one week before we landed here. You ought to get a copy. Hodge said that Korea, as part, of the Japanese empire, was our enemy and therefore subject to the terms of surrender. He said our troops would land in Korea to see that these terms were obeyed. He said that, at least in the beginning, it would be necessary to operate through the Jap administration. He said that during this period we would recognize the Japs as the lawful government of Korea. He admitted it was likely that the Koreans had hopes of freedom and independence. But he said that, as far as he knew, no Allied policy on

---

[72] Here, Gayn refers to Lieutenant Colonel Maurice Lutwack (1906–1979) of Buffalo, from November 1945 to May 1946 the U.S. military governor of Kyŏnggi Province. See Hoffmann's essay, 31 and 33, and Robinson's "Betrayal," 294.

[73] Brigadier General Charles S. Harris was appointed commander of the future U.S. Military Government on August 29—before U.S. troops even landed in Inch'ŏn—keeping that position until General Arnold was named USAMGIK's military governor on September 12, 1945. Arriving with a reconnaissance party at Kimp'o Airfield on September 4, Harris helped prepare for the formal surrender of Japanese military forces in southern Korea. Hodge's instructions to Harris are reproduced in Han Mu Kang, "The United States Military Government in Korea, 1945–1948: An Analysis and Evaluation of Its Policy" (PhD diss., University of Cincinnati, 1970), 34–35. See also p. 55 in this volume.

this had been formulated. Therefore, Hodge enjoined Harris to make no promises to the Koreans but to stress prompt and willing compliance with the surrender terms.

"I know of no excuse for the statement. It betrayed lack of instructions from Washington. It showed, to me anyway, that General Hodge had not read the Cairo Declaration, in which Britain, China, and we said that Korea would be 'free and independent.' It set the tone for the whole mess that followed. We were not an army of liberation. We had come to occupy, to see that the Koreans obeyed the terms of surrender. From the first day, we've behaved as enemies of the Korean people.

"Last spring Washington finally came through with a policy of moderation. But you must've found out that we honor it here only in the breach. To this day our allies are boys like Rhee, to whom moderation is anathema.

"You can say what you will of the Russians. You can justly call the People's Committees of North Korea [Pukchosŏn Inmin Wiwŏnhoe] a puppet regime. But the fact is that the Russians, from the outset, knew precisely what their policy was, they let the People's Committees do the job of governing, and they allowed the Koreans themselves to introduce reforms and wipe out collaborators. ..."

We were now on the subject of our relations with Russia, a worldwide problem that was especially acute in Korea. In Germany the issue was obfuscated by the presence of other Allied powers and other problems. Here the problem was clear cut. We faced Russia across an imaginary line on the map, and each of us controlled a chunk of a country in which we could practice what we said we believed in.

In this picture, I agreed with my visitor, the press should have played a major role. Yet, in this world ruled by the military, the press was an unwanted intruder. I was an American reporter who believed in what are generally known as American ideals. Economic democracy. Democratic politics. Free speech and assembly. Government by law. It may be, as the extreme leftists insist, that few of these concepts remain in our American structure, and a man who believes in them is a fool and a dreamer. On the other hand, it may be, as the conservatives assert, that the man who finds fault with American policy or personnel is a dangerous radical.

I did not think I was either a radical or a dreamer. I was a reporter, who had found, with shame and anguish, that under our flag—and often with our active encouragement—there had come into being a police state so savage in its suppression of man's elemental liberties that it was difficult to find a parallel for it. I had found in our zone only the shallow verbiage of democracy, and none of its practices. I had found administrative and political ineptness, and an alliance with the darkest reaction. I recalled Captain K., and his declaration that the army wanted no interference from the American people. I thought of Colonel Maglin, and his belief that "if the policeman did a good job for the Japanese, he will do a good job for us." I thought of my interpreter, Muk, hounded out of Seoul because he helped me to get at the facts; of Major Atkinson, who delayed action while men rotted in a dank police cell; of the officers who felt that Korea needed no reform; and of other officers who engaged in the practice of shadowing American correspondents.

Did an American reporter suppress this dark story because it would reflect on his country? Or would he serve his people better if he reported the blunders and the misdeeds? Was there a way of telling this shocking story without being attacked as a dreamer, or much worse?

The reporting was made doubly difficult because this was not a time of normalcy, and normal standards seemingly did not apply. Ordinarily, the foul mess in our zone would have been cleaned up as soon as the people back home learned the truth. But now the basis of our policy in Korea—or anywhere else—was fear of Russia, and many things that should not have happened were committed in the name of that fear.

Here was Hodge, an American general entrusted with the task of preparing Korea for statehood. His language should have been the language of reform. He had a busy Public Relations Office equipped to pass his decisions and his wisdom on to Korea and the world. Yet, day after dreary day, we had marched into the Public Relations Office to receive the announcement of yet another "intercepted Communist document," purporting to show the Communists did not like us, and Russia was prepared to sabotage the reforms we sponsored. But neither the Korean nor Russian Communists could wreck any bold and genuine reforms—if we had them. The real story of Korea was not the Communist dislike for us. The story was that we had had an opportunity to bring freedom and democracy to a people, and we had muffled our chance—partly because our policy was based on fear, and partly because we were represented here by the wrong people.

Korea is a problem for a diplomat and a reformer. We have handed its solution to a soldier, untrained in the devices of diplomacy and distrustful of social reform. What Hodge sees in Korea is primarily a military problem—the problem of a sudden and overwhelming Russian attack on our small and mal-equipped army. For the problem of Korea Hodge sees only a military man's solutions. A basic element in these is discipline. To Hodge and to his men, the peasant riots are not an outward expression of a deep-seated malady for which remedies have to be found. The riots are an act of extreme indiscipline, and only severe punishment can set things right again.

Both Russia and we made gestures at settling the Korean problem jointly. It is difficult to assess true merits in the feverish atmosphere of Seoul, but it would seem that neither side tried very hard. To the Russians this is a problem in security. Their Maritime Province adjoins Korea, and they are determined to have a friendly neighbor.

Thus, the Russians have been obdurate in insisting that the Joint Commission consult only supporters of Allied trusteeship for Korea, though a Korean could be a true liberal and yet oppose continued alien supervision. General Chistiakov, the Soviet counterpart of General Hodge, was described to me by a Russian in Tokyo as "a typical military man, no different from any of yours." I heard Dr. Bunce tell a Red Cross forum that he got along well with his Russian opposite number in a discussion of common economic problems—until the Russian suddenly reversed his stand, presumably on orders from Moscow. But in condemning the Russians, it is useful to think of our own attitude were we to learn that an unfriendly foreign power was establishing itself in Mexico or Canada.

There is also no evidence that we have been any more anxious than the Russians to reach an agreement. As our chief delegate we chose Major General Albert E. Brown, who is known to feel that war with Russia is not far away. His conduct has been colored by this belief. My visitor told me that Brown said, when it was suggested that a certain measure be discussed with the Koreans: "There's no need for discussing things with these fellows. Just tell them what we want done."

And if the Russians were mulish in refusing to consult Koreans opposed to trusteeship, we were equally mulish in insisting on consulting *all* the Korean groups. For, with the jails in our zone filled to the rafters, the word *all* can mean only the wide assortment of groups controlled by Syngman Rhee. Our union with this old man has led us to fight his cause in the Joint U.S.–Soviet Commission.

We discussed these facts of our relations with Russia, my nocturnal visitor and I, and we agreed that our policy was doubly wrong if we accepted the premise of an imminent war. For if one of the arts of war is the making of friends, we have followed a course which has won for us only a small band of allies and alienated the vast bulk of the Korean people. The Military Government's polls of public opinion are an inaccurate instrument. But they have the virtue of consistency, for they show the graph of the Korean dislike for us rising steadily. If war comes, our generals will be in an untenable position, for apart from the enemy rolling down from the north, they will have to reckon with native hostility in the rear. A program of reform alone could have made friends for us. To this day such a program is not even in blueprint form.

If we accept the generals' idea of a great ideological conflict with Russia, we have to confront the dynamic ideas of communism with our own vital concepts. But the tragic fact is that there are no ideas in our armory here. For vital ideas we have substituted an alliance with Korean groups, whose philosophy and methods have nothing in common with the philosophy and methods that we publicly espouse. And when this paucity of ideas was exposed by Korean popular unrest, we tried to conceal the bankruptcy of a policy with democratic clichés and talk of the red menace.

The men in command here neither have a constructive program of action nor are they willing to accept one. I am told that when Dr. Bunce and his State Department mission arrived in Korea last January, they were whisked from the airport directly to General Lerch's office, where approximately the following exchange took place:

Lerch: "You're not welcome here. We don't need any advice."

Bunce: "General, we don't accept your ultimatum."

Lerch (retreating): "What I mean is that you'll be part of our organization, and we'll call on you when needed."

Bunce: "General, I repeat, we don't accept your ultimatum. My staff and I will consider it, and will let you know our decision tomorrow."

Bunce and his mission stayed, and made a brave try at concealing their frustration. In discussing land reform with Charlotte, Hailey, and me, Bunce said he had drafted a reform plan providing for the redistribution of land formerly held by the Japanese. Bunce felt that although his plan was limited in scope (since it covered only Japanese holdings), it was superior in many provisions to the land reform law enforced in the Russian zone.

What Bunce did not tell us was that Military Government, from General Lerch down to the Korean interpreters, was opposed to any land reform. Thus a neat device was employed to kill what was called "Bunce's Folly." A public opinion poll was conducted by the Military Government, and it allegedly showed that *the sharecroppers did not want land now, but were anxious to wait for a future Korean Government to give it to them*. On the basis of this poll, the Bunce Plan was discarded. This was probably the end of the only major reform drafted by an American in the past fourteen months.

November 7, 1946 SEOUL

Charlotte and I received our Travel Orders and seat reservations for Tokyo for tomorrow. Williamson is sulking.

In the morning, guided by the Contact Man, we went calling on Kim Ku, one of the world's distinguished political assassins and a major figure in the Korean rightist camp. We were halted at the gate, examined by a crew of armed policemen and young men with pistols, and then escorted suspiciously to the pseudo-Grecian mansion in the back of an elaborate rock garden. Something had gone amiss, Kim Ku was away at a meeting, and a messenger was dispatched to fetch him.

We sat in the large, ornate, and cold reception room, and talked to a succession of slick young men and women, many of them speaking fluent English, and some of them known to me as among the sharpest political intriguers in Korea. These were a few of the small and politically ambitious band which thinks for Kim Ku and makes him utter the words it wants.

I recalled the story of a press conference at which Kim Ku, the irreconcilable enemy of Japan and of Korean collaborators, was asked what he would do with the latter. With characteristic bluntness, Kim Ku said:

"Practically everyone in Korea is a collaborator. They all ought to be in jail."

A young adviser doubling in brass as an interpreter did not even blink. "Mr. Kim Ku says," he translated, "that it's a problem to be studied carefully."

Now I am told Kim Ku has begun to make compromises, and this mansion, put at his disposal by the "mining king" of Korea,[74] is presumably one of them. But Kim Ku and Syngman Rhee differ in one major respect. While Rhee speaks for the collaborationists and landlords—for the "haves" of the extreme right—Kim Ku speaks for the rightist "have-nots" who refused to play along with the Japanese, spent decades in exile, and came back only to discover that the collaborators were still in control. There is little love lost between the two camps, though from time to time they work in alliance. Syngman Rhee's men hint that Kim Ku is a Chinese stooge. Kim Ku's men delight in listing the records of the collaborators working with Rhee.

A car rolled to a stop in front of the building, and the slick young men rushed out. They returned escorting a large, darkhaired man in a silk robe. Kim Ku gave us a surprisingly weak handshake, and settled down on a divan. He looked much younger than his seventy-two years, but his hands trembled. His palms were baby pink.

He brushed off our questions on political issues, saying that he would answer them if we gave him time to think. He was ready to talk of his life, beginning with his childhood in a family "of the poorest peasant stock, so poor that I had no schooling until I was eleven." Kim Ku began his revolutionary work at the age of eighteen, in a peasant revolt against the noblemen, and in 1896 switched to fighting the Japanese. By 1919 he had served three jail terms for three historic murders. ("In the last of them I wasn't even involved.")

---

[74] Referencing Ch'oe Ch'ang-hak (1891–1959), the Korean "gold mining king" and ambitious pro-Japanese entrepreneur who developed a mining company that he later sold to Mitsui Industries. Ch'oe had continued to invest in Japanese enterprises up through August 1945.

In 1919 he fled to Shanghai, and was made "Chief of Counter Intelligence" of the Provisional Korean Government. Terrorism became his profession. The climax came in 1932, when he organized the bombing of a group of Japanese dignitaries in Shanghai. Admiral Nomura [1877–1964],[75] who was Japanese ambassador to Washington on the eve of the attack on Pearl Harbor, lost an eye. Shigemitsu [1887–1957],[76] who signed Japan's surrender on the U.S.S. "Missouri," lost a leg. This bombing, as Bertsch put it, "thrust Kim Ku into the political big league." By 1941 he was president of the government-in-exile.

At this point we heard the unmistakable sound of a marching military unit. I looked out. A score of young men in civilian clothes, with white armbands, was marching past the house with military precision. I asked Kim Ku who the young men were, and he said, "A youth organization," and when I pressed, he said he knew nothing about it.

Later Kim Ku walked us out, and we saw the young men posted behind trees and rocks. Some men were watching us; others were scanning the fence. We said goodbye to Kim Ku, and walked over to the nearest youth. I had an interpreter translate the armband. It said simply: "Youth Organization." This, obviously, was Kim Ku's private army, like Syngman Rhee's Great Korea Democratic Young Men's Association.

We drove out, the gates slammed behind us, and the Contact Man said, "Mr. Kim Ku is a real gentleman, isn't he?"

In the afternoon, the Contact Man took us to another "gentleman"—General Yi Pŏm-sŏk [1900–1972], head of Korean National Youth Corps,[77] and a rising star in the rightist constellation. We kept

---

[75] The 1932 Hongkou Park bombing in Shanghai was executed by Yun Pong-gil (1908–1932). Nomura Kichisaburō was then vice admiral of the Navy and commander of the troops to fight the Chinese in Shanghai. Later he became Japan's Ambassador to the United States—and in December 1941 he thus became the man to deliver Japan's declaration of war to the White House seven and a half hours after the attack on Pearl Harbor had begun.

[76] Shigemitsu Mamoru was a career diplomat and later, at the end of the Pacific War, became the Japanese minister of foreign affairs.

[77] The name Korean National Youth, Inc., as Gayn rendered it, has been changed to Korean National Youth Corps here for consistency. See also Robinson's description of Yi Pŏm-sŏk and his youth organization in this volume, 260–61.

hearing his name all over the U.S. zone, and some Americans insisted that we see General Yi before we leave Korea.

We found him in the large, two-story headquarters of Korean National Youth Corps—a building assigned to it by the Military Government. There were U.S. Army trucks and jeeps in the yard, a few American soldiers upstairs, typing, and a flock of the tough young Koreans which had now become a familiar sight to me. General Yi was waiting for us in his small office.

Yi was slim and muscular, and his thin, hooked nose and a thin moustache gave him a strangely predatory look. Had he lived in California, he would have inevitably ended as an Oriental pirate in a Hollywood technicolor production. His career, as he unfolded it for us with much fist-waving, matched his looks. Born in a noble family, he left Korea for China at the age of fifteen. He entered a military academy under an assumed name, and on graduation went to Manchuria for some extracurricular anti-Japanese terrorism. After that his career was spectacular. He said he served as commander of a Soviet Russian International Cavalry Brigade; a colonel on the staff of a famous Chinese general fighting the Japanese in Manchuria; an inmate for eight months in a Siberian camp for Chinese troops who escaped from Manchuria; head of a Korean military academy set up by Chiang Kai-shek: a military adviser to a Chinese warlord, and the principal negotiator with the Japanese, who thought all along he was a Chinese; an associate of Dai Li [1897–1946], the dreaded chief of China's Secret Service; and, for a year, an agent of our own O.S.S.[78] He was flown into Korea four days after Japan's surrender with an O.S.S. team of twelve Americans and five Koreans.[79]

---

[78] O.S.S. is the Office of Strategic Services, the precursor of the CIA. From April 1945 it organized the China-based Eagle Project that trained Koreans in "unconventional operations" such as sabotage and espionage, to be carried out in Japan-occupied Korea. Yi was the leading member of the Koreans within that group. The Japanese surrendered before the Koreans could carry out their missions.

[79] The number of passengers that boarded the C-47 to embark on this mission varies from report to report. It was led by Willis H. Bird (1909–1983), Deputy Chief of the O.S.S. in China and Commander of Operation Eagle, who flew into Yŏŭido Airfield in Seoul on August 18, 1945, three days after the surrender, to check up on the POWs being kept in the area. The Japanese refused to allow him to complete this part of the mission.

"Korea today," he said, "is like Germany in 1919. There are ideological clashes, national discord, economic distress. National salvation lies in a united youth. It's our purpose to open schools for leaders. We shall teach them obedience to orders, ability to be practical, good morals—much like General Chiang Kai-shek's New Life Movement.[80]

"Fortunately, General Hodge and General Lerch understand the importance of the program, and they've assigned Lieutenant Colonel Ernest Voss [1895–1969],[81] of the Internal Security Department, to help us. General Lerch has given us 5,000,000 yen ($333,000) for the first six months of our work.

"We expect to open our School for Leaders this month, and graduate two hundred youths every thirty days. The trainees will then go into the country and set up branches of the Korean National Youth Corps. The applicants will have to be highly recommended by well-known patriots of good quality. To fulfill their duty, they'll also have to be absolutely healthy. Our purpose is to unify and purify the young men so that they can become leaders."

He talked on, and gradually I began to think that I was listening to a description not of a Korean democratic organization but one of Hitler's infamous "Leadership Schools."[82] The words were the same—the nation, destiny, discipline, endurance; the strange choice of teachers and subjects; the avowed kinship with other rightist strong-arm bands. And then the inspiration became clear.

Yi was telling us of the proposed curriculum: history, ethics (taught by himself), politics. "Also," he said, "methods of combating strikes. And history of *Hitler Jugend*." One of Yi's right-hand men, it appeared, had been an enthusiastic member of *Hitler Jugend* in Germany for three years.[83]

---

[80] Chiang's New Life Movement (Xin Shenghuo Yundong), launched in February 1934, popularized neo-Confucian teachings alongside Christian morals and fused them with fascist-inflected ideals of discipline and social hygiene, including eugenic ideas that were especially prominent in Nazi Germany and Hitler Youth pedagogy.

[81] Ernest E. Voss, National Councilman of the Boy Scouts of America and former head of the Philippine Boy Scouts.

[82] A reference to the SA's paramilitary NAPOLA boarding schools, where a few Korean and Korean American youths were trained as well—although Gayn could not have known this.

[83] Gayn refers to Kang Se-hyŏng (aka Sche-Hyong Kang, Sze Hyong Kang, 1899–1960); see "Betrayal of a Nation," 260–61, and Hoffmann's essay on fascism.

We were distracted by the appearance of an American officer in an adjoining office. He was talking on the phone. He wanted trucks. He had another printing order. He thought it was about time to have that building ready. ...

"That's Colonel Voss," said General Yi. "A very good man."

Colonel Voss opened the door and stepped in. We said hello. "You don't have to talk to me," said Voss. "My ideals and thoughts are the same as General Yi's. He's a great man."

Yi stuffed two pamphlets in our hands. "You must read these," he said. "They'll tell you of my work and hopes." I picked a sentence out of one of them. It was: "A strong leader who will put behind him all personal ambitions and work for the good of Korea is the need of the hour." The companion brochure met squarely the problem of finding such a leader:

"For the past thirty years, Yi Pŏm-sŏk has sacrificed all his time, energy, and all else in his life to his country. Despite physical pain, he has never been agitated, nor has he ever lost his iron will and ideas. He is awaiting the orders of his thirty million compatriots. If the nation desires him as a soldier ... "

The interview supplied a fitting climax to a fantastic visit. This topped it all—a Korean "School for Leaders," teaching the history of *Hitler Jugend*, operating on a subsidy from the American Military Government, and assisted by a colonel of the U.S. Army.

In the evening, we made discreet inquiries. "Oh, you finally found the 'Korean balilla,'" said one officer. "We've been wondering how long it'd take you. And have you met Voss? He calls his little hooligans 'boy scouts.'"

Another officer told us about the help General Yi has been receiving from the U.S. Army. The Army Engineers are building barracks for Korean National Youth in Pusan and Seoul. They are supplying American bulldozers for unspecified uses by General Yi. At the American taxpayers' expense they are doing a vast amount of printing for Yi, much of it political.

"The Korean National Youth Corps," he said, "is probably the most profitable enterprise in Korea. There are all kinds of donations from people who are afraid they'd be denounced as Jap collaborators if they didn't pay off. No one is quite sure who is behind Yi. He may be a political buccaneer, striking out on his own. But there is much talk of close contacts between him and Syngman Rhee. Yi is known to be planning to take over the National Assembly Independence Urge Youth Association, which includes eighteen of Rhee's youth bands. For the time being, Yi is trying to work quietly. But mark my words: he's going to be a big-time operator in another year—with our help.

"It's simple to dismiss his, or Rhee's, bands, as neighborhood gangs. This thing has gotten to be too big to be dismissed lightly. These boys have become the Storm Troopers of Korea. The Military Government has permitted the development of an integrated, large-scale movement much like Hitler's. And probably for the same purpose."

Tonight we also heard the story of Private Peevey[84] and his waterless paddy.

It seems that when the 38th Parallel was accepted as the dividing line between the United States and Soviet zones, it cut off a 70,000-acre Japanese farm from its reservoirs. We received the paddies; the Russians got the water. Private Peevey, who was placed in charge of the farm, soon discovered that rice needed water, and what there was of it was in the Soviet zone.

Thus it was that the relevant department of the Military Government here became increasingly aware of Private Peevey and his problem. There were few days when a plea for help was not received from Peevey. What he wanted was some sort of an understanding with the Russians so that he could have water for his fields. As days passed, and his rice stalks wilted, the messages became more urgent.

But a paddy, however large, could only be a small part of the broad problem of U.S.–Soviet relations. As long as the broad problem remained unsolved, Peevey could not have his water. So from time to time Seoul wired back comforting messages to Peevey, telling him that no local understanding was possible at the time, urging him to get along as best he could, and advising him, for Lord's sake, to keep his shirt on.

One day Peevey's messages stopped coming. Immersed in its own problems, the Military Government wondered mildly about Peevey for a week or so, and then proceeded to forget all about him and his paddies.

---

[84] Robinson spells Gayn's Private Peevey as Private Peavy (see Robinson, 147).

Not so long ago Peevey was ordered home after his appointed term of duty, and on his way to the embarkation point he stopped in Seoul, and called on the Military Government. "Peevey?" they said, "Peevey? Oh, wait a second, aren't you the chap that was up there at Ongjin, near the 38th?"

"Yes, sir," said Peevey, "that was me."

"Well, well," they said, "didn't you have some trouble with water or something? Whatever became of that?"

"Well, sir," said Private Peevey, "I had no water, and I just had to have some. It was an awful lot of rice going to waste, and the Russkys had all the water. So I made a treaty with them. I — "

"What?" said the colonel in command. "A treaty with the Russians? You're kidding?"

"No, sir, I'm not kidding. I told the Russians that if they gave me water I would give them 10,000 bags of rice at harvest time. So they gave me all the water I needed. ... "

"Christ, man," the colonel said. "That's impossible. You know what you've done? You're going to be court-martialed for this. *I* am going to be court-martialed. You had no right to enter into any negotiations with the Russians. You've exceeded your authority. Gaddamn it, you had no authority of *any* sort. Private Peevey!"

"Don't you worry none, sir," said Peevey. "I did sign a treaty with the Russians, and I did get the water. But I never meant to give them any rice."

One week after Private Peevey left Ongjin without having delivered the promised rice, a force of North Korean constabulary crossed the 38th Parallel with trucks and drove up to the rice storehouses at the farm. While trying to open the gates, they were challenged by some South Korean policemen and local officials. In the ensuing battle, four of the South Koreans were killed. The North Koreans piled their trucks high with rice and drove back across the line.

November 8, 1946 EN ROUTE TO TOKYO

We left Seoul for the airport at six in the morning. By the time we checked in our Travel Orders, the sun had come out, and it was crisply cold. A Red Cross truck was dispensing coffee and doughnuts, and there was a long line of waiting men, stamping their feet and slapping their bodies to keep warm. We drank coffee, and watched two small transport planes filling in with Korean policemen, with Japanese carbines and fur-lined coats. One plane took off, and the other taxied in in its place. I walked up and asked a crew member where the planes were going.

He said, "About 150 miles to the west. I hear some gooks have barricaded themselves in a farmhouse, and these boys are going to take it. We'll keep taxiing them all through the day."[85]

Hours passed. Something had happened to our plane, and more unscheduled, but high-priority, passengers kept arriving. We had more coffee, read old magazines, and talked to the other waiting men. One of them was a Military Government officer going home after nearly four years of service. "If we don't take off today," he said, "I'll go back to my room, and blow my brains out. I've come to feel I couldn't stand another day here."

We did take off around noon, in a four-engined transport. "Jesus," said the officer, "I thought the day would never come." His face kept breaking into a smile, and he knew it looked silly and tried to frown it off his face. After a while we started talking about Korea, and he calmed down. He has spent a year here and traveled widely.

"The solution of our differences with Russia is one of the dominant needs in Korea," he said. "If there's no solution, both the Russians and we will continue to keep our troops here and foster rival regimes. I seriously wonder if it isn't too late already. In the past few weeks I've talked to many Korean leaders, who for a year have been shouting their

---

[85] "150 miles to the west" would have brought them into the Yellow Sea. With the 38th parallel immediately to the north and the peninsula from coast to coast only being 120 miles wide, we are left with a destination in the south or southeast. These planes full of Korean policemen carrying their colonial period Japanese carbines were likely flown to some location in South Chŏlla Province, possibly Hwasun-gun. The Hwasun Coal Mine Strike had begun towards the end of October. During the early part of November U.S. Army CIC and Korean police made many arrests, resulting in a bloody conflict. It could also have been a number of other places, of course, given that over two million Koreans participated in the uprisings during the fall of 1946 all through southern Korea, often attacking police stations, local government offices, rice collection agencies, or big landlords. Local authorities in the provinces would then regularly be reinforced by Seoul-based police forces and CIC agents.

heads off, demanding our withdrawal. Now they're subdued. There're two new words in their vocabulary: Civil War. Now they want us and the Russians to stay on a while longer, for they think that our department will throw Korea into chaos and bloodshed.

"But it solves nothing for us to stay here any longer, for both in the north and the south the middle groups have been eliminated, and only the extremes remain. It's idle to hope that they won't jump at each other's throat at the first chance, next year or five years from now. Neither the men nor their ideas are compatible."

I myself had heard the words Civil War on more than one tongue, and I knew that the fear was real and growing. Probably without expecting or wanting it, Russia and we have hurt Korea far more than Japan did. For while the Japanese bled Korea, and made her an unhealthy adjunct to Japan's economy, they kept her as a unit. When Japan fell, Korea was a whole, ready to become an independent state. Then the two liberating powers moved in, split the country asunder, the industrial north from the agricultural south, snapped the railroads at the 38th Parallel, did their best to seal off the border, and then proceeded to foster political systems to their liking.

Now, fourteen months after liberation, the 38th has become a real frontier between two worlds. The moderate groups which shared authority in the Soviet zone in the first four or six months have been swallowed by the Communists. In our zone, the moderates have been wiped out or reduced to impotence, and the extremists like Rhee are in virtual control.

On both sides of the new frontier, feverish preparations are being made for the coming armed conflict. The Communists in the north are said to be training a militia of 150,000 men. On our side, there is a steadily expanding police force, a constabulary and a coast guard whose numbers are difficult to learn, and the tens of thousands of young men enrolled in the private armies of Syngman Rhee, Kim Ku, General Yi Pŏm-sŏk, all the way down to the local strong-arm bands organized by U.S. Army interpreters.

As important as the political dislocation is the economic crisis. Korea survived under the Japanese because it was an integral part of the Japanese economy, in which Manchuria was also a part. Now the whole elaborate system has fallen apart, and Korea herself has been split in two. The Soviet north hungers for the rice produced in our zone. What few industries we have in the south depend on the north for such items as coal. This means that as long as the 38th Parallel remains a frontier, South Korea must continue to be a drain on the American taxpayer.

These two problems, one political, the other economic, would tax the resources of a much abler man than Hodge. So would the uncertain policy directives from Washington, the desperate lack of trained American and Korean personnel, the arrival of Korean refugees from China, Manchuria, and Japan by the hundreds of thousands, the ingrained hostility of the Koreans to alien soldiery, and the sharecropper's reluctance to give up the rice to feed the cities.

But the crux of our failure, it is obvious, lies not in the complexity of the problems facing us, but in our failure to act constructively. It is probably true that our differences with Russia cannot be settled in Korea alone, but only as part of a world-wide settlement. But in our own zone there are urgent problems which should have been met, and have instead been ignored. Had constructive action been taken, our position in Korea would have been firmer, and it would not have been necessary to fly Japanese-trained policemen in American-piloted planes to suppress yet another Korean farmer uprising.

We were flying high now, and below us, through a hole in the clouds, we could see the coastline of Korea, a rugged brown mass of land holding back a gray sea. "Goodbye, Korea," said my neighbor, "and am I happy to be leaving!" I, too, was glad. It has been the blackest, the most depressing story I have ever covered. As an American I was ashamed of the facts that I kept digging up, of the ineptness of the men who spoke for my country, of the concerted effort to prevent the American people from learning what was happening in Korea.

But I was proud of the fact that, despite all the restrictions and precautions, in every town and village I visited there had always been Americans who had faith in the power of the press and its role in a democracy, and who tempted punishment by giving us information. Among the things I learned in Korea was the fact that censorship—especially when it is aimed at concealing official blunders—will not work well or long with Americans. And I was as happy with this discovery as I was with the fact that I was able to get some of the story of Korea.

Democracy, Authoritarianism, and Culpability in Southern Korea: Gayn and Robinson on the U.S. Military Government

Mark E. Caprio

The dreadful shortcomings of United States military occupations in Iraq and Afghanistan over the last two decades bear uncanny resemblance to the more distant occupation of southern Korea after Japan's defeat in the Pacific War. The occupation that was imposed on Korea was ill prepared to deliver the independence that Koreans had been promised earlier. Mark Gayn (1909–1981) and Richard D. Robinson (1921–2009) were astute observers of the policy failures of that occupation. Although they went to southern Korea under very different auspices, both arrived at the same assessment independently: U.S. policies in Korea were not advancing the development of a democratic sovereign nation—at least not in a way that served the interests of the Korean people.

The history of U.S. administration over southern Korea remains almost completely unknown to Americans, among whom little is known about Korea before the U.S. entered the Korean War (1950–1953). Most Americans blithely accept their government's reason for going to war: halting the so-called "domino effect" or the spread of Soviet communism across Asia and Eastern Europe. It was feared that if southern Korea fell to such forces, it would trigger communist revolutions across Asia. As recent scholarship has shown, U.S. failures during the occupation and war that followed helped sow the seeds of popular unrest that eventually evolved into the civil war that erupted between north and south. The "peace" that followed was only delicately protected by an unstable armistice signed in July 1953 by the U.S.,

China, and the Democratic People's Republic of Korea (DPRK)—excluding the Republic of Korea (ROK).[1]

The postwar trusteeship or "guidance" that Koreans would be forced to endure before they could claim true independence left deep divides within Korea. It was President Franklin D. Roosevelt (in office 1933–1945) who promoted the idea of trusteeship before and during the November 1943 Cairo Conference with British Prime Minister Winston Churchill (in office 1940–1945, 1951–1955) and Nationalist Chinese leader Chiang Kai-shek (Jiang Jieshi, in office 1928–1975). At the end of the meeting, they jointly entered into the Conference Communiqué a plan for a post-liberation occupation of Korea before it would gain independence. Although this document dealt exclusively with Asia's postwar fate, unfortunately, during the conference no real consideration was given to Korea's post-liberation plight—except a brief part of a dinner discussion between Roosevelt and Chiang on November 23. The three leaders and their staffs focused instead on military strategy in South Asia and Europe. Yet, on the final day of the conference, as they rushed to complete the document in time for Roosevelt and Churchill's scheduled departure for Teheran to meet with Joseph Stalin (in office 1922–1953), the British inserted a short imprecise phrase, "in due course," to qualify the timeframe in the promise for independence to Koreans. British intentions behind this insertion had more to do with protecting their colonial interests, in the face of burgeoning independence movements, than with Korea's future.[2]

---

[1] Most prominent among these scholars is Bruce Cumings who made this argument in his two-volume *Origins of the Korean War* (Princeton: Princeton University Press, 1981 and 1990). See also John Merrill, *Korea: The Peninsular Origins of the War* (Newark: University of Delaware Press, 1989).

[2] The complete sentence read "The aforesaid three great powers, mindful of the enslavement of the people of Korea, are determined that in due course Korea shall become free and independent." Previous versions of this document had offered the words "at the earliest possible moment," which President Roosevelt then changed to "at the proper moment," before the British replaced that with the phrase "in due course." For the two American drafts and the British draft of the Cairo Communiqué, see *Foreign Relations of the United States, Diplomatic Papers: The Conferences at Cairo and Teheran 1943*, comp. United States Department of State (Washington, DC: Government Printing Office, 1961), 399–404 (hereafter cited as *FRUS 1943*).

That phrase took on a life of its own when the Communiqué was released to the public in December, after Stalin had approved it. The duration of the trusteeship and designation of states to participate in it remained unclear at the time. Members of various Korean independence movements scattered throughout China, the U.S. and elsewhere made inquiries regarding this duration; but their concerns went unheeded, most probably because the Allies themselves did not know how long it would last. Postwar planning committees better understood the second issue. Prospective participants might include China, Great Britain (or a Commonwealth nation such as Australia), and possibly the Soviet Union—should it enter the Pacific War—in addition to the U.S.

Except for an occasional report on Korean matters and interviews that the State Department conducted with people familiar with Korea, there was very little tangible planning for Korea's post-liberation administration. The U.S. even had trouble deciding on the members of the occupation team. U.S. Government officers like Richard Robinson were deployed to Korea only at the very last minute, even after many had already boarded a ship bound for Japan, having been trained specifically for that occupation.[3] Robinson notes that when Lieutenant General John R. Hodge (1893–1963), the commanding officer of the forces entering Korea, assumed his duties in Korea in early September 1945, he had little information about Korea and little instruction on how it was to be administered,[4] much less how the U.S. would negotiate the peninsula's reunification with the Soviet administration occupying northern Korea.

---

[3] Donald Stone Macdonald (1919–1993) explained a similar experience in an interview. Macdonald made it to Japan only to learn that he was being transferred to southern Korea where he was stationed in Kwangju. To prepare for his Japan assignment he had taken a six-month Civil Affairs Training course at Harvard University. His efforts to inform himself about Korea were limited to a small part of a single volume that he found in the ship's library, an antiquated pre-World War I travel guide by T. Phillip Terry, *Terry's Japanese Empire, Including Korea and Formosa* (Boston: Houghton Mifflin, 1914). See Donald S. Macdonald, interview by Charles Stuart Kennedy, January 25, 1990, *Interview with Donald S. Macdonald*, Manuscript Division, Library of Congress, Washington, DC, https://www.loc.gov/item/mfdipbib000734 (hereafter cited as Macdonald, *Interview*).

[4] See Richard D. Robinson, "Betrayal of a Nation," in this volume, 70–71.

Franklin Roosevelt pushed trusteeship as a way of preparing formerly occupied peoples for admission into the international community as sovereign states. The president's disdain for colonialism, which he saw as a major cause of both world wars, fueled his crusade to bring it to an end. His support for a peoples' right to self-determination drew from the Fourteen Points speech of January 1918 by Woodrow Wilson (in office 1913–1921), its most famous proponent.

At the time, Wilson's speech spurred colonized peoples in a number of contexts to take to the streets to demand this right, which brought much bloodshed but little advancement toward their independence. The principles he included in this speech would later inform the text of the Atlantic Charter drafted by Roosevelt and Churchill at their initial summit in August 1941; they would in turn influence the Cairo Communiqué and future Allied declarations made at the Yalta and Potsdam conferences. Yet, Roosevelt concurred with Wilson that without a period of trusteeship, liberated peoples might likely revert to practices that were the basis for their being subjected to foreign occupation in the first place. This is how the necessity of trusteeship for Korea was explained by Sumner Welles (1892–1961), who served from 1937 to 1943 as Roosevelt's Undersecretary of State and was a prominent member of the president's brain trust:

> These words "in due course" have created much disquiet among certain Korean patriots. It must be clear, however, that, after a ruthless domination and exploitation such as the Korean people have suffered at the hands of Japan during the past thirty-seven [*sic*] years, a certain period of time must necessarily elapse before the last vestiges of Japanese rule can be wiped out and the independent economy of the country can once more be set up. The Korean people will need sufficient time to strengthen the atrophied muscles of self-government. It is equally clear that some friendly hands must be available to render the assistance required until all the mechanics of self-government can be supplied by the Korean people themselves.[5]

[5] Sumner Welles, *The Time for Decision* (New York and London: Harper & Brothers, 1944), 300.

As Welles indicated, Koreans deeply felt that trusteeship was unnecessary in their case. Even after foreign armies arrived on their shores, many Koreans believed that their presence on the peninsula would be short lived, or last just long enough to facilitate the evacuation of Japanese elements. The Korean people would then be able to determine their own fate as an independent state. This idea was reflected in a plan drafted by the *Voice of Korea*, a newspaper published by Koreans in Washington, D.C., just weeks after the U.S. 24th Corps arrived to assume its occupation duties in southern Korea. The newspaper, citing President Harry S. Truman's (in office 1945–1953) declaration that the building of a great nation had begun, reasoned that the sooner this nation is built the better for the Far East and the world. It continued by outlining the following schedule:

> [A]n unrestricted opportunity should be given to the leaders of the various Korean organizations to compose their differences and form a provisional government. Under proper conditions, it could be done within a month from now. Within 90 days of its formation a general election should be held to choose a permanent government under the supervision of the Allied Command. Within 60 days thereafter, with the exception of those who are hired by the Korean government, all occupation forces should be withdrawn.[6]

The two occupations in northern and southern Korea, however, lingered for three years until the two Korean states were formed on the peninsula in late 1948. Prior to this development, the Allied powers had drafted a plan in Moscow in December 1945 to consolidate northern and southern Korea into a unified government. This was at a meeting among the foreign ministers of the United States, Soviet Union, and Great Britain to discuss unresolved wartime issues. The three officials proposed that the two parties that occupied the Korea peninsula form a Joint Commission to initiate a process toward guiding the Korean people toward independence. An excerpt from the "Moscow Decision" reads as follows:

> The proposals of the Joint Commission shall be submitted, following consultation with the provisional Korean govern-

[6] "America's Responsibility," *Voice of Korea*, September 24, 1945.

> ment for the joint consideration of the Governments of the United States, Union of Soviet Socialist Republics, United Kingdom and China for the working out of an agreement concerning a four-power trusteeship of Korea for a period of up to five years.[7]

This period of trusteeship-assisted provisional administration was to help the Korean people form a permanent government as a sovereign state.

Most Koreans spoke out against the idea of trusteeship as soon as the Moscow Decision was made public. In particular, the southern Korean press overwhelmingly denounced it in their headlines.[8] However, Moscow declared that Korean political entities which objected to trusteeship would be ruled ineligible for consultation with the Joint Commission; this quickly generated support for the process among many of Korea's leftists and moderate rightists.

However, the extreme right continued to resist, and began to rally their constituents against it. Richard Robinson addresses the role of Syngman Rhee and other extreme right-wing Koreans in opposing the

---

[7] For a complete text of the Moscow Decision, see "The Ambassador in the Soviet Union (Harriman) to the Secretary of State" (December 27, 1945), in *Foreign Relations of the United States: Diplomatic Papers 1945*, comp. United States Department of State, vol. VI, *The British Commonwealth, The Far East* (Washington, DC: Government Printing Office, 1969), 1150–51 (this volume is hereafter cited as *FRUS 1945*). Robinson provides a full text of the provisions that concerned Korea in his "Betrayal of a Nation," 87–88.

[8] These are examples of the headlines that appeared in southern Korean newspapers following the release of the Moscow Decision on Korea: "Chŏn ilbon wiim t'ongch'ijie kukche sint'ak t'ongch'i" [From the Japanese Mandate to an international trusteeship], and "Sint'ak t'ongch'i sŭnginŭn maegugida! Maejogida!" [The recognition of trusteeship is a betrayal of the nation! Betraying one's own people!], *Chungang sinmun*, December 29, 1945; "Kwanggo, moyokchŏk sint'ak t'ongch'ie hyŏlchŏn haja!" [Public notice: Engage in a bloody battle against the scornful trusteeship], *Taegu sinbo*, December 31, 1945; and "Sint'ak t'ongch'inŭn chugŭmŭi kil!" [Trusteeship is the road to death], *Minju chungbo*, January 1, 1946. For a discussion of Korean reactions to the Moscow Decision see Sŏ Chung-sŏk, "Kungnae tongnip undong seryŏgŭi haebang hu kukka kŏnsŏl pangyang—Yŏ Un-hyŏngŭi Inmin Konghwaguk Inmindang sint'ak t'ongch'i kwallyŏn munjerŭl chungsimŭro" [The Influence of the domestic independence movement and trends in national reconstruction after liberation: With focus on Yŏ Un-hyŏng's People's Republic, the Korean People's Party and trusteeship issues], *Taedong munhwa yŏn'gu* 56 (2006): 289–321.

(Fig. 28)
Seoul Stadium, December 31, 1945. Citizens rally against the four-power trusteeship agreed to at the Moscow Conference of Foreign Ministers.

Moscow Decision.[9] Comments by General Hodge also did not help matters. In an attempt to explain the Moscow Decision to the Korean people, he presented a rather optimistic, but misleading, message in his December 1945 radio broadcast that directly refuted the Soviet view of absolute support.

> Despite the piecemeal so-called "Interpretative" releases written hurriedly by persons who never saw Korea except on a map and who do not know Korea or Koreans, there is

[9] Kim Haeng-sŏn discusses the influence of Syngman Rhee and the anti-trusteeship movement on the Joint Commission process in his article, "Miso Kongdong Wiwŏnhoe chaegaerŭl chŏnhuhan uikchinyŏngŭi tongyanggwa yang-myŏnjŏnsul" [Trends and two-faced tactics of right-wing groups around the time of the resumption of the U.S.–Soviet Joint Commission], *Hansŏng sahak* 14 (2002): 35–66.

> nothing in the communique that says that there has to be a "Trusteeship" established for Korea or that says that one definitely will be established. It does provide that after the establishment of the unity of Korea and after the Korean Government has been established, the two-power commission will consult with the Korean Government about and make recommendation to the four great powers concerning a four-power "Trusteeship" for a period of up to five years. There is nothing in the wording of the statement which leads me to believe that there will be a four-power "Trusteeship" forced upon the Koreans against their will. There is everything in the wording of the statement to make me believe that the plan set forth is designed to give full aid and protection to Korea in reestablishing itself as an independent nation. After careful study of the full statement in all its details I see nothing to the provisions that Koreans need to fear.[10]

To complicate matters further, Hodge's broadcast came at a time when rumors had spread that it was the Soviets, rather than the Americans, who had pushed for trusteeship at the Moscow meeting. The Soviets retorted that they had proposed an up to five-year trusteeship for Korea as a counterplan to an initial U.S. proposal that would have subjected Koreans to up to ten years of trusteeship.[11]

In May 1949, the *Voice of Korea* argued that the three years of divided occupation of the Korean peninsula was unnecessary because steps had already been taken to allow Koreans the chance to form their own transitional government at the time of Japan's surrender. The newspaper criticized the U.S. for disrupting this process by failing to

---

[10] "Text of Radio Broadcast Delivered by General Hodge on Moscow Pact" (December 30, 1945), included in the January 2, 1946 *Periodic Report*; reproduced in *HQ, USAFIK G-2 Periodic Report / Chuban Migun chŏngbo ilchi (1945.9.9–1946.2.12)*, vol. 1, comp. Hallim Taehakkyo, Asia Munhwa Yŏn'guso (Ch'unch'ŏn: Hallim Taehakkyo, Asia Munhwa Yŏn'guso, 1988), 506. Robinson discusses Hodge's speech in his "Betrayal of a Nation," 85–86. Hodge's statements had been preceded by a November 1945 report by his political advisor William R. Langdon (1891–1963) who argued that trusteeship was inappropriate for the Korean situation. For Langdon's report see "The Acting Political Advisor in Korea (Langdon) to the Secretary of State" (November 20, 1945), in *FRUS 1945*, 1130–33.

[11] The Soviet Union explained this and other inconsistencies in "TASS statement on the Korean Question" (January 23, 1946), reprinted in *The Soviet Union and the Korean Question (Documents)* (Moscow: Ministry of Foreign Affairs, 1948), 7–10.

recognize the efforts of Yŏ Un-hyŏng (aka Lyuh Woon Hyung, 1886–1947), whom the Japanese had chosen for this purpose.[12]

> There might have been no need at all for the Americans and Russians to occupy Korea. As a matter of fact, before the occupation forces entered the country, the Japanese in Korea had already surrendered the government to the late Lyuh Woon Hyung [Yŏ Un-hyŏng], a great liberal and the most popular leader throughout the country. Instead of allowing the people who survived the Japanese oppression at home to re-establish Korea as an independent state, the Allied Powers imported horses of different colors from abroad to dominate the political race in the North and the South.[13]

The newspaper continued by expressing a wistful aspiration that further destruction be prevented. As the "damage had already been done" the primary consideration at hand became finding a way to "prevent the Korean people from being thrown into a holocaust."[14]

Un-Democratic Military Administrations in Post-liberated Korea

Throughout the wartime period, the United States repeatedly withheld formal diplomatic recognition from any specific Korean political group living in exile, claiming that doing so would skew the Korean people's postwar determination for political leadership. This decision frustrated intensive efforts by Korean Provisional Government leaders, particularly Kim Ku (1876–1949) in Chongqing, China and Syngman Rhee in Washington, D.C. However, it became clear from the first day of occupation that the preferences of the U.S. and Soviet administrators

[12] It was actually the Japanese colonial administration in Korea that—believing that it would be the Soviet 25th Army that would occupy the peninsula—selected Yŏ to form a transitional government. Yŏ's leftist connections, it reasoned, might be useful in negotiating safe passage for Japanese nationals returning to Japan. But as soon as the Japanese learned that the U.S. would occupy southern Korea, they withdrew their support for Yŏ and the Preparatory Committee for the Establishment of a Korean State (Chosŏn Kŏn'guk Chunbi Wiwŏnhoe) that he had formed.

[13] "A Last Minute Appeal," *Voice of Korea*, May 31, 1949.

[14] Ibid.

would trump the will of the Korean people. U.S. forces entered Seoul on September 9, 1945 and, from early on, favored Koreans who held conservative (rightist) ideas, while the Soviet administration in the north, in juxtaposition, supported Koreans of leftist suasion from the earliest days of its occupation.

To Koreans throughout this period, decisions made by the United States Army Military Government in Korea (USAMGIK) indicated its interest in extending colonial rule under a different name, rather than make a clear break from previous Japanese rule.[15] This became evident at the very outset of the U.S. occupation, just after the Japanese had surrendered. Richard Robinson recounts that Americans who had arrived in Korea as an advance team to prepare for the occupation threw a big party for Japanese colonial officials. Koreans who tried to meet with them to discuss their country's future, on the other hand, were "summarily shown the door with a minimum of courtesy."[16] The arrival of the U.S. occupying force employed the Japanese soldiers for protection from the Koreans, yet they managed to shoot dead a number of the many Allied flag-waving Koreans who had lined the streets to greet their American liberators. Days earlier the Korean people as a whole had been warned of the general attitude that their liberators would assume. Article III of "Proclamation No. 1" that Commander in Chief, General Douglas MacArthur (1880–1964), delivered from Tokyo in September 1945 echoed the Peace Preservation legislation that Japan imposed on Koreans in 1925, a form of which would later appear in the ROK's National Security Act (*Kukka poan pŏp*) passed by the ROK National Assembly in December 1948. MacArthur's proclamation sternly warned: "All persons will obey promptly all my orders and orders issued under my authority. Acts of resistance to the

---

[15] This point is made by Kim Un-t'ae in his *Migunjŏngŭi Han'guk t'ongch'i* [The U.S. Military Government's administration of Korea] (Seoul: Pagyŏngsa, 1992).

[16] Robinson, "Betrayal of a Nation," 77. In a previous incident, Americans and Koreans, as part of an OSS operation named the Eagle Project, arrived in Seoul on August 18 to check on Allied POWs, and joined their Japanese "hosts" in a beer and song session that evening. For details on this incident see Mark E. Caprio, "The Eagle Has Landed: Groping for a Korean Role in the Pacific War," *Journal of American–East Asian Relations* 21, no. 1 (March 2014): 5–33.

occupying forces or any acts which may disturb public peace and safety will be punished severely."[17]

In essence, this statement gave the United States Military Government the same authority as the Japanese colonial government—the power to determine what would be considered "legal" and "authorized," and what would be considered threatening to the peace and security of southern Korea. As an important example of the exercise of U.S. power, financial and material limitations were imposed on the Koreans and Japanese who were returning to their homeland, which especially affected those who boarded "unauthorized" ships with "illegal" cargo (comprised of personal belongings that exceeded the paltry limits established by the U.S. and/or profits from supplying Japanese and Korean black markets).[18] Both Gayn and Robinson show how the USAMGIK made liberal use of this clause to carry out massive arrests of Koreans who challenged U.S. occupational rule, targeting those deemed to be leftists, in particular.

If Article III of MacArthur's proclamation captured the spirit of the continuity of foreign rule, Article II provided a direct and concrete means to ensure this by authorizing the Japanese and their Korean trainees to retain their positions of power for the foreseeable future. This article directed that, until further notification

> all governmental, public and honorary functionaries and employees, as well as all officials and employees, paid or voluntary, of all public utilities and services, including public welfare and public health, and all other persons engaged in essential services, shall continue to perform their usual functions and

[17] "Proclamation No. 1 by General of the Army Douglas MacArthur" (September 7, 1945), in *FRUS 1945*, 1043. John Barry Kotch notes that the "most egregious error" that the United States made during its tenure in Korea was the attitude that this power was absolute over all indigenous entities. See his "U.S. Occupations of Iraq Recalls Failure in Korea," *Japan Times*, June 18, 2003.

[18] For example, returnees were prohibited from bringing any more than a paltry 1,000 yen into either Korea or Japan. For an extensive report on repatriation in postwar Northeast Asia see "Foreign Affairs Section, Headquarters, United States Army Military Government in Korea, Repatriation from 25 September 1945 to 31 December 1945," prepared by William Gane (1946), Box 4, #41, Walter E. Monagan Papers, 1945–1948, Hoover Institution Library & Archives. Monagan (1911–2008) served as USAMGIK's legal advisor from 1945–1948.

> duties, and shall preserve and safeguard all records and property.[19]

Within days, Washington ordered that this directive be amended in response to the "unfavorable publicity" it had received through Korean protest: "For political reasons it is advisable that you should remove from office immediately: Governor-General Abe, Chiefs of all bureaus of the Government-General, provisional governors and provincial police chiefs. You should furthermore proceed as rapidly as possible with the removal of other Japanese and collaborationist Korean administrators."[20] USAMGIK found it difficult to carry out this revised directive to replace Japanese officials, thereby maintaining in office Koreans who had been trained by the Japanese.[21] As Yi Yŏn-sik has recently argued, even after the Japanese had been relieved of their duties, rumors spread among Koreans that the Japanese continued to influence the U.S. Military Administration.[22] Some U.S. officials in Seoul foresaw this development. General Hodge's political advisor, H. Merrill Benninghoff (1904–1995), predicted as much in a report he penned in response to his government's order to correct MacArthur's decree. He noted that the

> removal of Japanese officials is desirable from the public opinion standpoint but difficult to bring about for some time. They can be relieved in name but must be made to continue

---

[19] "Proclamation No. 1," in *FRUS 1945*, 1043.

[20] "Draft Message to General of the Army Douglas MacArthur" appended to "Memorandum by the Acting Chairman of the State-War-Navy Coordinating Committee" (September 10, 1945), in *FRUS 1945*, 1045.

[21] Regarding Korean collaboration, see Mark E. Caprio, "The Politics of Collaboration in Post-liberation Southern Korea," in *In the Ruins of the Japanese Empire: Imperial Violence, State Destruction, and the Reordering of Modern East Asia*, eds. Barak Kushner and Andrew Levidis (Hong Kong: Hong Kong University Press, 2020), 27–49; and Ahran Bae, "A Comprehensive Assessment of Korean Collaboration under Japanese Colonial Rule (1910–1945)" (PhD diss., Rikkyo University, 2018).

[22] Yi Yŏn-sik reports on rumors circulating among Koreans that the U.S. was allowing Japanese to return to Korea and preparing them to assume their dominant role in the region. Yi Yŏn-sik, "Haebang hu Ilbonin songhwan munjerŭl tullŏssan Namhan sahoewa migunjŏngŭi kaldŭng" [Conflict between southern Koreans and USAMGIK over the repatriation of Japanese nationals after liberation], *Hanil minjok munje yŏn'gu* 15 (2008): 5–47.

> [to] work. There are no qualified Koreans for other than the low-ranking positions, either in government or in public utilities and communications. Furthermore, such Koreans as have achieved high rank under the Japanese are considered pro-Japanese and hated almost as much as their masters.[23]

Both Gayn and Robinson document the effect of this directive on Korean society by focusing on the postwar police force. Robinson introduces the cases of two officials, Cho Pyŏng-ok (aka Chough Byung Ok, 1894–1960) and Chang T'aek-sang (1893–1969), who were chosen by USAMGIK to lead southern Korea's post-liberation police force. According to Robinson, both Cho and Chang had prospered under Japanese rule while conducting abusive and corrupt practices, practices that they then refined under the new regime. Robinson argues that by the end of 1946 southern Korea had become a Korean-led "police state."[24] Eradicating leftist influence in southern Korea was a primary task of this police state, a tactic Cho and Chang had honed while working for the Japanese.[25] John R. Hodge supported these efforts. When the commanding officer assumed his duties, he had suspicions that

---

[23] "The Political Adviser in Korea (Benninghoff) to the Secretary of State" (September 15, 1945), in *FRUS 1945*, 1049.

[24] Robinson, "Betrayal of a Nation," 185 and 194. In one memoir, a Japanese official remembers how USAMGIK solicited his advice on Korean matters. See Tsuboi Sachio, with Araki Nobuko, *Aru Chōsen Sōtokufu keisatsu kanryō no kaisō* [Memoirs of a Chōsen Government-General police bureaucrat] (Tokyo: Sōshisha, 2004), 149.

[25] In his interview Donald S. Macdonald explained one way that USAMGIK used to "reorganize" southern Korea's post-liberation police force: "The first step was to interview the Japanese. Following that, the Americans took over what the Japanese had been doing [...]. The next step was to dismiss all the Japanese and to install Korean personnel who had worked in the Japanese-led Korean government. [...] Then we, at least in name, turned the authority over to the Koreans. The Governor of South Cholla province, who was initially named, was a moderate physician who had been associated with the People's Committee. He was soon displaced by a Korean landowner who was famous for his conservative anti-Communist views and who spoke English very well and who was therefore attractive to the anti-Communist Americans. Under him, and a few other top people brought in from outside, continued all these ex-Japanese Government General Korean employees. What was done in effect was to continue the Japanese structure." Macdonald, *Interview*, [5–6].

communists harbored a "diabolical plot to seize power," according to James Matray.[26]

The U.S. position on pro-Japanese Koreans was manifested in a number of ways over the course of the occupation. At the local level, we see this in its reaction to an early warning that Yun Il (aka Yun T'aek-kŭn, 1893–?) of the South Kyŏngsang Province Branch of the People's Republic of Korea sent to the U.S. forces Military Administration, cautioning that USAMGIK was supporting "shameless and sly" traitors to the Korean people. An anonymous memo penned in at the bottom of his appeal read:

> Attempt to eliminate the bourgeois from all positions of responsibility. Even though no proof of being pro-Jap... The Communists wanted all educated men removed from competition with their "peasants and laborers" even though the leaders of the latter turned out to be more pro-Russian than pro-Korean. Our first contact with communist "double talk"![27]

A more direct display occurred in June 1947 when USAMGIK, responding in part to police pressure, squelched legislation passed by the South Korean Interim Government (Namjosŏn Kwado Chŏngbu) to bring colonial-era collaborators to trial. At the time the police threatened to seek retribution against any assembly member who supported the Law of Pro-Japanese, National Traitor and Profiteers that was then being debated in the Assembly. Robinson reports that the police even informed Hodge of the action that they would take should he fail to veto this legislation.[28] In the end, USAMGIK exercised its veto power over this legislation after it passed. Deputy Military Governor, Brigadier General Charles G. Helmick (1892–1991) gave four reasons for the veto: 1) the difficulty of determining guilt by law; 2) the probability that the law would be used for vengeance; 3) the fact that the assembly did not fully represent the "entire Korean

---

[26] James I. Matray, "Hodge Podge: American Occupation Policy in Korea, 1945–1948," *Korean Studies* 19 (1995): 27.

[27] A letter by Yun Il of the *Inmin haebangbo*, addressed to Brigadier General Harris (October 25, 1945), was found in Box 1, Folder 3, Francis E. Gillette Papers, Harvard-Yenching Library Special Collections.

[28] Robinson, "Betrayal of a Nation," 248.

nation;" and 4) the attempt to do too much with the law by lumping together colonial and post-colonial crimes.[29] Gayn and Robinson's writing suggests a potential fifth reason: the damage that such legislation might have caused to the population of Koreans on whom the Military Government most depended, to say nothing of the adverse effect it would have had on southern Korean conservative politics. Anti-traitor legislation was finally passed after the ROK National Assembly was formed in 1948; but even then, the legislation failed to eradicate this colonial-era legacy from ROK society.[30]

USAMGIK also preserved elements of the Japanese colonial legal code. One example was the USAMGIK administration's April 1946 ruling on the legality of simultaneously holding a government position while being in the National Bar Association and practicing law. In handing down its decision, USAMGIK courts, rather than interpret the law in postwar terms, cited a 1936 colonial-era law that made it illegal for practicing lawyers to hold office. The explanation for this ruling was that it is "not believed that an Order of the [Japanese] Governor can be repealed by an order of this Department."[31] The occupation's judicial branch made a similar judgement against "a certain newspaper," based on a "violation" of both the Ordinance of Military Government and the Japanese Criminal Code of "Crimes

[29] "Helmick to South Korean Interim Government" (November 20, 1947), in *Mi Kungmusŏng Han'guk kwan'gye munsŏ / Internal Affairs of Korea, 1940–1949*, vol. 11, comp. Han'guk Charyo Kaebarwŏn (Seoul: Arŭm Ch'ulp'ansa, 1995), 193–94.

[30] The collaborator issue has continued to remain a problem even after the efforts of the No Mu-hyŏn (aka Roh Moo-hyun) administration (in office, 2003–2008) that organized to identify collaborators and punish the families of those who had wrongfully acquired property. The committee that was established for this purpose produced a multi-volume series regarding the history of collaboration and the Koreans who were deemed guilty of having collaborated with their country's colonial subjugators: Ch'inil P'anminjok Haengwi Chinsang Kyumyŏng Wiwŏnhoe, ed., *Ch'inil panminjok haengwi kwan'gye saryojip* [Collection of documentary materials related to pro-Japanese collaboration activities], 16 vols. (Seoul: Ch'inil P'anminjok Haengwi Chinsang Kyumyŏng Wiwŏnhoe, 2007–2009). For a review of these efforts see Jeong-Chul Kim, "On Forgiveness and Reconciliation: Korean 'Collaborators' of Japanese Colonialism," in *Routledge Handbook of Memory and Reconciliation in East Asia*, ed. Mikyoung Kim (London: Routledge: 2016), 159–71.

[31] Department of Justice, *Selected Legal Opinions of the Department of Justice, United States Army Military Government in Korea,* Box 3, Opinion #198, Walter E. Monagan Papers, 1945–1948, Hoover Institution Library & Archives.

concerning peace and good order," which were yet to be repealed. Specifically, it found the newspaper guilty of "publishing false and defamatory statements regarding Military Government" for the "purpose of disturbing public peace."[32]

USAMGIK's reliance on Japanese and International law to justify censorship of the Korean press contradicted the position held by the American Delegation at the Joint Commission meetings that it convened with its Soviet counterparts. Here the two sides were to lay the groundwork for forming a unified Korean provisional government. The Soviet Delegation demanded that Korean democratic parties and social organizations that wished to participate in the Joint Commission process provide undivided support for the Moscow Decision. It targeted the anti-trusteeship groups in the American zone whose protests often turned violent.[33] Members of the American Delegation, ignoring the fact that they practiced censorship within their own zone of occupation, argued that it was within the Korean people's right of freedom of speech to voice opposition without forfeiting their eligibility to participate in the Joint Commission process. Perhaps a more accurate reason for the U.S. refusal to accept the Soviet's demands was that doing so would have decimated the Korean extreme right wing that formed the core of the anti-trusteeship movement.

USAMGIK also obstructed the press' right to free speech. As a reporter for the *Chicago Sun*, Mark Gayn felt direct pressure during his three-week stay in southern Korea, when the U.S. administration attempted to limit his ability to report on the more controversial elements of the occupation. Even before Gayn's arrival, Hodge had voiced his disapproval of press activities in the general's report on the "Conditions in Korea." Just days after the USAMGIK's arrival in Seoul, the commanding officer criticized the press for what he believed was irresponsible behavior:

[32] Department of Justice, *Selected Legal Opinions of the Department of Justice, United States Army Military Government in Korea*, Box 3, Opinion #239, Walter E. Monagan Papers, 1945–1948, Hoover Institution Library & Archives. The article in question had reported that "People came to the City Hall to ask for rice, but got guns and beating instead."

[33] For Robinson's description of right-wing anti-trusteeship plans and activities, see 212 and 262–64.

> The newspaper correspondents covering Korea as a group have behaved badly. They arrived by air after landing, most of them from Japan with no knowledge of the local situation and without orientation took advantage of the American uniform to run rampant over the area, committing acts of personal misbehavior that I have forbidden troops to do. There is reason to believe that by open sympathies with Korean radicals some of them have incited Korean group leaders to greater efforts at agitation for overthrow of everything and to have the Koreans take over all functions immediately. Before they got any glimmer of conditions as they existed, they were highly critical of all policies of the nation, of GHQ and of this headquarters relating to the occupation. This latter condition is now rectifying itself slowly as they begin to see the picture. One group arrived by air one afternoon, filed stories that evening and left the next morning, feeling that they knew all about the Korean occupation.[34]

Mark Gayn, who arrived in Korea just a month later, confronted this hostile attitude throughout his three weeks in the country. Officials attempted to keep him from conversing with more controversial Korean personalities and direct him toward more favorable ones. They inhibited his travel throughout the territory and refused to cooperate with his attempts to interview USAMGIK personnel in order to address its shortcomings. Those Americans who agreed to cooperate had to do so clandestinely, and often off the record. However, at the end of his stay in Korea in early November 1946, Gayn makes an upbeat observation: "Among the things I learned in Korea was the fact that censorship—especially when it is aimed at concealing official blunders—will not work well or long with Americans. And I was as happy with this discovery as I was with the fact that I was able to get some of the story of Korea."[35]

The election procedure USAMGIK introduced to the Korean people in October 1946 to seat Koreans in the Interim Legislative

---

[34] John R. Hodge, "Conditions in Korea" (September 13, 1945), in *Migunjŏnggi chŏngbo charyojip: Haji (John R. Hodge) munsŏjip: 1945.6–1948.8* [Collection of intelligence materials from the U.S. Military Government period: Hodge (John R. Hodge) Document Collection, June 1945–August 1948], vol. 3, comp. Asia Munhwa Yŏn'guso (Ch'unch'ŏn: Hallim Taehakkyo, Asia Munhwa Yŏn'guso, 1995), 7.

[35] Gayn, "Japan Diary: Korea," in this volume, 428.

Assembly (Namjosŏn Kwado Ippŏbŭiwŏn) also lacked democratic process. This body was made up of 90 members—half elected by the Korean people and half appointed by U.S. officials who sought balance across the political spectrum in the Assembly. Gayn and Robinson both noted the trouble USAMGIK had in reading southern Korea's political landscape. They criticized its handling of the election process, particularly its treatment of Korea's moderate and extreme left-wing elements. Hŏ Hŏn (1885–1951) explained this to Gayn as a problem of the USAMGIK committing blunders over its "inability to see that most of the Korean leftists are nationalists and not Communists. Yet, all of them are being oppressed alike."[36] We saw an example of this earlier in Yun Il's failed attempt to get U.S. military officials in South Kyŏngsang Province to support patriotic Koreans instead of those who collaborated with the Japanese. Yun opened his statement by acknowledging that Koreans felt "obliged" to the Americans for their values of "liberty and peace" and their faith in "international virtue," before attempting to suggest ways that it might correct some of the administration's problems—advice that a U.S. official dismissed as "communist 'double talk.'"[37] Americans summarily pigeonholed potentially constructive ideas of left-leaning moderate Koreans, such as Yŏ Un-hyŏng, as Soviet influenced and leftist to the extreme.

This attitude was reflected in the results of the October 1946 elections, lauded as the first free elections ever to be held in Korea. The occasion presented a golden opportunity for the USAMGIK to sell democracy to the Korean people. However, once elections were scheduled and held, all of the leftist candidates were either in prison or in hiding, and unable to participate, which skewed the results. Mark Gayn quotes Carl V. Bergstrom (1905–1962), Home Affairs Advisor to the Provincial Government of South Kyŏngsang Province, saying that this made it the "proper time for the rightists to hold the elections."[38] Robinson quotes from a letter that the Chairman of the Southern Korean Interim Legislative Assembly, Kim Kyu-sik (aka Kimm Kiusic,

---

[36] Ibid., 447.

[37] Marginal note in the translation of Yun Il's article of October 25, 1945 (see p. 443, footnote 27).

[38] Carl V. Bergstrom, quoted in Gayn, "Japan Diary: Korea," 382.

11. Appeals to vote are posted on village "town hall," which also serves as barber shop. With estimated illiteracy of 80%, voters in preceding election (with which these pix deal) usually had village headman write in names of two candidates, & almost invariably he was one of them. In last month's election (May), portraits of candidates & ballots which did not require writin were used.
CREDIT MARK GAYN

(Fig. 29) One of Mark Gayn's heretofore unpublished Korea photos from 1946 with his sharp analytical cutline. (See also Gayn, pp. 400–401.)

1881–1950), sent to Hodge that addressed flaws in the election process. Here Kim advised that due to "police investigations there was no chance for the leftist members in the elections. As a result, no competent patriot was elected. The results of the elections have produced impressions of an undemocratic nature and have caused disappointment to the people."[39] He appealed for the elections to be invalidated and held anew.

Mark Gayn, who had more intimate contacts among local Koreans, was able to report on the electoral process at a more personal level to uncover fundamental problems in it. He found, for example, that many people did not even know that the elections were being held. And many of those who cast ballots, Gayn discovered, were under the influence of conservative village headmen, as revealed in a discussion he had with illiterate farmers.

> Gayn: "How then did you write in the names of your candidates in the election?"
>
> Farmers: "Others wrote the names in for us."
>
> Gayn: "Was the headman one of the men who helped you?"
>
> Farmers: "Yes, he helped everyone."
>
> Gayn: "Was he himself elected?"
>
> They all caught on. They laughed and said, "Yes."[40]

Police law enforcement practices also relied on undemocratic measures, mostly to elicit confessions. Due to the record of police collaboration with the Japanese authorities, often at the people's expense, policemen who were largely trained under Japanese colonial rule, faced considerable difficulty gaining the respect and acceptance of the Korean people even if they acted ethically. Their actions under USAMGIK, as both Gayn and Robinson attest, were often even more brutal. Their treatment of fellow Koreans frequently involved torture to elicit confessions, even false confessions. Gayn gives us this example:

> In a village not far from [Seoul], sixty-two men were arrested on the charge of plotting to attack a police station. Among them was a doctor. The other day, the doctor's relatives finally got to an influential American officer and persuaded him to drive out to the jail and check the reports of brutal treatment. He did. He found the doctor dead of torture.

[39] Robinson, "Betrayal of a Nation," 206–7.
[40] Gayn, "Japan Diary: Korea," 400–401.

> Another man died later, with his face smashed to a pulp. The third had his back broken.[41]

Hodge brushed off this incident when it was reported to him, saying simply that it was the way "police have traditionally operated in the Orient. What can we do?"[42] Gayn took a particular interest in following the actions of Korean thugs that had formed into paramilitary police teams to "assist" the regular police force. He devoted considerable attention to the actions of a right-wing youth organization, which he identifies as the "Great Korea Young Men's Association."[43]

The idea of trusteeship emerged out of a concern that national peoples just released from foreign occupation, like the Koreans, were incapable of forming a democratic government without the guidance of developed nations, and that, without this assistance they would simply repeat incompetent practices that had led to their colonization. This process assumed, however, that the Allied occupiers would be capable of guiding the newly liberated people to sovereignty. Both accounts included here strongly suggest that USAMGIK was not up to this task, pointing to its lack of knowledge of Korea, its failure to practice democratic principles in its governance of southern Korea, as well as its mounting differences with the Soviet occupiers to the north. Richard Robinson warned of this as early as March 1946. In a report he authored in response to a public opinion survey that USAMGIK had recently completed, he noted the survey's results showing that the majority of Koreans favored an increase in government control over their economy in regard to land ownership and large industry. His suggestions for reform required a clear understanding of democracy, which he believed to be

> predicated on four concepts; (1) the obedience of the State to the will of the majority, (2) adequate political machinery to make that will effective, (3) the restraint of any force or

---

[41] Unidentified member of an American–Korean commission on police brutality, ibid., 408–9.
[42] Ibid., 409.
[43] Gayn refers to the Great Korea Democratic Young Men's Association (Taehan Minju Ch'ŏngnyŏn Ch'ongdongmaeng). See his October 20, 1946 diary entry, 353–59, and Robinson's observations in his "Betrayal," 183, 190–91.

> violence or threat of such which would make that will ineffective, and (4) the consideration and safeguard of the rights and freedoms of individuals and minority groups; *and further, that democracy prescribes no particular political structure or economic system.*[44]

Among his suggestions were the idea that the United States must refrain from prescribing a particular economic system on the Korean people, but rather to assure them that a system will be established "to the will of the people." This requires USAMGIK striving to "prevent *any* group from exercising control by force and violence, now, or ... in the foreseeable future." He further advised that USAMGIK "stop using such words as 'communism,' 'socialism' and 'democracy' without making certain that those to whom we speak know about *what* we speak; and that we stop using them in a manner which leads people to believe that we consider democracy to be necessarily incompatible with, and comparable to, socialism and communism."[45] He made these suggestions based on the assumption that "Military Government is interested in creating good will for itself so as to make more possible and probable the advancement of democratic ideals in the Korean mind."[46] As time progressed Robinson's understanding that USAMGIK's policy was advancing in a very undemocratic way, so much so as to encourage his drafting of his rather critical manuscript, "Betrayal of a Nation."

A Question of Culpability

As a warning of the potential consequences of a U.S. invasion and occupation of Iraq, almost two decades ago President George W. Bush's (in office 2001–2009) Secretary of State Colin Powell (1937–2021) invoked the Pottery Barn rule—you break it, you own it. "You will own all [the people's] hopes, aspirations and problems. You'll own

---

[44] Richard D. Robinson, "Suggested MG Public Relations Policy" (March 18, 1946), reprinted in *Haebang chŏnhusa charyojip*, 1: *Migunjŏng chunbi charyo* [Collection of historical materials from before and after the liberation, 1: Preparatory materials by the U.S. Military Government], comp. Yi Kil-sang (Seoul: Wŏnju Munhwasa, 1992), 381.

[45] Ibid., 382.

[46] Ibid., 381.

it all."[47] The U.S. lacked this sense of ownership during its occupation of Korea and it has been broken ever since. The texts published herein indicate that the Truman administration, which embarked on a mission that divided the Korean Peninsula and administered the southern half, lacked a sense of responsibility for its actions in Korea at that time.

Although Mark Gayn and Richard Robinson may not have employed Powell's stark rhetoric in their criticisms of the USAMGIK administration of southern Korea, the broken pot metaphor does ring true throughout their accounts. U.S. fingerprints can be found on the earliest events of this history, even before the arrival of occupation forces. In addition to being unprepared for the operation, the U.S. staffed the operation with incompetent people, who in turn employed incompetent people to perform their mission. After having taken the lead in insisting that Korea required a post-liberation occupation from as early as March 1943,[48] the U.S. found itself in a position of being unprepared to assume this responsibility in August 1945. Thus, the arrival of U.S. occupation forces on the peninsula was delayed for weeks, allowing the Japanese to continue the administration of Korea even after their defeat.[49] The continuation of Japanese rule during the first few weeks of the postwar period established the tone of U.S. rule, as seen in its favoritism toward conservative elements in Korean politics.

---

[47] Colin Powell, quoted in Bob Woodward, *Plan of Attack* (New York: Simon & Schuster, 2004), 150.

[48] The earliest mention I could find of President Roosevelt advocating trusteeship for Korea was during Roosevelt's discussion with Foreign Secretary Anthony Eden (1897–1977) during the British official's March 1943 visit to Washington. Herbert Feis, *Churchill, Roosevelt, Stalin: The War They Waged and the Peace They Sought*, 2nd ed. (Princeton: Princeton University Press, 1967), 124.

[49] Soon after the Japanese Emperor announced Japan's surrender in August 1945, Japanese officials in Korea established connections with the U.S. 24th Corps then preparing to depart Okinawa for the occupation of southern Korea. Between September 1 and 3, this U.S. Army Corps and the Japanese communicated seventeen and eighteen messages respectively. See Folder "Repatriation and Transfer of Control to US," RG 554, Box 33, National Archives and Records Administration. See also Bruce Cumings, *The Origins of the Korean War: Liberation and the Emergence of Separate Regimes, 1945–1947* (Princeton: Princeton University Press, 1981), 127–28.

The Soviet Union, as well, found itself ill-prepared for its duties in the north. Robinson is quick to assure his readers that his emphasis on the mistakes that the U.S. made in southern Korea does not excuse the failures of Soviet rule in northern Korea. Both superpower occupiers share responsibility for the predicaments that the Korean people came to face. As he explains:

> There is no doubt that the Soviet administration was harsh and unjust in much that it did. Being no apologist for the Soviet Union, I make that charge at the outset. With the same breath, however, I would hasten to condemn the American administration in South Korea on the same basis and almost as vigorously. Both regimes offended a democrat's sense of justice and humanity, not to mention intelligence.[50]

The USAMGIK rivaled its Soviet counterpart in its unwillingness to take responsibility for its shortcomings. Gayn would no doubt have agreed with Robinson's conclusion that "[m]istakes were rarely admitted to anyone."[51] This is particularly distressing, given that, across the sea in Japan, U.S. efforts are remembered for their contributions to the postwar success of Korea's erstwhile enemy.

Soviet–U.S. relations had deteriorated well before the two states took on the responsibilities of occupying a divided peninsula, and there was little to suggest that relations would improve once each settled into its administration. The 38th parallel, which the U.S. designated as the line of division, soon came to resemble a border where "unauthorized" crossings from either side, even by accident, came to be viewed as infiltrations. A May 1946 United States report criticized Soviet activities at the 38th parallel that included patrolling and establishing roadblocks south of 38°N, and inventorying and coercing civilian contributions of rice. This even extended to an incident involving the Soviets "hauling down a U.S. and Korean flag and tearing them up."[52]

---

[50] Robinson, "Betrayal of a Nation," 272.

[51] Ibid., 67.

[52] United States Army Forces in Korea, *Intelligence Summary Northern Korea (May 6, 1946), in HQ, USAFIK Intelligence Summary Northern Korea (1945.12.1–1947.3.31)*, vol. 1 (Ch'unch'ŏn: Hallim Taehakkyo, Asia Munhwa Yŏn'guso, 1989), 144.

People on the move:

(Fig. 30) Pusan Harbor, October 1945. Before boarding a ship, a Japanese soldier is searched in order to be repatriated to Japan. (Photo: Buker)

(Fig. 31) Kaesŏng refugee camp, May 1947, Koreans from northern Korea migrate southwards. (Photo: Warren T. Warnecke)

USAMGIK also pressured the Soviets on numerous occasions to assume more responsibility in Japanese repatriation efforts. Yet, Japanese trying to repatriate to their homeland from Manchuria and northern Korea were forced to cross the Korean peninsula to find passage back to Japan from the peninsula's southern-most ports.[53]

The two sides negotiated to allow for the exchange of goods, specifically chemical fertilizer from the North and rice from the South;

[53] Mizuno Naoki estimates that the remains of as many as 33,500 Japanese are scattered throughout North Korea. Mizuno Naoki and Mark E. Caprio, "Stories from Beyond the Grave: Investigating Japanese Burial Grounds in North Korea," *Asia-Pacific Journal: Japan Focus* 12, no. 9 (March 2, 2014): 6. Online: https://apjjf.org/2014/12/9/Mizuno-Naoki/4085/article.html.

but to no avail. Robinson casts blame on the U.S. for these failures. Having to import grain to feed starving Koreans south of the 38th parallel due to USAMGIK's inability to come to terms with the Soviets, he calculates, came at a much greater cost than having to pay northern Korea to obtain the fertilizer the South needed to grow rice locally.[54] The formation of the Joint Commission initially brought hope that the U.S. and Soviet Union together could work to resolve the Korean problem and put the North and the South on the road to reunification. This, of course, was not to be. Their failure to reach an agreement, instead, led to the formation of separate Korean governments and, within a few years, brutal confrontation between the two on the battlefield.

Gayn and Robinson also blame the Korean people, as well. They are particularly critical of the extremist elements in southern Korea's political landscape that were obsessed with impeding moderate forces, which offered better possibilities for reconciliation with the North, so they would remain weak and insignificant. While both the extreme left and right share blame, it was the latter that succeeded in grasping the reins of power in the South, largely through the support of the police, the emerging military elements, and eventually USAMGIK. As Robinson explains, the emergence of right-wing power was the product of unwise USAMGIK decisions, which limited its choices.

> [S]o many Korean politicos had been alienated in the early days of the occupation by roughshod American action in support of Kim Ku and [Syngman] Rhee that change was difficult. The extreme right wing was the only political faction friendly to the Americans. All other factions had been snubbed by General Hodge on one occasion or another. The sincerity of the Americans was openly doubted by the middle-of-the-roaders and moderate left-wingers due to the forced breakup of Yŏ Un-hyŏng's Korean People's Republic, the apparent sanction of the many excesses committed by the Korean police, and the appointment of many questionable characters to Military Government administrative posts. The Korean communists, of course, maintained a hostile attitude

[54] For U.S. negotiations with the Soviets to trade rice for fertilizer see Robinson's "Betrayal of a Nation," 126–32 and 150–52.

> toward the Americans from start to finish as matter of principle.[55]

Attempts by moderate groups to the left and right of center, and particularly by Kim Kyu-sik and Yŏ Un-hyŏng, to unite in cooperation never received the support they needed to make significant gains in the post-liberation politics of southern Korea. Extremist politics define much of the three-year occupations of both halves of the peninsula, politics supported by U.S. and Soviet administrations, but also pushed through manipulative efforts of certain Koreans, as well.

Finally, the defeated Japanese colonial occupiers also share responsibility for Korea's failure to successfully emerge as a unified state after its liberation from colonial rule. Many of the divisions that plagued wartime Koreans in exile carried over from the differences in their approaches to combating harsh Japanese rule. These differences prevented post-liberated Korea's smooth development as a state. In addition, Japan's economic policies in the last days of the war laid the foundation for rampant inflation. In a September 1945 report on "Conditions in Korea," Hodge criticized the colonial Bank of Chōsen (Chōsen Ginkō) for printing and distributing several billion yen following Japan's surrender for Japanese preparing to repatriate.[56] This contributed to surging inflation that gripped southern Korea in the immediate aftermath of the war.

A Third Perspective: George M. McCune on the United States Occupation

Mark Gayn and Richard Robinson both offer firsthand observations that are critical of the U.S. administration of southern Korea. As Richard Robinson notes, his work "is a reconstruction of the more complete version" that he felt compelled to destroy prior to his departure from Korea in 1947 "to avoid personal incarceration."[57] Fortunately for us, he was able to redraft it on the freighter that carried him to Turkey. For decades it remained an unpublished manuscript—except

[55] Ibid., 170.
[56] Hodge, "Conditions in Korea" (September 13, 1945), 3.
[57] Robinson, "Betrayal of a Nation," 68.

in Korean translation[58]—with very limited readership. Gayn, who retreated back to Japan after his stay, incorporated his Korea report in his book *Japan Diary*, which he published in 1948.

Another critical observer, the Korean historian, George M. McCune (1908–1948), assessed post-liberation Korean developments under U.S. administration, as well, but from his distant office at UC Berkeley. Today, McCune is best known for creating a useful Romanization system for the Korean language in collaboration with Harvard University Professor of Japanese Studies, Edwin O. Reischauer (1910–1990). The son of Presbyterian missionaries, McCune was born and raised in the city of P'yŏngyang. He remained in Korea until it was time to attend university, when he traveled to the United States. He completed his doctorate—writing his dissertation on "Korean Relations with China and Japan, 1800–1864"—and then joined the history department at Occidental College. After the United States entered the Pacific War, he left academia to serve in government as a Korean affairs expert, first with the Office of Strategic Services (OSS), then with the Board of Economic Warfare, and finally with the State Department. After Japan's defeat, he returned to academia but soon succumbed to ill health at the tender age of forty. His knowledge of Korean language, society, and history placed McCune in an ideal position to observe and comment on the peninsula both during and after the war.

While working in government services McCune assumed a major role in Korea's postwar planning. His drafts of position papers on Korea's future that he and others authored, transcripts of interview reports conducted with people returning from Korea, along with many other interesting items, are housed in the George M. McCune Collection at the University of Hawai'i, Manoa's Center for Korean Studies. In February 1946, after leaving government service, he published a position paper assessing the accomplishments of the U.S. Military Administration to that date. Written just prior to the start of U.S.–Soviet negotiations in the recently formed Joint Commission, McCune

[58] Rich'adŭ D. Robinsŭn, *Migugŭi paeban: Migunjŏnggwa Namjosŏn* [America's betrayal: The U.S. Military Government and southern Korea], trans. Chŏng Mi-ok (Seoul: Kwahakkwa Sasang, 1988).

conveys his doubts about Korea's left and right politics coming together, unless they are "given genuine freedom to solve their own practical political problems." While he saw a "hopeful sign" in the guarantee of Korean independence by the involved parties, he felt that the Joint Commission would have to "make allowances for minority opinions," rather than seek "complete agreement among the Korean leaders," if a sovereign Korean state were to prove successful. He criticized the United States' administration for its tendency to "drift without definite direction," an unfortunate situation in that he saw USAMGIK as a "testing ground of American postwar policies in the Far East." He believed that Commanding Officer Hodge was first a victim of circumstance who may have been "prepared militarily but not politically or economically,"[59] and second, only minimally equipped with the direction and personnel to carry out his important task. Hodge's entourage lacked personnel with experience and knowledge in Korean affairs. McCune predicted that the failure of U.S.–Soviet meetings would come not from the reluctance of the superpowers to negotiate, but from their inability to understand Koreans. His critique of the U.S. perspective follows:

> Korea is still looked upon as a step child in high government circles in Washington. The lack of preparation in the War Department and State Department for the occupation of Korea reflected this attitude. And now, even after five months of occupation, there is as yet no move toward meeting the Korean problem with the emphasis and care which it deserves. The success of the Joint Soviet–American Commission is imperiled unless the Korean situation is more seriously evaluated in Washington.[60]

McCune's final point proved to be prophetic. In the end, the Soviet and American delegations could not agree on which groups to consult with to plan for Korea's future government. The meetings ended in October 1947 with few positive results. There the process died, and Koreans were denied the chance to contribute their views

---

[59] George M. McCune, "Occupation Politics in Korea," *Far Eastern Survey* 15, no. 3 (February 13, 1946): 34.
[60] Ibid., 37.

directly to the Joint Commission. A later article by McCune in *Pacific Affairs*—itself under attack from the right—pinpoints the fundamental cause of Korea's travesty and argues that the hopeless outcome had been predictable from the start:

> [T]he lack of foresight that brought about the division of Korea (a liberated country) into two zones of occupation is hard to dismiss lightly; and the protracted occupation of a divided Korea by the military forces of two foreign powers, neither of which is governing with the consent of the governed, creates an intolerable situation. During the year and more since the occupation began, military rule has continued and the arbitrary division of the country has not been qualified in the least. Even as a temporary measure, foreign military control coupled with such a division would have been a serious blow to the Korean people; as an indefinite arrangement, it is an indefensible abrogation of justice.[61]

The U.S. and Soviets mostly heeded the voice of extreme right-wing groups that aimed to shut down the entire Moscow Decision process, which, of course, they eventually did. While the failure of the Joint Commission preceded the formal initiation of the Korean War by just under three years, relations between the two Koreas, now formed into formal states, continued to spiral into increased violence before escalating into full-scale war in June 1950.

As part of the legacy of the two occupations on the Korean peninsula, roughly 700,000 Koreans did not return to their ethnic homeland after liberation. Even well into the twenty-first century, the specter of "pro-Japanese" collaboration continues to haunt Korean society.[62] The accounts of Mark Gayn and Richard Robinson provide

---

[61] George M. McCune, "Korea: The First Year of Liberation," *Pacific Affairs* 20, no. 1 (March 1947): 4.

[62] For discussion on the difficulties that Koreans faced in returning to the peninsula after liberation, see Mark E. Caprio and Yu Jia, "Legislating Diaspora: The Contribution of Occupation-Era Administrations to the Preservation of Japan's Korean Community," in *Diaspora without Homeland: Being Korean in Japan*, eds. Sonia Ryang and John Lie (Berkeley: University of California Press, 2009), 21–38. For the legacy of collaboration, see Caprio, "The Politics of Collaboration" and Kim, "On Forgiveness and Reconciliation," 165–66.

a window into how a mis-administered occupation in southern Korea contributed to this tragic legacy. In this light, U.S. involvement in post-liberation Korea recalls Colin Powell's broken-pottery analolgy,[63] even though he later helped launch the Iraq War—a preemptive war widely regarded as unwarranted. In the Korean case, the U.S. and other associated parties must assume responsibility for the tragic history that Koreans have been made to endure over the decades that followed their "liberation" from Japanese colonial rule. For now, it involves seeing the problems of the Korean Peninsula as having deeper roots than simply brinkmanship by "rogue" states that periodically threaten neighbors and the security of the region. The solution requires that the U.S. join with other associated states to realize their part in this history and take positive steps to lessen regional tensions and resolve longstanding problems.

[63] See Woodward, *Plan of Attack*, 150.

Sprechen Sie Deutsch? Fascism in Korea

Frank Hoffmann

It is not true
that history
is being falsified
For the most part,
it truly
unfolded
false
I can attest to that:
I was there

— Erich Fried, "Die Engel der Geschichte"

The main discourse on fascism in Korea—kept at the margins of historiographic debate, despite decades of authoritarian rule in South Korea—dates back to a 1947 article. Between then and the publication of Fujii Takeshi's thought-provoking study *P'asijŭmgwa che-3 segyejuŭi saiesŏ* (Between fascism and Third-Worldism)[1] in 2012, post-liberation Korean fascism and its youth organizations were typically portrayed as an ephemeral political movement advised and funded by the U.S. Army Military Government in Korea (USAMGIK). Fujii's study shifts the vantage point, portraying Korean fascism as a nativist political movement—a Third-Worldist framing of the extreme right. A kind of decolonized brainchild of pan-Asianism, this reframing seeks distance from the Cold War's East–West divide between capitalism and communism.

---

[1] Hujii Tak'esi [Fujii Takeshi], *P'asijŭmgwa che-3 segyejuŭi saiesŏ: Chokch'ŏnggyeŭi hyŏngsŏnggwa mollagŭl t'onghae pon haebang 8-nyŏnsa* [Between fascism and Third-Worldism: An eight-year history of liberation viewed through the formation and fall of the Korean National Youth Corps]. Yŏkpi Han'gukhak yŏn'gu ch'ongsŏ, 34. 2nd ed. (Seoul: Yŏksa Pip'yŏngsa, 2016). The first edition appeared in 2012.

We ... women and their ... walls. I was introduced to ... National Youth Movement, which wears blue uniforms, and is recruited from husky young men of 18 to 35.

80,000 Marching. "This is the new Boy Scout movement—80,000 members already," explained Dr. Sze Hyong Kang, the school director, as we drove into the vast compound. He sat us down in a little room before a table set with sweet, black coffee.

"*Sprechen Sie Deutsch?*" he asked. "I studied in Germany, 1930 to 1934. We base our instruction on the German youth movement, because the Germans are the only people who really know how to organize young men."

We watched a squad of "Boy Scouts"

25

(Fig. 32)
Carl Mydans, "Korea: A Scout Is Militant," *Time* magazine, June 30, 1947; detail.

The acclaimed *Time-Life* photojournalist Carl Mydans (1907–2004), one of the foremost 20th-century American press photographers who would also cover the Yŏsu–Sunch'ŏn Rebellion for *Life* magazine the following year and later produce the most striking images of the Korean War (1950–1953), published a short article in *Time* magazine (see fig. 32). In that article, just two years after Nazi Germany's defeat, Mydans draws a direct line from the state-run Nazi youth movement and its Hitler Youth (Hitlerjugend) to the USAMGIK-funded Korean National Youth Corps

(Fig. 33)
Carl Mydans' slide, documenting his visit to Suwŏn, May 27, 1947: Mydans (left) with his colleague Joseph Fromm (middle) and Korean fascist Kang Se-hyŏng at Hwasŏng Fortress.

(Chosŏn Minjok Ch'ŏngnyŏndan, aka Chokch'ŏng) under "General" Yi Pŏm-sŏk (1900–1972).[2] Gregory Henderson (1922–1988) and many U.S. Army G-2 reports explicitly rendered *minjok* as "racial" (hence "Korean Racial Youth Corps")—then standard, now politically incorrect, but all too apt here.[3] The man who guides Mydans and his colleague Joseph

[2] See Carl Mydans, "Korea: A Scout Is Militant," *Time* 49, no. 26 (June 30, 1947): 25–26, and his Yŏsu–Sunch'ŏn photo essay "Revolt in Korea: A New Communist Uprising Turns Men into Butchers," *Life* 25, no. 20 (November 15, 1948): 55–58.

[3] Back in 1990, Bruce Cumings, in his own incisive overview on the topic, pointed out that the Korean National Youth Corps and other such youth groups were highly powerful *mass organizations* but remained "an unstudied phenomenon" (p. 194). Thirty-five years later, and despite hundreds of pages of USAMGIK G-2 military intelligence reports that document the formative role of right-wing youth groups and their sociopolitical, military, and terrorist activities in southern Korea, this is essentially still the case. Monica Kim's chapter on their crucial importance during the Korean War in her study *The Interrogation Rooms of the Korean War* is a commendable exception. This is complemented by shorter discussions in Sungik Yang's 2023 dissertation on "Korea's Fascist Moment" and Kornel Chang's 2025 study *A Fractured Liberation: Korea under US Occupation*. In Korea itself, Yi Sun-t'aek and Kim Si-hŭng published the first book on the topic in 1989—a very extensive study—which was later, in 2004, supplemented by a similarly extensive overview authored by Kim Haeng-sŏn. Also worth mentioning is Im Chong-myŏng's 1996 article on the relationship between the Korean National Youth Corps and USAMGIK. But apart from Fujii Takeshi's already mentioned book—his revised dissertation—and a few more articles and book chapters by him and others (Yi T'aek-sŏn and Ch'ae O-byŏng deserve mention), there is relatively little genuinely critical scholarship. A 2016 volume of interviews with former Korean National Youth Corps members, published alongside an exhibition catalog on the youth corps' Central Training Center in Suwŏn, leaves a disquieting aftertaste, suggesting that Suwŏn seeks to celebrate nearly anything historical as patriotic and glorious—even fascism.

See Bruce Cumings, *The Origins of the Korean War*, vol. II, *The Roaring of the Cataract, 1947–1950* (Princeton: Princeton University Press, 1990), esp. 193–203, 810–12; Monica Kim, *The Interrogation Rooms of the Korean War: The Untold History* (Princeton: Princeton University Press, 2019), 211–58, 391–96 (hereafter cited as Kim, *Interrogation Rooms*); Sungik Yang, "Korea's Fascist Moment: Liberation, War, and the Ideology of South Korean Authoritarianism, 1945–1979" (PhD diss., Harvard University, 2023); Kornel Chang, *A Fractured Liberation: Korea under US Occupation* (Cambridge: Belknap Press of Harvard University Press, 2025). Yi Sun-t'aek and Kim Si-hŭng, eds., *Taehan Min'guk kŏn'guk ch'ŏngnyŏn undongsa* [History of the youth movement during the founding period of the Republic of Korea] (Seoul: Kŏn'guk Ch'ŏngnyŏn Undong Hyŏbŭihoe, 1989); Kim Haeng-sŏn, *Haebang chŏngguk ch'ŏngnyŏn undongsa* [History of the liberation period youth movement] (Seoul: Sŏnin, 2004); Im Chong-myŏng, "Chosŏn Minjok Ch'ŏngnyŏndan (1946.10–1949.1) kwa Migunjŏngŭi 'changnae Han'gugŭi chido seryŏk' yangsŏng chŏngch'aek" [The Korean

Fromm (1920–2014) through Chokch'ŏng's headquarters, training camp, and historical sites in Suwŏn (see fig. 33) is Kang Se-hyŏng (1899–1960), rendered in his own transcription as Dr. Sze Hyong Kang. Nicknamed "Korea's Hitler" in the early years of the republic, the self-styled Berlin University doctor of philosophy, later a parliamentarian, who reportedly greeted Americans with "Sprechen Sie Deutsch?," seems at first glance to be the most obvious direct link between the Hitler Youth and the post-liberation fascist youth movement in Korea. But he was not alone. Yi Pŏm-sŏk himself, Chokch'ŏng's founder and the republic's future prime minister, was equally blunt about the main sources of inspiration for his militaristic, racist Weltanschauung. "After Auschwitz, to write a poem is barbaric,"[4] Adorno's dictum ran—a watchword across Europe. Yet halfway around the globe, the soon-to-be South Korean prime minister cast his country's youth in Hitler's ethno-fascist mold:

> We will remember that in Germany Hitler was compelled to initiate a movement to promote racial purity. But due to the complex historical circumstances surrounding the formation of the German nation, this goal was essentially unattainable.

Omitting the Holocaust, Yi continues in his essay dated June 1947:

> Despite this, the expulsion of the Jews had, in fact, a profound impact on the nation's solidarity. This single instance alone exemplifies how precious and important the purity of blood is, emphasizing the necessity for us to cherish and fully embrace this advantage ourselves.[5]

National Youth Corps (October 1946–January 1949) and its relationship with USAMGIK's 'Future Leaders of South Korea' training policy], *Han'guksa yŏngu* 95 (December 1996): 179–211; Suwŏn Pangmulgwan, *Haebang konggan Suwŏn, kŭ ttŭgŏun hamsŏng: 2016 Suwŏn pangmulgwan t'ŭkpyŏl kihoekchŏn* [Suwŏn after independence, the passionate shouts: 2016 Suwŏn Museum special exhibition] (Suwŏn: Suwŏn Pangmulgwan, 2016); Yu Sang-hŭi, Yi Sang-nok, Chŏng Tae-hun, et al., *Chosŏn Minjok Ch'ŏngnyŏndan Chungang Hullyŏnso* [Korean National Youth Corps Central Training Center] (Suwŏn: Suwŏn Pangmulgwan, 2016); Hujii Tak'esi [Fujii Takeshi], "Suwŏn Chokch'ŏng Chungang Hullyŏnsowa sae chŏngch'ijuch'eŭi saengsan" [The Korean National Youth Corps Suwŏn Central Training Center and the production of new political subjects], *Suwŏn yŏksa munhwa yŏn'gu* 6 (2016): 119–49.

[4] Theodor W. Adorno, *Prismen: Kulturkritik und Gesellschaft* [Prisms: Cultural criticism and society] (Frankfurt am Main: Suhrkamp, 1955), 31. The quote is from 1949.

[5] Yi Pŏm-sŏk, *Minjokkwa ch'ŏngnyŏn* [A people and its youth], Yi Pŏm-sŏk nonsŏljip, no. 1 (Seoul: Paeksusa, 1948), 30.

Yi Pŏm-sŏk titled his bold text "Minjongnon" (Theory of race). The piece tracks Nazi blood-and-soil ideology, recoded for East Asia, and its title pointedly echoes Yi Kwang-su's (1892–1950) infamous "Chosŏn minjongnon" (Theory of the Korean race), published in the June 1933 inaugural issue of the *Tonggwang ch'ongsŏ*, alongside excerpts from Hitler's *Mein Kampf* in Korean translation.

Other pieces in the same Yi Pŏm-sŏk booklet follow suit. Yi insists that Korea—unlike Germany—already possesses the monoethnic "advantage" the Nazis could only pursue, yet he folds this into an egalitarian language that blends proto-fascist and Confucian idioms. A year later, in an August 1948 interview, as if to leave no doubt about the décor of his political imagination, beneath portraits of Chiang Kai-shek (aka Jiang Jieshi, in office 1928–1975) and a Guomindang general, Yi explicitly invoked Hitler's autobiographical manifesto.[6] Speaking of *Mein Kampf*, he said: "This book is not just my favorite; it is also a book I will never forget, because it gave me the belief in and encouragement for the 'ethnie first, nation first' (*minjok chisang, kukka chisang*) principle."[7] His earlier "nation first, ethnie first" mirrors Chiang Kai-shek's *guojia zhishang, minzu zhishang* (often rendered "nation first, state first"),[8] but the 1948 reference to *Mein Kampf* fixes *minjok* as ethnie in an ethnonational sense. By reversing the order—"ethnie first, nation first"—Yi moves the phrase semantically closer to the Nazi slogan "Ein Volk, ein Reich, ein Führer!" than the Guomindang phrasing ever implied. At about the same time, Syngman Rhee (in office 1948–1960) and An Ho-

---

[6] Yi likely got to read the full version of *Mein Kampf* in its Chinese edition, first published in 1934 by a Shanghai publisher, immediately becoming a bestseller that was reprinted in several subsequent editions.

[7] Yi Pŏm-sŏk interview, "Ch'ŏrhyŏlch'ongni, taenae ch'onggyŏlsok, taeoegongjonŭl chŏlgyu: chogukchaegŏnŭi illyŏme yŏrhwagach'i pult'amyŏnsŏ" [An iron-willed prime minister, demanding internal unity and external coexistence: Burning like a raging fire at the thought of rebuilding the fatherland], *Samch'ŏlli* 31, no. 4 (August 1948): 9 (hereafter cited as Yi Pŏm-sŏk interview). Chokch'ŏng's official 1948 manifesto and organizational manual also sets it out as "nation first, state first"—in that order—as the youth group's "supreme ideals;" see Chosŏn Minjok Ch'ŏngnyŏndan Chojikpu, *Chojige kwanhan ch'amgo* [Organizational reference guide] (Seoul: Chosŏn Minjok Ch'ŏngnyŏndan Chojikpu, 1948), 4–5.

[8] See Brian Tsui, *China's Conservative Revolution: The Quest for a New Order, 1927–1949* (Cambridge: Cambridge University Press, 2018), esp. 127–28.

sang (1902–1999) developed the One-People's Doctrine (*ilminjuŭi*) in an attempt to Koreanize the underlying formula: neither communist nor capitalist-imperialist, but ethnonationalist—seasoned with proto-socialist motifs filtered through Sun Yat-sen's (1866–1925) Three Principles of the People (*sanmin zhuyi*) and its Korean offshoot, Cho So-ang's (1887–1958) Three Equalities Doctrine (*samgyunjuŭi*), both of which bore a family resemblance to interwar European "third way" projects.[9]

In that 1948 interview, we see how the future prime minister of the ROK—the second man in the state, and founder of the country's largest right-wing paramilitary youth movement—treats the Holocaust as a tactical overreach, offers only token disclaimers ("some of Hitler's writings and actions were wrong"[10]), and then returns to an unapologetic defense of ethno-fascist first principles. Circulated through a mass organization under U.S. patronage, this outlook helped normalize ethno-fascist assumptions in the postwar political culture. USAMGIK had helped uncork this force. It soon learned that Chokch'ŏng's nationalist-egalitarian rhetoric did not sit easily with the neocolonial logic of the occupation: a simplified capitalist order built on durable dependency.

Read in a larger historiographic context, American support for the far right in southern Korea has generally been treated as the product of confusion, haste, and anti-communist panic. This essay argues otherwise. Korea was not simply an aberration or the postwar era's accidental "original sin," but can be read as a revealing case of transition from U.S. colonial to neocolonial forms of rule. After 1945, older colonial techniques—tutelage, auxiliaries, racial hierarchy, and staged sovereignty—were not abandoned. They were repackaged in a neocolonial form inside a formally independent state and exercised through local anti-communist clients. What emerged in Seoul was thus a staged sovereignty: nominally sovereign, practically tutelary, and reliant on Korean far-right actors as local auxiliaries.

The Korean National Youth Corps—and the wider ecology of about 120 mostly right-wing political youth organizations that emerged

---

[9] Sun Yat-sen's Three Principles doctrine (1904, revised 1924), on which Cho's own theory was based, had already rejected capitalism in its third *minsheng* (social welfare) principle.

[10] Yi Pŏm-sŏk interview, 9.

under the U.S. occupation of southern Korea[11]—must be read in that light. These groups were not simply Korean copies of the Hitler Youth, nor were they merely American fabrications improvised under occupation. They were Korean far-right formations whose leaders had already been shaped elsewhere: by fascist youth mobilization under Japanese colonial rule, by militarized exile politics in Guomindang China, and by the appeal of German military modernity and efficiency—its doctrine, organization, technologies of mobilization, and models of youth discipline, politicized leisure, and communal labor—along with elements of Nazi racial science and eugenics.[12] What U.S. occupation power supplied was not the ideology itself, but the neocolonial framework in which such forces could be selected, financed, institutionalized, protected, and folded into the security architecture of the new state. In that sense, post-liberation Korean fascism did not arise from a vacuum. It was recombined under U.S. patronage.

On August 4, 1946, the U.S. Army Military Government in Korea formally installed Yi Pŏm-sŏk as leader of the Korean National Youth Corps, with Colonel Ernest E. Voss (1895–1969)—a U.S. Army intelligence officer and former organizer of the Philippine Boy Scouts—as his official advisor. Voss was supported by a small U.S. Army contingent: three officers and four enlisted men were assigned to assist him. Publicly inaugurated two months later, on October 9, the Corps was designed as a paramilitary, anti-communist mass movement. In a 1947 report to the Secretary of State, General Hodge's (1893–1963) political advisor in Korea made the chain of command explicit, describing the organization

---

[11] A 1947 annual report submitted to USAMGIK speaks "of the 119 political youth movements" which Chokch'ŏng "is beginning to influence." Ernest E. Voss, "Korean National Youth Inc.: Annual Report" [1947], January 13, 1948, reprinted in *Haebang chikhu chŏngch'i sahoesa charyojip*, 5: *Chŏngdang sahoe tanch'e charyo* (2) [Collection of political and social materials from the immediate post-liberation period, vol. 5: Materials on political parties and social organizations (2)], comp. Chŏng Yong-uk (Seoul: Tarakpang, 1994), 599.

[12] In a recent article on colonial Korea, Sin Sŭng-yŏp aptly describes "the increasing attention on the Nazis and the deepening emotional affinity that Koreans felt toward Hitler" (p. 30), and shows how Nazism could be seen, despite the apparent contradiction, by some as a means of career advancement within the Japanese colonial system, and by others as a way to overcome colonialism. See Shin Seungyop, "When Colonial Korea Met Fascism: Power, Desire, and Adolf Hitler in Public Discourse, 1931–1945," *Korea Journal* 63, no. 3 (Autumn 2023): 5–35.

(Fig. 34) Still shots from Colin Ross' 1940 movie *Das neue Asien* [The new Asia], showing an Imperial Japanese Army training camp for Korean volunteer soldiers near Seoul (Keijō). By 1943, over 800,000 Koreans had applied to enlist in the Japanese Army.

The Hitler Youth in Korea, October 1940

October 23

It has become very warm, the sun is shining in a clear blue sky. Every spot of land is cultivated, everywhere diligent farmers at work, the landscape is bright and colorful. In Heijō [P'yŏngyang], a brief stop, so out we go for some fresh air and a bit of exercise, but—there is an immense crowd and just as many flags, in our honor. We review the lines of assembled youth groups, amidst banzai shouts and Hitler salutes, a large banner with a heartfelt welcome greeting and an abundance of the finest Korean fruits as gifts to take on our journey. And again, green rice fields, dark groves, yellow or red soil, white-clad people, blue sky, such a neat color symphony. It gets hilly, with high mountains in the distance, fields, houses, huts, railway stations, and people who leave such a neat, clean, friendly impression, although everything is so plain and simple. Around noon arrival in Keijō [Seoul], the capital of Chōsen.

Again a warm welcome at the train station, followed by visits and tours. For the first time: a visit to a [Shintō] shrine. Reception at the governor-general's residence. What the Japanese have achieved in the development of Chōsen is truly amazing. We learn this at a large exhibition whose closure was postponed for three days until after our arrival.

October 24

Guided tour through the Government-General Museum of Chōsen and visit to a public elementary and middle school. Student workload and diligence, discipline, cleanliness, and courtesy caught our admiration. In the stairwell and in some classrooms, pictures of the Führer and of the German Luftwaffe. We then visit a training camp for Korean volunteers who are to be admitted to the Japanese Army. Military punctuality, orderliness, and cleanliness to high perfection. [...] At night, we depart for Kongō-san [Kŭmgang-san], the famous Diamond Mountains of Chōsen, in a special coach attached to the regular train.

October 25 and 26

[...] The Montserrat, the mountain of the Golden Fleece, must have looked just like the saw-toothed mountains of Kongō-san. A romantically situated Buddhist temple [i.e., Singye-sa] radiates peace and tranquility. The abbot hands us honey tea and apples from the temple garden. [...]

October 27

Back in Keijō. Participation in a large-scale youth rally, with us at its center; then departure to Fusan [Pusan] aboard the luxury train "Hope" [Nozomi]. [...] Along the way, on various stops, we step out of the train and onto the platforms, to walk along the fronts of the assembled youth organizations. In the evening, we board the ferry in Fusan that will take us across to Japan during the night.

Source: Heinrich Jürgens, "Reise nach Japan: Tagebuchaufzeichnungen von der Japanfahrt der HJ 1940" [Journey to Japan: Diary notes on the Hitler Youth's 1940 Japan trip], *Junge Welt* 3, no. 3 (March 1941): 22, and no. 4 (April 1941): 20.

草原ではちかった！

来朝の第一歩を
朝鮮に印して

語るH・ユーゲント

お伽噺の世
現實の

那智壽人

(Fig. 35) The Hitler Youth in Korea. *Kokumin shinpō*, November 10, 1940; detail. The photo shows Heinrich Jürgens' (1903–?) Hitler Youth delegation at a restaurant in Seoul (Keijō) with Itō Masakatsu of the Japanese Ministry of Education. The two-page article is signed by Nachi Hisato, a pen name that combines a phonetic pun on "Nazi" with an auspicious given name meaning "man of long life."

as "an office directly below and responsible to the Civil Administrator of Military Government," and adding that it had been "established by the Military Governor," and granted "a budget of five million yen [about $333,000 at the time] for current operations."[13] From the outset, Chokch'ŏng was financially distinct from other youth organizations. In 1947 alone, it received funding nearly equal to the entire budget of the South Korean Ministry of Labor. This funding enabled the Corps to maintain permanent headquarters in Seoul and to establish a flagship training facility in Suwŏn, while dues and patron donations supplied further resources. As one U.S. officer told Mark Gayn (1909–1981) in fall 1946, Chokch'ŏng was "probably the most profitable enterprise in Korea,"[14] fed in part by "donations" from people afraid they would otherwise be denounced as collaborators. The Central Training Camp in Suwŏn was housed in the compound of the former Japanese Army hospital and could hold about 500 trainees at a time. The military government placed the site at the Corps' disposal.

The Corps' program emphasized "citizen education" as a vehicle for reshaping Korea's political culture. While it presented itself as transcending ideological divisions, its deeper function was to manufacture a new moderate right-wing force that could replace discredited conservative factions and provide a reliable domestic base for U.S. policy. By 1947/48, Chokch'ŏng had become one of the largest youth organizations in Asia. By fall 1948, the *New York Times* estimated its membership at 1,250,000—"a potential source of military power."[15]

Richard D. Robinson (1921–2009) discusses Yi's fascist youth group and its Suwŏn leadership training center in unmistakable terms,[16] while Mark Gayn also points out that Hitler's NAPOLA leadership schools served Yi as a model for the center.[17] Mydans' *Time* article further points out that the center's teaching materials draw on Hitler Youth textbooks—apparently based on information from Kang Se-hyŏng,

[13] "From Wm. R. Langdon to the Secretary of State: Korean National Youth Movement," January 21, 1947, 1, Box 26, Folder B, James H. Hausman Archive, 1946–1981, Harvard-Yenching Library.
[14] Unnamed U.S. officer, quoted in Gayn, "Japan Diary: Korea," in this volume, 423.
[15] *New York Times*, October 10, 1948.
[16] See Richard D. Robinson, "Betrayal of a Nation," in this volume, 260–61, 319.
[17] See Mark Gayn, "Japan Diary: Korea," in this volume, 422–24.

whom Gayn calls "an enthusiastic member of *Hitler Jugend* in Germany for three years."[18] Joseph Fromm corroborates this, quoting Kang as he proudly advertises the school's "special lessons on the history of the *Hitler Jugend*."[19] Robinson adds that Chokch'ŏng, initiated and sponsored by the Americans, became a tool "to bring [Syngman] Rhee to power by intimidating and terrorizing the opposition."[20]

More than a decade after Yi Pŏm-sŏk's Chokch'ŏng group had been officially disbanded, Gregory Henderson—who had been in Korea since 1948 and was still working for the U.S. Foreign Service in Seoul in the early 1960s—wrote an extensive report on its influence and power. Although clearly diminished in political weight, "a small group of seven inner-core Chokch'ŏng men [was] planning assassinations of current government leaders"[21] as of November 1961, Henderson reported. American sponsors had expected anti-communist street power. But they were unsettled by the movement's egalitarian rhetoric and hostility to unfettered capitalism—one reason Fujii Takeshi reads these currents as a nativist, "Third-Worldist" extreme right.

Chokch'ŏng functioned as more than a patriotic youth movement: it was a paramilitary reserve, a propaganda arm, and a *neocolonial experiment*. Embedded in its very structure were the lessons of U.S. overseas rule—particularly in the Philippines. Even contemporaries could grasp how badly USAMGIK's tutelary language fit the realities of power. Stationed in Kwangju, E. Grant Meade (1914–1988) complained that the staffing system produced what he called "stupid or dishonest officers" who "wielded enormous local authority"[22] as U.S.

---

[18] Ibid., 422.

[19] Joseph Fromm, "Youth Training Center in Southern Korea Prepares Selected 'Boys' as Future Leaders," *World Report* 3, no. 40 (October 7, 1947): 26. The longer, 10-page type-written draft version of this article is among the Mark Gayn Papers in Toronto; see [Joseph] Fromm, "Suwon, Korea," typescript, draft of magazine article, June 18, 1947, Mark Gayn Papers, MS Coll. 215, Series 8 (Books), Box 100, Folder 24 (Korean National Youth), Thomas Fisher Rare Book Library, University of Toronto (hereafter cited as Fromm, "Suwon, Korea").

[20] Richard D. Robinson, "Betrayal of a Nation," in this volume, 319.

[21] G. Henderson, "The Racial Youth Corps and Yi Pom-Sok," May 31, 1962, 2, Foreign Service Despatch 463 to Dept. of State, Washington, Records of the U.S. Department of State Relating to Internal Affairs of Korea, 1960–1963, File 895B, RG 59, NARA.

[22] E. Grant Meade, *American Military Government in Korea* (New York: King's Crown Press, Columbia University, 1951), 48.

representatives; and in the same region a certain Major J. E. Dillon, meeting local Korean leaders, dispensed with the notion of trusteeship altogether: "Korea was captured by force of arms as an enemy country [...] we came here to kill all you people!"[23]

In 1945, occupation officers did not arrive in a conceptual void. The United States had long experience running military government and civil administration under its own sovereignty; the Philippines, Puerto Rico, and other "unincorporated territories" had functioned as laboratories of imperial rule. That institutional memory had now been codified into institutional doctrine. *Field Manual 27-5*, with its key terms "Military Government" and "Civil Affairs and Military Government,"[24] assumed a phased transition from seizure to garrison rule to "formal occupation." The familiar narrative—of well-intentioned U.S. officers overwhelmed by an ill-prepared mission—thus obscures more than it explains. Democracy operated less as the occupation's telos than as its legitimating idiom. What took shape in Seoul was thus not the absence of a policy but the redeployment of techniques forged in earlier U.S. "possessions," now translated into the language of anti-communism and democratization while securing strategic leverage and economic influence. The imperial world order was not simply shattered in 1945; in important respects, it was repackaged in a neocolonial idiom.

The contradiction had been visible from the start of the new American empire in 1898. Under McKinley (in office 1897–1901), the war with Spain produced colonial rule over Puerto Rico, Guam, and the Philippines, and a military occupation of Cuba that soon hardened into a protectorate, while "benevolent assimilation" framed coercion as a Christian mission to "civilize and uplift." In the 1901 Senate debates Senator Henry Teller (1830–1914) of Colorado, who had also argued for the self-rule of Cuba, put it bluntly:

[23] Ibid., 89. (The anecdote is also confirmed by another USAMGIK officer and later Korea specialist: Donald S. Macdonald, interview by Charles Stuart Kennedy, January 25, 1990, *Interview with Donald S. Macdonald*, [8], Manuscript Division, Library of Congress, Washington, DC, https://www.loc.gov/item/mfdipbib000734.)

[24] The 1940 *Field Manual 27-5* was revised in 1943 and again in 1947. See, for example, the December 22, 1943, edition: U.S. War Department and U.S. Navy Department, *United States Army and Navy Manual of Military Government and Civil Affairs (FM 27-5 / OPNAV 50E-3)* (Washington, DC: Government Printing Office, 1943).

> Imperialism has come; it is there in its worst form [...]. Are you going to keep up this imperialistic government? Are you going to continue to govern 12,000,000 people contrary to their wish, without a voice, without being heard, when your chief actor over there, General MacArthur, tells you that the people are a unit against this administration [...]?[25]

The general to whom Teller refers was Arthur MacArthur (1845–1912), the father of Douglas MacArthur (1880–1964), a career officer shaped by the Army's settler-colonial governance of Indigenous America. First as a field commander and soon after as military governor-general of the Philippine Islands, MacArthur helped direct the brutal conquest and counterinsurgency that followed the American takeover. For McKinley and MacArthur, the governance of Pacific and Asian territories was an extension of the settler wars in the American West, and it could be justified in the familiar idiom of Christianization, civilization, and democratic tutelage. Liberal newspapers and cartoonists warned that the republic was drifting into European-style colonialism, and Mark Twain (1835–1910), with his usual mordant clarity, spelled out the contradiction:

> There must be two Americas: one that sets the captive free, and one that takes a once-captive's new freedom away from him [...]; then kills him to get his land. [...] [W]e were only playing the American Game in public—in private it was the European.[26]

After the initial debates around 1900, U.S. colonialism was increasingly occluded in public discourse and recoded as tutelage. The title of a contemporary study captures this with disarming precision: *How to Hide an Empire*.[27]

In Senate testimony after his tenure as governor-general, Arthur MacArthur spoke of the "magnificent Aryan people" of North America

---

[25] Henry M. Teller (January 4, 1901), in *Congressional Record: The Proceedings and Debates of the Fifty-Sixth Congress, Second Session*, 34, pt. 1 (Washington, DC: Government Printing Office, 1901), 535.

[26] Mark Twain, "To the Person Sitting in Darkness," *North American Review* 531 (February 1901): 170–71.

[27] Daniel Immerwahr, *How to Hide an Empire: A History of the Greater United States* (New York: Farrar, Straus and Giroux, 2019).

and then described the Philippines as "an ideal strategical position" and "a means of protecting American interests," a "stepping-stone to commanding influence—political, commercial, and military supremacy in the East,"[28] all on the assumption of a "*permanent* [italics mine] occupation of the islands."[29] Auxiliary models such as the Philippine Scouts were explicitly segregated, largely closed to commissioned rank, and used against local insurgencies. While African American soldiers served in segregated U.S. Army units, the Scouts themselves consisted largely of Filipino men recruited into a racially stratified colonial force. Colonial manpower was thus made usable without conceding equality.

Without this imperial background and training in colonial administration, the political formation of Douglas MacArthur, who followed in his father's footsteps in the Philippine Islands in what reads as a textbook case of imperial nepotism, would be inconceivable. Douglas grew up inside the U.S. Army on frontier posts in the American West, where campaigns against Indigenous communities functioned as the domestic counterpart to his father's colonial war in the Philippines. Many of the high-ranking officers who later staffed his headquarters in Tokyo and helped direct U.S. policy toward Korea, like himself, had been professionally socialized through service in the colonial Philippines: Willoughby (1892–1972), Whitney (1897–1969), Almond (1892–1979), and Voss among them.

Manila in the 1930s and early 1940s became the staging ground for a cohort of officers and advisors who would later reappear across the Pacific. Even the man tasked by Hodge with building USAMGIK's administrative machinery from day one—Brigadier General Charles S. Harris (1894–1993)—came directly out of the Philippines' U.S.–Commonwealth civil-affairs world.[30] MacArthur served as military advisor to the Commonwealth Government of the Philippines in 1935 and

[28] Arthur MacArthur, on April 8, 1902, in a hearing of the 57th Congress, 1st Session, Senate, Committee on the Philippines, *Affairs in the Philippine Islands: Hearings before the Committee on the Philippines of the United States Senate*, Senate Doc. No. 331, pt. 2 (Washington, DC: Government Printing Office, 1902), 867 (hereafter cited as MacArthur, Senate Hearings).

[29] Ibid., 868.

[30] Harris was the de facto senior U.S. authority in Korea from September 4 to 12. See also pp. 55 and 413–14.

stayed in Manila until April 1942. Ernest E. Voss headed the Philippine Boy Scouts from 1930 to 1938 and returned in 1942 as an intelligence officer under MacArthur. The extreme-right, German-born Charles A. Willoughby became MacArthur's intelligence chief in June 1940; Courtney Whitney, in Manila since 1927, became his closest advisor in 1943. The operative models were colonial, racialized, and already institutionalized.

Albert C. Wedemeyer (1896–1989), for example, a veteran of several years' service in the Philippine Islands who succeeded Stilwell (1883–1946) in October 1944 as commander of U.S. forces in East Asia and as Chiang Kai-shek's chief of staff, remained deeply shaped by the colonial world in which he had been trained. As late as 1968, he described Filipinos as "just one huckleberry bush above the chimpanzee."[31] In 1947 he recommended building "a strong Korean military force *along the lines of the former Philippine Scouts* [italics mine]" that "should be under the control of the United States Military Commander"[32] and would "replace the present Constabulary."[33] Wedemeyer was thus, as we will see, recommending the very model of U.S.-directed right-wing Korean paramilitary youth formations that he himself had already helped instigate in February 1946. In this longer arc, U.S. sponsorship of far-right actors in Korea reads less as ad hoc Cold War panic than as the continuation of an established imperial toolkit—auxiliaries, hierarchy, and elite networks—repackaged in the language of "security" and "democratization." During the Korean War, such youth corps were "supplied with significant quantities of small arms,"[34] also for use as guerrilla fighters behind enemy lines. Yet U.S. reporting attributes the near-total failure of these units to inadequate professional training under Yi Pŏm-sŏk's supervision. The U.S. ambassador to the ROK at the time of the North

[31] Letter by General Albert C. Wedemeyer to Ernst E. F. von Helms, August 29, 1968, quoted in Joseph W. Bendersky, *The "Jewish Threat": Anti-Semitic Politics of the U.S. Army* (New York: Basic Books, 2000), 28 (hereafter cited as Bendersky).
[32] Albert C. Wedemeyer, *Report to the President Submitted September 1947: Korea* (Washington, DC: Government Printing Office, 1951), 26.
[33] Ibid., 27.
[34] "The Joint Chiefs of Staff to the Secretary of Defense (Marshall)" (January 17, 1951), *Foreign Relations of the United States, 1951*, vol. VII, *Korea and China*, part 1, comp. United States Department of State (Washington, DC: Government Printing Office, 1983), 107.

Korean invasion later recalled how Yi in his capacity as "Prime Minister and Minister of Defense and head of the National Youth Corps, came in joyfully exhaulting [*sic*; exulting] that his boys had just taken over Haeju," while "he didn't go on to say that practically every one of them" was "killed on the spot."[35]

With Ernest E. Voss—lower-ranking, but crucial as USAMGIK's liaison to Yi and his Chokch'ŏng corps—the picture is more complicated; a simple "pro-fascist" label would feel forced. Yet Voss' own writing reveals the colonial assumptions he carried. In his book-length fellowship thesis, "Scouting Among Primitive Boys," he paired romantic ideas about freedom and "real brotherhood"[36] with pseudo-scientific developmentalism, reproducing ranked IQ tables—Americans and Britons at 100, Germans under 89, Koreans under 84, Filipinos at 74[37]—and built staged "civilizational" comparisons ("Comparisons of Primitive and Civilized Youth"), insisting that "some races are considered to be as much as 3,000 years behind the white race in mental development."[38] Scouting in the Philippines was an instrument of colonial rule: a uniformed, disciplined body schooled in loyalty to the colonial state. It is telling that most Scoutmasters were U.S. soldiers, and that under MacArthur's watch obligatory military training for children was institutionalized.

The tension built into this colonial apartheid—segregation enforced by rank as well as race—periodically spilled into open protest; one of the larger mutinies came in early July 1924 at Fort McKinley, when about 380 men of the 57th Infantry refused to report for duty and more than 220 from the 12th Medical Regiment soon followed. The

---

[35] John J. Muccio, interview by Jerry N. Hess, February 10, 1971, *Oral History Interview with John J. Muccio*, [18], Harry S. Truman Library, NARA, https://www.trumanlibrary.gov/library/oral-histories/muccio1. Formally, though, Yi had stepped back from leadership of the youth corps upon taking ministerial office in 1948; at the instigation of Syngman Rhee, his Chokch'ŏng merged with other youth organizations in January 1949.

[36] Ernest E. Voss, "Scouting Among Primitive Boys," unpublished thesis (application for the Scout Executive's Fellowship), June 1939, 237, Kenneth Woltz Badgett Papers, 1900–2001, No. 4692, Box 004, Folder 35, Wilson Special Collections Library, University of North Carolina at Chapel Hill.

[37] See ibid., 95.

[38] Ibid., 144.

Army answered with sweeping courts-martial: 209 Scouts were tried on charges including mutiny and unbecoming conduct, and 103 were convicted. Douglas MacArthur chaired the court-martial board and oversaw these prosecutions.[39] Such practices belonged to a broader repertoire of rule—racial hierarchy, tutelary authority, auxiliary formations, and the management of sovereignty at one remove—that U.S. occupation authorities would later carry into Korea.

Nor were these colonial techniques confined to overseas rule. At the nadir of the Great Depression—an America of breadlines, foreclosures, and Hoovervilles, later etched in bleak precision by Steinbeck—tens of thousands of First World War veterans converged on Washington as the "Bonus Army" to demand early payment of promised bonuses. The president had authorized only a limited clearing operation, but MacArthur, as army chief of staff, escalated it into full-scale military action. On July 28, 1932, with his staff—among them his aide Dwight D. Eisenhower (later president, 1953–1961), who would then also serve as MacArthur's subordinate in the Philippines, George S. Patton (1885–1945), with tanks under his command, and Deputy Chief of Staff George Van Horn Moseley (1874–1960), MacArthur sent cavalry, infantry, and tanks against the camps; troops used gas, and the encampments were burned. The spectacle of regular troops attacking veterans on U.S. soil echoed tactics forged in the colonies. The political cast of MacArthur's circle was no less telling: by 1940, Moseley was advocating "selective breeding, sterilization, [and] the elimination of the unfit," and fantasizing about "breeding all Jewish blood out of the human race."[40]

Even within MacArthur's world, not all officers drew the same political conclusions. Major General Smedley Butler (1881–1940), one of the most highly decorated marines of his era, had fought under Arthur MacArthur in the Philippine–American War and spent much of his career in what would later be called the American "Banana Wars,"

---

39 See Christopher Capozzola, "The Secret Soldiers' Union: Labor and Soldier Politics in the Philippine Scout Mutiny of 1924," in *Making the Empire Work: Labor and United States Imperialism*, eds. Daniel E. Bender and Jana K. Lipman (New York: New York University Press, 2015), 85–103.

40 George Van Horn Moseley, unpublished memoir, quoted from a 1940 entry, in Bendersky, 255–56.

eventually broke with U.S. imperial rationale. "Our exploits against the American Indian, against the Filipinos, the Mexicans, and against Spain," Butler wrote, "are on a par with the campaigns of Genghis Khan, the Japanese in Manchuria and the African attack of Mussolini." He summed up: "I spent 33 years and 4 months in active military service as [...] a high-class muscle man for Big Business" and helped with "the raping of half a dozen Central American republics for the benefit of Wall Street."[41] Butler supported the veterans in the Bonus Army and later condemned their violent dispersal by MacArthur. In 1934, he alleged that intermediaries tied to major business interests attempted to recruit him for a coup d'état in Washington to install a "business government," at one point envisioning Douglas MacArthur as the strongman. Whatever one makes of the disputed details, the larger point stands: American elite circles were already entertaining the possibility of a homegrown fascist strongman in the wake of Hitler's rise.[42]

After 1945, formal possessions became less central as an American, surplus-driven informal empire took shape: imperialism without colonies, sustained by finance, intelligence, and elite alliances rather than territorial rule. William L. Clayton (1880–1966), one of the Marshall Plan's architects, explained the underlying economic logic: "[O]ur productive machine leaves us with great deficits and great surpluses, which we must trade out with the rest of the world. We need markets—big markets—around the world in which to buy and sell."[43] The problem was no longer how to hold territory, but how to hold markets—an Open Door problem of demand, convertibility, and political compliance without paying the full costs of colonial administration.

In Korea, as Roger Baldwin (1884–1981), then director of the American Civil Liberties Union, observed after a 1947 visit: "The main trouble lies in the policy of turning over to Koreans *an appearance of*

---

41 Smedley D. Butler, "America's Armed Forces, 2. 'In Time of Peace': The Army," *Common Sense* 4, no. 11 (November 1935): 8.

42 For Butler and the planned coup d'état, see Jules Archer, *The Plot to Seize the White House* (New York: Hawthorn Books, 1973); Jonathan M. Katz, *Gangsters of Capitalism: Smedley Butler, the Marines, and the Making and Breaking of America's Empire* (New York: St. Martin's Press, 2022), 305–39. The 1930s FBI file on the case is available online at https://archive.org/details/ButlerSmedleyHQ1/.

43 [William L.] Clayton, "The Foreign Economic Policy of the United States," *Department of State Bulletin* 20, no. 386 (November 24, 1946): 950.

authority [italics mine] they cannot in fact exercize [*sic*]. Korea thus falls between the occupation and the puppet Korean government."[44] What often appears as democratization gone wrong can also be read as constrained democracy by design—and Korea was not alone. As early as 1986, one study had already cataloged U.S. involvement in covert action and other major interventions—including government overthrows, electoral manipulation, and assassinations—across *more than fifty countries*.[45] Postwar Italy, from Il Duce to Bella Ciao in a blink, offers an even earlier case of supervised democracy.

In the run-up to the Italian parliamentary elections of April 1948, U.S. policymakers regarded a likely victory by the left as unacceptable.[46] James Angleton (1917–1987), raised in a family enmeshed in Fascist Italy's commercial networks and later the CIA's chief of counterintelligence, oversaw efforts to manipulate the vote and prepare contingency plans in case the socialists prevailed. Under NSC 4/A, U.S. agencies and the newly created CIA mounted a major propaganda campaign and funneled millions to De Gasperi's (in office 1945–1953) Italian Christian Democrats (DCI) and their neo-fascist allies. Francesco Cossiga, later Italy's prime minister and then its president (in office 1979–1980 and 1985–1992), revealed decades later that in 1948 a DCI-linked paramilitary unit—including himself—stood by for a possible coup d'état, "armed to the teeth" with a Sten machine gun, magazines, and "various hand grenades,"[47] ready to act if the election produced an "undesirable" result. The point of invoking Italy is not that it is identical—or even approximate—to Korea, but that it serves as an example of how, from 1945 onward, Washington had already assembled a repertoire—electoral

---

[44] Letter by Roger Baldwin, director of the American Civil Liberties Union, to Assistant Secretary of State John H. Hildring, May 28, 1947, reprinted in *Taehan Min'guksa charyojip* [Source materials on the history of the Republic of Korea], vol. 22, comp. Kuksa P'yŏnch'an Wiwŏnhoe (Kwach'ŏn: Kuksa P'yŏnch'an Wiwŏnhoe, 1994), 52.

[45] See William Blum, *The CIA: A Forgotten History* (London: Zed Books, 1986).

[46] The 1948 Italian election is one of the best documented cases of postwar U.S. interference operations. Today, even official U.S. government publications acknowledge it; see, for example, Thomas Boghardt, *Covert Legions: U.S. Army Intelligence in Germany, 1944–1949* (Washington, DC: Center of Military History, United States Army, 2022), 435.

[47] President Francesco Cossiga, quoted in the *Guardian*, January 15, 1992.

intervention, media campaigns, ready-made coups d'état, alliances with conservative (and at times neo-fascist) elites, enabling violent anti-communist actors—that advanced U.S. interests without direct rule.

With the end of World War II, anti-communism became the far right's master key and the legitimating idiom through which the United States could treat fascists as assets. As Jeffrey M. Bale, a scholar of modern extremism, explains, many European "fascists and elements of numerous non-fascist far right currents, including Catholic integralists, monarchists, and certain types of ultranationalists, were politically wedded to the Atlantic Alliance and its major sponsor, the United States." At the same time, "various revolutionary neo-fascist factions advocated the establishment of a strong, united Nation Europa, which would constitute a 'third force' opposed to the twin 'imperialisms' of international communism and international finance capitalism, both of which they perceived as being materialistic, exploitative, dehumanizing."[48] Their postwar neo-fascist vision sought to replace traditional nation-state nationalism with an authoritarian pan-European nationalism, imagined as a *third force* between the *twin imperialisms* of the United States and the USSR, even as other far-right currents aligned themselves more directly with the American camp. Fujii Takeshi's "Third-Worldist" reading of Korean fascists thus fits within this broader postwar ideological shift.

Set against this wider postwar configuration, the South Korean case reads as part of the same larger pattern. A few pages of PMAG minutes from August 1948 make that concrete.[49] With the Republic of Korea proclaimed on August 15 and U.S. troops preparing to leave, the Provisional Military Advisory Group (PMAG, later KMAG) was created to "advise" the new state. Five days after the ROK's founding, Prime Minister Yi Pŏm-sŏk met with PMAG chief Brigadier General William L. Roberts (1890–1968) and his staff, among them Ernest E. Voss. Roberts opens the meeting by handing Yi what he calls the "first draft of the National Security Act." Alongside it lies the draft of what will

---

[48] Jeffrey M. Bale, *The Darkest Sides of Politics*, vol. 1, *Postwar Fascism, Covert Operations, and Terrorism* (London: Routledge, 2018), 64.

[49] See "Conference between Lee Bum Suk, Premier of Korea, Gen Roberts, Col Wright, Capt Hausman, Col Voss, and Interpreter," August 20, 1948, Box 26, Folder R, James H. Hausman Archive, 1946–1981, Harvard-Yenching Library.

become the Armed Forces Organization Act (Kukkun chojikpŏp). The National Security Act, with its deliberately elastic provisions, especially Article 7, would remain one of the central instruments for crushing political opposition and censoring critical speech well into the twenty-first century. As the meeting shows, the Korean premier's role is not to initiate legislation but to receive U.S.-drafted laws and orders; Roberts' team even reveals a telling unfamiliarity with the newly promulgated ROK constitution under which these laws will operate.

The transcript of the meeting is striking in its tone as well as its content. Yi is not addressed as "Prime Minister" or "Mr. Yi Pŏm-sŏk," but reduced to "Suk" [Sŏk], a non-reciprocal, overfamiliar form of address—a colonial diminutive that reduces title and name to a convenient syllable. When Yi raises questions about the placement of intelligence functions or the title and authority of a "supreme chief of staff" position, PMAG officers explain what democratic civil–military relations should look like while making it equally clear that they expect to retain effective veto power. "It is our job," Roberts remarks to his colleagues in Yi's presence, "to keep Suk from making a mistake—to prevent him from making a mistake." Yi replies: "From your country we get help. [...] I like your idea, but I have no power." Even personnel discussion remains in the same register. When Yi asks whether Roberts' preferred candidate for a key military post is "not too young," Roberts snaps: "You damned Koreans think you have a lot of age before you have brains."

The same exchange also shows how U.S. advisors tried to domesticate Yi's fascist-inflected Korean National Youth Corps by folding it into state security. Roberts scolds Yi for parading the corps as his personal guard in Chokch'ŏng uniforms, then offers a fix that is at once administrative and performative: "We can fix it very easily by enlisting them in the Army," and afterwards present the move to the press as if it had been Yi's idea all along. Treated as dangerously independent yet useful for repression, the Youth Corps is thus pressed toward absorption into the Constabulary, the force-structure PMAG is drafting, rather than left as a private militia.

Seen from Seoul, this ninety-minute meeting lays bare the asymmetry of the new relationship in unusually naked form: Korea possesses the symbols of sovereignty—a flag, anthem, constitution, premier, president—while PMAG holds the operative levers: draft security laws, force design, decisive influence over appointments, and even the latitude to reduce Koreans to a racialized stereotype. In August 1948, the new republic reads less as an independent state than as a staged sovereignty: a partitioned former Japanese colony formally sovereign, yet guided by U.S. military officers socialized in colonial governance. Paramilitary youth formations, requested, financed, and backed by U.S. officers (Wedemeyer, Hodge, Voss), were built into the security architecture as Cold War instruments of neocolonial tutelage.

As discussed, many of the career U.S. Army officers who came ashore at Inch'ŏn in September 1945 brought with them a colonial repertoire of rule and repression forged in the conquest and administration of the Philippines, or otherwise carried a racist, reactionary political orientation. Korean fascists such as Yi Pŏm-sŏk, Kang Se-hyŏng, or An Ho-sang, however, had articulated their ideological convictions well before they ever met U.S. officers. Some of the Korean officers exiled in China and attached to Chiang Kai-shek's forces were trained at the Whampoa Military Academy[50] and elsewhere in contemporary tactics, weapons, doctrine, staff work, and even the German language, often by German advisors. From its founding in 1924 to the 22nd class, around 150 Koreans (in the early days often using pseudonyms and posing as Chinese natives, to avoid Japanese protests) were among the academy's trainees.[51] Song Myŏn-su (1910–1950), for example, who entered the academy in the early 1940s, apparently studied armored tactics there and learned German during the period when the German advisor Raimund von Imhof was teaching at the school[52] (Imhof arrived

---

[50] Founded in 1924, the academy relocated and was renamed several times, often known in this period as the Central Army Officer Academy (Zhongyang Lujun Junguan Xuexiao); for simplicity—and following common usage—I refer to it throughout as "Whampoa Military Academy."

[51] Of those officers, 51 entered the academy in 1948–49, which leaves pre-liberation Korean participation at roughly 100. For a detailed list, see Ye Quanhong, "Huangbu junxiao han ji xuesheng kao shi" [An examination of Korean students at the Whampoa Military Academy], *Hanguo xuebao* 14 (1996), 155–68.

[52] Erich Otto Stoelzner (1895–1991), a German military advisor to the Guomindang since 1928 and the intelligence operative who headed the Nazi intelligence network

soon after the official German military advisory group had left in July 1938). Song went on to serve as director of the Propaganda Department of the Korean Independence Party (Han'guk Tongniptang) in the circle around Kim Ku (1876–1949) and Cho So-ang. He also served under Yi Pŏm-sŏk, then chief of staff of the Korean Liberation Army (Han'guk Kwangbokkun),[53] founded in September 1940 in Chongqing and, from October 1942, commander of its 2nd Detachment in Xi'an. Song thus participated in cooperation with the OSS, including Wedemeyer and Yi's ultimately unsuccessful "Operation Eagle" project.

This Korean Chongqing circle reappeared almost intact after 1945. In the Korean National Youth Corps of 1946/47, Yi Pŏm-sŏk staffed key offices with men he had already worked with in wartime China. Song Myŏn-su, introduced above, now surfaces as director of Chok-ch'ŏng's Propaganda Department and then one of Yi's three deputy directors; the other two were Yi Chun-sik (1900–1966) and An Ch'un-saeng (1912–2011), a nephew of national hero An Chung-gŭn (1879–1910). Both, like Yi, had been senior officers in the Korean Liberation Army.

At the level of doctrine and political theory, the Chinese–Korean right was not simply a local mirror of the American right. Cho So-ang's extensive writings on his Three Equalities Doctrine, for example, could be read as frankly social-democratic—envisioning a planned economy, land nationalization, support for the poorest farmers, state-funded education, and equal rights across classes and between nations. Thus, anti-communism did not necessarily translate into laissez-faire capitalism. This is precisely what would catch U.S. policy-makers off guard: a political imagination trained on a two-point scale—then and now—treated anti-communism as automatic permission for market orthodoxy;

---

in Nationalist China, remained in the country after July 1938, later moved to California, and noted in his memoirs that the academy was headed by one of Wedemeyer's Berlin Kriegsakademie classmates. In his recollections Stoelzner also noted that apart from Imhof other German advisors had been teaching at the Whampoa Military Academy as early as the late 1920s. See Erich Stoelzner, "Period After the Departure of Most of the German Military Advisors from Wuhan (Hankow-Wuchang-Hanyang) in June 1938," [3], Erich Stoelzner Memoirs, 1964, Folder 1, Hoover Institution Library & Archives; and Stoelzner, "General Stoelzner's Personal Recollections," [10], same folder, same archive.

[53] The Korean Liberation Army was a small army that at its peak had only around 1,000 men.

a "third way" simply did not register. It is in this gap that certain affinities with proto- and early European fascist doctrines, likewise emphasizing equality, come into view.

Yi Pŏm-sŏk himself had spent most of his life in China, as a student and later instructor at Chinese military academies, and as an officer and commander of Korean troops within successive Chinese formations.[54] From 1940, he served as a company commander and instructor at the Central Training Corps (Zhongyang Xunlian Tuan). Guomindang authoritarian pedagogy shaped the world in which Korean exiles in the Chinese military apparatus came of age. Shao Yulin (1909–1984), earlier advisor to the Korean Provisional Government (Taehan Min'guk Imsijŏngbu) in Chongqing and liaison between Chiang Kai-shek and the Koreans, and later the first Chinese ambassador to the ROK, noted in his diary after Yi visited the new Chinese Embassy in Seoul that the premier had organized Chokch'ŏng to transplant the training methods of the Guomindang's Central Training Corps to South Korea.[55]

Seen from Nanjing, then Chongqing and Xi'an, fascism appeared less as a fixed doctrinal system than as a toolbox of techniques for state-building. Nationalist elites around Chiang Kai-shek borrowed from a global menu of authoritarian experiments: Mussolini's corporate state, Japanese military discipline, Soviet methods of cadre formation, and, increasingly, German military and statist models, above all those of Nazi Germany. Chiang was a pragmatic leader: even his anti-communism, real as it was, remained tactical rather than messianic—not the totalizing obsession that some Americans wanted to hear. As one contemporary journalist later recalled, an interview she conducted reappeared in print in New York with "questions I did not ask" and "answers Chiang Kai-shek did not give," retrofitted by *Time-Life* editors into "a massively anti-Communist diatribe."[56] In the mid-1920s, during

[54] For a solid biography of Yi Pŏm-sŏk, see Hwang Min-ho, *Ch'ŏlgi Yi Pŏm-sŏk p'yŏngjŏn* [A critical biography of Ch'ŏlgi Yi Pŏm-sŏk] (Seoul: Sŏnin, 2021).

[55] See Shao Yulin, *Shi Han huiyilu: Jindai Zhong-Han guanxi shihua / My Mission to Korea: A Personal Record of Modern Sino–Korean Relations* (Taipei: Zhuanji Wenxue Chubanshe, 1980), 109.

[56] Annalee Jacoby Fadiman, in *China Reporting: An Oral History of American Journalism in the 1930s and 1940s*, ed. Stephen R. MacKinnon and Oris Friesen (Berkeley: University of California Press, 1987), 138.

(Fig. 36) Wedemeyer (right), the future author of the American "Victory Plan" and commander of the Allied forces in China, as student of the Nazi Kriegsakademie Berlin, fall 1937, alongside an Argentine officer and two Chinese Guomindang majors: Zhou Jiabin (far left), trained in frontline command and strategy, and right next to the U.S. officer, Jiang Bi, specialized in engineering and military logistics.

(Fig. 37) Chiang Kai-shek's son, Chiang Wei-kuo (Jiang Weiguo), at the Munich Kriegsakademie in 1938, wearing a German Wehrmacht uniform.

the First United Front with the communists, Chiang even sent his older son to study in Stalin's Soviet Union. In the mid-1930s, as German military cooperation deepened, he dispatched his younger son, Chiang Wei-kuo (Jiang Weiguo, 1916–1997; see fig. 37), to Hitler's Germany, where he received training in a tank division and at a Nazi officers' school in Munich, studying German formations, staff methods, tactical planning, and field doctrine. In 1939—days before the invasion of Poland, and after most German military advisors had left China—Chiang then sent him to the U.S. Army Air Corps School in Alabama, as U.S. support against both Japan and the communists became a priority.[57]

[57] See Jiang Weiguo, with Liu Fenghan, *Jiang Weiguo koushu zizhuan* [Chiang Wei-kuo's oral autobiography], 2nd ed. (Beijing: Zhongguo Dabaike Quanshu Chubanshe, 2016), 70–87.

Half a century later, Chiang Wei-kuo would still call "the period between 1932 and 1937 the high point of Sino-German relations,"[58] and, tellingly, praise the Wehrmacht's staff ethos—"the individual is completely insignificant"[59]—as if its politics of erasure were a virtue.

Chinese Guomindang "developmental nationalism" fused industrialization, militarization, anti-communism, and a re-sacralized Confucian "national spirit" into an authoritarian project of national rescue, one that took the form of an *authoritarian modernism*: anti-liberal and anti-communist, yet openly committed to technology, mass media, and the large-scale mobilization of society. The Blue Shirts (Lanyishe) and allied networks gave that project institutional form, building concentric front organizations that ranged from elite conspiratorial cores to mass associations and extending it into political surveillance, internal security, cultural intervention, and the organized disciplining of the population.[60]

Sino–German ties fit easily into this picture. Long before the Nanjing Decade, Chiang Kai-shek had spent formative years in Japan, absorbing the prestige of the Meiji state and its Prussian-style command structures. From the late 1920s into the late 1930s, German officers and industrialists became the Nationalist regime's most important foreign partners. Sino–German cooperation peaked during the 1930s, when German military missions reorganized parts of the Nationalist army, oversaw the creation of "model divisions," and linked arms production to export deals that sent Chinese raw materials to the Reich and brought German machinery back to the Yangzi Delta. By the eve of the Second Sino-Japanese War, this cooperation had produced a sizeable "Germanized" core within the Nationalist forces: eight "model divisions," totaling approximately 80,000 men, had been trained to German standards and equipped as an elite striking force, while an additional two hundred thousand troops were undergoing German-style training—altogether some three hundred thousand soldiers shaped by German doctrine, organization, and materiel. These were not paper reforms. In 1937,

---

58 "Interview mit General Jiang Weiguo (16. April 1994 in Taibei)" [Interview with General Chiang Wei-kuo (April 16, 1994, in Taibei)], in *Deutsch-chinesische Beziehungen 1928-1937: "Gleiche" Partner unter "ungleichen" Bedingungen: Eine Quellensammlung*, eds. Bernd Martin and Susanne Kuß (Berlin: Akademie Verlag, 2003), 478.

59 Ibid., 477.

60 See Clinton, *Revolutionary Nativism*, 87–89.

Chiang committed precisely these elite formations to the set-piece defense of Shanghai—against the advice of at least some German advisors—and the battle consumed a significant share of the very troops the mission had been designed to create. China absorbed 37 percent of Germany's arms exports that year, compared with 13 percent for Japan. Despite Japan's protests, German military advisors continued to work in China—forty-six at the outbreak of the Second Sino-Japanese War—alongside nearly fifteen hundred German civilian specialists.

Yet armies and procurement were only half the story; the same drive toward discipline and mobilization also targeted youth. Youth politics were central to this effort, and here, too, the Chinese case dovetailed with the broader fascist repertoire. The Scouts of China, reorganized in 1934 as a national association, offered Nationalist elites a ready-made instrument to channel students away from unions and street protest into hierarchized "character building." Scout training privileged obedience over debate, self-cultivation over collective demands, and national solidarity over class consciousness. As Brian Tsui has shown, the movement's rituals and routines left ample room for statism and militarism to be projected onto it: Scouts patrolled the streets to enforce Chiang Kai-shek's New Life Movement (Xin Shenghuo Yundong), inspecting hygiene, dress, and comportment and turning everyday urban space into an arena of moral policing. Yi Pŏm-sŏk treated this Guomindang program of youth discipline less as background than as a template for post-1945 Korea. Speaking to Mark Gayn in 1946 about his Suwŏn leadership school, he put the borrowing plainly: "It's our purpose to open schools for leaders. We shall teach them obedience to orders, ability to be practical, good morals—much like General Chiang Kai-shek's New Life Movement."[61]

Some of the Koreans who would later play prominent roles in southern Korea's right-wing youth groups and armed forces were not just embedded in the Guomindang army but also steeped in its fascistized political culture (even if Japanese-trained officers remained far more numerous). German-trained officers such as Ch'oe Tŏk-sin (1914–1989) thus foreshadowed a broader Cold War pattern—anti-communist cadres whose political imagination was shaped less by parliamentary

[61] Yi Pŏm-sŏk, November 7, 1946, quoted by Mark Gayn, in this volume, 422.

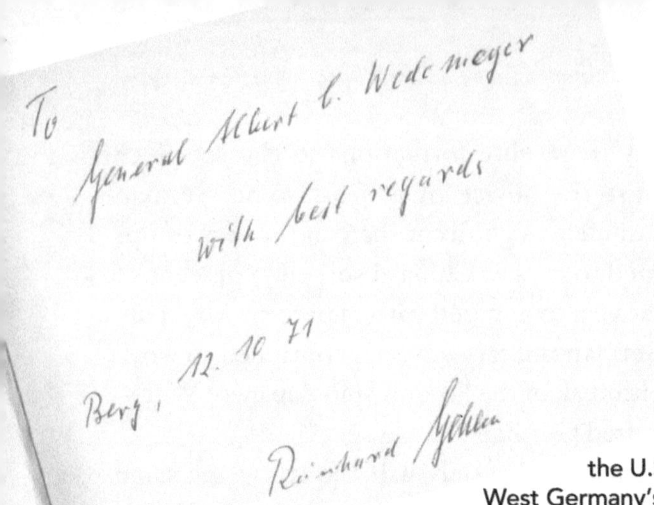

(Fig. 38) Reinhard Gehlen's inscription to Wedemeyer in his memoir *Der Dienst* [The service], 1971, a book formerly in the general's private library. Gehlen had been the chief of Hitler's Fremde Heere Ost (FHO), in charge of military intelligence on the Red Army. In 1946 the U.S. installed him as head of West Germany's intelligence agency, the Gehlen Org, and in 1956 as president of the Federal Intelligence Service (BND). His book was quickly translated into English by the infamous British historian and later Holocaust denier David Irving.

liberalism than by military academies, security services, and youth organizations already retooled along fascist lines.

In February 1938, Hitler announced in the Reichstag that Germany would recognize the Japanese puppet state of Manchukuo, a declaration that signaled a strategic realignment. Berlin had now pivoted toward Japan. The German advisory commission had expanded to well over 130 advisers, yet withdrawal followed swiftly in July 1938. This "end," however, did not dissolve the institutional residue of Sino–German collaboration. The bureau of the Trading Company for Industrial Products (HAPRO) remained open during World War II—an index of how procurement channels, industrial linkages, and Nazi–Guomindang relations could outlive formal alliance. Nor did admiration for fascist doctrines and techniques evaporate with Germany's diplomatic turn. In 1943, major wartime intellectuals such as Lin Tongji (1906–1980) and Lei Haizong (1902–1962), both U.S.-trained, invoked Erich Ludendorff's (1865–1937) concept of "total war"—to be discussed below—as a model of mobilization just as Goebbels' Sportpalast speech was thrusting it to the center of Nazi wartime propaganda. A Taiwanese semi-official history of the military academies, published in 2015, notes that years later, after the war and the Guomindang's retreat to Taiwan, Chiang Kai-shek still sought German military advisors, beginning with Walther Wenck (1900–1982), "jointly recommended by Major General Reinhard Gehlen, the first director of West Germany's intelligence service, and General Chiang Wei-kuo."[62] All of these actors were closely connected to General Wedemeyer (see fig. 38): Gehlen (1902–1979) knew him well, Wenck had been his classmate at the Kriegsakademie (German General Staff School), and Chiang Kai-shek's Wehrmacht-trained son had worked with him in Chongqing. The job finally went to Oskar Munzel (1899–1992), "classified as a war criminal and imprisoned by the Allied forces for two years,"[63] as the Taiwanese volume matter-of-factly notes; the same book reproduces a photograph of him in Wehrmacht uniform without any apparent unease.

On the American side, General Albert C. Wedemeyer personifies the bridge between Nationalist China and the U.S. occupation of Korea. A 1956 historian bluntly captured the premise of that role: "it was Wedemeyer's brilliant record in the German Kriegsakademie which was chiefly responsible for his warm reception in China."[64] Wedemeyer aligned himself with the German advisors, crediting them for "China's gallant three months' stand against Japan in 1937 at Shanghai and then at Nanking [Nanjing]," while harshly criticizing his predecessor Stilwell for his alleged inefficiency and "dictatorial attitude toward Chiang Kai-shek."[65] (Stilwell, who in turn dismissed Wedemeyer as "the world's most pompous prick,"[66] was later considered for the Korea occupation command, but his friction with Chiang helped push MacArthur toward the politically less encumbered Hodge.) Upon arriving in Chongqing, the Berlin-trained American general quickly sidelined liberal-minded U.S. advisors and officers, including John S. Service (1909–1999; see my Robinson/Gayn biographical essay)—a fluent Chinese speaker who had visited the communist leaders in Yan'an. Wedemeyer was, after all, one

---

[62] Jia Zhongwei, *Weiguo zhanshi de yaolan: Sanjun guanxiao de caochuang yu yange* [Cradle of national defenders: The founding and evolution of the three military academies] (Taipei: Cangbi Chuban Youxian Gongsi, 2015), 89.

[63] Ibid. West German military advisors remained active in Taiwan into the mid-1970s. For related materials, see the Wang Yue-che papers (1960s–2020s), Hoover Institution Library & Archives.

[64] F. F. Liu, *A Military History of Modern China, 1924–1949* (Princeton: Princeton University Press, 1956), 61.

[65] Albert C. Wedemeyer, *Wedemeyer Reports!* (New York: Henry Holt, 1958), 324.

[66] Joseph Stilwell, diary entry of May 14, 1944, Stilwell Papers, quoted in Michael Schaller, *The U.S. Crusade in China, 1938–1945* (New York: Columbia University Press, 1979), 164.

of the very few American officers to have studied at the German General Staff School: Wedemeyer arrived in Berlin on July 2, 1936, during the Olympic Games, and stayed for two and a half years. As a student at the Berlin Kriegsakademie he "met some high-ranking Nazis like Hess, Goebbels, Göring, Ley, Bormann,"[67] and, as one of his biographers noted, immediately "recognized the superiority of what he was being taught at the Kriegsakademie over what he had learned at West Point and Leavenworth [...]: economic factors in war, the use of propaganda, and long-range strategic post-war objectives. [...] Mobility and aggressiveness were the new concepts."[68] The school's training also steeped him in the geopolitics circulating in German officer education, including the Haushoferian concepts of *Lebensraum* and the strategic "heartland" imagination that made continental buffer states and anti-Soviet positioning feel like first principles rather than policy choices. He not only observed but absorbed the operational art of the Wehrmacht and the worldview that underwrote it, in which Bolshevism was the supreme global enemy and "Judeo-Bolshevism" a civilizational threat. Wedemeyer's papers at the Hoover Institution Library & Archives make plain that he became a lifelong anti-Semite and segregationist who treated racial hierarchy and authoritarian discipline as natural foundations of order. His correspondence shows that after the war—and especially after his retirement—Wedemeyer appears as a co-organizer and active participant in several extreme right-wing, segregationist movements: a major player in the China Lobby, the John Birch Society ("Ku Kluxers out of nightshirts,"[69] as a later U.S. president called them), right-wing radio circles, the For America policy committee, and others. (The clearer visibility of these commitments in the later record may owe less to any change in Wedemeyer's views or activities than to the waning of military censorship once he was no longer in uniform.) He also fed documents from U.S. government files into the McCarthyian ecosystem. He copied, for example, a letter from the U.S. ambassador to

---

[67] John J. McLaughlin, "General Albert Coady Wedemeyer 1897–1989: Soldier, Scholar, Statesman" (PhD diss., Drew University, 2008), 53 (hereafter cited as McLaughlin).

[68] Ibid., 19–20.

[69] Harry Truman (in office 1945–1953), quoted by Robert H. Terte in the *New York Times*, November 14, 1961.

China to Alfred Kohlberg (1887–1960), who was actively targeting Gayn, Robinson, and many other liberals (see pp. 18–19 in this volume), with the explicit instruction to "destroy this letter"[70] after reading. McCarthy himself, in turn, devotes nearly forty pages of his *America's Retreat from Victory* to canonizing Wedemeyer and the *Wedemeyer Report*.[71]

Wedemeyer's racialized anti-communism was so fervent that some right-wing civilians recoiled.[72] By the 1980s, he was hosting and corresponding with figures straight out of Kubrick's *Dr. Strangelove*, such as James von Brunn (1920–2010), an open white supremacist widely regarded as a nutball—yet treated sympathetically by more than one U.S. general. Fantasizing about World War III, Brunn warned Wedemeyer that "Germans who escape nuclear holocaust" would face a "negro invasion" that would "destroy the irriplacable [*sic*] white gene pool." He then complimented Mrs. Wedemeyer on her "lovely blue eyes."[73] Wedemeyer raised no objection and continued the correspondence. Brunn would later carry out two armed attacks, culminating in June 2009, when, at 88, he entered the U.S. Holocaust Memorial Museum and murdered a security guard.

---

[70] Letter by Albert C. Wedemeyer to Alfred Kohlberg, October 10, 1947, Box 93, Folder 18, Albert C. Wedemeyer Papers, Hoover Institution Library & Archives.

[71] Joseph McCarthy, *America's Retreat from Victory: The Story of George Catlett Marshall* (New York: Devin-Adair, 1951). Wedemeyer's report, which called for greater U.S. support for the Chinese Guomindang regime and the emerging South Korean right, made the general an icon in McCarthyite circles and the China Lobby, all the more because it was suppressed by Wedemeyer's former mentor, General George C. Marshall (1901–1953), and by President Truman; McCarthy made that suppression one of the central counts in his indictment of the administration, arguing that the disregard of Wedemeyer's recommendations had helped bring about the "loss" of China and, as Wedemeyer had warned, had left an opening for North Korea to attack the South. Wedemeyer's 1947 report reached the public only belatedly and in separate publications, under pressure from the political right: the China section appeared in 1949, and the Korea section was issued separately in 1951, after the Korean War had begun.

[72] After receiving one of Wedemeyer's propaganda pamphlets, Victor Emanuel (1898–1967)—a wealthy industrialist, military contractor, financier, and hardline anti-communist associated with the *Time-Life* orbit—wrote back at length to explain how "completely useless" such material, full of false claims, was. See Letter by Victor Emanuel to Albert C. Wedemeyer, September 11, 1952, 1, Box 105, Folder 11, Albert C. Wedemeyer Papers, Hoover Institution Library & Archives.

[73] Letter by James von Brunn to Albert C. Wedemeyer, June 14, 1981, Box 105, Folder 11, Albert C. Wedemeyer Papers, Hoover Institution Library & Archives.

That outlook had not developed in a vacuum. In the United States from the late 1930s until Pearl Harbor in December 1941, foreign-policy debate can be broadly framed as a struggle between *isolationists*, many of them gathering under the banner of America First and seeking to keep the country out of another overseas war, and *interventionists*, who argued that fascist expansion had to be confronted before it was too late. In significant parts of the America First movement, this stance was bound up with racial hierarchy, antisemitism, and eugenicist thinking—an entanglement with clear echoes in the United States today; this helps explain why sympathy for Nazi Germany was often closer to the surface than later memory allowed. In Berlin, Wedemeyer had moved in circles where the Third Reich's war planners intersected with prominent American isolationists. These circles included U.S. Military Attaché Truman Smith (1893–1970) and, at their celebrity edge, the aviation hero Charles Lindbergh (1902–1974), who accepted a military decoration from Luftwaffe chief Göring (1893–1946).[74] Although Wedemeyer was no Nazi party man, his worldview was so closely aligned with core elements of Nazi ideology—race, authoritarian order, anti-Bolshevism, *Lebensraum* logic of expansion, and contempt for liberal democracy—that the distinction between "Third Reich" and "American" became a matter of flag rather than fundamentals. He remained a fierce opponent of Roosevelt and the New Deal and carried the Kriegsakademie's imprint back into American war planning. As the architect of the 1941 "Victory Plan," widely credited with shaping the strategic framework for defeating Nazi Germany, he drew on the Wehrmacht's operational planning and *Blitzkrieg* methods in preparing the Normandy landings. As one account put it, "It is ironic that the plan for the defeat of Germany was provided *by the Nazis to the Allies* through Albert C. Wedemeyer."[75]

---

[74] Lindbergh was a fervent Nordicist, eugenicist, and prominent Nazi-sympathizing America First voice; he later maintained secret families in Germany and Switzerland (fathering seven children—his own "Nordic" gene pool in miniature). Retired San Francisco judge Lise Pearlman argues that the 1932 "kidnapping" narrative concealed the aviation hero's own role in the death of his son, whom she portrays as possibly disabled. See Lise Pearlman, *The Lindbergh Kidnapping Suspect No. 1: The Man Who Got Away* (Berkeley: Regent Press, 2020).

[75] McLaughlin, 32.

For Wedemeyer, Korean exiles in China mattered less as agents of an independent national project than as deployable anti-communist auxiliaries. Long before 1945, Koreans had been drawn into the intelligence world under Dai Li (1897–1946)—routinely described as anything from a "ruthless henchman"[76] to "China's combination of Himmler and J. Edgar Hoover"[77]—where informants, smugglers, couriers, and political operatives of every stripe were mobilized for counterinsurgency. Korean military personnel moving through Nationalist Chinese command structures and intelligence channels thus belonged to the same orbit. With Chiang Kai-shek's approval, Wedemeyer folded these exile circles into the OSS, beginning his collaboration with Yi Pŏm-sŏk and other Korean officers in 1944.[78] Once he took direct control of OSS and U.S. military intelligence organizations in the China–Burma–India command, Wedemeyer also approved and oversaw Project Eagle, one of eight POW rescue missions dispatched to Vietnam, Manchukuo, and elsewhere in the immediate aftermath of Japan's surrender.[79] Eagle was the Korea mission, and under Wedemeyer's authority Yi Pŏm-sŏk served as its principal Korean partner, entering Korea with OSS officers and three Korean Liberation Army officers. In August 1945, Yi entered southern Korea with an OSS team; the operation collapsed at once, exposing the limits of this improvised fusion of wartime intelligence, exile militarism, and occupation planning. Even so, Yi remained on Wedemeyer's radar. On February 12, 1946, Wedemeyer visited Seoul, met General John R. Hodge, and pressed for Yi's placement in the Constabulary. The next day Wedemeyer met with Chiang Kai-shek in Shanghai—where Yi also resided[80]—before returning to Seoul on March 20/21 amid repatriation

---

[76] William C. Spracher, "The OSS in Support of the Chinese Communists," *American Intelligence Journal* 3, no. 3 (Winter 1980/81): 17.

[77] Barbara Tuchman, *Stilwell and the American Experience in China, 1911–1945* (London: Phoenix Press, 2001), 261.

[78] See also Gayn on Yi Pŏm-sŏk's ties to Dai Li, in this volume, 421. Hugh Deane also reported that Yi worked for Dai Li; see the *China Weekly Review*, March 22, 1947.

[79] For English-language publications on Eagle Project, see Mark E. Caprio, "The Eagle Has Landed: Groping for a Korean Role in the Pacific War," *Journal of American–East Asian Relations* 21, no. 1 (March 2014): 5–33; Robert S. Kim, *Project Eagle: The American Christians of North Korea in World War II* (Lincoln: Potomac Books, 2017).

[80] See Kukpangbu, Chŏnsa P'yŏnch'an Wiwŏnhoe, *Han'guk chŏnjaengsa*, 1: *Haebang-gwa kŏn'gun* [History of the Korean War, vol. 1: Liberation and founding of the armed forces] (Seoul: Kukpangbu, 1967), 307; *Chayu sinmun*, February 15, 1946.

discussions about Koreans still in China.[81] Yi returned to Korea on June 3, 1946, and on October 9 formally established the Korean National Youth Corps, initiated, planned, and funded by USAMGIK. The military government backed its Central Training Center in Suwŏn and its headquarters in Ŭljiro, Seoul, with five million yen for the first six months of operations, as mentioned, along with U.S.-supplied equipment. By early 1950, the State Department was still debating whether to keep supporting the National Youth movement or only the "Leaders' School of National Defense Corps (National Guard), which is made up of National Youth members only."[82]

What mattered here was less a chain of national influences than the movement of people through connected institutions. German advisers, Guomindang security men, Korean exiles, OSS officers, and later U.S. occupation planners moved through overlapping worlds of intelligence, youth mobilization, and authoritarian statecraft. From the mid-1920s into the late 1930s, Chinese Nationalist politics generated what Maggie Clinton has called a "revolutionary nativism": an *authoritarian modernization* project that fused anti-colonial nationalism and industrial development with a violently anti-communist, hierarchical reordering of society.[83] Some of the Korean exiles who later re-entered Korea as anti-communist cadres were formed in precisely that world.

Walter Stennes (aka Walther Stennes, 1895–1983) offers a revealing point of entry. His trajectory alone shows how porous the borders were between proto-fascism, authoritarianism, and the anti-communist worlds in which figures such as Yi Pŏm-sŏk moved. The television mini series *Babylon Berlin* recently resurrected Stennes in all his chilling brutality[84] (S04-E12, 2022): the man who had been a senior Berlin police officer

---

[81] See *Chayu sinmun*, March 19 and 21, 1946; *Seoul sinmun*, March 20 and 22, 1946.
[82] "The Chargé in Korea (Drumright) to the Secretary of State" (February 10, 1950), in *Foreign Relations of the United States, 1950*, vol. VII, *Korea*, comp. United States, Department of State (Washington, DC: Government Printing Office, 1976), 27.
[83] See Maggie Clinton, *Revolutionary Nativism: Fascism and Culture in China, 1925–1937* (Durham: Duke University Press, 2017; hereafter cited as Clinton, *Revolutionary Nativism*).
[84] At the time Stennes commanded 25,000 SA men. In 1931, a Berlin newspaper alleged that for years he had been responsible for "forming *Rollkommandos* which carried out systematically organized raids with the aim of carrying out deliberate,

(Fig. 39) Kwangju, summer 1947. Members of the fascist, paramilitary Korean National Youth Corps (Chokch'ŏng), financed by the U.S. Army and headed by former Guomindang general and future ROK prime minister Yi Pŏm-sŏk, at the inaugural ceremony for the organization's Chŏnnam division. Standing in the center, on the left in the front row, is Kim Nog-yŏng, later a politician who actively fought against Rhee and subsequent autocratic regimes. (Photo: Yi Kyŏng-mo)

and, from 1928, head of the Berlin SA—the storm troopers, or Brown Shirts—openly defied Goebbels and Hitler in spring 1931 in the so-called Stennes Revolt. Stennes' break with Hitler was not a rejection of fascism; it was a quarrel within it: between a plebeian, anti-bourgeois radicalism and Hitler's increasingly pragmatic alliance with industrial capital.[85]

premeditated killings of political opponents" (*Welt am Abend*, April 17, 1931). Until the split, Stennes was to Hitler what Kim Tu-han (1918–1972) would later be to Syngman Rhee. For a detailed account of Stennes' activities in the fascist movement, see Bernhard Sauer, "Goebbels 'Rabauken': Zur Geschichte der SA in Berlin-Brandenburg" [Goebbels' "hooligans": On the history of the SA in Berlin-Brandenburg], *Berlin in Geschichte und Gegenwart: Jahrbuch des Landesarchivs Berlin* 25 (2006): 107–64.

[85] A survey of the Stennes files (1933–1972) at Munich's Institute of Contemporary History reveals a fascist movement far removed from the monolithic myth. These

After Hitler came to power, Stennes left Germany and from December 1933 to 1949 served Chiang Kai-shek in China: first as head of Chiang's 400-man bodyguard unit and of a 3,000-man special regiment guarding Chiang's headquarters, and later also as head of his personal Air Transport Squadron and as a political advisor involved in reorganizing Guomindang police forces.[86] He remained in China even after the official German military mission was withdrawn in 1938, thus spanning the German, Stilwell, and Wedemeyer phases of foreign military influence on Nationalist China.

The Harvard University Archives preserve Stennes' long postwar correspondence with Heinrich Brüning (in office 1930–1932), the democratic former chancellor of the Weimar Republic.[87] Oddly enough, the former SA deputy chief even sought recognition as a "victim of the Nazi regime" and tried to secure reparations from West Germany, asking Brüning to testify for him. That strange intimacy suggests that by 1930 the democratic center may already have been trying to survive the fascist challenge by bargaining with parts of the radical right rather than confronting it outright. Serving Chiang Kai-shek as chief of his European intelligence service during the war and moving in the orbit of his secret service chief Dai Li, Stennes, like Yi Pŏm-sŏk, cultivated overlapping intelligence relationships with the major Allied powers—including the Soviets. "As Chiang Kai-shek's intelligence chief, I exchange information with intelligence agents from the U.S., England, and France," Stennes told the Soviets. "I could, on a gentlemanly basis, share information with the Soviet Union as well."[88] Documents released

---

records, bolstered by contemporary accounts and personal recollections, show a fractured and ideologically inconsistent movement that achieved a semblance of cohesion only once it secured control of the state. Stennes thus shows that the German case was, in fact, little different from, say, the Chinese or Korean cases. See esp. these files: ZS-1147, https://www.ifz-muenchen.de/archiv/zs/zs-1147_1.pdf and https://www.ifz-muenchen.de/archiv/zs/zs-1147_2.pdf.

[86] See Charles Drage, *The Amiable Prussian* (London: Anthony Blond, 1958), 108–109, 115, 130 (hereafter cited as Drage, *Amiable Prussian*).

[87] See the correspondence between Walther Stennes and Heinrich Brüning (1949–1964), Heinrich Brüning Personal Archive and Brüning Family Archive, HUGFP 93.10, Box 38, Folder 2, Harvard University Archives.

[88] Walter Stennes, as reported in a January 1939 memorandum by NKVD agent Nikolai Tishchenko and reproduced in Aleksandr Pronin, "Sovetnik Chan Kaishi"

by the Russians in the late 1990s show him, from early 1939, cooperating in Shanghai with the NKVD/NKGB under the codename DRUG ("friend"). Stennes' British biographer notes, incidentally, that he also used Korean couriers.[89]

As in Korea, the move from occupation to formal sovereignty did not break old anti-communist networks but reembedded them in new U.S.-backed security states. After relocating to West Germany, Stennes inserted himself into the new intelligence landscape. The NKVD already knew by 1947—when he was still working for Chiang in Shanghai—that "the Americans had offered him a job in the newly created West German Intelligence Service (the future BND, under Reinhard Gehlen)"[90]—Hitler's former head of Fremde Heere Ost, responsible for military intelligence on the Red Army. We do not know for sure whether General Wedemeyer—later involved in advising on German personnel for sensitive positions, and close to Gehlen (both were Berlin Kriegsakademie graduates)—played any role in Stennes' appointment (see fig. 36). Yet Stennes did join the new West German service amid its massive recruitment of former Nazis, choreographed in detail by the occupying U.S. Army and, soon after, the newly formed CIA,[91] while he also continued to cooperate with Soviet intelligence until Moscow dropped him in 1952. In West Germany no less than in South Korea, the United States folded fascist personnel into new security structures under its tutelage.

Kim Hong-il (1898–1980)—German-speaking and, for decades, the most senior Korean officer inside Chiang Kai-shek's National Revolutionary Army (NRA)—shows especially clearly how German military advisors shaped Nationalist China and how that influence later resurfaced in early South Korean doctrine. That advisory channel was politically marked from the outset. It opened under Colonel Max

---

[Advisor to Chiang Kai-shek], *Trud*, no. 045 (March 11, 2000) (hereafter cited as Pronin, "Sovetnik Chan Kaishi"). Multiple later Russian, German, and American studies, including published document collections, corroborate the account.

[89] See Drage, *Amiable Prussian*, 150.

[90] Pronin, "Sovetnik Chan Kaishi."

[91] See Gerhard Sälter, *NS-Kontinuitäten im BND: Rekrutierung, Diskurse, Vernetzungen* [Nazi continuities in the Federal Intelligence Service (BND): Recruitment, discourses, networks] (Berlin: Ch. Links, 2022), esp. 455.

Bauer (1869–1929), a close confidant of Erich Ludendorff, whom Chiang brought to China in 1927 as his first German advisor. After Bauer's death in 1929, the role passed to Hermann Kriebel (1876–1941), a Bavarian officer of the radical right who had been convicted for his role in the failed 1923 Hitler–Ludendorff putsch, had shared Landsberg Prison with Hitler, and had been present there when Hitler wrote *Mein Kampf*. This informal and politically radical advisory mission was then systematized under General Hans von Seeckt (1866–1936), Chiang's chief military advisor from 1933 to 1935, who reorganized and trained the elite core of the NRA. Von Seeckt, architect of the Reichswehr's mobile-warfare doctrine later associated with the Blitzkrieg label, embedded its central features—centralized command, speed, and combined arms—into the Chinese military establishment. Between 1935 and 1937, Nationalist China was also the largest importer of German military equipment. In this German-shaped NRA environment, Kim Hong-il, assisted by Yi Pŏm-sŏk and others, trained around 100 Korean cadets at Whampoa's Luoyang branch campus in 1934/35. A former student and later high military officer recalled that

> the Luoyang Military Academy adopted the then-advanced German military education system. Many textbooks and reference materials were translations of German military manuals and publications, reflecting the advanced military theories and technologies of the era. The instructors were highly qualified and fluent in foreign languages, and the academy also brought in German military instructors. Core curriculum included: military courses—German-translated tactical lectures, combined arms tactics tutorials, weaponry tutorials, fortification tutorials, transportation tutorials, topography tutorials, military system tutorials [...] and political training courses.[92]

What traveled through this educational channel was, however, more than military instruction. It was a political grammar of hierarchy, obedience, and command, combined with the introduction of modern technology. Even figures on the Korean left were drawn to this image

[92] Han Shengtao, "Zhongyang Lujun Junguan Xuexiao junguan xunlianban di san qi xueyuan Han Shengtao huiyilu" [Han Shengtao's memoir: A cadet of the Central Army Officer Academy's third officer-training cohort], August 9, 2018, online at: https://m.krzzjn.com/show-1183-78877.html.

of *military modernity*—the military face of a broader authoritarian modernism in East Asia, with its promise of discipline, technological power, hierarchy, and national regeneration. The militarist-anarchist Kim Wŏn-bong (aka Yaksan, 1898–1958), another Whampoa graduate, learned German in his youth and at one point hoped to study at a military academy in Germany. Even his Ŭiyŏltan (Righteous Brotherhood), for all its anarchist and anti-colonial militancy, relied on a German bomb maker whose close associate later recalled him as "sympathetic with the Italian movement"[93]—that is, with fascism.

In the fall of 1944, Kim Hong-il met General Wedemeyer when Chinese authorities adopted Wedemeyer's reorganization plan for a Chinese Youth Army (Zhongguo Qingnianjun).[94] Because most soldiers in the Guomindang Army remained illiterate, Wedemeyer wanted to recruit students and educated youth into a new formation. Modeled in part on the Philippine Scouts and, more unsettlingly, on the Hitler Youth, the plan revived Nationalist youth-mobilization logics of the Blue Shirts type. Kim Hong-il, still operating under the name Wang Yishu, directed the general staff office of the Youth Training Department (Qingnian Xunlian Zongjianbu), while Huang Wei (1904–1989), Wedemeyer's Berlin Kriegsakademie classmate, implemented the training program. The structural affinity was obvious enough that a later Taiwanese alumnus could compare this Youth Army, with disarming candor, to the SS Hitler Youth division: "At the mention of a 'youth army,' many military enthusiasts may first think of Nazi Germany's SS-12—the Waffen-SS 'Hitler Youth' Division—whose defense of Normandy left lasting scars in the memories of Allied troops landing there."[95] Wilhelm Daniel (1916–2002), who toured Korea in 1940 as

[93] Nym Wales and Kim San, *Song of Ariran: The Life Story of a Korean Rebel* (New York: John Day, 1941), 59. A prominent former anarchist and later ROK parliamentarian identified him as a German Jew named Marcell (transcribed "Machäll"). See Frank Hoffmann, *Berlin Koreans and Pictured Koreans*, Koreans and Central Europeans: Informal Contacts up to 1950, vol. 1, ed. Andreas Schirmer (Vienna: Praesens, 2015), 70 (hereafter cited as Hoffmann, *Berlin Koreans*).

[94] See Kim Hong-il, *Taeryugŭi punno: nobyŏngŭi hoesanggi* [The continent's indignation: a veteran's memoir] (Seoul: Munjosa, 1972), 360–62.

[95] Wang Jian, in *Qingnianjun di er qi tongxue tongxunlu* [Youth Army, Second Cohort classmates' directory], comp. Minguo Junxi Tongxuehui Bubing di-208-shi Mofan

part of a Hitler Youth delegation in their stylish Hugo Boss uniforms (see fig. 35), met Korean youth, and was introduced by Kang Se-hyŏng to Governor-General Minami Jirō (in office 1936–1942), would a few years later serve as a high-ranking officer and unit doctor alongside thousands of seventeen-year-olds in exactly that tank division. The 12th SS Hitler Youth Division he later joined left a record in Normandy of extreme brutality and multiple war crimes, including the massacre of POWs.[96] The Chinese Youth Army, organized too late in the war to be sent into combat against Japan, was spared that fate. The same could not be said of many youths in Yi Pŏm-sŏk's Chokch'ŏng and other far-right youth groups during the Korean War.

Later, back in Korea—as an ROK Army general and principal of the new Korea Military Academy—Kim Hong-il distilled this Guomindang inheritance in his booklet *Kukpang kaeron* (Outline of national defense): mechanization, combined arms, and air–ground cooperation, explicitly linked to German "modern" doctrine. The main concept was still the *Wehrstaat*, the "national-defense state," organized around "total war" as whole-of-society mobilization and peacetime preparation. As Kim presented it, the intellectual lineage ran back to Erich Ludendorff. Ludendorff's 1935 pamphlet *Der totale Krieg* (Total war), often treated as a blueprint for Nazi military strategy, was translated into Chinese in 1936 by Zhang Junmai (Carsun Chang, 1887–1969). The Germanophile Hegelian philosopher rejected both capitalism and communism and had co-founded the National Socialist Party of China (Zhongguo Guojia Shehuidang), explicitly modeled on Hitler's NSDAP. What traveled with Ludendorff's text was not merely "total war" as strategy. It came packaged with ethnic racism and the call for a fascist state. Kim Hong-il's program for ROK national defense carried that package forward. In the same register, he presented "defense economics" (*Wehrwirtschaft*) with striking explicitness, closely tracking Kurt Hesse (1894–1976), a Wehrmacht officer, military economist, and propagandist who systema-

---

Lian Daduihui (Taipei: Minguo Junxi Tongxuehui Bubing di-208-shi Mofan Lian Daduihui, 1987), [1].

96 See Wilhelm Daniel, *Aus meinem Lebensbuch* [From my book of life] ([Vienna: Self-published], 1985), 72–76. To be sure, Daniel records these experiences without a trace of contrition; his memoir reads as an unabashed celebration of himself, the Hitler Youth, and fascist perpetrators.

tized Nazi war-economy doctrine: state control of key industries, prices, currency, and labor, paired with unity behind the leader.[97]

Yi Pŏm-sŏk's own biography brings these Chinese and German lineages into especially clear focus. His path ran through Chinese military academies, Guomindang command structures, Berlin encounters, and OSS collaboration, making him less an isolated zealot than a nodal figure in the transimperial field sketched here. Yi had a long career as an exiled army officer. In rapid succession he entered the Yunnan Military Academy (class of 1919), fought at Qingshanli (Ch'ŏngsan-ri in Korean memory), taught at the Sinhŭng Military Academy, commanded Korean units in Manchuria, served as a staff officer under Ma Zhanshan (1885–1950), and eventually chief of staff of the small Korean Liberation Army. But the political utility of his résumé depended less on its factual coherence than on its narratability. In the winter of 1941, Kim Ku and the Guomindang paired Yi with the young Chinese writer Bu Naifu, better known as Wumingshi (literally "Anonymous," 1917–2002) in a straightforward propaganda commission: Yi supplied the raw materials—campaigns, retreats, exile talk, set-pieces—and Wumingshi supplied plot, pacing, and voice. The arrangement produced flattering portraits of Korean fighters for wartime audiences. Decades later, however, the collaboration took a stranger turn. In 1971, Yi published his autobiography, *Udungbul* (Bonfire). Within it, some previously published Wumingshi stories returned. "Love of Russia" (Luxiya zhi lian), a 1933 Berlin story,[98] "The Knight's Lament" (Qishi di aiyuan), and at least one other short story now resurfaced under Yi Pŏm-sŏk's name, recasting these "fictions" as "memoir." Whole sequences are redeployed with the third-person narrator swapped for a first-person "I," as if the border between invention and testimony were only a matter of pronoun and cover page. Chapter 3 of *Udungbul*, "My

---

[97] See Kim Hong-il, *Kukpang kaeron* [Outline of national defense] (Seoul: Koryŏ Sŏjŏk, 1949), esp. 39–41. For a detailed discussion, see Kim Chi-hun, "Kim Hong-irŭi Chungguk Kungminhyŏngmyŏnggun'gwa *Kukpang kaeron* chŏsul" [Kim Hong-il's experience in the Chinese National Revolutionary Army and the writing of *Outline of National Defense*], *Kunsa* 112 (September 2019): 1–44.

[98] See https://commons.wikimedia.org/wiki/File:SSID-12582590_露西亞之戀.pdf, 96–124, a scan of the fourth (1948) edition of Wumingshi's short-story collection *Luxiya zhi lian*.

Beloved Horse Mujŏn" (Aema 'Mujŏn'), is a lightly reworked version of "The Knight's Lament." Chapter 6, "Nostalgia for the Volga" (Pulgaŭi hyangsu), performs the same operation on "Love of Russia," the Berlin story.[99] Wumingshi is mentioned in the introduction to the Berlin chapter, but just as a proofreader. Yi's appropriation was not merely personal fraud. It placed him in distinctively modern company—MacArthur, Wedemeyer, and a generation of military leaders who understood that narrative, no less than deeds, now made generals into politicians. Contemporaries noticed the same dynamic. An American OSS officer (later one of Nixon's Watergate plotters) who worked with Yi and the Korean Liberation Army in Xi'an offered the neatest deflation: he cast Yi as a grandiose phrasemonger, "an interesting character who spun a colorful yarn" about operations he meant to undertake, yet was "quite satisfied to preserve his current lifestyle" and had "done virtually nothing."[100]

All through the 1930s, life was difficult for Korean independence activists in exile. After the Wilsonian promise of self-determination collapsed in the wake of the March First Movement of 1919, liberal democracy no longer appeared to many Koreans as a credible road to liberation. Communism, too, increasingly appeared to many activists less as a viable politics of national emancipation than as another regime of discipline, repression, and internal coercion. Japan's occupation and remaking of Manchuria into Manchukuo, together with the wider Chinese nationalists' flirtation with fascism as a "third way" beyond both liberal democracy and communism, made that option look brutally modern and politically effective. In the world of Korean resistance after 1931, meanwhile, rival armies, rival political groups, rival personalities, collapsing fronts, and opportunistic "patriots" produced a constant fog of improvisation. Yi drifted into the orbit of the Chinese warlord General Ma Zhanshan, who managed—in the space of a single year—

[99] See Yi Pŏm-sŏk, *Udungbul* [Bonfire] (Seoul: Sasangsa, 1971), 93–124 (ch. 3), and 303–36 (ch. 6); Kim Chae-uk, "Chungguk hyŏndae Hanin chejae chakp'um yŏn'guesŏ Han'gukchŏk kwanjŏm hwakribŭi p'iryosŏng koch'al: Mumyŏngssiwa Yi Pŏm-sŏgŭi munhakchŏk kwan'gye yŏn'gurŭl chungsimŭro" [A Study on the need to establish Korean perspectives in research on modern Chinese works featuring Koreans: With focus on the literary relationship between Wumingshi and Yi Pŏm-sŏk], *Chungguk ŏmun hakchi* 73 (2020): 163–83.

[100] E. Howard Hunt, with Greg Aunapu, *American Spy: My Secret History in the CIA, Watergate, and Beyond* (Hoboken: John Wiley & Sons, 2007), 25.

to be denounced as a Manchukuo collaborator, then celebrated as China's anti-Japanese hero, and quietly rewarded for both roles.[101] In the defeats and retreats that followed, Yi was pushed across borders with Ma Zhanshan and his forces and, like many anti-Japanese fighters in the region, ended up in the Soviet Union—at one point interned in Tomsk, deep in Siberia.

Yi Pŏm-sŏk, as part of Ma's group, now rebranded as a Military Affairs Commission for the Guomindang, pulled into Berlin's Schlesischer Bahnhof on April 20, 1933—Hitler's forty-fourth birthday.[102] After eight months of internment in Siberia, Ma was allowed to leave the Soviet Union with sixty-five of his officers and their family members. While one might expect the new regime to still be wearing its honeymoon face, the aftermath of the Reichstag fire had already seen thousands of communists, socialists, and political opponents arrested; SA stormtroopers had dismantled trade unions; and Jewish professionals had been forced from their jobs. Yet these anti-Japanese resistance fighters were enthusiastically received. Public sympathy (and that of the nascent Nazi regime) lay firmly with the Chinese, who were viewed through the romanticized lens of a nation fighting for self-determination. The next day, Berlin's morning paper ran a photograph of the balding Yi Pŏm-sŏk in round nickel-rimmed glasses, seated between Ma and his three top generals at a meeting with the press in the Chinese Legation.[103]

The Wumingshi–Yi Pŏm-sŏk tale of émigré nostalgia, staged in a Russian café in midnight Berlin, tells us little about Yi's actual visit except for one detail: his meeting with a certain Myŏng. In *Udungbul*, Yi notes that Myŏng is a pseudonym and describes him as a philosophy lecturer at Berlin University. Fujii Takeshi later identified this figure as the already mentioned Kang Se-hyŏng, the liaison between the Hitler Youth and Japanese and Korean youth organizations. Kang would go on to serve as director of operations at the Japanese–German Cultural Institute (Nichi–Doku Bunka Kyōkai) in Tokyo and to act as an or-

---

[101] For a critical discussion of Ma Zhanshan, see Jianda Yuan, *Chinese Government Leaders in Manchukuo, 1931–1937: Intertwined National Ideals* (London: Routledge, 2023), 109–39.
[102] See *Deutsch-Chinesische Nachrichten*, April 22, 1933.
[103] See *Berliner Morgenpost*, April 21, 1933.

ganizer and guide during the Hitler Youth delegation's visit to Korea in October 1940. After liberation, he reappears in yet another setting: Yi's Korean National Youth Corps Central Training Center in Suwŏn, where he was in charge of much of the training program, modeled on the Hitler Youth, and taught Nazi ideology. Robinson and Gayn both noted him, and Joseph Fromm memorably described him as "a pudgy, round-faced Korean with an ingratiating manner and an oily handshake."[104]

Kang Se-hyŏng was by no means an eccentric exception. As my earlier Berlin study showed, the Korean presence in Berlin in the 1930s and 1940s reached deep into the operational life of the Axis: cultural propaganda, espionage, war technology, and race science. That circle included the composer An Ik-t'ae (1906–1965), who came from the United States into the Third Reich and completed the future South Korean national anthem in Berlin; the dancer Kuni Masami (aka Pak Yŏng-in, 1908–2007), who let himself be used in Goebbels' cultural propaganda while spying on the Nazis for their Japanese allies; engineer Chang Kŭk (1913–2008), brother of a later ROK prime minister, who worked within German–Japanese technological cooperation to assist in the construction of wartime bomber engines; the anthropologist and physician Kim Paek-p'yŏng (1900–1990), who joined the core Nazi eugenics and race research institute; and Kang Se-hyŏng himself, trained in philosophy, an avowed blood-and-soil propagandist who fused Nazism with Japanese colonial ideology and later resurfaced in Yi's post-liberation youth apparatus before becoming a member of parliament.[105]

An Ik-t'ae's case adds another layer. He lived for years in the villa of Ehara Kōichi (1896–1969), which from the fall of 1943 would become the Manchukuo Legation.[106] Ehara, officially the number two man at the Manchukuo Legation in Berlin, was in practice the Kwantung

[104] Fromm, "Suwon, Korea," 1.

[105] For detailed discussions, see Hoffmann, *Berlin Koreans*, 106–153.

[106] On the night of November 22–23, 1943, Allied bombing destroyed the Manchukuo Legation at Lessingstraße 1 in Berlin's affluent Hansaviertel. Its official emergency quarters were then transferred to the requisitioned Jewish-owned Grunewald villa of Ehara Kōichi. From that point on, the Legation and its diplomats are listed at Ehara's address in *Verzeichnis der Mitglieder des Diplomatischen Korps in Berlin, Januar 1945* [Directory of the diplomatic corps in Berlin, January 1945], comp. Auswärtiges Amt (Berlin: Reichsdruckerei, 1945), 38.

Army's intelligence chief in Europe. The legation functioned not merely as a diplomatic mission but as a Japanese intelligence node, cooperating with the Polish underground, the Home Army (Armia Krajowa), to pass information to the London-based Polish government-in-exile while gathering intelligence on the German administration of the occupied territories in the East and especially on the war against the Soviet Union. Numerous Polish underground agents such as the leading officer Major Michał Rybikowski (1900–1991) received Manchukuo citizenship,[107] and agents such as the Home Army Captain Alfons Jerzy Jakubianiec (aka Kuba, 1905–1945), and Sabina—her real name being Salomea Łapińska (1914–?)—and several others even worked and lived directly in the Manchukuo Legation.[108] From spring 1939 until the Soviet route closed in June 1941, thousands of Jews also received Manchukuo visas for travel to or through East Asia. As the former legation secretary Wang Tifu (1911–2001) recalled, the head of the mission "instructed me [...] to issue Manchukuo entry visas to Jews departing Germany" and "then described in detail how Ribbentrop and State Secretary Weizsäcker had summoned him two days earlier"[109] to secure exactly that cooperation.[110] An Ik-t'ae thus appears not simply as a career-driven,

---

[107] Rybikowski's Manchukuo passport is on display at the Polish Army Museum in Warsaw. See also "German Passport of a Jewish Consul Widow–Wang Tifu 王替夫," accessed December 19, 2025, https://www.passport-collector.com/passport-of-a-jewish-widow-of-a-german-consul/.

[108] Of the six Polish agents employed at the Manchukuo Legation, three were arrested by the Gestapo on July 6–7, 1941, among them Jakubianiec and Łapińska; Jakubianiec was later shot by a guard in Sachsenhausen concentration camp. See also Halina Czarnocka, ed., *Armia Krajowa w dokumentach, 1939-1945* [The Home Army in documents, 1939–1945], vol. 1 (London: Studium Polski Podziemnej, 1970), 460, 495; vol. 2 (London: Studium Polski Podziemnej, 1973), 81–82; Andrzej Suchcitz et al., eds., *Armia Krajowa w dokumentach 1939-1945* [The Home Army in documents, 1939–1945], vol. 1, pt. 2, 2nd ed. (Warsaw: Instytut Pamięci Narodowej, Komisja Ścigania Zbrodni przeciwko Narodowi Polskiemu, 2015), 522–23.

[109] Wang Tifu, with Yang Mingsheng, *Jianguo Xitele yu jiuguo Youtairen de Wei Man waijiaoguan* [I met Hitler and saved Jews: A Manchukuo puppet state diplomat] (Harbin: Heilongjiang Renmin Chubanshe, 2002), 159; see also 160–65.

[110] A key document, a detailed twelve-page memorandum sent by Reich Security Main Office chief Reinhard Heydrich (1904–1942) to Foreign Minister von Ribbentrop (1893–1946) shortly after the arrests, confirms that by July 1941, and in some respects as early as the fall of 1940, German counterintelligence was fully aware of the role played by the Manchukuo Legation in Berlin, the Manchukuo Consulate

opportunistic musician in fascist Europe, but as another Korean figure lodged within a world in which Japanese militarism, German fascism, propaganda, espionage, and personal advancement converged. In his case, ideological commitment and self-interest seem less opposed than mutually reinforcing.

These trajectories also warn against reading political identities as fixed. Under the pressure of anti-communism, elements that might seem irreconcilable—collaboration, anti-Japanese resistance, fascist admiration, and later Cold War allegiance—could be retrospectively reordered and made to coexist within a single political career. One of the better-known German-speaking Whampoa graduates was the aforementioned Ch'oe Tŏk-sin, a hardline anti-communist and career officer who rose to general in the South Korean Army. He later bore command responsibility for the 1951 Kŏch'ang Massacre, in which hundreds of villagers were murdered in southeastern Korea, and later still served as ROK foreign minister under the country's new, Japanese-trained military dictator.[111] I recall that around the time of the Chernobyl disaster, Ch'oe appeared—unannounced and uninvited—at our small Korean Studies seminar at Tübingen University, conversing with us in German. Later that year, the classmate who had served him tea shoved an issue of the *Rodong sinmun* in my face: "Oh gee—look who's on the front page!" Ch'oe had just resettled in P'yŏngyang. Political ideology was not fixed; it was rearranged.

After liberation, such rearrangements did not remain matters of biography alone; they were built into the institutions of policing, intelli-

---

in Hamburg, and the broader scope of Polish–Japanese cooperation against Nazi interests. Yet, in order not to upset its Japanese ally, the German side lodged no strong protest. A letter by Karl Ritter (1883–1968), the Foreign Office's liaison to the Wehrmacht High Command, dated January 15, 1942, attached to Heydrich's archived memorandum (RZ 214, R 101.091, sheets 031 and 032), quotes the head of military intelligence (Abwehr), Admiral Canaris (1887–1945), as recommending that the matter still not be raised with the Japanese ambassador in Berlin. Canaris himself, of course, was by then cooperating with the Polish government-in-exile and the British through his lover Halina Szymańska (1906–1989), a Polish MI6 agent. See Heydrich to Ribbentrop, "Japanische Spionage im Reich" [Japanese Espionage in the Reich], August 7, 1941, together with related correspondence, SD-Berichte betr. Irland und Japan, Berlin, RZ 214, R 101.091, Politisches Archiv des Auswärtigen Amts, Berlin.

[111] On Ch'oe, see the footnotes to the Robinson account, 103, footnote 37, and 232, footnote 79.

gence, and war. During the Korean War, the organization of local units of the Korean Youth Corps into "defense forces to support the police"[112] was only one way these groups became entangled in the conflict.[113] Their manhunts and killings left little doubt about their ideological inheritance. In December 1950, Reuters reported that 800 political prisoners had just been shot by South Korean firing squads. A British captain serving with UN forces, who witnessed one such mass execution in a gully beside the British barracks, said he was no longer willing to fight for the South Koreans: "These people have no democratic rights or liberties, and I am no longer prepared to encourage my men to risk their lives to champion a cause which, to say the least, is highly doubtful."[114] Elsewhere, a right-wing youth group massacred villagers, including women and children; the local youth leader justified killing the children on the grounds that "the parents were Communists, therefore when they grew up they too would be Communists."[115] After the first recapture of Seoul, rightist youth corps organized street courts and lynched thousands accused of having "collaborated" with the North Koreans (see

[112] *Washington Post*, August 3, 1950.

[113] With the establishment of the ROK in August 1948, Chokch'ŏng was renamed the South Korean National Youth Corps (Taehan Minjok Ch'ŏngnyŏndan). In November 1948, Syngman Rhee pushed the integration of youth groups; after resisting at first, the corps was dissolved and absorbed into the newly organized South Korean Youth Corps (Taehan Ch'ŏngnyŏndan) in early 1949. Its former members nonetheless continued to operate as the Chokch'ŏng group (Chokch'ŏng-gye).

[114] Unnamed British Army captain of the UN forces in Korea, quoted in the *Sydney Morning Herald*, December 18, 1950. (See also *Manchester Guardian*, December 19, 1950.)

[115] Unnamed local leader of a South Korean youth organization, quoted in ibid. Of the many similar mass atrocities, these two were among the very few reported in the international press, while news about most of the others was suppressed by U.S. military censorship. Once military censors lost control of the story, as in the case of this Reuters report, American follow-up coverage still omitted facts that would have raised basic political questions—like the British officer's statement undermining the UN's military engagement—while casting the U.S. military's role as heroic. *The Boston Globe* of December 18, 1950, thus abbreviated the story, cut all references to several other massacres Australian and British papers mentioned, and ran it under a headline suggesting that the U.S. Army, which was under the UN umbrella but actually in command and responsible, had "saved" the massacre's sole survivor. In other cases in which the U.S. and ROK military failed to suppress news about massacres, the killings were simply blamed on North Korean troops, as, e.g., in the case of the Taejŏn Prison Massacre (*Taejŏnhyŏngmuso haksal sagŏn*) right after the outbreak of the Korean War, which had been observed and photographed by American CIC officers who watched passively.

(Fig. 40) On their last ride, just outside Seoul, mid-November 1950: South Korean civilians, labeled communist sympathizers for not having fled the northern invasion, are forced to crouch on a truck. By June 1949, the Syngman Rhee regime had imprisoned 36,000 ROK citizens, and by late 1952—supported by right-wing youth groups and often operating under the guidance of KMAG and U.S. CIC agents—it had massacred between 100,000 and 200,000 compatriots. (Photo: I. R. Lorwin)

also fig. 40). The victims of rape, torture, murder, lynching, and summary execution committed by South Korean paramilitary youth leagues on both sides of the 38th parallel—often in conjunction with Korean police combat units or U.S. Army Counter Intelligence Corps (CIC) teams—ran into the hundreds of thousands.[116] As Callum MacDonald notes,

[116] Still highly insightful on politically motivated Southern atrocities in both halves of Korea during the first year of the war, and especially attentive to the role of right-wing youth groups, is a 1991 article by the Scottish historian Callum MacDonald, "'So Terrible a Liberation'—the UN Occupation of North Korea," *Bulletin of Concerned Asian Scholars* 23, no. 2 (April–June 1991): 3–19 (hereafter cited as MacDonald, "'So Terrible a Liberation'"). For more recent studies, see especially Dong-Choon Kim, "Forgotten War, Forgotten Massacres—the Korean War (1950–1953) as Licensed Mass Killings," *Journal of Genocide Research* 6, no. 4 (December 2004): 523–44; Dong-Choon Kim, "The War against the 'Enemy within': Hidden Massacres in the Early Stages of the Korean War," in *Rethinking Historical Injustice and Reconciliation in Northeast Asia: The Korean Experience*, eds. Gi-Wook Shin, Soon-Won Park, and Daqing Yang (London: Routledge, 2007), 75–93; Chinsil Hwahaerŭl wihan Kwagŏsa Chŏngni Wiwŏnhoe, *Chinsil Hwahae Wiwŏnhoe chonghap pogosŏ* [Truth

when P'yŏngyang was occupied by UN forces in October 1950, it was effectively run by youth groups.[117] The violence these groups had already inflicted in the South was thus repeated in the North. Monica Kim's recent *The Interrogation Rooms of the Korean War* confirms that such youth groups had indeed "become key to the rightist regime and US counterintelligence network"[118] on the peninsula.

More than fifty years after his collaboration with the Japanese colonizers, Wang Tifu could still claim in his memoirs that, by following Nazi and Japanese directives, he had saved Jews—and find moral comfort in that claim. Activists like Kang Se-hyŏng and Yi Pŏm-sŏk likewise screened out nearly everything that did not fit their selective memories. The Yi–Kang story, like the An Ik-t'ae–Manchukuo Legation story, poses a puzzle at the heart of this essay: how could a Korean collaborator be praised in the autobiography of an anti-Japanese fighter known for armed resistance, and why would that officer work with him after 1945, when by the late 1930s he had publicly promoted Japan's *naisen ittai* ("Japan and Korea as one body") campaign? One possibility is not espionage but political re-sorting, in which anti-communism becomes the master key reorganizing reputations, alliances, and even retroactive claims to legitimacy.

The career of Yŏm Tong-jin (1909?–1950) makes the pattern legible. In 1933/34, Yŏm studied at the Luoyang Branch of the Central Army Military Academy (Luoyang Junguan Xuexiao) and went on to found and command the terroristic White Shirts Society (Paegŭisa), modeled on Dai Li's Blue Shirts. After liberation, the White Shirts operated in both southern and northern Korea and was implicated in the assassinations of Kim Ku and Yŏ Un-hyŏng (aka Lyuh Woon Hyung, 1886–1947), along with numerous other political attacks; and from January 1946 to 1948, "there were anti-North Korean espionage and intelligence-gathering activities carried out in coordination with the U.S. Counter

---

and Reconciliation Commission, comprehensive report], vol. 3, Civilian massacres (Seoul: Chinsil Hwahaerŭl wihan Kwagŏsa Chŏngni Wiwŏnhoe, 2010); Su-kyoung Hwang, *Korea's Grievous War* (Philadelphia: University of Pennsylvania Press, 2016).

[117] See MacDonald, "'So Terrible a Liberation'," 12.

[118] Kim, *Interrogation Rooms*, 27. Chapter 5 of the book provides an in-depth look at the role of rightist youth groups and their close cooperation with the CIC.

Intelligence Corps (CIC)."[119] Under Donald P. Whitaker (1900?–1987),[120] head of the CIC Seoul District (971 CIC), the CIC worked closely with the group, co-sponsoring its spy and terrorist activities and training its personnel. In 1949 this personnel stream reappeared in KLO, the Korean Liaison Office (aka Kelo Unit), a U.S.–financed special unit under U.S. Far East Command, a successor formation that likewise ran intelligence-gathering and infiltration operations against North Korea.[121] The White Shirts and KLO drew heavily on youth recruited from the Northwest Youth Association (Sŏbuk Ch'ŏngnyŏnhoe), largely northern young men who had moved south after 1945; the association was the main competitor of Yi's Chokch'ŏng group, though some of Yi's youth also joined the White Shirts. (Interestingly enough, during the Korean War, the U.S. Army provided KLO units with former Nazi Waffen-SS camouflage uniforms, with SS insignia still attached.[122]) Celebrated in some rightist circles after 1945, White Shirt founder Yŏm Tong-jin later proved to have been a paid informant for the Japanese, working for the Kwantung Army's military police from March 1936 to March 1944.[123] As the historian who worked on the Yŏm case explains, many collaborators "clearly engaged in pro-Japanese activity, but subjectively they rationalized it as anti-communist activism,"

---

[119] Chŏng Pyŏng-jun, "Kwandonggun miljŏng Yŏm Tong-jin'gwa tongnipt'usa Kim Hyŏk: Nagyanggun'gwanhakkyo tonggisaengŭi ŏtkallin unmyŏnggwa paegŭisaŭi kiwŏn" [Kwantung Army informant Yŏm Tong-jin and independence fighter Kim Hyŏk: Divergent fates of Luoyang Military Academy classmates and the origins of the White Shirts Society], *Yŏksa pip'yŏng* 135 (Summer 2021): 293 (hereafter cited as Chŏng, "Yŏm Tong-jin").

[120] On Whitaker, later a leading CIA agent in South Korea, see this volume, 356–57, footnote 31, and 358–59.

[121] See Chŏng Yong-uk, "Haebang chikhu Chuhan Migun pangch'ŏptaeŭi chojik ch'egyewa hwaldong" [Organization and activities of the USAFIK Counter Intelligence Corps in the immediate post-liberation period], *Han'guk saron* 53 (June 2007): 443–84; Yi Wan-bŏm, "Paegŭisawa KLOŭi hwaldongŭl t'onghaesŏ pon Namhan Taebuk chŏngbohwaldongŭi wŏllyu (1945-1953)" [The origins of South Korea's intelligence activities against North Korea through the activities of the White Shirts Society and KLO (1945–1953)], *Kukka chŏngbo yŏn'gu* 3, no. 1 (August 2010), 47–82.

[122] For photographs of KLO personnel wearing German uniforms, see "KLO," accessed December 19, 2025, https://namu.wiki/w/KLO. By the 1960s, Korean cartoonists had registered the eccentric iconography and depicted KLO troops—swastika emblems, German shepherds, and all—fighting People's Army soldiers.

[123] For details, see Chŏng, "Yŏm Tong-jin," 304–5.

insisting that what mattered was "not cooperation with Japan but the struggle against the Communist Party."[124]

Yi Pŏm-sŏk may or may not belong in that category, but his praise of Kang Se-hyŏng before liberation and Kang's post-liberation reintegration into Yi's youth-mobilization world point in the same direction: anti-communism could be made to read as the higher loyalty, and anti-Japanese credentials could become negotiable—even redeemable in retrospect—so long as anti-communism was prioritized over everything else. Ōgushi Ryūkichi's work sharpens the point: from the late 1930s, and especially from 1940 onward, Japan's centralized wartime youth mobilization developed in explicit exchange with the Hitler Youth, while colonial Korea's Alliance of Korean Youth Leagues (Chosŏn Yŏnhap Ch'ŏngnyŏndan) and, from 1941, the Chosŏn Youth Corps (Chosŏn Ch'ŏngnyŏndan) were folded into the same fascist-imperial orbit.[125] After liberation, these already connected Japanese, German, and colonial Korean repertoires of youth discipline and political mobilization did not disappear; they were recombined inside the South Korean far right under U.S. patronage. Seen from this perspective, Fujii's nativist Third-Worldism captures a rhetoric of self-description rather than the actual genealogy of the formation. What emerges instead is not a decolonized Third-Worldist exception but a transimperial fascist formation. It was forged in Japanese colonial fascist pedagogy in Korea and intensified through direct Hitler Youth–Korea connections and the militarized youth apparatus of Korea's Alliance of Korean Youth Leagues and the Chosŏn Youth Corps. It was also shaped through the Korean exile military world formed within Guomindang command structures, where fascist ideology and militarized statecraft had their own powerful appeal, and after 1945 it was recombined within a U.S.-backed order that was not merely anti-communist but neocolonial and racialized, governing through Korean fascists as auxiliaries behind the façade of sovereignty. Fascism thus supplied a modern political idiom for racialized rule under neocolonial conditions.

---

[124] Ibid., 304.

[125] See Ōgushi Ryūkichi, "Senji taiseika Nihon seinendan no kokusai renkei: Hitorā Yūgento to Chōsen Rengō Seinendan no aida" [The Japan Youth League's wartime international ties: Between Hitler Youth and the Alliance of Korean Youth Leagues], parts 1 and 2, *Jinbun gakuhō: kyōikugaku* 31 (March 1996): 153–75; 32 (March 1997): 1–36.

References

Adorno, Theodor W. *Prismen: Kulturkritik und Gesellschaft* [Prisms: Cultural criticism and society]. Frankfurt am Main: Suhrkamp, 1955.

Archer, Jules. *The Plot to Seize the White House*. New York: Hawthorn Books, 1973.

Arimitsu Kyōichi 有光教一. "1945–46-nyŏne issŏttŏn naŭi kyŏnghŏmdam" 一九四五-四六 년에 있었던 나의 경험담 [My personal account of 1945–46]." Translated by Kim Sŏng-nam 김성남. *Han'guk kogo hakpo* 韓國考古學報 34 (May 1996): 7–27.

Bae Ahran. "A Comprehensive Assessment of Korean Collaboration under Japanese Colonial Rule (1910–1945)." PhD diss., Rikkyo University, 2018.

Bale, Jeffrey M. *The Darkest Sides of Politics*, vol. 1, *Postwar Fascism, Covert Operations, and Terrorism*. London: Routledge, 2018.

Bendersky, Joseph W. *The "Jewish Threat": Anti-Semitic Politics of the U.S. Army*. New York: Basic Books, 2000.

Bertsch, Leonard M. "UN Victory in Korea Poses Question of Rhee's Future." *Foreign Policy Bulletin* 30, no. 2 (October 20, 1950): 2–3.

Blum, William. *The CIA: A Forgotten History*. London: Zed Books, 1986.

Boghardt, Thomas. *Covert Legions: U.S. Army Intelligence in Germany, 1944–1949*. Washington, DC: Center of Military History, United States Army, 2022.

Bolles, Blair. "Can U.S. Quarantine Korean Conflict?" *Foreign Policy Bulletin* 29, no. 37 (July 14, 1950): 1–2.

Bradshaw, Graham, and Margery Pearson. "Journey from the East: The Life and Times of Mark Gayn." Exhibition pamphlet. Toronto: Thomas Fisher Rare Book Library, University of Toronto, 1986.

Bricmont, Jean. *Impérialisme humanitaire: droits de l'homme, droit d'ingérence, droit du plus fort?* [Humanitarian imperialism: Human rights, right of intervention, right of the strongest?]. 2nd rev. ed., with a new preface by Noam Chomsky. Brussels: Aden, 2009.

"Britain's Postwar Plans: The Case of Thailand." *Amerasia* 9 (January 26, 1945), 19–29.

Butler, Smedley D. "America's Armed Forces, 2. 'In Time of Peace': The Army." *Common Sense* 4, no. 11 (November 1935): 8–12.

Capozzola, Christopher. "The Secret Soldiers' Union: Labor and Soldier Politics in the Philippine Scout Mutiny of 1924." In *Making the Empire Work: Labor and United States Imperialism*, edited by Daniel E. Bender and Jana K. Lipman, 85–103. New York: New York University Press, 2015.

Caprio, Mark E. "The Eagle Has Landed: Groping for a Korean Role in the Pacific War." *Journal of American–East Asian Relations* 21, no. 1 (March 2014): 5–33.

———. "The Politics of Collaboration in Post-liberation Southern Korea." In *In the Ruins of the Japanese Empire: Imperial Violence, State Destruction, and the Reordering of Modern East*

Asia. Edited by Barak Kushner and Andrew Levidis, 27–49. Hong Kong: Hong Kong University Press, 2020.

————, and Yu Jia. "Legislating Diaspora: The Contribution of Occupation-Era Administrations to the Preservation of Japan's Korean Community." In *Diaspora without Homeland: Being Korean in Japan*. Edited by Sonia Ryang and John Lie, 21–38. Berkeley: University of California Press, 2009.

Chang, Kornel. *A Fractured Liberation: Korea under US Occupation*. Cambridge: Belknap Press of Harvard University Press, 2025.

Ch'inil P'anminjok Haengwi Chinsang Kyumyŏng Wiwŏnhoe 친일반민족행위 진상규명 위원회, ed. *Ch'inil panminjok haengwi kwan'gye saryojip* 친일 반민족 행위 관계 사료집 [Collection of documentary materials related to pro-Japanese collaboration activities]. 16 vols. Seoul: Ch'inil P'anminjok Haengwi Chinsang Kyumyŏng Wiwŏnhoe, 2007–2009.

Chinsil Hwahaerŭl wihan Kwagŏsa Chŏngni Wiwŏnhoe 진실·화해를위한과거사 정리 위원회. *Chinsil Hwahae Wiwŏnhoe chonghap pogosŏ*. III, *Min'ganin chiptanhŭisaeng sagŏn* 진실 화해 위원회 종합 보고서 III: 민간인 집단희생 사건 [Truth and Reconciliation Commission, comprehensive report. Vol. 3, Civilian massacres]. Seoul: Chinsil Hwahaerŭl wihan Kwagŏsa Chŏngni Wiwŏnhoe, 2010.

Chŏng Pyŏng-jun 정병준. "Kwandonggun miljŏng Yŏm Tong-jin'gwa tongnipt'usa Kim Hyŏk: Nagyanggun'gwanhakkyo tonggisaengŭi ŏtkallin unmyŏnggwa paegŭisaŭi kiwŏn" 관동군 밀정 염동진과 독립투사 김혁: 낙양군관학교 동기생의 엇갈린 운명과 백의사의 기원 [Kwantung Army informant Yŏm Tong-jin and independence fighter Kim Hyŏk: Divergent fates of Luoyang Military Academy classmates and the origins of the White Shirts Society]. *Yŏksa pip'yŏng* 역사비평 135 (Summer 2021): 289–331.

Chŏng Yong-uk 鄭容郁, comp. *Haebang chikhu chŏngch'i sahoesa charyojip*, 1: *Yaksayu (1)* 解放直後政治·社會史資料集, 1: 略史類(1) [Collection of political and social materials from the immediate post-liberation period. Vol. 1: An outline history (1)]. Seoul: Tarakpang, 1994.

————, comp. *Haebang chikhu chŏngch'i sahoesa charyojip*, 5: *Chŏngdang sahoe tanch'e charyo (2)* 解放直後政治·社會史資料集, 5: 政黨·社會團體 資料 (2) [Collection of political and social materials from the immediate post-liberation period. Vol. 5: Materials on political parties and social organizations (2)]. Seoul: Tarakpang, 1994.

————, comp. *Haebang chikhu chŏngch'i sahoesa charyojip*, 7: *Chuhan Migun pangch'ŏptae charyojip (2)* 解放直後政治·社會史資料集, 7: 주한미군 방첩대 자료집 (2) [Collection of political and social materials from the immediate post-liberation period. Vol. 7: USAFIK Counter Intelligence Corps resource collection (2)]. Seoul: Tarakpang, 1994.

————, comp. *Haebang chikhu chŏngch'i sahoesa charyojip*, 10: *Chuhan Migun pangch'ŏptae charyojip (5)* 解放直後政治·社會史資料集, 7: 주한미군 방첩대 자료집 (5) [Collection of political and social materials from the immediate post-liberation period. Vol. 10: USAFIK Counter Intelligence Corps resource collection (5)]. Seoul: Tarakpang, 1994.

————. "Rich'adŭ Robinsŭnŭi Han'guk hyŏndaesa ihae" 리차드 로빈슨의 한국현대사 이해 [Richard Robinson's understanding of contemporary Korean history]. In *Haeoe hakcha Han'guk hyŏndaesa yŏn'gu punsŏk* 해외학자 한국현대사 연구분석, vol. 2. Edited by Han'guk Chŏngsinmunhwa Yŏn'guwŏn, 11–46. Seoul: Paeksan Sŏdang, 1999.

————. *Migunjŏng charyo yŏn'gu* 미군정자료연구 [Research on U.S. Military Government source materials]. Seoul: Sŏnin, 2003.

————. "Haebang chikhu Chuhan Migun pangch'ŏptaeŭi chojik ch'egyewa hwaldong" 해방 직후 주한미군 방첩대의 조직 체계와 활동 [Organization and activities of the

USAFIK Counter Intelligence Corps in the immediate post-liberation period]. *Han'guk saron* 韓國史論 53 (June 2007): 443–84.

————. "*Chuhan Migunsa*ŭi p'yŏnch'an kyŏngwiwa naeyong kusŏng" '주한미군사'의 편찬 경위와 내용 구성 [Compilation process and content composition of *History of the United States Army Forces in Korea*]. In *Chuhan Migunsa* 주한미군사 / *History of the United States Army Forces in Korea*, vol. 1. Edited by Kuksa P'yŏnch'an Wiwŏnhoe, 25–46. Seoul: Sŏnin, 2014.

[————] Chung Yong Wook. "From Occupation to War: Cold War Legacies of US Army Historical Studies of the Occupation and Korean War." *Korea Journal* 60, no. 2 (Summer 2020): 14–54.

————, and Yi Kil-sang 李吉相, comps. *Haebang chŏnhu Migugŭi taehan chŏngch'aeksa charyojip* 解放前後 美國의 對韓政策史 資料集 [Source materials on the history of the U.S. Korea policy before and after liberation]. 13 vols. Seoul: Tarakpang, 1995.

Chosŏn Minjok Ch'ŏngnyŏndan Chojikpu 朝鮮民族青年團組織部. *Chojige kwanhan ch'amgo* 組織에 關한 參考 [Organizational reference guide]. Seoul: Chosŏn Minjok Ch'ŏngnyŏndan Chojikpu, 1948.

Clayton, [William L.] "The Foreign Economic Policy of the United States." *Department of State Bulletin* 20, no. 386 (November 24, 1946): 950–53.

Clinton, Maggie. *Revolutionary Nativism: Fascism and Culture in China, 1925–1937*. Durham: Duke University Press, 2017.

Communist International. *Blueprint for World Conquest*. With an introduction by William Henry Chamberlain. Washington, DC: Human Events, 1946.

Congressional Record: The Proceedings and Debates of the Fifty-Sixth Congress, Second Session. Vol. 34, 4 parts. Washington, DC: Government Printing Office, 1901.

Congressional Record: The Proceedings and Debates of the 81st Congress, Second Session. Vol. 96, 20 parts. Washington, DC: Government Printing Office, 1950.

Cumings, Bruce. *The Origins of the Korean War*. 2 vols. Princeton: Princeton University Press, 1981 and 1990.

————. *Parallax Visions: Making Sense of American–East Asian Relations at the End of the Century*. Durham and London: Duke University Press, 1999.

Czarnocka, Halina, ed. *Armia Krajowa w dokumentach, 1939-1945*. 6 vols. [The Home Army in documents, 1939–1945]. London: Studium Polski Podziemnej, 1970–1989.

Daniel, Wilhelm. *Aus meinem Lebensbuch* [From my book of life]. [Vienna: Self-published], 1985.

Deane, Hugh. *The Korean War 1945–1953*. San Francisco: China Books, 1999.

Dennett, Tyler. "'In Due Course.'" *Far Eastern Survey* 14, no. 1 (January 17, 1945): 1–4.

Dickson, Paul, and Thomas B. Allen. *The Bonus Army: An American Epic*. New York: Walker, 2004.

Drage, Charles. *The Amiable Prussian*. London: Anthony Blond, 1958.

Dower, John W. *Embracing Defeat: Japan in the Wake of World War II*. New York: W.W. Norton, 1999.

[Ebener, Charlotte.] "Korea: Master Plan." *Newsweek* 28, no. 19 (November 4, 1946): 50.

————. *No Facilities for Women*. New York: Alfred A. Knopf, 1955.

Eckert, Carter J. *Offspring of Empire: The Koch'ang Kims and the Colonial Origins of Korean Capitalism, 1876–1945*. 2nd ed. Seattle: University of Washington Press, 2014.

Elliot, Oliver. *The American Press and the Cold War: The Rise of Authoritarianism in South Korea, 1945–1954*. Cham: Palgrave Macmillan, 2018.

Feis, Herbert. *Churchill, Roosevelt, Stalin: The War They Waged and the Peace They Sought*. 2nd ed. Princeton: Princeton University Press, 1967.

Fromm, Joseph. "Youth Training Center in Southern Korea Prepares Selected 'Boys' as Future Leaders." *World Report* 3, no. 40 (October 7, 1947): 26.

Gayn, Mark J. *Journey from the East: An Autobiography*. New York: Alfred A. Knopf, 1944.

———. "Cold War: Two Police States in Korea." *New Republic* 117, no. 11 (September 15, 1947): 15–16.

———. *Japan Diary*. New York: William Sloane Associates, 1948.

[———] Mark Gein. *Iaponskii dnevnik* [Japan diary]. An abridged translation by I. Boronos, D. Kunina, and N. Loseva, with an introduction by A. Varshavskii. Moscow: Izdatel'stvo inostrannoi literatury, 1951.

[———] Māku Gein マーク·ゲイン. *Nippon nikki* ニッポン日記 [Japan diary]. Translated by Imoto Takeo 井本威夫. 2 vols. Tokyo: Chikuma Shobō, 1951.

———. *Dziennik japoński* [Japan diary]. Translated by Kazimierz Błeszyński. Warsaw: Książka i Wiedza, 1954.

———. "The Cult of Kim." *New York Times Magazine* (October 1, 1972): 16–17, 20, 24, 26, 28, 31–32, and 34.

[———] Māku Gein マーク·ゲイン. *Shin Nippon nikki: Aru jānarisuto no ikō* 新ニッポン日記: あるジャーナリストの遺稿 [New Japan diary: The posthumous writings of a journalist]. Translated by Kuga Toyō 久我豊雄. Tokyo: Nippon Hōsō Shuppan Kyōkai, 1982.

[———] Mak'ŭ Kein 마크 게인. *Haebanggwa migunjŏng: 1946.10–11* 해방과 미군정: 1946.10–11 [Liberation and the U.S. Army: October–November 1946]. Translated by Kkach'i Editorial Board. Seoul: Kkach'i, 1986.

———, with Suzanne Gayn. "Why We Chose Canada." *Star Weekly Magazine* (May 9, 1959): 10–11.

Germany, Auswärtiges Amt, and United States Department of State, comps. *Documents on German Foreign Policy, 1918–1945, from the Archives of the German Foreign Ministry*. Series D (1937–1945), Vol. XII, *The War Years, February 1–June 22, 1941*. Washington, DC: Government Printing Office, 1962.

Gillette, F. E. *Migunjŏnggi chŏngbo charyojip: Chillet'ŭ (F.E. Gillette) pogosŏ, chŏnbŏmdae chaep'an kirok, 1946–1948* 美軍政期情報資料集: 질레트 (F.E. Gillette) 보고서 · 전범대 재판기록, 1946-1948 [Collection of intelligence materials from the U.S. Military Government period: Gillette (F.E. Gillette) reports and war crimes tribunal records, 1946–1948]. 2 vols. Compiled by Hallim Taehakkyo, Asia Munhwa Yŏn'guso. Ch'unch'ŏn: Hallim Taehakkyo, Asia Munhwa Yŏn'guso, 1996.

Ginsbourg, Sam. *My First Sixty Years in China*. Beijing: New World Press, 1982.

Hailey, Foster. *Half of One World*. New York: Macmillan, 1950.

Hallim Taehakkyo, Asia Munhwa Yŏn'guso 翰林大學 아시아文化硏究所, comp. *HQ, USAFIK G-2 Periodic Report / Chuhan Migun chŏngbo ilchi* 駐韓美軍情報日誌 *(1945.9.9–1946.2.12)*. Vol. 1. Ch'unch'ŏn: Hallim Taehakkyo, Asia Munhwa Yŏn'guso, 1988.

———, comp. *Migunjŏnggi chŏngbo charyojip: Haji (John R. Hodge) munsŏjip, 1945.6–1948* 美軍政期情報資料集: 하지 (John R. Hodge) 문서집, 1945.6–1948.8 [Collection of intelligence materials from the U.S. Military Government period: Hodge (John R. Hodge) Document Collection, June 1945–August 1948]. 3 vols. Ch'unch'ŏn: Hallim Taehakkyo, Asia Munhwa Yŏn'guso, 1995.

———, comp. *Migunjŏnggi chŏngbo charyojip: Simin soyo, yŏron chosa pogosŏ, 1945.9–1948.6* 美軍政期情報資料集: 시민소요·여론조사 보고서, 1945.9–1948.6 [Collection of intelligence materials from the U.S. Military Government period: Reports on civil unrest and opinion polls, September 1945–June 1948]. Vol. 2. Ch'unch'ŏn: Hallim Taehakkyo, Asia Munhwa Yŏn'guso, 1995.

Hamlin, Will [pseud., Richard D. Robinson]. "Korea: An American Tragedy." *Nation* 164, no. 9 (March 1, 1947): 245–47.

Han'guk Charyo Kaebarwŏn 한국자료개발원, comp. *Mi Kungmusŏng han'guk kwan'gye munsŏ* 美國務省韓國關係文書 / *Internal Affairs of Korea, 1940–1949*. Vol. 11. Seoul: Arŭm Ch'ulp'ansa, 1995.

Han Shengtao 韩声涛, "Zhongyang Lujun Junguan Xuexiao junguan xunlianban di san qi xueyuan Han Shengtao huiyilu" 中央陆军军官学校军官训练班第三期学员韩声涛回忆录 [Han Shengtao's memoir: A cadet of the Central Army Officer Academy's third officer-training cohort], August 9, 2018, https://m.krzzjn.com/show-1183-78877.html.

Henderson, Gregory. *Korea: The Politics of the Vortex*. Cambridge: Harvard University Press, 1968.

Herman, Edward S., and Noam Chomsky. *Manufacturing Consent: The Political Economy of the Mass Media*. New York: Pantheon Books, 1988.

[Historical Section, Headquarters XXIV Corps, US Army Forces in Korea.] *Chuhan Migunsa* 駐韓美軍史 / *HUSAFIK*. 3 parts in 4 vols. Seoul: Tolbegae, 1988.

Hoffmann, Frank. *Berlin Koreans and Pictured Koreans*. Koreans and Central Europeans: Informal Contacts up to 1950, vol. 1. Edited by Andreas Schirmer. Vienna: Praesens, 2015.

Hujii Tak'esi 후지이 다케시 [Fujii Takeshi 藤井豪]. *P'asijŭmgwa che-3 segyejuŭi saiesŏ: Chokch'ŏnggyeŭi hyŏngsŏnggwa mollagŭl t'onghae pon haebang 8-nyŏnsa* 파시즘과 제 3 세계주의 사이에서: 족청계의 형성과 몰락을 통해 본 해방 8 년사 [Between fascism and Third-Worldism: An eight-year history of liberation viewed through the formation and fall of the Korean National Youth Corps]. Yŏkpi Han'gukhak yŏn'gu ch'ongsŏ, 34. 2nd ed. Seoul: Yŏksa Pip'yŏngsa, 2016.

———— . "Suwŏn Chokch'ŏng Chungang Hullyŏnsowa sae chŏngch'ijuch'eŭi saengsan" 수원 족청 중앙훈련소와 새 정치주체의 생산 [The Korean National Youth Corps Suwŏn Central Training Center and the production of new political subjects]. *Suwŏn yŏksa munhwa yŏn'gu* 水原歷史文化研究 6 (2016): 119–49.

Hunt, E. Howard, with Greg Aunapu. *American Spy: My Secret History in the CIA, Watergate, and Beyond*. Hoboken: John Wiley & Sons, 2007.

Hwang Min-ho 황민호. *Ch'ŏlgi Yi Pŏm-sŏk p'yŏngjŏn* 鐵驥 李範奭 평전 [A critical biography of Ch'ŏlgi Yi Pŏm-sŏk]. Seoul: Sŏnin, 2021.

Hwang, Su-kyoung. *Korea's Grievous War*. Philadelphia: University of Pennsylvania Press, 2016.

Im Chong-myŏng 林鍾明. "Chosŏn Minjok Ch'ŏngnyŏndan (1946.10–1949.1) kwa Migunjŏngŭi 'changnae Han'gugŭi chido seryŏk' yangsŏng chŏngch'aek" 조선민족청년단(1946.10-1949.1)과 미군정의 '장래 한국의 지도세력'양성정책 [The Korean National Youth Corps (October 1946–January 1949) and its relationship with USAMGIK's 'Future Leaders of South Korea' training policy]. *Han'guksa yŏn'gu* 韓國史硏究 95 (December 1996): 179–211.

Immerwahr, Daniel. *How to Hide an Empire: A History of the Greater United States*. New York: Farrar, Straus and Giroux, 2019.

Im Sŏng-uk 임성욱. "Migunjŏnggi Chosŏn Chŏngp'ansa 'wijojip'ye' sagŏn yŏn'gu" 미군정기 조선정판사 '위조지폐' 사건 연구 [A study of the Chosŏn Chŏngp'ansa 'Counterfeit

Banknotes' case during the U.S. Military Government]. PhD diss., Hankuk University of Foreign Studies, 2015.

"Interview mit General Jiang Weiguo (16. April 1994 in Taibei)" [Interview with General Chiang Wei-kuo (April 16, 1994, in Taibei)]. In *Deutsch-chinesische Beziehungen 1928-1937: "Gleiche" Partner unter "ungleichen" Bedingungen: Eine Quellensammlung*. Edited by Bernd Martin and Susanne Kuß, 471–79. Berlin: Akademie Verlag, 2003.

Isaacs, Harold R. *No Peace for Asia*. New York: Macmillan, 1947.

Jiang Weiguo 蒋纬国, with Liu Fenghan 刘凤翰. *Jiang Weiguo koushu zizhuan* 蒋纬国口述自传 [Chiang Wei-kuo's oral autobiography]. 2nd ed. Beijing: Zhongguo Dabaike Quanshu Chubanshe, 2016.

Jia Zhongwei 賈忠偉. *Weiguo zhanshi de yaolan: Sanjun guanxiao de caochuang yu yange* 衛國戰士的搖籃: 三軍官校的草創與沿革 [Cradle of national defenders: The founding and evolution of the three military academies]. Taipei: Cangbi Chuban Youxian Gongsi, 2015.

Jürgens, Heinrich. "Reise nach Japan: Tagebuchaufzeichnungen von der Japanfahrt der HJ 1940" [Journey to Japan: Diary notes on the Hitler Youth's 1940 Japan trip]. Parts 1–3. *Junge Welt* 3, no. 3 (March 1941): 20–22; no. 4 (April 1941): 20–22; no. 5 (May 1941): 21–23.

Kang, Han Mu. "The United States Military Government in Korea, 1945–1948: An Analysis and Evaluation of Its Policy." PhD diss., University of Cincinnati, 1970.

Katz, Jonathan M. *Gangsters of Capitalism: Smedley Butler, the Marines, and the Making and Breaking of America's Empire*. New York: St. Martin's Press, 2022.

Keeley, Joseph. *The China Lobby Man: The Story of Alfred Kohlberg*. New Rochelle: Arlington House, 1969.

Kim Chae-uk 金宰旭. "Chungguk hyŏndae Hanin chejae chakp'um yŏn'guesŏ Han'gukchŏk kwanjŏm hwakribŭi p'iryosŏng koch'al: Mumyŏngssiwa Yi Pŏm-sŏgŭi munhakchŏk kwan'gye yŏn'gurŭl chungsimŭro" 중국 현대 한인제재 작품 연구에서 한국적 관점 확립의 필요성 고찰: 無名氏와 李範奭의 문학적 관계 연구를 중심으로 [A Study on the need to establish Korean perspectives in research on modern Chinese works featuring Koreans: With Focus on the literary relationship between Wumingshi and Yi Pŏm-sŏk]. *Chungguk ŏmun hakchi* 中國語文學誌 73 (2020): 163–83.

Kim Chi-hun 김지훈. "Kim Hong-irŭi Chungguk Kungminhyŏngmyŏnggun'gwa *Kukpang kaeron* chŏsul" 김홍일의 중국 국민혁명군 경험과 '국방개론' 저술 [Kim Hong-il's experience in the Chinese National Revolutionary Army and the writing of *Outline of National Defense*]. *Kunsa* 軍史 112 (September 2019): 1–44.

Kim Dong-Choon. "Forgotten War, Forgotten Massacres—the Korean War (1950–1953) as Licensed Mass Killings." *Journal of Genocide Research* 6, no. 4 (December 2004): 523–44.

———. "The War against the 'Enemy within': Hidden Massacres in the Early Stages of the Korean War." In *Rethinking Historical Injustice and Reconciliation in Northeast Asia: The Korean Experience*. Edited by Gi-Wook Shin, Soon-Won Park, and Daqing Yang, 75–93. London: Routledge, 2007.

Kim Haeng-sŏn 김행선. "Miso Kongdong Wiwŏnhoe chaegaerŭl chŏnhuhan uikchinyŏngŭi tongyanggwa yangmyŏnjŏnsul" 미소공동위원회 재개를 전후한 우익진영의 동향과 양면전술 [Trends and two-faced tactics of right-wing groups around the time of the resumption of the U.S.–Soviet Joint Commission]. *Hansŏng sahak* 漢城史學 14 (2002): 35–66.

———. *Haebang chŏngguk ch'ŏngnyŏn undongsa* 해방정국 청년운동사 [History of the liberation period youth movement]. Seoul: Sŏnin, 2004.

Kim Hong-il 金弘一 [金弘壹]. *Kukpang kaeron* 國防概論 [Outline of national defense]. Seoul: Koryŏ Sŏjŏk, 1949.

——— 金弘壹. *Taeryugŭi punno: nobyŏngŭi hoesanggi* 大陸의憤怒: 老兵의回想記 [The continent's indignation: a veteran's memoir]. Seoul: Munjosa, 1972.

Kim Hwan-gyun 김환균. *Pigŭgŭn haengjinŭrobut'ŏ sijak toenda: tak'yument'ŏrisŭt'ŭ Kim Hwan-gyunŭn malhanda* 비극은 행진으로부터 시작된다: 다큐멘터리스트 김환균은 말한다 [A tragedy begins with a march: Documentarian Kim Hwan-gyun speaks]. Koyang: Tŭllin Ach'im, 2004.

Kim, Jeong-Chul. "On Forgiveness and Reconciliation: Korean 'Collaborators' of Japanese Colonialism." In *Routledge Handbook of Memory and Reconciliation in East Asia*. Edited by Mikyoung Kim, 159–71. London: Routledge: 2016.

Kim, Joungwon Alexander. *Divided Korea: The Politics of Development, 1945–1972*. Cambridge: East Asian Research Center, Harvard University, 1975.

Kim, Monica. *The Interrogation Rooms of the Korean War: The Untold History*. Princeton: Princeton University Press, 2019.

Kim, Robert S. *Project Eagle: The American Christians of North Korea in World War II*. Lincoln: Potomac Books, 2017.

Kim Un-t'ae 金雲泰. *Migunjŏngŭi Han'guk t'ongch'i* 美軍政의 韓國統治 [The U.S. Military Government's administration of Korea]. Seoul: Pagyŏngsa, 1992.

Korea, 1945 to 1948: A Report on Political Developments and Economic Resources with Selected Documents. Compiled by Department of State. Washington, DC: U.S. Government Printing Office, 1948.

Korea's Independence. Washington, DC: Government Printing Office, 1947.

"Korea: The Russians Came." *Time* 47, no. 4 (January 28, 1946): 33–34.

Kukpangbu, Chŏnsa P'yŏnch'an Wiwŏnhoe 國防部, 戰史編纂委員會. *Han'guk chŏnjaengsa, 1: Haebanggwa kŏn'gun* 韓國戰爭史, 1: 解放과 建軍 [History of the Korean War. Vol. 1: Liberation and founding of the armed forces]. Seoul: Kukpangbu, 1967.

Kuksa P'yŏnch'an Wiwŏnhoe 國史編纂委員會, comp. *Taehan Min'guksa charyojip* 大韓民國史資料集 [Source materials on the history of the Republic of Korea]. Vol. 22. Kwach'ŏn: Kuksa P'yŏnch'an Wiwŏnhoe, 1994.

———, ed. *Chuhan Migunsa* 주한 미군사 / *History of the United States Army Forces in Korea*. Vol. 1. Seoul: Sŏnin, 2014.

Kuzmarov, Jeremy. *Modernizing Repression: Police Training and Nation-Building in the American Century*. Amherst and Boston: University of Massachusetts Press, 2012.

"Labour Law for the Factory and Office Workers in North Korea." In *Kim Il Sung: Works*, vol. 2, 247–51. P'yŏngyang: Foreign Languages Publishing House, 1980.

"Law on Agrarian Reform in North Korea." In *Kim Il Sung: Works*, vol. 2, 93–95. P'yŏngyang: Foreign Languages Publishing House, 1980.

Liu, F. F. *A Military History of Modern China, 1924–1949*. Princeton: Princeton University Press, 1956.

Liu Xiaoyuan. *A Partnership for Disorder: China, the United States, and Their Policies for the Postwar Disposition of the Japanese Empire, 1941–1945*. Cambridge: Cambridge University Press, 1996.

MacArthur, Arthur. "Annual Report of Maj. Gen. Arthur MacArthur, U.S.V., Commanding Division of the Philippines, Military Governor in the Philippine Islands." In *Annual Reports of the War Department, 1900*, vol. 1, pt. 5, *Report of the Lieutenant-General Commanding the Army*, pt. 3, 59–195. Compiled by the United States War Department. Washington, DC: Government Printing Office, 1900.

MacDonald, Callum, "'So Terrible a Liberation'—the UN Occupation of North Korea." *Bulletin of Concerned Asian Scholars* 23, no. 2 (April–June 1991): 3–19.

Macdonald, Donald S. *Interview with Donald S. Macdonald.* Interview by Charles Stuart Kennedy, January 25, 1990. Manuscript Division, Library of Congress, Washington, DC, https://www.loc.gov/item/mfdipbib000734.

MacKinnon, Stephen R., and Oris Friesen. *China Reporting: An Oral History of American Journalism in the 1930s and 1940s.* Berkeley: University of California Press, 1987.

Masuda Hajimu. *Cold War Crucible: The Korean Conflict and the Postwar World.* Cambridge: Harvard University Press, 2015.

Matray, James I. "Hodge Podge: American Occupation Policy in Korea, 1945–1948." *Korean Studies* 19 (1995): 17–38.

McCarthy, Joseph. *America's Retreat from Victory: The Story of George Catlett Marshall.* New York: Devin-Adair, 1951.

McCune, George M. "Occupation Politics in Korea." *Far Eastern Survey* 15, no. 3 (February 13, 1946): 33–37.

———. "Korea: The First Year of Liberation." *Pacific Affairs* 20, no. 1 (March 1947): 3–17.

McLaughlin, John J. "General Albert Coady Wedemeyer 1897–1989: Soldier, Scholar, Statesman." PhD diss., Drew University, 2008.

Meade, E. Grant. *American Military Government in Korea.* New York: King's Crown Press, Columbia University, 1951.

Menon, K. P. S. *Many Worlds Revisited: An Autobiography.* 4th enl. ed. Bombay: Bharatiya Vidya Bhavan, 1981.

Merrill, John. *Korea: The Peninsular Origins of the War.* Newark: University of Delaware Press, 1989.

Migunjŏng ch'ŏng kwanbo 美軍政廳官報 / *Official Gazette, United States Army Military Government in Korea.* 4 vols. Seoul: Wŏnju Munhwasa, 1991.

Minguo Junxi Tongxuehui Bubing di-208-shi Mofan Lian Daduihui 民國軍系同學會步兵第二〇八師模範連大隊會, comp. *Qingnianjun di er qi tongxue tongxunlu* 青年軍第二期同學通訊錄 [Youth Army, Second Cohort classmates' directory]. Taipei: Minguo Junxi Tongxuehui Bubing di-208-shi Mofan Lian Daduihui, 1987.

Mitchell, Richard H. "Japan's Peace Preservation Law of 1925: Its Origins and Significance." *Monumenta Nipponica* 28, no. 3 (Autumn 1973): 317–45.

Mizuno Naoki, and Mark E. Caprio. "Stories from Beyond the Grave: Investigating Japanese Burial Grounds in North Korea." *Asia-Pacific Journal: Japan Focus* 12, no. 9 (March 2, 2014): 1–13. Online: https://apjjf.org/2014/12/9/Mizuno-Naoki/4085/article.html.

Muccio, John J. *Oral History Interview with John J. Muccio.* Interview by Jerry N. Hess, February 10, 1971, Harry S. Truman Library, NARA, https://www.trumanlibrary.gov/library/oral-histories/muccio1.

Mydans, Carl. "Korea: A Scout Is Militant." *Time* 49, no. 26 (June 30, 1947): 25–26.

———. "Revolt in Korea: A New Communist Uprising Turns Men into Butchers." *Life* 25, no. 20 (November 15, 1948): 55–58.

Nachi Hisato 那智壽人 [pseud.]. "Chōsen wa sōgen de wa nakatta, raichō no daiippo o Chōsen ni shirushite, kataru H. Yūgento" 朝鮮は草原ではなかった, 来朝の第一歩を朝鮮に印して, 語る H·ユーゲント [Korea was not a steppe, Korea marks the first stop on the trip to Japan, said the Hitler Youth]. *Kokumin shinpō* 國民新報 85 (November 10, 1940): 4–5.

Ōgushi Ryūkichi 大串隆吉. "Senji taiseika Nihon seinendan no kokusai renkei: Hitorā Yūgento to Chōsen Rengō Seinendan no aida" 戦時体制下日本青年団の国際連携: ヒトラー・ユーゲントと朝鮮連合青年団の間 [The Japan Youth League's wartime international ties: Between Hitler Youth and the Alliance of Korean Youth Leagues]. Parts 1 and 2. *Jinbun gakuhō: kyōikugaku* 人文学報: 教育学 31 (March 1996): 153–75; 32 (March 1997): 1–36.

Pearlman, Lise. *The Lindbergh Kidnapping Suspect No. 1: The Man Who Got Away*. Berkeley: Regent Press, 2020.

Rebedep'ŭ pimangnok 레베데프 비망록 [The Lebedev memorandum]. Edited by Kim Yŏng-jung 김영중. Cheju: Haedong, 2016.

Reporters Without Borders (RSF). "2025 World Press Freedom Index." Accessed May 8, 2025. https://rsf.org/en/index?year=2025.

Robinson, Richard D. "Betrayal of a Nation." Unpublished manuscript, 1960. Harvard-Yenching Library, Harvard University.

[———] Rich'adŭ D. Robinsŭn 리차드 D. 로빈슨. *Migugŭi paeban: Migunjŏnggwa Namjosŏn* 미국의 배반: 미군정과 남조선 [America's betrayal: The U.S. Military Government and southern Korea]. Translated by Chŏng Mi-ok 정미옥. Seoul: Kwahakkwa Sasang, 1988.

———. "A Personal Journey through Time and Space." *Journal of International Business Studies* 25, no. 3 (Fall 1994): 435–65.

———, and Patricia Elliott Swanson, eds. *In the Process of Creation: The Spiritual Philosophy of Dr. William Dunlop Robinson, 1873–1965*. Gig Harbor: Hamlin Publications, 2004.

Robinson, W. Dunlop. *An Idealist at Large*. Boston, New York, and Chicago: Pilgrim Press, 1913.

Rosinger, Lawrence K. "Election Leaves Korea's Future in Doubt." *Foreign Policy Bulletin* 27, no. 31 (May 14, 1948): 1–3.

Roth, Andrew. "Korea's Heritage." *Nation* 162, no. 5 (February 2, 1946): 122–24.

———. "Cross-Fire in Korea." *Nation* 162, no. 8 (February 23, 1946): 220–23.

Russell, Dick. *The Man Who Knew Too Much: Hired to Kill Oswald and Prevent the Assassination of JFK*. New York: Carroll & Graf / Richard Gallen, 1992.

Sälter, Gerhard. *NS-Kontinuitäten im BND: Rekrutierung, Diskurse, Vernetzungen* [Nazi continuities in the Federal Intelligence Service (BND): Recruitment, discourses, networks]. Berlin: Ch. Links, 2022.

Satō Tomoya 佐藤知也. *Heijō de sugoshita jūninen no hibi* 平壌で過ごした 12 年の日々 [My daily life over twelve years in P'yŏngyang]. Tokyo: Kōyō, 2009.

Sauer, Bernhard. "Goebbels 'Rabauken': Zur Geschichte der SA in Berlin-Brandenburg" [Goebbels' "hooligans": On the history of the SA in Berlin-Brandenburg]. *Berlin in Geschichte und Gegenwart: Jahrbuch des Landesarchivs Berlin* 25 (2006): 107–64.

Schaller, Michael. *The U.S. Crusade in China, 1938–1945*. New York: Columbia University Press, 1979.

———. *The United States and China: Into the 21st Century*. 3rd ed. Oxford: Oxford University Press, 2002.

Scher, Mark J. "U.S. Policy in Korea 1945–1948: A Neo-Colonial Model Takes Shape." *Bulletin of Concerned Asian Scholars* 5, no. 4 (December 1973): 17–27.

Senate Reports, No. 2108, 81st Congress, 2nd Session, Serial 11375. *State Department Employee Loyalty Investigation: Report of the Committee on Foreign Relations Pursuant to S. Res. 231*. Washington, DC: U.S. Government Printing Office, 1950.

Shao Yulin 邵毓麟. *Shi Han huiyilu: Jindai Zhong-Han guanxi shihua* 使韓回憶錄: 近代中韓關係史話 / *My Mission to Korea: A Personal Record of Modern Sino-Korean Relations*. Taipei: Zhuanji Wenxue Chubanshe, 1980.

Shepherd, William, Iyanatul Islam, and Sankaran Raghunathan, eds. *Who's Who in International Business Education and Research*. Cheltenham and Northampton: Edward Elgar, 1999.

Shin Seungyop. "When Colonial Korea Met Fascism: Power, Desire, and Adolf Hitler in Public Discourse, 1931–1945." *Korea Journal* 63, no. 3 (Autumn 2023): 5–35.

Shwittŭikkop'ŭ ilgi, 1946–1948 쉬띄꼬프 일기, 1946-1948 [The Shtykov diary, 1946–1948]. Compiled by Chŏn Hyŏn-su 전현수. Kwach'ŏn: Kuksa P'yŏnch'an Wiwŏnhoe, 2004.

Snow, Edgar. "We Meet Russia in Korea." *Saturday Evening Post* 218, no. 39 (March 30, 1946): 18–19, 117–18.

Sŏ Chung-sŏk 서중석. "Kungnae tongnip undong seryŏgŭi haebang hu kukka kŏnsŏl pangyang—Yŏ Un-hyŏngŭi Inmin Konghwaguk Inmindang sin'tak t'ongch'i kwallyŏn munjerŭl chungsimŭro" 국내 독립운동세력의 해방 후 국가건설방향—여운형의 인민공화국 인민당 신탁통치 관련 문제를 중심으로 [The Influence of the domestic independence movement and trends in national reconstruction after liberation: With focus on Yŏ Un-hyŏng's People's Republic, the Korean People's Party and trusteeship issues]. *Taedong munhwa yŏn'gu* 大東文化硏究 56 (2006): 289–321.

Song Chae-gyŏng 송재경. "Migunjŏng yŏronjosaro pon Han'gugŭi chŏngch'i-sahoe tongyang (1945–1947) 미군정 여론조사로 본 한국의 정치·사회동향 (1945-1947)" [Political and social trends in Korea as seen through the U.S. Military Government Opinion Poll (1945–1947)]. M.A. thesis. Seoul National University, 2014.

Spracher, William C. "The OSS in Support of the Chinese Communists." *American Intelligence Journal* 3, no. 3 (Winter 1980/81): 14–20, 11.

"Statement of the Military Governor." *Summation: United States Army Military Government Activities in Korea* 20 (May 1947): 14–15.

Suchcitz, Andrzej, et al., eds. *Armia Krajowa w dokumentach 1939-1945* [The Home Army in documents, 1939–1945]. Vol. 1, pt. 2, 2nd ed. Warsaw: Instytut Pamięci Narodowej, Komisja Ścigania Zbrodni przeciwko Narodowi Polskiemu, 2015.

Sugg, Harold. "Watch Korea." *Harper's Magazine* 194, no. 1160 (January 1947): 38–44.

Suwŏn Pangmulgwan 수원 박물관. *Haebang konggan Suwŏn, kŭ ttŭgŏun hamsŏng: 2016 Suwŏn pangmulgwan t'ŭkpyŏl kihoekchŏn* 해방 공간 수원, 그 뜨거운 함성: 2016 수원 박물관 특별 기획전 [Suwŏn after independence, the passionate shouts: 2016 Suwŏn Museum special exhibition]. Suwŏn: Suwŏn Pangmulgwan, 2016.

"TASS statement on the Korean Question" (January 23, 1946). Reprinted in *The Soviet Union and the Korean Question (Documents)*, 7–10. Moscow: Ministry of Foreign Affairs, 1948.

Terry, T. Phillip. *Terry's Japanese Empire, Including Korea and Formosa*. Boston: Houghton Mifflin, 1914.

Truman, Harry S. *Memoirs: Years of Trial and Hope*. Vol. 2. Garden City: Doubleday, 1956.

Tsuboi Sachio 坪井幸生, with Araki Nobuko 荒木信子. *Aru Chōsen Sōtokufu keisatsu kanryō no kaisō* ある朝鮮総督府警察官僚の回想 [Memoirs of a Chōsen Government-General police bureaucrat]. Tokyo: Sōshisha, 2004.

Tsui, Brian. *China's Conservative Revolution: The Quest for a New Order, 1927–1949*. Cambridge: Cambridge University Press, 2018.

Tuchman, Barbara. *Stilwell and the American Experience in China, 1911–1945*. London: Phoenix Press, 2001.

Twain, Mark. "To the Person Sitting in Darkness." *North American Review* 531 (February 1901): 161–76.

United States, 57th Congress, 1st Session, Senate, Committee on the Philippines. *Affairs in the Philippine Islands: Hearings Before the Committee on the Philippines of the United States Senate*. Senate Doc. No. 331, pt. 2. Washington, DC: Government Printing Office, 1902.

United States Army Forces in Korea. *Intelligence Summary Northern Korea* (May 6, 1946), in *HQ, USAFIK Intelligence Summary Northern Korea (1945.12.1–1947.3.31)*. Vol. 1. Ch'unch'ŏn: Hallim Taehakkyo, Asia Munhwa Yŏn'guso, 1989.

United States Department of State, comp. *Foreign Relations of the United States, 1947*, vol. I, *General; The United Nations*. Washington, DC: Government Printing Office, 1973.

———, comp. *Foreign Relations of the United States, Diplomatic Papers: The Conferences at Malta and Yalta 1945*. Washington, DC: Government Printing Office, 1955.

———, comp. *Foreign Relations of the United States, Diplomatic Papers: The Conference of Berlin 1945*. 2 vols. Washington, DC: Government Printing Office, 1960.

———, comp. *Foreign Relations of the United States, Diplomatic Papers: The Conferences at Cairo and Teheran 1943*. Washington, DC: Government Printing Office, 1961.

———, comp. *Foreign Relations of the United States, Diplomatic Papers 1945*. Vol. VI: *The British Commonwealth, The Far East*. Washington, DC: Government Printing Office, 1969.

———, comp. *Foreign Relations of the United States, Diplomatic Papers 1945*. Vol. VII: *The Far East: China*. Washington, DC: Government Printing Office, 1969.

———, comp. *Foreign Relations of the United States, 1946*. Vol. VIII: *The Far East*. Washington, DC: Government Printing Office, 1971.

———, comp. *Foreign Relations of the United States, 1950*. Vol. VII: *Korea*. Washington, DC: Government Printing Office, 1976.

———, comp. *Foreign Relations of the United States, 1951*. Vol. VII: *Korea and China*. Part 1. Washington, DC: Government Printing Office, 1983.

U.S. War Department and U.S. Navy Department. *United States Army and Navy Manual of Military Government and Civil Affairs (FM 27-5 / OPNAV 50E-3)*. Washington, DC: Government Printing Office, 1943.

Verzeichnis der Mitglieder des Diplomatischen Korps in Berlin, Januar 1945 [Directory of the diplomatic corps in Berlin, January 1945]. Compiled by Auswärtiges Amt. Berlin: Reichsdruckerei, 1945.

Voss, Ernest E. "Scouting Among Primitive Boys." Unpublished thesis submitted when applying for the Scout Executive's Fellowship, June 1939. Kenneth Woltz Badgett Papers, 1900–2001, No. 4692, Box 004, Folder 35, Wilson Special Collections Library, University of North Carolina at Chapel Hill.

Wales, Nym, and Kim San. *Song of Ariran: The Life Story of a Korean Rebel*. New York: John Day, 1941.

Wang Tifu 王替夫, with Yang Mingsheng 杨明生. *Jianguo Xitele yu jiuguo Youtairen de Wei Man waijiaoguan* 见过希特勒与救过犹太人的伪满外交官 [I met Hitler and saved Jews: A Manchukuo puppet state diplomat]. Harbin: Heilongjiang Renmin Chubanshe, 2002.

Wedemeyer, Albert C. *Report to the President Submitted September 1947: Korea*. Washington, DC: Government Printing Office, 1951.

———. *Wedemeyer Reports!* New York: Henry Holt, 1958.

Welles, Sumner. *The Time for Decision*. New York and London: Harper & Brothers, 1944.

Woodward, Bob. *Plan of Attack*. New York: Simon & Schuster, 2004.

Wu, Anthony. "Reporting East Asia: The Collection of Suzanne and Mark Gayn." Updated April 17, 2021. Accessed August 28, 2023. https://anthonywuart.com/post/reporting-east-asia-the-collection-of-suzanne-and-mark-gayn.

Yang Sungik. "Korea's Fascist Moment: Liberation, War, and the Ideology of South Korean Authoritarianism, 1945–1979." PhD diss., Harvard University, 2023.

Ye Quanhong 葉泉宏. "Huangbu junxiao han ji xuesheng kao shi" 黃埔軍校韓籍學生考實 [An examination of Korean students at the Whampoa Military Academy]. *Hanguo xuebao* 韓國學報 14 (1996), 155–68.

Yi Chŏng-sik 이정식. *Taehan Min'gugŭi kiwŏn: haebang chŏnhu hanbando kukche chŏngsewa minjok chidoja 4-inŭi chŏngch'ijŏk kwejŏk* 대한민국의 기원: 해방전후 한반도 국제정세와 민족 지도자 4 인의 정치적 궤적 [The origins of the Republic of Korea: The international situation on the Korean peninsula before and after liberation and the political trajectory of four national leaders]. Seoul: Ilchogak, 2006.

Yi Kil-sang 李吉相, comp. *Haebang chŏnhusa charyojip*, 1: *Migunjŏng chunbi charyo* 解放前後史資料集 1: 美軍政準備資料 [Collection of historical materials from before and after the liberation, 1: Preparatory materials by the U.S. Military Government]. Seoul: Wŏnju Munhwasa, 1992.

Yi Pŏm-sŏk 李範奭. *Minjokkwa ch'ŏngnyŏn* 民族과青年 [A people and its youth]. Yi Pŏm-sŏk nonsŏljip, no. 1. Seoul: Paeksusa, 1948.

——— interview. "Ch'ŏrhyŏlch'ongni, taenae ch'onggyŏlsok, taeoegongjonŭl chŏlgyu: chogukchaegŏnŭi illyŏme yŏrhwagach'i pult'amyŏnsŏ" 鐵血總理, 對內總結束, 對外共存을 絶叫: 祖國再建의 一念에 熱火같이 불타면서 [An iron-willed prime minister, demanding internal unity and external coexistence: Burning like a raging fire at the thought of rebuilding the fatherland]. *Samch'ŏlli* 三千里 31, no. 4 (August 1948): 8–9.

———. *Udungbul* 우둥불 [Bonfire]. Seoul: Sasangsa, 1971.

Yi Sun-t'aek 李順澤 and Kim Si-hŭng 金時興, eds. *Taehan Min'guk kŏn'guk ch'ŏngnyŏn undongsa* 大韓民國建國青年運動史 [History of the youth movement during the founding period of the Republic of Korea]. Seoul: Kŏn'guk Ch'ŏngnyŏn Undong Hyŏbŭihoe, 1989.

Yi Wan-bŏm 이완범. "Paegŭisawa KLOŭi hwaldongŭl t'onghaesŏ pon Namhan Taebuk chŏngbohwaldongŭi wŏllyu (1945–1953)" 백의사와 KLO 의 활동을 통해서 본 남한 대북 정보활동의 원류 (1945–1953) [The origins of South Korea's intelligence activities against North Korea through the activities of the White Shirts Society and KLO (1945–1953)]. *Kukka chŏngbo yŏn'gu* 국가정보연구 3, no. 1 (August 2010), 47–82.

Yi Yŏn-sik 李淵植. "Haebang hu Ilbonin songhwan munjerŭl tullŏssan Namhan sahoewa Chosŏn Minjok Ch'ŏngnyŏndan Chungang migunjŏngŭi kaldŭng" 解放 後 日本人 送還問題를 둘러싼 南韓社會와 美軍政의 葛藤 [Conflict between southern Koreans and USAMGIK over the repatriation of Japanese nationals after liberation]. *Hanil minjok munje yŏn'gu* 韓日民族問題研究 15 (2008): 5–47.

Yuan, Jianda. *Chinese Government Leaders in Manchukuo, 1931–1937: Intertwined National Ideals*. London: Routledge, 2023.

Yu Sang-hŭi 유상희, Yi Sang-nok 이상록, Chŏng Tae-hun 정대훈, et al. *Chosŏn Minjok Ch'ŏngnyŏndan Chungang Hullyŏnso* 조선민족청년단중앙훈련소 [Korean National Youth Corps Central Training Center]. Suwŏn: Suwŏn Pangmulgwan, 2016.

Newspapers

Berliner Morgenpost
Boston Globe
Chayu sinmun 自由新聞
China Weekly Review
Chosŏn ilbo 朝鮮日報
Christian Advocate
Christian Science Monitor
Chungang sinmun 中央新聞
Deutsch-Chinesische Nachrichten
Gazette (Montreal)
Haebang ilbo 解放日報
Japan Times
Korean Independence (Los Angeles)
Kyŏnghyang sinmun 京鄉新聞
Maeil sinbo 每日申報
Manchester Guardian
Minju chungbo 民主衆報 (Pusan)
New York Times
PM Daily (New York)
Seoul sinmun 서울신문
Sydney Morning Herald
Taegu sinbo 大邱新報
Tonga ilbo 東亞日報
Trud (*Труд*)
Voice of Korea
Wall Street Journal
Washington Post

Archival Collections

Archiv der sozialen Demokratie, Bibliothek der Friedrich-Ebert-Stiftung
Beinecke Rare Book and Manuscript Library, Yale University
Harvard University Archives
Harvard-Yenching Library Special Collections
Hoover Institution Library & Archives, Stanford University
Imperial War Museum, London
National Archives and Records Administration, College Park (NARA)
National Archives at New York City
National Library of Korea, Digital Collection
National Security Archive, George Washington University
Personal Collection of Carol A. Robinson
Politisches Archiv des Auswärtigen Amts (PAAA), Berlin
Thomas Fisher Rare Book Library, University of Toronto
Wilson Special Collections Library, U of North Carolina at Chapel Hill

Image Credits

Cover; p. v: Photo by Mark Gayn: The Seoul Metropolitan Police halted three students and tied their wrists with twine, fall 1946. Mark Gayn Papers, MS Coll. 00215, Series 20: Photographs, Korea, Thomas Fisher Rare Book Library, University of Toronto. **Frontispiece:** Crowds cheering as U.S. troops pull in at Seoul Station on Sept. 9, 1945. RG 111, Records of the Office of Chief Signal Officer, 1860–1985, Signal Corps Photographs of American Military Activity, 1754–1954 [111-SC], part 3, National Archives and Records Administration. **(Fig. 1)** The Robinsons in 1936: William D. Robinson, Richard, Marion H. Robinson, and oldest son Hamlin. Richard Dunlop Robinson and Patricia Elliott Swanson, eds., *In the Process of Creation: The Spiritual Philosophy of Dr. William Dunlop Robinson, 1873–1965* (Gig Harbor: Hamlin Publications, 2004), 1. Copyright Carol A. Robinson. **(Fig. 2)** Richard D. Robinson with Soviet soldiers at the 38th parallel, winter 1945/46. Personal Collection of Carol A. Robinson. Copyright Carol A. Robinson. **(Fig. 3)** Letter by Chief of Military Intelligence Division L. R. Forney to Commanding General, Korean Base Command, APO, 901, "Richard D. Robinson" (January 6, 1948), RG 319, Army - Intelligence Project Decimal Files, 1946–1948, Box 243, Identification of 'Will Hamlin,' National Archives and Records Administration. **(Fig. 4)** Cover of the 1988 Korean edition of Richard D. Robinson's book, published as *Migugŭi paeban: Migunjŏnggwa Namjosŏn* [America's betrayal: The U.S. Military Government and southern Korea]. **(Fig. 5)** Still from a TV interview of Richard D. Robinson with Korean journalist Kim Hwan-gyun, aired on KBS TV1 in January 2004. **(Fig. 6)** Richard D. Robinson's summary of an "Interview with Dr. Arthur C. Bunce, Member of the American Delegation to the Joint–Soviet–American Commission, Economic Advisor to the CG" (January 23, 1946), RG 332, USAFIK, XXIV Corps, G-2, Historical Section, Box 69, Records Regarding the Okinawa Campaign, U.S. Military Government in Korea, U.S.–U.S.S.R. Relations in Korea, and Korean Political Affairs, 1945–48, National Archives and Records Administration. **(Fig. 7)** Part of the first page of part 2, vol. 1, chapter 4: "American–Soviet Relations: The First Year" in the "History of the United States Army Forces in Korea, 1945–1948," National Archives and Records Administration. **(Fig. 8)** Mark Julius Gayn, Declaration of Intention for Citizenship (April 1940), 1/19/1842 – 10/29/1959; NAI Number 4713410; Record Group Title: *Records of District Courts of the United States, 1685-2009*; Record Group Number: 21, National Archives at New York City. **(Fig. 9)** The Ginsbourg family in Shanghai in the late 1920s. From: Sam Ginsbourg, *My First Sixty Years in China* (Beijing: New World Press, 1982), photo page following the foreword, unpaginated. Photo now in public domain, licensed under CC BY 2.0. **(Fig. 10)** Amerasia case newspaper report with photos of *Amerasia* journalists. *Pittsburgh Press*, May 1, 1950. **(Fig. 11)** Handwritten entry for October 19, 1946 in Mark Gayn's journal. Mark Gayn Papers, MS Coll. 00215, Series 4, Box 44, Notebook 4 (entry for October 19, 1946), Thomas Fisher Rare Book Library, University of Toronto. **(Fig. 12)** Covers of various editions of Mark Gayn's *Japan Diary*, in English and in other languages. **(Fig. 13)** August 26, 1945, Koreans look on as Soviet troops parade through P'yŏngyang. From: P'al-iro Haebang Ilchunyŏn Kinyŏm Chungang Chunbi Wiwŏnhoe, comp., *P'al-iro haebang ilchunyŏn Pukchosŏn Minjujuŭi kŏnsŏl sajinch'ŏp* [P'yŏngyang, 1946], [photo no. 6]. The album is part of record group 242, Korean, Chinese, and Russian Language Documents Captured in Korea, ca. 09/1953–01/1958, National Archives and Records Administration. **(Fig. 14)** P'yŏngyang, July 1946, procession to celebrate the implementation of the new Labor Law. Same source as fig. 13, [photo no. 41]. **(Fig. 15)** September 8, 1945, a first U.S. Army M8 armored car enters Seoul. Photo: Alexander Roberts, U.S. Army Signal Corps. RG 111, Records of the Office of Chief Signal Officer, 1860–1985, Signal Corps Photographs of American Military Activity, 1754-1954 [111-SC], part 3, National Archives and Records Administration. **(Fig. 16)** Oil portraits of Stalin, British premier Clement Attlee, U.S. president Truman, and Chiang Kai-shek displayed on the wall of the Chosŏn Misul Kŏnsŏl Ponbu / Corean Association for the Progress of Fine Arts, fall of 1945. Photographer unknown, photo in public domain, licensed under CC BY 2.0. **(Fig. 17)** Taegu, October 1, 1946, post office workers in sympathy with the railroad strikers demand the "Elimination of Japanese telegrams!" and the use of Korean language. Photo: Yi Yun-su, 1946. Photo in public domain, licensed under CC BY 2.0. **(Fig. 18)** Taegu, October 2, 1946, the 10.1 Taegu Uprising of 1946 is in full swing. Protesters and police are firing at each other while the U.S. Army supervises mass arrests of protesters. Photographer unknown, photo in public domain, licensed under CC BY 2.0. **(Fig. 19)** Seoul, May 1946, members of the militant right-wing P'yŏngan Youth Association (P'yŏngan Ch'ŏngnyŏnhoe). Photographer unknown, photo in public domain, licensed under CC BY 2.0. **(Fig. 20)** Seoul Stadium, March 1, 1947, members of the right-wing Founding Youth (Kŏn Ch'ŏng) and other groups are demonstrating against trusteeship. Photo: Pang; U.S. Army Signal Corps. RG 111, Records of the Office of Chief Signal Officer, 1860–1985, Signal Corps Photographs of American Military Activity, 1754–1954 [111-SC], part 3, National Archives and Records Administration. **(Fig. 21)** A still from the "World at Your Elbow" section of *Pathé News*. Right-wing nationalist forces clash with Korean communists in Seoul on March 1, 1947. *Pathé News*, Film ID 1181.22, April 4, 1947, British Pathé Archive, London. **(Fig. 22)** Seoul, June 14, 1947, Generals Hodge, Shtykov, and Lebedev convene at a Joint U.S.–Soviet Commission meeting. Photo: Acme Newspictures. **(Fig. 23)** Photo by Mark Gayn: Dr. Syngman Rhee, 1946. Mark Gayn Papers, MS Coll. 00215, Series 20: Photographs, Korea, Thomas Fisher Rare Book Library, University of Toronto. **(Fig. 24)** Photo by Mark Gayn: Kim Ku, 1946. Mark Gayn Papers, MS Coll. 00215, Series 20: Photographs, Korea, Thomas Fisher Rare Book Library, University of Toronto. **(Fig. 25)** Photo by Mark Gayn: Kim Kyu-sik, 1946. Mark Gayn Papers, MS Coll. 00215, Series 20: Photographs, Korea, Thomas Fisher Rare Book Library, University of Toronto. **(Fig. 26)** Photo by Mark Gayn: Korean county police chief, 1946. Mark Gayn Papers, MS Coll. 00215, Series 20: Photographs, Korea, Thomas Fisher Rare Book Library, University of Toronto. **(Fig. 27)** Photo by Mark Gayn: Korean landlord who owns 20,000 acres of land, 1946. Mark Gayn Papers, MS Coll. 00215, Series 20: Photographs, Korea, Thomas Fisher Rare Book Library, University of Toronto. **(Fig. 28)** Citizens rally against the four-power trusteeship agreed to at the Moscow Conference of Foreign Ministers, Seoul Stadium, December 31, 1945. Seoul Sinmun Archive. Photo in public domain, licensed under CC BY 2.0. **(Fig. 29)** Photo by Mark Gayn, Appeals to vote are posted on village 'town halls,' with a reproduction of Gayn's original cutline; photo 1946, cutline 1948. Mark Gayn Papers, MS Coll. 00215, Series 20: Photographs, Korea, Thomas Fisher Rare Book Library, University of Toronto. **(Fig. 30)** Pusan Harbor, October 12, 1945. Before boarding a ship, a Japanese soldier is searched in order to be repatriated to Japan. Photo: Buker; U.S. Army Signal Corps. RG 111, Records of the Office of Chief Signal Officer, 1860–1985, Signal Corps Photographs of American Military Activity, 1754–1954 [111-SC], part 3, National Archives and Records Administration. **(Fig. 31)** Kaesŏng refugee camp, May 25, 1947. Photo: Warren T. Warnecke; U.S. Army Signal Corps. RG 111, Records of the Office of Chief Signal Officer, 1860–1985, Signal Corps Photographs of American Military Activity, 1754–1954 [111-SC], part 3, National Archives and Records Administration. **(Fig. 32)** Detail of page 25 from an article by Carl Mydans, "Korea: A Scout Is Militant," *Time* 49, no. 26 (June 30, 1947). **(Fig. 33)** Carl Mydans' slide, documenting his visit to Suwŏn on May 27, 1947. Carl and Shelley Smith Mydans Papers, Box 38, Beinecke Rare Book and Manuscript Library, Yale University. **(Fig. 34)** Still shots from Colin Ross' travel movie *Das neue Asien* [The new Asia], 1940, showing a Korean *yangban*, the Japanese Government-General Building, and an Imperial Japanese Army training camp for Korean volunteer soldiers near Seoul (Keijō). **(Fig. 35)** Detail from the article: Nachi Hisato [pseud.], "Chōsen wa sōgen de wa nakatta" [Korea, after all, is not a steppe], *Kokumin shinpō* 5, no. 85 (November 10, 1940): 4–5. **(Fig. 36)** Wedemeyer, right, as student of the Kriegsakademie Berlin, summer 1937, with an Argentinian and two Chinese Guomindang officers at a maneuver in southern Germany (detail). Hoover Institution Library & Archives, Stanford University. **(Fig. 37)** Chiang Kai-shek's son, Chiang Wei-kuo (Jiang Weiguo), at the Kriegsakademie Munich in 1938, wearing a Wehrmacht's Unterfeldwebel (Junior Sergeant) uniform. Photographer unknown, photo in public domain, licensed under CC BY 2.0. **(Fig. 38)** Reinhard Gehlen's inscription to Wedemeyer in his memoir *Der Dienst* [The service], dated October 12, 1971. The book was formerly in the general's private library. Collection Frank Hoffmann. **(Fig. 39)** Kwangju, summer 1947, members of the right-wing, paramilitary Korean National Youth Corps at the inaugural ceremony for the organization's Chŏnnam division. Photo: Yi Kyŏng-mo, 1947. Photo in public domain, licensed under CC BY 2.0. **(Fig. 40)** ROK citizens accused of being communist sympathizers on the way to their execution by the ROK Army in a valley near Seoul, mid-November 1950. Photo: I. R. Lorwin (Pix, Inc., New York). Collection Frank Hoffmann.

Glossary and Index

Contributors

Mark E. Caprio is professor emeritus at Rikkyo University in Tokyo and currently the Kim Ku Visiting Professor at Harvard University. He received his PhD from the University of Washington in 2001 and is the author of *Japanese Assimilation Policies in Colonial Korea, 1910–1945* (University of Washington Press, 2009). He has published widely on colonial-era Korea, including "Abuse of Modernity: Japanese Biological Determinism and Identity Management in Colonial Korea" (*Cross-Currents*, 2014). Caprio has been researching Korean overseas activity during the Pacific War in pursuit of postwar national sovereignty and has published articles on related themes, including "The Politics of Trusteeship and the Perils of Korean Reunification" (*Seoul Journal of Korean Studies*, 2019). Presently, he is translating a memoir by a Japanese resident of P'yŏngyang, chronicling twelve years in the city, 1936–48. He is also co-editing a collection on modern Korea–Japan relations.

Mark Gayn (1909–1981) was born in Manchuria as the oldest of three sons in a Russian–Jewish family. He grew up in a small settlement at a Manchurian railway station close to the Mongolian border, but then moved with his family to Harbin, and later to Shanghai, witnessing revolutions, hunger, and war. In 1929 he left China to study journalism in the United States. *The Washington Post* then hired him as a special correspondent and he returned to Shanghai. During the war, back in New York, he wrote for several liberal papers, and in 1943 he became a U.S. citizen. In June 1945 Gayn and other journalists were arrested by the FBI for having used classified government documents for their work—the so-called Amerasia case that became the foundation for McCarthyism. In December 1945 Gayn settled in Tokyo as the *Chicago Sun*'s bureau chief for Japan and Korea, and in October and November the following year he visited Korea. His journalistic *Japan Diary* that dealt with postwar U.S. occupation politics, published in 1948, became a bestseller. Because of the continuous hostilities during the McCarthy era, he relocated to Canada in late 1952, where he worked for the *Toronto Daily Star* and other newspapers and magazines.

Frank Hoffmann studied Korean studies and art history at the University of Tübingen. He continued his research on modern Korean art and intellectual history at Harvard University and taught at IIC in

San Francisco and Hamburg University, among other institutions. For several years, he served as a co-owner and moderator of the academic Moderated Korean Studies Internet Discussion List. He is currently a senior IT systems administrator at UC Berkeley and the founder of Academia Publishers, LLC. His articles have appeared in specialized journals such as the *Korea Journal* and *Korean Studies*, as well as acclaimed popular magazines, including *Art in America*. He also compiled *The Harvard Korean Studies Bibliography* (Harvard University Press, 2000) and is the author of *Berlin Koreans and Pictured Koreans* (Praesens, 2015). His latest publication delves into fin-de-siècle Hamburg and the history of Korean art history (forthcoming).

John Merrill is a visiting scholar at the Institute of Korean Studies, George Washington University. He retired from the State Department as chief of INR's Northeast Asia Division. Merrill has taught at Georgetown University, George Washington University, Lafayette College, and the University of Delaware. He is the author of *Korea: The Peninsular Origins of the War* (1989) as well as numerous articles, reviews, and op-eds. His recent pieces include "Inside the White House: The Future of US–DPRK Policy" (*Korea Observer*, Winter 2016), as well as op-eds and articles for *SisaIN*, *Tonga ilbo*, and *Nikkei Asian Review*.

Richard D. Robinson (1921–2009) was trained as an officer for the future administration of the U.S. occupation forces in preparation for Japan's surrender. In November 1945, he was sent to Korea, where he served as the officer-in-charge of the U.S. Army Military Government in Korea's (USAMGIK) Office of Public Opinion. In his second year there, now as a civilian working for USAMGIK, he became one of a handful of historians working on an official history of the U.S. occupation of southern Korea. Witnessing the army's support for ultra right-wing Korean politicians, the suppression of democracy and abuses on all levels of the administration, as well as the censorship of the official history he worked on, he published a critical article in the popular *Nation* magazine and wrote a book-length alternative occupation history, "Betrayal of a Nation." Being investigated by the army for his article and for speaking out in support of Korean democracy, he fled the country in the summer of 1947, then stayed on in Turkey for almost a decade, becoming a Turkish area specialist. After his return to the United States in 1956 Robinson worked as a lecturer at the Harvard Graduate School of Business, and later became Professor of Management at the Alfred P. Sloan School of Management at MIT (1962–86). He authored or edited about twenty books and numerous articles.

www.ingramcontent.com/pod-product-compliance
Lightning Source LLC
LaVergne TN
LVHW040824090826
845145LV00001BA/33

9781956067910